The Pension Answer Book

Ninth Edition

Revised by: Stephen J. Krass
Krass & Lund, P.C.
New York City

(Original Edition by Krass and Keschner)

THE PANEL ANSWER BOOK SERIES

A PANEL PUBLICATION
ASPEN PUBLISHERS, INC.

Copyright © 1994

by
PANEL PUBLISHERS
A division of Aspen Publishers, Inc.
A Wolters Kluwer Company

36 West 44th Street
Suite 1316
New York, NY 10036
(212) 790-2000

ISBN 1-56706-021-8

Printed in the United States of America

About Panel Publishers

Panel Publishers derives its name from a panel of business professionals who organized in 1964 to publish authoritative, timely books, information services, and journals written by specialists to assist business professionals in the areas of human resources, compensation and benefits management, and pension planning and compliance, as well as owners of small to medium-sized businesses and their legal and financial advisors. Our mission is to provide practical, solution-based "how-to" information to business professionals.

Also available from Panel Publishers:

The Pension Answer Book: Forms & Worksheets
401 (k) Answer Book
401 (k) Answer Book: Forms & Worksheets
Individual Retirement Account Answer Book
Nonqualified Deferred Compensation Answer Book
Employee Benefits Answer Book
Executive Compensation Answer Book
Health Insurance Answer Book
ERISA Fiduciary Answer Book
Journal of Pension Planning & Compliance
Journal of Pension Benefits
Pension Benefits Newsletter

PANEL PUBLISHERS
A division of Aspen Publishers, Inc.
Practical Solutions for Business Professionals

To my sister, Ellen M. Krass
With love and affection

About the Authors

STEPHEN J. KRASS, ESQ., is a member of the law firm of Krass & Lund, P.C. in New York City. Mr. Krass received his B.S. (Accounting) from The Ohio State University and LL.B. and LL.M. (Taxation) from New York University School of Law. Mr. Krass is one of the original co-authors of *The Pension Answer Book*. He is a member of the American Bar Association Sections on Taxation (Member, Committee on Employee Benefits) and Real Property, Probate and Trust Law (Member, Employee Benefits Committee) and the New York State Bar Association Sections on Trusts and Estates, and Taxation (Member, Employee Benefits Committee and Committee on Estates and Trusts). He has served on the Board of Directors of the Estate Planning Council of New York City and is a member of the Advisory Boards of the *CCH Financial and Estate Planning Reporter*, the *Journal of Pension Planning & Compliance*, and *Pension Benefits*. Mr. Krass has been a panelist on AICPA and New York State Bar Association programs and The C.P.A. Report. He has spoken at the N.Y.U. Institute on Federal Taxation; The Ohio State University College of Law; Fordham Law School; UJA-Federation Annual Tax and Estate Planning Conference; The American College-CCH National Conference on Financial Planning; Institute of Certified Financial Planners Annual Conference; International Association for Financial Planning; American Academy of Matrimonial Lawyers; Hofstra University-Center for Business Studies; New York Law School; C. W. Post Tax Institute; Iona College Tax Institute; and New York State Society of Certified Public Accountants. Mr. Krass has been an instructor in the Long Island University Paralegal Program. He has contributed articles to *The Journal of Taxation of Estates and Trusts*; *Estate Planning*;

Taxes—The Tax Magazine; *Journal of the Institute of Certified Financial Planners*; *The Pension Actuary*; *The Practical Accountant*; *CLU Journal*; *CCH Financial and Estate Planning Reporter*; *The Journal of Financial Planning*; *Journal of Pension Planning & Compliance*; *Taxation for Accountants*; and *Taxation for Lawyers*. Mr. Krass is a frequent lecturer on employee benefit plans, estate planning, and taxation.

STEVEN SCHMUTTER, ESQ., is a member of the law firm of Krass & Lund, P.C. Mr. Schmutter received his B.S. (*magna cum laude*) from the State University of New York at Binghamton, his J.D. from St. John's University School of Law, and his LL.M. (Taxation) from New York University School of Law. He has written on employee benefit plan topics.

RICHARD L. KESCHNER, ESQ. (1945-1989), was a sole practitioner in New York City. Mr. Keschner received his B.S. from Brooklyn College, his M.B.A. from Baruch College, and his J.D. from Brooklyn Law School.

Acknowledgments

As with previous editions of *The Pension Answer Book*, this *Ninth Edition* incorporates the efforts of many people. Again, I express my appreciation to my partner, Steven Schmutter, my co-author-in-residence, who always provides invaluable assistance; and I also thank my partner, Daniel P. Lund, and our associate, William A. Palomo, for their contributions.

As before, I express my extreme gratitude to my personal secretary, Susan Busani-Halevi, who has now read every word of four editions. I also thank our secretary, Stella Chin, for her efforts.

I never fail to thank my wife, Sallie, for her continued, but strained, patience and understanding.

Thanks again to my editor, Ellen Ros, and to all the people at Panel Publishers, without whose efforts this *Ninth Edition* would not be in your hands.

Usually, I have completed the acknowledgments at this point, but I realize that I have not thanked the most important people—you, the reader. I receive many letters during the year from you with suggestions, comments and, of course, criticisms. I attempt to respond to your enquiries and incorporate in the next edition your suggestions. I thank all of you very, very much and hope that you find this edition of *The Pension Answer Book* again to be a useful and welcome addition to your library.

S J K

Preface

To achieve our goal of providing the most up-to-date information to our readers, *The Pension Answer Book, Ninth Edition,* incorporates and discusses all of the pertinent provisions of the Revenue Reconciliation Act of 1993. RRA '93, which became law on August 10, 1993, contains provisions that significantly affect qualified retirement plans.

A new annual compensation limit of $150,000 is imposed, which will affect the calculation of plan benefits and contributions and also tax deductions. This change will also affect 401(k) plans and plans that provide for matching employer contributions. Such plans must meet specific tests, and the new annual compensation limitation will make these tests more difficult to pass. Although the $150,000 limit is subject to cost-of-living adjustments, if the rate of inflation continues at the same pace as in 1992 and 1993, there will be no increase in this new limit until 1997.

Lastly, RRA '93 repeals the dollar limitation on the Medicare base. This provision does not, on its face, appear to affect qualified retirement plans, but it does. The criterion for calculating contributions to a qualified retirement plan covering a self-employed individual is earned income. Earned income is determined after deducting one-half of the individual's self-employment taxes and the contribution to the plan on behalf of that individual. Hence, repeal of the dollar limitation on the Medicare base reduces earned income with a potential concomitant reduction in the amount of the deductible contribution on behalf of the self-employed individual.

In addition, *The Pension Answer Book, Ninth Edition*, covers the recently issued final regulations relating to the nondiscrimination requirements, permitted disparity, minimum coverage, and definition of compensation. Also covered are the new proposed regulations relating to separate lines of business along with a complete discussion of how both the final and proposed regulations may ease compliance for employers and plan administrators.

Other specific additions to this book include:

- A new chapter on highly compensated employees
- Expanded coverage of eligible rollover distributions and mandatory income tax withholding
- Coverage of the IRS Voluntary Compliance Resolution Program
- New inroads on *Patterson v. Shumate,* including enforcement of IRS tax liens.

How to Use This Book

The Ninth Edition of *The Pension Answer Book* integrates the most recent changes in pension practice into a single-volume reference. It is designed for professionals who need quick and authoritative answers to help them decide whether to institute or continue pension and other retirement plans, how to choose the plans most suited to their needs, and how to comply with the morass of federal requirements. This book uses simple, straightforward language and avoids technical jargon when possible. Citations of authority are provided as research aids for those who need to pursue particular items in greater detail.

The question-and-answer format, with its breadth of coverage and its plain-language explanations (plus numerous illustrative examples), offers a clear and useful guide to understanding the complex but extremely important area of qualified pension and profit sharing plans.

Numbering System: The questions are numbered consecutively within each chapter (e.g., 2:1, 2:2, 2:3).

Detailed List of Questions: The detailed List of Questions that follows the Table of Contents in the front of this book helps the reader locate areas of immediate interest. This list is like a detailed table of contents that provides both the question number and the page on which it appears.

Glossary: Because the pension area is replete with technical terms that have specific legal meanings, a special glossary of terms is

provided following the question-and-answer portion of this book. Expressions not defined elsewhere, and abbreviations used throughout the book, are defined in the glossary, which is arranged in alphabetical order.

Tables: In order to facilitate easy access to a particular section of the Internal Revenue Code, Treasury Regulations, ERISA, Revenue Rulings, Letter Rulings, and to pertinent legal cases, tables of all of the sections and cases referenced in the text and their appropriate question number have been included.

Index: At the back of this book is an index provided as a further aid to locating specific information. Key words included in the glossary are used in the index as well. All references in the index are to question numbers rather than page numbers.

Use of Abbreviations: Because of the breadth of subject area, a number of terms and statutory references are abbreviated throughout *The Pension Answer Book*. Among the most common of these shorthand references are:

- Code—The Internal Revenue Code of 1986.

- ERISA—The Employee Retirement Income Security Act of 1974, as amended.

- IRS—The Internal Revenue Service.

- DOL—The U.S. Department of Labor.

- COBRA—The Consolidated Omnibus Budget Reconciliation Act of 1985.

- PBGC—Pension Benefit Guaranty Corporation.

- TRA '86—The Tax Reform Act of 1986.

- TAMRA—The Technical and Miscellaneous Revenue Act of 1988.

For explanations of other abbreviations consult the Glossary.

Contents

Contents

List of Questions

Chapter 1 Overview

Chapter 2 Types and Choices of Plans

Chapter 3 Highly Compensated Employees

Chapter 4   Requirements for Qualification

Chapter 5   Eligibility and Participation

Chapter 6 Contribution and Benefit Limitations

Chapter 7 Permitted Disparity

Chapter 8 Funding Requirements

Chapter 9   Vesting

Chapter 10 General Distribution Requirements

Chapter 11 Minimum Distribution Requirements

Chapter 12 Tax Deduction Rules

Chapter 13 Taxation of Distributions

Chapter 14 Insurance and Death Benefits

Chapter 15   Determination Letters

Chapter 16 Operating the Plan

Chapter 17 Reporting to Government Agencies

Chapter 18   Summary Plan Descriptions

Chapter 19   Fiduciary Responsibilities

Chapter 20 Prohibited Transactions

Chapter 21 Termination of the Plan

Chapter 22 Top-Heavy Plans

I

Chapter 23   401(k) Plans

Chapter 24 Employee Stock Ownership Plans

Chapter 25 Multiemployer Plans

Chapter 26 Individual Retirement Plans

Chapter 27   Simplified Employee Pensions

Chapter 28 Rollovers

Chapter 29 Business Owners

Chapter 30 Qualified Domestic Relations Orders

Chapter 1

Overview

There is no better way for a company to accumulate a substantial nest egg for its loyal employees—and the working owner—than to establish a tax-favored retirement plan. This chapter examines qualified retirement plans—what they are, their tax advantages, the types of costs involved, and the kinds of benefits that can be provided.

Q 1:1 Why should a company adopt a qualified retirement plan?

A qualified retirement plan is one of the best tax shelters available. The company is allowed a current deduction for its contributions to the plan; the employee pays no tax on money contributed for the employee's benefit until a distribution is made; earnings from investments made with funds in the plan accumulate tax-free; and distributions from the plan may be afforded favorable income tax treatment.

A qualified retirement plan is especially attractive to working owners of closely held corporations and to self-employed individuals. Their long-term service with their companies gives them the best opportunity to accumulate large sums of money through the tax-free build-up of capital. Although benefits must be provided for other employees as well, the owner usually receives a much larger benefit than the other employees.

The nontax reasons for adopting a qualified retirement plan include the following: (1) attracting employees; (2) reducing employee turnover; (3) increasing employee incentive; and (4) accumulating funds for retirement.

Q 1:2   What is a qualified retirement plan?

There are two distinct elements embodied in the term qualified retirement plan. The main element is the term "retirement plan." A retirement plan means any plan or program maintained by an employer or an employee organization (or both) that (1) provides retirement income to employees or (2) results in a deferral of income by employees for periods extending generally to the end of employment or beyond, regardless of how plan contributions or benefits are calculated or how benefits are distributed. [ERISA § 3(2)]

The other element is the term "qualified," which means that the retirement plan is afforded special tax treatment for meeting a host of requirements of the Internal Revenue Code (the Code). Qualified retirement plans fall into two basic categories: defined contribution plans and defined benefit plans. A defined contribution plan provides benefits based on the amount contributed to an employee's individual account, plus any earnings and forfeitures of other employees that are allocated to the account. A defined benefit plan provides a definitely determinable annual benefit; that is, the benefits are determined on the basis of a formula contained in the plan.

When the term qualified retirement plan is used in this book, it refers to both defined contribution and defined benefit plans.

Q 1:3   What are the basic tax advantages of a qualified retirement plan?

A qualified retirement plan is afforded special tax treatment. These tax advantages include the following:

1. The sponsoring company is allowed an immediate tax deduction for the amount contributed to the plan for a particular year. [IRC § 404]

2. Participants pay no current income tax on amounts contributed by the company on their behalf. [IRC §§ 402, 403]

3. Earnings of the plan are tax-exempt—permitting the tax-free accumulation of income and gains on investments. [IRC §§ 401, 501]

4. Reduced tax rates may apply to lump-sum distributions to certain participants. [IRC § 402(d)]

5. Income taxes on certain types of distributions may be deferred by rolling over the distribution to an individual retirement account (IRA) or to another qualified retirement plan. [IRC §§ 402(c), 403(a)(4), 403(a)(5)]

6. Income taxes on certain types of distributions to a deceased participant's spouse may be deferred by rolling over the distribution to an IRA. [IRC § 402(c)(9)]

7. Installment or annuity payments are taxed only when they are received. [IRC §§ 72, 402(a), 403(a)]

Q 1:4   Must a company incorporate to have a qualified retirement plan?

No. The benefits of a qualified retirement plan are available to incorporated and unincorporated businesses alike. Sole proprietorships and partnerships can have retirement plans that are comparable to corporate retirement plans.

Q 1:5   How does the deductibility of employer contributions differ between qualified and nonqualified plans?

Qualified retirement plans are given favorable tax treatment for meeting special requirements of the Code. There is no special tax treatment for nonqualified retirement plans. The basic difference between a qualified plan and a nonqualified plan is that contributions by the company to the nonqualified plan are not deductible until they are includible in the participant's income. This means the company does not get a current deduction for contributions made to a nonqualified plan. In contrast, contributions to a qualified plan are immediately deductible. [IRC §§ 83, 162, 404]

Q 1:6   How do qualified and nonqualified plans differ with regard to the taxation of employer contributions?

A participant in a qualified plan is not taxed until the benefits are distributed to the participant. This is also true in a nonqualified, unfunded plan. If the nonqualified plan is funded, however, the participant generally is taxed in the first year that the participant's rights are transferable or are not subject to a substantial risk of forfeiture. [IRC §§ 83, 402(b)]

Q 1:7 How do qualified and nonqualified plans differ with regard to coverage of employees and benefit or contribution limitations?

The nonqualified plan is designed primarily to provide retirement income for essential employees. Such a plan does not have to cover a broad spectrum of employees, as the qualified plan does. Furthermore, there are no limits on benefits or contributions, nor are there any reporting or bookkeeping requirements in connection with the nonqualified plan so long as it is not funded. [IRC § 401(a)]

Q 1:8 How is the employee affected by the employer's choice of a qualified or nonqualified plan?

From the employee's standpoint, benefits paid under a non-qualified plan will usually be taxed at and after retirement when, presumably, the employee will be in a lower tax bracket. This same income tax advantage is available to those who participate in a qualified plan, but there are some additional tax benefits in that case. If the benefits are paid in a lump sum, for example, the distribution might qualify for forward averaging tax treatment (see Q 13:13), which is a special method of tax computation that is unavailable for distributions from IRAs, simplified employee pensions (SEPs), and nonqualified plans. [IRC § 402(d)]

Q 1:9 What is the Employee Retirement Income Security Act?

The Employee Retirement Income Security Act of 1974 (ERISA) became law on September 2, 1974. ERISA completely overhauled the federal pension law after Congress found that:

1. Employees with long years of service were losing anticipated retirement benefits due to the lack of plan provisions relating to the vesting of benefits;

2. Many plans lacked adequate funds to pay employees promised retirement benefits; and

3. Plans were being terminated before enough funds had been accumulated to pay employees and their beneficiaries promised retirement benefits.

To protect the interests of retirement plan participants and their beneficiaries, ERISA (1) established a new set of rules for participation in retirement plans, (2) added mandatory schedules for the vesting of benefits, (3) fixed minimum funding standards, (4) set standards of conduct for administering the plan and handling plan assets, (5) required disclosure of plan information, and (6) established a system for insuring the payment of pension benefits.

Q 1:10   What other acts have affected retirement plans?

The following acts have affected retirement plans:

- The Multiemployer Pension Plan Amendments Act of 1980 (MPPAA)
- The Economic Recovery Tax Act of 1981 (ERTA)
- The Tax Equity and Fiscal Responsibility Act of 1982 (TEFRA)
- The Tax Reform Act of 1984 (TRA '84)
- The Retirement Equity Act of 1984 (REA)
- The Single-Employer Pension Plan Amendments Act of 1986 (SEPPAA)
- The Tax Reform Act of 1986 (TRA '86)
- The Omnibus Budget Reconciliation Act of 1986 (OBRA '86)
- The Pension Protection Act (PPA), attached to The Omnibus Budget Reconciliation Act of 1987 (OBRA '87)
- The Technical and Miscellaneous Revenue Act of 1988 (TAMRA)

- The Revenue Reconciliation Act (RRA), Title VII of The Omnibus Budget Reconciliation Act of 1989 (OBRA '89)
- The Omnibus Budget Reconciliation Act of 1990 (OBRA '90)
- The Unemployment Compensation Amendments of 1992 (UC '92)

Q 1:11 What is the Unemployment Compensation Amendments of 1992?

The Unemployment Compensation Amendments of 1992 (UC '92) became law on July 3, 1992. UC '92 contained provisions affecting qualified retirement plans that:

1. Expanded the rules relating to rollovers of qualified retirement plan distributions; and

2. Required income tax withholding on eligible rollover distributions not transferred directly to another eligible retirement plan.

Q 1:12 What is the Revenue Reconciliation Act of 1993?

The Revenue Reconciliation Act of 1993 (RRA '93) is an outgrowth of the Clinton Administration's proposals that were sent to Congress on April 30, 1993. RRA '93 (Title XIII of The Omnibus Budget Reconciliation Act of 1993—OBRA '93), which became law on August 10, 1993:

1. Increases income tax rates;

2. Repeals the dollar limitation on the Medicare base;

3. Reduces the amount of compensation for purposes of calculating benefits, contributions, and deductions; and

4. Modifies cost-of-living adjustments.

Except for tax rate increases, the above changes will become effective for years beginning *after* 1993.

Q 1:13   What is the Tax Simplification Bill of 1993?

The Tax Simplification Bill of 1993 (TSB '93) was introduced by House Ways and Means Committee Chairman Dan Rostenkowski on January 5, 1993 but has not yet been enacted into law. Title II-Pension Simplification, if enacted, will:

1. Repeal five-year income averaging for lump-sum distributions;
2. Repeal the $5,000 employee death benefit exclusion;
3. Simplify the method for taxing installment distributions;
4. Expand the availability of SEPs;
5. Extend 401(k) plans to nongovernmental tax-exempt employers;
6. Ease nondiscrimination testing for 401(k) plans;
7. Simplify the definition of highly compensated employee;
8. Repeal the family aggregation rule;
9. Limit the minimum participation requirement to defined benefit plans;
10. Round cost-of-living adjustments to the nearest $1,000 or $100; and
11. Eliminate the special vesting rule for multiemployer plans.

The changes listed above will become effective for years beginning *after* 1993. Similar legislation has been introduced in the Senate.

Q 1:14   Does the adoption of a qualified retirement plan by an employer constitute a contractual obligation to maintain the plan?

No. Although a qualified retirement plan must be a permanent plan (see Qs 1:16, 21:1), continuance of the plan is voluntary. It is not a contractual obligation of the company, except in the case of certain collectively bargained plans.

A carefully drafted plan and trust will specifically limit the company's obligation to maintain and fund the plan. In addition, the company should expressly retain the right to reduce, suspend, or discontinue contributions and the right to terminate the plan (see Q 21:2).

Q 1:15   What costs will the company incur in adopting a qualified retirement plan?

Professional fees vary, depending on the type of plan adopted by the company. However, the following types of services are generally required:

1. Legal services for drafting the plan and trust, and for submitting those and other required documents to IRS to obtain tax qualification;
2. Accounting services; and
3. Actuarial services to provide cost and benefit computations if a defined benefit plan is adopted.

It is also possible to adopt a master or prototype plan designed by an insurance company, a bank, or other investment-oriented company (a mutual fund, for example). (See Q 2:24.) These institutions generally charge less for their services because they expect to profit from the products (e.g., life insurance policies) whose purchase may be required.

Q 1:16   Must the company contribute to the plan each year once it adopts a qualified retirement plan?

It depends on the type of plan adopted. IRS says that the adoption of a qualified retirement plan commits the company to maintaining the plan on a permanent basis. For this purpose, permanent means that, from the plan's inception, the company must intend to support the plan over a number of years. [Treas Reg § 1.401-1(b)(2)]

Annual contributions to a pension plan are required. Although there are exceptions to this rule, a company considering the adoption of a pension plan must recognize that it is undertaking a commitment to maintain and fund the plan. For details on funding requirements, see Chapter 8.

Annual contributions to a profit sharing plan are not usually required. Further, a company that has not done well in a particular year may decide to make either a minimal contribution or no contribution at all for that year (unless the plan itself mandates a contribution each year). Nevertheless, a profit sharing plan is not permanent unless contributions are "recurring and substantial." [Treas Reg § 1.401-1(b)(2)]

Q 1:17   Must a qualified retirement plan include all employees?

No. A company is permitted to exclude certain categories of employees from participation in its qualified retirement plan. These exclusions are optional and apply only if they are specified in the plan. [IRC § 410]

Q 1:18   What are the most common eligibility requirements for participation in a qualified retirement plan?

The most common eligibility requirements are those relating to minimum age and length of service with the company.

A plan may exclude any employee who has not yet reached age 21. Plans of certain educational institutions may exclude employees who are under age 26. [IRC §§ 410(a)(1)(A)(i), 410(a)(1)(B)(ii)]

In most instances, the plan requires an employee to complete a certain period of service before being eligible to participate. This service requirement usually does not exceed one year; otherwise, the plan must provide full and immediate vesting of benefits. Under no circumstances may the service requirement exceed two years. The service requirement for 401(k) plans cannot exceed one year. [IRC §§ 401(k)(2)(D), 410(a)(1)(A)(ii), 410(a)(1)(B)(i)]

Q 1:19   What statutory exclusions from participation in a qualified retirement plan are permitted?

The two most common statutory exclusions from plan participation are minimum age and length of service requirements (see Q 1:18).

Other than these exclusions, the most common statutory exclusion applies to union employees on whose behalf negotiations for retirement benefits have been conducted with the company. The company may exclude union employees from coverage, whether or not they are covered under a separate retirement plan, as long as retirement benefits were the subject of good-faith bargaining. Statutory exclusions for air pilots and nonresident aliens are also available. [IRC § 410(b)(3)]

Q 1:20   What other exclusions from participation in a qualified retirement plan are permitted?

Other exclusions—so-called plan exclusions—usually fall into the following categories: (1) classification by job description, (2) classification by geographic location of employment or by specific division of the company, and (3) classification by method of compensation (e.g., hourly as opposed to salaried). Bear in mind, however, that regardless of the plan's eligibility provisions, coverage of a sufficient number of employees not excluded by statute (see Q 1:19) is needed to satisfy the minimum coverage requirements of the Code. The minimum coverage requirements have become stricter, and a minimum participation requirement has been introduced (see Qs 5:15, 5:24). [IRC §§ 401(a)(26), 410(b)]

Q 1:21   Can a company establish two qualified retirement plans?

Yes. The Code permits a company to maintain as many qualified retirement plans as it chooses, provided that all the plans meet the Code's requirements, including limitations on benefits and contributions.

Quite often, large companies establish separate plans for individual subsidiaries or divisions. These plans need not be comparable in all cases. Indeed, as explained in Questions 5:30 through 5:33, not all divisions or subsidiaries of the same company or members of the controlled group must adopt a plan in order for another division, subsidiary, or member to maintain a plan for its employees.

The minimum participation requirements severely curtail an employer's ability to maintain separate plans for individual subsidiaries or divisions and essentially eliminate the practice of establishing comparable plans. [IRC § 401(a)(26)]

Q 1:22 What kinds of benefits may be provided under a qualified retirement plan?

Qualified retirement plans are primarily intended to provide retirement benefits. Nevertheless, qualified retirement plans also frequently provide benefits upon death, disability, early retirement, or some other termination of employment. These benefits are usually funded by a trust fund, insurance contracts, or a combination of the two.

A profit sharing plan need not be limited to retirement benefits; it may also provide for hardship distributions, for example. In addition, a profit sharing plan may permit distribution of all or part of a participant's vested interest that has remained in the plan for at least two years prior to the distribution. It may also permit a participant with at least five years of participation in the plan to withdraw all or part of the participant's vested interest, including any amount contributed within the last two years. [Rev Rul 68-24, 1968-1 CB 150; Rev Rul 71-224, 1971-1 CB 124; Rev Rul 71-295, 1971-2 CB 184; Rev Rul 73-553, 1973-2 CB 130]

A 10 percent excise tax applies to most premature distributions from qualified retirement plans and IRAs. Consequently, a profit sharing plan can provide for in-service distributions of plan benefits after the passage of at least two years or because of hardship, but the distribution may be subject to the 10 percent excise tax, in addition to ordinary income tax. [IRC § 72(t)]

Q 1:23 May a qualified retirement plan provide life insurance benefits for participants?

Yes. However, different limits may apply to life insurance policies acquired under defined contribution plans and those acquired under defined benefit plans (see Q 14:4). The following general rules also apply:

1. The policies can be ordinary life, term life, universal life, retirement income, or endowment;

2. The insurance must be incidental to the primary purpose of the plan (i.e., to provide benefits at retirement); and

3. The participant pays tax on the cost of the current life insurance protection that is received each year.

Q 1:24 May a qualified retirement plan provide health insurance?

Yes, although the rules governing how much health insurance can be acquired and for whom vary, depending on whether the plan is a pension plan or a profit sharing plan.

A pension plan may provide health insurance, but only for retired employees and their families. [IRC § 401(h); Treas Reg § 1.401-14]

A contribution allocated to an individual medical account under a pension plan is treated as part of an annual addition (see Q 6:1) to a defined contribution plan. [IRC § 15(l)]

A profit sharing plan may provide health insurance benefits for all plan participants and their families. If this insurance is purchased with funds that have been in the plan for more than two years, there is no limit on how much the plan may pay for insurance coverage. If the plan uses other funds to buy the insurance, the amount of the premiums must be incidental; that is, the premiums may not exceed 25 percent of the funds allocated to the participant's account that have not been in the plan for at least two years. [Treas Reg § 1.401-1(b)(1)(ii); Rev Rul 61-164, 1961-2 CB 99]

Q 1:25 Is a contribution to a qualified retirement plan adopted on the last day of the taxable year fully deductible?

Yes, if the plan and trust are executed by the end of the year and other procedural requirements established by IRS are met, then contributions made by the due date for filing the company's income tax return for that year (including extensions) are fully deductible. [IRC § 404(a)(6); Rev Rul 81-114, 1981-1 CB 207]

Example: Sallie Corp., a calendar-year corporation, adopts a pension plan to become effective December 31, 1993. If the documents are executed by December 31, 1993, and the contribution is made by March 15, 1994 (or as late as September 15, 1994, if the company has received an extension until that time for filing its tax return), a full deduction will be allowed for 1993.

Q 1:26   May excess contributions made to a qualified retirement plan be returned to the company?

If the company makes an excess contribution to its qualified retirement plan, that excess may be returned to the company only in the following circumstances:

1. An actuarial error caused the excess funds to remain in the trust after the plan's termination and after the payment of all benefits to participants or their beneficiaries. [Treas Reg § 1.401-2]

2. The contribution was conditioned on the initial qualification of the plan, the plan did not qualify, and the plan was submitted to IRS for a determination letter (see Q 15:1) within the remedial amendment period. [ERISA § 403(c)(2)(B); IRC § 401(b)]

3. The contribution was conditioned on its deductibility and the deduction was denied. [ERISA § 403(c)(2)(C)]

4. The excess contribution was made due to a mistake of fact. [ERISA § 403(c)(2)(A)]

In any event, the plan itself must permit the return of the excess contribution; and, in either of the last two situations, earnings attributable to the excess contribution may not be returned to the company. Losses attributable to the excess contribution will reduce the amount to be returned. Further, returns to the employer must be made within one year of the mistaken contribution, denial of qualification, or denial of the deduction. [Rev Rul 91-4, 1991-1 CB 57]

A 10 percent excise tax is now imposed on nondeductible contributions to a qualified retirement plan (see Q 12:8). [IRC § 4972]

Special rules apply to excess contributions made to a 401(k) plan. See Chapter 23.

Chapter 2

Types and Choices of Plans

The range of retirement plan alternatives is extensive. There are defined contribution plans and defined benefit plans; there are pension plans and profit sharing plans. But before the employer can evaluate the relative merits of the various types of plans and choose the most appropriate plan, the employer must know what each type of plan offers. This chapter describes the categories of retirement plans, examines the basic choices available to a company, and offers guidelines for choosing the appropriate plan.

Q 2:1 What are the basic choices among qualified retirement plans?

Qualified retirement plans generally fit into one of two categories: defined contribution plans (see Q 2:2) and defined benefit plans (see Q 2:3).

Q 2:2 What is a defined contribution plan?

A defined contribution plan is a retirement plan that "provides for an individual account for each participant and for benefits based solely upon the amount contributed to the participant's account, and any income, expenses, gains and losses, and any forfeitures of accounts of other participants which may be allocated to such participant's account." [ERISA § 3(34); IRC § 414(i)]

Defined contribution plans include the following:

- Money purchase pension plans (see Q 2:4)
- Target benefit plans (see Q 2:5)
- Profit sharing plans (see Qs 2:6–2:7)
- Thrift or savings plans (see Q 2:10)
- 401(k) plans (see Q 2:11)
- Stock bonus plans (see Q 2:12)
- Employee stock ownership plans (ESOPs) (see Q 2:13)
- Simplified employee pensions (SEPs) (see Q 2:14)

Three major consequences result when a retirement plan is classified as a defined contribution plan: (1) plan contributions are determined by formula and not by actuarial requirements (except for target benefit plans); (2) plan earnings and losses are allocated to each participant's account and do not affect the company's retirement plan costs; and (3) plan benefits are not insured by the Pension Benefit Guaranty Corporation (PBGC).

Q 2:3   What is a defined benefit plan?

A defined benefit plan is a retirement plan "other than an individual account plan." In other words, a plan that is not a defined contribution plan is classified as a defined benefit plan. Under a defined benefit plan, retirement benefits must be definitely determinable. For example, a plan that entitles a participant to a monthly pension for life equal to 30 percent of monthly compensation is a defined benefit plan. [ERISA § 3(35); IRC § 414(j)] The most common types of defined benefit plans are flat benefit plans (see Q 2:15) and unit benefit plans (see Q 2:16).

If a plan is categorized as a defined benefit plan: (1) plan formulas are geared to retirement benefits and not to contributions (except for cash balance plans); (2) the annual contribution is usually actuarially determined; (3) certain benefits may be insured by PBGC; (4) early termination of the plan is subject to special rules; and (5) forfeitures reduce the company's cost of providing retirement benefits.

Q 2:4   What is a money purchase pension plan?

A money purchase pension plan is a defined contribution plan in which the company's contributions are mandatory and are usually based solely on each participant's compensation.

The obligation to fund the plan makes a money purchase pension plan different from most profit sharing plans. In most profit sharing plans, there are generally no unfavorable consequences for the company if it fails to make a contribution. However, if the company maintains a money purchase pension plan, its failure to make a contribution can result in the imposition of a penalty tax (see Q 8:18). Contributions must be made to a money purchase pension plan even if the company has no profits.

Forfeitures that occur because of employee turnover may reduce future contributions of the company or may be used to increase the benefits of remaining participants. [IRC § 401(a)(8)]

Retirement benefits are based on the amount in the participant's account at the time of retirement; that is, whatever pension the money can purchase.

The following is an example of a money purchase pension plan formula:

> The company shall contribute each plan year during which the plan is in effect on behalf of each participant an amount equal to 10 percent of compensation.

Under the formula, an equal percentage of compensation is allocated to each participant's account. The age and length of service of the participant are irrelevant for both contribution and allocation purposes, although length of service could be considered. [IRC § 411(b)(2); Treas Reg § 1.401-1(b)(1)(i)]

This concept is illustrated in the following example. The allocation in column (d) reflects a contribution formula that does not include permitted disparity. When permitted disparity is considered, differences in compensation become more relevant. See Chapter 7 for more details.

L & Y Corporation
Schedule of Contributions to
Money Purchase Pension Plan
for
Plan Year Ended December 31, 1993

(a)	(b)	(c)	(d)
			Allocation of Company
Participant	Age	Compensation	Contributions
Leonard	45	$200,000	$20,000
Yvette	30	50,000	5,000
Total		$250,000	$25,000

For plan years beginning *after* December 31, 1993, the amount of compensation on which contributions or benefits may be based is reduced from $200,000 to $150,000 (see Qs 6:21, 6:22). With the same 10-percent-of-contribution formula, Leonard's contribution for the 1994 plan year will be reduced to $15,000 [10% × $150,000]. To maintain the same amount of contribution for Leonard, the contribution formula must be increased to 13⅓ percent of compensation [13⅓% × $150,000 = $20,000], and this will increase the contribution for Yvette to $6,667 [13⅓% × $50,000]. [RRA '93, Act § 13212]

Q 2:5   What is a target benefit plan?

A target benefit plan is a hybrid or cross between a defined benefit plan and a money purchase pension plan. It is like a defined benefit plan in that the annual contribution is determined by the amount needed each year to accumulate (at an assumed rate of interest) a fund sufficient to pay a projected retirement benefit (the target benefit) to each participant on reaching retirement age. Thus, if a target benefit plan contains a target formula, such as 40 percent of compensation, that is identical to the benefit formula in a defined benefit plan and is based on identical actuarial assumptions (e.g., interest rates, mortality, employee turnover), the employer's initial contribution for the same group of employees will be the same.

However, this is where the similarity ends. In a defined benefit plan, if the actual experience of the plan differs from the actuarial assumptions used (for example, if the interest earned is higher or lower than the assumptions), then the employer either increases or decreases its future contributions to the extent necessary to provide the promised benefits. In a target benefit plan, however, the contribution, once made, is allocated to separate accounts maintained for each participant. Thus, if the earnings of the fund differ from those assumed, this does not result in any increase or decrease in employer contributions; instead, it increases or decreases the benefits payable to the participant.

In this regard, the target benefit plan operates like a money purchase pension plan. In fact, the only difference between a money purchase pension plan and a target benefit plan is that, in a money purchase pension plan, contributions are generally determined and allocated as a percentage of current compensation; in a target benefit plan, contributions are determined as if the plan were to provide a fixed benefit. In a money purchase pension plan, contributions for identically compensated employees are the same even though their ages differ; in a target benefit plan, age is one of the factors that determines the size of the contributions.

Since target benefit plans are defined contribution plans, they are subject to the limit on annual additions to a participant's account (see Q 6:1).

Q 2:6   What is a profit sharing plan?

A profit sharing plan is a defined contribution plan to which the company agrees to make "substantial and recurring," though generally discretionary, contributions (see Q 1:16). Amounts contributed to the plan are invested and accumulate (tax-free) for eventual distribution to participants or their beneficiaries either at retirement, after a fixed number of years, or upon the occurrence of some specified event (e.g., disability, death, or termination of employment) (see Q 1:22).

Unlike contributions to a pension plan, contributions to a profit sharing plan are usually keyed to the existence of profits. However, neither current nor accumulated profits are required for a company to contribute to a profit sharing plan. [IRC § 401(a)(27)]

Even if the company has profits, it can generally forgo or limit its contribution for a particular year if the plan contains a discretionary formula. The following is an example of such a formula:

> The company shall contribute each plan year during which the plan is in effect out of its earnings for its taxable year, or out of its accumulated earnings, an amount decided upon by the Board of Directors [or owner, partners, etc., as appropriate]. The contribution shall be allocated among the participants in the proportion that the compensation of each participant bears to the aggregate compensation of all the participants.

Under the allocation formula (the second sentence in the example), each participant receives the same percentage of the contribution as the participant's compensation bears to total compensation. The participant's length of service is irrelevant, although this factor can be considered in the allocation formula if prohibited discrimination does not result. However, note that, in a discretionary profit sharing plan, the actual amount to be allocated to each participant cannot be determined until the company decides upon its contribution for the year. [Treas Reg § 1.401-1(b)(1)(ii)]

Although many profit sharing plans adopt a discretionary contribution formula, others adopt a fixed formula. For example, a company may obligate itself to contribute to its profit sharing plan a specified percentage of each participant's compensation if profits exceed a specified level.

As with other defined contribution plans, retirement benefits in profit sharing plans are based on the amount in the participant's account at retirement. Unlike defined benefit plans, forfeitures in profit sharing plans arising from employee turnover may be reallocated among the remaining participants.

Q 2:7 What is an age-based profit sharing plan?

An age-based profit sharing plan is a profit sharing plan (see Q 2:6) that uses both age and compensation as a basis for allocating employer contributions among plan participants. This concept is similar to a target benefit plan (see Q 2:5), where age and compensation are factors used to determine the amount of the employer contribution.

All of the basic requirements that apply to regular profit sharing plans also apply to an age-based profit sharing plan. An age-based profit sharing plan can have a discretionary contribution formula and provide the employer with flexibility over the amount of the contribution to be made each year. Because age is a factor, this type of plan favors older employees who have fewer years than younger employees to accumulate sufficient funds for retirement (see Q 2:8). [Treas Reg § 1.401(a)(4)-8]

Q 2:8 How does an age-based profit sharing plan benefit older employees?

The basis for allocating employer contributions under an age-based profit sharing plan is determined by calculating the present value of a straight (i.e., single) life annuity beginning at the testing age (see Q 2:9). A standard interest rate, which may not be less than 7.5 percent nor more than 8.5 percent, compounded annually, and a straight life annuity factor that is based on a standard annuity table and on the same or a different standard interest rate, must be used. [Treas Reg §§ 1.401(a)(4)-8(b)(2), 1.401(a)(4)-12]

The following is an example of an allocation formula under an age-based profit sharing plan:

> The contribution shall be allocated among the participants in the proportion that the allocation factor of each participant bears to the aggregate allocation factors of all the participants. The allocation factor of a participant for the plan year shall be the product of (a) the participant's compensation for the plan year, multiplied by (b) the present value of $1.00, discounted with interest at 8.5 percent from the testing age to the participant's age as of the last day of the plan year. The following scenario provides a practical application of this allocation formula:

Example. For 1993, Ess-UU-Kay Corporation adopts an age-based profit sharing plan with a calendar year plan year. The following six employees are eligible to participate in the plan:

Participant	Age	Compensation
A (owner)	50	$100,000
B	40	50,000
C	35	50,000
D	35	40,000
E	30	35,000
F	25	25,000
Total		$300,000

Ess-UU-Kay contributes $39,000 to the plan. The plan uses a testing age of 65. The contribution is allocated among the participants based upon each participant's allocation factor, as follows:

Participant	Present Value (PV) of $1.00	Allocation Factor (PV x Compensation)	Contribution
A	.294	29,400	$24,547
B	.130	6,500	5,427
C	.087	4,350	3,632
D	.087	3,480	2,906
E	.058	2,030	1,695
F	.038	950	793
Total		46,710	$39,000

If the contribution is allocated among the participants in proportion to compensation, A's allocation would be only $13,000 ($100,000/$300,000 x $39,000). If the allocation formula is integrated with Social Security, A would receive $14,611 (see Chapter 7 for details). Because A is the oldest participant, A benefits most under the age-based profit sharing plan.

Q 2:9 What is the testing age for an age-based profit sharing plan?

The testing age is the age from which present value is calculated. If the testing age is 65, the present value of $1.00 at age 65 will be $1.00 and the present value of $1.00 at any lesser age will be a lesser amount. The standard interest rate currently used must not be less than 7.5 percent nor more than 8.5 percent, compounded annually. [Treas Reg §§ 1.401(a)(4)-8(b)(2), 1.401(a)(4)-12]

An example of a present value table is set forth below:

Present Value Table
8.5% Interest
Testing Age of 65

Age	Present Value	Age	Present Value
65	1.000	44	.180
64	.922	43	.166
63	.849	42	.153
62	.783	41	.141
61	.722	40	.130
60	.665	39	.120
59	.613	38	.111
58	.565	37	.102
57	.521	36	.094
56	.480	35	.087
55	.442	34	.080
54	.408	33	.073
53	.376	32	.068
52	.346	31	.062
51	.319	30	.058
50	.294	29	.053
49	.271	28	.049
48	.250	27	.045
47	.230	26	.042
46	.212	25	.038
45	.196		

If the testing age is 65, the factor for a 50-year-old participant is .294. The testing age is the participant's normal retirement age (see Q 10:55) under the plan if the plan provides the same uniform normal retirement age for all participants, or is age 65 if the plan does not provide a uniform normal retirement age—even if the participant is beyond the testing age. For example, if the uniform normal retirement age under the plan is 65 and Bernard is age 70, Bernard's testing age is 65. [Treas Reg § 1.401(a)(4)-12]

Q 2:10 What is a thrift or savings plan?

A thrift or savings plan is a defined contribution plan in which employees are directly involved in contributing toward the ultimate benefits that will be provided. The plan can be in the form of a money purchase pension plan or a profit sharing plan.

These plans are contributory in the sense that employer contributions on behalf of a particular employee are geared to mandatory contributions by the employee. Employees can participate in the plan only if they contribute a part of their compensation to the plan.

Employer contributions are made on a matching basis—for example, 50 percent of the contribution made by the employee. The plan may permit the employer, at its discretion, to make additional contributions and may also permit employees to make voluntary contributions.

A contributory plan must satisfy a new nondiscrimination test that compares the relative contribution percentages of highly compensated employees with those of nonhighly compensated employees (see Q 6:17).

Q 2:11 What is a 401(k) plan?

A 401(k) plan is a qualified profit sharing or stock bonus plan that offers participants an election to receive company contributions in cash or to have these amounts contributed to the plan. A participant in a 401(k) plan does not have to include in income any company contributions to the plan merely because an election could have been made to receive cash instead. [IRC §§ 401(k)(2), 402(a)(8)]

A 401(k) plan may also be in the form of a salary reduction agreement. Under this type of arrangement, each eligible employee may elect to reduce current compensation or elect to forgo a salary increase and have these amounts contributed to the plan. [Treas Reg § 1.401(k)-1(a)(3)(i)]

Benefits attributable to employer contributions to a 401(k) plan generally may not be distributed without penalty until the employee retires, becomes disabled, dies, or reaches age 59½. Contributions made by the employer to the plan at the employee's election are nonforfeitable (i.e., 100 percent vesting is required at all times). For a complete discussion of 401(k) plans, see Chapter 23.

Q 2:12   What is a stock bonus plan?

A stock bonus plan is similar to a profit sharing plan except that benefit payments must be made in stock of the company. However, a stock bonus plan may distribute cash to a participant, subject to the participant's right to demand a distribution of employer securities. Further, if the plan permits cash distributions and the employer securities are not readily tradable on an established market, participants must be given the right to require the company to repurchase the stock it distributes to them under a fair valuation formula. [IRC § 401(a)(23); Treas Reg §§ 1.401-1(a)(2)(iii), 1.401-1(b)(1)(iii)]

Q 2:13   What is an employee stock ownership plan?

An ESOP is a special type of defined contribution plan (usually profit sharing or stock bonus) that can qualify for favorable tax treatment. For a discussion on ESOPs, see Chapter 24.

Q 2:14   What is a simplified employee pension?

A SEP is a defined contribution plan that takes the form of an individual retirement account (IRA) but is subject to special rules. A SEP may be adopted by both incorporated and unincorporated businesses. For a discussion on SEPs, see Chapter 27.

Q 2:15   What is a flat benefit plan?

Under this type of defined benefit plan, the benefit for each participant depends solely on compensation. The following is a typical formula used in a flat benefit plan:

Each participant shall be entitled to a monthly pension, commencing at normal retirement age and thereafter payable for life, of an amount equal to 30 percent of monthly compensation.

Under this formula, a participant whose monthly compensation is $1,000 would receive a monthly pension of $300; a participant whose monthly compensation is $2,000 would receive a monthly pension of twice as much (i.e., $600).

Q 2:16   What is a unit benefit plan?

This type of defined benefit plan recognizes service with the company by providing greater benefits for a long-service employee than for a short-term employee with the same average compensation. The following formula represents a type of unit benefit plan:

Each participant shall be entitled to a monthly pension, commencing at normal retirement age and thereafter payable for life, of an amount equal to one percent of monthly compensation multiplied by the number of years of service with the company.

Under this formula, a participant with a monthly compensation of $1,000 and 30 years of employment at retirement would receive a monthly pension of $300, while a participant with the same monthly compensation but only ten years of employment would receive a monthly pension of $100.

These examples and those in Question 2:15 reflect plan formulas that are not integrated with Social Security. When Social Security integration is considered, differences in compensation become more relevant. See Chapter 7 for more details on this issue.

Q 2:17   How is the cost of providing benefits under a defined benefit plan determined?

The cost of funding the plan (other than a fully insured plan; see Q 2:22) is determined actuarially. An actuary (generally one enrolled under the auspices of the Joint Board for the Enrollment of Actuaries) may take into consideration many factors in determining each year's plan contribution needed to fund the benefits the plan is to provide. [IRC § 412(c)] Among the most common actuarial assumptions are the following:

- Interest
- Mortality
- Employee turnover
- Salary scale

Each individual actuarial assumption is required to be reasonable or, if not, the assumptions, in the aggregate, must result in a total contribution equivalent to that which would be determined if each assumption were reasonable. Also, the actuarial assumptions must, in combination, offer the actuary's best estimate of anticipated experience under the plan (see Q 2:3). [IRC § 412(c)(3); Rhoades, McKee and Boer v United States, No. 1:91:CV:540 (WD Mich 1993); Vinson & Elkins, 99 TC 9 (1992); Citrus Valley Estates, Inc, 99 TC No. 21 (1992); Wachtell, Lipton, Rosen & Katz, 64 TCM 128 (1992); but see Jerome Mirza & Assocs Ltd v United States, 882 F 2d 229 (7th Cir 1989); Ltr Ruls 9226001, 9119007]

Q 2:18   Must the actuarial assumptions be set forth in the plan?

The actuarial assumptions used to determine the cost of funding a defined benefit plan need not be set forth in the plan. However, the actuarial assumptions used to determine the value of a benefit (e.g., postretirement interest and mortality) must be set forth in the plan in a manner that precludes employer discretion. In other words, the lump-sum value of a participant's benefit and the present value of the monthly benefit must be the same (i.e., actuarially equivalent). If the postretirement actuarial assumptions are not specified, the benefits under the defined benefit plan are not considered to be definitely determinable (see Q 2:3). [IRC § 401(a)(25)]

Q 2:19   What is a Keogh plan?

A Keogh, or H.R. 10, plan is a qualified retirement plan maintained by a self-employed individual, either a sole proprietor or a partner. The self-employed individual may take a tax deduction for annual contributions to the plan made on behalf of the individual and on behalf of any eligible employees. A Keogh plan may be either a defined contribution plan (see Q 2:2) or a defined benefit plan (see Q 2:3).

For more details, see Chapter 29.

Q 2:20 What is a floor offset plan?

A floor offset plan is a hybrid arrangement in which the employer maintains a defined benefit plan and a defined contribution plan, and the benefits provided under the defined benefit plan will be reduced by the value of the participant's account in the defined contribution plan. In essence, the defined benefit plan provides a guaranteed floor benefit, but the amount is offset by the benefit provided under the defined contribution plan. [ERISA § 407(d)(9); Treas Reg § 1.401(a)(4)-8(d); Rev Rul 76-259, 1976-2 CB 111]

If the value of the participant's account in the defined contribution plan declines, the participant will be insulated from the risk of investment loss because the full amount of pension benefits will be received under the defined benefit plan. Alternatively, if the value of the participant's account exceeds the amount of the benefit under the defined benefit plan, the participant will receive benefits exclusively from the defined contribution plan. In other words, the participant has the best of both worlds: the participant is protected against any risk of adverse investment experience under the defined benefit plan and receives the favorable investment experience under the defined contribution plan.

The defined contribution plan component of this type of arrangement may be subject to certain restrictions that are not imposed on freestanding defined contribution plans (see Q 19:41).

Q 2:21 What is a cash balance plan?

A cash balance plan is a defined benefit plan (see Q 2:3), but it exhibits features of both defined benefit and defined contribution plans (see Q 2:2). The most recognizable feature of the cash balance plan is its use of a separate account for each participant. A cash balance account is established for each employee upon the employee's becoming a member of the plan. [Treas Reg § 1.401 (a) (4)-8(c) (3)]

If the plan is replacing an existing defined benefit plan, employees are credited with an opening balance, typically the actuarial present value of their accrued prior plan benefits. Thereafter, the employee's cash balance account receives additional credits. These are likely to be computed as a flat percentage of the employee's pay, such as 4 percent or 5 percent. In addition, employees' balances grow based on interest credits. The rate varies from year to year and is communicated to employees before the start of the year. As an example, it might be the yield on one-year Treasury bills. The interest rate is not tied to the actual investment performance of the plan's assets and is determined independently, based on specific provisions in the plan document. The plan may also set forth a minimum and/or maximum rate; but the minimum cannot be more than the lowest standard interest rate, and the maximum cannot be less than the highest standard interest rate. [Treas Reg §§ 1.401 (a) (4)-8(c) (3) (iv) (C), 1.401 (a) (4)-12]

The amounts an employer contributes to the plan are determined actuarially to ensure sufficient funds to provide for the benefits promised by the plan. The minimum funding standards apply to cash balance plans, as is the case with other types of defined benefit plans. [IRC § 412]

From the employee's perspective, one of the cash balance plan's advantages is that investment risks are borne by the employer as in any other defined benefit plan. This differs from a defined contribution plan.

Cash balance plans provide higher benefits for younger employees and lower benefits for older employees, in contrast to traditional defined benefit plans. However, the costs of providing these benefits are also correspondingly higher for younger employees and lower for older employees, as compared with traditional defined benefit plans.

An employee's monthly pension is not determined solely by the amount in the employee's individual account at the time of retirement. If the balance in the account is less than the pension benefit promised, the employee will receive the higher promised benefit. However, if the cash balance account is greater than the promised benefit, the employee will receive a greater monthly benefit.

Q 2:22   What is an insured qualified retirement plan?

An insured plan is a qualified retirement plan that is funded in whole or in part through the purchase of life insurance policies. The plan can be either split-funded or fully insured.

In a split-funded plan, there is partial funding of retirement benefits through insurance policies, with the balance of the retirement benefit coming from an investment fund. The portion of the plan's assets accumulated in the investment fund can be invested as the trustee determines.

In a fully insured plan, all company contributions are directed toward the purchase of insurance, normally in the form of retirement income policies or annuity contracts. One advantage of a fully insured plan is that the plan may qualify for an exemption from the minimum funding requirements (see Q 8:4).

Qualified retirement plans can be attractive vehicles for acquiring life insurance. Premiums indirectly paid by the company in the form of plan contributions are deductible. Each insured participant reports taxable income, as determined under IRS tables, representing the cost of current life insurance protection. For further details, see Chapter 14.

Q 2:23   What is a custom-designed retirement plan?

A custom-designed (or individually designed) retirement plan is a plan tailored to meet the needs of the client. The custom-designed plan reflects the company's desires and needs more fully than a master or prototype (see Q 2:24) because the client has a greater variety of available options.

Q 2:24   What are master and prototype retirement plans?

A master plan is a form of retirement plan in which the funding organization (trust, custodial account, or insurer) is specified in the sponsor's application. A prototype plan is a form of retirement plan in which the funding organization is specified in the adoption agreement.

Insurance companies, mutual funds, banks, brokerage firms, and other investment management firms have created IRS-approved master and prototype plans. The client adopts the plans by executing an adoption agreement and electing certain available options. Any change in the preapproved plan provisions causes the plan to lose its master or prototype status. [Rev Proc 93-10, 1993-5 IRB, Rev Proc 89-9, 1989-1 CB 780]

Q 2:25 How does a company's cash position affect its choice of a qualified retirement plan?

Because adoption of a pension plan entails a commitment to fund the plan even if the company has no profits, a company experiencing a weak cash position would be ill-advised to establish that type of plan. Generally, it does not make good sense for a company to borrow funds to meet its pension obligations. In this situation, a profit sharing plan would be more appropriate.

Q 2:26 What type of retirement plan should a company adopt if profits fluctuate from year to year?

A profit sharing plan is the only type of plan that can afford a company significant flexibility with respect to the contributions it makes from year to year. The typical profit sharing plan—probably more than 95 percent of all profit sharing plans maintained by small companies—specifies that the company's contribution is to be determined annually by its board of directors (or owners, partners, etc., as appropriate). The amount contributed in any year may vary from zero to 15 percent of the total compensation of all plan participants.

Q 2:27 Are profit sharing plans best for small companies?

There is no general answer to this question. The decision about the type of retirement plan best suited for a small company must be made on the basis of all the facts and circumstances, including the owner's goals.

Profit sharing plans are usually recommended for recently formed companies because no profit pattern exists. Often, both a discretionary profit sharing plan and a 10 percent money purchase pension plan are recommended for the company. This combination permits a total contribution of 25 percent of compensation (as opposed to the 15 percent limitation for a profit sharing plan alone), but entails only a 10 percent of compensation commitment by the company, allowing some flexibility. [IRC §§ 404(a)(3)(A), 404(a)(7)]

Remember, however, that a company's size is not always a factor in choosing the best plan. In many cases, a small company may decide to maximize its tax-deductible contributions. For example, a company with an older work force that adopts a defined benefit plan increases the amount of the contribution that must be made each year to fund retirement benefits, which in turn increases the company's tax deduction (see Q 2:28).

Q 2:28   What type of qualified retirement plan is best for a company whose essential employees have reached an advanced age?

For a company whose essential employees have reached an advanced age, a defined benefit plan (see Q 2:3) is a better choice than a defined contribution plan (see Q 2:2) for the following reasons:

1. A defined contribution plan limits the company's tax-deductible contributions on behalf of each employee regardless of age. Except for a target benefit plan (see Q 2:5) and an age-based profit sharing plan (see Q 2:7), age is not a factor in determining the company's contribution or the allocation of the company's contribution to plan participants. Contributions on behalf of older employees are based on the same percentage of compensation as those made on behalf of younger employees. Since contributions are limited, there may not be sufficient time left before retirement to accumulate a desired amount for older employees.

2. A defined benefit plan allows a company with older essential employees to make larger contributions to accumulate sufficient funds for retirement. The limit on contributions under a defined benefit plan is the amount necessary to fund the annual

pension, and this may far exceed the allowable contribution to a defined contribution plan. [IRC §§ 404(a)(1), 415(b), 415(c)]

Q 2:29   How can an ESOP or a stock bonus plan benefit a corporation and its shareholders?

An ESOP (see Q 2:13) or a stock bonus plan (see Q 2:12), like all other qualified retirement plans, must be organized and operated for the exclusive benefit of the employees or their beneficiaries. This does not mean that the company and its shareholders cannot also derive a benefit from the plan. In fact, an ESOP or a stock bonus plan can benefit the company and its shareholders by:

1. Providing a market for the owner's closely held stock as a tax-favored alternative to a stock redemption;
2. Giving the company tax deductions without affecting its cash flow; and
3. Keeping company stock in what is generally considered friendly hands in the event of a hostile takeover of the company.

See Chapter 24 for more details.

Q 2:30   Can the company take Social Security wage tax payments or benefits into consideration in its qualified retirement plan?

Yes. The company can combine (integrate) its qualified retirement plan with Social Security and thereby reduce the cost of maintaining its plan. This is referred to as permitted disparity. For details on how this works, see Chapter 7.

Q 2:31   After an employer has chosen a type of qualified retirement plan, what options are available?

After the employer has determined the most suitable qualified retirement plan, consideration must be given to the actual plan provisions. Among the employer's choices are the following:

1. Eligibility requirements (see Chapter 5), including:
   a. Length of service (Q 5:2)
   b. Minimum age (Q 5:2)
   c. Exclusion of union employees (Q 1:19)
   d. Other classification exclusions (Q 5:18).
2. Contributions or benefits, including:
   a. Defined contribution plan formula
   b. Defined benefit plan formula
   c. Permitted disparity (i.e., integration with Social Security) (Q 7:1)
   d. Voluntary contributions (Q 6:18)
   e. Mandatory contributions (Q 6:17)
   f. Minimum benefits or contributions (Qs 22:37, 22:43)
   g. 401(k) features (Q 23:1).
3. Vesting (see Chapter 9), including:
   a. Cliff vesting
   b. Graded vesting
   c. Full and immediate vesting
   d. Top-heavy vesting (Q 22:32).
4. Investment provisions (see Chapter 19), including:
   a. Participant-directed accounts
   b. Insurance benefits (Q 14:2)
   c. Loan provisions (Qs 13:44–13:48).
5. Methods of payment of benefits, including:
   a. Lump-sum distributions
   b. Annuities
   c. Installment distributions.
6. Miscellaneous provisions, including:
   a. Designation of plan administrator (Q 16:1)
   b. Definition of compensation
   c. Choice of plan year

d. Normal retirement age (Q 10:55)
e. Rollover provision (Q 28:6)
f. Death benefits.

Chapter 3

Highly Compensated Employees

One of the most important terms in the Code is highly compensated employee. The definition of this term is incorporated in many of the nondiscrimination requirements applicable to qualified retirement plans, and is also incorporated in other Code provisions relating to the qualified retirement plan area. This chapter analyzes which employees are considered highly compensated.

Q 3:1 To what qualified retirement plan provisions does the definition of highly compensated employee apply?

The term "highly compensated employee" is relevant in determining if a plan satisfies the general nondiscrimination requirements that apply to all qualified retirement plans (see Q 4:9), the actual deferral percentage test applicable to 401(k) plans (see Q 23:8), the actual contribution percentage test applicable to employer matching contributions and employee contributions (see Q 23:48), certain requirements applicable to SEPs (see Q 27:3), the minimum coverage requirements (see Qs 5:16, 5:17), and the minimum vesting standards (see Q 9:5). The definition also applies in determining if an organization is a member of an affiliated service group (see Q 29:31) and if a loan is exempt from the tax on prohibited transactions (see Q 13:48). [IRC §§ 401(a)(4), 401(a)(5), 401(k)(3), 401(m), 408(k), 410 (b)(1), 411(d)(1), 414(m), 414(q), 4975(d); Temp Reg § 1.414(q)-1T, Q&A 1(b)(1)]

The definition of highly compensated employee is applicable *only* to those qualified retirement plan provisions that incorporate the definition by reference, and the definition does *not* apply to provisions that do not incorporate it. For example, the definition of highly compensated employee generally has no application to the limitation on plan contributions and benefits (see Chapter 6). [IRC § 415; Temp Reg § 1.414(q)-1T, Q&A 1(a) and (b)(2)]

Q 3:2   Who is a highly compensated employee?

Highly compensated employees are divided into two groups: highly compensated active employees (see Q 3:3) and highly compensated former employees (see Q 3:12). In certain circumstances, highly compensated active employees and highly compensated former employees are considered separately in applying the provisions for which the definition of highly compensated employee is applicable (see Q 4:19). [IRC § 414(q); Temp Reg § 1.414(q)-1(T), Q&A 2]

Q 3:3   Who is a highly compensated active employee?

To determine if an employee is a highly compensated active employee for the determination year, two calculations are required: the look-back year calculation and the determination year calculation (see Q 3:11).

For the look-back year calculation, a highly compensated active employee is an employee who performs services for the employer (see Q 3:10) during the determination year, and who during the look-back year:

1. Was a 5 percent owner of the employer (see Q 3:4);

2. Received compensation from the employer of more than $75,000 (see Qs 3:8, 3:9);

3. Received compensation from the employer of more than $50,000 (see Qs 3:8, 3:9) and was a member of the top-paid group (see Q 3:5) of employees; or

4. Was an officer (see Q 3:6) of the employer who received compensation of more than $45,000 (one-half of the defined benefit plan maximum dollar amount; see Qs 3:8, 3:9, 6:8).

For the determination year calculation, an employee is a highly compensated active employee only if, during the determination year, the employee is either (a) a 5 percent owner; or (b) both described in paragraph 2, 3, or 4 above (substituting determination year for look-back year) *and* one of the 100 employees paid the most compensation.

[IRC §§ 414(q)(1), 414(q)(2); Temp Reg § 1.414(a)-1T, Q&A 3(a)]

Example 1. During the years specified below, Jack, who commenced employment with the employer in 1989, was not a 5 percent owner, an officer, or one of the top 100 paid employees; but, during each year, Jack was a member of the top-paid group. For the purpose of this example, the dollar amounts in paragraphs 2, 3, and 4 above are not increased for inflation. For each of the following years, Jack is included in, or excluded from, the highly compensated group as specified below:

Year	Compensation	Status
1989	$45,000	Excluded
1990	$80,000	Excluded
1991	$80,000	Included
1992	$45,000	Included
1993	$45,000	Excluded

For 1989, Jack was excluded because he was not in any of the applicable categories (i.e., paragraphs 1 through 4 above) during the look-back year (1988); for 1990, Jack was excluded because he was not within any of the applicable categories for the look-back year (1989); for 1991, Jack was included because he was described in paragraphs 2 and 3 for the look-back year (1990); for 1992, Jack was included again because he was described in paragraphs 2 and 3 for the look-back year (1991); but, for 1993, Jack again became excluded because he was not in any of the applicable categories for the look-back year (1992).

Example 2. The facts are the same as in Example 1, except that Jack was one of the top 100 paid employees in 1990 and 1993. For

1990, Jack is included because he was described in paragraphs 2 and 3 for the determination year (1990) and was one of the top 100 paid employees that year. In 1993, even though Jack was in the top 100 that year, he would still be excluded because he was not described in paragraph 2, 3, or 4 for the look-back year (1992) or the determination year (1993).

[Temp Reg § 1.414(q)-1T, Q&A 3(e)]

Q 3:4 Who is a 5 percent owner?

An employee is a 5 percent owner of the employer for the determination or look-back year (see Q 3:11) if, at any time during the year, the employee is a 5 percent owner for top-heavy plan purposes (see Q 22:28). [IRC §§ 414(q)(3), 416(i)(1)(B)(i)]

If the employer is not a corporation, the ownership test is applied to the person's capital or profits interest in the employer. In determining ownership percentages, each employer, whether related or unrelated (see Q 5:30), is treated as a separate entity. For example, an individual who is a 5 percent owner of a subsidiary corporation that is part of a controlled group of corporations (see Q 5:32) is treated as a 5 percent owner for purposes of determining which employees are highly compensated employees (see Q 3:2). [Temp Reg § 1.414(q)-1T, Q&A 8]

Q 3:5 What is the top-paid group?

An employee is in the top-paid group of employees for the determination or look-back year (see Q 3:11) if the employee is in the group consisting of the top 20 percent of the employer's employees when ranked on the basis of compensation (see Q 3:8) received from the employer (see Q 3:10) during the year. The identification of the employees who are in the top-paid group for a year involves a two-step procedure:

1. The determination of the number of employees that corresponds to 20 percent of the employer's employees; and

2. The identification of the employees who are among the number of employees who receive the most compensation during the year.

Employees who perform no services for the employer during the year are not included in making either of these determinations. [IRC § 414(q)(4); Temp Reg § 1.414(q)-1T, Q&A 9(a)]

For purposes of determining the number of employees in the top-paid group for a year, the following employees are excluded:

1. Employees who have not completed 6 months of service by the end of the year;
2. Employees who normally work less than 17½ hours per week during the year;
3. Employees who normally work 6 months or less during any year;
4. Employees who are not age 21 by the end of the year; and
5. Certain nonresident aliens.

Union employees (see Qs 1:19, 4:5) are excluded only if they constitute 90 percent of the employer's work force and the retirement plan covers only nonunion employees. Including union employees has the effect of expanding the number of employees in the top-paid group. [IRC §§ 414(q)(8), 414(q)(11); Temp Reg § 1.414(q)-1T, Q&A 9(b)(1)]

The employer may elect to reduce the period of service or lower the age specified above, including a zero service or age requirement, provided the election applies to all plans of the employer. [IRC § 414(q)(8); Temp Reg. § 1.414(q)-1T, Q&A 9(b)(2)]

Q 3:6   Who is an officer?

To determine if an employee is an officer of the employer for highly compensated employee purposes (see Q 3:3), the same general test used in determining who is an officer for top-heavy plan purposes is applied (see Q 22:25). [IRC § 414(q)(1)(D); Temp Reg § 1.414(q)-1T, Q&A 10(a)]

For an officer to be a member of the group of highly compensated employees, the officer must receive compensation (see Q 3:8) during the determination year or look-back year (see Q 3:11) that is more than one-half of the defined benefit plan maximum dollar amount (see Qs 3:9, 6:8). If no officer satisfies the compensation requirement, the highest paid officer for the year is treated as a highly compensated employee by reason of being an officer without regard to the amount of compensation. This is true whether or not the employee is also a highly compensated employee on any other basis. For example, if no officer of the employer meets the compensation requirement and an employee is both the highest paid officer and a 5 percent owner (see Qs 3:3, 3:4), the employee is treated as an includible officer for this minimum inclusion rule. [IRC § 414(q)(5)(B); Temp Reg § 1.414(q)-1T, Q&A 10(a) and (c)]

The number of employees that can be considered officers is equal to 10 percent of all employees, or three, whichever is greater. In no case, however, can the total number of officers exceed 50. Thus, if the employer has fewer than 30 employees, no more than three can be considered officers. [IRC § 414(q)(5)(A); Temp Reg § 1.414(q)-1T, Q&A 10(b)]

Q 3:7 Can an employee be described in more than one highly compensated employee category?

Yes. An individual who is a highly compensated active employee (see Q 3:3) for a determination year (see Q 3:11) by reason of being described in one category, during either the look-back year (see Q 3:11) or the determination year, is not disregarded in determining whether another individual is a highly compensated active employee by reason of being described in another category. An individual who is a highly compensated active employee for a determination year by reason of being a 5 percent owner (see Q 3:4) during that year, and who receives compensation in excess of $50,000 (see Qs 3:8, 3:9) during both the look-back year and the determination year, is taken into account in determining the group of employees who are highly compensated active employees for the determination year by reason of (1) receiving more than $50,000 and (2) being in the top-paid group (see Q 3:5) during either or both the look-back year or the determination year. [Temp Reg § 1.414(q)-1T, Q&A 3(d)]

Example. Elaine is the sole shareholder and officer of The Pearlmans of Wisdom, Inc. and, in 1993, earns $200,000. There are nine other employees, and the two next highly compensated are Fred ($95,000) and Tami ($70,000). Even though Elaine is a highly compensated active employee by reason of being a 5 percent owner, she is not disregarded for purposes of determining the top-paid group. Consequently, Tami is not a highly compensated active employee even though she earns more than $50,000 (adjusted for inflation) because she is not in the top-paid group.

Q 3:8 How is compensation defined for purposes of determining who is a highly compensated employee?

The definition of compensation is the same as is used for purposes of the annual addition limitation applicable to defined contribution plans (see Q 6:3). However, in addition, elective or salary reduction contributions to a 401(k) plan (see Q 23:13), a cafeteria plan, or a tax-sheltered annuity are included. Only compensation received by an employee during the determination year or during the look-back year (see Q 3:11) is considered in determining whether the employee is a highly compensated employee under either the look-back year calculation or the determination year calculation (see Q 3:3). Compensation is not annualized for purposes of determining an employee's compensation in the determination year or the look-back year. [IRC § 414(q)(7); Temp Reg § 1.414(q)-1T, Q&A 13]

Example. Janeth earns $5,000 a month and is employed for five months during 1993. Janeth's compensation for 1993 is $25,000 and not $60,000 ($5,000 × 12).

Q 3:9 Are the highly compensated employee dollar thresholds adjusted for inflation?

Yes. The dollar amounts in paragraphs 2, 3, and 4 of Question 3:3 are adjusted for inflation. The first adjustment occurred in 1989, and the adjusted amounts are:

Year	Paragraph 2 Amount	Paragraph 3 Amount	Paragraph 4 Amount
1993	$96,368	$64,245	$57,821
1992	$93,518	$62,345	$56,111
1991	$90,803	$60,535	$54,482
1990	$85,485	$56,990	$51,291
1989	$81,720	$54,480	$49,032

[IR 93-2 (Jan 15, 1993); IRC § 414(q)(1); Temp Reg § 1.414(q)-1T, Q&A 3(c)(1)]

The applicable dollar amount for a determination year or look-back year (see Q 3:11) is the dollar amount for the calendar year in which the determination year or look-back year begins. The dollar amount for purposes of determining the highly compensated active employees (see Q 3:3) for a particular look-back year is based on the calendar year in which this look-back year begins, not the calendar year in which the look-back year ends or in which the determination year with respect to that look-back year begins. [Temp Reg § 1.414(q)-1T, Q&A 3(c)(2)]

Q 3:10   Who is the employer for purposes of determining highly compensated employees?

The employer is the entity employing the employees and includes all other entities aggregated with the employing entity under the aggregation rules. The following entities must be treated as a single employer for purposes of determining the employees who are highly compensated employees (see Q 3:2):

1. All corporations that are members of a controlled group of corporations that includes the employing entity (see Q 5:32). [IRC § 414(b)]

2. All trades or businesses (whether or not incorporated) that are under common control, which group includes the employing entity (see Q 5:30). [IRC § 414(c)]

3. All organizations (whether or not incorporated) that are members of an affiliated service group that includes the employing entity (see Q 29:31). [IRC § 414(m)]

4. Any other entities required to be aggregated with the employing entity pursuant to Section 414(o). [IRC § 414(q)(10); Temp Reg § 1.414(q)-1T, Q&A 6(a)]

The separate lines of business rules (see Q 5:33) do not apply in determining the group of highly compensated employees; an employer with separate lines of business is still treated as a single employer. [IRC § 414(r); Temp Reg § 1.414(q)-1T, Q&A 6(c)]

Q 3:11 What are the determination year and the look-back year?

The determination year is generally the plan year, and the look-back year is the 12-month period immediately preceding the determination year. [Temp Reg § 1.414(q)-1T, Q&A 14]

Example. The Rube Corporation has two qualified retirement plans, Plan R and Plan J. If Plan R has a calendar year plan year and Plan J has a July 1 to June 30 plan year, the determination year calculation and look-back year calculation for Plan R are made on the basis of the calendar year, and the determination year calculation and look-back year calculation for Plan J are made on the basis of the July 1 to June 30 year.

Q 3:12 Who is a highly compensated former employee?

A highly compensated former employee for a determination year (see Q 3:11) is a former employee who had a separation year prior to the determination year and was a highly compensated active employee (see Q 3:3) for either (1) the employee's separation year or (2) any determination year ending on or after the employee's 55th birthday. The separation year generally is the determination year during which the employee separates from service with the employer. For example, an employee who is a highly compensated active employee for the employee's separation year is a highly compensated former employee for determination years after the separation year. Under an alternative rule, the employer may elect to include as a highly compensated former employee any former employee who separated from service prior to 1987 and was either a 5 percent owner (see Q 3:4) or received compensation (see Q 3:8) in excess of $50,000 in the year of separation or any determination year ending on or after the employee attained age 55. [IRC § 414(q)(9); Temp Reg §§ 1.414(q)-1T, Q&A 4(a), Q&A 4(d), and Q&A 5]

The term "highly compensated former employee" is relevant only if a provision of the Code makes a specific reference to the term (see Q 4:19). [Temp Reg § 1.414(q)-1T, Q&A 4(e)(1)]

Q 3:13   Who is a nonhighly compensated employee?

A nonhighly compensated employee is any employee who is not a highly compensated employee (see Q 3:2). Therefore, a nonhighly compensated active employee is an employee who is not a highly compensated active employee (see Q 3:3), and a nonhighly compensated former employee is an employee who is not a highly compensated former employee (see Q 3:12).

Q 3:14   Does a family aggregation rule apply?

Yes. If an individual, during the determination year or look-back year (see Q 3:11), is a member of the family of either (1) a 5 percent owner (see Q 3:4) who is an active or former employee, or (2) a highly compensated employee (see Q 3:2) who is one of the ten most highly compensated employees, the individual is not considered a separate employee and any compensation paid to such individual (and any plan contribution or benefit of such individual) is treated as if it were paid to the 5 percent owner or highly compensated employee. [IRC §§ 414(q)(6)(A), 414(q)(6)(C); Temp Reg § 1.414(q)-1T, Q&A 11(a)]

The determination of which employees are highly compensated employees, which highly compensated employees are among the ten most highly compensated employees, the number and identity of employees in the top-paid group (see Q 3:5), and the identity of individuals in the top 100 (see Q 3:3) employees is made prior to the application of the family aggregation rule. [Temp Reg § 1.414(q)-1T, Q&A 11(c)]

Individuals who are family members include the employee's spouse and lineal ascendants or descendants and the spouses of such lineal ascendants and descendants. If an individual is a family member on any day during the year, the individual is treated as a family member for the entire year so that, if an individual is a family member on the first day of a year, the individual continues to be a family member throughout the year even if the relationship changes as a result of death or divorce. [IRC § 414(q)(6)(B); Temp Reg § 1.414(q)-1T, Q&A 12]

> **Example.** Irv is the sole shareholder and an employee of Le Group Singer, Inc. Among its other employees are his wife, Iris, and his children, Adam, Jonathan, and Jennifer. Irv and his four family members are treated as a single employee.

Q 3:15   How will the Tax Simplification Bill of 1993 affect the determination of highly compensated employees?

If enacted, TSB '93 (see Q 1:13) will simplify the definition of a highly compensated employee. The term will mean any employee who (1) was a 5 percent owner (see Q 3:4) during the determination year or the look-back year (see Q 3:11), or (2) received compensation (see Q 3:8) during the look-back year of more than $50,000 (adjusted for inflation). If no employee comes within the new definition, the highest paid officer (see Q 3:6) will be treated as a highly compensated employee. In addition, the family aggregation rule (see Q 3:14) would be repealed. These changes would be effective for plan years beginning *after* 1993. [TSB '93, Act § 221]

Chapter 4

Requirements for Qualification

A company's retirement plan will receive favorable tax treatment only if the plan is qualified. The Code sets out a host of requirements that a retirement plan must meet in order to qualify. This chapter analyzes those requirements.

Q 4:1 What basic requirements must all retirement plans meet to qualify for favorable tax treatment?

The four fundamental requirements for a qualified retirement plan are the following:

1. The plan must be a definite written program.
2. The plan must be communicated to the employees.
3. The plan must be permanent.
4. The plan must prohibit the use or diversion of funds for purposes other than the exclusive benefit of employees or their beneficiaries.

[IRC §§ 401(a)(1), 401(a)(2); Treas Reg §§ 1.401-1, 1.401-2]

When a retirement plan made 22 unsecured loans, representing 75 percent of plan assets, to the sole shareholder of the employer and the sole trustee of the plan over a two-year period, IRS ruled that the loans violated the exclusive benefit rule. IRS has also ruled that an ESOP (see Q 24:1) that permits a trustee to consider *nonfinancial* employment-related factors, such as continuing job security and employment opportunities, before acting upon tender offers violates the exclusive benefit rule. [Ltr Rul 9145006; GCM 39870]

The following requirements must also be met before a retirement plan qualifies for favorable tax treatment:

1. The plan must satisfy minimum coverage and minimum participation requirements. For details, see Chapter 5. [IRC §§ 401(a)(3), 401(a)(26)]

2. Contributions or benefits under the plan may not discriminate in favor of highly compensated employees (see Q 3:2). For details, see Questions 4:9 through 4:23. [IRC § 401(a)(4)]

3. The plan must meet requirements for the vesting of benefits. For details, see Chapter 9. [IRC § 401(a)(7)]

4. The plan must provide for required minimum distribution of benefits. For details, see Chapter 11. [IRC § 401(a)(9)]

5. Additional requirements apply to top-heavy plans. These additional requirements include minimum vesting rules and, for employees who are not key employees, minimum benefits and/or minimum contributions. A retirement plan can qualify only if it contains provisions satisfying the top-heavy plan requirements that automatically take effect if the plan becomes top-heavy. For details, see Chapter 22. [IRC § 401(a)(10)(B)]

6. With few exceptions, plans must provide for the payment of benefits in the form of a joint and survivor lifetime annuity, and death benefits in the form of a preretirement survivor annuity. For details, see Chapter 10. [IRC § 401(a)(11)]

7. The plan must provide that benefits may not be assigned or alienated. For details, see Question 4:24. [IRC § 401(a)(13)]

8. The plan must comply with rules regarding the commencement of benefit payments. For details, see Question 10:53. [IRC § 401(a)(14)]

9. The plan must limit the contributions that can be made to the plan on behalf of an employee (in the case of a defined contribution plan) or it must limit the benefits that can be paid to an employee (in the case of a defined benefit plan). For details, see Chapter 6. [IRC § 401(a)(16)]

10. The plan must impose a $200,000 cap (subject to cost-of-living adjustments that began in 1990) on the amount of compensation that can be taken into account (see Q 6:21). [IRC § 401(a)(17)]

11. A defined benefit plan must specify the actuarial assumptions that are used to determine the value of a benefit (see Q 2:18). [IRC § 401(a)(25)]

12. The plan must permit certain types of distributions to be made by a direct trustee-to-trustee transfer to another eligible retirement plan. For details, see Questions 28:8–28:29. [IRC § 401(a)(31), as added by UC '92, Act § 522]

Q 4:2 Does a 401(k) plan qualify for favorable tax treatment?

Yes, provided certain special requirements are met in addition to the regular retirement plan qualification requirements. For details, see Chapter 23.

Q 4:3 Can an oral trust created in a state that recognizes its validity be used for a qualified retirement plan?

No. Since a qualified retirement plan must be a definite written program (see Q 4:1), an oral trust, which may be valid under local law, will not meet the Code requirements for favorable tax treatment. [Rev Rul 69-231, 1969-1 CB 118; Attardo, 62 TCM 313 (1991)]

Q 4:4 Can a trust that is not valid under local law be part of a qualified retirement plan?

No. Contributions to a qualified retirement plan's trust must be made to a trust that is valid under local law. [Rev Rul 69-231, 1969-1 CB 118; Rev Rul 81-114, 1981-1 CB 207]

Q 4:5 Must all qualified retirement plans have trustees?

No. The most common type of qualified retirement plan that has no trustee is an annuity plan funded solely through contracts issued by an insurance company (see Q 2:22).

Q 4:6   Does a retirement plan have to be submitted to IRS for approval?

A retirement plan may qualify for tax-favored status without first being submitted to IRS. Nevertheless, it is prudent to submit the retirement plan for IRS approval since this is the most important step that can be taken to preserve a retirement plan's qualified status. If, upon review of the application for a determination letter, IRS finds defects in the retirement plan, the timely filing of the application allows the plan to be corrected retroactively (see Q 4:7). The procedure for submitting a retirement plan to IRS is discussed in Chapter 15. [IRC § 401(b); Treas Reg § 1.401(b)-1]

There is another reason for applying for a determination letter from IRS with regard to the initial qualification of a retirement plan. If IRS does not approve the retirement plan, the employer may recover its contribution only if the employer made a timely request for the determination. In that case, the return of the employer's contribution must be made within one year after receipt of the adverse determination. [ERISA § 403(c)(2)(B); Rev Rul 60-276, 1960-2 CB 150]

Q 4:7   Even if a retirement plan is not submitted to IRS for approval, must it nevertheless be amended periodically?

Yes. A retirement plan must be amended to comply with changes in laws, regulations, and rulings that affect retirement plans in general, or the specific type of retirement plan in particular, even if it is not submitted to IRS for approval. A retirement plan's qualification can be revoked if the employer fails to make required plan amendments timely to comply with changes in law, even if such changes would not affect the operation of the plan. [Mills, Mitchell & Turner, TCM 1993-99; Hamlin Development Company, TCM 1993-89; Kollipara Rajsheker, MD, Inc, 64 TCM 1153 (1992); Attardo, 62 TCM 313 (1991); Stark Truss Company, Inc, 62 TCM 169 (1991); Basch Eng'g, Inc, 59 TCM 482 (1990); Halligan, 51 TCM 1203 (1986); Bollinger, 77 TC 1353 (1981); Tionesta Sand & Gravel, Inc, 73 TC 758 (1980)] (See also Qs 13:23, 28:37.)

The Voluntary Compliance Resolution Program (VCRP) introduced by IRS in 1992 applies to a plan *only* if it has received a favorable determination letter for TEFRA, TRA '84, and REA (see Qs 1:10, 15:17).

Formal amendments required as a result of TRA '86 (and other laws) need not be made until the last day of the plan year beginning in 1994. However, retirement plans must operate in conformity with the new rules as of each rule's effective date; and plan amendments, when made, must be retroactive to the applicable effective date. [Notice 92-36, 1992-2 CB 364; Ann 92-81, 1992-22 IRB 56; Ann 92-29, 1992-9 IRB 37; IRS Field Office Directive on Good-Faith Compliance (June 12, 1992)]

Q 4:8 May an employee's benefits be reduced after retirement to reflect Social Security benefit increases?

No. A qualified retirement plan must provide that benefits cannot be reduced because of increases in Social Security benefits or wage base levels after (1) benefit payments commence to a participant or beneficiary or (2) a participant who has vested benefits under the plan separates from service. [IRC § 401(a)(15)]

Q 4:9 What is the general nondiscrimination rule that applies to every qualified retirement plan?

A retirement plan is a qualified plan only if the contributions or the benefits provided under the plan do not discriminate in favor of highly compensated employees (see Q 3:2). A plan will satisfy this nondiscrimination rule only if it complies *both* in form and in operation with the requirements promulgated by IRS. [IRC § 401(a)(4); Treas Reg § 1.401(a)(4)-1(a)]

There are three requirements a plan must meet to satisfy the nondiscrimination rule. The first requirement is that either the contributions or the benefits provided in the plan must be nondiscriminatory in amount (see Q 4:10). A plan generally is permitted to satisfy this requirement on the basis of either contributions or benefits, regardless of whether the plan is a defined contribution plan (see Q 2:2) or a defined benefit plan (see Q 2:3). Thus, a plan is *not* required to establish nondiscrimination in amount with respect to both the contributions and the benefits provided. [Treas Reg § 1.401(a)(4)-1(b)(2)(i)]

The second requirement is that the benefits, rights, and features provided under the plan must be available to participants in a nondiscriminatory manner (see Q 4:18). The benefits, rights, and features subject to this requirement are the optional forms of benefit (e.g., retirement annuities and single-sum payments), ancillary benefits (e.g., disability benefits), and other rights and features (e.g., loans and investment options) available to participants. [Treas Reg § 1.401(a)(4)-1(b)(3)]

The third requirement is that the effect of plan amendments, including grants of past service credit, and of plan terminations must be nondiscriminatory (see Q 4:19). [Treas Reg § 1.401(a)(4)-1(b)(4)]

Q 4:10   What does nondiscrimination in amount of contributions or benefits mean?

The first requirement a retirement plan must satisfy is that either the contributions (see Q 4:11) or the benefits (see Q 4:13) provided under the plan must be nondiscriminatory in amount. [Treas Reg §§ 1.401(a)(4)-2, 1.401(a)(4)-3]

A defined contribution plan (see Q 2:2) generally will satisfy the nondiscriminatory amount requirement by showing that the *contributions* provided under the plan are nondiscriminatory in amount. However, a defined contribution plan also is permitted to satisfy the nondiscriminatory amount requirement by showing that the *equivalent benefits* provided under the plan are nondiscriminatory in amount (see Q 4:20). 401(k) plans are deemed to satisfy this requirement because such a plan must contain a qualified cash-or-deferred arrangement which incorporates a nondiscriminatory amount requirement; however, plans providing for employee or matching contributions must satisfy special rules (see Chapter 23). [Treas Reg § 1.401(a)(4)-1(b)(2)(ii)(B)]

A defined benefit plan (see Q 2:3) generally will satisfy the nondiscriminatory amount requirement by showing that the employer-provided *benefits* under the plan are nondiscriminatory in amount. However, a defined benefit plan also is permitted to satisfy the nondiscriminatory amount requirement by showing that the *equivalent contributions* provided under the plan are nondiscriminatory in amount (see Q 4:20).

Plans may use certain alternative methods to demonstrate that contributions or benefits are nondiscriminatory in amount.

Q 4:11 How is the nondiscrimination in amount of contributions requirement satisfied?

To determine whether the contributions provided under a defined contribution plan (see Q 2:2) are nondiscriminatory in amount (see Q 4:10), two safe harbor tests are permitted. [Treas Reg § 1.401(a)(4)-2(b)(1)]

The first safe harbor is design based. A defined contribution plan complies with this safe harbor if the plan allocates all employer contributions and forfeitures (see Q 9:17) for the plan year under a single uniform formula that allocates to each participant the same percentage of compensation, the same dollar amount, or the same dollar amount for each uniform unit of service (not to exceed one week) performed by the participant. Differences in allocations attributable to permitted disparity (see Chapter 7) do not cause the plan to fail to satisfy this safe harbor. The following is an example of a defined contribution plan formula that satisfies this safe harbor:

> The company shall contribute each plan year during which the plan is in effect on behalf of each participant an amount equal to 10 percent of compensation.

[Treas Reg § 1.401(a)(4)-2(b)(2)]

The second safe harbor permits a defined contribution plan to have a uniform allocation formula weighted for age or service if the average rate of allocations for highly compensated employees (see Q 3:2) under the plan does not exceed the average rate of allocations for nonhighly compensated employees (see Q 3:13) under the plan. A single uniform formula weighted for age or service is one that would allocate to each participant the same percentage of compensation or the same dollar amount if every participant was the same age and had the same number of years of service or plan participation. A uniform allocation formula need not grant points for both age and service, but must grant points for at least one of them. If points are granted for years of service, the number of years taken into account may be limited to a maximum number. Plans using this second safe harbor need not grant points for units of compensation, but, if the allocation formula takes compensation into account, the plan must provide the same number of points for each unit of compensation, and each unit of compensation must not exceed $200. This type of plan is known as a uniform points plan.

> **Example.** KSL Corporation adopts a profit sharing plan that allocates its plan contribution among the participants based on points awarded to each participant. Each participant is awarded one point for each $200 of compensation earned during the plan year and ten points for each year of service with KSL. The contributions allocated to highly compensated employees average 8 percent of compensation, and the allocations to the nonhighly compensated employees average 10 percent of compensation. The second safe harbor is satisfied.

[Treas Reg § 1.401(a)(4)-2(b)(3)]

The safe harbors are available even though the plan contains, in addition to other permitted provisions, the following provisions:

1. The plan limits allocations to employees in accordance with Section 415 (see Chapter 6).
2. The plan limits allocations otherwise provided under the formula to a maximum dollar amount or a maximum percentage of compensation, or limits the dollar amount of compensation or the number of years of service or plan participation taken into account in determining the amount of allocations.
3. The plan provides that an allocation to an employee for the plan year is conditioned on the employee's employment on the last day of the plan year or on the employee's completion of a minimum number of hours of service during the plan year (not to exceed 1,000).

[Treas Reg § 1.401(a)(4)-2(b)(4)]

Plans that do not satisfy either of the safe harbors must satisfy the general test for nondiscrimination in the amount of contributions (see Q 4:12).

Q 4:12 Is there a general test for the nondiscrimination in amount of contributions requirement?

Plans that do not satisfy either of the safe harbors (see Q 4:11) generally comply with this nondiscrimination requirement only if each rate group under the plan satisfies the minimum coverage requirements (see Q 5:15). Each rate group consists of a highly compensated employee (see Q 3:2) participating in the plan and all other participants (both highly and nonhighly compensated) who have an allocation rate greater than or equal to that highly compensated employee's allocation rate. In determining allocation rates, permitted disparity may be taken into account. [Treas Reg § 1.401(a)(4)-2(c)(1)]

The allocation rate for an employee equals the sum of the allocations to the employee's account for the plan year expressed either as a percentage of compensation or as a dollar amount. The amounts taken into account in determining allocation rates include all employer contributions and forfeitures that are allocated to the employee's account for the plan year. [Treas Reg § 1.401(a)(4)-2(c)(2)]

For purposes of determining whether a rate group satisfies the minimum coverage requirements, the rate group is treated as if it were a separate plan that benefits only the employees included in the rate group for the plan year. Generally, the rules that apply in determining whether a rate group satisfies the minimum coverage requirements are the same as apply in determining whether a plan satisfies those requirements. For example, if the rate group does not satisfy the ratio percentage test (see Q 5:16), the rate group must satisfy the average benefit test (see Q 5:17). [Treas Reg §§ 1.401(a)(4)-2(c)(3), 1.401(a)(4)-2(c)(4)]

Example 1. (a) Employer Y has only six nonexcludible employees, all of whom benefit under Plan D. The highly compensated employees are H1 and H2, and the nonhighly compensated employees are N1 through N4. For the 1994 plan year, H1 and N1 through N4 have an allocation rate of 5 percent of plan year compensation. For the same plan year, H2 has an allocation rate of 7.5 percent of plan year compensation.

(b) There are two rate groups under Plan D. Rate group 1 consists of H1 and all those employees who have an allocation rate greater than or equal to H1's allocation rate (5 percent). Thus, rate group 1 consists of H1, H2, and N1 through N4. Rate group 2 consists only of H2 because no other employee has an allocation rate greater than or equal to H2's allocation rate (7.5 percent).

(c) The ratio percentage for rate group 2 is zero percent; i.e., zero percent (the percentage of all nonhighly compensated excludible employees who are in the rate group) divided by 50 percent (the percentage of all highly compensated nonexcludible employees who are in the rate group). Therefore, rate group 2 does not satisfy the ratio percentage test. Rate group 2 also does not satisfy the nondiscriminatory classification test and, therefore, does not satisfy the minimum coverage requirements. As a result, Plan D does not satisfy the general test even though the ratio percentage for rate group 1 is 100 percent.

Example 2. (a) The facts are the same as in Example 1, except that N4 has an allocation rate of 8 percent.

(b) There are two rate groups in Plan D. Rate group 1 consists of H1 and all those employees who have an allocation rate greater than or equal to H1's allocation rate (5 percent). Thus rate group 1 consists of H1, H2, and N1 through N4. Rate group 2 consists of H2 and all those employees who have an allocation rate greater than or equal to H2's allocation rate (7.5 percent). Thus, rate group 2 consists of H2 and N4.

(c) Rate group 1 satisfies the ratio percentage test because the ratio percentage of the rate group is 100 percent; i.e., 100 percent (the percentage of all nonhighly compensated nonexcludible employees who are in the rate group) divided by 100 percent (the percentage of all highly compensated nonexcludible employees who are in the rate group).

(d) Rate group 2 does not satisfy the ratio percentage test because the ratio percentage of the rate group is 50 percent, i.e., 25 percent (the percentage of all nonhighly compensated nonexcludible employees who are in the rate group) divided by 50 percent (the percentage of all highly compensated nonexcludible employees who are in the rate group).

(e) However, rate group 2 does satisfy the nondiscriminatory classification test because the ratio percentage of the rate group

(50 percent) is greater than the safe harbor percentage applicable to the plan (45.5 percent).

(f) If rate group 2 satisfies the average benefit percentage test, then rate group 2 satisfies the minimum coverage requirements. In that case, Plan D satisfies the general test because each rate group under the plan satisfies the minimum coverage requirements.

Q 4:13   How is the nondiscrimination in amount of benefits requirement satisfied?

The basic rules for determining whether a plan is nondiscriminatory with respect to the amount of benefits generally apply to defined benefit plans (see Q 2:3). They may, however, also be applied to defined contribution plans (see Q 2:2) in testing nondiscrimination on the basis of equivalent benefits (see Qs 4:10, 4:20). [Treas Reg § 1.401(a)(4)-3(a)]

There are five safe harbors under which a plan is considered nondiscriminatory with respect to the amount of benefits (see Qs 4:14–4:16). Four of the safe harbors are design based and require no determination or comparison of actual benefits under the plan. All of the safe harbors require that the plan have a uniform benefit formula, that each subsidized optional form of benefit (see Q 10:42) be provided on similar terms to substantially all participants, that the plan not require employee contributions, that the plan have a uniform normal retirement age for all employees, and that each employee's benefit be accrued over the same years of service that are taken into account in applying the plan's benefit formula to that employee. The definition of uniform normal retirement age has been expanded to provide generally that a plan's normal retirement provisions will not fail to be uniform merely because benefits commence on different dates for different employees, provided that each employee's normal retirement date does not differ by more than six months from a uniform normal retirement age. [Treas Reg §§ 1.401(a)(4)-3(b)(2), 1.401(a)(4)-12]

Plans that do not satisfy any of the five safe harbors must satisfy the general test for nondiscrimination in the amount of benefits (see Q 4:17).

The safe harbors are available even though the plan contains, in addition to other permitted provisions, the following:

1. The plan provides for benefits that were previously accrued under a formula that does not satisfy any of the safe harbors.

2. The plan limits accruals in accordance with Section 415 (see Chapter 6) or provides for increases in accrued benefits based solely on adjustments to the dollar limitation.

3. The plan limits accruals to a maximum dollar amount or a maximum percentage of compensation or limits the dollar amount of compensation or the number of years of service or participation taken into account in determining the amount of accruals.

4. The plan takes permitted disparity into account (see Chapter 7).

[Treas Reg §§ 1.401(a)(4)-3(b)(6)]

Q 4:14   What safe harbors apply to unit credit plans for the requirement of nondiscrimination in amount of benefits?

The first two safe harbors enable *unit credit plans* (see Q 2:16) to satisfy the nondiscrimination requirement with respect to the amount of benefits on the basis of plan design. A unit credit plan is a defined benefit plan (see Q 2:3) that contains a formula under which all employees accrue a fixed benefit (either as a percentage of compensation or as a dollar amount) for each year of service, and all employees with the same number of years accrue the same benefit. For example, a plan constitutes a unit credit plan for this purpose if it provides a benefit of (1) 1 percent of final average compensation (see Q 7:23) times years of service up to 20, and (2) 1.25 percent of final average compensation times years of service in excess of 20 but not in excess of 30.

The first safe harbor applies to unit credit plans that accrue benefits under the 133⅓ percent rule (i.e., the benefit accrued in a plan year does not exceed by more than 133⅓ percent the benefit accrued in any prior plan year). [IRC § 411(b)(1)(B); Treas Reg § 1.401(a)(4)-3(b)(3)(i)]

Example. Plan A provides a specific annual accrual for each employee in the plan payable at normal retirement age. For each of the first five years of service, the annual accrual is 1.5 percent of compensation. For the next five years of service, the annual accrual is 1.75 percent; and, for each additional year of service, the annual accrual is 2 percent. Plan A satisfies this safe harbor because the benefit accrued in a later year (2 percent) does not exceed the lowest benefit accrual in a prior year (1.5 percent) by more than 133⅓ percent (1.5% × 133⅓% = 2%).

The second safe harbor applies to unit credit plans that accrue benefits under the fractional rule; that is, the employee's accrued benefit (see Q 9:2) as of a given year equals the benefit projected as of normal retirement age (see Q 10:55) multiplied by the ratio of the employee's years of service as of the year to the employee's projected years of service as of normal retirement age. [IRC § 411(b)(1)(C)]

A plan under which benefits are calculated under a unit credit formula but accrue under the fractional accrual rule may also satisfy the unit credit safe harbor even though all employees with the same number of years of service may not accrue the same benefit. Such a plan satisfies the safe harbor only if the benefit (expressed as a percentage of compensation or a dollar amount) that any employee may accrue in any year is not more than one-third larger than the benefit that any other employee can accrue (disregarding employees with more than 33 years of projected service under the plan). [Treas Reg § 1.401(a)(4)-3(b)(4)(i)(C)(1)]

Example. Plan B provides for a benefit equal to 1.6 percent of compensation times each year of service up to 25. Plan B further provides that the plan benefits accrue under the fractional rule. The greatest benefit that an employee can earn in any one year is 1.6 percent of compensation(this is the case for any employee in the plan who will have 25 or fewer years of projected service at normal retirement age). The lowest benefit that will accrue for an employee in the plan with no more than 33 projected years of service is 1.212 percent (this is the case for any employee in the plan with 33 years of projected service under the formula: 1.6% × 25 ÷ 33). Since 1.6 percent is not more than one-third larger than 1.212 percent, Plan B satisfies this safe harbor.

Q 4:15   What safe harbors apply to flat benefit plans for the requirement of nondiscrimination in amount of benefits?

The third safe harbor is a design-based safe harbor for *flat benefit plans* (see Q 2:15) that satisfy the fractional accrual rule (for example, a defined benefit plan (see Q 2:3) that provides a benefit of 50 percent of compensation, accrued ratably over all years of service). Such a plan satisfies the safe harbor only if the plan provides that the maximum flat benefit will be accrued over a period of at least 25 years. The 25-year rule reduces the potential differences in the rates at which benefits accrue between those employees who enter the plan at younger ages and those who enter at older ages. In this way, this safe harbor applies nondiscrimination rules to flat benefit plans in a manner that takes into account the rate of benefit accrual.

The 25-year rule does not mean, however, that an employee must participate in a plan for 25 years to accrue the maximum annual retirement benefit (see Q 6:8). Rather, the maximum annual retirement benefit can be accrued in less than 25 years if the plan formula would produce a maximum calculated benefit in 25 years that is higher than the maximum annual retirement benefit permitted. The plan must still limit actual benefits to the maximum amount. For example, assume an employee is age 55, earns $220,000 (see Q 6:21), and the maximum annual retirement benefit permitted is $110,000 (50 percent of the employee's compensation). To satisfy the safe harbor while permitting this employee to accrue the maximum annual retirement benefit in ten years, the employer could establish a plan that provides a benefit of 125 percent of compensation at normal retirement age, accrued ratably over all years of service (thereby satisfying the fractional accrual rule). The benefit would be proportionately reduced for years of service less than 25, and the accrued benefit at any time would be limited to the maximum annual retirement benefit. Under this plan, at age 65, the employee would have ten years of service and would therefore accrue a benefit of 10/25 of 125 percent of compensation, or 50 percent of compensation. [Treas Reg § 1.401(a)(4)-3(b)(4)(i)(C)(2)]

The fourth safe harbor, also for *flat benefit plans*, requires that the average accrual rate of nonhighly compensated employees (see Q 3:13) as a group be at least 70 percent of the average accrual rate of highly compensated employees (see Q 3:2) as a group. This safe harbor is applied by taking into account all nonexcludible employees of the employer whether they are covered under the plan or not. [Treas Reg § 1.401(a)(4)-3(b)(4)(i)(C)(3)]

Q 4:16   What safe harbor applies to insurance contract plans for the requirement of nondiscrimination in amount of benefits?

The fifth and final safe harbor is for *insurance contract plans* (see Q 8:5). Because these plans are subject to special accrual rules and deliver benefits in the form of insurance contract cash values, they are not designed in a way that accords with any of the four safe harbors discussed above (see Qs 4:14, 4:15). An insurance contract plan generally satisfies this safe harbor if it satisfies a special accrual rule and certain funding requirements, and if the stated benefit formula under the plan would satisfy either the unit credit fractional accrual safe harbor (see Q 4:14) or the flat benefit fractional accrual safe harbor (see Q 4:15) if the stated normal retirement benefit were accrued ratably over each employee's period of plan participation through normal retirement age (see Q 10:55). [Treas Reg § 1.401(a)(4)-3(b)(5)]

Q 4:17   Is there a general test for the nondiscrimination in amount of benefits requirement?

Those plans that do not satisfy any of the five safe harbors (see Qs 4:14–4:16) must satisfy the general test for nondiscrimination with respect to the amount of benefits. Under this test, the employer must identify, for each highly compensated employee (see Q 3:2) benefiting under the plan, the group of employees consisting of that highly compensated employee and all other employees (both highly compensated and nonhighly compensated) with equal or greater normal and most valuable accrual rates (a rate group). Thus, depending on their accrual rates, employees may be included in more than one rate group. A rate group must be determined for each highly compensated employee benefiting under the plan. Each rate group so identified must satisfy the minimum coverage requirements (see Q 5:15) as though it were a separate plan. [Treas Reg §§ 1.401(a)(4)-3(c)(1), 1.401(a)(4)-3(c)(4)]

Example 1. (a) Employer X has 1,100 nonexcludible employees: N1 through N1000 are nonhighly compensated employees, and H1 through H100 are highly compensated employees. Employer X maintains Plan A, a defined benefit plan that benefits all 1,100 nonexcludible employees. The normal and most valuable accrual rates (determined as a percentage of average annual compensation) for the employees in Plan A for the 1994 plan year are listed in the following table.

Employee	Normal Accrual Rate	Most Valuable Accrual Rate
N1 through N100	1.0	1.4
N101 through N500	1.5	3.0
N501 through N750	2.0	2.65
N751 through N1000	2.3	2.8
H1 through H50	1.5	2.0
H51 through H100	2.0	2.65

(b) There are 100 rate groups in Plan A because there are 100 highly compensated employees in Plan A.

(c) Rate group 1 consists of H1 and all those employees who have a normal accrual rate greater than or equal to H1's normal accrual rate (1.5 percent) and who also have a most valuable accrual rate greater than or equal to H1's most valuable accrual rate (2.0 percent). Thus rate group 1 consists of H1 through H100 and N101 through N1000.

(d) Rate group 1 satisfies the ratio percentage test (see Q 5:16) because the ratio percentage of the rate group is 90 percent; i.e., 90 percent (the percentage of all nonhighly compensated nonexcludible employees who are in the rate group) divided by 100 percent (the percentage of all highly compensated nonexcludible employees who are in the rate group).

(e) Because H1 through H50 have the same normal accrual rates and the same valuable accrual rates, the rate group with respect to each of them is identical. Thus, because rate group 1 satisfies the minimum coverage requirements, rate groups 2 through 50 also satisfy the minimum coverage requirements.

(f) Rate group 51 consists of H51 and all those employees who have a normal accrual rate greater than or equal to H51's normal accrual rate (2.0 percent) and who also have a most valuable accrual rate greater than or equal to H51's most valuable accrual rate (2.65 percent). Thus, rate group 51 consists of H51 through H100 and N501 through N1000. (Even though N101 through N500 have a most valuable accrual rate [3.0 percent] greater than H51's most valuable accrual rate [2.65 percent], they are not included in this rate group because their normal accrual rate [1.5 percent] is less than H51's normal accrual rate [2.0 percent].)

(g) Rate group 51 satisfies the ratio percentage test because the ratio percentage of the rate group is 100 percent; i.e., 50 percent (the percentage of all nonhighly compensated nonexcludible employees who are in the rate group) divided by 50 percent (the percentage of all highly compensated nonexcludible employees who are in the rate group).

(h) Because H51 through H100 have the same normal accrual rates and the same most valuable accrual rates, the rate group with respect to each of them is identical. Thus, because rate group 51 satisfies the minimum coverage requirements, rate groups 52 through 100 also satisfy the minimum coverage requirements.

(i) The benefits under Plan A are nondiscriminatory in amount because each rate group under the plan satisfies the minimum coverage requirements.

A plan that fails the general test discussed above may demonstrate that, on the basis of all relevant facts and circumstances, the plan is not discriminatory. This demonstration is available only to a plan that fails the general test with respect to 5 percent or less of the highly compensated employees (i.e., the plan could pass the test were it allowed to disregard the participation of not more than 5 percent of the highly compensated employees). For this purpose, 5 percent of the number of highly compensated employees may be determined by rounding to the nearest whole number (e.g., 1.4 rounds to 1 and 1.5 rounds to 2). Among the relevant factors that will be considered in determining nondiscrimination are:

1. The extent to which the plan fails the general test;
2. The extent to which the failure is for reasons other than the design of the plan;
3. Whether the highly compensated employees causing the failure are 5 percent owners (see Q 3:4) or are among the highest paid nonexcludible employees;

4. Whether the failure is attributable to a nonrecurring event (e.g., a plant closing); and

5. The extent to which the failure is attributable to benefits accrued under a prior benefit structure or when a participant was not a highly compensated employee. [Treas Reg §§ 1.401(a)(4)-3(c)(3), 1.401(a)(4)-3(c)(4)]

Example 2. The facts are the same as in Example 1, except that H96 has a most valuable accrual rate of 3.5. Each of the rate groups is the same as in Example 1, except that rate group 96 consists solely of H96 because no other employee has a most valuable accrual rate greater than 3.5. Because the plan would satisfy the general test by disregarding H96 (who constitutes less than 5 percent of the highly compensated employees in the plan), IRS may determine that, on the basis of all of the relevant facts and circumstances, the plan does not discriminate with respect to the amount of benefits.

The normal accrual rate for a plan year is the increase in the employee's accrued benefit (see Q 9:2) during the measurement period (current plan year, current plan year and all prior years, or current plan year and all prior and future years), divided by the employee's testing service (the employee's years of service as defined in the plan for purposes of applying the benefit formula under the plan) during the measurement period, and expressed either as a dollar amount or as a percentage of the employee's average annual compensation. [Treas Reg § 1.401(a)(4)-3(d)]

The most valuable accrual rate for a plan year is the increase in the employee's most valuable optional form of payment of the accrued benefit during the measurement period, divided by the employee's testing service during the measurement period, and expressed either as a dollar amount or as a percentage of the employee's average annual compensation. It reflects the value of all benefits accrued or treated as accrued that are payable in any form and at any time under the plan, including early retirement benefits, retirement-type subsidies, early retirement window benefits, etc. Alternatively, an employee's most valuable accrual rate for the current plan year may be determined as the employee's highest most valuable accrual rate determined for any prior plan year. This option may be used only if the employee's normal accrual rate has not changed significantly from the normal accrual rate for such prior plan year and there has been no plan amendment in the interim period that affects the determination of the most valuable accrual rate. [Treas Reg §§ 1.401(a)(4)-3(d)(1)(ii), 1.401(a)(4)-3(d)(1)(iv)]

Q 4:18   What is the nondiscriminatory availability requirement?

The second nondiscrimination requirement a qualified retirement plan must satisfy is that the benefits, rights, and features provided under the plan must be made both currently and effectively available to the participants in a nondiscriminatory manner. The benefits, rights, and features that must satisfy this requirement are the optional forms of benefits, ancillary benefits, and other rights and features provided under the plan. Each optional form of benefit, each ancillary benefit, and each other right or feature provided under a plan must separately satisfy the nondiscrimination requirements with respect to its availability. Two or more benefits, rights, and features may be permissively aggregated if one of the benefits, rights, or features is inherently of equal or greater value than the other, and if the more valuable benefit, right, or feature, standing alone, satisfies the current and effective availability requirements. [Treas Reg §§ 1.401(a)(4)-4(a), 1.401(a)(4)-4(b), 1.401(a)(4)-4(c), 1.401(a)(4)-4(d)(4)]

The term "optional form of benefit" (see Q 10:42) means a distribution alternative that is available under a qualified retirement plan. Different optional forms of benefit exist if the distribution alternative is not payable on substantially the same terms. The relevant terms include all terms affecting the value of the optional form, such as the actuarial assumptions used to determine the amount distributed or the method of benefit calculation (see Q 2:18). Different optional forms of benefit may result from differences in payment schedule, timing, commencement, medium of distribution (e.g., in cash or in kind), election rights, or the portion of the benefit to which the distribution alternative applies. [Treas Reg § 1.401(a)(4)-4(e)(1)]

> **Example.** Plan A is a defined benefit plan that benefits all employees of Divisions S and T. The plan offers a qualified joint and survivor annuity at normal retirement age, calculated by multiplying an employee's single life annuity payment by a factor. For an employee of Division S whose benefit commences at age

65, the plan provides a factor of 0.90; but, for a similarly situated employee of Division T, the plan provides for a factor of 0.85. The qualified joint and survivor annuity is not available to employees of Division S and T on substantially the same terms and constitutes two separate optional forms of benefit.

The term "ancillary benefit" includes the following:

- Social Security supplements described in Section 411(a)(9)
- Disability benefits not in excess of a qualified disability benefit described in Section 411(a)(9)
- Ancillary life insurance and health insurance benefits
- Death benefits under a defined contribution plan (see Q 2:2)
- Preretirement death benefits under a defined benefit plan (see Q 2:3), and
- Other similar benefits

Different ancillary benefits exist if an ancillary benefit is not available on substantially the same terms as another ancillary benefit. [Treas Reg § 1.401(a)(4)-4(e)(2)]

The term "other right or feature" means any right or feature applicable to participants, other than a right or feature taken into account as part of an optional form of benefit or ancillary benefit provided under the plan, and other than a right or feature that cannot reasonably be expected to be of meaningful value to an employee (e.g., administrative details). Different rights or features exist if the right or feature is not available on substantially the same terms as another right or feature. Other rights and features include, but are not limited to, the following:

- Plan loan provisions
- The right to direct investments [Ltr Rul 9137001]
- The right to a particular form of investment, including, for example, a particular class or type of employer securities (taking into account any difference in conversion, dividend, voting, liquidation preference, or other rights conferred under the security), and

- The right to make rollover contributions and transfers to and from the plan

[Treas Reg § 1.401(a)(4)-4(e)(3)]

A plan must satisfy the nondiscriminatory availability requirement not only with respect to employees who are currently benefiting under the plan but also with respect to employees with accrued benefits (see Q 9:2) who are not currently benefiting under the plan (i.e., frozen participants). A plan satisfies the availability requirement with respect to this latter group of employees if *any* of the following requirements is met:

1. The benefit, right, or feature must be one that would satisfy the current and effective availability requirements if it were not available to any employee currently benefiting under the plan.

2. The benefit, right, or feature must be one that would satisfy the current and effective availability requirements if all frozen participants were treated as employees currently benefiting under the plan.

3. No change in the availability of the benefit, right, or feature may have been made that is first effective in the current plan year with respect to a frozen participant.

4. Any change in the availability of the benefit, right, or feature that is first effective in the current plan year with respect to a frozen participant must be made in a nondiscriminatory manner. Thus, any expansion in the availability of the benefit, right, or feature to any highly compensated frozen participant must be applied on a consistent basis to all nonhighly compensated frozen participants. Similarly, any contraction in the availability of the benefit, right, or feature that affects any nonhighly compensated frozen participant must be applied on a consistent basis to all highly compensated frozen participants. [Treas Reg § 1.401(a)(4)-4(d)(2)]

Certain corrective amendments to the availability of benefits, rights, and features are permitted. Because it is difficult or impossible, in many cases, to make a benefit, right, or feature meaningfully available on a retroactive basis, a corrective amendment increasing availability is required only on a prospective basis. However, in order to take the correction into account for a plan year, the group of employees to whom the benefit, right, or feature is available (after taking the amendment into account) generally must satisfy a nondiscriminatory requirement. In addition, the amendment must remain in effect until the end of the plan year following the year in which the amendment is effective, and must not be part of a pattern of amendments used to correct repeated failures of the same benefit, right or feature. Other rules relating to retroactive correction also apply (e.g., the requirement that the correction be made no later than the 15th day of the tenth month after the close of a plan year).

As an alternative to increasing availability, an employer may make a corrective amendment by the last day of the plan year eliminating the benefit, right, or feature (to the extent permitted under Section 411(d)(6)). In that case, the amendment will be treated as if it were in effect throughout the plan year for purposes of nondiscrimination testing. [Treas Reg § 1.401(a)(4)-11(g)]

Q 4:19 What is the nondiscriminatory requirement for plan amendments?

The third nondiscrimination requirement a qualified retirement plan must satisfy is that the effect or timing of plan amendments must be nondiscriminatory. Under this requirement, plan amendments must not have the effect of discriminating significantly in favor of highly compensated active employees (see Q 3:3) or highly compensated former employees (see Q 3:12). A plan amendment includes the establishment or termination of the plan, and any change in the benefits, rights, or features, benefit formulas, or allocation formulas under the plan. Whether a plan meets this requirement depends on the relevant facts and circumstances. [Treas Reg § 1.401(a)(4)-5(a)(1)]

A plan does not satisfy this requirement if the timing of a plan amendment or series of amendments (including amendments terminating the plan) discriminate significantly in favor of highly compensated active or former employees at the time the amendment first becomes effective. Relevant facts and circumstances include the relative numbers of highly and nonhighly compensated active and former employees affected by the plan amendment, the relative accrued benefits (see Q 9:2) of the highly and nonhighly compensated active and former employees before and after the effective date of the plan amendment, the relative length of service of the highly and nonhighly compensated active and former employees, the length of time the plan or plan provisions have been in effect, and the turnover of employees prior to the plan amendment. [Treas Reg §§ 1.401(a)(4)-5(a)(2), 1.401(a)(4)-5(a)(4)]

> **Example.** Plan D is a defined benefit plan that covered both highly compensated and nonhighly compensated employees for most of its existence. The employer decides to wind up the business. Shortly thereafter, at a time when the plan covers only highly compensated employees, Plan D is amended to increase benefits and thereafter is terminated. Plan D does not satisfy this requirement because the timing of the amendment increasing benefits discriminates significantly in favor of highly compensated employees.

A plan does not satisfy this requirement if plan provisions that provide past service credit have the effect of discriminating significantly in favor of highly compensated active and former employees. Past service credit includes benefit accruals for an employee's service prior to the time a plan is established, increases in existing accrued benefits resulting from an employee's service prior to the effective date of a plan amendment, and benefit accruals for service with another employer. Relevant facts and circumstances include the amount of benefits that former employees would have received had the plan or benefit increase been in effect throughout the period to which the past service credit applies. In addition, those facts and circumstances that are generally relevant to other plan amendments are taken into account. A safe harbor is provided under which a grant of up to five years of past service credit is deemed to be nondiscriminatory. The existence of this safe harbor does not mean that a grant of past service credit for a longer period violates the nondiscrimination rules. [Treas Reg §§ 1.401(a)(4)-5(a)(2), 1.401(a)(4)-5(a)(3), 1.401(a)(4)-5(a)(4), 1.401(a)(4)-11(d)(3)]

> **Example 1.** Employer X currently has six employees, two of whom, A and B, are highly compensated employees, and the remaining four of whom, C, D, E, and F, are nonhighly compensated employees. The ratio of highly compensated employees to highly compensated former employees is significantly higher than the

ratio of nonhighly compensated employees to nonhighly compensated former employees. Employer X establishes a defined benefit plan providing a 2 percent benefit for each year of service with the employer, including service rendered before the plan is established. A and B each has 15 years of prior service, C has nine years of past service, D has five years, E has three years, and F has one year. The plan violates the special effect requirement because the grant of past service discriminates significantly in favor of highly compensated employees.

Example 2. Assume the same facts as in Example 1, except that the plan limits the past service credit to five years. The grant of past service credit does not discriminate significantly in favor of highly compensated employees and is within the safe harbor.

The requirement that a plan must be nondiscriminatory also covers plan terminations. Existing rules (see Q 21:8) that restrict distributions to highly compensated active and former employees upon termination of a defined benefit plan have been liberalized. These restrictions are inapplicable if the payment is less than 1 percent of plan assets or, after the payment of the benefit, the value of plan assets is at least 110 percent of the plan's current liabilities (see Q 8:2). [Treas Reg § 1.401(a)(4)-5(b)]

Q 4:20 What does cross-testing mean?

A qualified retirement plan may not discriminate in favor of highly compensated employees (see Q 3:2) with respect to the amount of contributions or benefits. Whether a defined contribution plan (see Q 2:2) satisfies this requirement is generally determined with respect to the amount of contributions (see Q 4:11). As an alternative, however, a defined contribution plan (other than an ESOP [see Q 24:1]) may be tested with respect to the equivalent amount of benefits. Similarly, whether a defined benefit plan (see Q 2:3) satisfies this requirement is generally determined with respect to the amount of benefits (see Q 4:13). As an alternative, however, a defined benefit plan may be tested with respect to the equivalent amount of contributions. [Prop Reg § 1.401(a)(4)-8]

An age-based profit sharing plan is an example of a defined contribution plan being tested with respect to an equivalent amount of benefits (see Qs 2:7–2:9).

A defined contribution plan that is cross-tested by using the current plan year as the measurement period under the general test (see Q 4:12) may disregard income, expenses, gains, and losses allocated during the current plan year that are attributable to the allocation for the current plan year. Thus, only contributions and forfeitures allocated during the current plan year are taken into account. [Treas Reg §§ 1.401(a)(4)-8(b)(2)(i), 1.401(a)(4)-8(b)(2)(ii)]

Q 4:21 Do special rules apply to target benefit plans?

A target benefit plan (see Q 2:5) is generally subject to the alternative cross-testing method applicable to defined contribution plans (see Q 4:20). However, a target benefit plan will be deemed to satisfy the nondiscrimination requirement with respect to the amount of equivalent benefits if each of the following requirements is satisfied:

1. Each employee's stated benefit is determined as the straight life annuity commencing at the employee's normal retirement age (see Q 10:55);

2. The same benefit formula applies to all employees, and the benefit formula provides all employees with an annual benefit payable in the same form commencing at the same uniform normal retirement age;

3. The stated benefit under the plan complies with one of the defined benefit plan safe harbors that uses the fractional accrual rule (see Qs 4:14, 4:15);

4. Contributions necessary to fund the stated benefit for an employee are determined under the individual level premium funding method and are based on the employee's theoretical reserve. An employee's theoretical reserve generally consists of prior contributions with interest accumulated at the plan's assumed interest rate used for funding purposes for prior years;

5. Generally, an employee's stated benefit may not take into account service prior to the first plan year that the employee benefited under the plan;

6. Forfeitures under the plan are applied to reduce contributions;

7. Employee contributions are not used to fund the stated benefit; and

8. Stated benefits and contributions after normal retirement age satisfy certain additional requirements.

[Treas Reg §§ 1.401(a)(4)-8(a), 1.401(a)(4)-8(b), 1.401(a)(4)-12]

Q 4:22 When are the new nondiscrimination requirements effective?

The new nondiscrimination requirements (see Q 4:9) are generally effective for plan years beginning on or after January 1, 1994. For plan years beginning before 1994, a retirement plan must be operated in accordance with a reasonable, good-faith interpretation of the new requirements. Whether compliance is reasonable and in good faith will generally be determined on the basis of facts and circumstances, including the extent to which the employer has consistently resolved all unclear issues in its favor. Reasonable, good-faith compliance will be deemed to exist, however, if a plan is operated in accordance with the final August 1993 regulations, the January 1993 proposed regulations, the September 1991 regulations, or the 1990 proposed regulations. [Treas Reg § 1.401(a)(4)-13(a); Rev Proc 93-42, 1993-31 IRB; Ann 93-130, 1993-31 IRB; Notice 92-36, 1992-2 CB 364; Ann 92-81, 1992-22 IRB 56; Ann 92-29, 1992-9 IRB 37; IRS Field Office Directive on Good-Faith Compliance (June 12, 1992)]

Q 4:23 What happens if a retirement plan fails to satisfy the new nondiscrimination requirements?

If a retirement plan fails to satisfy any of the qualification requirements of Section 401(a) (see Q 4:1), including the new nondiscrimination requirements (see Q 4:9), the tax-exempt status of plan earnings is revoked, employer deductions for contributions may be deferred or eliminated, and all employees must include the value of their vested plan contributions in income. [IRC § 402(b)(1)]

However, if the plan fails to satisfy the minimum coverage requirements (see Q 5:15), each highly compensated employee (see Q 3:2) must include in income an amount equal to the employee's entire vested accrued benefit not previously included in income, not just current vested plan contributions. If, however, the plan is not qualified solely because it fails to satisfy the minimum coverage requirements, no adverse tax consequences are imposed on nonhighly compensated employees. [IRC § 402(b)(2)]

IRS has opined that, with the integrated approach underlying the new nondiscrimination requirements and the minimum coverage requirements, any failure to satisfy the nondiscrimination requirements can be viewed as failure to satisfy the minimum coverage requirements. Consequently, failure to meet the nondiscrimination requirements will subject highly compensated employees to the special sanctions. [Preamble to final regulations (Sept 19, 1991)]

Q 4:24 May a participant assign his or her vested interest in a qualified retirement plan?

As a general rule, benefits provided under a qualified retirement plan may not be assigned or alienated. There are, however, exceptions to this rule.

A participant or beneficiary whose benefits are in pay status may assign or alienate the right to future benefit payments provided the following conditions are satisfied: (1) the assignment or alienation is voluntary and revocable; (2) the amount does not exceed 10 percent of any benefit payment; and (3) there is no direct or indirect defraying of plan administration costs. [IRC § 401(a)(13)(A); Treas Reg § 1.401(a)-13(d)(1)]

A loan made to a participant or beneficiary is generally not treated as an assignment or alienation if the loan is secured by the participant's vested interest and is not a prohibited transaction (see Qs 13:44–13:48, 20:7, 29:25). [IRC §§ 401(a)(13)(A), 4975(d)(1); Treas Reg § 1.401(a)-13(d)(2)] Even though a loan may be secured by the participant's vested interest, the secured loan could not be accorded priority status in a bankruptcy proceeding, concluded one court. [In re Scott, No. 91-34119 (Bankr ED Va 1992)]

If a participant designates a beneficiary to receive benefits under a qualified retirement plan upon the participant's death, a disclaimer of the death benefits by the designated beneficiary does not constitute a prohibited assignment or alienation of benefits. [GCM 39858]

Although some courts have held that the prohibition against the assignment or alienation of retirement plan benefits does not preclude the enforcement of a federal tax levy or the collection by IRS on a judgment resulting from an unpaid tax assessment [IRC § 6331; Treas Reg § 1.401(a)-13(b)(2); In re Raihl, No. 91-2200-RMJ (9th Cir US Bankr App Panel 1993); In re Anderson, 1992 Bankr Lexis 2197 (9th Cir US Bankr App Panel 1992); In re Jacobs, Sr, No. 91-00748E (Bankr WD Pa 1992); In re Palmore, 1993 US Dist Lexis 4517 (ND Okla 1993); In re Taylor, No. 90-4-3273-PM (Bankr D Md 1991); United States v Weintraub, No. C-1-76-0032 (SD Ohio 1990)], another court has ruled that IRS could not levy against the participant's benefits because they were exempt under ERISA [ERISA § 206(d); In re Lewis, No. 90 B 02776 D (Bankr D Col 1990)]. Another court has held that a state statute that allows tax levies against pension benefits to collect delinquent state income taxes was preempted by ERISA as a violation of the anti-alienation rule and the benefits were protected from attachment. [Retirement Fund Trust of the Plumbing, Heating and Piping Industry of S California v Franchise Tax Bd, Nos. 88-6355 and 88-6415 (9th Cir 1990)]

Even though the United States Supreme Court has held that a participant's interest in a qualified retirement plan is exempt from the claims of creditors in a bankruptcy proceeding, the enforcement of a federal tax levy against, or the collection by IRS of an unpaid tax assessment from, plan benefits may be permitted. It remains the position of IRS that such levies are permissible. IRS agents have been instructed to levy qualified retirement plan benefits only in flagrant and aggravated cases; and, generally, IRS will not levy benefits if the annual benefits are $6,000 or less. [Patterson v Shumate, 112 S Ct 2242 (1992); In re Jacobs, Sr, No. 91-00748E (Bankr WD Pa 1992); IRM 536(14).5 and .22] See Question 29:40 for more details.

If a qualified domestic relations order (QDRO; see Q 30:1) requires the distribution of all or part of a participant's benefits to another individual, even though the participant is still employed, the distribution is not considered an assignment or alienation. [IRC §§ 401(a)(13)(B), 414(p); Treas Reg § 1.401(a)-13(g)]

Q 4:25   May a participant's qualified retirement plan benefits be attached or garnished?

According to IRS, an attachment, garnishment, levy, execution, or other legal or equitable process of or against a participant's qualified retirement plan benefits is not a voluntary assignment or alienation (see Q 4:24) and, therefore, violates the anti-alienation rule. IRS has also held that a transfer of a participant's plan benefits, which violates the anti-alienation rule, results in the disqualification of the plan. [Treas Reg § 1.401(a)-13(d)(1); Ltr Ruls 9011037, 8829009] However, if benefits have been distributed to the participant, the attachment or assignment of the distributed plan benefits will not violate the anti-alienation provisions. [Trucking Employees of North Jersey Welfare Fund, Inc v Colville, No. 92-5241 (3rd Cir 1993); Brosamer v Mark, No. 27S02-9011-CV-700 (S Ct Ind 1990)]

In 1992, the United States Supreme Court held that a participant's interest in a qualified retirement plan is exempt from the claims of creditors in a bankruptcy proceeding. [Patterson v Shumate, 112 S Ct 2242 (1992)] See Q 29:40 for more details.

Chapter 5

Eligibility and Participation

A company's retirement plan does not qualify for tax-favored status unless certain minimum standards for coverage of, and participation by, employees are met. This chapter examines those standards, describes the consequences of owning more than one company, and discusses important terms.

Q 5:1 Must a company's qualified retirement plan cover all of its employees?

No. Certain minimum coverage and participation requirements, in terms of a percentage or a number of the company's work force (see Qs 5:15, 5:24), must be satisfied. A retirement plan that meets the minimum coverage and participation requirements may qualify for favorable tax treatment even though some employees are excluded.

It is important to recognize that the coverage and participation requirements are minimum standards that must be satisfied by a qualified retirement plan. A company may use more liberal standards than those discussed in this chapter. [IRC §§ 401(a)(26), 410(b)]

In the first instance, a determination must be made as to whether or not an individual is an employee. ERISA Section 3(b) defines an employee as any individual employed by an employer. Concluding that the ERISA definition is completely circular and explains nothing, the Supreme Court adopted a common-law test for determining employee status. Under the test, the following should be considered:

- The right of the hiring party to control the manner and means by which the product is accomplished
- The skill required
- The source of the instrumentalities and tools
- The work location
- The duration of the parties' relationship
- Whether the hiring party has the right to assign more projects to the hired party
- The extent to which the hired party may decide when and how long to work
- The payment method
- The role of the hired party in hiring and paying assistants
- Whether the work is part of the hiring party's regular business
- Whether the hiring party is in business
- The provision of employee benefits, and
- The tax treatment of the hired party

All incidents of the relationship must be taken into account, and no single factor will be decisive. [Nationwide Mutual Ins Co v Darden, 112 S Ct 1344 (1992); Keleher v Dominion Insulation, Inc, 1992 US App Lexis 25561 (4th Cir 1992); Community for Creative Non-Violence v Reid, 490 US 730 (S Ct 1989)]

Q 5:2 What minimum age and service requirements may be set by a qualified retirement plan?

A qualified retirement plan may require an employee to reach age 21 before becoming eligible to participate in the plan. A plan may also require an employee to complete one year of service (see Q 5:8) with the company before becoming eligible to participate. [IRC § 410(a)(1)(a)]

For qualified retirement plans that provide full and immediate vesting (see Q 9:12), an employer may condition participation on completion of more than one year of service. The maximum period for such plans is two years; however, for 401(k) plans, the maximum period is only one year (see Qs 5:4, 23:4). [IRC §§ 410(a)(1)(B), 401(k)(2)(D)]

Q 5:3 May a qualified retirement plan set a maximum age limit for participation?

No. A qualified retirement plan may not exclude from participation employees who are hired after reaching a specified maximum age. Previously, defined benefit and target benefit plans (see Qs 2:3, 2:5) could exclude employees who were hired within five years of the plan's normal retirement age (see Q 10:55). [IRC § 410(a)(2); Prop Reg §§ 1.410(a)-4A, 1.411(b)-2]

Although a plan may not exclude older employees by its terms, an older employee may waive plan participation, provided the waiver is knowingly and voluntarily made. A refusal to allow waivers of participation by older employees would be equivalent to imposing mandatory plan participation on that group of employees. [Finz v Schlesinger, 957 F 2d 78 (2d Cir 1992); Laniok v Advisory Committee of the Brainerd Mfg Co Pension Plan, 935 F 2d 1360 (2d Cir 1991)]

Q 5:4 May a qualified retirement plan require two consecutive years of service for participation?

Qualified retirement plans that provide for immediate 100 percent vesting and require more than one year of service, but not more than two years of service, to be eligible to participate (see Qs 5:2, 9:12) may provide that years of service preceding a one-year break in service (see Q 5:10) be disregarded if the employee has not yet met the service eligibility criterion. Thus, an employee who completes one year of service and then incurs a one-year break in service starts over again, either the next year or when the employee is rehired. However, the plan cannot require that the two years of service be consecutive. [IRC § 410(a)(5)(B); Temp Reg § 1.410(a)-8T]

Example. CeeKay Corp. established a profit sharing plan in 1992 that operates on a calendar year basis. The plan provides that an employee must complete two years of service before becoming a participant and that the employee will be 100 percent vested upon completion of the two-year eligibility requirement. The following three employees all became employed by CeeKay on December 31, 1991:

	Hours of Service Completed		
Plan Year	*Stephanie*	*Caroline*	*James*
1992	1,000	1,000	1,000
1993	1,000	700	500
1994	1,000	1,000	1,000
1995	1,000	1,000	700
1996	1,000	1,000	1,000

Stephanie will have satisfied the plan's service requirement at the end of 1993; Caroline at the end of 1994 because 1992 may not be disregarded, since she did not have a one-year break in service in 1993; and James at the end of 1996 because 1992 may be disregarded, since he did have a one-year break in service in 1993.

Q 5:5 May conditions other than age and service be set for participation in a qualified retirement plan?

Yes. A qualified retirement plan can impose other conditions for participation, provided that the minimum coverage and minimum participation requirements are satisfied (see Qs 5:15, 5:24). For example, a plan could require that an employee not be employed within a specified job description (e.g., sales representative) to be eligible to participate (see Q 1:20). [Treas Reg § 1.410(a)-3(d)]

The most common exclusion, other than exclusions based upon age and service, applies to union employees on whose behalf negotiations for retirement benefits have been conducted with the company. The company may exclude union employees from coverage, whether or not they are covered under a separate retirement plan, as long as retirement benefits were the subject of good-faith bargaining. Exclusions for air pilots and nonresident aliens are also permitted. [IRC § 410(b)(3)]

Q 5:6 May the company require employee contributions as a condition of plan participation?

Yes. A company may adopt a plan—commonly called a thrift or savings plan (see Q 2:10)—that gears employer contributions on behalf of an employee to contributions made by the employee. Other types of plans may also require contributions to be made by the employees (e.g., defined benefit plans). Since participation in these plans is usually limited to those employees who contribute, if required employee contributions are so burdensome that nonhighly compensated employees cannot afford to participate, the plan may fail to satisfy the minimum coverage and participation requirements (see Qs 5:15, 5:24, 6:17).

Q 5:7   When must an employee who meets the plan's eligibility requirements begin to participate?

An employee who meets the minimum age and service requirements of the Code (see Q 5:2), and who is otherwise eligible to participate in the qualified retirement plan, must commence participation no later than the earlier of (1) the first day of the first plan year beginning after the date the employee met the eligibility requirements or (2) the date six months after these requirements were met. [IRC § 410(a)(4)]

> **Example.** Ken began working for Danielle Corporation on October 1, 1992. He was 30 years old at that time. Danielle Corporation's qualified retirement plan operates on a calendar-year basis and requires that employees be at least age 21 and complete one year of service. Since Ken met the plan's eligibility requirements on October 1, 1993, he must start to participate in the plan no later than January 1, 1994. This is because January 1, 1994, the first day of the first plan year beginning after Ken has met the eligibility requirements, is earlier than April 1, 1994, the date six months after he has met these requirements.

Q 5:8   What is a year of service for a plan's service eligibility requirement?

A year of service for eligibility purposes means a calendar year, a plan year, or any other consecutive 12-month period (the eligibility computation period) specified in the qualified retirement plan during which the employee completes at least 1,000 hours of service (see Q 5:9). The period starts on the date employment commences. [IRC § 410(a)(3)(A)]

If the employee does not complete 1,000 hours of service during the initial eligibility computation period, the next period commences on the anniversary date of employment or, if provided in the plan, on the first day of the plan year during which the anniversary date falls. If the plan's service eligibility requirement is two years and the plan provides for the second year to start from the first day of the plan year, the employee will be credited with two years of service if 1,000 hours of service are completed during both the initial eligibility computation period and the plan year.

Q 5:9   What is an hour of service?

An hour of service is any hour for which an employee is paid or is entitled to payment by the employer. An hour of service includes any hour for which payments are made due to an employee's vacation, sickness, holiday, disability, layoff, jury duty, military duty, or leave of absence, even if the employee no longer works for the company. An hour of service also includes any hour for which back pay is awarded. [Keleher v Dominion Insulation, Inc, 1992 US App Lexis 25561 (4th Cir 1992); DOL Reg § 2530.200b-2]

Q 5:10   What is a one-year break in service?

A one-year break in service means a calendar year, a plan year, or any other consecutive 12-month period designated in the plan during which an employee does not complete more than 500 hours of service (see Q 5:9). [IRC §§ 410(a)(5)(C), 411(a)(6)(A); DOL Reg § 2530.200b-4]

An employee who works over 500 hours during the designated 12-month period does not incur a one-year break in service. An employee's one-year break in service has significance in terms of eligibility (see Qs 5:4, 5:12) and vesting of benefits (see Q 9:11).

Q 5:11   What years of service must be taken into account for eligibility purposes?

In general, all years of service with the employer must be counted. For the exceptions, see Question 5:12. [IRC § 410(a)(5)]

Service with a predecessor of the employer must be counted if the successor-employer maintains the predecessor's qualified retirement plan. If the successor adopts a new retirement plan, recognition of service with the predecessor-employer is supposed to be decided under as-yet-unissued IRS regulations. [IRC § 414(a)]

Service with any member of a controlled group of corporations or with a commonly controlled entity (see Q 5:30), whether or not incorporated, must be counted for eligibility purposes. Similarly, service with any member of an affiliated service group (see Q 29:31) must be counted. [IRC §§ 414(b), 414(c), 414(m)]

Q 5:12   May any years of service be disregarded for eligibility purposes?

Yes. Most qualified retirement plans may require up to two years of service as a prerequisite to participation (see Q 5:2). For plans that require two years of service as an eligibility requirement, a year of service (see Q 5:8) preceding a one-year break in service (see Q 5:10) need not be considered in determining whether an employee is eligible to participate (see Q 5:4). [IRC §§ 410(a)(1)(B), 410(a)(5)(B)]

Q 5:13   May past service with a former employer be used for eligibility purposes in the qualified retirement plan of the present employer?

If the present employer maintains the qualified retirement plan of a predecessor employer, an employee's service with the predecessor counts as service for the present employer (see Q 5:11).

A qualified retirement plan may provide that service as an employee with a predecessor business counts for purposes of meeting the service eligibility requirement, even if the predecessor business had no qualified retirement plan (see Q 4:19) . Furthermore, service as a partner of a partnership may be counted in meeting the service requirement for participation in the plan of a successor corporation. [Ltr Rul 7742003; Farley Funeral Homes, Inc, 62 TC 150 (1974)]

Q 5:14 Is a maternity or paternity period of absence treated as a break in service?

For purposes of determining whether a one-year break in service (see Q 5:10) has occurred for both participation and vesting purposes, an employee who is absent from work due to the birth or adoption of a child is treated as having completed, during the absence, the number of hours that normally would have been credited but for the absence, up to a maximum of 501 hours, so as to prevent a one-year break in service.

The hours of service are credited only in the year in which the absence begins (if necessary to prevent a break in service in that year) or in the following year. [IRC §§ 410(a)(5)(E), 411(a)(6)(E)]

Example. Before taking an approved maternity leave, Susan completed 750 hours of service during the 1993 plan year. Since the credit is not needed in 1993 to prevent a break in service, Susan is entitled to up to 501 hours of credited service in 1994.

Q 5:15 What coverage requirements must a retirement plan satisfy to qualify for favorable tax treatment?

A retirement plan must satisfy one of two coverage tests in order to qualify for favorable tax treatment:

1. The ratio percentage test (see Q 5:16), or
2. The average benefit test (see Q 5:17)

A plan maintained by an employer that benefits only nonhighly compensated employees (see Q 3:13) or by an employer that has only highly compensated employees (see Q 3:2) will automatically satisfy the coverage requirements. [IRC §§ 410(b)(1), 410(b)(2), 410(b)(6)(F); Treas Reg §§ 1.410(b)-2(a), 1.410(b)-2(b); Rev Proc 93-42, 1993-31 IRB; Ann 93-130, 1993-31 IRB; Ann 92-81, 1992-22 IRB 56]

A separate line of business exception may apply for the minimum coverage requirements (see Q 5:33).

Q 5:16 What is the ratio percentage test for the minimum coverage requirements?

Under the ratio percentage test, the percentage of the nonhighly compensated employees (see Q 3:13) who benefit under the retirement plan must equal at least 70 percent of the percentage of the highly compensated employees (see Q 3:2) who benefit under the plan. Percentages are rounded to the nearest one-hundredth of 1 percent. [IRC § 410(b)(1); Treas Reg §§ 1.410(b)-2(b)(2), 1.410(b)-9]

Example 1. For a plan year, Debi Corporation's defined benefit plan covers 60 percent of its nonhighly compensated employees and 80 percent of its highly compensated employees. The plan's ratio percentage for the year is 75 percent (i.e., 60% ÷ 80%) and thus satisfies the ratio percentage test.

Example 2. For a plan year, Danielle Ltd.'s defined contribution plan covers 40 percent of its nonhighly compensated employees and 60 percent of its highly compensated employees. The plan fails to satisfy the ratio percentage test because the ratio percentage is only 66.67 percent (i.e., 40% ÷ 60%).

For purposes of satisfying the minimum coverage requirements, employees who do not meet the plan's minimum age or service requirement (see Q 5:2) are not counted. In addition, nonresident aliens who receive no earned income from sources within the United States and union members whose retirement benefits have been the subject of good-faith bargaining between the employer and the union do not count (see Q 5:5). [IRC §§ 410(b)(3), 410(b)(4); Treas Reg §§ 1.410(b)-6(a), 1.410(b)-6(b)(1), 1.410(b)-6(b)(2), 1.410(b)-6(c), 1.410(b)-6(d)]

Q 5:17 What is the average benefit test for the minimum coverage requirements?

Under the average benefit test, (1) the plan must benefit such employees as qualify under a classification set up by the employer and found by IRS not to be discriminatory in favor of highly compensated employees (see Q 3:2), and (2) the average benefit percentage for nonhighly compensated employees (see Q 3:13) of the employer must equal at least 70 percent of the average benefit percentage for highly compensated employees of the employer. [IRC § 410(b)(2); Treas Reg §§ 1.410(b)-2(b)(3), 1.410(b)-4, 1.410(b)-5]

The classification test is described in Question 5:18, and the average benefit percentage test in Question 5:19.

Q 5:18 What is the classification test?

The classification test is satisfied if, based on all the facts and circumstances, the classification set up by the employer is reasonable and is established under objective business criteria. In addition, the classification must be found to be nondiscriminatory based on either a safe harbor rule or a facts and circumstances test. The safe harbor rule is satisfied only if the plan's ratio percentage (see Q 5:16) is equal to or greater than the employer's safe harbor percentage. The safe harbor rule looks at the percentage (concentration percentage) of all of the employer's employees who are nonhighly compensated employees (see Q 3:13) and then creates both a safe harbor percentage and an unsafe harbor percentage. The employer's safe harbor percentage is 50 percent reduced by .75 percent for each whole percentage point by which the concentration percentage exceeds 60 percent, and the unsafe harbor percentage is 40 percent reduced by .75 percent for each whole percentage point by which the concentration percentage exceeds 60 percent (but in no event less than 20 percent). [Treas Reg §§ 1.410(b)-4(b), 1.410(b)-4(c)]

The following table illustrates the safe harbor and unsafe harbor percentages at each concentration percentage:

Nonhighly Compensated Employee Concentration Percentage	Safe Harbor Percentage	Unsafe Harbor Percentage
0-60	50.00	40.00
61	49.25	39.25
62	48.50	38.50
63	47.75	37.75
64	47.00	37.00
65	46.25	36.25
66	45.50	35.50
67	44.75	34.75
68	44.00	34.00

(*Table continues.*)

Nonhighly Compensated Employee Concentration Percentage	Safe Harbor Percentage	Unsafe Harbor Percentage
69	43.25	33.25
70	42.50	32.50
71	41.75	31.75
72	41.00	31.00
73	40.25	30.25
74	39.50	29.50
75	38.75	28.75
76	38.00	28.00
77	37.25	27.25
78	36.50	26.50
79	35.75	25.75
80	35.00	25.00
81	34.25	24.25
82	33.50	23.50
83	32.75	22.75
84	32.00	22.00
85	31.25	21.25
86	30.50	20.50
87	29.75	20.00
88	29.00	20.00
89	28.25	20.00
90	27.50	20.00
91	26.75	20.00
92	26.00	20.00
93	25.25	20.00
94	24.50	20.00
95	23.75	20.00
96	23.00	20.00
97	22.25	20.00
98	21.50	20.00
99	20.75	20.00

Example 1. Mikey Corp. has 200 employees; 120 are nonhighly compensated employees and 80 are highly compensated employees. The nonhighly compensated employee concentration percentage is 60 percent (120/200). Mikey Corp. maintains a retirement plan that excludes employees of a specified geographic location. The plan benefits 72 highly compensated employees and 60 nonhighly compensated employees. The plan's ratio percentage is 55.56 percent [(60/120) ÷ (72/80) = (50% ÷ 90%)]. Since the

concentration percentage is 60 percent, the safe harbor percentage is 50 percent and the unsafe harbor percentage is 40 percent. Because the ratio percentage (55.56 percent) is greater than the safe harbor percentage (50 percent), the plan's classification satisfies the safe harbor rule.

Example 2. The facts are the same as in Example 1 except that the plan benefits 45 nonhighly compensated employees. The plan's ratio percentage is 41.67 percent [(45/120) ÷ (72/80) = (37.50% ÷ 90%]. Because the ratio percentage (41.67 percent) is below the safe harbor percentage (50 percent), but above the unsafe harbor percentage (40 percent), IRS may determine that the classification is nondiscriminatory based on all the facts and circumstances.

Q 5:19   What is the average benefit percentage test?

In order for a qualified retirement plan to satisfy the average benefit percentage test, the benefits provided to nonhighly compensated employees (see Q 3:13) under all plans of the employer (expressed as a percentage of compensation) must generally be at least 70 percent as great, on average, as the benefits provided to the employer's highly compensated employees (see Q 3:2). [Treas Reg § 1.410(b)-5(a)]

Satisfaction of the average benefit percentage test requires that the employer determine an employee benefit percentage for each employee taken into account for testing purposes and then separately average the percentages of all employees in the highly compensated and nonhighly compensated groups. Employee benefit percentages may be determined on either a contributions or a benefits basis, and employee contributions and benefits attributable to employee contributions are not taken into account. Generally, the employee benefit percentage for an employee is the rate that would be determined for that employee for purposes of applying the general nondiscrimination tests (see Qs 4:12, 4:17, 4:20). [Treas Reg §§ 1.410(b)-5(b), 1.410(b)-5(c), Prop Reg §§ 1.410(b)-5(d), 1.410(b)-5(e)]

Q 5:20   When does an employee benefit under the qualified retirement plan?

For purposes of the minimum coverage rules, an employee must benefit under the qualified retirement plan to be taken into account for the percentage tests (see Qs 5:16, 5:17). An employee is treated as benefiting under the plan for a plan year:

1. In the case of a defined contribution plan (see Q 2:2), only if the employee receives an allocation of contributions or forfeitures.

2. In the case of a defined benefit plan (see Q 2:3), only if the employee receives a benefit accrual (see Q 9:2).

3. In the case of a 401(k) plan, if the employee is eligible to make an elective contribution (see Q 23:13), whether or not the employee actually does so.

4. If the employee fails to accrue a benefit solely because of the Section 415 limits on benefits and annual additions (see Qs 6:1, 6:5, 6:15), except that, in the case of a defined benefit plan, this exception does not apply if benefits in excess of the Section 415 limits are used to determine accrual rates for the general nondiscrimination test (see Q 4:17).

5. If the employee fails to accrue a benefit solely because of a uniformly applicable benefit limit under the plan.

6. If the current benefit accrual is offset by the contributions or benefits under another plan.

7. In the case of a target benefit plan (see Q 2:5), the employee's theoretical reserve is greater than or equal to the actuarial present value of the fractional rule benefit (see Q 4:21).

8. If the employee has attained normal retirement age (see Q 10:55) under a defined benefit plan and fails to accrue a benefit solely because of the provisions regarding adjustments for delayed retirement. [Treas Reg §§ 1.410(b)-3(a)(1), 1.410(b)-3(a)(2)(i)-(iv); Rev Proc 93-42, 1993-31 IRB; Ann 93-130, 1993-31 IRB; Ann 92-81, 1992-22 IRB 56]

In the case of a defined contribution plan, if no employee receives an allocation of contributions or forfeitures, the plan is treated as satisfying the minimum coverage requirements for the plan year because the plan benefits no highly compensated employees (see Q 3:2). Thus, a defined contribution plan for which contributions cease and for which no forfeitures can be allocated satisfies the requirements. In the case of a defined benefit plan, if no employee accrues any additional benefits under the plan, the plan is treated as satisfying the requirements for the plan year because no highly compensated employees benefit under the plan during that plan year. However, this special rule is not available with respect to a top-heavy plan that has required minimum contributions or benefit accruals (see Qs 22:37, 22:43), or to a plan where future compensation increases are taken into account in determining the accrued benefit under the plan.

An employee is treated as benefiting under a defined benefit plan for a plan year only if there is an increase in the employee's accrued benefit (see Q 9:2). Final regulations published by IRS on August 31, 1993, clarify that increases in the dollar amount of the accrued benefit merely because of the passage of time or because of a change in indices affecting the accrued benefit do not cause an employee to be treated as benefiting. In certain situations, however, an employee in a defined benefit plan will be treated as benefiting for a plan year even though the employee does not receive an accrual for the plan year. One of these situations is where an employee's accrued benefit would have increased if a previously accrued benefit were disregarded. An increase in covered compensation or a decrease in the employee's compensation for the plan year are other examples of situations where this might occur.

For the treatment of terminated employees, see Question 5:21; and, for a discussion of the family aggregation rule, see Question 5:22.

Q 5:21 How are employees who terminated employment during the plan year treated for minimum coverage purposes?

At the option of the employer, an employee is not taken into account for purposes of the minimum coverage tests (see Q 5:15) if:

1. The employee does not benefit (see Q 5:20) under the plan for the plan year;

2. The employee is eligible to participate in the plan;

3. The plan has a minimum hours of service requirement or a requirement that an employee be employed on the last day of the plan year (last-day requirement) in order to accrue a benefit or receive an allocation for the plan year;

4. The employee fails to accrue a benefit or receive an allocation under the plan solely because of the failure to satisfy the minimum hours of service or last-day requirement; and

5. The employee terminates employment during the plan year with not more than 500 hours of service (see Q 5:9) and the employee is not an active employee as of the last day of the plan year. (A plan that uses the elapsed time method of determining years of service may use either 91 consecutive calendar days or three consecutive calendar months instead of 500 hours of service, provided it uses the same rule for all employees during a plan year).

If the employer elects to use this option with respect to any employee for a plan year, it must be applied to all employees for that plan year. [Treas Reg § 1.410(b)-6(f)]

Example. Norman of New Mexico, Inc. has 30 employees who are eligible under its profit sharing plan. The plan requires the employee to complete 1,000 hours of service during the plan year to receive an allocation of contributions or forfeitures. Ten employees do not receive an allocation because of their failure to complete 1,000 hours of service. Three of the ten employees completed less than 501 hours of service and terminated their employment. Two of the employees completed between 501 and 999 hours of service and terminated their employment. The remaining five employees did not terminate employment. The three terminated employees who completed less than 501 hours of service are not taken into account unless the employer elects to do so. The other seven employees who do not receive an allocation are taken into account but are treated as not benefiting under the plan.

Q 5:22   What is the family aggregation rule?

A highly compensated employee (see Q 3:2) who is a 5 percent owner (see Q 3:4) or one of the ten most highly compensated employees and all family members of such highly compensated employee who are also employees of the employer are treated as a single highly compensated employee for purposes of the minimum coverage requirements.

If any member of such group is benefiting (see Q 5:20) under the plan, the deemed single employee is treated as benefiting under the plan. If no member of such group is benefiting under the plan, the deemed single employee is treated as not benefiting under the plan.

Family includes the highly compensated employee's spouse, lineal descendants and ascendants, and spouses of lineal descendants or ascendants (see Q 3:14). [IRC §§ 410(b)(6)(A), 414(q)(6); Treas Reg § 1.410(b)-8(b)]

If enacted, TSB '93 (see Q 1:13) will repeal the family aggregation rule for years beginning *after* 1993. [TSB '93, Act § 221(c)]

Q 5:23   When are the new minimum coverage rules effective?

The new rules (see Qs 5:15–5:22) are generally effective for plan years beginning on or after January 1, 1989. However, the final regulations published by IRS on August 31, 1993 by IRS, are effective for plan years beginning on or after January 1, 1994.

For plan years beginning before January 1, 1994, the plan must be operated in accordance with a reasonable, good-faith interpretation of the minimum coverage requirements. Whether compliance is reasonable and in good faith will be determined on the basis of all the facts and circumstances, including the extent to which the employer has resolved unclear issues in its favor. A reasonable, good-faith interpretation will be deemed to exist, however, if a plan is operated in accordance with the regulations published by IRS prior to August 31, 1993. [Treas Reg § 1.410(b)-10; Notice 92-36, 1992-2 CB 364; Ann 92-29, 1992-9 IRB 37; IRS Field Office Directive on Good-Faith Compliance (June 12, 1992); Ltr Rul 9214002]

Q 5:24   What is the minimum participation requirement?

In addition to the minimum coverage requirements (see Q 5:15), a minimum participation requirement must be met by each retirement plan of the employer in order to be qualified. To satisfy this latter requirement, a qualified retirement plan must benefit at least the lesser of (1) 50 employees, or (2) 40 percent of all employees. This requirement may not be satisfied by aggregating different plans of the employer. [IRC § 401(a)(26); Treas Reg §§ 1.401(a)(26)-1(a), 1.401(a)(26)-2(a)]

Example 1. S&C Professional Law Corporation employs two attorneys and no other employees. Each attorney may participate in a separate qualified retirement plan because each plan will cover 40 percent or more of the employees.

Example 2. SC&J Professional Law Corporation employs three attorneys and no other employees. Each attorney may not participate in a separate qualified retirement plan because each plan will cover less than 40 percent of the employees.

Among the plans that are deemed to meet the minimum participation requirements automatically are the following:

1. A plan that is not a top-heavy plan (see Qs 22:1, 22:3), benefits no highly compensated employee (see Q 3:2), and is not aggregated with any other plan to enable such other plan to satisfy the nondiscrimination requirements (see Q 4:9) or the minimum coverage requirements (see Q 5:15). [Treas Reg § 1.401(a)(26)-1(b)(1)]

2. Certain multiemployer plans (see Q 25:2). [Treas Reg § 1.401(a)(26)-1(b)(2)]

3. Certain underfunded defined benefit plans (see Q 2:3). [Treas Reg § 1.401(a)(26)-1(b)(3)]

4. Certain 401(k) plans (see Q 23:1) maintained by employers that include governmental or tax-exempt entities. [IRC § 401(k)(4)(B); Treas Reg § 1.401(a)(26)-1(b)(4)]

5. Certain plans of an employer involved in an acquisition or disposition. [Treas Reg § 1.401(a)(26)-1(b)(5)]

6. Defined contribution plans (see Q 2:2) under which no employee receives an allocation of either contributions or forfeitures for the plan year. [Treas Reg § 1.401(a)(26)-2(b)]

7. Defined benefit plans under which no employee accrues any additional benefit for a plan year (other than those minimum benefits provided for non-key employees under top-heavy plans) but which satisfy the prior benefit structure requirements (see Qs 5:26, 22:37). [Treas Reg § 1.401(a)(26)-2(b)]

Generally, an employee is deemed to benefit under the plan if the employee is deemed to benefit under the plan for the minimum coverage tests (see Q 5:20), and the family aggregation rule (see Q 5:22) does not apply for purposes of the minimum participation requirement. [Treas Reg § 1.401(a)(26)-5]

If TSB '93 (see Q 1:13) is enacted, the minimum participation requirement will apply *only* to defined benefit plans commencing with the first plan year beginning *after* 1993. In addition, the 40 percent requirement will be changed to the *greater* of (1) 40 percent of all employees, or (2) two employees (or if there is only one employee, that employee). In Example 1 above, if a plan was a defined benefit plan, that plan would not satisfy the minimum participation requirement because the plan will not cover *two* employees. In Example 2 above, if each plan was a defined contribution plan, the minimum participation requirement would not be applicable to any of the plans. [TSB '93, Act § 222]

Q 5:25 Which employees are not counted for the minimum participation requirements?

For purposes of applying the minimum participation test, all employees other than excludible employees must be taken into account. Generally, these requirements are applied separately to each qualified retirement plan of the employer and must be applied on a uniform and consistent basis. [Treas Reg § 1.401(a)(26)-6(a)]

An employee, if covered by one of the following exclusions, is an excludible employee:

1. The employee does not meet the plan's minimum age or service requirement (see Q 5:2).

2. The employee is a nonresident alien who receives no earned income from sources within the United States.

3. The employee is a union member whose retirement benefits have been the subject of good-faith bargaining between the employer and the union (see Q 5:5).

[Treas Reg § 1.401(a)(26)-6(b)]

Example 1. Jerry of Lawrence Ltd. maintains a defined benefit plan under which employees who have not completed one year of service are not eligible to participate. Jerry of Lawrence Ltd. has six employees. Two of the employees participate in the plan. The other four employees have not completed one year of service and are not eligible to participate. The four employees who have not completed one year of service are excludible employees and may be disregarded for purposes of applying the minimum participation test. Therefore, the test is satisfied because both of the employees who must be considered are participants in the plan.

Example 2. Busy Bea Corporation has 100 employees and maintains two defined benefit plans, Plan A and Plan B. Plan A provides that employees who have not completed one year of service are not eligible to participate. Plan B has no minimum age or service requirement. Twenty of Busy Bea's employees do not meet the minimum service requirement under Plan A. Each plan satisfies the ratio percentage test (see Q 5:16). In testing Plan A to determine whether it satisfies the minimum participation requirements, the 20 employees not meeting the minimum age and service requirement under Plan A are treated as excludible employees. In testing Plan B, no employees are treated as excludible employees because Plan B does not have a minimum age or service requirement.

In addition, certain terminated employees may be excluded (see Q 5:21), and a separate line of business exception may apply (see Q 5:33). [Treas Reg §§ 1.401(a)(26)-6(b)(7), 1.401(a)(26)-6(b)(8)]

Q 5:26 What is a prior benefit structure?

Defined benefit plans (see Q 2:3), but not defined contribution plans (see Q 2:2), must also satisfy the minimum participation requirements (see Q 5:24) with respect to a prior benefit structure. The prior benefit structure under a defined benefit plan for a plan year includes all benefits accrued to that time; therefore, the plan can have only one prior benefit structure. [Treas Reg §§ 1.401(a)(26)-3(a), 1.401(a)(26)-3(b)]

Generally, the prior benefit structure satisfies the minimum participation requirement if at least 50 employees or 40 percent of the employees currently accrue meaningful benefits (see Q 5:24).

Whether a plan is providing meaningful benefits is determined on the basis of all the facts and circumstances. This determination is intended to ensure that a plan functions as an ongoing defined benefit plan providing meaningful benefits to at least 50 employees of the employer or 40 percent of the employer's employees. A plan does not satisfy this requirement if it exists primarily to preserve accrued benefits for a small group of employees and thereby functions more as an individual plan for the small group of employees or for the employer. The relevant factors in making this determination include the following:

1. The level of current benefit accruals;
2. The comparative rate of accruals under the current benefit formula compared to prior rates of accrual under the plan;
3. The projected accrued benefits under the current benefit formula compared to accrued benefits as of the close of the immediately preceding plan year;
4. The length of time the current benefit formula has been in effect;
5. The number of employees with accrued benefits under the plan; and
6. The length of time the plan has been in effect.

[Treas Reg § 1.401(a)(26)-3(c)]

Q 5:27 May a retirement plan that does not satisfy the minimum participation requirements be retroactively corrected?

The minimum participation requirements are generally effective for plan years beginning on or after January 1, 1989 (see Q 5:24). [Treas Reg § 1.401(a)(26)-9(a)]

To satisfy the requirements, the plan must satisfy the test on each day of the plan year. However, the plan will be treated as satisfying the requirements if it satisfies the test on any single day during the plan year, but only if that day is reasonably representative of the employer's work force and the plan's coverage. A plan does not have to be tested on the same day each plan year. [Treas Reg §§ 1.401(a)(26)-7(a), 1.401(a)(26)-7(b)]

If a plan fails to satisfy the minimum participation requirements for a plan year, the plan may be retroactively amended by the last day of the plan year to satisfy the requirements by expanding coverage, improving benefits or contributions, modifying eligibility conditions under the plan, or merging plans and deeming the merger to be effective retroactively to the first day of the 1989 plan year. In addition, because the minimum participation requirements were added by TRA '86, retroactive correction may be accomplished as late as the end of the last day of the 1994 plan year. [Treas Reg § 1.401(a)(26)-7(c); Notice 92-36, 1992-2 CB 364; IRS Field Office Directive on Good-Faith Compliance (June 12, 1992)]

Q 5:28 Can an employee's waiver of participation in the employer's qualified retirement plan jeopardize the tax-favored status of the plan?

Yes. For example, an employee who is otherwise eligible to participate in the employer's defined benefit plan that requires mandatory employee contributions as a condition of participation may be unable or unwilling to contribute and would therefore waive participation in the plan (see Qs 5:3, 5:6). That employee is included in determining whether the company's retirement plan satisfies the minimum coverage and minimum participation tests (see Qs 5:15, 5:24). Therefore, the plan may lose its tax-favored status if too many employees waive participation.

An employee's decision not to make an elective contribution (see Q 23:13) to a 401(k) plan is not a waiver of participation that would jeopardize the tax-favored status of the plan for purposes of the minimum coverage and minimum participation requirements (see Qs 5:20, 5:24). [Treas Reg §§ 1.410(b)-3(a)(2)(i), 1.401(a)(26)-5(a)(1)]

Q 5:29 What happens if a retirement plan fails to satisfy the minimum coverage or minimum participation requirements?

If a retirement plan fails to satisfy the qualification requirements of Section 401(a) (see Q 4:1), the tax-exempt status of plan earnings is revoked, employer deductions for contributions may be deferred or eliminated, and all employees must include the value of vested (see Q 9:1) plan contributions in income. [IRC § 402(b)(1)]

However, if the plan fails to satisfy the minimum coverage or minimum participation requirements (see Qs 5:15, 5:24), each highly compensated employee (see Q 3:2) must include in income an amount equal to the employee's entire vested accrued benefit (see Q 9:2) not previously included in income, not just current vested plan contributions. If, however, the plan is not qualified solely because it fails to satisfy either of the requirements, no adverse tax consequences are imposed on nonhighly compensated employees (see Q 3:13). [IRC § 402(b)(4)]

Q 5:30 Do special coverage and participation rules apply to commonly controlled businesses?

For purposes of determining whether a retirement plan covers a sufficient number of employees to meet the minimum coverage requirements (see Q 5:15) and the minimum participation requirements (see Q 5:24), as well as other plan-related requirements, all employees of corporations that are members of a controlled group of corporations (see Q 5:32) are treated as if they were employed by a single employer. A comparable requirement applies to affiliated service groups (see Q 29:31), partnerships, sole proprietorships, and other businesses that are under common control. [IRC §§ 414(b), 414(c), 414(m)]

However, the Tax Court has held that the employees of two failing corporations should not be aggregated with the employees of a sole proprietorship, all three of which were commonly controlled, when, under the circumstances, neither corporation was able, in good faith, to adopt a permanent retirement plan. IRS did not acquiesce in this decision. [Sutherland, 78 TC 395 (1982); non-acq., 1986-1 CB 1]

A separate line of business exception may apply, for purposes of the minimum coverage and participation requirements, to commonly controlled businesses but not to affiliated service groups (see Q 5:33). [IRC § 401(a)(26)(G), 410(b)(5), 414(r)]

Q 5:31   If an individual owns two corporations, each of which has employees, can a qualified retirement plan be adopted by only one of the corporations?

Perhaps. For example, assume Herman owns all of the stock of Herman Corporation and Mabel Corporation. Herman Corporation maintains a retirement plan for its employees; Mabel Corporation does not.

The composition of Herman's employees is as follows:

Employee	Age	Service	Compensation
1	50	10 years	$150,000
2	35	6 years	20,000
3	30	4 years	10,000
4	28	less than 1 year	10,000

The composition of Mabel's employees is as follows:

Employee	Age	Service	Compensation
5	45	2 years	$100,000
6	43	2 years	20,000
7	18	less than 1 year	10,000

Employees 1, 2, 3, 5, and 6 satisfy the plan's eligibility requirements (age 21 and one year of service), and employees 1 and 5 are highly compensated employees (see Q 3:3). Employees 4 and 7 need not be counted for purposes of the minimum participation and minimum coverage tests since they have not satisfied the plan's age and service requirements.

Since the retirement plan covers 60 percent of the employees who satisfy the eligibility requirements (i.e., 3 ÷ 5), the plan satisfies the minimum participation requirement (see Q 5:24). In addition, the plan satisfies the ratio percentage test (see Q 5:16) because the plan's ratio percentage is 70 percent or more (i.e., the coverage percentage of nonhighly compensated employees, 66.67 percent (2 ÷ 3), divided by the coverage percentage of highly compensated employees, 50 percent (1 ÷ 2)).

Q 5:32 When does common ownership result in a controlled group of corporations or businesses?

A controlled group of corporations exists if there is:

1. A parent-subsidiary group of corporations connected through at least 80 percent stock ownership, or

2. A brother-sister group in which

    a. Five or fewer people own 80 percent or more of the stock value or voting power of each corporation, and

    b. The same five or fewer people together own more than 50 percent of the stock value or voting power of each corporation, taking into account the ownership of each person only to the extent such ownership is identical with respect to each organization.

[IRC § 1563(a); United States v Vogel Fertilizer Co, 102 S Ct 821 (1982)]

Q 5:33 Is there a separate line of business exception to the minimum coverage and minimum participation requirements?

All employees of a single employer (see Q 5:30) are taken into account for purposes of applying the minimum coverage requirements (see Q 5:15) and the minimum participation requirements (See Q 5:24). However, if an employer is treated as operating qualified separate lines of business (see Q 5:36), the employer is permitted to apply the minimum coverage requirements separately with respect to the employees of each qualified separate line of business. A similar exception (but only with IRS consent) is provided for purposes of applying the minimum participation requirements. The separate line of business exception does not apply to an affiliated service group (see Q 29:31). [IRC §§ 410(b)(5), 401(a)(26)(G), 414(r)]

If the employer operates qualified separate lines of business, the employer need not satisfy the ratio percentage test (see Q 5:16) or the average benefit percentage test (see Q 5:19) on an employer-wide basis. However, even if an employer is treated as operating qualified separate lines of business, every plan of the employer must satisfy the nondiscriminatory classification test (see Q 5:18) on an employer-wide basis. [Prop Reg §§ 1.414(r)-8, 1.414(r)-9]

An employer is treated as operating qualified separate lines of business during any year if the employer operates separate lines of business (see Q 5:35) for *bona fide* business reasons and satisfies certain other conditions. An employer is treated as operating qualified separate lines of business only if: (1) the employer identifies all the property and services it provides to customers and designates the property and services provided by each of its lines of business (see Q 5:34); (2) each line of business is organized and operated separately from the remainder of the employer and is therefore a separate line of business; and (3) each separate line of business meets additional statutory requirements (see Q 5:36) and thus constitutes a qualified separate line of business.

An employer is treated as operating qualified separate lines of business only if all the property and services provided by the employer to its customers are provided exclusively by qualified separate lines of business. Therefore, if an employer is treated as operating qualified separate lines of business, no portion of the employer may remain that is not included in a qualified separate line of business. [Prop Reg § 1.414(r)-1]

Q 5:34   What is a line of business?

In order to demonstrate that it maintains qualified separate lines of business (see Q 5:36), an employer must initially determine its lines of business. A line of business is a portion of an employer that is identified by the property or services it provides to customers of the employer. [Prop Reg § 1.414(r)-2]

In determining its lines of business, the employer first identifies all the property and services it provides to its customers and then designates the property and services provided by each of its lines of business. Therefore, an employer may use its discretion to determine its lines of business in a manner that conforms to its business operations.

Example 1. Rancho Krevat Corporation is a domestic conglomerate engaged in the manufacture and sale of consumer food and beverage products and the provision of data processing services to private industry. The corporation provides no other property or services to its customers. Rancho Krevat Corporation apportions all the property and services it provides to its customers among three lines of business, one providing all its consumer food products, a second providing all its consumer beverage products, and a third providing all its data processing services. Rancho Krevat Corporation has three lines of business.

Example 2. The facts are the same as in Example 1, except that Rancho Krevat Corporation determines that neither the consumer food products line of business nor the consumer beverage products line of business would satisfy the separateness criteria for recognition as a separate line of business. Accordingly, Rancho Krevat Corporation apportions all the property and services it provides to its customers between only two lines of business, one providing all its consumer food and beverage products and a second providing all its data processing services. Rancho Krevat Corporation has two lines of business.

See Question 5:35 for the rules pertaining to vertically integrated lines of business.

Q 5:35   What is a separate line of business?

In order to demonstrate that it maintains qualified separate lines of business (see Q 5:36), an employer must show that its lines of business (see Q 5:34) are organized and operated separately from one another and therefore are separate lines of business. [Prop Reg §§ 1.414(r)-3, 1.414(r)-11(b)(2), 1.414(r)-11(b)(3)]

Whether a line of business is a separate line of business is determined by satisfying each of the following objective criteria.

Separate organizational unit. Each line of business must be formally organized by the employer as a separate organizational unit within the employer (i.e., a corporation, a partnership, a division, or other similar unit).

Separate financial accountability. Each line of business must be a separate profit center within the employer. For this purpose, the employer's books and records must indicate separate revenue and expense information for each profit center comprising the line of business.

Separate work force. Each line of business must have its own separate work force. Satisfaction of this test will depend upon the degree to which each line shares personnel with other portions of the employer. A line of business has its own separate work force if at least 90 percent of the employees of the employer who provide any services to the line of business are substantial-service employees (see Q 5:43) with respect to the line of business and are not substantial-service employees with respect to any other line of business.

Separate management. Each line of business must have its own separate management. A line of business has its own separate management only if at least 80 percent of the top-paid work force who provide services to the line of business are substantial-service employees with respect to the line of business. The top-paid work force is the top 10 percent, by compensation, of all employees who provide at least 25 percent of their services to the line of business and who are not substantial-service employees with respect to any other line of business. In addition, in determining the group of top-paid employees, the employer may choose to disregard all employees who provide less than 25 percent of their services to the line of business.

Employees of a line of business (the upstream line) that provides property or services to another line of business of the employer (the downstream line) generally are also considered to be providing services to the downstream line of business. Since this presents difficulties for vertically integrated employers desiring to satisfy the separateness tests, an optional rule permits employers to treat these employees as not necessarily providing services to the downstream line. This rule is available only if certain conditions are satisfied, including a requirement that the upstream line provide at least 25 percent of its total output to outside customers of the employer. The optional rule can now apply in the case of an upstream manufacturer that provides all of its product to a downstream line and has few, if any, outside customers. Under this alternative, the vertical integration rule will also apply if, with respect to the downstream line, the business of the upstream line consists primarily of producing or manufacturing tangible property, and the same type of tangible property is provided to unrelated customers by some entities engaged in a business similar to the upstream line. The alternative would apply also for purposes of satisfying the requirement that a line of business provide property to customers of the employer. [Prop Reg §§ 1.414(r)-2(b)(2)(i), 1.414(r)-3(d)]

> **Example.** El Glucko Corporation operates two lines of business, one engaged in upholstery textile manufacturing and the other in furniture manufacturing. The upholstery textile line of business provides its entire output of upholstery textiles to the furniture line of business. The furniture line of business uses the upholstery textiles in the manufacture of upholstered furniture for sale to the customers of El Glucko Corporation. The furniture line of business substantially modifies the upholstery textiles provided to it by the upholstery textile line of business in providing upholstered furniture products to cus-tomers of the corporation. In addition, although the upholstery textile line of business does not provide upholstery textiles to customers of the corporation, some entities engaged in upholstery textile manufac-turing provide upholstery textiles to customers outside their controlled groups. Under these facts, El Glucko Corporation's two lines of business satisfy the requirements for the optional rule. Thusly, the employees of the upholstery textile line of business will be deemed to provide services only to that line of business for purposes of the separate work force and separate management requirements, the 50-employee requirement (see Q 5:37), and the determination of the employees of each qualified separate line of business (see Q 5:43).

Q 5:36   What is a qualified separate line of business?

To demonstrate that the employer maintains qualified separate lines of business, the following requirements must be satisfied: (1) each separate line of business must have at least 50 employees (see Q 5:37); (2) the employer must notify IRS that it treats itself as operating qualified separate lines of business (see Q 5:38); and (3) the line must satisfy administrative scrutiny (see Q 5:39). [Prop Reg § 1.414(r)-1(b)(2)(iv)]

Q 5:37   What is the 50-employee requirement?

One of the requirements to establish that the employer maintains qualified separate lines of business (see Q 5:36) is that each separate line of business (see Q 5:35) must have 50 or more employees. [IRC § 414(r)(2)(A); Prop Reg § 1.414(r)-1(b)(2)(iv)(B)]

The 50-employee requirement must be satisfied on each day of the testing year (see Q 5:44). All employees who provide services exclusively to the separate line of business (see Q 5:43), *including* employees who are covered under a collective bargaining agreement, are counted. However, employees who normally work less than 17½ hours per week, who normally work six months or less during the year, who are under age 21, or who have not completed six months of service are not taken into account. [Prop Reg § 1.414(r)-4(b)]

Q 5:38 What is the notice requirement?

To satisfy the notice requirement, the employer must notify IRS that it treats itself as operating qualified separate lines of business (see Q 5:36). [IRC § 414(r)(2)(B); Prop Reg § 1.414(r)-1(b)(2)(iv)(C)]

The notice is given with respect to all the qualified separate lines of business of the employer and with respect to all retirement plans of the employer for plan years beginning in the testing year (see Q 5:44). [Prop Reg § 1.414(r)-4(c)]

Notice that the employer wishes to be treated as operating qualified separate lines of business is given by filing Form 5310-A, Notice of Merger, Consolidation or Transfer of Plan Assets or Liabilities. A revised Form 5310-A will be available early in 1994. Until the revised form is ready, an employer should print "QSLOB NOTICE" in bold letters on the top of Form 5310-A and submit an attachment with the form containing the following information:

1. The identification of each qualified separate line of business;

2. The identity of each plan maintained by the employer;

3. The qualified separate lines of business that have employees benefiting under each separate plan; and

4. The Code sections for which the employer is testing on a qualified separate line of business basis (i.e., minimum coverage (see Q 5:15) or minimum participation (see Q 5:24)). [Rev Proc 93-40, 1993-31 IRB]

Q 5:39   What is the administrative scrutiny requirement?

To satisfy the administrative scrutiny requirement that the employer maintains qualified separate lines of business (see Q 5:36), a separate line of business (see Q 5:35) must meet either the statutory safe harbor test (see Q 5:40) or one of the administrative safe harbors (see Q 5:41). A separate line of business that does not satisfy any of these safe harbors may still satisfy this requirement if the employer requests and receives from IRS an individual determination that the separate line of business satisfies administrative scrutiny (see Q 5:42). Each separate line of business of an employer must satisfy the administrative scrutiny requirement but need not satisfy this requirement in the same manner as the employer's other separate lines of business. [IRC § 414(r)(2)(C); Prop Reg § 1.414(r)-1(b)(2)(iv)(D)]

Q 5:40   What is the statutory safe harbor?

A qualified separate line of business (see Q 5:36) satisfies the statutory safe harbor for administrative scrutiny (see Q 5:39) if the percentage of highly compensated employees (see Q 3:2) of the separate line of business (see Q 5:35) falls within a range that is at least 50 percent but no more than 200 percent of the highly compensated employee percentage of the employer as a whole (see Q 5:43). The highly compensated employee percentage ratio of a separate line of business is calculated by determining a fraction (expressed as a percentage), the numerator of which is the percentage of the employees of the separate line of business who are highly compensated employees, and the denominator of which is the percentage of all employees of the employer who are highly compensated employees.

Additionally, if at least 10 percent of all highly compensated employees of the employer perform services exclusively for a particular separate line of business, that separate line of business will be deemed to satisfy the 50 percent requirement of the statutory safe harbor. However, a separate line of business that satisfies this special 10 percent rule still must satisfy the 200 percent requirement of the statutory safe harbor. [IRC § 414(r)(3); Prop Reg § 1.414(r)-5(b)]

Q 5:41 What are the administrative safe harbors?

There are five administrative safe harbors for the administrative scrutiny requirement (see Q 5:39). To permit the application of the minimum coverage and minimum participation standards (see Qs 5:15, 5:24) on a qualified separate line of business basis, these administrative safe harbors delineate situations that IRS has determined pass administrative scrutiny without the need for an individual determination (see Q 5:42). [IRC § 414(r)(2)(C); Prop Reg §§ 1.414(r)-5(c)–1.414(r)-5(g)]

Industry category safe harbor. This administrative safe harbor is satisfied only if the separate line of business (see Q 5:35) is in a different industry or industries from every other separate line of business of the employer. An employer may disregard foreign operations in determining whether a separate line of business is in a different industry or industries from every other separate line of business of the employer. For purposes of this administrative safe harbor, there are 12 industry categories:

1. *Food and Agriculture.* Food, beverages, tobacco, food stores and restaurants.
2. *Textiles and Clothing.* Textile mill products, apparel and other finished products made from fabrics and other similar materials (including leather and leather products), and general merchandise stores.
3. *Forest Products.* Pulp, paper, lumber and wood products (including furniture).
4. *Transportation.* Transportation equipment and services.
5. *Finance.* Banking, insurance, and financial industries.
6. *Utilities.* Public utilities and other regulated industries and communications.
7. *Coal and Metals.* Metal industries and coal mining and production.
8. *Machinery and Electronics.* Industrial and commercial machinery; computers and other electronic and electrical equipment and components.
9. *Petroleum and Chemicals.* Oil and gas extraction, production and distribution (including gasoline service stations);

petroleum refining and related industries; chemicals and allied products; rubber and miscellaneous plastic products.

10. *Construction and Real Estate.* Construction industry, real estate, stone, clay, and glass products.

11. *Leisure.* Entertainment, sports, and hotels.

12. *Printing and Publishing.* Printing, publishing, and allied industries.

[Rev Proc 91-64, 1991-2 CB 866]

Merger and acquisition safe harbor. This second administrative safe harbor is satisfied if (1) the employer designates the acquired business as a line of business; (2) the line of business satisfies the separateness criteria; and (3) there are not any significant changes in the work force of the acquired separate line of business.

FAS 14 safe harbor. The third administrative safe harbor (the reportable business segments safe harbor) requires that a separate line of business be reported as one or more reportable industry segments in accordance with the Statement of Financial Accounting Standards No. 14, Financial Reporting for Segments of a Business Enterprise (FAS 14).

Average benefits safe harbor. If the highly compensated employee percentage ratio (see Q 5:40) of the separate line of business is less than 50 percent, the separate line of business will satisfy this administrative safe harbor if the actual benefit percentage of the nonhighly compensated employees (see Q 3:13) of the separate line of business is at least equal to the actual benefit percentage of all other nonhighly compensated employees of the employer (see Q 5:19). Similarly, if the highly compensated employee percentage ratio of the separate line of business is greater than 200 percent, the separate line of business will satisfy this safe harbor if the actual benefit percentage of the highly compensated employees (see Q 3:2) of the separate line of business does not exceed the actual benefit percentage of all other highly compensated employees of the employer.

Minimum or maximum benefits safe harbor. The fifth and last administrative safe harbor is the minimum or maximum benefits safe harbor. If the highly compensated employee percentage ratio of the separate line of business is less than 50 percent, then, under the minimum benefit requirement, at least 80 percent of the nonhighly compensated employees (excluding those who do not meet the lowest age and service eligibility requirements of any plan that benefits employees in the separate line of business) in that separate line of business must benefit under a retirement plan, and each of these employees must receive at least a specified minimum benefit. The minimum benefit standard can be satisfied on the basis of the average benefit accruals or allocations provided to nonhighly compensated employees; but, in contrast to the 80 percent requirement, the averaging must be based on 100 percent of such nonhighly compensated employees. If the highly compensated employee percentage ratio of the separate line of business is more than 200 percent, then, under the maximum benefit requirement, each highly compensated employee who benefits under a retirement plan in that separate line of business must receive no more than a specified maximum benefit.

Q 5:42   Can the administrative scrutiny requirement be satisfied if the safe harbors are not?

Yes. A separate line of business (see Q 5:35) that does not satisfy either the statutory safe harbor (see Q 5:40) or any of the administrative safe harbors (see Q 5:41) may still satisfy the administrative scrutiny requirement if the employer requests and receives from IRS an individual determination that the separate line of business satisfies administrative scrutiny. [IRC § 414(r)(2)(C); Prop Reg § 1.414(r)-6]

This determination process applies to those situations in which the separate line of business does not satisfy any of the administrative scrutiny safe harbors (see Q 5:41). Effective October 12, 1993, IRS began accepting requests for individual determinations. An employer cannot make a request for a testing year (see Q 5:44) that ended prior to the date of the request.

In determining whether a separate line of business will receive an individual determination, IRS will consider all relevant facts and circumstances. Among the factors that may be considered in analyzing whether separate lines of business exist are the following, no one of which will necessarily be determinative:

- Differences in property or services provided
- Separateness of organization and operation
- Nature of business competition
- History of the separate lines of business
- Geographic area in which the businesses are operated
- Degree to which the separate line of business fails to satisfy the applicable safe harbors
- Size and composition of the separate lines of business
- Allocation method used for residual shared employees (see Q 5:43)
- Level of benefits provided by each separate line of business
- Other separate lines of business and
- Whether the separate line of business operates in a regulated industry.

[Rev Proc 93-41, 1993-31 IRB]

If the separate line of business does not satisfy any of the safe harbors and does not obtain a favorable individual determination, the separate line of business will not satisfy administrative scrutiny.

Q 5:43　Who are the employees of each qualified separate line of business?

For purposes of testing retirement plans (see Qs 4:9, 5:15, 5:24) benefiting employees of a qualified separate line of business (see Qs 5:35, 5:36) and for purposes of applying the statutory safe harbor (see Q 5:40) and the minimum or maximum benefits safe harbor (see Q 5:41), an employer must determine which employees are treated as employees of each qualified separate line of business. [Prop Reg § 1.414(r)-7]

All employees must be assigned among the employer's qualified separate lines of business. The employees of a qualified separate line of business consist of all employees who provide substantial services to the qualified separate line of business and all other employees who are allocated to the qualified separate line of business. An employee is a substantial-service employee with respect to a line of business

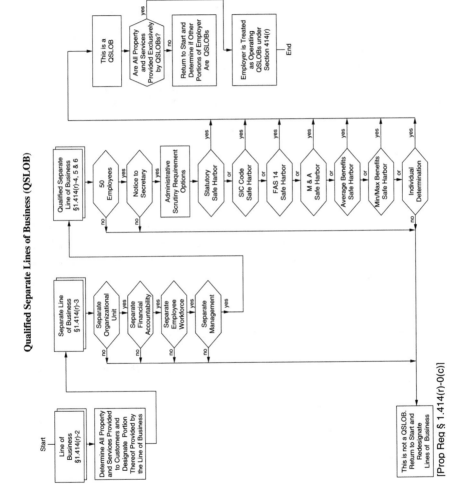

Qualified Separate Lines of Business (QSLOB)

[Prop Req § 1.414(r)-0(c)]

(see Q 5:34) for a testing year (see Q 5:44) if at least 75 percent of the employee's services are provided to that line of business for that testing year. Employers may treat employees who provide between 50 percent and 75 percent of their services to a particular qualified separate line of business as substantial-service employees with respect to that line of business and assign those employees to that qualified separate line of business for all purposes. This option may be exercised by the employer on an employee-by-employee basis; and, if not elected, that employee is treated as a residual shared employee. [Prop Reg §§ 1.414(r)-11(b)(2), 1.414(r)-11(b)(4)]

Employees who are not substantial-service employees with respect to any line of business are referred to as residual shared employees. All residual shared employees must be assigned under the same allocation method, and each residual shared employee must be allocated to only one qualified separate line of business.

There are three permissible allocation methods:

Dominant line of business method. Under the first method for allocating residual shared employees, an employer is permitted to allocate all its residual shared employees to its dominant line of business.

Pro-rata method. The second method permits the employer to allocate residual shared employees among its qualified separate lines of business in proportion to the percentage of all substantial-service employees who provide their services to each qualified separate line of business.

HCE percentage ratio method. The third method of allocation permits the employer to allocate residual shared employees among its qualified separate lines of business in a manner generally consistent with the statutory safe harbor for satisfying administrative scrutiny (see Q 5:40).

Q 5:44   What is the testing year?

For purposes of determining whether an employer operates qualified separate lines of business for *bona fide* business reasons (see Q 5:33), the employer must apply the requirements (see Qs 5:34–5:43) on the basis of the testing year. The testing year is the calendar year. Similarly, an employer's retirement plans are tested for discrimination (see Q 4:9), minimum coverage (see Q 5:15), and minimum participation (see Q 5:24) separately with respect to the employees of each qualified separate line of business for all plan years that begin in the testing year. [Prop Reg §§ 1.414(r)-1(d)(6), 1.414(r)-11(b)(5); Rev Proc 93-42, 1993-31 IRB; Ann 93-130, 1993-31, IRB]

Q 5:45 What are the averaging rules for the separate lines of business requirements?

For purposes of determining certain percentages (see Qs 5:35, 5:40) for testing whether lines of business satisfy separate lines of business requirements, the employer is permitted to use up to a five-year moving average, absent large fluctuations. In determining whether specific percentages have been satisfied, this rule permits the employer to average the results for the current testing year (see Q 5:44) with the results for the immediately preceding one, two, three, or four testing years. The purpose of this rule is to provide stability from year to year in the application of the separate lines of business requirements. [Prop Reg § 1.414(r)-11(c)]

Q 5:46 Is there a flowchart to show how the qualified separate lines of business requirements work?

Yes. IRS has created the flowchart on page 5-35 to show how the major provisions of the qualified separate lines of business requirements (see Qs 5:34–5:43) are applied.

Q 5:47 What is the effective date of the new qualified separate lines of business requirements?

The new qualified separate lines of business requirements (see Qs 5:34–5:43) apply to plan years beginning on or after January 1, 1992. With respect to plan years beginning before October 12, 1993 (see Q 5:42), an employer is treated as operating qualified separate lines of business if the employer reasonably determines that it meets the requirements (other than the administrative scrutiny requirement; see Q 5:39). Whether an employer reasonably determines that it meets these requirements will generally be determined on the basis of all relevant facts and circumstances, including the extent to which the employer has resolved unclear issues in its favor. [Prop Reg § 1.414(r)-1(d)(9); Notice 92-36, 1992-2 CB 364; Ann 92-29, 1992-9 IRB 37; IRS Field Office Directive on Good-Faith Compliance (June 12, 1992)]

Q 5:48 Who is a leased employee?

A leased employee is an individual who performs services for another person (the recipient) under an arrangement between the recipient and a third person (the leasing organization) who is otherwise treated as the individual's employer. The services performed by an individual for the recipient must be of a type that is historically performed by employees (see Q 5:49). [IRC §§ 414(n)(1), 414(n)(2)]

In 1987, IRS issued proposed regulations relating to leased employees. However, in 1993, as part of the Regulatory Burden Reduction Initiative, IRS withdrew these proposed regulations because IRS did not plan to finalize them. [TD 8474]

Q 5:49 Who is the employer of a leased employee?

The leased employee (see Q 5:48) is treated as the recipient's employee if the leased employee has performed services for the recipient pursuant to an agreement with the leasing organization on a substantially full-time basis for a period of at least one year and the services are of a type historically performed by employees in the recipient's business field. [IRC §§ 414(n)(1), 414(n)(2)

If TSB '93 (see Q 1:13) is enacted, for years beginning *after* 1993, the requirement that the services provided to the recipient be of a type historically performed by employees will be changed to a requirement that such services be performed under significant direction or control by the recipient. [TSB '93, Act § 231]

Q 5:50 When is the leased employee first considered an employee of the recipient?

The leased employee (see Q 5:48) is treated as the recipient's employee after the leased employee has performed services for the recipient for a period of one year. Once this occurs, the leased employee's years of service for the recipient include the entire period for which the leased employee performed services for the recipient. [IRC § 414(n)(4)

Q 5:51 What happens if the leased employee participates in the leasing organization's qualified retirement plan?

If the leasing organization maintains a qualified retirement plan, contributions or benefits for the leased employee (see Q 5:48) are treated as if provided by the recipient to the extent those contributions or benefits are attributable to services performed by the leased employee for the recipient. [IRC § 414(n)(1)(B)]

Q 5:52 When will the leased employee not be treated as an employee of the recipient?

A leased employee (see Q 5:48) will not be treated as the recipient's employee if leased employees do not constitute more than 20 percent of the recipient's nonhighly compensated work force and each leased employee is covered by a qualified money purchase pension plan (see Q 2:4) maintained by the leasing organization that provides the following:

- Immediate participation
- Full and immediate vesting
- A nonintegrated contribution rate of 10 percent of compensation

The immediate participation requirement does not apply to (1) employees who perform substantially all of their services for the leasing organization and (2) employees whose compensation from the leasing organization for each of the four preceding plan years is less than $1,000. A money purchase pension plan meeting these requirements is referred to as a safe harbor plan. The term nonhighly compensated work force means the aggregate number of individuals other than highly compensated employees (see Qs 3:2, 3:13) who are employees of the recipient and have performed services for the recipient on a substantially full-time basis for one year or who are leased employees with respect to the recipient. [IRC § 414(n)(5)]

Q 5:53 Can an employer utilizing the services of leased employees obtain IRS approval of its qualified retirement plan?

Yes. An employer utilizing one or more leased employees (see Q 5:48) may be able to obtain a favorable determination letter (see Q 15:1) by following an application procedure developed by IRS. [Rev Proc 85-43, 1985-2 CB 501]

Chapter 6

Contribution and Benefit Limitations

ERISA set limits on the amount that could be allocated to an employee under a defined contribution plan and on the amount of the annual retirement benefit that could be provided to an employee under a defined benefit plan. These limits were subject to cost-of-living increases; and, because of the high rates of inflation in the late 1970s, these limits rose significantly. Congress reduced these limits in TEFRA and again in TRA '86. This chapter examines limitations now in effect for both defined contribution and defined benefit plans.

Q 6:1   How much may the company contribute to a defined contribution plan on behalf of a participant?

The Code sets limits on contributions and other additions made to a participant's account in a defined contribution plan (see Q 2:2). Contributions and other additions are referred to as the annual addition to a participant's account. The annual addition is the sum of the following:

1. Employer contributions;
2. Employee contributions;
3. Forfeitures;
4. Amounts allocated to an individual medical account that is part of a pension or annuity plan maintained by the employer; and

5. Amounts derived from contributions that are attributable to post-retirement medical benefits allocated to the separate account of a key employee (see Q 22:24) under a welfare benefit fund maintained by the employer.

[IRC §§ 415(c)(2), 415(l), 419(e), 419A(d)]

The annual addition with respect to a participant's account during any limitation year (see Q 6:14) may not exceed the *lesser* of $30,000 (see Q 6:2) or 25 percent of the participant's compensation (see Q 6:3). [IRC § 415(c)(1)]

The annual addition limitation is best explained by an example:

Participant's compensation for 1993	$80,000
Employer contribution	16,000
Employee contribution	4,000
Forfeitures allocated to participant's account	2,000

Computation of Annual Addition

Employer contribution	$16,000
Employee contribution	4,000
Forfeitures	2,000
Annual Addition	$22,000

The total amount to be allocated to the participant under the defined contribution plan will be $22,000 unless it exceeds the limitation amount, which is the lesser of $30,000 or 25 percent of the participant's compensation. Since the limitation for 1993 is $20,000 (25% of $80,000), the annual addition of $22,000 ($16,000 + $4,000 + $2,000) exceeds the limitation amount. The contributions and other additions to this participant's account therefore may not exceed $20,000.

Employee contributions distributed to correct an excess annual addition are treated as corrective disbursements and are not includible in the employee's gross income. However, if earnings on the returned contributions are distributed to the employee, the earnings are includible in income in the year distributed. If the plan returns employee contributions but not the earnings attributable to the returned contributions, the earnings are treated as additional employee contributions and must be taken into account for annual addition limitation purposes. [Treas Reg § 1.415-6(b)(6)(iv); Rev Proc 92-93, 1992-47 IRB]

See Question 6:27 for a discussion of the family aggregation rule.

Q 6:2 Will the $30,000 ceiling on the annual addition rise?

The dollar limitation on the annual addition is set at the *greater* of $30,000 or one-quarter of the dollar limitation applicable to defined benefit plans (see Q 6:8). Therefore, the $30,000 ceiling cannot increase until the defined benefit plan ceiling increases to more than $120,000. [IRC § 415(c)(1)]

Q 6:3 What does compensation mean for purposes of the annual addition limitation?

For annual addition limitation purposes (see Q 6:1), compensation means the total compensation received from the employer for the limitation year (see Q 6:14). For a self-employed individual (see Q 29:8), compensation means earned income (see Q 29:10). This is commonly referred to as Section 415 compensation. [IRC § 415(c)(3); Treas Reg § 1.415-2(d)(4)]

Items treated as compensation include:

1. Wages, salaries, fees for professional services, and other amounts received (without regard to whether or not an amount is paid in cash) for personal services actually rendered in the course of employment to the extent that the amounts are includible in income (including, but not limited to, commissions paid to sales representatives, compensation for services on the basis of a percentage of profits, commissions on insurance premiums, tips, bonuses, fringe benefits, reimbursements, and expense allowances), whether earned from sources inside or outside the United States;

2. Employer-provided accident and health insurance benefits and medical reimbursement plan benefits, but only to the extent includible in the income of the employee [American Family Mutual Ins Co v US, 71 AFTR 2d (WD Wis 1993)];

3. Moving expenses paid by an employer, but only to the extent not deductible by the employee under Section 217;

4. The value of a nonqualified stock option granted to an employee by the employer, but only to the extent includible in the income of the employee for the taxable year in which it was granted; and

5. The amount includible in income that results when an employee who receives restricted property makes an election to be taxed on it under Section 83(b). [Treas Reg § 1.415-2(d)(2)]

If the qualified retirement plan defines Section 415 compensation to include only those items specified in paragraph 1 above and to exclude all items not treated as compensation as set forth below, the plan will contain a definition of compensation that satisfies Section 415. [Treas Reg § 1.415-2(d)(10)]

Items not treated as compensation include the following:

1. Elective or salary reduction contributions to a 401(k) plan to the extent not includible in the income of the employee for the year in which they are contributed (see Q 23:5);

2. Employer contributions to a tax-sheltered annuity whether or not excludible from the income of the employee;

3. Certain deferred compensation payments [Licciardi v Kropp Forge Div Employees' Retirement Plan, No. 92-2731 (7th Cir 1993)];

4. SEP contributions that are excludible from the income of the employee (see Q 27:16);

5. Amounts realized from the exercise of a nonqualified stock option or when restricted stock or property held by an employee becomes freely transferrable or is no longer subject to a substantial risk of forfeiture; and

6. Amounts realized from the sale, exchange, or other disposition of stock acquired under a qualified stock option. [Treas Reg § 1.415-2(d)(3)]

In lieu of defining Section 415 compensation as set forth above, a qualified retirement plan may utilize alternative definitions of Section

415 compensation (see Q 6:4). The definition of Section 415 compensation applies only to the calculation of the annual addition limitation; a different definition of compensation may be used for the allocation or crediting of contributions under a defined contribution plan (see Qs 6:28–6:36).

The annual compensation of an employee taken into account under a qualified retirement plan may not exceed $200,000, with adjustments for inflation. The $200,000 limitation is reduced to $150,000 for benefits accruing in plan years beginning *after* December 31,1993. For details, see Questions 6:21 through 6:26, and also see Question 6:27 for a discussion of the family aggregation rule.

Q 6:4   Can an alternative definition of Section 415 compensation be used for annual addition limitation purposes?

In lieu of defining Section 415 compensation to include and exclude certain specified forms of compensation (see Q 6:3), a qualified retirement plan may define Section 415 compensation (except in the case of self-employed individuals; see Q 29:8) using either of the following wage reporting definitions:

1. Wages under Section 3401(a) and all other payments of compensation to an employee by the employer for which the employer is required to furnish the employee a written statement under Sections 6041(d), 6051(a)(3), and 6052. This definition may be modified to exclude amounts paid or reimbursed by the employer for moving expenses incurred by an employee, but only to the extent that at the time of the payment it is reasonable to believe that these amounts are deductible by the employee under Section 217. Compensation must be determined disregarding any rules that limit remuneration based on the nature or location of employment or services performed.

2. Wages under Section 3401(a) for purposes of income tax withholding, disregarding any rules that limit remuneration based on the nature or location of employment or services performed.

[Treas Reg § 1.415-2(d)(11)]

Q 6:5 Can a qualified retirement plan include accrued compensation for annual addition limitation purposes?

For limitation years (see Q 6:14) beginning after December 31, 1991, an employer may *not* use accrued compensation. Any election previously made to use accrued compensation is not valid for limitation years beginning after December 31, 1991.

However, an employer may include in compensation amounts earned but not paid in a year because of the timing of pay periods and pay days if these amounts are paid during the first few weeks of the next year, the amounts are included on a uniform and consistent basis with respect to all similarly situated employees, and no compensation is included in more than one limitation period. No formal election is required to include the accrued compensation permitted under this *de minimis* rule. [Treas Reg § 1.415-2(d)(5)]

Q 6:6 Does a withdrawn employee voluntary contribution that is replaced during the same year constitute part of the annual addition?

Yes. If employee voluntary contributions (see Q 6:18) are withdrawn and then replaced during the same limitation year (see Q 6:14), they are treated as part of the annual addition (see Q 6:1).

Example. Sallie made employee voluntary contributions of $3,000 in January, 1993 and withdrew $2,000 in June. If she replaced the $2,000 within the same limitation year of the $3,000 contribution, she will be deemed to have made a total of $5,000 of employee voluntary contributions. [Ltr Rul 8622044]

Q 6:7 Is a transfer of benefits from one qualified retirement plan to another considered an annual addition in the year of transfer?

IRS has ruled that a trustee-to-trustee transfer of plan benefits by a participant in a defined benefit plan (see Q 2:3) to a 401(k) plan (see Q 2:11) was not an annual addition (see Q 6:1). IRS has also ruled that amounts held in a trust under a frozen profit sharing plan (see Qs 2:6, 22:15) that were transferred to a second trust, which trust then held the assets of both the frozen plan and another profit sharing plan maintained by the employer, did not constitute an annual addition for the limitation year (see Q 6:14) in which the transfer occurred. [Treas Reg § 1.415-6(b)(2)(iv); Ltr Ruls 9221045, 9111046, 9052058]

Q 6:8   What is the maximum annual retirement benefit that a defined benefit plan may provide?

The annual benefit (see Q 6:9) that may be paid to a participant under a defined benefit plan (see Q 2:3) is limited to the *lesser* of (1) $90,000, with cost-of-living adjustments, or (2) 100 percent of the participant's average compensation (see Q 6:10). [IRC § 415(b)(1)]

Cost-of-living adjustments to the $90,000 limit are calculated in a manner similar to the annual cost-of-living increases in Social Security benefits. To calculate the cost-of-living increases for any particular year, the Consumer Price Index for All Urban Consumers (CPI-U) must be obtained from the Department of Labor for the last three months (i.e., October, November, and December) of the previous year. The sum of the three indices is then divided by the sum of the indices for the last three months of the base year. The quotient of these sums is truncated to five decimal places. This result is then rounded to four decimal places. Finally, this result is multiplied by the dollar limitation, which is then rounded to the nearest dollar to obtain the new dollar limitation for a particular year.

For a limitation year ending in 1993, the $90,000 limit has been increased to $115,641. [IRC § 415(d); Treas Reg § 1.415-1(f)(1); IR 93-2 (Jan 15, 1993)] For prior limitation years, the adjusted limit was:

Limitation Year Ending In	Adjusted Limit
1992	$112,221
1991	$108,963
1990	$102,582
1989	$ 98,064
1988	$ 94,023

Example. FSB Corp. maintains a defined benefit plan with a plan year beginning on February 1 and ending on January 31. The limitation year is the same as the plan year; and Fred and Sue, who are participants in the plan, both have compensation of $120,000 for the limitation year ended January 31, 1993. The maximum annual retirement benefit for both Fred and Sue is $115,641 even though the limitation year began in 1992.

If TSB '93 (see Q 1:13) is enacted, this adjustment will be rounded to the nearest $1,000 for calendar years beginning *after* 1993. [TSB '93, Act § 232]

See Question 6:27 for a discussion of the family aggregation rule.

Q 6:9   What does annual benefit mean?

The term "annual benefit" means a retirement benefit payable annually in the form of a straight life annuity (with no ancillary or incidental benefits) under a defined benefit plan (see Q 2:3) to which employees do not contribute and to which no rollover contributions are made. (Under a straight life annuity, payments terminate upon the death of the annuitant.) [IRC § 415(b)(2)(A)]

If benefits under a defined benefit plan are payable in a form other than a straight life annuity, the limits (see Q 6:8) are adjusted to a benefit that is equivalent to a straight life annuity. But if benefits under the plan are payable in the form of a joint and survivor annuity (see Q 10:8), no reduction in the annual benefit is required. IRS has ruled that, if the disability benefit under a retirement plan exceeds the retirement benefit, the disability benefit is subject to the annual benefit limits. [IRC § 415(b)(2)(B); Ltr Rul 9237042]

If benefits under a defined benefit plan commence before the participant attains Social Security retirement age (see Q 6:12), the $90,000 limit is *reduced* to the actuarial equivalent of a $90,000 annual benefit commencing at the Social Security retirement age. Similarly, if benefits commence after the Social Security retirement age, the $90,000 limit is *increased* to the actuarial equivalent of a $90,000 annual benefit commencing at the Social Security retirement age. [IRC §§ 415(b)(2)(C), 415(b)(2)(D)]

In adjusting the benefit limits for payment in a form other than a straight life annuity or for payments commencing before the Social Security retirement age, the interest rate assumption cannot be less than the *greater* of 5 percent or the interest rate specified in the plan. The interest rate for an adjustment if the payments commence after the Social Security retirement age cannot exceed the *lesser* of 5 percent or the rate specified in the plan. [IRC § 415(b)(2)(E)]

Q 6:10   What does average compensation mean for purposes of the annual retirement benefit limitation?

For purposes of the limitation on a participant's annual retirement benefit under a defined benefit plan (see Q 6:8), average compensation means the average compensation for the high three years. A participant's high three years is the period of consecutive years (not more than three) during which the participant both was an active participant in the plan and had the greatest aggregate compensation from the employer. It should be noted that IRS regulations use the high three years of service, not years of participation. [IRC § 415(b)(3); Treas Reg § 1.415-3(b)(3)]

For purposes of calculating average compensation, the definition of compensation parallels the definition of Section 415 compensation used to calculate the annual addition limitation, and the $200,000 annual compensation limitation, with adjustments for inflation, also applies (see Qs 6:3, 6:4, 6:21–6:26). The definition of Section 415 compensation applies only to the calculation of the maximum annual retirement benefit; a different definition of compensation may be used to calculate the accrued benefit (see Q 9:2) under a defined benefit plan (see Qs 6:28–6:36).

See Question 6:27 for a discussion of the family aggregation rule.

Q 6:11   Is there a minimum number of years of participation or service required before a participant in a defined benefit plan qualifies for the maximum annual benefit?

If a participant has less than ten years of participation with the employer at retirement, the dollar limitation ($90,000; see Q 6:8) is reduced by 10 percent for each year of *participation* less than ten. The maximum percentage limitation (100 percent of the participant's average compensation; see Q 6:10) is reduced by 10 percent for each year of *service* less than ten. In both cases, the reduction in the limitation is never more than 90 percent. [IRC § 415(b)(5); Rev Proc 92-42, 1992-1 CB 872]

Example 1. Stephanie has seven years of service but only five years of plan participation at retirement in 1993, and her average compensation is $115,641. Stephanie's maximum annual benefit is $57,821 [the lesser of $57,821 (5/10 × $115,641) or $80,949 (7/10 × 100% × $115,641)].

Example 2. If Stephanie's average compensation is $70,000, the maximum annual benefit is $49,000 [the lesser of $57,821 (5/10 x $115,641) or $49,000 (7/10 × 100% × $70,000)].

In any event, the annual benefit payable to a participant under a defined benefit plan does not exceed the limitation (see Q 6:8) if the following conditions are met:

1. The annual benefit payable to a participant under the plan (and under all other defined benefit plans of the employer) does not exceed $10,000 for the plan year or for any prior plan year; and

2. The employer has not at any time maintained a defined contribution plan in which the participant participated.

Therefore, if a participant's average compensation is less than $10,000, the annual benefit under the plan could be $10,000—more than the participant's average compensation. If the participant has less than ten years of service with the employer, however, the $10,000 amount is reduced by 10 percent for each year less than ten (the reduction is never more than 90 percent). [IRC § 415(b)(4)]

Q 6:12   What is the Social Security retirement age?

For purposes of calculating adjustments to the dollar limitation ($90,000) on benefits payable under a defined benefit plan (see Q 6:9), Social Security retirement age means the age used as the retirement age under the Social Security Act (rounded to the next lower whole number) and depends on the calendar year of birth.

| | *Social Security* |
Year of birth	*retirement age*
Before 1938	65
After 1937 but before 1955	66
After 1954	67

[IRC § 415(b); Social Security Act § 216(1)]

Q 6:13   What happens if the employee's accrued benefit under a defined benefit plan exceeded the TRA '86 limitations?

If the defined benefit plan was in existence on May 6, 1986, the employee was a participant as of the first day of the first plan year beginning after 1986, and the employee's accrued benefit (see Q 9:2) as of the end of the plan year beginning before 1987 exceeded the TRA '86 maximum allowable benefit (see Qs 6:8, 6:9), the higher accrued benefit is preserved. [TRA '86 § 1106(i)]

Q 6:14   What is the limitation year?

The limitation year, with respect to any qualified retirement plan maintained by the employer, is the calendar year. However, instead of using the calendar year, an employer may elect to use any other consecutive 12-month period as the limitation year. The election is made by the adoption of a written resolution by the employer. This requirement is satisfied if the election is made in connection with the adoption of the plan or any amendments to the plan. [Treas Reg § 1.415-2(b)]

In the case of a group of employers that constitutes either a controlled group of corporations or trades or businesses (whether or not incorporated) under common control (see Q 5:30), the election to use a consecutive 12-month period other than the calendar year as the limitation year must be made by all members of the group that maintain a qualified retirement plan.

Once established, the limitation year may be changed only by making the election described above. Any change in the limitation year must be a change to a 12-month period commencing with any day within the current limitation year. The limitations are applied in the normal manner to the new limitation year and are separately applied to a limitation period that begins with the first day of the current limitation year and ends on the day before the first day of the first limitation year for which the change is effective. The dollar limitation with respect to this limitation period is determined by multiplying (1) the applicable dollar limitation for the calendar year in which the limitation period ends by (2) a fraction, the numerator of which is the number of months (including any fractional part of a month) in the limitation period, and the denominator of which is 12. This adjustment of the dollar limitation *only* applies to a defined contribution plan (see Q 2:2).

> **Example.** In 1993, Sil-Fen, Inc., an employer with a profit sharing plan using the calendar year as the limitation year elects to change the limitation year to a period beginning July 1 and ending June 30. Because of this change, the plan must satisfy the limitations for the limitation period beginning January 1, 1993 and ending June 30, 1993. In applying the limitations to this limitation period, the amount of compensation taken into account may only include compensation for this period. Furthermore, the dollar limitation for this period is $15,000 ($30,000 × 6/12).

Q 6:15   What happens if an employee participates in both a defined benefit plan and a defined contribution plan?

If an employee participates in both a defined benefit plan (see Q 2:3) and a defined contribution plan (see Q 2:2) that are maintained by the same employer, a special formula is used to determine the combined maximum limit on benefits and contributions. [IRC § 415(e)]

For an employee who participates in both plans, the sum of the defined benefit plan fraction and the defined contribution plan fraction cannot exceed 1.0. To arrive at the overall maximum limitation, take the following steps:

1. Compute a defined benefit plan fraction. The numerator of this fraction is the projected annual retirement benefit determined at year end. The denominator is the *lesser* of 1.25 times the

dollar limitation for the current year or 1.4 times the percentage limitation for the current year. [IRC § 415(e)(2)]

2. Compute a defined contribution plan fraction. The numerator of this fraction is the total of the annual additions to the participant's account for all years determined at year end. The denominator is the *lesser* of 1.25 times the dollar limitation or 1.4 times the percentage limitation for the current year and all years of prior service. [IRC § 415(e)(1)]

Each plan may contain a fail-safe provision that freezes the annual addition or benefit accrual at a level that prevents the limitation from being exceeded. For purposes of the 1.0 rule, the reduction, if any, in the defined benefit plan dollar limitation is based upon years of service, not years of participation (see Q 6:11). [IRC § 415(b)(5)(B)]

Example. Mr. James, age 45, incorporates his business in January, 1993. The corporation adopts a 100 percent defined benefit plan and a 10-percent-of-compensation money purchase pension plan. Mr. James earns $115,641 in 1993. Here is how the 1.0 rule works:

1. The defined benefit plan fraction is .8 [$115,641/$144,551 (the lesser of 1.25 × $115,641 or 1.4 × $115,641)].

2. The defined contribution plan fraction is .308 [$11,564/$37,500 (the lesser of 1.25 × $30,000 or 1.4 × $28,910)].

3. The two fractions total 1.108.

At this point, the 1.0 rule comes into play—one of the fractions must be reduced. If the 10-percent-of-compensation contribution formula under the defined contribution plan is reduced to 6.485 percent, the defined contribution plan fraction will be .2 [$7,500 (6.485% × $115,641)/$37,500]. Then, the total of the fractions will be 1.0.

The cost to fund the 100-percent-of-compensation defined benefit plan varies from participant to participant. Note that contributions under a defined benefit plan depend upon the participant's age and the actuarial assumptions, such as interest and retirement age, used by the actuary to calculate that cost. Thus, the combination of a defined benefit plan and a defined contribution plan may provide the employer with a greater tax deduction.

IRS has ruled that, if benefit accruals under a defined benefit plan are frozen (see Q 22:15), the accrued benefit (see Q 9:2) as of the date benefits are frozen becomes the projected annual retirement benefit and is, therefore, the numerator of the defined benefit plan fraction. [Ltr Rul 8936053]

For details on tax deduction rules, see Chapter 12; and, for details on top-heavy combined plans, see Questions 22:51 through 22:58.

Q 6:16 At what level of compensation will the 1.0 rule affect an employee?

If the employee's annual compensation (see Qs 6:3, 6:4, 6:10) exceeds $102,804, the 1.0 rule requires a reduction in one of the plans (see Q 6:15). Under the rule, at $102,804 of compensation, the total of the fractions of a 100 percent defined benefit plan ($102,804/$143,926 = .714) plus a 10 percent defined contribution plan ($10,280/$35,981 = .286) equals 1.0.

If the maximum dollar limits increase (see Qs 6:1, 6:8), the threshold level of compensation for equivalency will also increase, but not necessarily in proportion to the percentage increase in the dollar limits.

Q 6:17 What limits apply to employee contributions required under a qualified retirement plan?

A special nondiscrimination test, the actual contribution percentage (ACP) test, applies to required (i.e., mandatory) employee contributions under all qualified defined contribution plans (see Qs 2:2, 23:48–23:55). If the plan satisfies the special requirements regarding such employee contributions, the plan will not be discriminatory. [Prop Reg § 1.401(a)(4)-1(b)(2)(ii)(B)]

Since a defined benefit plan does not separately account for required employee contributions (such contributions are not allocated or credited to separate accounts), the special nondiscrimination test does not apply, but the plan will generally be deemed nondiscriminatory only if such employee contributions are made at the same rate, expressed as a percentage of compensation, by all employees under the plan. [Prop Reg § 1.401(a)(4)-6]

If required employee contributions are so burdensome that non-highly compensated employees (see Q 3:13) cannot afford to participate, the plan may fail to satisfy the coverage requirements (see Chapter 5) and not be a qualified retirement plan.

Required employee contributions made to a defined contribution plan are considered employee contributions that must satisfy the annual addition limitation (see Q 6:1).

Q 6:18   Is any limit set on the amount that a participant can voluntarily contribute to a qualified retirement plan?

The same special nondiscrimination test (see Q 6:17) applies to employee voluntary contributions. Since employee voluntary contributions under a defined benefit plan (see Q 2:3) will be separately accounted for, there is no limit on the amount of employee voluntary contributions made to either a defined contribution plan or a defined benefit plan as long as the ACP test and other special requirements are satisfied. (see Qs 23:48–23:55).

However, under all circumstances, whether the employee voluntary contributions are made to a defined contribution plan or a defined benefit plan, these contributions are considered employee contributions that must satisfy the annual addition limitation (see Q 6:1).

Q 6:19   What tax advantages are gained when a qualified retirement plan permits participants to make voluntary contributions?

Although participants cannot deduct their voluntary contributions to the plan, they do get the advantage of having their contributions build up free of tax under the protection of the qualified retirement plan's tax shelter (see Qs 1:1, 1:3).

Q 6:20   May a qualified retirement plan permit deductible employee contributions?

The law permitting deductible employee contributions was repealed. [TRA '86 § 1101(b)]

Although deductible employee contributions are no longer permitted, separate accounting by the employer or plan administrator is required with respect to any such contributions that were ever made to the plan to ensure that an employee who later receives a distribution from the plan is able to compute the tax due correctly. However, assets purchased by the plan with deductible employee contributions need not be segregated from other plan assets. [Notice 82-13, 1982-1 CB 360]

Distributions of deductible employee contributions (including earnings) are taxed as ordinary income in the year received unless they are rolled over (that is, transferred tax-free) to an IRA or to another qualified retirement plan. Distributions of deductible employee contributions may also be subject to the early distribution tax (see Q 13:39).

Q 6:21   Is there an annual compensation limit under a qualified retirement plan?

Yes. For each employee who participates in a qualified retirement plan, an annual limit on compensation is required. [IRC § 401(a)(17); Treas Reg § 1.401(a)(17)-1]

This limit applies to a qualified retirement plan in two ways. First, a plan many not base allocations (see Q 2:6), in the case of a defined contribution plan (see Q 2:2), or benefit accruals (see Q 9:2), in the case of a defined benefit plan (see Q 2:3), on compensation in excess of the annual limit. Second, the amount of an employee's annual compensation that may be taken into account in applying certain specified nondiscrimination rules is subject to the annual limitation. [Treas Reg § 1.401(a)(17)-1(a)(1)]

The annual compensation limit is $200,000; however, the $200,000 limitation is reduced to $150,000 for benefits accruing in plan years beginning *after* December 31, 1993. (see Q 6:22). [IRC § 401(a)(17); Treas Reg § 1.401(a)(17)-1(a)(2); RRA '93, Act § 13212]

See Question 6:27 for a discussion of the family aggregation rule.

Q 6:22   Will the $200,000 ceiling on annual compensation rise?

Yes. The amount of the annual limit, $200,000 (see Q 6:21), is adjusted annually for increases in cost-of-living. For 1993, the annual compensation limit is $235,840. [IRC § 401(a)(17); IR 93-2 (Jan 15, 1993)] For prior years, the annual compensation limit was:

Year	Annual Compensation Limit
1992	$228,860
1991	$222,220
1990	$209,200

The adjustment applies to plan years *beginning* in the calendar year in which the adjustment is effective. In addition, any increase in the annual limit applies only to compensation taken into account for the year of the increase and subsequent years and does not apply to compensation for prior years that are used in determining an employee's benefit.

Example 1. L & L Corp. maintains a defined contribution plan with a plan year beginning on July 1 and ending on June 30. For the plan year ended June 30, 1993, Larry's compensation was $235,840. Because the plan year began in 1992, the annual compensation limit in effect on January 1, 1992 ($228,860) applies to the plan for the entire plan year and Larry's excess compensation of $6,980 ($235,840 – $228,860) is disregarded.

Example 2. K & K Corp. maintains a defined benefit plan with a calendar-year plan year. The plan became effective on January 1, 1989, and bases benefits on the average of an employee's compensation for the five highest consecutive years. For each plan year, 1989 through 1993, Leona had compensation of $235,840. The plan cannot base benefits for Leona in 1993 on compensation in excess of $219,224, the average of Leona's annual compensation capped by the limit for the applicable year ($235,840 + $228,860 + $222,220 + $209,200 + $200,000). Each year used in the average is subject to the applicable annual compensation limit for that year.

[Treas Reg §§ 1.401(a)(17)-1(a)(2), 1.401(a)(17)-1(b)(1), 1.401(a)(17)-1(b)(2), 1.401(a)(17)-1(b)(3), 1.401(a)(17)-1(b)(6)]

The annual compensation limit is reduced to $150,000 for the plan year beginning in 1994 (Q 6:21). Although the first cost-of-living adjustment could occur in the plan year beginning in 1995, it probably will not because an adjustment will be made only if it is $10,000 or greater and then will be made in multiples of $10,000 (i.e., rounded down to the next lowest multiple of $10,000). For example, an increase in the cost-of-living of $9,999 will result in no adjustment, and an increase of $19,999 will create an upward adjustment of $10,000. Therefore, the cost-of-living must increase by 6⅔ percent before the first adjustment to the annual compensation limit will occur [6⅔% × $150,000 = $10,000]. [RRA '93, Act § 13212]

Q 6:23 Can a qualified retirement plan use a 12-month period other than the plan year to determine compensation?

Yes. Alternatively, a qualified retirement plan may determine compensation used in determining allocations or benefit accruals for the plan year for all employees on the basis of a 12-consecutive-month period, or periods, ending no later than the last day of the plan year. If compensation is based on these alternative 12-month periods, the annual compensation limit (see Qs 6:21, 6:22) applies to compensation for each of those periods based on the annual compensation limit in effect for the respective calendar year in which each 12-month period *begins*. [Treas Reg § 1.401(a)(17)-1(b)(3)(ii)]

If compensation for a period of less than 12 months is used for a plan year, then the otherwise applicable annual compensation limit is reduced in the same proportion as the reduction in the 12-month period. Furthermore, if the period for determining compensation used in calculating an employee's allocation or accrual for a plan year is a short plan year (i.e., shorter than 12 months), the annual compensation limit is an amount equal to the otherwise applicable annual compensation limit multiplied by the fraction, the numerator of which is the number of months in the short plan year and the denominator of which is 12. [Treas Reg § 1.401(a)(17)-1(b)(3)(iii)(A)]

Example. B & S Corp. adopts a profit sharing plan on October 1, 1993, and the first plan year is the short period of October 1, 1993 to December 31, 1993. Barbra's compensation from B & S Corp. for calendar year 1993 is $235,840. The annual compensation limit for the plan for the short period is $58,960 (3/12 × $235,840), and Barbra's excess compensation of $176,880 ($235,840 – $58,960) is disregarded.

However, no proration is required if the plan formula provides that the allocation or accrual for each employee is based on compensation for the portion of the plan year during which the employee is a participant. [Treas Reg. § 1.401(a)(17)-1(b)(3)(iii)(B)]

Example. S & B Corp. adopts a calendar-year money purchase pension plan on January 1, 1993. Steven, whose compensation is $25,000 per month, commences participation in the plan on July 1, 1993. For purposes of allocating employer contributions, only compensation earned after an employee becomes a participant is used. Steven's entire compensation of $150,000 earned from July 1, 1993 to December 31, 1993 may be used because there is no proration of the annual compensation limit.

Q 6:24 How is the annual compensation limit applied if an employee participates in a qualified retirement plan sponsored by more than one employer?

If the employers are part of a controlled group or an affiliated service group (see Qs 5:30, 5:32, 29:31), the annual compensation limit is applied on an aggregate basis to compensation received from all members of the group. But, if the employers are not related, the annual compensation limit applies separately with respect to the compensation received by an employee from each unrelated employer maintaining the plan rather than to the total compensation from all employers maintaining the plan. [IRC §§ 413(c), 414(b), 414(c), 414(m); Treas Reg § 1.401(a)(17)-1(b)(4)]

Example. Maxine Corp., Sooper-Max Inc., and Maxfly Ltd., which are each unrelated to the others, all adopt a single profit sharing plan for calendar year 1993. Bob is employed by all three corporations and has compensation from each of $100,000. The plan is permitted to take into account the full $300,000 of Bob's compensation from the three corporations for the plan year without violating the annual compensation limit.

Although compensation need not be aggregated in the above example, for purposes of applying the annual addition limitation (see Q 6:1) and the annual retirement benefit limitation (see Q 6:8), contributions or benefits attributable to the employee from all three corporations must be taken into account. Consequently, under the profit sharing plan in the above example, Bob's annual addition limitation is $30,000 in the aggregate. [Treas Reg § 1.415-1(e)]

Q 6:25   Does the annual compensation limit affect the Code's nondiscrimination requirements?

The annual compensation limit (see Qs 6:21, 6:22) applies for purposes of applying the nondiscrimination rules under Sections 401(a)(4), 401(a)(5), 401(l), 401(k)(3), 401(m)(2), and 410(b)(2). The limit also applies in determining whether an alternative method of determining compensation impermissibly discriminates in favor of highly compensated employees (see Qs 3:2, 6:28–6:35). [Treas Reg § 1.401(a)(17)-1(c)]

Q 6:26   When is the annual compensation limit effective?

The annual compensation limit (see Qs 6:21, 6:22) is generally effective for plan years beginning on or after January 1, 1989, but the final regulations published by IRS on September 19, 1991, are effective for plan years beginning on or after January 1, 1994.

For plan years beginning before January 1, 1994, but on or after January 1, 1989, the plan must be operated in accordance with a reasonable, good-faith interpretation of the annual compensation limit requirement. Whether compliance is reasonable and in good faith will be determined on the basis of all the facts and circumstances, including the extent to which the employer has resolved unclear issues in its favor. A reasonable, good-faith interpretation will be deemed to exist, however, if a plan is operated in accordance with the proposed regulations published on May 14, 1990, the final regulations published on September 19, 1991, or the proposed regulations or the proposed amendments to regulations published by IRS in 1993. [Treas Reg § 1.401(a)(17)-1(d); Notice 92-36, 1992-2 CB 364;

Ann 92-29, 1992-9 IRB 37; IRS Field Office Directive on Good-Faith Compliance (June 12, 1992)]

The new $150,000 annual compensation limit is generally effective for plan years beginning on or after January 1, 1994 (see Qs 6:21, 6:22). [RRA '93, Act § 13212(d)(1)]

Q 6:27   What is the family aggregation rule?

If an individual is a member of the family of either a 5 percent owner (see Q 3:4); or a highly compensated employee (see Q 3:3) who is one of the ten most highly compensated employees, the compensation of that individual is treated as if paid to (or on behalf of) a single 5 percent owner or highly compensated employee. Family members include the employee's spouse and any lineal descendant who has not attained age 19 before the close of the year. [IRC §§ 401(a)(17), 414(q)(6); Treas Reg § 1.401(a)(17)-1(b)(5)]

Example. The Ezratty Golfing Group Ltd. adopts a 25-percent-of-compensation money purchase pension plan for calendar year 1993. There are two participants, Marty, who earns $235,840, and his wife, Rona, who also earns $235,840. Because of the family aggregation rule, their combined compensation cannot exceed $235,840 (see Q 6:3). The contribution for each is calculated as follows:

1. Each is deemed to earn $117,920 ($235,840 ÷ 2).
2. The contribution for each is $29,480 (25% × $117,920).
3. The total contribution is $58,960 ($29,480 + $29,480).

If the family aggregation rule did not apply, the total contribution would be $60,000 [(lesser of $30,000 or 25% × $235,840) × 2]. The family aggregation rule does not apply to the annual addition limitation (see Q 6:1), nor does it apply to the limitation on the annual retirement benefit that a defined benefit plan may provide (see Q 6:8).

The reduction in the annual compensation limitation to $150,000 in 1994 (see Q 6:21) will reduce Marty and Rona's total contribution to $37,500 [($150,000 ÷ 2) × 25% × 2]. However, TSB '93 (see Q 1:13) contains a provision repealing the family aggregation rule and, if enacted, will increase Marty and Rona's total contribution in 1994 to

$60,000 [(lesser of $30,000 or 25% × $150,000) × 2]. [TSB '93, Act § 221(c)]

Q 6:28   Can the definition of compensation used in a qualified retirement plan cause prohibited discrimination?

Section 414(s) provides rules for defining compensation for purposes of applying any provision that specifically refers to Section 414(s). For example, Section 414(s) is explicitly referred to in many of the nondiscrimination provisions applicable to qualified retirement plans. The amount of plan benefits or contributions, expressed as a percentage of compensation (see Qs 6:29–6:35), is generally one of the key factors in determining whether these nondiscrimination provisions are satisfied. [IRC § 414(s); Treas Reg § 1.414(s)-1(a)]

Q 6:29   May different definitions of compensation be used if an employer maintains more than one qualified retirement plan?

An employer may use any definition of compensation that satisfies Section 414(s) to determine if an applicable provision is satisfied with respect to a qualified retirement plan. This rule is designed to permit an employer, whenever possible, to use the definition used under the plan for calculating contributions or benefits to determine if an applicable nondiscrimination provision is satisfied. Consequently, an employer that maintains more than one qualified retirement plan may generally use one definition of compensation that satisfies Section 414(s) in determining whether one of the plans satisfies a particular nondiscrimination requirement (such as the general nondiscrimination requirements of Section 401(a)(4)) and use the same or a different definition of compensation in determining whether another plan satisfies the same nondiscrimination requirement. The definition of compensation selected generally must be used consistently to define the compensation of all employees taken into account in determining whether a plan satisfies the nondiscrimination provision. [Treas Reg §§ 1.414(s)-1(b)(1), 1.414(s)-1(b)(2)(i), 1.414(s)-1(b)(2)(ii)]

Q 6:30 Are there specific definitions of compensation that will satisfy Section 414(s)?

A definition of compensation that includes all compensation within the meaning of Section 415(c)(3) and excludes all other compensation will automatically satisfy Section 414(s) (see Q 6:3). In addition, Section 414(s) will be satisfied if either of the Section 415(c)(3) safe harbor definitions is used (see Q 6:4). [Treas Reg § 1.414(s)-1(c)(2)]

A safe harbor alternative definition of compensation that will automatically satisfy Section 414(s) without further testing is permitted. Under the safe harbor, compensation may be defined as set forth in the preceding paragraph but may be reduced by *all* of the following items (even if includible in income): (1) reimbursements or other expense allowances; (2) fringe benefits (cash and noncash); (3) moving expenses; (4) deferred compensation; and (5) welfare benefits. [Treas Reg § 1.414(s)-1(c)(3)]

A definition of compensation as set forth in either of the two preceding paragraphs will still satisfy Section 414(s) even though it is modified to include *all* elective contributions that are made by the employer on behalf of its employees that are not includible in income under Section 125, Section 402(a)(8), Section 402(h), or Section 403(b) and *all* compensation deferred under a Section 457 plan. [Treas Reg § 1.414(s)-1(c)(4)]

Any of the safe harbor definitions may be modified to permit additional items or amounts of compensation to be excluded from the compensation of highly compensated employees (see Q 3:2), but not from the compensation of any nonhighly compensated employees (see Q 3:13). This modification is permitted to be made after the inclusion of elective contributions and deferred compensation. For example, a definition of compensation under Section 415(c)(3) could be first modified to include all elective contributions and Section 457 deferred compensation, but then be further modified to exclude Section 457 deferred compensation from the compensation of highly compensated employees. Highly compensated employees need not be treated consistently. A safe harbor definition will continue to satisfy Section 414(s) automatically even if the definition is modified to exclude any portion of the compensation of some or all of the highly compensated employees. [Treas Reg § 1.414(s)-1(c)(5)]

Q 6:31 Are there any alternative definitions of compensation that may satisfy Section 414(s)?

A definition of compensation will satisfy Section 414(s) with respect to employees if the definition of compensation is reasonable, does not by design favor highly compensated employees (see Q 3:2), and satisfies the nondiscrimination requirement (see Q 6:32). A reasonable definition of compensation is permitted to exclude, on a consistent basis, all or any portion of irregular or additional compensation, including one or more of the following:

1. Any type of additional compensation for employees working outside their regularly scheduled tour of duty (such as overtime pay, premiums for shift differential, and call-in premiums);

2. Bonuses; or

3. Any type of compensation excluded under the safe harbor alternative definition (see Q 6:30).

Whether a type of compensation is irregular or additional is determined based upon all the relevant facts and circumstances. A reasonable definition of compensation is also permitted to include, on a consistent basis, all or any portion of certain types of elective contributions (see Q 6:30). [Treas Reg §§ 1.414(s)-1(d)(1), 1.414(s)-1(d)(2)(i), 1.414(s)-1(d)(2)(ii)]

A definition of compensation is *not* reasonable if the definition includes an item or amount not includible under a safe harbor definition (e.g., business expenses substantiated to the payor under an accountable plan). In addition, a definition is *not* reasonable if it provides that each employee's compensation is a specified portion of the employee's total compensation (such as 90 percent). However, a definition of compensation is not unreasonable merely because it excludes all compensation in excess of a specified dollar amount. [Treas Reg § 1.414(s)-1(d)(2)(iii)]

Q 6:32   Must an alternative definition of compensation be nondiscriminatory?

Yes. An alternative definition of compensation is nondiscriminatory if the average percentage of total compensation included under the alternative definition for an employer's highly compensated employees (see Q 3:2) as a group does not exceed by more than a *de minimis* amount the average percentage included under the alternative definition for the employer's nonhighly compensated employees (see Q 3:13) as a group. Self-employed individuals (see Q 29:8) and employees with zero compensation (see Q 6:34) are disregarded for purposes of this nondiscrimination test (see Q 6:35). [Treas Reg §§ 1.414(s)-1(d)(3)(i), 1.414(s)-1(d)(3)(iii), Rev Proc 93-42, 1993-31 IRB; Ann 93-130, 1993-31 IRB; Ann 92-81, 1992-22 IRB 56]

To calculate the average percentage, total compensation means all compensation within the meaning of Section 415(c)(3) and excludes all other compensation (see Qs 6:3, 6:4). However, an employer is permitted to increase this amount by including certain types of elective contributions (see Q 6:30). If a portion of the compensation of some highly compensated employees is excluded (see Q 6:30), the total compensation of such affected highly compensated employees is reduced; but, if the exclusion applies consistently to all highly compensated employees, the adjustment is not required. Total compensation taken into account for each employee (including, if added, the elective contributions) may not exceed the annual compensation limit (see Qs 6:21, 6:22). [Treas Reg § 1.414(s)-1(d)(3)(ii)]

To determine whether the average percentage requirement is satisfied, the employer must calculate individual percentages for each employee in a group and then average the percentages. However, the employer may use any other reasonable method to determine the average percentages. Thus, an employer may calculate an aggregate compensation percentage for each group of employees by dividing the aggregate amount of compensation of all employees in that group that is included under the alternative definition by the aggregate amount of total compensation of all employees in that group. Alternatively, the individual-percentage method may be used for one group and the aggregate-percentage method may be used for the other group. An alternative method is considered reasonable only if the percentage is not reasonably expected to vary significantly from the average percentage produced using the individual-percentage method because of the extra weight given employees with higher compensation in the relevant group. [Treas Reg § 1.414(s)-1(d)(3)(iv)]

The determination of whether the average percentage of total compensation included for the employer's highly compensated employees as a group exceeds by more than a *de minimis* amount the average percentage of total compensation included for the employer's nonhighly compensated employees as a group is based on the applicable facts and circumstances. The differences between the percentages for prior periods may be considered in determining whether the amount of the difference between the percentages for a given period is more than *de minimis*. In addition, an isolated instance of a more than *de minimis* difference between the compensation percentages that is due to an extraordinary, unforeseeable event (such as overtime payments due to a major hurricane) will be disregarded if the amount of the difference in prior determination periods was *de minimis*. [Treas Reg § 1.414(s)-1(d)(3)(v)]

Q 6:33 Can a rate-of-pay definition of compensation be used?

Rate-of-pay is permitted as an alternative definition of compensation (see Q 6:31). Therefore, compensation may be defined as the amount of each employee's basic or regular compensation using the employee's basic or regular *rate* of compensation rather than using the employee's *actual* basic or regular compensation. For this purpose, the employee's rate of compensation must be determined using an hourly pay scale, weekly salary, or similar unit of basic or regular compensation applicable to the employee. It is permissible to define compensation as (1) including each employee's basic or regular compensation, the amount of which is determined using each employee's basic or regular rate of compensation, plus actual amounts of irregular or additional compensation, such as overtime or bonuses, or (2) the greater of the employee's actual compensation or basic or regular compensation using the employee's basic or regular rate of compensation. Of course, the rate-of-pay definition must be nondiscriminatory. [Treas Reg § 1.414(s)-1(e)(1)]

A rate-of-pay definition cannot be used to determine if elective contributions (see Q 23:13), matching contributions (see Q 23:48), or employee contributions (see Qs 6:17, 6:18) satisfy, for example, the ADP test (see Q 23:8) or the ACP test (see Q 23:48). [Treas Reg § 1.414(s)-1(e)(2)]

The amount of each employee's basic or regular compensation for the determination period must be determined using the employee's basic or regular rate of compensation as of a designated date in the determination period. If the determination period is a calendar year, this requirement would be satisfied if the amount of each employee's basic or regular compensation for the calendar year is determined using the basic or regular rate of compensation as of January 1. Alternatively, the amount of each employee's basic or regular compensation for a determination period can be the sum of the amounts separately determined for shorter specified periods (e.g., weeks or months) within the determination period, provided that the amount of each employee's basic or regular compensation for each specified period is determined using the employee's basic or regular rate of compensation as of a designated date within the specified period. [Treas Reg §§ 1.414(s)-1(e)(3)(ii), 1.414(s)-1(h)(2)]

One or more dates may be used to determine employees' rates of compensation for a determination period or specified period provided that, if the same date is not used for all employees, the dates selected are designed to determine the rates of compensation for that period on a consistent basis for all employees taken into account for the determination period. For example, if annual compensation increases are provided to different groups of employees on different dates during the year, it would be consistent to choose a different date for each group in order to include the annual increase in the employees' rates of compensation for the determination period. [Treas Reg § 1.414(s)-1(e)(3)(iii)]

An employee's compensation may generally only be determined using the rate of compensation for employment periods during which the employer actually compensates the employee. However, if an employee terminates employment or otherwise stops performing services (such as for a leave of absence, layoff, or similar event), either without compensation or with reduced compensation during a determination period, the employer may continue to credit the employee with compensation based on the employee's rate of compensation for a period of up to 31 days after the event, but not beyond the end of the determination period (see Q 6:34). [Treas Reg § 1.414(s)-1(e)(3)(iv)]

Q 6:34 Can prior-employer compensation and imputed compensation be used?

Solely for purposes of determining whether a defined benefit plan (see Q 2:3) satisfies certain requirements (see Qs 4:9, 5:15), an alternative definition of compensation that includes prior-employer compensation or imputed compensation may be a reasonable alternative definition (see Q 6:31). Prior-employer compensation is compensation from an employer other than the employer (determined at the time that the compensation is paid) maintaining the defined benefit plan that is credited for periods prior to the employee's employment with the current employer maintaining the plan, and during which periods the employee performed services for the other employer. Imputed compensation is compensation credited for periods after an employee has commenced or recommenced participation in a defined benefit plan while the employee is not compensated by the employer maintaining the plan, or is compensated at a reduced rate by that employer because the employee is not performing services as an employee for the employer (including a period in which the employee performs services for another employer, e.g., a joint venture) or because the employee has a reduced work schedule. [Treas Reg §§ 1.414(s)-1(f)(1), 1.414(s)-1(f)(4)]

Crediting prior-employer compensation or imputed compensation must apply on the same terms to all similarly situated employees; there must be a legitimate business purpose, based on all of the relevant facts and circumstances, for crediting such compensation to an employee; and, based on all of the relevant facts and circumstances, crediting such compensation must not by design or in operation discriminate significantly in favor of highly compensated employees (see Q 3:2). Subject to certain requirements, any reasonable method may be used to determine the amount of prior-employer compensation or imputed compensation. [Treas Reg §§ 1.414(s)-1(f)(2), 1.414(s)-1(f)(3)]

Q 6:35 Are there any special rules for self-employed individuals?

If an alternative definition of compensation (see Q 6:31) is used, an equivalent alternative compensation amount must be determined for any self-employed individual (see Q 29:8) who is in the group of employees for whom the consistency requirement (see Q 6:29) requires a single definition of compensation to be used. This equivalent alternative compensation amount is determined by multiplying the self-employed individual's total earned income (see Q 29:10) by the percentage of total compensation (see Q 6:32) included under the alternative definition for the employer's nonhighly compensated common-law employees as a group. For purposes of this determination, highly compensated common-law employees (see Q 3:2) must be disregarded. This equivalent alternative compensation amount will be treated as compensation determined using the alternative definition of compensation. [Treas Reg §§ 1.414(s)-1(b)(3), 1.414(s)-1(g)(1)(i), 1.414(s)-1(g)(1)(iii)]

If the alternative definition of compensation includes any types of elective contributions (see Q 6:30), the self-employed individual's earned income for this determination must be increased by the amount of elective contributions made by the employer on behalf of the self-employed individual, and the definition of total compensation for this determination must include all such types of elective contributions made by the employer on behalf of common-law employees (other than highly compensated employees). An alternative definition may provide that compensation for some or all self-employed individuals who are highly compensated employees is a specified portion of, rather than equal to, equivalent compensation amount. [Treas Reg § 1.414(s)-1(g)(1)(ii)]

Q 6:36 When are the new nondiscriminatory compensation rules effective?

The new rules (see Qs 6:28–6:35) are generally effective for plan years beginning on or after January 1, 1987. However, the final regulations published by IRS on September 1, 1993, are effective for plan years beginning on or after January 1, 1994.

For plan years beginning before January 1, 1994, but on or after January 1, 1987, the plan must be operated in accordance with a reasonable, good-faith interpretation of the nondiscriminatory compensation requirement. Whether compliance is reasonable and in good faith will be determined on the basis of all the facts and circumstances, including the extent to which the employer has resolved unclear issues in its favor. A reasonable, good-faith interpretation will be deemed to exist, however, if a plan is operated in accordance with the regulations that were previously published. [Treas Reg § 1.414(s)-1(j); Notice 92-36, 1992-2 CB 364; Ann 92-29, 1992-9 IRB 37; IRS Field Office Directive on Good-Faith Compliance (June 12, 1992)]

Chapter 7

Permitted Disparity

A company can make its qualified retirement plan part of an overall retirement scheme that includes Social Security; this combination is called permitted disparity. (Prior to TRA '86, this was called integration.) This chapter examines how permitted disparity works in light of the extensive changes brought about by TRA '86 and the opportunity it affords a company to provide benefits favorable to shareholder-employees and key personnel without running afoul of the prohibition against discrimination.

Q 7:1 What does permitted disparity mean?

Every employer is already paying for a retirement plan for its employees—Social Security. By providing for permitted disparity in its qualified retirement plan (i.e., combining its private retirement plan with Social Security), the employer gets the benefit of its Social Security tax payments. The employer in effect makes its qualified retirement plan part of one overall scheme that combines both Social Security and the employer's private plan.

Technically, a plan that provides for permitted disparity means a qualified retirement plan that is not considered discriminatory merely because the benefits provided under the plan favor highly compensated employees (see Q 3:2), as long as the difference in benefits is attributable to what IRS refers to as permitted disparity (i.e., Social Security integration). Permitted disparity may be taken into account to demonstrate that the amount of contributions or benefits does not discriminate in favor of highly compensated employees (see Qs 4:10, 4:11, 4:13).

Permitted disparity (called integration prior to TRA '86) can mean a substantial saving for the employer because the cost of the employer's qualified retirement plan can be reduced.

[IRC §§ 401(a)(5), 401(l); Treas Reg § 1.401(l)-1]

Q 7:2 What types of qualified retirement plans can provide for permitted disparity?

Both defined contribution plans (see Q 2:2) and defined benefit plans (see Q 2:3) can provide for permitted disparity.

A defined contribution excess plan is a defined contribution plan under which the rate at which employer contributions (and forfeitures) are allocated to the accounts of participants with respect to compensation above a level specified in the plan (expressed as a percentage of such compensation) is greater than the rate at which employer contributions (and forfeitures) are allocated with respect to compensation at or below such specified level (expressed as a percentage of such compensation). [Treas Reg § 1.401(l)-1(c)(16)(ii)]

A defined benefit excess plan is a defined benefit plan under which the rate at which employer-provided benefits are determined with respect to average annual compensation (see Q 7:21) above a level specified in the plan (expressed as a percentage of such compensation) is greater than the rate with respect to compensation at or below such specified level (expressed as a percentage of such compensation). [Treas Reg § 1.401(l)-1(c)(16)(i)]

A defined benefit offset plan is a defined benefit plan that is not a defined benefit excess plan and that provides that each participant's employer-provided benefit is reduced by a specified percentage of the participant's final average compensation (see Q 7:23) up to the offset level under the plan. [Treas Reg § 1.401(l)-1(c)(25)]

For purposes of the permitted disparity rules, target benefit plans (see Q 2:5) are generally treated like defined benefit plans. [Treas Reg § 1.401(l)-2(a)(1)]

Q 7:3 What general rules apply to a defined contribution excess plan?

A defined contribution excess plan (see Q 7:2) will meet the permitted disparity rules only if the excess contribution percentage (ECP; see Q 7:4) does not exceed the base contribution percentage (BCP; see Q 7:5) by more than the lesser of (1) the BCP or (2) the greater of 5.7 percentage points, or the percentage equal to the rate of tax attributable to the old age insurance portion of the Old-Age, Survivors, and Disability Insurance (OASDI) as of the beginning of the plan year. [IRC § 401(l)(2); Notice 89-70, 1989-1 CB 730]

For purposes of the permitted disparity rules, target benefit plans (see Q 2:5) are generally treated like defined benefit plans. [Treas Reg § 1.401(l)-2(a)(1)]

Q 7:4 What is the excess contribution percentage?

The excess contribution percentage (ECP) is the percentage of compensation at which employer contributions (and forfeitures) are allocated to the accounts of participants with respect to compensation of participants above the integration level (see Q 7:6) specified in the defined contribution plan (see Q 2:2) for the plan year. [IRC § 401(l)(2)(B)(i); Treas Reg § 1.401(l)-1(c)(15)]

Q 7:5 What is the base contribution percentage?

The base contribution percentage (BCP) is the percentage of compensation at which employer contributions (and forfeitures) are allocated to the accounts of participants with respect to compensation of participants at or below the integration level (see Q 7:6) specified in the defined contribution plan (see Q 2:2) for the plan year. [IRC § 401(l)(2)(B)(ii); Treas Reg § 1.401(l)-1(c)(4)]

Q 7:6   What is the integration level?

The integration level is the amount of compensation specified in the defined contribution or defined benefit excess plan (see Q 7:2) at or below which the rate of contributions or benefits provided under the plan is less than the rate with respect to compensation above such level. [Treas Reg § 1.401(l)-1(c)(20)]

For defined contribution excess plans, the integration level must meet one of the following requirements:

1. The integration level for each participant is the taxable wage base (TWB; see Q 7:7) in effect as of the beginning of the plan year.
2. The integration level for all employees is a single dollar amount (either specified in the plan or determined under a formula specified in the plan) that does not exceed 20 percent of the TWB in effect as of the beginning of the plan year.
3. The integration level for all employees is a single dollar amount (either specified in the plan or determined under a formula specified in the plan) that is greater than the amount in (2) above and less than the TWB in effect as of the beginning of the plan year, provided the limitation of 5.7 percentage points (see Q 7:3) is reduced. If the integration level is more than 20 percent of the TWB but not more than 80 percent of the TWB, the 5.7 percentage points factor is reduced to 4.3 percentage points. If the integration level is more than 80 percent but less than 100 percent of the TWB, the 5.7 percentage points factor is reduced to 5.4 percentage points.

[Treas Reg § 1.401(l)-2(d)]

See Question 7:15 for a discussion of the integration level in defined benefit excess plans.

Q 7:7   What is the taxable wage base?

The taxable wage base (TWB) is the maximum amount of earnings in any calendar year that may be considered wages for Social Security purposes. For 1993, this amount is $57,600.

For the four prior calendar years, the TWB was:

Year	Taxable Wage Base
1992	$55,500
1991	$53,400
1990	$51,300
1989	$48,000

Q 7:8 How are the permitted disparity rules applied to contribution formulas under defined contribution excess plans?

The following examples illustrate whether or not a defined contribution excess plan meets the permitted disparity rules (see Qs 7:2, 7:3):

Example 1. J. T. Corporation has a money purchase pension plan with a calendar year plan year. For the 1993 plan year, the plan provides that each participant will receive a contribution of 5 percent of compensation up to the TWB (see Q 7:7) and 10 percent of compensation in excess of the TWB. The plan meets the permitted disparity rules because the ECP (see Q 7:4), 10 percent, does not exceed the BCP (see Q 7:5), 5 percent, by more than the lesser of 5 percentage points or 5.7 percentage points.

Example 2. Assume the same facts as in Example 1 except that the plan provides that, with respect to compensation in excess of the TWB, each participant will receive a contribution for the plan year of 10.7 percent of such excess compensation. The plan does not meet the permitted disparity rules because the ECP, 10.7 percent, exceeds the BCP, 5 percent, by more than the lesser of 5 percentage points or 5.7 percentage points.

Example 3. For the 1993 plan year, a profit sharing plan uses an integration level of $30,000, which is less than 80 percent of the taxable wage base of $57,600 but more than $11,520 (20% × $57,600). Consequently, the 5.7 percentage points factor must be replaced by 4.3 percentage points.

Q 7:9   What general rules apply to a defined benefit excess plan?

A defined benefit excess plan (see Q 7:2) will meet the permitted disparity rules if the excess benefit percentage (EBP; see Q 7:10) does not exceed the base benefit percentage (BBP; see Q 7:11) by more than the maximum excess allowance (MEA; see Q 7:12). Also, benefits must be based on average annual compensation (see Q 7:21).

Furthermore, any optional form of benefit, preretirement benefit, actuarial factor, or other benefit or feature provided with respect to compensation above the integration level (see Q 7:15) must also be provided with respect to compensation below the integration level. Thus, for example, if a lump-sum distribution option, calculated using particular actuarial assumptions, is available for benefits relating to compensation above the integration level, the same lump-sum option must be available on an equivalent basis for benefits based on compensation up to the integration level. [IRC § 401(l)(3); Treas Reg § 1.401(l)-3]

For purposes of the permitted disparity rules, target benefit plans (see Q 2:5) are generally treated like defined benefit plans. [Treas Reg § 1.401(l)-2(a)(1)]

Q 7:10   What is the excess benefit percentage?

The excess benefit percentage (EBP) is the percentage of compensation at which employer-provided benefits are determined with respect to average annual compensation (see Q 7:21) of participants above the integration level (see Q 7:15) specified in the defined benefit plan for the plan year. [IRC § 401(l)(3)(A); Treas Reg § 1.401(l)-1(c)(14)]

Q 7:11   What is the base benefit percentage?

The base benefit percentage (BBP) is the percentage of compensation at which the employer-provided benefits are determined with respect to average annual compensation (see Q 7:21) of participants at or below the integration level (see Q 7:15) specified in the defined benefit plan for the plan year. [IRC § 401(l)(3)(A); Treas Reg § 1.401(l)-1(c)(3)]

Q 7:12   What is the maximum excess allowance?

The maximum excess allowance (MEA) for a plan year is the lesser of either the BBP (see Q 7:11) or .75 percentage point. [IRC § 401(l)(4)(A); Treas Reg § 1.401(l)-3(b)(2)]

Q 7:13   How are the permitted disparity rules applied to benefit formulas under defined benefit excess plans?

The following examples illustrate whether or not a defined benefit excess plan meets the permitted disparity rules (see Qs 7:2, 7:9):

Example 1. M.P. Corporation maintains a defined benefit excess plan. The formula is .5 percent of the participant's average annual compensation (see Q 7:21) up to covered compensation (see Q 7:22) for the plan year plus 1.25 percent of the participant's average annual compensation for the plan year in excess of the participant's covered compensation for the plan year, multiplied by the participant's years of credited service with the company up to a maximum of 35 years. The plan formula provides a benefit that exceeds the MEA (see Q 7:12) because the EBP (see Q 7:10), 1.25 percent, for the plan year exceeds the BBP (see Q 7:11), .5 percent, for the plan year by more than the BBP.

Example 2. If the BBP in Example 1 was .75 percent, the plan would meet the permitted disparity rules because the EBP (1.25 percent) would not exceed the BBP (.75 percent) by more than the MEA (.75 percentage point).

[Treas Reg § 1.401(l)-3(b)(5)]

Q 7:14   Can benefits commence prior to Social Security retirement age in a defined benefit excess plan?

Yes; but, if benefits commence prior to the Social Security retirement age (see Q 6:12), the .75 percentage point factor (see Q 7:12) is reduced depending on the age at which benefits commence and the participant's Social Security retirement age. [Treas Reg § 1.401(l)-3(e)]

Q 7:15 What integration levels can be used in a defined benefit excess plan?

For defined benefit excess plans, the integration level must meet one of the following requirements:

1. The integration level for each participant is the participant's covered compensation (see Q 7:22).

2. The integration level for each participant is a uniform percentage (greater than 100 percent) of each participant's covered compensation, does not exceed the TWB (see Q 7:7) in effect for the plan year, and the .75 percent factor is adjusted.

3. The integration level for all participants is a single dollar amount that does not exceed the greater of $10,000 or one-half of the covered compensation of an individual who attains Social Security retirement age (see Q 6:12) in the calendar year in which the plan year begins.

4. The integration level for all participants is a single dollar amount that is greater than the amount determined in (3) above, does not exceed the TWB, satisfies special demographic requirements, and the .75 percent factor is adjusted.

5. The integration level for all participants is a single dollar amount described in (4) above, and the .75 percent factor in the MEA (see Q 7:12) is reduced to the lesser of an adjusted factor or 80 percent of the otherwise applicable factor.

[Treas Reg § 1.401(l)-3(d)]

Q 7:16 What general rules apply to a defined benefit offset plan?

A defined benefit offset plan (see Q 7:2) will meet the permitted disparity rules if the participant's accrued benefit (see Q 9:2) is not reduced by reason of the offset by more than the maximum offset allowance (MOA; see Q 7:17) and benefits are based on average annual compensation (see Q 7:21). [IRC § 401(l)(3)(B); Treas Reg § 1.401(l)-3(b)]

A defined benefit plan may offset a participant's benefit by a percentage of the participant's primary insurance amount under Social Security. [Treas Reg § 1.401(l)-3(c)(2)(ix); Notice 92-32, 1992-2 CB 362]

For purposes of the permitted disparity rules, target benefit plans (see Q 2:5) are generally treated like defined benefit plans. [Treas Reg § 1.401(l)-2(a)(1)]

Q 7:17   What is the maximum offset allowance?

The maximum offset allowance (MOA) for a plan year is the lesser of (1) .75 percentage point, or (2) one-half of the gross benefit percentage, multiplied by a fraction (not to exceed one), the numerator of which is the participant's average annual compensation (see Q 7:21), and the denominator of which is the participant's final average compensation (see Q 7:23) up to the offset level (see Q 7:20). The gross benefit percentage is the percentage of employer-provided benefits (before application of the offset) with respect to a participant's average annual compensation. [IRC § 401(l)(4)(B); Treas Reg §§ 1.401(l)-1(c)(18), 1.401(l)-3(b)(3)]

Q 7:18   How are the permitted disparity rules applied to benefit formulas under defined benefit offset plans?

The following example illustrates whether or not a defined benefit offset plan meets the permitted disparity rules (see Qs 7:2, 7:16):

Example. Jill Corporation maintains a defined benefit offset plan. The formula provides that, for each year of credited service with the company up to a maximum of 35 years, a participant receives a normal retirement benefit equal to 2 percent of the participant's average annual compensation (see Q 7:21), reduced by .75 percent of the participant's final average compensation up to covered compensation (see Qs 7:22, 7:23). The plan meets the permitted disparity rules because the MOA is equal to .75 percent, the lesser of .75 percent or one-half of the gross benefit percentage [1% (1/2 × 2%)].

If the formula in the above example provided for a normal retirement benefit equal to one percent of the participant's average annual compensation, the plan would not meet the permitted disparity rules because the MOA would be equal to .5 percent, the lesser of .75 percent or one-half of the gross benefit percentage [.5% (1/2 × 1%)]. [Treas Reg § 1.401(l)-3(b)(5)]

Q 7:19   Can benefits commence prior to Social Security retirement age in a defined benefit offset plan?

Yes; but, if benefits commence prior to Social Security retirement age (see Q 6:12), the .75 percentage point factor (see Q 7:17) is reduced depending on the age at which benefits commence and the participant's Social Security retirement age. [Treas Reg § 1.401(l)-3(e)]

Q 7:20   What is the offset level?

The offset level is the dollar limit specified in the defined benefit offset plan (see Q 7:2) on the amount of each participant's final average compensation (see Q 7:23) taken into account in determining the offset. [Treas Reg § 1.401(l)-1(c)(22); Treas Reg § 1.401(l)-1(c)(23)]

For defined benefit offset plans, the offset level must meet one of the following requirements:

1. The offset level for each participant is the participant's covered compensation (see Q 7:22).

2. The offset level for each participant is a uniform percentage (greater than 100 percent) of each participant's covered compensation, does not exceed the participant's final average compensation, and the .75 percent factor is adjusted.

3. The offset level for all participants is a single dollar amount that does not exceed the greater of $10,000 or one-half of the covered compensation of an individual who attains Social Security retirement age (see Q 6:12) in the calendar year in which the plan year begins.

4. The offset level for all participants is a single dollar amount that is greater than the amount determined in (3) above, does not exceed the participant's final average compensation, satis-

fies special demographic requirements, and the .75 percent factor is adjusted.

5. The offset level for all participants is a single dollar amount described in (4) above, and the .75 percent factor in the MOA (see Q 7:17) is reduced to the lesser of an adjusted factor or 80 percent of the otherwise applicable factor.

[Treas Reg § 1.401(l)-3(d)]

Q 7:21 What is average annual compensation?

Average annual compensation means the participant's highest average annual compensation for (1) any period of at least three consecutive years, or (2) if shorter, the participant's full period of service. The plan may limit the period of years taken into account in determining average annual compensation to the current plan year and the nine years beginning before the current plan year. [IRC § 401(l)(5)(C); Treas Reg §§ 1.401(a)(4)-3(e)(2), 1.401(l)-1(c)(2)]

Q 7:22 What does covered compensation mean?

Covered compensation means the average (without indexing) of the taxable wage bases (TWB; see Q 7:7) for the 35 calendar years ending with the year an individual attains Social Security retirement age (see Q 6:12). A defined benefit plan can provide for permitted disparity on the basis of each individual employee's covered compensation. Covered compensation does not refer to the amount of compensation that the employee actually earned, but reflects the ceiling for Social Security wages (TWBs) over the years.

1993 Covered Compensation Tables

Calendar Year of Birth	Year of Social Security Retirement Age	Table I	Table II
1924	1989	$16,800	$16,968
1925	1990	18,600	18,312
1926	1991	19,800	19,728
1927	1992	21,000	21,192

Calendar Year of Birth	Year of Social Security Retirement Age	Table I	Table II
1928	1993	22,800	22,716
1929	1994	24,000	24,228
1930	1995	25,800	25,728
1931	1996	27,000	27,240
1932	1997	28,800	28,752
1933	1998	30,000	30,252
1934	1999	31,800	31,764
1935	2000	33,000	33,276
1936	2001	34,800	34,728
1937	2002	36,000	36,192
1938	2004	39,000	39,036
1939	2005	40,200	40,452
1940	2006	42,000	41,880
1941	2007	43,200	43,272
1942	2008	44,400	44,604
1943	2009	45,600	45,876
1944	2010	47,400	47,112
1945	2011	48,600	48,324
1946	2012	49,800	49,500
1947	2013	50,400	50,640
1948	2014	51,600	51,636
1949	2015	52,800	52,536
1950	2016	53,400	53,340
1951	2017	54,000	54,060
1952	2018	54,600	54,684
1953	2019	55,200	55,248
1954	2020	55,800	55,764
1955	2022	56,400	56,604
1956	2023	57,000	56,964
1957	2024	57,000	57,240
1958	2025	57,600	57,420
1959	2026	57,600	57,540
1960 or later	2027 or later	57,600	57,600

IRS permits alternative definitions of covered compensation. In lieu of using the tables set forth above, defined benefit plans may use alternative definitions of covered compensation, including the following table that rounds the actual amounts of covered compensation for different years of birth.

1993 Rounded Table

Year of Birth	Covered Compensation
1924-1925	$18,000
1926-1927	21,000
1928-1929	24,000
1930-1931	27,000
1932-1933	30,000
1934-1935	33,000
1936-1937	36,000
1938-1939	39,000
1940-1941	42,000
1942-1943	45,000
1944-1945	48,000
1946-1948	51,000
1949-1953	54,000
1954-1959	57,000
1960 or later	57,600

[IRC § 401(l)(5)(E); Treas Reg § 1.401(l)-1(c)(7); Rev Rul 93-20, 1993-12 IRB]

Q 7:23　What is final average compensation?

Final average compensation means the average of the participant's annual compensation for (1) the three consecutive year period ending with or within the plan year, or (2) if shorter, the participant's full period of service; but it does not include compensation for any year in excess of the TWB (see Q 7:7) in effect at the beginning of such year. [IRC § 401(l)(5)(D); Treas Reg § 1.401(l)-1(c)(17)]

Q 7:24   What does compensation mean?

Compensation means compensation as defined under the plan, provided that such definition is nondiscriminatory and satisfies Section 414(s) (see Qs 6:28–6:36). [IRC §§ 401(l)(5)(B), 414(s); Treas Reg §§ 1.401(l)-1(c)(2), 1.401(l)-1(c)(17)]

Q 7:25   Can the termination of a defined benefit plan affect permitted disparity?

Yes. If a defined benefit plan providing for permitted disparity is terminated and the plan assets exceed the present value of the accrued benefits (see Q 9:2), the use of the excess funds to increase benefits under the plan must not violate the permitted disparity rules. [Rev Rul 80-229, 1980-2 CB 133] The termination of a qualified retirement plan may not discriminate in favor of highly compensated employees (see Qs 3:2, 21:44). [Treas Reg § 1.401(a)(4)-5(a)(1)]

Q 7:26   What special restrictions on permitted disparity apply to top-heavy plans?

A top-heavy defined benefit plan (see Q 22:1) must provide each participant who is a non-key employee (see Q 22:29) with a minimum annual retirement benefit, and a top-heavy defined contribution plan (see Q 22:3) must provide each participant who is a non-key employee with a minimum annual contribution. A top-heavy plan cannot take into account Social Security benefits or contributions to satisfy these minimum requirements (see Qs 22:37, 22:43, 22:47). [IRC § 416(e); Treas Reg § 1.416-1, Question M-11]

Chapter 8

Funding Requirements

To ensure that sufficient money will be available to pay promised retirement benefits to employees when they retire, certain qualified retirement plans are subject to minimum funding requirements. This chapter examines the funding requirements—which qualified retirement plans must meet them, how they work, and how they are enforced.

Q 8:1 What are the minimum funding standards?

To ensure that sufficient money will be available to pay promised retirement benefits to employees when they retire, minimum funding standards have been established for defined benefit plans (see Q 2:3), money purchase pension plans (see Q 2:4), and target benefit plans (see Q 2:5). [ERISA §§ 301, 302; IRC § 412; Prop Reg § 1.412(a)-1]

For defined benefit plans, employers are required each year to fund the retirement benefits earned that year by the employees (the normal cost). In addition, formulas are established for amortizing over stated periods (1) the cost of retirement benefits for employees' services in the past for which funds have not yet been set aside (past service liabilities), (2) the cost of retroactively raising the level of benefits by plan amendments, and (3) the cost of making up experience losses (see Q 8:13) and increases in liabilities attributable to changes in actuarial assumptions.

For a money purchase pension plan, the amount required to be contributed each year is based on the plan's contribution formula. For example, if the employer has a money purchase pension plan with a 10-percent-of-compensation formula and the participants' aggregate compensation for the year totals $80,000, the employer's required contribution is $8,000.

In a target benefit plan, the required contribution is based on the participant's compensation, age, and an assumed interest rate that is specified in the plan document.

Certain qualified retirement plans are not subject to minimum funding standards (see Q 8:4).

Q 8:2 Are there funding requirements in addition to the minimum funding standards?

Yes. There is an additional funding requirement that generally applies to defined benefit plans (other than multiemployer plans or defined benefit plans having 100 or fewer participants) with assets less than their current liability for the plan year. For this purpose, current liability means all liabilities to participants and their beneficiaries under the plan. [ERISA § 302(d); IRC § 412(1)]

Q 8:3 Are there special funding rules for multiple employer plans?

Yes. The minimum funding requirements for a multiple employer plan (a plan maintained by more than one employer) established after December 31, 1988, are generally determined by treating each employer as maintaining a separate plan. Multiple employer plans established before that date generally must be funded as if all participants in the plan were employed by a single employer. However, the plan administrator of a pre-1989 multiple employer plan was permitted to elect to have the new rules apply and fund the plan as if each employer maintains a separate plan. The election was required to be attached to Schedule B of Form 5500 (see Q 17:4) for the first plan year beginning after November 10, 1988. If the election was made, the funding requirements for that first plan year and all subsequent plan years are determined in accordance with the new rules. The election may be revoked only with the consent of IRS. [IRC § 413(c)(4); Ann 90-3, 1990-3 IRB 36]

Q 8:4 Which qualified retirement plans are not subject to the minimum funding standards?

The minimum funding standards do not apply to profit sharing (see Q 2:6), stock bonus (see Q 2:12), 401(k) (see Chapter 23), or employee stock ownership plans (ESOPs; see Chapter 24). Pension plans funded exclusively by the purchase of certain insurance contracts (insurance contract plans; see Q 8:5) are also exempt from the funding standards. [IRC §§ 412(h), 412(i)]

Other retirement plans that are not subject to the minimum funding standards include:

1. Plans that do not provide for employer contributions after September 2, 1974 (such as plans to which only employees contribute);
2. Unfunded nonqualified plans that are maintained by the employer primarily to provide deferred compensation for selected management or highly compensated employees;
3. Supplemental plans that provide benefits in excess of the limits on contributions and benefits under the Code;
4. Governmental plans; and
5. Certain church plans.

[ERISA § 301(a); IRC §§ 412(h), 414(d), 414(e)]

Q 8:5 What is an insurance contract plan?

An insurance contract plan is a pension plan that is funded exclusively by individual insurance contracts and meets the following requirements:

1. The insurance contracts provide for level annual premiums from the time the employee commences plan participation until retirement age.
2. Benefits under the plan are equal to the benefits provided under the contracts.
3. Benefits are guaranteed by an insurance company licensed to do business in the state in which the plan is located.

4. Premiums are paid timely or the contracts have been reinstated.

5. No rights under the contracts were subject to a security interest during the plan year.

6. No policy loans were outstanding during the plan year.

A pension plan that is funded exclusively by group insurance contracts having the same characteristics as those listed above is also considered to be an insurance contract plan. [ERISA § 301(b); IRC § 412(i); Treas Reg § 1.412(i)-1]

Q 8:6 Can a pension plan be converted to an insurance contract plan?

Yes. Although the conversion of an existing pension plan to a plan that is funded exclusively by insurance contracts might cause the premium payments to begin after an employee commences participation in the plan (see Q 8:5), the converted plan may be considered to be an insurance contract plan for future years. [Rev Rul 81-196, 1981-2 CB 107]

Where a defined benefit plan (see Q 2:3) was terminated, all benefit accruals ceased, and the trustee purchased annuity contracts to provide plan benefits, IRS concluded that the plan had not been converted to an insurance contract plan because a conversion must provide for continued meaningful premium level accruals. [Ltr Rul 9234004]

Q 8:7 Should the employer contribute more than the amount needed to meet the minimum funding standards?

Only if the additional amount is deductible. If the additional amount is not deductible, a tax is imposed on the employer equal to 10 percent of the nondeductible contributions to the plan (see Qs 12:9, 12:16, 12:17). [IRC §§ 412(c)(6), 412(c)(7), 4972]

Q 8:8 Must actuarial assumptions used in determining plan costs be reasonable?

Yes. In the case of a defined benefit plan (see Q 2:3), all plan costs, liabilities, interest rates, and other factors must be determined on the basis of actuarial assumptions and methods (1) each of which is reasonable (taking into account the experience of the plan and reasonable expectations), or which, when taken together, produce a total contribution that is the same as if each assumption and method were reasonable; and (2) which, in combination, offer the actuary's best estimate of anticipated experience under the plan. [ERISA § 302(c)(3); IRC § 412(c)(3)]

The actuarial assumptions used to determine the cost of funding a defined benefit plan need not be set forth in the plan (see Q 2:18). However, even if the actuarial assumptions and methods are set forth in the plan, that does not mean they will always be reasonable or acceptable. [Rev Rul 78-48, 1978-1 CB 115]

In one case, the court agreed with IRS that use of a 5 percent interest rate was not reasonable and that an 8 percent interest rate was appropriate at a time when safe investments were yielding approximately 12 percent or more. The court concluded that "the reasonableness of an actuary's assumption must be evaluated in light of the plan's experience and reasonable expectations." [Jerome Mirza & Assocs, Ltd v United States, 882 F 2d 229 (7th Cir 1989); see also Ltr Ruls 9111004, 9031001]

In another case, IRS recalculated a corporation's tax deduction by rejecting the actuarial assumptions contained in its defined benefit plan. IRS concluded that the actuarial assumptions contained in the plan did not reflect current plan experience. IRS determined that a more appropriate interest rate was 8 percent (instead of the plan's assumed 5½ percent rate) and that the normal retirement age for this one-participant plan should have been age 65, rather than age 55 as provided for in the plan. As a result of these modifications by IRS, no deduction for the taxable year involved was allowable. [Ltr Rul 8552001] In a similar case, IRS determined that the plan's normal retirement age of 60 was not reasonable and, based on plan experience and other investments available at the time, the 5 percent preretirement interest rate assumption was too low; therefore, the entire deduction for two years was disallowed. [Ltr Rul 9244006]

In yet another case, IRS disallowed the entire contribution made to a defined benefit plan after recalculation of the plan's liabilities and costs. The assumed 6 percent preretirement interest rate and 6½ percent postretirement interest rate were determined to be unreasonable in the aggregate when the actual investment rate of return over a five-year period exceeded 15 percent. [Ltr Rul 9226001] Similarly, IRS determined in another case that the actuarial assumptions used were not reasonable in the aggregate in view of the experience of the plan. The assumed rate of interest was 7 percent, but the average annual investment return over the prior five plan years was over 12 percent. [Ltr Rul 9226004] In another ruling, IRS determined that a 7.5 percent assumed rate of interest was not reasonable because the plan's investment returns far exceeded 7.5 percent and could reasonably be expected to continue to do so. [Ltr Rul 9250002] IRS, in yet another ruling, determined that the funding method and actuarial assumptions used were unreasonable and therefore disallowed the entire deduction. The actuary failed to explain in any detail the funding method used and did not furnish proper evidence that the owner would likely retire at age 55. [Ltr Rul 9119007] In a different case, although IRS concluded that interest and mortality assumptions were not reasonable, the poor health of the participant justified a normal retirement age of 55. Therefore, only a portion of the contribution was disallowed. [Ltr Rul 9249003]

IRS had expanded its defined benefit plan actuarial examination program and questioned the funding of defined benefit plans if the annual contribution per participant indicated that the actuaries may have exceeded the contribution limits for any of the following reasons:

1. Using an inappropriate funding method;
2. Exceeding the maximum benefit limitation under Section 415;
3. Using an unreasonably low interest rate not supported by the facts and circumstances of the plan; or
4. Employing an unreasonably low retirement age not supported by the facts and circumstances of the plan.

Recently, however, IRS's actuarial examination program experienced a major setback when the Tax Court, in a number of cases, ruled in favor of the employers, finding that an interest rate assumption of less than 8 percent and a retirement age assumption of below age 65 were, among other assumptions, reasonable actuarial assumptions. [Vinson & Elkins, 99 TC 9 (1992); Citrus

Valley Estates, Inc, 99 TC 21 (1992); Wachtell, Lipton, Rosen & Katz, 64 TCM 128 (1992)]

With regard to the interest rate assumption, the Tax Court considered the following:

1. The deference Congress gave to enrolled actuaries under ERISA for defined benefit pension plans;
2. The tendency of actuaries to be conservative in adopting actuarial assumptions;
3. That the plans were designed for a long-term time frame during which available rates of returns on plan investments were likely to fluctuate;
4. That the plans' investments were self-directed, which could reduce the rate of return;
5. That the plans, due to their recent adoption, lacked credible experience;
6. The risk that the use of too optimistic an interest rate assumption would create a funding deficit that would require increased contributions in later years;
7. The relatively slight differences between the actuarial experts' suggested ranges for proper interest rate assumptions and the rate used by the plans' actuaries; and
8. That most small defined benefit plans used interest rate assumptions of between 5 percent and 6 percent for the years at issue.

The Tax Court also found that a retirement age earlier than age 65 was justifiable under the circumstances. Most importantly, the Tax Court concluded that, since the assumptions used were not "substantially unreasonable" and represented the actuary's best estimate of anticipated experience under the plans based on actuarial assumptions used by similar plans, IRS was precluded from requiring a retroactive change of assumptions.

The reasoning of the Tax Court has been adopted by another court, which ruled against IRS. [Rhoades, McKee and Boer v United States, No. 1:91:CV:540 (WD Mich 1993)]

IRS has filed an appeal in at least one of the Tax Court cases and continues to contest this issue. However, IRS has advised that it will no longer follow its initial inflexible approach and will allow, on a selective basis, less than 8 percent interest assumptions and retirement ages of less than 65 in order to settle cases and avoid the costs and hazards of litigation.

Q 8:9   Must a change in a plan's funding method be approved?

Generally, IRS must approve a change in a defined benefit plan's funding method. [IRC § 412(c)(5); Ltr Rul 9044001] However, subject to certain restrictions, automatic approval will be granted for a change to another acceptable funding method. Changes for which automatic approval will be granted include changes to a method such as the entry age normal cost method, the unit credit cost method, changes in the asset valuation date, and changes to or from the shortfall funding method. Automatic approval will not be granted with respect to plan years beginning on or after January 1, 1994. [Rev Proc 92-48, 1992-1 CB 987; Rev Proc 85-29, 1985-1 CB 51]

Q 8:10   Is there any penalty for overstatement of pension liabilities?

Yes. Effective for returns due after December 31, 1989 (determined without regard to extensions), a penalty tax is imposed on the underpayment of tax created by a substantial overstatement of pension liabilities. A 20 percent penalty tax is imposed if the actuarial determination of pension liabilities is between 200 percent and 399 percent of the amount determined to be correct; if the actuarial determination is 400 percent or more of the correct amount, the penalty tax is increased to 40 percent. No penalty will be imposed if the underpayment attributable to the substantial overstatement is $1,000 or less. [IRC §§ 6662(a), 6662(f), 6662(h)]

For pension liabilities that are overstated after October 22, 1986, but before the above penalty tax became effective, and that result in an underpayment of tax, a percentage of the underpayment is added to the tax as follows:

If the claimed pension liability is the following percentage of the correct valuation	*The applicable percentage is:*
150% or more, but not more than 200%	10%
More than 200%, but not more than 250%	20%
More than 250%	30%

[IRC § 6659A prior to repeal]

Q 8:11 Can a pension plan's normal retirement age affect the minimum funding standards?

Yes. Each actuarial assumption used to determine pension plan costs should be reasonable and must offer the actuary's best estimate of anticipated experience under the plan. [ERISA § 302(c)(3); IRC § 412(c)(3)] Therefore, an assumption that employees will retire at the normal retirement age specified in the plan, ignoring the fact that employees normally retire at earlier or later ages, would not be reasonable (see Q 8:8).

Q 8:12 How are past service costs funded?

If a defined benefit plan was adopted after January 1, 1974, costs relating to an employee's service before the adoption of the plan must be amortized over not more than 30 years from the date the plan was adopted. Increases or decreases in past service costs resulting from an amendment to the plan must be amortized over not more than 30 years from the time the amendment takes effect.

For plans in existence on January 1, 1974, past service liabilities on the first day of the plan year beginning after December 31, 1975, may be amortized over not more than 40 years. Increases or decreases in past service liabilities arising thereafter must be amortized over not more than 30 years. [IRC § 412(b)(2)]

There is an additional funding requirement for many plans (see Q 8:2) that generally requires the amortization of unfunded old liability over 18 plan years. Unfunded old liability is generally the unfunded current liability of the plan as of the beginning of the first plan year beginning after December 31, 1987. [IRC § 412(l)(3)]

Q 8:13   Do the pension plan's investment earnings affect the funding requirement?

Yes. Experience gains and losses—that is, when the defined benefit plan's actual investment growth and earnings are either higher or lower than was actuarially estimated—must be amortized over a period of not more than five years from the time the gain or loss is determined. For experience gains and losses occurring in plan years beginning before 1988, the period for amortizing experience gains and losses was 15 years. The 15-year amortization period is retained for multiemployer plans (see Q 25:2). [IRC §§ 412(b)(2)(B)(iv), 412(b)(3)(B)(ii)]

An experience gain reduces the amount of funding required, and an experience loss increases the amount of funding required. Increases or decreases in costs resulting from a change in the Social Security law or from changes in the amount of wages taken into account under a pension plan providing for permitted disparity (see Q 7:1) are treated as experience gains or losses. [IRC § 412(c)(4)]

Q 8:14   How are assets valued in a defined benefit plan?

For funding purposes, assets in a defined benefit plan (see Q 2:3) must be valued every year on the basis of any reasonable actuarial method of valuation that takes into account fair market value. To be considered a reasonable actuarial method of valuation, the method must result in an actuarial value between 80 percent and 120 percent of the current fair market value. Special rules apply to the valuation of bonds or other evidences of indebtedness. [IRC §§ 412(c)(2), 412(c)(9); Treas Reg § 1.412(c)(2)-1]

If TSB '93 is enacted (see Q 1:13), assets in a multiemployer plan (see Q 25:2) will be required to be valued at least once every three years. This change will be effective for years beginning *after* December 31, 1993. [TSB '93, Act § 235]

IRS has announced that it intends to focus on retirement plans that improperly value non-publicly traded assets (e.g., partnerships, real estate). The Form 5500 series, Annual Return/Report of Employee Benefit Plan (see Q 17:1), now requires information regarding assets that have a fair market value that is not readily determinable on an established market and the date these assets were valued by an independent third-party appraiser. [Forms 5500, 5500 C/R 1992]

Q 8:15 What is the funding standard account?

Each pension plan subject to the minimum funding standards (see Q 8:1) must maintain a funding standard account, which is a device used to ease the administration of the funding rules. Each year, the funding standard account is charged with amounts that must be paid to satisfy the minimum funding standards and is credited with the plan contributions made, any decrease in plan liabilities, and experience gains. If the pension plan meets the minimum funding standards (the charges equal the credits) at the end of any plan year, the funding standard account will show a zero balance. If the employer has contributed more than the minimum amount required for any year (the credits exceed the charges), the account will show a positive balance and the employer is credited with interest on the excess. If the employer contributed less than the minimum amount required for any year (the charges exceed the credits), the account will show an accumulated funding deficiency. An excise tax is imposed on that deficiency (see Q 8:18). [IRC § 412(b)]

The following examples illustrate how the funding standard account works.

Example 1. In 1992, MuMu Corporation established a defined benefit plan that is subject to the minimum funding requirements. For the plan's first year, the normal cost (the cost of benefits earned during the year) is $80,000. Past service costs (the cost of benefits for employees' services before the plan was adopted) are $1,000,000. The actuarially assumed rate of interest is 6 percent. MuMu contributed $148,537 to the plan. The funding standard account is charged with $80,000 of normal cost and with $68,537, which represents amortization of the past service costs of $1,000,000 at 6 percent over 30 years. Since the total charges ($148,537) equal the contribution, the funding standard account has a zero balance.

Example 2. In 1993, MuMu amends its defined benefit plan to increase benefits, so that past service costs rise by $100,000. The plan's normal cost is now $85,000. In addition, the plan had an experience gain (the plan's actual investment growth was higher than that actuarially estimated) of $5,000. MuMu contributed $170,000 to the plan in 1993. The funding standard account for 1993 is credited with the $170,000 contribution plus $1,120 (representing amortization of the $5,000 experience gain at 6 percent over five years), for a total credit of $171,120. The funding standard account is charged with $85,000 normal cost and $68,537 for amortizing past service costs over 30 years, plus $6,854 for amortizing past service costs resulting from the plan amendment over 30 years, for a total charge of $160,391. Since the account's credits exceed the charges by $10,729 [$171,120 – $160,391], the funding standard account has a positive balance of $10,729. Add to this $644, representing interest on the $10,729 at 6 percent, and the account has a balance of $11,373 to be credited to future years.

Q 8:16   What is the full funding limitation?

The term full funding limitation means the excess, if any, of the lesser of (1) 150 percent of current liability, or (2) the accrued liability (including normal cost) under the defined benefit plan, over the value of plan assets. If plan assets equal or exceed plan liabilities, the plan is fully funded and no contribution is required. Furthermore, because of the full funding limitation, there may be no contribution or a decreased contribution even if the accrued liability under the plan exceeds plan assets. In any case, no deduction is allowed for a contribution made when the plan is fully funded. In future years, if plan liabilities (for full funding limitation purposes) increase and exceed the value of plan assets, the employer will have to make contributions to satisfy the minimum funding requirements. [IRC §§ 404(a)(1)(A), 412(c)(6), 412(c)(7)]

If TSB '93 is enacted (see Q 1:13), the 150 percent of current liability limitation will not apply to multiemployer plans (see Q 25:2). This change will be effective for years beginning *after* December 31, 1993. [TSB '93, Act § 235]

In addition, if TSB '93 is enacted, certain employers will be allowed to elect an alternative full funding limitation and disregard the 150 percent limitation, provided the plan is not top-heavy (see Q 22:1). This change would be retroactively effective to January 1, 1993. [TSB '93, Act § 236]

Q 8:17   Must separate funding standard accounts be maintained for each pension plan established by a controlled group of companies?

Yes. Even though identical, but separate, pension plans are established by members of a controlled group of companies (see Q 5:32), separate funding standard accounts (see Q 8:15) must be maintained for each plan. [ERISA § 302(b)(1); IRC § 412(b)(1); Rev Rul 81-137, 1981-1 CB 232]

Q 8:18   What happens if the company fails to make the required contribution to its pension plan?

There is an excise tax for failure to comply with the minimum funding standards (see Q 8:1) equal to 10 percent (5 percent for multiemployer plans; see Q 25:2) of the amount of the accumulated funding deficiency. If the accumulated funding deficiency is not corrected, an excise tax equal to 100 percent of such uncorrected amount is imposed. Accumulated funding deficiency means the excess of the total charges to the funding standard account for all plan years over the total credits to such account for such years. [IRC §§ 412(a), 4971(a), 4971(b), 4971(c)]

An accumulated funding deficiency caused by an employer's failure to make timely contributions due to his reliance on the erroneous advice of his plan consultant could not be excused even though the employer had set aside the necessary amount in a segregated checking account. The court ruled that the imposition of the excise tax was mandatory and not subject to an exception that would excuse an employer's unintentional or inadvertent failure to meet the minimum funding requirements. However, the court noted that IRS may waive the 100 percent tax and is also authorized to grant an employer any reasonable period in order to correct the accumulated funding deficiency. [DJ Lee, MD, Inc v Comm'r, 931 F 2d 418 (6th Cir 1991)]

In another case, no excise tax for underfunding was imposed when a bookkeeping error caused contributions to pension and profit sharing plans of the employer to be misallocated between them. [Ahlberg, 780 F Supp 625 (DC Minn 1991)]

In one case, excise taxes imposed by IRS for failure to meet the minimum funding standards were *not* considered to be penalties for bankruptcy purposes, and, therefore, the excise taxes had priority over the claims of general creditors. [In re The Mansfield Tire and Rubber Co, No 90-4103 (6th Cir 1991)] However, in another case, excise taxes relating to the minimum funding standards were considered penalties (not claims for failure to pay taxes) and, therefore, did *not* have priority status. [In re CF&I Fabricators of Utah, Inc, No 90B-6721-6730 (Bankr D Utah 1993)]

The failure to meet minimum funding standards triggers a reportable event notice requirement to PBGC if the present value of unfunded vested benefits under the pension plan equals or exceeds $250,000 (see Q 21:16). [ERISA § 4043; PBGC Reg § 2615.16]

In addition, if a quarterly payment (see Q 8:28) or any other payment required by the minimum funding standards is not made, PBGC must be notified within ten days of the due date of the payment if the unpaid balance exceeds $1 million (see Q 17:25). Furthermore, a lien is created in favor of the plan upon all property of the employer if the delinquency exceeds $1 million. [ERISA § 302(f); IRC § 412(n)]

Q 8:19 Who is liable for failure to make contributions?

Liability for contributions to a pension plan (other than a multi-employer plan; see Q 25:2) is joint and several among the employer-sponsor and the members of the controlled group (see Q 5:32) of which the employer is a member. Also, all members of the controlled group are subject to the lien (see Q 8:18) in favor of a pension plan maintained by any member if the contributions are late. [IRC §§ 412(c)(11), 412(n)]

Furthermore, if an employer fails to make a required payment to meet minimum funding requirements or a required quarterly payment (see Qs 8:27, 8:28) within 60 days after it is due, the employer must notify each participant and beneficiary of such failure. This notice requirement does not apply to multiemployer plans or if the employer has a funding waiver request pending with IRS. This notice requirement is in addition to the requirement that participants be notified of the filing of an application for a funding waiver (see Q 8:22). [ERISA § 101(d)]

Q 8:20 May IRS waive the minimum funding standards for a particular company?

Yes. IRS may grant a waiver of the minimum funding standards for any year in which the employer is unable to make the necessary contributions without "temporary substantial business hardship" ("substantial business hardship" for multiemployer plans; see Q 25:2) and if meeting the funding requirement would harm the interests of the plan's participants. [IRC § 412(d)(1)]

IRS examines several factors in deciding whether to waive the funding standards, including the following:

1. Is the employer operating at a loss?
2. Is there substantial unemployment or underemployment in the industry?
3. Are sales and profits of the industry depressed or declining?
4. Will the pension plan be continued only if the waiver is granted?

These factors are not all-inclusive. Furthermore, IRS must be convinced that the employer's business hardship is temporary. IRS has granted a conditional waiver of the minimum funding standards to a company that has experienced net losses, but whose financial situation was improving. [Ltr Ruls 9310050, 9309051, 9224052, 9223055] IRS granted a conditional funding waiver although a company had both a very large negative working capital and a negative tangible net worth, when a substantial payment—enough to pay the required pension plan contribution—was expected from the state. [Ltr Rul 9216034] In another case, IRS granted a conditional funding waiver where the employer had taken a number of steps to improve its financial condition, including expansion into new and profitable product lines and markets, consolidation of company functions to streamline operations, and refinancing its debt on longer and more favorable repayment terms [Ltr Rul 9304032; see also Ltr Ruls 9313029, 9308049, 9248042] However, IRS has denied requests for waivers of the minimum funding standards to companies whose prospects of recovery were tenuous. [Ltr Ruls 9317057, 9316053, 9226075] In one ruling, IRS granted waivers for two plans sponsored by a member of a controlled group but denied waivers for two other plans sponsored by another group member. The controlled group, on a consolidated basis, suffered severe business hardship; but one of the subsidiaries, considered alone, had not demonstrated economic hardship and appeared capable of satisfying the minimum funding standards. [Ltr Ruls 9226054, 9219041]

The legislative history indicates that a waiver should not be granted to an employer if it appears that the employer will not recover sufficiently to make its waived contributions. Chances for a waiver are improved if the plan's assets are greater than the benefits to which the participants are entitled. [IRC § 412(d)(2)]

As a practical matter, IRS, in its efforts to avert plan terminations, generally approves a hardship waiver request if it can find reasonable grounds for doing so. In one case, IRS required the owner, as a condition for granting the waiver, to reduce his accrued benefit until plan assets became sufficient to meet plan liabilities. [Ltr Rul 7945047] In another case, IRS granted a conditional waiver of the minimum funding standards subject to the adoption of an amendment ceasing the accrual of benefits for participants who were also shareholders. [Ltr Rul 8847079]

There are other rules with respect to funding waivers. They include:

1. The number of waivers allowed within a 15-year period is three (five for multiemployer plans).

2. If the employer applying for a funding waiver is a member of a controlled group, not only must the employer-applicant meet the standards, but the standards must be met as if all members of the controlled group are treated as a single employer.

3. The amortization period of a waived funding deficiency is five years (15 years for multiemployer plans).

4. The interest rate used for computing the amortization charge is the greater of (1) 150 percent of the federal midterm rate, or (2) the plan interest rate.

5. IRS is authorized to require security when outstanding waived amounts are $1 million or more.

[ERISA § 303(a); IRC §§ 412(b), 412(d), 412(f)]

Q 8:21 What is the procedure for obtaining a waiver of the minimum funding standards?

The request for a waiver of the minimum funding standards is made to the IRS National Office and not to the local IRS Key District Office.

The employer must furnish evidence that (1) the minimum funding standards cannot be satisfied without temporary substantial business hardship, and (2) meeting the funding standards would adversely affect the interests of the plan's participants in the aggregate. The request should include the following items:

1. A statement concerning the employer's business, its history and ownership, any recent or contemplated changes that might affect its financial condition, and whether the employer is to be aggregated with any other entity (see Q 5:32).

2. The current and preceding two years' financial statements (the balance sheets and profit and loss statements). Uncertified statements are acceptable if certified statements have not been prepared. If the employer files financial reports with the Securities and Exchange Commission, the most recent ones should be submitted. If neither the statements nor reports are available, copies of federal income tax returns may be submitted.

3. A comprehensive discussion of the nature and extent of the business hardship, and statements that (1) discuss the prospects of recovery and why recovery is likely, (2) describe actions taken or planned to effect recovery, and (3) explain

when and to what extent it is anticipated that required contributions can reasonably be expected to resume.

4. Facts concerning the plan and its coverage of employees (e.g., the name of the plan, the date it was adopted).

5. Copies of the current plan document and summary plan description.

6. A description of any plan amendments that affected plan costs.

7. Actuarial reports for the preceding two plan years.

8. A statement of how the plan is funded (e.g., trust funds, insurance policies).

9. The contribution history for the current plan year and prior two plan years.

10. The plan year for which the waiver is requested and the approximate contribution required to meet the minimum funding standards.

11. Copy of the most recent annual report, with appropriate schedules attached.

12. A statement as to whether the plan is subject to PBGC jurisdiction (see Q 21:12).

13. A statement as to whether any other matters are currently or about to be pending before any court, IRS, DOL, or PBGC.

14. Information concerning the granting of any prior waivers.

15. Information concerning any other plans maintained by the employer.

[Rev Proc 88-29, 1988-1 CB 828; Rev Proc 83-41, 1983-1 CB 775]

In addition to the above, a defined contribution plan subject to the minimum funding standards must adopt an amendment to the plan specifying how the waived contribution will be made up and allocated to the plan participants. [Rev Rul 78-223, 1978-1 CB 125; Ltr Ruls 9309051, 9224052]

If, in addition to the waiver request, the employer wants to receive a determination letter with respect to the amendment, it should submit the waiver request as part of the determination letter request to the IRS Key District Office and include all of the above information. For more details, see Chapter 15.

The application for a waiver generally should be submitted no earlier than 180 days prior to the beginning of the plan year for which the waiver is being requested, because the evidence required to support the request may not be available. Furthermore, requests must be submitted no later than the 15th day of the third month following the close of the plan year for which the waiver is required. This deadline may be extended upon a showing of good cause for the late filing. [IRC § 412(d)(4); Rev Proc 88-29, 1988-1 CB 828; Rev Proc 83-41, 1983-1 CB 775; Ltr Rul 9310050]

Requests for a waiver only should be addressed to:

> Commissioner of Internal Revenue
> Attention: OP:E:A
> 1111 Constitution Avenue, N.W.
> Washington, DC 20224

Q 8:22 Are there any notice requirements when a funding waiver request is filed?

Yes. The applicant must give advance notice of the waiver application to (1) each participant in the plan, (2) each beneficiary under the plan, (3) each alternate payee (see Q 30:3), and (4) each employee organization representing participants in the plan. The notice must include a description of the extent to which the plan is funded for benefits that are guaranteed by PBGC and the extent to which the plan is funded for benefit liabilities. [ERISA § 303(e)(1); IRC § 412(f)(4)(A); Rev Proc 88-29, 1988-1 CB 828]

Q 8:23 Is any additional information required to be filed along with the funding waiver request?

Yes. The employer must provide a list of all prior plan years for which IRS has granted it a waiver. This list must include the amount waived for each plan year, the outstanding balance of the amortization base established by the waiver, and any conditions regarding the waiver.

The employer must also provide a copy of the letter that was sent to each union representing plan participants and indicate whether the letter was mailed or hand delivered to the union, to enable IRS to verify this notice requirement. [Rev Proc 88-29, 1988-1 CB 828; Rev Proc 88-5, 1988-1 CB 587]

Q 8:24 May a pension plan be amended if a waiver of the funding standards is in effect for a particular year?

Yes, but the funding waiver automatically ends if one of the following types of plan amendments is adopted:

1. An amendment increasing plan benefits;

2. An amendment changing the accrual of benefits if the change would increase the plan's liabilities; or

3. An amendment changing the rate at which benefits become nonforfeitable if the change would increase the plan's liabilities.

These amendments will not cause a funding waiver to cease if (1) DOL decides that the amendment is reasonable and has only a small impact on plan liabilities, (2) the amendment merely repeals a retroactive plan amendment reducing benefits, or (3) the amendment must be made for the plan to remain qualified for tax-favored status. [IRC §§ 412(f)(1), 412(f)(2)]

IRS ruled that amendments increasing benefits were neither reasonable nor *de minimis*; therefore, previously granted waivers no longer applied. [Ltr Ruls 9226075, 9224051] IRS has also ruled that an amendment increasing benefits was not reasonable merely because the amendment was agreed to in collective bargaining; and, therefore, the previously granted waivers ceased to apply. [Ltr Rul 9244040]

In one case, an employer proposed that a plan that had previously been granted a waiver of the minimum funding standards be converted to a 401(k) plan. IRS ruled that, since the contributions under the new plan would represent an impermissible increase in contribution levels, the previously granted funding waiver would be revoked. [Ltr Rul 9036037] However, in another case involving a plan that had previously been granted a waiver, the employer adopted a 401(k) plan, but IRS ruled the waiver would not be revoked because the contributions to the new plan were equal to the waived amount. [Ltr Rul 9036050]

Q 8:25 What alternative is available if IRS will not waive the minimum funding standards?

To keep the pension plan in compliance with the minimum funding standards, owners of the company may have to waive their benefits irrevocably. In small pension plans, the costs attributable to the owners' benefits are usually a large portion of the required contribution. Thus, if the owners are permitted to waive their contributions or benefits, the amount that has to be contributed to the pension plan to meet the minimum funding standards may be reduced substantially. IRS has ruled that an accumulated funding deficiency could not be corrected by the waiver of a key employee's benefits upon plan termination. [Ltr Rul 9146005]

Q 8:26 May an employer obtain an extension of an amortization period to help it meet the minimum funding standards?

Yes. An extension may be granted by IRS if the employer shows that the extension would provide adequate protection for participants and their beneficiaries and denial of the extension would (1) risk the continuation of the pension plan or might cause a curtailment of retirement benefits or employee compensation, and (2) be adverse to the interests of the participants. (Extending an amortization period reduces each year's pension outlay by spreading out the cost of funding benefits over a greater number of years.) [IRC § 412(e)(1); Rev Rul 79-408, 1979-2 CB 191; Rev Proc 79-61, 1979-2 CB 575]

In addition to the information required when a waiver is sought (see Q 8:21), an application for an extension must include the following information:

1. The unfunded liability (past service costs, for example) for which the extension is sought;
2. The reasons an extension is being sought;
3. The length of the desired extension (up to a maximum of ten years); and

4. A numerical illustration showing how annual plan costs will be affected.

A request for a ten-year extension of the time to amortize the unfunded liability for a pension plan was denied where there was no indication that the hardship was temporary or that there was a fair chance of recovery. [Ltr Rul 9216029]

Q 8:27 May a contribution be timely for the minimum funding standards but not for tax deduction purposes?

Yes. Contributions made after the close of a plan year may relate back to that year if they are made within 8½ months (2½ months for multiemployer plans; see Q 25:2) after the close of the plan year. This special deadline does not extend the time limit for making a contribution for tax deduction purposes; that is, payment by the due date, including extensions, for filing the employer's federal income tax return (see Q 12:3). [ERISA § 302(c)(10)(A); IRC § 412(c)(10); Treas Reg § 1.412(c)-12]

This special deadline applies only for purposes of minimum funding and the excise tax (see Q 8:18) imposed for failure to meet the funding requirements. Employer contributions to its plan after the due date for filing its federal income tax return (including extensions) but within 8½ months after the close of the plan year are not deductible as contributions for the closed year. Although the minimum funding standards may be met, the tax deduction requirements are not. [Ltr Rul 7949018]

Q 8:28 Must quarterly contributions be made to a defined benefit plan?

Yes. Quarterly contribution payments are required to be made to a defined benefit plan (other than a multiemployer plan; see Q 25:2). The quarterly payments are due 15 days after the end of each quarter of the plan year. The percentage of each required quarterly payment is equal to 25 percent of the required annual payment. (Prior to 1992, the percentage of each required quarterly payment was phased in.) The required annual payment is the lesser of (1) 90 percent of the amount required to be contributed to the plan for the plan year in order to meet minimum funding, or (2) 100 percent of the amount so required for the preceding plan year. Quarterly contributions are not required for the first plan year. [ERISA § 302(e); IRC § 412(m); Notice 89-52, 1989-1 CB 692]

An underpayment of a required quarterly payment requires that the funding standard account (see Q 8:15) be charged with interest at a rate equal to the greater of (1) 175 percent of the federal mid-term rate, or (2) the rate of interest used to determine costs by the plan. However, the interest is offset by the assumed interest rate under the plan. [IRC § 412(m); Notice 89-52, 1989-1 CB 692]

The required quarterly payments may result in nondeductible contributions (see Q 8:7). IRS has instituted procedures for the return of nondeductible contributions. Generally, before nondeductible contributions may be returned, the contributions must be disallowed by obtaining a ruling letter from IRS, but a formal ruling is not necessary for nondeductible contributions of less than $25,000. The procedures are effective for contributions made to satisfy the quarterly installment requirement for plan years commencing on or after January 1, 1990. [Rev Proc 90-49, 1990-2 CB 620]

Q 8:29 Does the minimum funding requirement cease once a pension plan terminates?

Generally, the minimum funding standards apply to a pension plan until the end of the plan year in which the plan terminates and do not apply to the plan in later years. Therefore, the funding standard account (see Q 8:15) must be maintained through the end of the plan year in which the pension plan terminates, even if the termination occurs before the last day of the plan year. [JP Jeter Co, Inc, TCM 1993-231]

If plan assets are not distributed as soon as administratively feasible after the date of plan termination, the plan will not be treated as terminated and, therefore, such a plan remains subject to the minimum funding standards (see Q 21:61). [Rev Rul 89-87, 1989-2 CB 81; Rev Rul 79-237, 1979-2 CB 190]

For details on plan terminations, see Chapter 21.

Chapter 9

Vesting

One of the major features of a qualified retirement plan is the requirement that it provide for the vesting of benefits according to one of several schedules set by law. Thus, at a certain point, an employee acquires a nonforfeitable interest in benefits under the plan. This chapter examines what vesting means, the minimum requirements set by law, and how vesting works.

Q 9:1 What does vesting mean?

Vesting represents the nonforfeitable interest of participants in their (1) account balances under a defined contribution plan (see Q 2:2) or (2) accrued benefits under a defined benefit plan (see Q 2:3).

Example. Assume a participant is 40 percent vested (that is, the participant has a nonforfeitable right to 40 percent of the benefit accrued in the plan). In a defined contribution plan, the participant's vested accrued benefit is equal to 40 percent of the balance in the account. In a defined benefit plan, the participant has a nonforfeitable right to 40 percent of the normal retirement benefit that has been accrued. Thus, if the accrued normal retirement benefit is $150 a month, the participant has a nonforfeitable right to $60 a month.

Vesting is directly related to an employee's length of service with the employer or group of employers (see Q 9:3).

Special vesting rules apply to top-heavy plans (see Q 22:32).

Q 9:2   What is an accrued benefit?

A participant's accrued benefit is the benefit that has accumulated up to a particular point in employment. Earning accrued benefits does not mean that a participant has a nonforfeitable (i.e., vested) right to those benefits. The nonforfeitability of an accrued benefit is determined by the retirement plan's vesting schedule.

Defined contribution plans (see Q 2:2) must provide separate accounts with respect to each participant's accrued benefit. This means that a participant's accrued benefit is the balance of the participant's individual account (see Q 9:24). [IRC § 411(a)(7)(A)(ii)]

Defined benefit plans (other than those funded solely through insurance contracts) are required to include a procedure for determining a participant's accrued benefit that satisfies one of three alternative benefit accrual formulas. Generally, accrued benefits are determined with reference to the benefits that are payable at normal retirement age (see Q 10:55) and that accrue over the period of the employee's participation in the plan or service with the employer. The alternative formulas limit the amount of back loading (providing a higher rate for accrual of benefits for later years of service than for earlier years); however, they do not require the same rate of benefit accrual each year. Front loading (providing a higher rate for accrual of benefits for earlier years of service than for later years) is permitted, although such front loading also may be limited. [IRC § 411(b)(1); Prop Reg § 1.411(b)-2(b)(3); Rev Rul 85-131, 1985-2 CB 138; Notice 87-21, 1987-1 CB 458 (Q&A 16); Notice 89-45, 1989-1 CB 684; Jerome Mirza & Assocs, Ltd v United States, 882 F 2d 229 (7th Cir 1989)]

Q 9:3   Are minimum vesting standards set by law?

Yes. Two minimum vesting schedules apply to a participant's accrued benefit (see Q 9:2) derived from employer contributions. [IRC § 411(a)(2); Temp Reg §§ 1.411(a)-3T(b), 1.411(a)-3T(c), 1.411(a)-3T(e)] These schedules, either one of which may be used, are as follows:

Five-Year Vesting

Years of service	Nonforfeitable percentage
Less than 5	0%
5 or more	100%

Seven-Year Graded Vesting

Years of service	Nonforfeitable percentage
Less than 3	0%
3	20%
4	40%
5	60%
6	80%
7 or more	100%

Example 1. Stanley Corporation's retirement plan provides for plan participation after the completion of one year of service and provides for 100 percent vesting after five years of plan participation rather than service. The plan does not satisfy the minimum vesting standards because, under the plan, an employee becomes 100 percent vested only after completion of more than five years of service. Vesting based upon years of participation is permitted as long as the minimum vesting standards are satisfied. [Ferrara v Allentown Physician Anesthesia Assocs, Inc, 711 F Supp 206 (DC ED Pa 1989)]

Example 2. Marjorie Corporation's retirement plan contains the following vesting schedule:

Years of service	Nonforfeitable percentage
1 or less	0%
2	10%
3	25%
4	45%
5	65%
6	75%
7 or more	100%

The plan does not satisfy the minimum vesting standards because the nonforfeitable percentage after six years of service (75 percent) is less than the percentage required at that time (80 percent). The fact that the nonforfeitable percentage for years prior to the sixth year of service is greater than the percentage required is immaterial.

These new minimum vesting standards apply to plan participants who perform an hour of service in any plan year beginning after 1988.

Q 9:4 Do the minimum vesting standards apply to multiemployer plans?

A multiemployer plan (see Chapter 25) may use a ten-year cliff vesting schedule (that is, an employee with at least ten years of service is 100 percent vested), but only for participants covered under the plan pursuant to a collective bargaining agreement.

Employees are not covered under a collective bargaining agreement *unless* they are represented by a *bona fide* employee representative who is a party to the agreement. Consequently, an employee of the multiemployer plan or an employee of the union is not covered under the collective bargaining agreement, even though the employee participates in the plan pursuant to an agreement with the plan or with the union.

Plan participants not covered pursuant to a collective bargaining agreement must have a nonforfeitable right to accrued benefits derived from employer contributions under either the five-year cliff or the seven-year graded vesting schedule (see Q 9:3).

For employees covered by a multiemployer plan pursuant to a collective bargaining agreement ratified before March 1, 1986, the effective date of the new minimum vesting standards is the plan year beginning on or after the earlier of: (1) January 1, 1991, or (2) the later of (a) January 1, 1989, or (b) the date the last such collective bargaining agreement terminates.

Example. A calendar-year multiemployer plan is maintained pursuant to a three-year collective bargaining agreement, which expired on February 28, 1989. The plan must be in compliance with the new vesting rules for its plan year commencing on January 1, 1990—the first plan year beginning after February 28, 1989. However, the new vesting rules apply to plan participants who are employees of the plan or of the union as of the plan year beginning after December 31, 1988, if they have an hour of service after that date.

[IRC §§ 411(a)(2)(C), 414(f)(1)(B); Temp Reg §§ 1.411(a)-3T(d), 1.411(a)-3T(e)]

TSB '93 (see Q 1:13), if enacted, will eliminate this special vesting rule for multiemployer plans so that all qualified retirement plans will be subject to the same vesting standards. The effective date of this change would be the first plan year beginning on or after the earlier of: (1) January 1, 1996, or (2) the later of (a) January 1, 1994, or (b) the date the last such collective bargaining agreement terminates. [TSB '93, Act § 234]

Q 9:5 Does the adoption of one of the minimum vesting schedules guarantee the retirement plan's qualification?

Unless there has been a pattern of abuse or actual misuse in the operation of a retirement plan, the use of one of the two minimum vesting schedules (see Q 9:3) will satisfy the plan's qualification requirements. The intentional dismissal of employees to prevent vesting may indicate a pattern of abuse. See Chapter 22 for details relating to vesting under a top-heavy plan. [IRC § 411(d)(1); Prop Reg § 1.411(d)-1(b); Rev Proc 89-29, 1989-1 CB 893]

When an employee was discharged by the employer shortly before his qualified retirement plan benefits would have become vested, courts have found that the proximity of the termination date and the vesting date was sufficient to infer that the employer's purpose in discharging the employee was to deprive him of his retirement benefits. [Hazen Paper Co v Biggins, No. 91-1600 (S Ct 1993); Olitsky v Spencer Gifts, Inc, No. 91-1010 (5th Cir 1992)] One court ruled that the prevention of further benefit accruals or additional vesting must be a motivating factor in the employer's decision to discharge an employee. [Clark v Coats & Clark, Inc, No. 92-8024 (11th Cir 1993)] However, in another case, the court upheld the plan's vesting schedule even though a significant number of participants never became vested because of the transient nature of their employment. [Phillips v Alaska Hotel and Restaurant Employees Pension Fund, Nos. 89-35735 and 90-35144 (9th Cir 1991)]

Q 9:6   May a qualified retirement plan's vesting schedule be changed?

Yes. Like other provisions in a qualified retirement plan, the vesting schedule may be amended by the employer, even after IRS has approved the plan as initially adopted.

If the vesting schedule is amended, however, each participant in the qualified retirement plan on the date the amendment is adopted or becomes effective (whichever is later) who has completed at least three years of service may elect, during the election period (see Q 9:7), to stay under the old vesting schedule. A participant's failure to make that election means that the participant is subject to the new schedule—provided that the participant was notified of the right to elect. An amendment of the vesting schedule may not cause any participant to forfeit (directly or indirectly) vested benefits regardless of length of service. [IRC § 411(a)(10); Temp Reg § 1.411(a)-8T(b)(1)]

A new determination letter should be obtained, particularly if the plan's vesting schedule has been made less liberal (see Q 21:5). See Chapter 15 for details.

Q 9:7   What is the period within which a participant may elect to stay under the old vesting schedule?

A participant must have at least 60 days to elect the old vesting schedule. In addition, the election period must begin no later than the date on which the amendment is adopted and end no earlier than the latest of the following:

- 60 days after the amendment is adopted
- 60 days after the amendment becomes effective or

- 60 days after the participant "is issued written notice of the plan amendment by the employer or plan administrator"

[IRC § 411(a)(10)(B); Temp Reg § 1.411(a)-8T(b)(2)]

Q 9:8 What vesting standards apply to an employee's own contributions?

Whether contributions are mandatory or voluntary (see Qs 6:17, 6:18), the employee at all times must have a nonforfeitable right to 100 percent of the benefits derived from the employee's own contributions. [IRC § 411(a)(1); Treas Reg §§ 1.411(a)-1(a)(2), 1.411(c)-1]

Q 9:9 What is a year of service for vesting purposes?

For purposes of determining a participant's vested benefits, a year of service means a 12-month period specified in the qualified retirement plan during which the participant completes at least 1,000 hours of service (see Q 5:9). [IRC § 411(a)(5)]

Q 9:10 What years of service must be taken into account for vesting purposes?

In general, all years of service with the employer must be counted. For the exceptions, see Question 9:11. [IRC § 411(a)(4)]

Service with a predecessor of the employer must be counted if the successor-employer maintains the predecessor's qualified retirement plan. If the successor adopts a new retirement plan, recognition of service with the predecessor-employer is supposed to be decided under as-yet-unissued IRS regulations. IRS has said that, in the case of a predecessor-partnership, service with the partnership could be counted for vesting purposes under the successor-corporation's retirement plan, even though the corporation did not continue the partnership's retirement plan. [IRC § 414(a); Ltr Rul 7742003]

Service with any member of a controlled group of corporations or with a commonly controlled entity (see Q 5:32), whether or not incorporated, must be counted for vesting purposes. Similarly, service with any member of an affiliated service group (see Q 29:31) must be counted. [IRC §§ 414(b), 414(c), 414(m)]

A multiple-employer defined benefit plan that does not credit vesting service attributable to periods for which an employer does not make required contributions to the plan does not satisfy the minimum vesting requirements. [Rev Rul 85-130, 1985-2 CB 137]

Q 9:11 May any years of service be disregarded for vesting purposes?

Yes. There are limited exceptions to the general rule that all years of service with an employer must be counted for vesting purposes (see Q 9:10). [IRC § 411(a)(4)]

The following years of service may be disregarded:

1. Years of service before the employee reached age 18;
2. Years of service before the qualified retirement plan went into effect;
3. Years of service during which the employee declined to make required (mandatory) contributions; and
4. Years of service before a one-year break in service (see Q 5:10) if the number of consecutive one-year breaks in service equals or exceeds the greater of five or the number of prebreak years of service, and the participant did not have any nonforfeitable right to the accrued benefit (see Q 9:14).

Q 9:12 Is an employee's length of service ever irrelevant in determining the degree of vesting?

Yes. In any of the following circumstances an employee is fully vested (that is, has a nonforfeitable right to 100 percent of the employer-provided account balance or accrued benefit) regardless of how many years of service the employee has completed:

1. The employee reaches normal retirement age (see Q 10:55). [IRC §§ 411(a), 411(a)(8)]

2. The qualified retirement plan is terminated, a partial termination of the plan has occurred (see Q 21:5), or plan contributions are completely discontinued. [IRC § 411(d)(3)]

3. The minimum service requirement for participation is more than one year of service (see Qs 5:4, 23:4). [IRC § 410(a)(1)(B)(i)]

4. The plan is a qualified 401(k) plan and the accrued benefit is derived from employer contributions made pursuant to the employee's election. See Chapter 23 for details. [IRC § 401(k)(2)(C)]

The plan may also provide for full vesting under any of these circumstances:

1. The employee reaches the early retirement age set by the qualified retirement plan.

2. The employee becomes disabled.

3. The employee dies.

Q 9:13   What vesting schedule is best for the employer?

It depends on how long employees usually stay with the employer.

Example. Keren Corporation adopted a 5-percent-of-compensation money purchase pension plan on January 1, 1992. Sharon completes a year of service on January 1, 1993 and joins the plan. Sharon earns $20,000 a year. Below is a calculation of Sharon's benefits under the seven-year graded and five-year cliff vesting schedules (see Q 9:3):

	Seven-Year		Five-Year	
Plan Year	Contribution/ Account Balance	Vesting Percentage/ Vested Benefits	Contribution/ Account Balance	Vesting Percentage/ Vested Benefits
1	0 / 0		0 / 0	
2	$1,000 / $1,000	0% / $0	$1,000 / $1,000	0% / $0
3	$1,000 / $2,000	20% / $400	$1,000 / $2,000	0% / $0
4	$1,000 / $3,000	40% / $1,200	$1,000 / $3,000	0% / $0
5	$1,000 / $4,000	60% / $2,400	$1,000 / $4,000	100% / $4,000
6	$1,000 / $5,000	80% / $4,000	$1,000 / $5,000	100% / $5,000
7	$1,000 / $6,000	100% / $6,000	$1,000 / $6,000	100% / $6,000

In plan years 3 and 4, less vested benefits are provided under the five-year cliff vesting schedule; and, in plan years 5 and 6, less vested benefits are provided under the seven-year graded vesting schedule. Thus, if employees customarily leave before completing five years of service, five-year cliff vesting is more favorable to the employer; but, if they leave after completing five or six years of service, the seven-year graded schedule is more favorable to the employer. After seven years of service, both schedules provide equal benefits.

As an alternative, Keren Corporation could require employees to complete two years of service to become eligible, but then employees must be 100 percent vested immediately (see Q 9:12). With a two-year service requirement and 100 percent immediate vesting, Sharon's benefits would be as follows:

Plan Year	Contribution/ Account Balance	Vesting Percentage/ Vested Benefits
1	$\dfrac{0}{0}$	
2	$\dfrac{0}{0}$	
3	$\dfrac{\$1,000}{\$1,000}$	$\dfrac{100\%}{\$1,000}$
4	$\dfrac{\$1,000}{\$2,000}$	$\dfrac{100\%}{\$2,000}$
5	$\dfrac{\$1,000}{\$3,000}$	$\dfrac{100\%}{\$3,000}$
6	$\dfrac{\$1,000}{\$4,000}$	$\dfrac{100\%}{\$4,000}$
7	$\dfrac{\$1,000}{\$5,000}$	$\dfrac{100\%}{\$5,000}$

In plan years 3 and 4, the least vested benefits still occur under five-year cliff; in plan year 5, the least vested benefits still occur under seven-year graded; in plan year 6, the most vested benefits are still created under five-year cliff; and, in plan year 7 and in all subsequent plan years, the least vested benefits occur with the two-year service requirement. Therefore, if employees customarily leave after completing seven or more years of service, the two-year service requirement will be most favorable to the employer.

Q 9:14 How does a one-year break in service affect a previously nonvested participant's right to benefits?

A nonvested participant's years of service before any period of consecutive one-year breaks in service (see Q 5:10) may be disregarded for vesting purposes if the number of consecutive one-year breaks in service equals or exceeds the greater of five or the participant's years of service before the break. [IRC § 411(a)(6)(D)]

Example. Yehiel Corporation's profit sharing plan, which operates on a calendar-year basis, requires an employee to complete one year of service to become a participant. Under the plan's vesting provision, a participant becomes 100 percent vested after five years of service. Lauren began working for Yehiel on January 1, 1989, separated from service on December 15, 1990, and was rehired on January 12, 1994. Lauren's two years of service before her break in service must be counted because her consecutive one-year breaks in service are less than five.

A participant's prebreak years of service do not have to be taken into account until a year of service is completed after reemployment. [IRC § 411(a)(6)(B)]

Q 9:15   How does a one-year break in service affect an employee if the qualified retirement plan requires the employee to have more than one year of service in order to be eligible to participate?

Qualified retirement plans that provide for immediate 100 percent vesting but require more than one year of service to be eligible to participate (see Qs 5:12, 9:12) may provide that years of service preceding a one-year break in service (see Q 5:10) be disregarded if the employee has not yet met the service eligibility criterion. Thus, an employee who completes one year of service and then incurs a one-year break in service starts over again when rehired. [IRC § 410(a)(5)(B)]

Q 9:16   How does a one-year break in service affect a vested participant's right to benefits?

The years of service of a vested participant in a defined contribution plan (see Q 2:2) or a fully insured defined benefit plan (see Q 2:22) completed after a one-year break in service (see Q 5:10) need not be counted for purposes of computing the participant's right to benefits derived from employer contributions accruing before the one-year break in service if the participant has at least five consecutive one-year breaks in service. [IRC § 411(a)(6)(C)]

Example. Jay-Kay Corporation has a profit sharing plan in which James participated. At the time James separated from service, he had a nonforfeitable right to 20 percent of his accrued benefit, but no distribution was made. In 1993, after incurring a one-year break in service, James is rehired and becomes an active participant in the plan once again. The plan is not permitted to disregard James's post-break service for purposes of computing the vested percentage of his pre-break accrued benefit.

If a participant's pre-break years of service are required to be taken into account, such years of service need not be counted until the participant completes a year of service after resuming employment. [IRC § 411(a)(6)(B)]

Q 9:17 What is a forfeiture of benefits?

If an employee terminates employment before becoming 100 percent vested, the employee may be entitled to some benefits. This will usually depend on the number of years the employee worked for the company. Thus, if, at the time of termination, the employee's account balance in a profit sharing plan is $10,000 and the employee is 60 percent vested, the vested benefit is $6,000 (60 percent of $10,000). The balance in the account that is not vested at the time of termination generally will be forfeited at the earlier of (1) when the employee receives a distribution or (2) after the employee incurs five consecutive one-year breaks in service (see Q 5:10). [IRC § 411(a)(6)(C)]

Q 9:18 What happens to amounts forfeited by participants?

Only defined benefit plans (see Q 2:3) are restricted in the application of forfeitures. Forfeitures under a defined benefit plan must be used to reduce future employer contributions and may not be used to provide additional benefits for remaining participants. Defined contribution plans (see Q 2:2) may provide that forfeitures be used either to reduce contributions or to increase benefits provided under the plan. [IRC § 401(a)(8)]

IRS has ruled that a profit sharing plan may provide for the allocation of forfeitures to participants on the basis of their account balances provided such allocation does not discriminate in favor of highly compensated employees (see Q 3:2). [Rev Rul 81-10, 1981-1

CB 172; Treas Reg §§ 1.401-4(a)(1)(iii), 1.401(a)(4)-1(c)(1), 1.401(a)(4)-11(c)]

Q 9:19   May a nonforfeitable benefit ever be forfeited?

The courts have differed on whether forfeitures can be imposed because of employee dishonesty (so-called bad boy clauses) or violation of a promise not to compete. Some courts say such forfeitures are not permitted. Other courts have ruled that if the forfeiture provisions do not cause a forfeiture of an amount greater than what would result under the minimum vesting standards (see Q 9:3), the forfeiture is allowed. [Noell v American Design, Inc Profit Sharing Plan, 764 F 2d 827 (8th Cir 1985); Montgomery v Lowe (DC ED Texas 1981); Hepple v Roberts & Dybdahl, Inc (8th Cir 1980); Marshall v Edison Bros, 593 F 2d 30 (8th Cir 1979); Nedrow v MacFarlane and Hays Co (DC Mich 1979)]

According to IRS, vested benefits in excess of the benefits required to be nonforfeitable under the statutory alternatives (see Q 9:3) may be forfeited because of an employee's misconduct or dishonesty. The qualified retirement plan must provide the specific criteria for application of this bad boy clause, and its use cannot be discriminatory in operation.

Example 1. Nephew Mikey Corporation's retirement plan provides that an employee is fully vested after the completion of three years of service. The plan also provides that, if the employee works for a competitor, he forfeits his rights in the plan. Such a provision could result in a prohibited forfeiture; but, if the plan limited the forfeiture to employees who completed less than five years of service, the plan would not fail to satisfy the minimum vesting requirements.

Example 2. Aunt Sallie Corporation's retirement plan has a seven-year graded vesting provision and provides for forfeiture of benefits if an employee with less than five years of service terminates employment and works for a competitor. This is permissible because the plan could have had five-year cliff vesting.

[Temp Reg § 1.411(a)-4T(c); Treas Reg § 1.411(d)-4, Q&A 6; Rev Rul 85-31, 1985-1 CB 153]

Q 9:20 Does a distribution (cash-out) of benefits affect how many years of service must be taken into account?

Yes. Upon termination of the employee's participation in a qualified retirement plan, the plan may disregard service for which the employee has received (1) an involuntary distribution of the present value of the employee's nonforfeitable benefit up to a maximum of $3,500, or (2) a voluntary distribution of the present value of the nonforfeitable benefit. [IRC §§ 411(a)(7)(B), 411(a)(11); Treas Reg § 1.411(a)-7(d)(4)]

In order to disregard the prior service of a participant who resumes employment and participation under the qualified retirement plan and who previously received a distribution of less than the present value of the accrued benefit, the plan must provide the participant with the opportunity to repay the entire amount of the distribution (see Q 9:21). [IRC § 411(a)(7)(C); Treas Reg § 1.411(a)-7(d)(4)]

Q 9:21 How can a reemployed participant restore (buy-back) forfeited benefits?

In most situations, upon reemployment, a participant is entitled to repay a prior distribution from the qualified retirement plan and to have any forfeited benefits restored. This buy-back provision must permit the employee to pay back the full amount distributed. The plan can require repayment by the reemployed participant before the earlier of (1) five years after reemployment, or (2) when the participant incurs a period of five consecutive one-year breaks in service commencing after the distribution. Thus, the employer is not required to offer this buy-back right to a participant who has five consecutive one-year breaks in service after the distribution. [IRC § 411(a)(7)(C)]

A defined benefit plan may require that any repayment include interest on the full amount of the distribution. The maximum interest rate that may be charged upon repayment is 120 percent of the federal midterm rate in effect on the first day of the plan year during which repayment occurs. [IRC §§ 411(a)(7)(C), 411(c)(2)(C), 1274; Treas Reg § 1.411(a)-7(d)(2)(ii)(B)]

Q 9:22 May a qualified retirement plan provide for the forfeiture of vested benefits on the death of an employee?

Yes, with the following exception: the surviving spouse of a participant in a qualified retirement plan subject to the survivor annuity requirements must be paid an annuity based on the participant's vested accrued benefit unless the participant waived the coverage with the spouse's consent (see Q 10:20). [IRC § 401(a)(11)]

A qualified retirement plan may not provide for the forfeiture of vested benefits derived from employee contributions, whether mandatory or voluntary (see Q 9:8). However, a forfeiture does not occur merely because benefits derived from contributions of both the employer and the employee are paid out in the form of an annuity that stops on the employee's death. [Treas Reg § 1.411(a)-4(b)(1)(ii)]

Q 9:23 May any years of service be disregarded for accrual purposes?

Yes. A qualified retirement plan may impose a limitation on the amount of benefits an employee may accrue or the number of years of service that will be taken into account in determining an employee's accrued benefit (see Q 9:2). Therefore, a qualified retirement plan may disregard an employee's service that occurs after the specified benefit level or the specified number of years of service has been reached. However, a retirement plan may not cease an employee's accrual of benefits (or reduce the rate of accrual) solely because the employee attains a certain age. [IRC § 411(b)(1)(H); Prop Reg § 1.411(b)-2; Atkins v Northwest Airlines, Inc, No. 91-3179MN (8th Cir 1992); American Assn of Retired Persons v Farmers Group, Inc, No. 90-55872 (9th Cir 1991)]

> **Example.** Stephanie Corporation maintains a defined benefit plan under which the participant's normal retirement benefit will be based on the highest annual salary earned by the participant during the time of employment. The plan further provides that each participant will accrue an interest in the benefit at the rate of 4 percent per year of service. The plan does, however, limit the number of years of service that will be taken into account in determining each participant's retirement benefit to 20. Therefore, a participant's normal retirement benefit will be limited to 80

percent of the participant's highest annual salary. This type of accrual scheme is permissible despite the fact that an older participant is more likely to be affected by the plan provision.

Q 9:24 Can a qualified retirement plan be amended to reduce accrued benefits?

Generally, no. A qualified retirement plan may not be amended to eliminate or reduce a Section 411(d)(6) protected benefit (see Q 10:42) that has already accrued, unless IRS approves a request to amend the plan or the elimination or reduction satisfies certain requirements (see Q 9:25). This is the rule even if such elimination or reduction is contingent upon the employee's consent. However, a plan may (subject to certain notice requirements) be amended to eliminate or reduce Section 411(d)(6) protected benefits with respect to benefits not yet accrued as of the later of the amendment's adoption date or effective date (see Q 9:26). [IRC §§ 411(d)(6), 412(c)(8); ERISA §§ 204(g), 302(c)(8), 4281; Treas Reg § 1.411(d)-4, Q&A 2; Production and Maintenance Employees' Local 504 v Roadmaster Corp, Nos. 89-1464 and 90-2698 (7th Cir 1992)]

One court has held that a defined contribution plan (see Q 2:2) could not be retroactively amended to change the plan's valuation date where the effect of the amendment was to reduce the amount of benefits payable to a terminated plan participant. In this case, the value of the terminated participant's account balance in the plan decreased markedly from the prior valuation date. Under the plan in effect on his termination date, the terminated participant was entitled to a distribution of his account balance valued as of the nearest prior valuation date. After the participant's termination, the plan was amended (retroactive to the beginning of the plan year) to provide for interim valuation dates. An interim valuation resulted in a much smaller account balance for the terminated participant. The court held that, in a defined contribution plan, the accrued benefit is the participant's account balance (see Q 9:2). Thus, the participant's account balance could not be reduced by a retroactive plan amendment adopted after the participant terminated employment. [Pratt v Petroleum Production Mgmt, Inc Employee Savings Plan and Trust, No. 88-2190 (10th Cir 1990); also see Kay v Thrift and Profit Sharing

Plan for Employees of Boyertown Casket Co, 780 F Supp 1447 (ED Pa 1991)]

Amendments eliminating participants' rights to elect lump-sum distributions or delaying the right to payment of retirement benefits constitute prohibited elimination or reduction in accrued benefits. [Counts v Kissack Water and Oil Service, Inc Profit Sharing Plan, No. 92-8036 (10th Cir 1993); Davis v Burlington Industries, Inc, No. 91-1725 (4th Cir 1992); Auwarter v Paper Sales Corp Defined Benefit Pension Plan, No. 91-3082 (ED NY 1992)] It has also been held that the elimination of a post-retirement cost-of-living adjustment in monthly retirement benefits constitutes a prohibited reduction in accrued benefits. [Hickey v Chicago Truck Drivers, Helpers and Warehouse Workers Union, 1992 US App Lexis 30961 (7th Cir 1992)]

Q 9:25   Can accrued benefits be eliminated or reduced?

It is permissible to eliminate or reduce accrued benefits (see Q 9:2) if any of the following circumstances is present:

1. The amendment constitutes timely compliance with a change in law affecting plan qualification (IRS gives Section 7805(b) relief), and the elimination or reduction is made only to the extent necessary to comply with the plan qualification rules. An amendment will not be treated as necessary if it is possible to satisfy the applicable qualification requirement through other modifications to the plan (e.g., by expanding the availability of an optional form of benefit to additional employees).

2. A qualified retirement plan that provides a range of three or more actuarially equivalent joint and survivor annuity options may be amended to eliminate any of such options, other than the options with the largest and smallest optional survivor payment percentages. The amendment is permissible even if the effect of such amendment is to change the option that is the qualified joint and survivor annuity (QJSA) (see Q 10:8).

Example. A retirement plan provides three joint and survivor annuity options with survivor payments of 50 percent, 75 percent, and 100 percent, respectively. The options are uniform with respect to age and are actuarially equivalent. The employer may eliminate the option with the 75 percent survivor payment, even if this option had been the QJSA under the plan.

3. If a qualified retirement plan includes an optional form of benefit under which benefits are distributed in specified property (other than cash), such optional form may be modified for distributions after plan termination by substituting cash for the property, but only to the extent that, on plan termination, an employee has the opportunity to receive the optional form of benefit in the specified property. However, if the employer that maintains the terminating plan also maintains another plan that provides an optional form of benefit in the specified property, this exception is not available.

Example. Ess-Kay Corporation maintains a stock bonus plan under which a participant, upon termination from employment, may elect to receive benefits in a lump-sum distribution in the company's stock. This is the only plan maintained by Ess-Kay under which distributions in employer stock are available. Ess-Kay decides to terminate the stock bonus plan. If such plan is amended to make available a lump-sum distribution in employer stock on plan termination, the plan will not fail the anti-cutback rule solely because the optional form of benefit providing a lump-sum distribution in employer stock on termination of employment is modified to provide that such distribution is available only in cash.

[Treas Reg § 1.411(d)-4, Q&A 2(b)]

Other circumstances permitting elimination or reduction of accrued benefits include amendments to provide for certain involuntary distributions, to eliminate provisions authorizing loans and certain plan-to-plan transfers, and to make a *de minimis* change in the timing of an optional form of benefit (see Q 10:33). In addition, special rules have been provided for amendments to employee stock ownership plans (ESOPs) (see Q 24:1). [Treas Reg § 1.411(d)-4, Q&A 2(d)]

Q 9:26   Can a qualified retirement plan be amended to reduce future accruals of benefits?

Yes. However, an amendment to a qualified retirement plan subject to the minimum funding requirements (see Q 8:1) that provides for a "significant reduction in the rate of future benefit accrual" will not be effective unless the plan administrator (see Q 16:1) provides written notice to all participants, any alternate payee under a qualified domestic relations order (QDRO) (see Q 30:1), and each employee organization representing participants. That notice, which must set forth the amendment and its effective date, is required to be sent to such parties after adoption of the amendment and at least 15 days prior to its effective date. The reduction may result in either a termination or partial termination of the plan. See Chapter 21 for details. [ERISA § 204(h)]

In a case in which an employer amended its qualified retirement plan to cease benefit accruals retroactively and gave notice of the amendment to its employees before the amendment was adopted and after the amendment's effective date, the court held that the amendment violated the prohibition against reducing accrued benefits and thus was ineffective. [Production and Maintenance Employees' Local 504 v Roadmaster Corp, Nos. 89-1464 and 90-2698 (7th Cir 1992)] In another case, the court ruled that an amendment to the employer's qualified retirement plan that excluded certain income from the plan's definition of compensation, the effect of which was to reduce future benefit accruals, was ineffective because prior written notice was not given to plan participants. [Davidson v Canteen Corp, Nos. 91-1270 and 91-1348 (7th Cir 1992)]

Q 9:27   What benefits are not Section 411(d)(6) protected benefits?

The following are examples of benefits that are not Section 411(d)(6) benefits and, therefore, may be reduced or eliminated by an amendment to a qualified retirement plan:

1. Ancillary life insurance protection;
2. Accident or health insurance benefits;

3. Social Security supplements described in Section 411(a)(9) [Cattin v General Motors Corp, Nos. 90-1016, 90-1051, and 90-1052 (6th Cir 1992);

4. The availability of loans (other than the distribution of an employee's accrued benefit upon default under a loan);

5. The right to make certain after-tax employee contributions or elective deferrals;

6. The right to direct investments;

7. The right to a particular form of investment (for example, investment in employer stock or securities, or investment in certain types of securities, commercial paper, or other investment media);

8. The allocation dates for contributions, forfeitures, and earnings, the time for making contributions (but not the conditions for receiving an allocation of contributions or forfeitures for a plan year after such conditions have been satisfied), and the valuation dates for account balances;

9. Administrative procedures for distributing benefits, such as provisions relating to the particular dates on which notices are given and by which elections must be made; and

10. Rights that derive from administrative and operational provisions, such as mechanical procedures for allocating investment experience among accounts in defined contribution plans.

[Treas Reg § 1.411(d)-4, Q&A 1(d)]

Q 9:28 What happens to a participant's benefits if the qualified retirement plan merges with another plan?

In case of a merger or consolidation of qualified retirement plans, or a transfer of assets or liabilities from one qualified retirement plan to another, each participant must be entitled to receive a benefit after the merger that is at least equal to the value of the benefit the participant would have been entitled to receive before the merger. (The before-and-after merger benefits are determined as if the plan had been terminated.) [IRC § 401(a)(12); Treas Reg §§ 1.401(a)-12, 1.414(l)-1]

Generally, the plan sponsor or plan administrator (see Q 16:1) of a merged plan must apprise the appropriate IRS District Director of the merger by completing Form 5310-A and filing the form, in duplicate, at least 30 days before the event. Form 5310-A should be filed for each plan involved in the merger. Although IRS will not issue a determination letter (see Q 15:1) when a Form 5310-A is filed, an actuarial statement of valuation must be submitted, and, of course, IRS may request additional documentation with regard to any filing.

There is a penalty for late filing; the penalty is $25 a day for each day Form 5310-A is late (up to a maximum of $15,000). For exceptions to the requirement for filing Form 5310-A, see Question 9:29.

Q 9:29   Must Form 5310-A always be filed if there is a merger of qualified retirement plans?

No. Form 5310-A is *not* required to be filed in the following four situations:

1. Two or more defined contribution plans are merged, and all of the following conditions are met:

    a. The sum of the account balances (see Q 9:2) in each plan prior to the merger equals the fair market value of the entire plan assets (e.g., each plan has no unallocated suspense account or outstanding waiver balances (see Q 8:21)).

    b. The assets of each plan are combined to form the assets of the plan as merged.

    c. Immediately after the merger, each participant in the plan as merged has an account balance equal to the sum of the account balances the participant had in the plans immediately prior to the merger. [Treas Reg § 1.414(l)-1(d)]

2. There is a spinoff of a defined contribution plan, and all of the following conditions are met:

    a. The sum of the account balances in the plan prior to the spinoff equals the fair market value of the entire plan assets (e.g., the plan has no unallocated suspense account or outstanding waiver balances).

   b. The sum of the account balances for each participant in the resulting plans equals the account balance of each participant in the plan before the spinoff.

   c. The assets in each of the plans immediately after the spinoff equal the sum of the account balances for all participants in the plan (e.g., there is no unallocated suspense account or outstanding waiver balances in any of the plans spun off). [Treas Reg § 1.414(l)-1(m)]

3. Two or more defined benefit plans (see Q 2:3) are merged into one defined benefit plan, and both of the following conditions are met:

   a. The total liabilities (the present value of benefits, whether or not vested; see Q 9:1) that are merged into the larger plan involved in the merger are less than 3 percent of the assets of the larger plan. This condition must be satisfied on at least one day in the larger plan's plan year during which the merger occurs.

   b. The provisions of the larger plan that allocate assets upon termination must provide that, in the event of a spinoff or termination of the plan within five years following the merger, plan assets will be allocated first for the benefits of the participants in the other plan(s) to the extent of the present value of their benefits as of the date of the merger. [Treas Reg § 1.414(l)-1(h)]

4. There is a spinoff of a defined benefit plan into another defined benefit plan, and both of the following conditions are met:

   a. With respect to each resulting spinoff plan, other than the spinoff plan with the greatest value of plan assets after the spinoff, the value of the assets spun off is not less than the present value of the benefits spun off (whether or not vested).

   b. The value of the assets spun off to all the resulting spinoff plans (other than the spinoff plan with the greatest value of plan assets after the spinoff) plus other assets previously spun off during the plan year in which the spinoff occurs is less than 3 percent of the assets of the plan before the spinoff as of at least one day in that plan's plan year. [Treas Reg § 1.414(l)-1(n)(2)]

A transferor of assets or liabilities is considered to be a combination of separate mergers and spinoffs; and, unless the parts of the transaction that are deemed to be a spinoff or merger conform to one of the situations described above, Form 5310-A must be filed. A transferor plan in a spinoff of a defined contribution plan need not account for changes in the value of assets between the spinoff date and the actual date of transfer if there is no undue or intentional delay in transferring the assets. [The John Blair Consulting, Inc Profit Sharing Plan v Telemundo Group, Inc Profit Sharing Plan, No. 90 Civ 5499 (MGC) (SDNY 1993)]

Chapter 10

General Distribution Requirements

Numerous rules govern the timing and form of benefit distributions. This chapter examines qualified joint and survivor annuity (QJSA) requirements, qualified preretirement survivor annuity (QPSA) requirements, limits on optional forms of benefit, and related matters.

Q 10:1 Must a qualified retirement plan provide benefits to a participant's surviving spouse?

If a married participant with vested benefits dies before the annuity starting date (see Q 10:3), a QPSA (see Q 10:9) must, with certain exceptions, be provided to the participant's surviving spouse. A QPSA must be provided whether or not the participant separated from service before death. If a married participant survives until the annuity starting date, all vested benefits must, with certain exceptions, be paid in the form of a QJSA (see Q 10:8). The QPSA and the QJSA must be provided by all qualified retirement plans except certain profit sharing plans (see Q 10:6), but may be waived if the applicable notice, election, and spousal consent requirements are satisfied (see Qs 10:20–10:26). Also, the automatic survivor benefit requirements do not apply to a payment of the benefit before the annuity starting date if the present value of the married participant's benefit is $3,500 or less (see Q 10:60). [IRC §§ 401(a)(11), 417]

It is possible that one portion of a married participant's benefit may be subject to a QJSA and another portion to a QPSA at the same time. For example, a participant in a money purchase pension plan may have separate accounts for employer contributions and employee contributions. An in-service withdrawal of all or part of the employee contribution account would be subject to the QJSA. The QPSA would apply to the employer contribution account if the participant died prior to the annuity starting date. [Treas Reg § 1.401(a)-20, Q&A 9]

Q 10:2 Must a qualified retirement plan continue to pay benefits to a surviving spouse who remarries?

Yes. The remarriage of a surviving spouse does not affect a qualified retirement plan's obligation to continue to pay benefits to the surviving spouse under the QPSA or QJSA. The plan must continue to pay benefits to the surviving spouse as long as the participant and surviving spouse are married on the date of the participant's death with respect to a QPSA, and on the annuity starting date with respect to a QJSA (see Q 10:19). [Treas Reg § 1.401(a)-20, Q&A 25(b)]

Q 10:3 What is the annuity starting date?

The annuity starting date is the first day of the first period for which a benefit is payable as an annuity. For benefits payable in any other form, it is the first day on which all events have occurred that entitle the participant to the benefit. For example, if an annuity is scheduled to begin on January 1,1994, the annuity starting date is January 1,1994, even though the first payment is not made until July 1,1994. If the benefit is a deferred annuity, the annuity starting date is the date on which the annuity payments are scheduled to commence, not the date that the deferred annuity is elected or the date the deferred annuity contract is distributed. [IRC § 417(f)(2)(A); Treas Reg § 1.401(a)-20, Q&A 10(b)]

There is a special rule that applies to disability benefits. The annuity starting date of a disability benefit is the first day of the first period for which the disability benefit becomes payable, unless it is an auxiliary benefit. An auxiliary disability benefit is disregarded in determining the annuity starting date. A disability benefit is considered auxiliary if it is not taken into account in determining the disabled participant's retirement benefit under the plan. [IRC § 417(f)(2)(B); Treas Reg § 1.401(a)-20, Q&A 10(c)]

Q 10:4 What is the significance of the annuity starting date to survivor benefit requirements?

The annuity starting date (see Q 10:3) determines whether benefits are payable as a QJSA, QPSA, or any other selected optional form of benefit. If a participant is living on the annuity starting date, the benefits must be payable as a QJSA. If the participant dies before the annuity starting date, the surviving spouse must receive a QPSA.

The annuity starting date is also relevant in determining when a participant may waive a QJSA and when a spouse may consent to the waiver. Such waivers and consents are effective only if made within 90 days before the annuity starting date. Since, under a deferred annuity, the annuity starting date is the date on which the payments are to commence (see Q 10:3), the QJSA cannot be waived until 90 days before such time. [Treas Reg § 1.401(a)-20, Q&A 10(a)]

Q 10:5 How do the automatic survivor benefit requirements apply to unmarried participants?

A QJSA (see Q 10:8) for an unmarried participant is a life annuity (i.e., payments cease on the participant's death). Thus, an unmarried participant must be provided with a life annuity unless the participant elects another form of benefit.

There is no requirement to provide a QPSA (see Q 10:9) with respect to an unmarried participant who dies before the annuity starting date. [Treas Reg § 1.401(a)-20, Q&A 25(a)]

Q 10:6 Are all qualified retirement plans required to provide automatic survivor benefits?

The automatic survivor benefit requirements (see Q 10:1) apply to defined benefit plans (see Q 2:3) and also to defined contribution plans subject to minimum funding requirements (i.e., money purchase pension and target benefit plans; see Q 8:1).

The automatic survivor benefit requirements also apply to participants in a profit sharing plan, stock bonus plan, or a 401(k) plan *unless*:

1. The plan provides that, upon the participant's death, the participant's vested benefit (reduced by any security interest held by the plan by reason of a loan outstanding to such participant) is payable in full to the participant's surviving spouse (unless the participant has elected with spousal consent that such benefit be paid instead to a designated beneficiary) (see Q 10:18);

2. The participant does not elect the payment of benefits in the form of a life annuity; and

3. With respect to the participant, the plan is not a direct or indirect transferee plan (see Q 10:13) or a floor offset arrangement (see Q 10:14).

[IRC § 401(a)(11); Treas Reg § 1.401(a)-20, Q&A 3(a)]

If a participant elects a life annuity option provided by a plan otherwise exempt from the automatic survivor benefit requirements, the participant's benefits under the plan will be subject to automatic survivor requirements thereafter. Generally, plans eligible to avoid the automatic survivor benefit requirements will offer benefits only in the form of a single-sum distribution or over a fixed period that is less than the participant's life expectancy. [Treas Reg § 1.401(a)-20, Q&A 4]

Q 10:7 Are there any other conditions that must be satisfied, with respect to a participant, to be exempt from the automatic survivor rules?

Yes. In order for a participant in a profit sharing plan (or other defined contribution plan not subject to the minimum funding standards) (see Q 10:6) to be exempt from the automatic survivor rules:

1. The benefit payable to the participant's surviving spouse must be available within a reasonable period after the participant's death (whether the period is reasonable will be determined on the basis of facts and circumstances; however, 90 days will be deemed to be reasonable); and

2. The benefit must be adjusted for gains or losses occurring after the participant's death in accordance with plan provisions specifying the adjustment of account balances for other plan distributions.

[Treas Reg § 1.401(a)-20, Q&A 3(b)]

Q 10:8   What is a qualified joint and survivor annuity?

A QJSA is an immediate annuity for the life of the participant, with a survivor annuity for the life of the participant's spouse. The amount of the survivor annuity may not be less than 50 percent, nor more than 100 percent, of the amount of the annuity payable during the time that the participant and spouse are both alive. The QJSA must be at least the actuarial equivalent of an annuity for the life of the participant only. [IRC § 417(b)]

A qualified retirement plan may have more than one form of joint and survivor annuity satisfying the QJSA requirements. In that event, the joint and survivor annuity with the greatest actuarial value is the QJSA. If one or more are actuarially equivalent, the plan must designate which one is the automatic form of payment. In any event, the QJSA for a married participant must be at least equal to the most valuable optional form of benefit payable to the participant at the time of the election. [IRC § 417(b); Treas Reg § 1.401(a)-20, Q&A 16]

A participant must be allowed to receive a QJSA at the participant's earliest retirement age, which is generally the earliest date on which the participant could receive a distribution from the plan. The participant (but not the participant's spouse) must consent to the distribution in the form of a QJSA before the participant's benefits are immediately distributable. A participant's benefits are immediately distributable at the later of normal retirement age (see Q 10:55) or age 62. Once benefits are immediately distributable, a QJSA may be distributed without the participant's consent (but see Qs 10:33–10:50 on optional forms of benefit). Distributions may not be made at any time in a form other than a QJSA unless the participant so elects and the participant's spouse consents. [Treas Reg §§ 1.401(a)-20, Q&A 17, 1.417(e)-1(b)]

Q 10:9 What is a qualified preretirement survivor annuity?

A QPSA is an immediate annuity for the life of the surviving spouse of a participant who dies before the annuity starting date (see Q 10:3). Under a QPSA, each payment to the surviving spouse will be the same as (or the actuarial equivalent of) the payment that would have been made to the surviving spouse under the plan's QJSA (see Q 10:8) if:

1. In the case of a participant who dies after attaining the earliest retirement age (see Q 10:8) under the plan, the participant had retired with an immediate QJSA on the day before the participant's death; or

2. In the case of a participant who dies upon or before attaining the earliest retirement age under the plan, the participant had: (a) separated from service on the date of death, (b) survived to the earliest retirement age, (c) retired with an immediate QJSA at the earliest retirement age, and (d) died on the day after the day on which the earliest retirement age would have been attained. (If the participant had separated from service prior to death, the amount of the QPSA is calculated by reference to the actual date of separation from service rather than the date of death to prevent the participant from accruing benefits after separation from service.)

Example. Dan, who is married, participates in a pension plan, and early retirement age under the plan is age 50. The plan must provide automatic survivor coverage in the form of a QJSA and a QPSA. In 1993, Dan reached age 50 but did not elect early retirement. Although Dan continues to work after age 50, a QPSA must be provided for his wife in the event that he dies before he retires.

The QPSA may be payable from a defined benefit plan (see Q 2:3) to the surviving spouse at any time, but must be available to the surviving spouse no later than the month in which the participant would have reached the earliest retirement age under the plan. A defined benefit plan may provide that the QPSA is forfeited if the surviving spouse does not survive until the QPSA is payable under the plan. Similarly, the plan may provide that the QPSA is forfeited if the surviving spouse elects to defer payment of the QPSA but does not survive until the deferred commencement date. [IRC § 417(c); Treas Reg § 1.401(a)-11, Q&A 18, 19, 22(a)]

The QPSA provided under a defined contribution plan (see Q 2:2) must be available to the surviving spouse within a reasonable time after the participant's death (see Q 10:7). The QPSA may not be less valuable than 50 percent of the vested account balance of the participant as of the date of the participant's death. [IRC § 417(c)(2); Treas Reg § 1.401(a)-20, Q&A 20, 22(b)]

Q 10:10 How is a survivor annuity treated for estate tax purposes?

The value of a surviving spouse's interest in a QPSA or QJSA is included in the participant's gross estate for estate tax purposes. The marital deduction is allowable unless the deceased participant's executor elects not to take the deduction (see Qs 14:18, 14:20). [IRC §§ 2039, 2056(b)(7)(C)]

Q 10:11 What is the effect of a loan on the amount of a QPSA or QJSA?

In determining the amount of the QPSA or QJSA, the accrued benefit (see Q 9:2) is reduced by any security interest held by the plan by reason of a loan outstanding to the participant if, at the date of death or benefit payment, the security interest is treated as payment of the loan under the plan. The plan may offset any loan outstanding at the participant's death that is secured by the participant's account balance against the spousal benefit. [IRC § 417(c); Treas Reg § 1.401(a)-20, Q&A 24(d)]

Q 10:12 Is spousal consent necessary for plan loans?

Yes, if the participant's accrued benefit (see Q 9:2) is used as security for the loan. Consent is required even if the accrued benefit is not the primary security for the loan. Spousal consent is not required, however, if the total accrued benefit subject to the security is $3,500 or less. Spousal consent must be obtained within 90 days of the date that the loan is so secured in the same manner as the consent to the waiver of the QJSA or QPSA is obtained (see Q 10:21).

For purposes of spousal consent, any renegotiation, extension, renewal, or other revision of a loan is treated as a new loan. [Treas Reg § 1.401(a)-20, Q&A 24]

Q 10:13   What is a transferee plan?

Although profit sharing plans, stock bonus plans, and 401(k) plans are generally not subject to the automatic survivor benefit requirements (see Qs 10:1, 10:6), these plans become subject to such requirements to the extent the plan is a transferee plan with respect to any participant. A plan is a transferee plan with respect to a participant if it is a direct or indirect transferee of that participant's benefits held on or after January 1, 1985, by:

- A defined benefit plan
- A defined contribution plan subject to the minimum funding standards (see Q 8:1), or
- A defined contribution plan that is subject to the automatic survivor benefit requirements with respect to that participant

Neither a transfer made before 1985 nor a rollover contribution (see Q 28:1) made by a participant at any time is treated as a transfer that subjects a plan to the survivor benefit rules with respect to the participant. Even if a plan is a transferee plan with respect to a participant, the automatic survivor benefit requirements apply only to benefits attributable to the transferred assets, as long as there is an acceptable separate accounting between the transferred assets and other plan benefits. If a separate accounting is not maintained for the transferred assets, the survivor benefit requirements apply to all benefits payable with respect to the participant under the plan. [IRC § 401(a)(11)(B)(iii)(III); Treas Reg § 1.401(a)-20, Q&A 5]

Q 10:14   Do the automatic survivor annuity requirements apply to floor offset plans?

Yes. If benefits of a plan not otherwise subject to the survivor annuity requirements (see Qs 10:1, 10:6) are used to offset benefits that would otherwise accrue under a plan subject to the survivor annuity requirements (e.g., a defined benefit plan), the floor offset plan (see Q 2:20) will be subject to the survivor annuity requirements. [Treas Reg § 1.401(a)-20, Q&A 5; ERISA § 407(d)(9)]

Q 10:15   Must annuity contracts distributed to a participant or spouse by a plan satisfy the automatic survivor benefit requirements?

Yes. If a plan is required to provide automatic survivor benefits (see Q 10:1), such benefits may not be eliminated or reduced because the plan uses annuity contracts to provide benefits or because such a contract is held by a participant or spouse instead of a plan trustee. [Treas Reg § 1.401(a)-20, Q&A 2]

Q 10:16   Must a frozen or terminated plan provide automatic survivor benefits?

Benefits under a plan that is subject to the survivor benefit requirements must be provided in the form of a QJSA (see Q 10:8) or QPSA (see Q 10:9) even if the plan is frozen or terminated. [Treas Reg § 1.401(a)-20, Q&A 6]

Q 10:17   Does it make any difference if PBGC is administering the plan?

No. If PBGC (see Q 21:10) is administering a plan, it will pay benefits in the form of a QPSA or QJSA. [Treas Reg § 1.401(a)-20, Q&A 7]

Q 10:18   To which benefits do the automatic survivor rules apply?

Benefits derived from both employer and employee contributions are subject to the automatic survivor benefit requirements (see Q 10:1).

For defined benefit plans (see Q 2:3), the automatic survivor benefit requirements apply only to benefits in which the participant was vested immediately before death. They do not apply to benefits to which the participant's beneficiary becomes entitled by reason of death or to the proceeds of a life insurance contract maintained by the plan for the participant to the extent such proceeds exceed the present value of the participant's vested benefits existing immediately before death.

For defined contribution plans (see Q 2:2), the survivor annuity requirements apply to all vested benefits, whether vested before or upon death, including the proceeds of insurance contracts. This rule also applies in determining the vested benefits that must be paid to the surviving spouse under a defined contribution plan exempt from the survivor annuity requirements since such a plan is required to pay all death benefits to the surviving spouse (see Q 10:6). [IRC §§ 401(a)(11), 417(f)(1); Treas Reg § 1.401(a)-20, Q&A 11, 12, 13]

Q 10:19 Can a qualified retirement plan treat married participants as not married under any circumstances?

Yes. A qualified retirement plan is not required to treat a participant as married unless the participant was married throughout the one-year period ending on the earlier of the participant's annuity starting date (see Q 10:3) or date of death. The one-year marriage requirement is optional, and the plan need not contain this one-year provision. However, if the plan contains a one-year marriage requirement and if the participant marries within one year of the annuity starting date and dies after that date, the participant's spouse is still entitled to the QJSA, provided the marriage lasted for at least one year. This is true even if the spouse and the participant are not married on the date of the participant's death, except as may be provided in a qualified domestic relations order (QDRO) (see Q 30:1). [IRC § 417(d); Treas Reg § 1.401(a)-20, Q&A 25(b)(2), 25(b)(3); Hinkel v Navistar International Corp, No. 90-3992 (6th Cir 1992); Kyrouac v Northern Illinois Gas Co, No. 91 C 0364 (ND Ill 1991); Enlow v Fire Protection Systems, Inc, No. 91-04080 (ED Mo Ct of App 1991)]

Also, a qualified retirement plan can refuse payment of a survivor annuity to a participant's surviving spouse who pleaded guilty to the murder of the participant. [New Orleans Electrical Pension Fund v Newman, No. 90-1935 (ED La 1992); Ltr Rul 9008079]

Q 10:20   May a participant waive the automatic survivor benefits?

A plan required to provide automatic survivor benefits must also provide the participant with an opportunity to waive the QJSA (see Q 10:8) or the QPSA (see Q 10:9) during the applicable election period. In addition, the participant is permitted to revoke any election during this period. There is no limit on the number of times the participant may waive the QJSA or QPSA or revoke a waiver. [IRC § 417(a)(1)]

The applicable election period is:

1. In the case of a QJSA, the 90-day period ending on the annuity starting date (see Q 10:3), or
2. In the case of a QPSA, the period beginning on the first day of the plan year in which the participant attains age 35 and ending on the date of the participant's death.

[IRC § 417(a)(6); Treas Reg § 1.401(a)-20, Q&A 10, 33]

Q 10:21   Must the participant's spouse consent to the waiver of the QJSA or QPSA?

Yes. A spouse's consent to the participant's waiver of the QJSA or the QPSA is effective only if:

1. The spouse consents to the waiver in writing;
2. The election designates a beneficiary (or a form of benefit) that may not be changed without spousal consent (unless the consent expressly allows such amended designations);
3. The spouse's consent acknowledges the effect of the election; and
4. The consent is witnessed by a plan representative or notary public. [Howard v Branham & Baker Coal Co, No. 91-5913 (6th Cir 1992); Farris v Farris Chemical Co Inc, No. 91-5530 (6th Cir 1992)]

The consent must be given within the applicable election period (see Q 10:20). Spousal consent is not required if the participant establishes to the satisfaction of the plan representative that there is no spouse or the spouse cannot be located, or if there is a court order stating that the participant is legally separated or has been abandoned unless a QDRO (see Q 30:1) provides otherwise. Without a court order, the estrangement of a participant and spouse is *not* sufficient reason to avoid the QPSA requirement. A participant's notarized letter alleging that his spouse could not be located was not sufficient because the plan administrator (see Q 16:1) should have protected the spouse's rights by further questioning the participant and trying to contact the spouse at her last known address or telephone number. [IRC § 417(a)(2); Treas Reg § 1.401(a)-20, Q&A 27; Lefkowitz v Arcadia Trading Co Ltd Benefit Pension Plan, 1993 US App Lexis 15138 (2d Cir 1993); Lester v Reagan Equipment Co Profit Sharing Plan & Employee Savings Plan, US Dist Lexis 12872 (ED La 1992)]

A spouse's consent to the waiver of the QJSA or QPSA is binding only on that spouse; it is not binding on a subsequent spouse of the participant. A plan may preclude a spouse from revoking the consent to the waiver once it has been given, but a plan may also permit a spouse to revoke the consent and render ineffective the participant's prior election to waive the QJSA or QPSA. [Treas Reg § 1.401(a)-20, Q&A 29, 30]

Spousal consent is also required for distributions made in the form of a direct trustee-to-trustee transfer from a qualified retirement plan to an eligible retirement plan (see Q 28:26).

Q 10:22   Is spousal consent contained in an antenuptial agreement effective?

An agreement entered into *prior* to marriage does not satisfy the consent requirement (see Q 10:21) even if the agreement is executed within the applicable election period (see Q 10:20). [Treas Reg § 1.401(a)-20, Q&A 28]

Courts have held the purported waiver to be invalid because the agreement was not signed by the participant's "spouse" since the agreement predated the marriage, another beneficiary was not specified (see Q 10:23), and the agreement did not acknowledge the effect of the waiver (see Q 10:21). [Hurwitz v Sher, 982 F 2d 778 (2d Cir 1992); Nellis v Boeing Co, No. 91-1011-K (DC Kan 1992); but see In re Estate of Hopkins, Nos. 2-90-0894 and 2-90-1007 (2d Dist, App Ct of Ill 1991)]

Q 10:23 Must the waiver of the QPSA or QJSA specify an alternate beneficiary?

Yes. The participant's waiver of a QPSA and QJSA, and the spouse's consent, must specify the nonspouse beneficiary (or class of beneficiaries) who will receive the benefit. For example, if the spouse consents to the participant's election to have benefits payable upon the participant's death before the annuity starting date (see Q 10:3) paid to the participant's children, the participant may not subsequently change beneficiaries (to someone other than a child) without the consent of the spouse unless the change is back to a QPSA or the spouse gave a general consent (see Q 10:26). If the spouse consents only to the designation of a trust as beneficiary, no further spousal consent to the designation of trust beneficiaries is required. [Treas Reg § 1.401(a)-20, Q&A 31(a)]

Q 10:24 Must the waiver of a QJSA specify the optional form of benefit chosen?

Yes. Both the participant's waiver of a QJSA and the spousal consent must specify the particular optional form of benefit (see Q 10:42). A participant who has waived a QJSA with spousal consent in favor of another form of benefit may not subsequently change the optional form of benefit without the spouse's consent unless the change is back to a QJSA or the spouse gave a general consent (see Q 10:26). If the plan so provides, the participant may change the optional form of benefit after the spouse's death or a divorce (other than as provided in a QDRO; see Q 30:1). [Treas Reg § 1.401(a)-20, Q&A 31(b)(1)]

Q 10:25 Must the waiver of a QPSA specify the optional form of benefit chosen?

No. A participant's waiver of a QPSA and the spouse's consent need not specify the optional form of any preretirement benefit. A participant may subsequently change the form of the preretirement benefit without obtaining further spousal consent. However, the participant may not change the nonspouse beneficiary without spousal consent unless there was a general consent (see Qs 10:23, 10:26). [Treas Reg § 1.401(a)-20, Q&A 31(b)(2)]

Q 10:26 May a plan allow a spouse to give general consent to waive a QPSA or QJSA?

Yes, a plan may permit a spouse to execute a general consent. A general consent will enable the participant to waive a QPSA or QJSA and change a designated beneficiary or the optional form of benefit without further spousal consent. Alternatively, the spouse may give a limited general consent; that is, the spouse consents only to changes with respect to certain beneficiaries or forms of benefits.

A general consent executed after October 21, 1986, will not be valid unless the general consent acknowledges that the spouse (1) has the right to limit consent to a specific beneficiary and a specific optional form of benefit, and (2) voluntarily elects to relinquish both such rights. A general consent, including a limited general consent, is effective only if it is made during the applicable election period (see Q 10:20). [Treas Reg § 1.401(a)-20, Q&A 31(c)]

Q 10:27 Does the nonparticipant spouse's consent to the waiver of a QJSA or a QPSA by the participant result in a taxable gift?

No. Such consent by the nonparticipant spouse before the participant's death does not result in a taxable transfer for purposes of the gift tax. After the participant's death, the surviving spouse may be able to disclaim the survivor benefit and avoid the gift tax. [IRC §§ 2503(f), 2518]

Q 10:28 Should the plan document specifically set forth the spousal consent rules?

It is highly recommended to ensure that plan representatives obtain valid spousal consents. One court ordered a plan to pay the QPSA to the surviving spouse because the plan "by its own terms" did not require that spousal consent meet the requirements of the Code and ERISA. [Profit-Sharing Plan for Employees of Republic Financial Servs, Inc v MBank Dallas, NA, 683 F Supp 592 (ND Tex 1988)]

Q 10:29   Must participants be notified of the QJSA?

A plan that is required to provide a QJSA (see Qs 10:6, 10:8) must give each participant a written explanation of:

1. The terms and conditions of the QJSA;
2. The participant's right to make, and the effect of, an election to waive the QJSA;
3. The rights of the participant's spouse; and
4. The right to make, and the effect of, a revocation of an election.

Participants must also be furnished with a general description of the eligibility conditions and other material features of the optional forms of benefit, as well as sufficient information to explain the relative values of the optional forms of benefit. This explanation must be given to the participant within a reasonable period before the annuity starting date (see Q 10:3). The plan must provide this explanation to both vested and nonvested participants. [IRC § 417(a)(3)(A); Treas Reg §§ 401(a)-11(c), 1.401(a)-20, Q&A 34, 36]

Q 10:30   Must participants be notified of the QPSA?

A plan that is required to provide a QPSA (see Qs 10:6, 10:9) must give each participant a written explanation of the QPSA similar to the explanation required for the QJSA (see Q 10:29). This explanation must be given to both vested and nonvested participants within whichever of the following applicable periods ends last with respect to a participant:

1. The period beginning with the first day of the plan year in which the participant attains age 32 and ending at the end of the plan year preceding the plan year in which the participant attains age 35;
2. The period beginning one year before and ending one year after the individual becomes a participant;
3. The period beginning one year before and ending one year after the survivor benefit applicable to the participant is no longer subsidized (see Q 10:31);

4. The period beginning one year before and ending one year after the survivor benefit requirements become applicable to the participant; or

5. In the case of a participant who separates from service before age 35, the period beginning one year before and ending one year after the separation.

[IRC § 417(a)(3)(B); Treas Reg § 1.401(a)-20, Q&A 35, 36]

Q 10:31   What happens if the plan fully subsidizes the cost of the QJSA or QPSA?

If a plan fully subsidizes a QJSA (see Q 10:8) or QPSA (see Q 10:9) and does not permit a participant to waive the benefit or to designate another beneficiary, it need not provide the required written explanation (see Qs 10:29, 10:30). If a plan that subsidizes the cost of the QJSA or QPSA offers such election, the plan must satisfy the election, consent, and notice requirements. [IRC § 417(a)(5); Treas Reg § 1.401(a)-20, Q&A 37]

A fully subsidized QJSA is one under which no increase in cost or decrease in benefits to the participant could possibly result from the participant's failure to elect another benefit. For example, if a plan provides a joint and survivor annuity and a lump-sum option, the plan does not fully subsidize the joint and survivor annuity (even if the actuarial value of the joint and survivor annuity is greater than the amount of the lump-sum payment) because, in the event of the participant's early death, the participant would have received less under the annuity than under the lump-sum option. Similarly, if a plan provides for a life annuity of $100 per month and a joint and 100 percent survivor benefit of $99 per month, the plan is not fully subsidizing the joint and survivor benefit.

A QPSA is fully subsidized if the participant's benefit is not reduced because of the QPSA coverage and the participant is not charged for the QPSA coverage. Therefore, a QPSA is fully subsidized in a defined contribution plan because the participant's account balance is not reduced by the QPSA coverage and no charge is made against the account for such coverage. [Treas Reg § 1.401(a)-20, Q&A 38]

Q 10:32   When did the survivor annuity benefit requirements become effective?

The survivor annuity benefit provisions generally became effective for plan years beginning after 1984, but the spousal-consent rules (see Q 10:21) became effective on January 1, 1985. Thus, a waiver by a participant made in 1985, but before the first day of the first plan year to which the survivor annuity benefit provisions apply, is not effective unless the participant's spouse subsequently consents to the election. A participant's election to waive the QPSA (see Q 10:9), and spousal consent to the waiver made before August 23, 1984 (the effective date of REA), are not valid; a new election and consent must be executed by the participant and the participant's spouse. [REA §§ 302(a), 303(c)(3); Treas Reg § 1.401(a)-20, Q&A 39, 43, 44; Ltr Rul 9008003; Lucaskevge v Mollenberg, 11 EBC 1355 (WD NY 1989); The Manitowac Eng'g and Salaried Employees' Deferred Profit Sharing Plan v Powalisz, 8 EBC 1094 (D Wis 1987)]

Q 10:33   Can a qualified retirement plan provide optional ways in which to pay benefits?

Yes. However, the optional forms of benefit provided by a qualified retirement plan must comply with IRS guidelines. Generally, each optional form of benefit must (1) be provided in a way that does not discriminate in favor of highly compensated employees (see Qs 3:2, 4:9, 4:18, 10:34–10:41), and (2) be available to eligible employees without employer discretion (see Qs 10:42–10:50). [IRC §§ 401(a)(4), 411(d)(6); Treas Reg §§ 1.401(a)(4)-4, 1.401(a)-4, 1.411(d)-4]

If a plan offers optional forms of benefit, the different forms must be actuarially equivalent and the plan must specify the actuarial assumptions to be used in calculating the equivalent benefits. [IRC § 401(a)(25); Rev Rul 79-90, 1979-1 CB 155]

Q 10:34   Can a plan permit optional forms of benefit payment that favor highly compensated employees?

No. A qualified retirement plan must provide benefits that do not discriminate in favor of highly compensated employees (see Qs 3:2, 4:9). If a plan provides for optional forms of benefit payment, for example, different forms of distribution commencing at the same time or the same form of distribution commencing at different times, the availability of each of these optional forms of benefit payment is subject to this nondiscrimination requirement (see Q 4:18). This is true whether or not the particular benefit option is the actuarial equivalent (see Qs 2:17, 2:18) of any other form of benefit under the plan. To meet the nondiscrimination requirement, the optional form of benefit must be both currently available (see Q 10:35) and effectively available (see Q 10:36) in a nondiscriminatory manner. It is not necessary, however, to apply a nondiscriminatory test to the actual receipt of each optional form of benefit. [IRC § 401(a)(4); Treas Reg §§ 1.401(a)(4)-4(b), 1.401(a)(4)-4(c), 1.401(a)-4, Q&A 1, 2]

Q 10:35 How is the determination made as to whether the current availability of an optional form of benefit is nondiscriminatory?

An optional form of benefit must be currently available to a group of employees that satisfies one of the minimum coverage tests (see Q 5:15). Generally, current availability is determined on the basis of current facts and circumstances. However, certain specified conditions on the availability of an optional form of benefit (e.g., minimum age or service, disability, hardship, vesting, family status, or waiver of rights under federal or state law) are disregarded in determining whether a benefit is currently available to an employee.

If an employer eliminates an optional form of benefit with respect to *future* benefit accruals, the current availability test is treated as satisfied for all years after the elimination if the optional form satisfied the nondiscrimination requirement immediately prior to its elimination.

Example. A profit sharing plan that provides for a lump-sum distribution available to all employees on termination of employment is amended in 1993 to eliminate the lump-sum option with respect to benefits accrued after December 31,1993. As of December 31,1993, the lump-sum optional form of benefit is available to a group of employees that satisfies the ratio percentage test (see Q 5:16). As of January 1,1996, all nonhighly compensated employees (see Q 3:13) who were entitled to the lump-sum optional form of benefit have terminated employment and taken a distribution of their benefits. The only remaining employees who are eligible to take a portion of their benefits in a lump sum on termination of employment are highly compensated employees (see Q 3:2). Because the availability of the lump-sum optional form of benefit satisfied the current availability test as of December 31, 1993, the availability of such optional form of benefit will be deemed to continue to satisfy the current availability test.

[Treas Reg §§ 1.401(a)(4)-4(b), 1.401(a)-4, Q&A 2(a), 2(b)]

Q 10:36   How is the determination made as to whether the effective availability of an optional form of benefit is nondiscriminatory?

This determination must be based on all the surrounding facts and circumstances of the employer maintaining the plan. A condition with respect to the availability of a particular optional form of benefit payment violates the effective availability test if it substantially favors highly compensated employees (see Q 3:2).

> **Example.** Gaby Corporation maintains a qualified retirement plan in which all of its eligible employees participate. Under the plan, a participant is entitled to receive a retirement benefit at age 65. Also, an employee who terminates employment after age 55 with at least 30 years of service may also receive early retirement benefits. Both of Gaby Corporation's highly compensated employees, but only two of Gaby Corporation's eight nonhighly compensated employees (see Q 3:13), may become eligible to receive early retirement benefits because they were hired before age 35. Even though the early retirement benefit is currently available to all participants, because age and service requirements are disregarded, it does not meet the effective availability test because the availability conditions substantially favor highly compensated employees.

[Treas Reg §§ 1.401(a)(4)-4(c), 1.401(a)-4, Q&A 2(a)(3)]

Q 10:37 May a qualified retirement plan deny a participant an optional form of benefit payment for which the participant is otherwise eligible?

No. Even though this type of provision may satisfy the nondiscrimination requirements in certain circumstances, such a provision impermissibly results in the employer or some person other than the participant having discretion as to the optional form of benefit payment (see Q 10:44). [IRC § 411(d)(6)]

Q 10:38 Will a qualified retirement plan be considered discriminatory if it requires that an involuntary distribution be made?

No. A qualified retirement plan will not be treated as discriminatory merely because it provides for an involuntary distribution if the present value of an employee's benefit is $3,500 or less (see Q 10:60). Thus, a plan may require a lump-sum distribution to terminating employees whose benefits have a present value of $3,500 or any lower amount. However, this rule does not permit employer discretion in deciding whether or not to cash out involuntarily a terminating employee. [IRC §§ 411(a)(11), 417(e); Treas Reg §§ 1.401(a)(4)-4(b)(2)(ii)(C), 1.401(a)-4, Q&A 4, 1.411(d)-4, Q&A 2(b)(2)(V)]

Q 10:39 What are the effective dates for the optional forms of benefit payment nondiscrimination rules?

The old Section 1.401(a)-4 regulations on discrimination in optional forms of benefit payment became effective January 30, 1986, with respect to new plans (i.e., plans either adopted or made effective on or after such date).

With respect to existing plans—i.e., plans both adopted and in effect prior to January 30, 1986—the old regulations were effective for the first day of the first plan year commencing on or after January 1, 1989. The delayed effective date for existing plans is applicable only if the optional form of benefit and any condition causing the availability of such optional form of benefit to be discriminatory were both adopted and in effect before January 30, 1986. Otherwise, the rules became effective with respect to such optional form of benefit payment as if the plan were a new plan. [Treas Reg § 1.401(a)-4, Q&A 6]

The new Section 1.401(a)(4)-4 regulations become effective for plan years beginning on or after January 1, 1994. Plans must comply with the old regulations until the 1994 plan year and the reasonable, good-faith standard (see Q 4:22) does not apply with respect to the old regulations during the transition years (1989–1993).

For plan years beginning on or after January 1, 1994, the new regulations will apply with respect to plan benefits, rights, and features. In addition to incorporating the relevant rules concerning optional forms of benefit provided in the old regulations, the new regulations require that each optional form of benefit subject to different terms affecting the value of the optional form of benefit (such as actuarial assumptions or the method of benefit calculation) separately satisfy Section 401(a)(4) with respect to its availability. This standard does not apply to the transition years. Similarly, the new regulations provide rules with respect to nondiscriminatory availability of ancillary benefits and other rights and features that are not effective until 1994. During the transition years, provisions relating to these benefits, rights, and features are subject to the general nondiscrimination requirements of Section 401(a)(4) and the good-faith standard is applicable. [Treas Reg § 1.401(a)(4)-13; Notice 92-36, 1992-2 CB 364; Ann 92-29, 1992-9 IRB 37; IRS Field Office Directive on Good-Faith Compliance (June 12, 1992)]

Q 10:40 Can a qualified retirement plan containing discriminatory optional forms of benefits be amended?

Yes. If the availability of an optional form of benefit in an existing qualified retirement plan is discriminatory, the plan must be amended either to eliminate the optional form or to make the availability of the optional form nondiscriminatory. The availability of an optional form of benefit may be made nondiscriminatory by making the benefit available to a sufficient number of additional nonhighly compensated employees (see Q 3:13) or by imposing nondiscriminatory objective criteria on its availability so that the group of employees to whom the benefit is available is nondiscriminatory. The plan sponsor may also amend the plan in that manner if the availability of an optional form of benefit may reasonably be expected to discriminate.

The plan sponsor must have selected one of the alternatives with respect to each affected optional form on or before the applicable effective date (see Q 10:39) for the plan. This is an operational requirement and does not require a plan amendment prior to the date the plan must be amended to meet the requirements of TRA '86. [Treas Reg § 1.401(a)-4, Q&A 5]

Certain corrective amendments to the availability of an optional form of benefit are permitted. Because it is difficult or impossible, in many cases, to make an optional form of benefit meaningfully available on a retroactive basis, a corrective amendment increasing availability is required only on a prospective basis. However, in order to take the correction into account for a plan year, the group of employees to whom the optional form is available (after taking the amendment into account) generally must satisfy a nondiscriminatory requirement. In addition, the amendment must remain in effect until the end of the plan year following the year in which the amendment is effective, and must not be part of a pattern of amendments used to correct repeated failures. Other rules relating to retroactive correction also apply (e.g., the requirement that the correction be made no later than the 15th day of the tenth month after the close of a plan year).

As an alternative to increasing availability, an employer may make a corrective amendment by the last day of the plan year eliminating the optional form of benefit (to the extent permitted under Section 411(d)(6)). In that case, the amendment will be treated as if it were in effect throughout the plan year for purposes of nondiscrimination testing.

[Treas Reg § 1.401(a)(4)-11(g)]

Q 10:41 Should the plan administrator provide any notice that the qualified retirement plan's optional forms of benefit are being modified?

Yes. Although there is no special reporting requirement regarding modification of a qualified retirement plan's optional forms of benefit, a plan administrator (see Q 16:1) is required to file with DOL and to furnish to participants a summary of material modifications within 210 days after the close of the plan year in which the modification is adopted (see Qs 18:8, 18:9).

However, even before a modification is formally adopted, it is prudent for the plan administrator to give prompt notice of any such modification to participants. Giving prompt notice to participants would reconcile the conflict between ERISA's mandate that the plan be administered in accordance with the terms of its plan documents and IRS's operational requirement that the plan be administered consistent with a conforming plan amendment that has not yet been adopted. [ERISA §§ 104, 404(a)(1)(D); DOL Reg § 2520.104b-3]

Q 10:42   What are Section 411(d)(6) protected benefits?

Accrued benefits, early retirement benefits, retirement-type subsidies, and optional forms of benefit are Section 411(d)(6) protected benefits that may not be eliminated, reduced, or made subject to employer discretion except to the extent permitted by regulations (see Q 10:40). [IRC § 411(d)(6); Treas Reg § 1.411(d)-4, Q&A 1(a); Counts v Kissack Water and Oil Service, Inc, No. 92-8036 (10th Cir 1993); Davis v Burlington Industries, Inc, No. 91-1725 (4th Cir 1992); Auwarter v Donohue Paper Sales Corp Defined Benefit Pension Plan, No. 91-3082 (ED NY 1992); Costantino v TRW Inc, No. C86-3368 (ND Ohio 1991); Rev Proc 92-10, 1992-1 CB 661] See Question 9:27 for examples of benefits that are not Section 411(d)(6) protected benefits.

An optional form of benefit is a form of distribution of benefits from a qualified retirement plan that is identical with respect to all features relating to the specified distribution form. The plan provides separate optional forms of benefit to the extent there are any differences in any features relating to the form of distribution, including payment schedule, timing, commencement, medium of distribution, portion of the benefit to which such distribution features apply, and election rights with respect to such features. [Treas Reg §§ 1.411(d)-4, Q&A 1(b), 1.401(a)(4)-4(e)]

Example 1. A plan permits each participant to receive a benefit under the plan as a lump-sum distribution, a level monthly distribution over ten years, a single life annuity, a joint and 50 percent survivor annuity, a joint and 75 percent survivor annuity, a joint and 50 percent survivor annuity with a benefit increase for the participant if the beneficiary dies before a specified date, or a joint and 50 percent survivor annuity with a ten-year certain feature. Each of these forms of benefit payment is an optional form of benefit, whether or not their values are actuarially equivalent.

Example 2. A plan provides a single life annuity that begins in the month of termination of employment and a single life annuity that begins after five consecutive one-year breaks in service (see Q 5:10). They are optional benefit forms because they begin at different times.

Example 3. A profit sharing plan permits loans that are secured by an employee's account balance. In the event of default on such a loan, there is an execution on the account balance. Such execution is a distribution of the employee's accrued benefit under the plan. A distribution of an accrued benefit contingent on default under a plan loan secured by such accrued benefits is an optional form of benefit under the plan.

Q 10:43 Can a pattern of plan amendments result in an optional form of benefit?

Yes. Generally, benefits are considered to be provided as an optional form of benefit only if such optional form is provided under the terms of the qualified retirement plan. If, however, an employer establishes a pattern of repeated plan amendments providing for similar benefits in similar situations for limited periods of time, those benefits may be treated as provided under the terms of the plan without regard to the limited periods of time. For example, a pattern of repeated plan amendments making single-sum distributions available only to certain participants for a limited period may result in single-sum distributions being treated as provided under the terms of the plan to all participants, without regard to any restrictions provided by the terms of the plan. However, where an employer amended its plan in each of four consecutive plan years to provide an early retirement window benefit, IRS held that the recurrence of the plan amendments did not convert this benefit to a permanent plan feature because the amendments were made in connection with the employer's efforts to reorganize its business, decrease operating costs, and reduce its work force. [Rev Rul 92-66, 1992-2 CB 92; Treas Reg § 1.411(d)-4, Q&A 1(c)]

Q 10:44   Can a plan provide that the employer may, through the exercise of discretion, deny a participant an optional form of benefit?

Generally, no. A qualified retirement plan that permits an employer, through the exercise of discretion, to deny a participant a Section 411(d)(6) protected benefit (see Q 10:42) violates the anti-cut-back rule (see Q 9:24). In other words, to the extent benefits have accrued, the discretionary denial of the optional form of the benefit is not permitted. In addition, a pension plan that permits employer discretion to deny the availability of a Section 411(d)(6) protected benefit will fail to satisfy the requirement that all benefits be definitely determinable. This is so even if the plan specifically limits the employer's discretion to choose among optional forms of benefit that are actuarially equivalent. However, a plan may permit limited administrative discretion (see Q 10:46). [Treas Reg § 1.411(d)-4, Q&A 1, 4(a)]

Q 10:45   When is the exercise of discretion by persons other than the employer treated as employer discretion?

For the purposes of determining impermissible employer discretion, the employer is considered to include a plan administrator (see Q 16:1), fiduciary (see Q 19:1), trustee, actuary, independent third party, and other persons. Thus, if a qualified retirement plan permits any person—other than the participant and the participant's spouse—to exercise discretion to limit or deny the availability of an optional form of benefit, the plan violates these rules. [IRC §§ 401(a), 411(d)(6); Treas Reg § 1.411(d)-4, Q&A 5]

Q 10:46   What is the scope of the administrative discretion exception?

A qualified retirement plan may permit limited discretion with respect to the ministerial or mechanical administration of the plan, including the application of objective plan criteria specifically set forth in the plan. The following are examples of permissible provisions of limited administrative discretion:

1. Commencement of benefit payments as soon as administratively feasible after a stated date or event;
2. Employer authority to determine whether objective criteria specified in the plan (see Q 10:47) have been satisfied; and
3. Employer authority to determine, pursuant to specific guidelines set forth in the plan, whether the participant or spouse is dead or cannot be located.

[Treas Reg § 1.411(d)-4, Q&A 4(b)]

Q 10:47   May a plan condition the availability of a Section 411(d)(6) protected benefit on objective criteria that are specifically set forth in the plan?

The availability of a Section 411(d)(6) protected benefit (see Q 10:42) may be limited to employees who satisfy certain objective conditions. The conditions must be ascertainable, clearly set forth in the qualified retirement plan, and not subject to the employer's discretion, except to the extent reasonably necessary to determine whether the objective conditions are met. In addition, the availability of the Section 411(d)(6) protected benefit must meet the nondiscrimination requirements. [Treas Reg §§ 1.411(d)-4, Q&A 6, 1.401(a)(4)-4, 1.401(a)-4]

For example, a plan may provide that the lump-sum benefit distribution option is not available to participants for whom life insurance is not available at standard rates. A plan may also provide that an otherwise permissible lump-sum distribution option may be available only in the event of extreme financial need, determined under standards specifically set forth in the plan. Another example is a provision making a lump-sum distribution available only upon the execution of a covenant not to compete, provided that the plan sets forth objective conditions with respect to employees required to execute a covenant, its terms, and the circumstances requiring execution of the covenant.

On the other hand, a plan may not condition the availability of Section 411(d)(6) protected benefits on factors that are within the employer's control. For example, the availability of an optional form of benefit payment from a defined benefit plan may not be conditioned on the level of the funding of the plan because the amount of plan funding is within the employer's discretion.

A plan may limit the availability of a Section 411(d)(6) protected benefit (e.g., a lump-sum distribution) in an objective manner. For example, a plan may provide that lump-sum distributions of $25,000 and less are available without limit, and lump-sum distributions in excess of $25,000 are available for a given year only to the extent that the total amount of such distributions for that year does not exceed $5 million. However, the plan must then also provide an objective and nondiscriminatory method for determining which particular lump-sum distributions will and will not be distributed because of the $5 million limitation.

In a case decided before the IRS regulations were issued, a "good health standard" in terms of expected mortality for determining eligibility for lump-sum payments was satisfactory. [Medei v Bethlehem Steel Corp and General Pension Bd, 617 F Supp 372 (ED Pa 1985)]

Q 10:48 May a plan be amended to add employer discretion or other conditions restricting the availability of a Section 411(d)(6) protected benefit?

No. The addition of employer discretion or restrictive conditions with respect to a Section 411(d)(6) protected benefit that has already accrued violates the anti-cutback rule (see Q 9:24). The addition of conditions, even if they are objective conditions, is impermissible if it results in any further restrictions. However, conditions and restrictions may be imposed prospectively to benefits accrued after the later of the adoption or effective date of the amendment. [Treas Reg § 1.411(d)-4, Q&A 7]

Q 10:49 What are the effective dates of the Section 411(d)(6) protected benefit rules?

The final rules relating to Section 411(d)(6) protected benefits are effective January 30, 1986, but there are significant exceptions.

For existing plans, these rules became effective for the first day of the first plan year commencing on or after January 1, 1989. Plans that were adopted and in effect prior to August 1, 1986, are existing plans for this purpose.

For new plans, these rules are effective August 1, 1986. Plans that were adopted or made effective on or after August 1, 1986, are considered new plans for purposes of these rules. However, a new plan that received a favorable determination letter (see Q 15:1) with respect to an application submitted prior to July 11, 1988, is treated as an existing plan with respect to Section 411(d)(6) protected benefits. [Treas Reg § 1.411(d)-4, Q&A 9]

Q 10:50 Is there a transitional rule allowing amendment of plans containing prohibited discretion or consent provisions?

Yes. If an existing plan (see Q 10:49) provides for employer discretion with respect to the availability of an optional form of benefit payment, the plan must be amended to eliminate such discretion or to eliminate the optional form of benefit payment subject to a consent or discretion provision.

Any amendment to eliminate employer discretion or an optional form of benefit payment must be applied in operation beginning on the applicable effective date (see Q 10:49). If the plan satisfies the operational requirement, the plan amendment conforming to the operational procedure selected need not be adopted until the time plan amendments for TRA '86 must be adopted, which is the last day of the first plan year beginning on or after January 1, 1994. [Notice 92-36, 1992-2 CB 364; Treas Reg § 1.411(d)-4, Q&A 8]

Q 10:51 May participants choose the way benefits will be paid to them?

Yes, if the qualified retirement plan itself provides alternatives, although the participant's spouse may have to consent (see Q 10:21). Retirement benefits are taxed when paid, not if merely made available to the participant. Thus, a deferral of the receipt of benefits also defers the taxation of the benefits. [IRC § 402(a)(1)]

Q 10:52 Is there a limitation on the amount of benefits that may be distributed to an individual in any one year?

No. However, there is a 15 percent tax on the amount of any excess distributions (see Qs 13:27–13:38) made to any individual during any calendar year. [IRC § 4980A(a)]

Q 10:53 When must benefit payments to a participant begin?

The plan must provide that, unless the participant elects to defer payment, payment of benefits to the participant will begin not later than the sixtieth day after the close of the plan year in which the latest of the following events occurs:

1. The participant reaches the plan's normal retirement age (see Q 10:55) or age 65, whichever is earlier;
2. The tenth anniversary of the employee's participation in the plan is reached; or
3. The participant terminates service with the employer.

[IRC § 401(a)(14); Treas Reg § 1.401(a)-14(a); Rev Proc 92-10, 1992-1 CB 661]

See Chapter 11 for details on minimum distribution requirements.

Q 10:54 May a participant defer payment of benefits indefinitely?

No. The qualified retirement plan must provide that (1) the entire interest of the participant be distributed to the participant not later than the required beginning date, or (2) the participant's interest be paid out in installments that start on or before the required beginning date. The installments must be paid over (1) the life of the participant, (2) the lives of the participant and the participant's designated beneficiary, or (3) a period not extending beyond the life expectancy of the participant or the joint life expectancy of the participant and the participant's designated beneficiary. [IRC § 401(a)(9)(A)]

See Chapter 11 for details on minimum distribution requirements.

Q 10:55   What does the term normal retirement age mean?

Normal retirement age means the earlier of (1) the time specified in the plan as the normal retirement age, or (2) the later of the time a participant attains age 65 or the fifth anniversary of the participant's date of initial plan participation. A qualified retirement plan must provide that an employee's right to benefits is nonforfeitable once the employee reaches the plan's normal retirement age (see Q 9:12). [IRC §§ 411(a), 411(a)(8)]

Previously, a participant's normal retirement age could be deferred until the *tenth* anniversary of the participation commencement date. OBRA '86 first modified the definition of normal retirement age but created an anomalous result in which a younger employee could have a retirement age later than that of an older employee. To overcome this result, the following may be added to the definition of normal retirement age contained in the first paragraph:

> If, for plan years beginning before January 1, 1988, normal retirement age was determined with reference to the anniversary of the participation commencement date (more than five but not to exceed ten years), the anniversary date for participants who first commenced participation under the plan before the first plan year beginning on or after January 1, 1988, shall be the earlier of (1) the tenth anniversary of the date the participant commenced participation in the plan (or such anniversary as had been elected by the employer, if less than ten) or (2) the fifth anniversary of the first day of the first plan year beginning on or after January 1, 1988. The participation commencement date is the first day of the first plan year in which the participant commenced participation in the plan.

Ordinarily, a defined benefit plan uses a normal retirement age of 65. However, a plan will not fail to qualify merely because it provides for a normal retirement age earlier than 65. (Planning aspects relating to the use of a normal retirement age earlier than 65 are discussed in Question 29:20.) [Rev Rul 78-120, 1978-1 CB 117]

Unlike defined benefit plans, the normal retirement age used by a defined contribution plan (see Q 2:2) other than a target benefit plan does not affect the company's plan contribution. Thus, for example, a profit sharing plan may permit a participant to retire at age 55 and receive full benefits under the plan at that time even if employees in the particular industry involved customarily retire at a later age. [Rev Rul 80-276, 1980-2 CB 131]

Q 10:56 May benefits commence earlier than the deadlines required under the law?

Yes. The law and regulations establish only the time by which the plan must begin paying benefits (see Qs 10:53, 10:54). As long as participants are not treated in a discriminatory manner (see Qs 10:34–10:41), benefits may begin earlier.

Generally, defined benefit plans (see Q 2:3) and certain defined contribution plans, including money purchase pension plans (see Q 2:4) and target benefit plans (see Q 2:5), may not make distributions to employees who have not reached normal retirement age (see Q 10:55) or qualified for early retirement benefits (see Q 10:59). However, an employee may receive a distribution if a severance from employment has occurred. A severance from employment occurs during an employer's reorganization (e.g., sale, merger, or liquidation) only if the employee no longer works for an employer sponsoring the plan after the reorganization. An employee who works at the same job for a new employer may receive a distribution from the former employer's plan because the employee's employment has been severed, but the employee may not have had a "separation from service" for the purpose of treating the distribution as a lump-sum distribution (see Qs 13:4, 13:9). [Treas Reg § 1.401-1(b)(1)(i); GCM 39824 (July 6, 1990)]

Plan benefits are taxed only when they are paid to the employee or a beneficiary. They are not taxed if they are merely made available (see Q 10:51). It is not necessary, therefore, to draft a plan so that a participant does not have an absolute, unrestricted right to demand payment of benefits upon satisfying certain plan provisions. [IRC § 402(a)(1)]

Q 10:57 What type of election by the participant is required to postpone the commencement of benefits?

A qualified retirement plan that permits an election by a participant to postpone the receipt of benefits beyond the latest of the three dates referred to in Question 10:53 must require that the election be made by submitting to the plan administrator a written statement (signed by the participant) describing the benefit and the date payments will begin. [Treas Reg § 1.401(a)-14(b)(2)]

However, an election to postpone the payment of benefits cannot be made if it would cause benefits payable under the plan, with respect to the participant, to begin after the required beginning date or to violate the incidental death benefits rule. [Treas Reg § 1.401(a)-14(b)(3)] For details, see Chapter 11.

Q 10:58 May a participant receive benefit payments from a plan while still employed by the plan sponsor?

Yes, provided the participant has reached the plan's normal or early retirement age. [Rev Rul 80-276, 1980-2 CB 131; Ltr Ruls 8311071, 8137048]

Q 10:59 Can a qualified retirement plan provide early retirement benefits?

Yes. However, if a defined benefit plan permits a participant to receive an early retirement benefit if the participant meets certain age and service requirements (e.g., age 55 and 30 years of service), the plan must also permit a former participant who fulfilled the service requirement, but separated from service before meeting the age requirement, to receive benefit payments when the former participant meets the age requirement. [IRC § 401(a)(14); Treas Reg § 1.401(a)-14(c)]

> **Example.** A defined benefit plan provides a benefit of $100 a month at age 65, or an actuarially reduced benefit at age 55 for employees with 30 years of service who are still employed when they reach age 55. An employee who separates from service at age 50 with 30 years of service would have the right to an actuarially reduced benefit at age 55.

A plan was permitted to pay a more valuable early retirement benefit to participants electing periodic payments than to participants electing single-sum distributions. Those electing single-sum distributions received the benefits they were entitled to, but they did not receive the supplemental payments made to the early retirees who elected to receive periodic payments. [DeNobel v Vitro Corp, 885 F 2d 1180 (4th Cir 1989)]

Q 10:60   Can a qualified retirement plan make immediate distributions without the participant's consent?

A qualified retirement plan may provide for an involuntary, immediate distribution of the present value of the benefits under either a QJSA (see Q 10:8) or a QPSA (see Q 10:9) if the present value does not exceed $3,500. The plan may pay benefits in the form of a QJSA or a QPSA at any time after the benefits are no longer immediately distributable (see Q 10:8), whether or not the present value exceeds $3,500. A plan may provide that a participant may elect a QJSA at any time without spousal consent. [Treas Reg § 1.417(e)-1(b)(1)]

If the distribution exceeds $3,500, the participant must consent in writing before a distribution may be made. [Franklin v Thornton, Nos. 90-16274 and 91-15375 (9th Cir 1993)]

No single-sum distribution may be made after the annuity starting date (see Q 10:3) unless the participant (and spouse or surviving spouse, if applicable) consents in writing to the distribution, whether or not the present value exceeds $3,500. [IRC §§ 411(a)(11), 417(e); Treas Reg §§ 1.411(a)-11(c)(3), 1.417(e)-1(b)(2)]

Q 10:61   What interest rate must be used to value benefits?

Generally, the interest rate used to value benefits is the applicable interest rate, which is the interest rate that would be used by PBGC for purposes of determining the present value of a lump-sum distribution on plan termination. [IRC § 417(e)(3)(B)] If a defined benefit plan uses interest rates in addition to the applicable interest rate to value benefits, the interest rate producing the greatest benefit must be used. [Treas Reg § 1.417(e)-1(d)(4)]

The applicable interest rate is used to value the participant's vested benefit if the present value of the benefit does not exceed $25,000, and 120 percent of that rate is used if the present value exceeds $25,000. (If 120 percent of the applicable interest rate is used, the present value cannot be less than $25,000.) Note that the applicable interest rate may be a series of interest rates. For example, the applicable interest rate could be 5 percent for the first five years over which the benefits are valued, 5.25 percent for the next ten years, and 5.5 percent for the following years. [Treas Reg § 1.417(e)-1(d)(2)]

Q 10:62   Does a participant have to formally apply for benefits?

No. However, failure to apply for benefits would result in the participant receiving the benefit in the form of a QJSA, if applicable, or in the normal form of benefit under the terms of the plan, rather than an optional form of benefit that the participant might have preferred. If the participant has received notice of the QJSA and optional forms of benefit no less than 30 days and no more than 90 days after the annuity starting date (see Q 10:3), a QJSA can be distributed without the participant's consent after the participant reaches normal retirement age (see Q 10:55), or age 62, if later. [Treas Reg § 1.411(a)-11(c)(2)]

ERISA requires that every plan establish and maintain reasonable claims procedures, which must be described in the summary plan description (SPD) (see Q 18:1). DOL regulations further provide that a claim is filed when the requirements of a "reasonable claim filing procedure" of a plan have been met. [DOL Reg § 2560.503-1]

Q 10:63   What are the participant's rights if a claim for benefits is denied?

If the claim for benefits is denied, either in part or in full, the plan administrator must furnish written notice to the participant or beneficiary explaining why the claim was denied. Moreover, the plan must afford a reasonable opportunity to the participant or beneficiary to have a full and fair review of that decision. [ERISA § 503]

Chapter 11

Minimum Distribution Requirements

The primary purpose of a qualified retirement plan is to provide retirement income to employees when they retire from employment. This objective will not be satisfied if employees can defer the receipt of benefits indefinitely. This chapter discusses when retirement benefits must be distributed, how much must be distributed each year, and the penalty for failure to satisfy these requirements.

Q 11:1 What plans are subject to the minimum distribution requirements?

All qualified retirement plans are subject to the minimum distribution requirements. [IRC § 401(a)(9); Prop Reg § 1.401(a)(9)-1, A-1]

The required minimum distribution rules also apply to IRAs (see Q 26:1), SEPs (see Q 27:1), and tax-sheltered annuities. [IRC §§ 403(b)(3), 408(a)(6); Prop Reg §§ 1.403(b)-2, Q&A-1–Q&A-3, 1.408-8, A-1–A-8] (Also see Qs 26:31, 27:18.)

Q 11:2 How must the participant's benefits be distributed?

To satisfy the minimum distribution requirements, the entire interest of a participant (1) must be distributed to the participant not later than the required beginning date (see Q 11:3), or (2) must be distributed, in installments, beginning not later than the required beginning date. The installments must be paid over (1) the life of the participant, (2) the lives of the participant and the participant's designated beneficiary (see Q 11:8), or (3) a period not extending beyond the life expectancy (see Q 11:12) of the participant or the joint life expectancy of the participant and the participant's designated beneficiary. [IRC § 401(a)(9)(A); Prop Reg § 1.401(a)(9)-1, B-1]

Q 11:3 What is the required beginning date?

For participants who reach age 70½ after 1988, the required beginning date is April 1 of the calendar year following the calendar year in which the participant reaches age 70½. [IRC § 401(a)(9)(C)]

For participants who reached age 70½ before 1989, the determination of the required beginning date depends on whether the participant was a 5 percent owner (see Q 22:28). For 5 percent owners, the required beginning date was the April 1 following the calendar year in which age 70½ was reached; for all other participants who attained age 70½ before 1988, the required beginning date is deferred until the April 1 following the calendar year in which the participant retires or becomes a 5 percent owner. A transitional rule applied to participants who were not 5 percent owners and who attained age 70½ in 1988. Those participants were treated as having retired in 1989, and their required beginning date was April 1, 1990. [Prop Reg § 1.401(a)(9)-1, B-2; Notice 89-42, 1989-1 CB 683]

A participant attains age 70½ as of the date six months after the participant's 70th birthday. For example, a participant whose date of birth is June 30, 1923 attains age 70½ on December 30, 1993 , and a participant whose date of birth is August 31, 1923 attains age 70½ on February 28, 1994. [Prop Reg § 1.401(a)(9)-1, B-3]

If TSB '93 (see Q 1:13) is enacted, the required beginning date for a *non-5 percent owner* will revert to the old rule; that is, April 1 of the calendar year following the *later* of the calendar year in which the participant attains age 70½ or retires. This change will be effective for years beginning *after* 1993. [TSB '93, Act § 204]

Q 11:4 Must distributions made before the required beginning date satisfy the minimum distribution requirements?

Lifetime distributions made *both* before the participant's required beginning date (see Q 11:3) and before the participant's first distribution calendar year (see Q 11:15) need *not* satisfy the minimum distribution requirements. However, if distributions commence under a particular distribution option, such as in the form of an annuity, before the participant's required beginning date for the participant's first distribution calendar year, the distribution option will fail to satisfy the minimum distribution requirements when distributions commence if, under the particular distribution option, distributions to be made for the participant's first distribution calendar year or any subsequent distribution calendar year will not satisfy the minimum distribution requirements. [Prop Reg § 1.401(a)(9)-1, B-3A]

Q 11:5 If distributions have begun before the participant's death, how must distributions be made after death?

If distribution of the participant's benefit has begun (see Q 11:6) and the participant dies before the entire benefit is distributed, the remaining portion of the participant's benefit must be distributed at least as rapidly as under the distribution method in effect on the date of the participant's death (see Q 11:14). [IRC §§ 401(a)(9)(A)(ii), 401(a)(9)(B)(i); Prop Reg § 1.401(a)(9)-1, B-4]

Example. Jane retired in 1990 and elected to receive her qualified retirement plan benefits in annual installments over 15 years. Jane dies in 1993 after receiving four installment payments (1990–1993). Jane's remaining benefit must be distributed to Jane's beneficiary over no more than the next 11 years (1994–2004).

Q 11:6 When are distributions considered to have begun?

Distributions are treated as having begun to the participant on the participant's required beginning date (see Q 11:3) even though payments may actually have been made before that date. [Prop Reg § 1.401(a)(9)-1, B-5]

Example 1. Jack retired in 1991 at age 65½ and began receiving installment distributions from a qualified retirement plan over the joint life expectancy of Jack and his wife, Jill. Distributions will not be treated as having begun until April 1, 1997 (the April 1 following 1996, the calendar year in which Jack will attain age 70½). Thus, if Jack dies before April 1, 1997 (his required beginning date), distributions to Jill must be made in accordance with the rules regarding distributions that begin after a participant has died (see Q 11:7). However, if Jack made an irrevocable election at retirement to receive his distribution in the form of an annuity, distribution will be considered to have begun on the actual date payments started (see Q 11:4), even if Jack dies before his required beginning date.

Example 2. Assume the same facts as in Example 1, except that Jack dies on July 1, 1997 without having received his required minimum distribution for 1997. If Jill elects to receive the entire remaining benefit in 1997, she may roll over the entire distribution into her own IRA, except the amount of the 1997 required minimum distribution (see Qs 28:30, 28:31). [Ltr Rul 9005071]

Q 11:7 If the participant dies before distributions are treated as having begun, how must the participant's benefit be distributed?

To satisfy the minimum distribution requirements, distributions must be made under one of two methods. The first method (the five-year rule) requires that the entire interest of the participant be distributed within five years of death regardless of to whom or to what entity the distribution is made. The second method (the exception to the five-year rule) requires that any portion of the participant's interest that is payable to a designated beneficiary (see Q 11:8) be distributed, commencing within one year of the participant's death, over the life of such beneficiary or over a period not extending beyond the life expectancy (see Q 11:12) of such beneficiary. [IRC §§ 401(a)(9)(B)(ii), 401(a)(9)(B)(iii); Prop Reg § 1.401(a)(9)-1, C-1]

To satisfy the five-year rule, the participant's entire interest must be distributed no later than December 31 of the calendar year that contains the fifth anniversary of the date of the participant's death. For example, if the participant died on January 1, 1990, the entire interest must be distributed by December 31, 1995. [Prop Reg § 1.401(a)(9)-1, C-2]

To satisfy the exception to the five-year rule, if the designated beneficiary is *not* the participant's surviving spouse, distributions must commence on or before December 31 of the calendar year immediately following the calendar year in which the participant died. This rule also applies if an individual is designated as a beneficiary in addition to the surviving spouse. If the designated beneficiary is the surviving spouse, distributions must commence on or before the *later* of (1) December 31 of the calendar year immediately following the calendar year in which the participant died, or (2) December 31 of the calendar year in which the participant would have attained age 70½. [IRC § 401(a)(9)(B)(iv); Prop Reg § 1.401(a)(9)-1, C-3]

The plan may adopt a provision specifying which method will apply to distributions after the participant's death. Alternatively, the plan may permit participants or beneficiaries to elect the method of distribution. If, however, the plan is silent as to which method applies if no election is made, distributions must be made in accordance with the exception to the five-year rule if the participant's beneficiary is the surviving spouse and, in all other cases, in accordance with the five-year rule. [Prop Reg § 1.401(a)(9)-1, C-4]

Q 11:8 Who is a designated beneficiary?

A person's status as a designated beneficiary is not dependent upon being selected by the participant. For example, if the terms of the plan specify the beneficiary, then whoever is so specified is the designated beneficiary and is treated as having been designated by the participant. [IRC § 401(a)(9)(E); Prop Reg § 1.401(a)(9)-1, D-1]

An individual may be designated as a beneficiary under the plan either by the terms of the plan or, if the plan provides, by an affirmative election by the participant specifying the beneficiary. A designated beneficiary need not be specified by name in the plan or by the participant to be a designated beneficiary so long as the individual who will be the beneficiary is identifiable under the plan as of the participant's required beginning date (see Q 11:3), or as of the date of the participant's death, and at all subsequent times. The members of a class of beneficiaries capable of expansion or contraction (e.g., the participant's children) will be treated as being identifiable if it is possible at the applicable time to identify the class member with the shortest life expectancy (see Qs 11:12, 11:13). [Prop Reg § 1.401(a)(9)-1, D-2]

Example. Stanley attains age 70½ in calendar year 1993. As of April 1, 1994, Stanley designates as his beneficiaries under the plan his spouse and his children. Stanley does not specify them by name. Even though Stanley did not specify his spouse, Susan, and his children, Hollie and Amy, by name, they are identifiable based on their relationship to Stanley as of his required beginning date. It is irrelevant that additional children of Stanley may be born after his required beginning date and that the class of beneficiaries is capable of expansion.

Q 11:9 May a person other than an individual be a designated beneficiary?

No. Only individuals may be designated beneficiaries (see Q 11:8) for purposes of the minimum distribution requirements. A person who is not an individual, such as the participant's estate, may not be a designated beneficiary.

If a person other than an individual is designated as a beneficiary, the participant will be treated as having no designated beneficiary. In that event, distribution must be made over the participant's life or over a period not exceeding the participant's life expectancy (see Q 11:10). Furthermore, if, upon the participant's death, distribution has not commenced, distribution must be made in accordance with the five-year rule (see Q 11:7). [Prop Reg § 1.401(a)(9)-1, D-2A]

Q 11:10 For purposes of calculating the distribution period, when is the designated beneficiary determined?

For purposes of calculating the distribution period for distributions before death, the designated beneficiary (see Q 11:8) will be determined as of the participant's required beginning date (see Q 11:3). If, as of that date, there is no designated beneficiary to receive the benefit upon death, the distribution period is limited to the participant's life or a period not extending beyond the participant's life expectancy (see Q 11:12). If there is a beneficiary, such as the participant's estate, who is not designated, there is deemed to be no designated beneficiary (see Q 11:9). [Prop Reg § 1.401(a)(9)-1, D-3]

The designated beneficiary can be determined *after* the required beginning date. [Ltr Rul 9311037]

Example. Dick and his wife, Jane, are both age 73. Dick dies in 1994, and Jane rolls over the entire distribution from his qualified retirement plan to a newly established IRA. Jane designates her child as beneficiary. Even though Jane's required beginning date had passed when she established her IRA, she is not required to take a distribution until December 31, 1995. Jane's child may be treated as a designated beneficiary because the designation occurred prior to the first required distribution date. (See Chapter 28 for details on rollovers.)

For purposes of calculating the distribution period for distributions beginning after death in accordance with the exception to the five-year rule (see Q 11:7), the designated beneficiary will be determined as of the participant's date of death. If, as of the date of death, there is no designated beneficiary, distribution must be made in accordance with the five-year rule. If there is a beneficiary, such as the participant's estate, who is not designated, there is deemed to be no designated beneficiary. [Prop Reg § 1.401(a)(9)-1, D-4(a)]

Q 11:11   Can the beneficiary of a trust be a designated beneficiary?

If a trust is named as a beneficiary of the participant, all beneficiaries of the trust are treated as having been designated (see Q 11:8) as beneficiaries during the participant's lifetime if, as of the later of the date on which the trust is named as a beneficiary or the participant's required beginning date (see Q 11:3), and as of all subsequent periods during which the trust is named as a beneficiary, the following requirements are met:

1. The trust is a valid trust under state law, or would be but for the fact that there is no corpus.

2. The trust is irrevocable.

3. The beneficiaries of the trust are identifiable (see Q 11:8).

4. A copy of the trust instrument is provided to the plan.

[Prop Reg § 1.401(a)(9)-1, D-5(a); Rev Rul 89-89, 1989-2 CB 231; Ltr Ruls 9052015, 9038015]

Since only an individual may be a designated beneficiary, a trust itself may not be the designated beneficiary even though the trust is named as a beneficiary (see Q 11:9). However, if the above requirements are met, distributions made to the trust will be treated as paid to the trust beneficiaries. If, as of any date on or after the participant's required beginning date, a trust is named as a beneficiary and the above requirements are *not* met, the participant will be treated as not having a designated beneficiary. Consequently, for calendar years subsequent to such date, distribution must be made over the participant's life or over the period that would have been the participant's remaining life expectancy (see Q 11:12) determined as if no beneficiary had been designated as of the required beginning date. [Prop Reg § 1.401(a)(9)-1, D-5(b)]

With respect to distributions commencing after the participant's death, all beneficiaries of the trust will be treated as designated beneficiaries if the above requirements are satisfied as of the participant's death. However, if the above requirements are *not* satisfied, the participant will be treated as not having a designated beneficiary, and distribution must be made in accordance with the five-year rule (see Q 11:7). [Prop Reg § 1.401(a)(9)-1, D-6(a)]

Q 11:12   What age is used to calculate life expectancy?

Life expectancy is calculated using the participant's and the designated beneficiary's attained age as of the participant's birthday and the designated beneficiary's birthday in the calendar year in which the participant attains age 70½ (see Q 11:3). If life expectancy is being recalculated (see Q 11:14), the life expectancy of the participant, the life expectancy of the participant's spouse, or the joint life expectancy of the participant and spouse will be recalculated using the participant's and the spouse's attained age as of the participant's birthday and the spouse's birthday in each succeeding calendar year in which recalculation is provided for purposes of calculating the minimum distribution for that distribution calendar year (see Q 11:15).

If the participant's required beginning date (see Q 11:3) is April 1 of the year following the calendar year in which the participant retires, that calendar year is substituted for the calendar year in which the participant attains age 70½. [Prop Reg § 1.401(a)(9)-1, E-1(a), (b)]

In the case of any installment distribution to a designated beneficiary (see Qs 11:7, 11:8), the life expectancy of the designated beneficiary is calculated based on the beneficiary's attained age as of the beneficiary's birthday in the calendar year in which distributions are required to commence to such beneficiary. [Prop Reg § 1.401(a)(9)-1, E-2]

> **Example.** An unmarried participant, A, dies at age 50 on January 31, 1993. A's designated beneficiary is A's brother, B, and B will receive A's interest over B's life expectancy. The date on which distributions are required to commence to B is December 31, 1994. Therefore, B's life expectancy is calculated based on B's attained age as of B's birthday in calendar year 1994.

Life expectancy for purposes of determining required minimum distributions must be computed by use of the expected return multiples in Tables V (single life) and VI (joint lives) of Treasury Regulations Section 1.72-9. [Prop Reg § 1.401(a)(9)-1, E-3 & 4]

Q 11:13   If the participant has more than one designated beneficiary, which designated beneficiary's life expectancy is used to determine the distribution period?

If more than one individual is designated as a beneficiary (e.g., the participant's children) as of the applicable date for determining the designated beneficiary (see Q 11:8), the designated beneficiary with the shortest life expectancy (see Q 11:12) will be the designated beneficiary for purposes of determining the distribution period.

If a person other than an individual is designated as a beneficiary, the participant will be treated as not having any designated beneficiaries even if there are also individuals designated as beneficiaries (see Q 11:9). The date for determining the designated beneficiary is the applicable date (see Q 11:10). The period for distributions commencing before the participant's death or for distributions over a life expectancy commencing after the participant's death, whichever is applicable, is the distribution period. [Prop Reg § 1.401(a)(9)-1, E-5(a)(1)]

Q 11:14   Can life expectancy be recalculated?

The life expectancy (see Q 11:12) of the participant and/or the participant's spouse can be recalculated *annually*. The life expectancy of a designated beneficiary (see Q 11:8) other than a spouse *cannot* be recalculated. The plan can either specify whether life expectancy will be recalculated or allow the participant to elect whether to recalculate life expectancy. The election becomes irrevocable as of the date of the first required distribution. [Prop Reg § 1.401(a)(9)-1, E-6, E-7]

Life expectancy or joint life expectancy is recalculated annually by using the appropriate table (see Q 11:12) to redetermine the life expectancy of the participant or the participant's spouse, or the joint life expectancy of the participant and the participant's spouse, using the attained ages on their birthdays in that year. Upon the death of the participant or the participant's spouse, the recalculated life expectancy of the deceased participant or deceased spouse is reduced to *zero* in the year following the year in which death occurred, *and* the participant's entire remaining interest must be distributed in the year in which the last life expectancy is reduced to zero. [IRC § 401(a)(9)(D); Prop Reg § 1.401(a)(9)-1, E-8]

Q 11:15   How much must be distributed each year?

If the participant's benefit is in the form of an individual account (e.g., a defined contribution plan; see Q 2:2) and will be distributed (1) over a period not extending beyond the life expectancy (see Q 11:12) of the participant or the joint life expectancy of the participant and the designated beneficiary (see Q 11:8) or (2) over a period not extending beyond the life expectancy of the designated beneficiary, the amount required to be distributed for each calendar year, beginning with the first calendar year for which distributions are required and then for each succeeding calendar year, must at least equal the quotient obtained by dividing the participant's applicable account balance by the applicable life expectancy. The applicable account balance is the account balance as of the plan's last valuation date in the calendar year immediately preceding the calendar year for which the distribution is being made. The applicable life expectancy is the life expectancy of the participant, the joint life expectancy of the participant and the participant's designated beneficiary, or the life expectancy of the designated beneficiary. [Prop Reg § 1.401(a)(9)-1, F-1]

A year for which a distribution must be made is called a distribution calendar year. Generally, the first distribution calendar year is the year in which the participant reaches age 70½ (see Q 11:3). The distribution for the first distribution calendar year must be made by April 1 of the following year (see Q 11:3). Distributions for subsequent distribution calendar years must be made by December 31 of such year. Thus, if the participant attained age 70½ in 1993 and deferred the initial distribution until 1994, two minimum distributions must occur in 1994. The minimum distribution for 1993 must occur by April 1, 1994, and the minimum distribution for 1994 must occur by December 31, 1994. However, for purposes of calculating the December 31, 1994 minimum distribution, the applicable account balance is reduced by the amount of the required distribution for the first distribution calendar year actually made in 1994 by April 1, 1994. Taking two distributions in a single calendar year could subject the participant to the excise tax on excess distributions (see Q 13:27). [Prop Reg § 1.401(a)(9)-1, F-1, F-5]

The amount distributed in satisfaction of the minimum distribution requirement is determined annually. No credit is given for amounts distributed in previous years that exceeded the required amount. [Prop Reg § 1.401(a)(9)-1, F-2]

Annuity distributions under a defined benefit plan must be paid in periodic payments at intervals not longer than one year, over (1) the life of the participant, (2) the lives of the participant and the participant's designated beneficiary, or (3) a period certain not extending beyond the life expectancy of the participant or the joint life expectancy of the participant and the participant's designated beneficiary. Once payment begins over a period certain, the period certain cannot be extended. Payments under the annuity must either be nonincreasing or increase only under certain circumstances (e.g., in accordance with a specified cost-of-living index). The annuity may vary with the investment performance of the underlying assets. [Prop Reg § 1.401(a)(9)-1, F-3]

Q 11:16   How does a rollover affect the required minimum distribution rules?

If an amount distributed by one plan (distributing plan) is rolled over to another plan (receiving plan), the amount distributed is still treated as a distribution by the distributing plan notwithstanding the rollover. However, a required minimum distribution may not be rolled over to another qualified retirement plan or to an IRA. [IRC § 402(c)(4)(B); Prop Reg § 1.401(a)(9)-1, G-1] See Chapter 28 for a discussion of rollovers.

The participant's benefit under the receiving plan is increased by the amount of the rollover. However, the rollover has no impact on the minimum distribution required to be made by the receiving plan for the calendar year in which the rollover is received. But if a minimum distribution is required to be made by the receiving plan for the following calendar year, the rollover amount must be considered to be part of the participant's benefit under the receiving plan. Consequently, for purposes of determining any minimum distribution for the calendar year immediately following the calendar year in which the rollover is received by the receiving plan, the participant's benefit will be increased by the rollover amount. [Prop Reg § 1.401(a)(9)-1, G-2]

In the case of a *transfer* of the participant's benefit from one plan (transferor plan) to another (transferee plan), the transfer is not treated as a distribution by the transferor plan for required minimum distribution purposes. Instead, the benefit of the participant under the transferor plan is decreased by the amount transferred. However, if any portion of the participant's benefit is transferred in a distribution calendar year, then, in order to satisfy the minimum distribution requirement, the transferor plan must determine the amount of the minimum distribution with respect to the participant for the calendar year of the transfer using the participant's benefit under the transferor plan *before* the transfer. [Prop Reg § 1.401(a)(9)-1, G-3]

However, the participant's benefit under the transferee plan is increased by the amount transferred. The transfer has no impact on the minimum distribution required to be made by the transferee plan in the calendar year in which the transfer is received. But if a minimum distribution is required from the transferee plan for the following calendar year, the transferred amount must be considered to be part of the participant's benefit under the transferee plan. Consequently, for purposes of determining any minimum distribution for the calendar year immediately following the calendar year in which the transfer occurs, the participant's benefit under the transferee plan will be increased by the amount transferred. [Prop Reg § 1.401(a)(9)-1, G-4]

Q 11:17   What distribution rules apply if the individual is a participant in more than one plan?

If the individual is a participant in more than one qualified retirement plan, the individual must receive a minimum distribution from *each* plan. [Prop Reg § 1.401(a)(9)-1, H-1]

Separate accounts under a plan are generally aggregated for purposes of the minimum distribution requirements. Aggregation is not required if different beneficiaries are designated for each separate account; in that event, each separate account may separately satisfy the requirements. [Prop Reg § 1.401(a)(9)-1, H-2]

Q 11:18   What happens if the participant has not attained normal retirement age?

A plan will not fail to qualify solely because the plan permits distributions to commence to a participant on or after April 1 of the calendar year following the calendar year in which the participant attains age 70½ (see Q 11:3) even though the participant has not retired or attained normal retirement age (see Q 10:55) as of the date on which such distributions commence. [Prop Reg § 1.401(a)(9)-1, H-5]

Q 11:19   Can distributions be delayed until after the required beginning date?

Yes, but only if the participant made a valid election under Section 242(b)(2) of TEFRA before 1984. In that case, the participant can defer distributions until the participant actually retires. An election is valid only if it designated a distribution method that would not have disqualified the plan under pre-TEFRA law. IRS ruled that elections that deferred distributions until one year prior to the expiration of the electing participant's life expectancy or until ten years after retirement were invalid because the distribution methods did not satisfy the incidental death benefits rule (see Q 11:21). Also, elections that did not explicitly set forth the form of payment and beneficiary of death benefits were valid with regard to lifetime distributions to the electing participant but were not applicable with regard to the distribution of death benefits. [Prop Reg § 1.401(a)(9)-1, J-1; Notice 83-23, 1983-2 CB 418; Ltr Rul 9042063]

However, if the Section 242(b)(2) election is revoked after the participant's required beginning date (see Q 11:3), the total amount of distributions that would have been required by the revocation date must be distributed by the end of the calendar year after the year of revocation. [Prop Reg § 1.401(a)(9)-1, J-4; Notice 83-23, 1983-2 CB 418]

A revocation of a Section 242(b)(2) election does not result from (1) the change in the employer's form of business from a corporation to a partnership or (2) the revocation of the election with respect to another plan within a commingled trust. An employee's Section 242(b)(2) election under a terminated profit sharing plan will not be revoked by the employer's transfer of the employee's account balance, without the employee's consent, to a segregated account in a 401(k) plan sponsored by the employer. The election will continue to apply only to the transferred account and not to the employee's other accounts in the 401(k) plan. When one plan was merged into another plan and the participant had made identical Section 242(b)(2) elections under each plan, the transferee plan could make distributions in accordance with the elections even though the transferee plan did not account separately for the transferred funds. An employee's election was not revoked when he withdrew a portion of his voluntary contributions (see Q 6:19) because the withdrawal was not inconsistent with the election and the terms of the plan both before and after the election. [Ltr Ruls 9310026, 9215040, 9052058, 9013011, 8938073]

Q 11:20 Is there a penalty for failure to make a required minimum distribution?

Yes. A nondeductible excise tax is imposed on the payee (e.g., participant or beneficiary) equal to 50 percent of the difference between the amount required to be distributed (see Q 11:15) and the amount actually distributed in any year. IRS may waive the excise tax if the payee establishes that the shortfall was due to reasonable error and that reasonable steps are being taken to correct the deficiency. The tax will not apply to distributions made in accordance with a properly executed Section 242(b)(2) election (see Q 11:19). [IRC § 4974; Prop Reg § 54.4974-2, Q&A-1, Q&A-2, Q&A-8]

IRS has issued guidelines for plans that are unable to make required minimum distributions due to investments in insolvent insurance companies. [Rev Proc 92-16, 1992-1 CB 673; Rev Proc 92-10, 1992-1 CB 661]

Q 11:21 How does the incidental death benefit rule affect benefit distributions?

Any benefits payable to a beneficiary because of the participant's death must be incidental to the qualified retirement plan's primary purpose of providing retirement benefits to the participant (see Q 14:4). [Treas Reg § 1.401-1(b)(1); Prop Reg § 1.401(a)(9)-2, Q&A-1]

A qualified retirement plan is generally required to provide a QPSA (see Q 10:9) to the surviving spouse of a vested participant who dies before the annuity starting date. Since a QPSA is considered a part of the preretirement death benefit, both the QPSA and any other death benefit must be considered together to determine whether the total death benefits provided are incidental. If a plan provides a preretirement death benefit equal to both 100 times the participant's projected monthly benefit and a QPSA, the incidental death benefits rule will be violated. This problem may be remedied by:

1. Eliminating the preretirement death benefit; or
2. Offsetting the preretirement death benefit by the value of the QPSA.

[Rev Rul 85-15, 1985-1 CB 132]

Q 11:22   What is the minimum distribution incidental benefit requirement?

Distributions made during or after a participant's first distribution calendar year (see Q 11:15) must satisfy a minimum distribution incidental benefit (MDIB) requirement as well as the minimum distribution requirements. Thus, distributions must satisfy the MDIB requirement even if the amount required to be distributed under this requirement exceeds the amount required under the general minimum distribution rules. The MDIB requirement only applies to distributions during the participant's lifetime; this requirement does *not* apply to distributions after the participant's death.

For individual account and annuity distributions, the amount that must be distributed to meet the MDIB requirement is determined by dividing the participant's benefit by the applicable divisor specified in the proposed regulations. The applicable divisor is based on the joint life expectancy (see Q 11:12) of the participant and a hypothetical individual ten years younger than the participant. However, if the participant's beneficiary on the required beginning date (see Q 11:3) is the participant's spouse, satisfaction of the minimum distribution requirement will automatically satisfy the MDIB requirement. [IRC § 401(a)(9)(G); Prop Reg § 1.401(a)(9)-2, Q&A-1–Q&A-7]

> **Example 1.** Bob, who has attained age 70½, is a participant in The Laitman Group Ltd. Profit Sharing Plan. Bob designates his twin daughters, Bonnie and Cathy, age 35, as his beneficiaries. The joint life expectancy of Bob and his daughters is 47.5 years. But, to satisfy the MDIB requirement, the applicable divisor is 26.2—the equivalent joint life expectancy of a 70-year old and a 60-year old.

> **Example 2.** Instead of designating his daughters as beneficiaries, Bob designates his wife, Pegge, age 55, as his beneficiary. The joint life expectancy of Bob and Pegge is 29.9 years. The applicable divisor is 29.9, not 26.2, because Pegge, the designated beneficiary, is Bob's wife, and satisfaction of the minimum distribution requirement automatically satisfies the MDIB requirement.

Q 11:23   Must a qualified retirement plan set forth the minimum distribution requirements?

A qualified retirement plan must include several written provisions reflecting the minimum distribution requirements. First, the plan must generally set forth the statutory rules, including the incidental death benefit requirement (see Q 11:22). Second, the plan must provide that distributions will be made in accordance with the proposed regulations. The plan document must also provide that these provisions override any distribution options in the plan inconsistent with the minimum distribution requirements. Finally, the plan must include any other provisions as may be prescribed in the future by IRS. [Prop Reg § 1.401(a)(9)-1, A-3]

The plan need not be amended to reflect the minimum distribution requirements until the last day of the plan year beginning on or after January 1, 1994, provided that:

1. The plan complies in operation with the requirements, and
2. The amendment applies retroactively.

[Prop Reg § 1.401(a)(9)-1, A-4; Notice 92-31, 1992-2 CB 359, 1992-29 IRB 6; Ann 92-29, 1992-9 IRB 37]

A plan will *not* satisfy the general qualification requirements (see Q 4:1) unless all required minimum distributions are made for the calendar year ending with or within the plan year. However, a plan will not fail to satisfy the qualification requirements if there are isolated instances when the minimum distribution requirements are not satisfied in operation. But a pattern or regular practice of failing to meet the minimum distribution requirements with respect to one or more participants will not be considered an isolated instance even if each instance is *de minimis*. [Prop Reg § 1.401(a)(9)-1, A-5]

Chapter 12

Tax Deduction Rules

One of the primary tax advantages of a qualified retirement plan is that a current deduction is allowed for the company's contributions to a plan that provides future benefits. This chapter examines when a contribution must be made in order to be deductible on a current basis and the limits set on the amount of a tax-deductible contribution.

Q 12:1 What are the basic requirements for deducting employer contributions to a qualified retirement plan?

For such a contribution to be tax deductible, it must be an "ordinary and necessary" business expense and must be compensation for services actually rendered. Thus, for example, a contribution on behalf of a shareholder may be made only if the shareholder is also an employee actually rendering services to the corporation. Also, the contribution, when considered together with the employee's regular compensation, must be "reasonable in amount" for the services rendered. Reasonable current compensation and the plan contribution may include additional amounts for previously uncompensated prior services. [IRC §§ 162, 404; Treas Reg § 1.404(a)-1(b); Bianchi, 66 TC 324 (1976), aff'd, 533 F 2d 93 (2d Cir 1977); Richlands Medical Assn, 60 TCM 1572 (1990); aff'd, unpublished opinion (4th Cir 1992); M & E Shindler, Inc, 63 TCM 3039 (1992)]

A contribution on behalf of a self-employed individual (see Q 29:8) satisfies the ordinary-and-necessary business expense requirement if it does not exceed the individual's earned income for the year determined without regard to the deduction for the contribution (see Q 29:10). [IRC § 404(a)(8); Temp Reg § 1.404(a)(8)-1T; but see Gale v United States, 768 F Supp 1305 (ND Ill 1991)]

Q 12:2 When must contributions be made to be currently deductible?

Tax-deductible contributions to a qualified retirement plan may be made at any time during the taxable year and even after the end of the taxable year up to the due date (including valid extensions) for the filing of the employer's federal income tax return for the particular year. Timely contributions made after the end of the taxable year are deductible for that taxable year if either (1) the employer designates in writing to the plan administrator or trustee that the contribution is for the preceding year, or (2) the employer claims the contribution as a deduction on its tax return for the preceding year. Such a designation, once made, is irrevocable. [IRC § 404(a)(6); Rev Rul 76-28, 1976-1 CB 106]

A contribution is timely if it is made before the income tax return extended due date even if it is made after the return is filed. An employer must obtain a valid extension to file the return in order to extend the time to make a contribution. IRS has ruled that a request for an automatic extension of time to file the employer's tax return was invalid because the employer failed to pay the balance of tax due shown on extension request Form 7004. An application for an extension of time to file is invalid if the employer fails to comply with all requirements of the regulations. [Rev Rul 66-144, 1966-1 CB 91; IRC § 6081(b); Treas Reg § 1.6081-3; Ltr Rul 9033005]

The employer's timely mailing of the contribution is adequate. Thus, a contribution mailed and bearing a postage cancellation date no later than the due date of the employer's tax return, including extensions, is timely even if the trust received it after such due date. [Ltr Rul 8536085]

A bookkeeping entry showing that a portion of the employer's certificate of deposit (CD) belonged to a qualified retirement plan as of the deadline for tax-deductible contributions is not timely payment of the contribution. [Rollar Homes, Inc, 53 TCM 471 (1987)]

In another case, an employer mistakenly made out and mailed its plan contribution check for the taxable year to PBGC. The check was returned by PBGC, and the contribution was paid late. IRS ruled that the contribution was not timely made and, therefore, was not deductible for that taxable year. [Ltr Rul 9031033]

Q 12:3 May a contribution be timely for tax deduction purposes but not for the minimum funding standards?

Yes. The rules regarding timeliness for tax deduction purposes are based on the employer's taxable year and are independent of the rules regarding timeliness for purposes of the minimum funding standards (see Q 8:1), which are based on the plan year. Tax-deductible plan contributions may be made after the end of the taxable year if payment is made by the due date (including extensions) for filing the employer's federal income tax return for that taxable year (see Q 12:2). For purposes of the minimum funding standards, contributions made after the end of the plan year may relate back to that year if they are made within $8\frac{1}{2}$ months after the end of the plan year. [IRC § 412(c)(10)(A); Rev Rul 77-82, 1977-1 CB 121]

Q 12:4 May an employer deduct the fair market value of property other than money contributed to its qualified retirement plan?

Yes. If property is contributed, the employer may deduct the fair market value of the property at the time of the contribution. However, if the fair market value exceeds the employer's basis in the property, the employer has a taxable gain equal to the excess; but, if the basis exceeds the fair market value, there is no recognizable loss to the employer. [IRC §§ 267, 1001; Rev Rul 75-498, 1975-2 CB 29; Rev Rul 73-583, 1973-2 CB 146; Rev Rul 73-345, 1973-2 CB 11]

If an employer purchases real estate from its qualified retirement plan for an amount in excess of the real estate's fair market value, such excess is considered a contribution to the plan. [Ltr Rul 8949076]

DOL may consider an employer's contribution of property to or the purchase of property from its qualified retirement plan to be a prohibited transaction (i.e., a transfer, sale, or exchange of assets between a party in interest and the plan) in some circumstances (see Q 20:8).

Q 12:5 May an employer make a timely contribution to the qualified retirement plan by check?

Yes. The contribution will be considered timely even if the plan trustee receives payment after the deadline for a deductible contribution (see Q 12:2) if the employer mails the check to the plan trustee before such deadline, the check is promptly presented for payment, and it is paid in the regular course of business. However, the contribution is not timely if the trustee delays presentation of the check because of the employer's financial problems. Also, the contribution was not considered timely in one case because the employer could not explain why the check was not negotiated until two weeks after the contribution deadline. [Flomac, Inc, 53 TCM 305 (1987); Walt Wilger Tire Co, Inc, 38 TCM 287 (1979); Cain-White & Co, Inc, 37 TCM 1829 (1978)]

If the check bounces, no contribution is deemed to have been made. [Springfield Productions, Inc, 38 TCM 74 (1979)]

Q 12:6 Is a contribution of the employer's promissory note a deductible payment?

No. The employer must make a timely contribution in cash or its equivalent to obtain a tax deduction for its contribution for the current or preceding taxable year (see Q 12:2). Since the contribution by the employer of its own promissory note is merely a promise to pay, it is not considered a payment of cash or its equivalent. [Don E Williams Co v United States, 429 US 569 (1977); Rev Rul 80-140, 1980-1 CB 89]

A contribution of the employer's own promissory note is also a prohibited transaction (see Q 20:1).

Q 12:7 What is the primary limitation on tax-deductible contributions to a profit sharing plan?

The primary limitation on tax-deductible contributions to a profit sharing plan is 15 percent of the total compensation (see Q 12:14) paid to all participants during the taxable year. [IRC § 404(a)(3)(A); Treas Reg § 1.404(a)-9(c)]

Q 12:8 How are excess amounts contributed to a profit sharing plan treated for tax purposes?

There is an excise tax imposed on the employer equal to 10 percent of the portion of any contribution to any qualified retirement plan that is not deductible (see Qs 12:9–12:12). [IRC § 4972]

Amounts contributed in excess of the primary limitation (see Q 12:7) are generally carried forward and may be deducted in later years. However, the total amount deductible in a later taxable year, including the contribution to the profit sharing plan for that year, is limited to 15 percent of the compensation of the participants in the later taxable year. [IRC § 404(a)(3)(A); Treas Reg § 1.404(a)-9(e); Rev Rul 83-48, 1983-1 CB 93; Rev Rul 73-608, 1973-2 CB 147]

> **Example.** Joel Corporation contributes $30,000 to its profit sharing plan in 1991, $32,000 in 1992, and $36,000 in 1993. If $27,000 is 15 percent of the total compensation paid to all participants in 1991, Joel's deduction for 1991 would be limited to $27,000, and $3,000 ($30,000 – $27,000) would be carried over to later years. Joel would be subject to an excise tax of $300 (10% × $3,000). If $33,000 is 15 percent of compensation in 1992, Joel's deduction for 1992 is $33,000 ($32,000 + $1,000 carried over from 1991) and the excise tax would be $200 [10% × ($3,000 – $1,000)]. If $38,000 is 15 percent of compensation in 1993, Joel's deduction for 1993 is $38,000 ($36,000 plus the remaining $2,000 carried over from 1991).

Q 12:9 How is the amount of nondeductible contributions computed?

Nondeductible contributions are defined as the sum of (1) amounts contributed by an employer to a qualified retirement plan for a taxable year in excess of the amount allowable as a deduction for that taxable year, plus (2) the unapplied amounts from the preceding taxable year.

The unapplied amounts from the preceding taxable year are the amounts subject to the excise tax in the preceding taxable year reduced by the sum of (1) the portion that is returned to the employer during the taxable year, plus (2) the portion that is deductible during the current taxable year.

> **Example.** Nan Corporation makes a nondeductible contribution of $100,000 for its 1991 taxable year. Nan contributes $75,000 in 1992 when its deductible limit is $150,000. In 1993, it contributes $75,000 when its deductible limit is $100,000. Nan must pay an excise tax of $10,000 for 1991 (10% × $100,000) and $2,500 for 1992 [10% x ($100,000 + $75,000 − $150,000)]. It owes no excise tax for 1993 [10% × ($25,000 + $75,000 − $100,000)]. [IRC § 4972(c)]

Q 12:10 When are nondeductible contributions for a given taxable year determined?

Nondeductible contributions for purposes of the excise tax are determined as of the close of the employer's taxable year. If, however, a nondeductible contribution is returned by the last day on which a deductible contribution could be made for that year (see Qs 1:26, 12:2), the returned amount is not treated as a nondeductible contribution and is not subject to the tax (see Q 12:9). [IRC § 4972(c)(3)]

Q 12:11 What happens if a deduction for plan contributions is subsequently disallowed?

The excise tax applies to contributions for which the deduction is disallowed. [General Explanation of TRA '86, Title XI, D2, p 748]

Q 12:12 Does the excise tax imposed on nondeductible contributions apply to tax-exempt organizations?

No. The 10 percent excise tax imposed on an employer for making nondeductible plan contributions (see Qs 12:8–12:11) does not apply to an employer that has, *at all times*, been exempt from tax. [IRC §§ 4972(d)(1)(B), 4980(c)(1)(A)]

IRS has ruled, however, that a tax-exempt organization that had been subject to tax on unrelated business taxable income (UBTI) was not subject to the excise tax because the portion of the nondeductible contribution attributable to the UBTI was *de minimis*. [Ltr Rul 9304033]

In another ruling, IRS concluded that plan contributions made by a tax-exempt organization, which was a member of a controlled group (see Qs 5:30, 5:32) that contained at least one nonexempt employer whose employees were covered under the plan, was subject to the 10 percent excise tax whether or not the organization had UBTI. When one of the controlled group members maintaining the plan is nonexempt, the whole group is considered nonexempt; and, therefore, the exempt organization does not qualify for the exception. [Ltr Rul 9236026]

Q 12:13   Can the employer make up a missed profit sharing plan contribution?

If an employer made less than the full 15 percent contribution (see Q 12:7) in a taxable year beginning before January 1, 1987, it may carry over the unused difference, known as the unused pre-1987 limitation carryforward, and make a larger tax-deductible contribution in a subsequent year, provided the plan is still qualified.

However, the combined regular deduction and unused pre-1987 limitation carryforward may not exceed the lesser of (1) 25 percent of that year's total compensation (see Q 12:14), or (2) 15 percent of that year's total compensation plus the amount of the unused pre-1987 limitation carryforward. Also, to avoid disqualifying the plan, the employer's contribution must be limited so that the amount allocated to any participant's account does not exceed the annual addition limitation (see Q 6:1). [IRC §§ 401(a)(16), 404(a)(3)(A)]

Q 12:14   What does compensation mean for purposes of the limits on deductible contributions to a profit sharing plan?

Compensation generally includes the total compensation of all plan participants paid or accrued during the taxable year. Even if, for purposes of allocating employer contributions, the plan defines compensation as base salary only, other forms of compensation (e.g., overtime, bonuses, and commissions) are included for purposes of the profit sharing plan deduction limitations (see Qs 6:28–6:32). Elective contributions (see Q 23:13) to a 401(k) plan (see Q 23:1) are not compensation for purposes of determining the limitation on deductible contributions. [Treas Reg § 1.404(a)-9(b); Rev Rul 80-145, 1980-1 CB 89; Ltr Rul 9225038]

The deduction for contributions to a 401(k) plan that are attributable to services rendered by participants after the end of the employer's taxable year will not be allowed because compensation must be earned before it can be deferred and contributed to the plan. [Treas Reg § 1.404(a)-1(b); Rev Rul 90-105, 1990-2 CB 69]

> **Example.** PDB Corp.'s taxable year ended June 30, 1993, and the plan year of its 401(k) plan is the calendar year. Barbara, an employee of PDB Corp. whose salary is $1,000 per week, became a 401(k) plan participant on January 1, 1993. She elected to defer 5 percent of her salary ($50) each week. Thus, she deferred $2,600 ($50 × 52) during the 1993 plan year. However, PDB Corp. can deduct only $1,300 ($50 × 26) on its income tax return for the taxable year ended June 30, 1993, which is the portion of the deferral attributable to Barbara's services through June 30, 1993. The $1,300 deferred by Barbara during the second half of 1993 will be deductible by PDB Corp. on its income tax return for the taxable year ending June 30, 1994.

If a terminated employee does not receive a share of the employer's contribution for the year of termination, such employee's compensation is not included for deduction limitation purposes. [Dallas Dental Labs, 72 TC 117 (1979); Rev Rul 65-295, 1965-2 CB 148]

There is a $200,000 per participant compensation cap that applies to the computation of deductions for contributions to all qualified retirement plans. The $200,000 limit is adjusted for inflation and is $235,840 for 1993. [IRC § 404(l); IR 93-2 (Jan 15, 1993)] For prior years, the adjusted amount was:

Year	Adjusted Amount
1992	$228,860
1991	$222,220
1990	$209,200

The $200,000 limitation is reduced to $150,000 for the plan year beginning in 1994. Although the first cost-of-living adjustment could occur in the plan year beginning in 1995, it probably will not because an adjustment will be made only if it is $10,000 or greater and then will be made in multiples of $10,000 (i.e., rounded down to the next lowest multiple of $10,000). For example, an increase in the cost-of-living of $9,999 will result in no adjustment, and an increase of $19,999 will create an upward adjustment of $10,000. Therefore, the cost-of-living must increase by 6⅔ percent before the first adjustment to the annual compensation limit will occur [6⅔% × $150,000 = $10,000]. [RRA '93, Act § 13212]

See Question 12:25 for a discussion of the family aggregation rule.

Q 12:15   May a company make a deductible contribution to the profit sharing plan of an affiliated company?

Yes. Although contributions to a profit sharing plan are not required to be based on profits (see Q 2:6), a profit sharing plan may require profits in order to make a contribution. If a member of an affiliated group of corporations cannot make a contribution to its profit sharing plan because it has no current or accumulated earnings or profits, another member of the affiliated group may make a contribution for the employees of the unprofitable member. However, the contribution is deductible only if both members participate in the same profit sharing plan; the contribution is not deductible if they maintain separate plans. [IRC §§ 404(a)(3)(B), 1504; Treas Reg § 1.404(a)-10(a)(1)]

Q 12:16   What is the limit on tax-deductible contributions to defined contribution plans other than profit sharing plans?

Generally, the deduction for defined contribution plans that are pension plans (e.g., money purchase and target benefit plans; see Qs 2:4, 2:5) is the amount necessary to meet minimum funding standards (see Q 8:1). Thus, the deductible amount of the employer's contribution to a money purchase pension plan or a target benefit plan is ordinarily the sum of amounts required to be contributed on behalf of each plan participant. [IRC § 404(a)(1)(A); Prop Reg § 1.412(b)-1(a)]

However, in computing the amount deductible for contributions to any type of defined contribution plan (see Q 2:2), if the annual addition (see Q 6:1) of any participant under the plan is more than the amount allowed by law, the excess amount of the company contribution will not be deductible (see Q 12:24). [IRC § 404(j)(1)(B)]

> **Example.** B&P Corp. established a money purchase pension plan in 1993 for its only employee, Alexis. The plan provides a 25-per-cent-of-compensation contribution formula. Alexis's compensation is $150,000, and the contribution under the formula is $37,500. The excess portion of B&P Corp.'s contribution for 1993 of $7,500 ($37,500 − $30,000) will not be deductible. In addition, the nondeductible contribution will be subject to a nondeductible 10 percent excise tax penalty (see Qs 12:8–12:10).

For a discussion of the per participant limitation on compensation for making tax-deductible contributions, see Question 12:14.

Q 12:17   What is the limit on tax-deductible contributions to a defined benefit plan?

Under the level cost method, the employer may deduct the amount needed to fund each employee's past and current service credits distributed as a level amount over the employee's remaining years of future service. If the amount attributable to three or fewer employees is more than 50 percent of the remaining costs, the unfunded costs for these employees must be spread over a period of at least five years. [IRC § 404(a)(1)(A)(ii)]

Under the normal cost method, the employer may deduct the normal cost of the plan plus the amount needed to amortize the unfunded portion of past service costs equally over ten years. [IRC § 404(a)(1)(A)(iii)]

If the contribution needed to satisfy the minimum funding requirement (see Q 8:1) exceeds the amount calculated under either of these two methods (whichever the plan adopts), the deductible limit is the minimum funding amount. [IRC § 404(a)(1)(A)(i)]

No deduction is allowed for any contribution to fund a retirement benefit in excess of any participant's annual benefit limit (see Q 12:24). [IRC § 404(j)(1)(A)] For a discussion of the per participant limitation on compensation for making tax-deductible contributions, see Question 12:14.

In any event, the deductible limit cannot exceed the full funding limitation (see Q 8:16). [IRC § 404(a)(1)(A)]

For details, see Chapter 8.

Q 12:18   How does a defined benefit plan's funding method affect its tax-deductible contributions?

The amount of deductible contributions cannot exceed the cost based on reasonable funding methods and actuarial assumptions. [IRC § 412(c)(3); Treas Reg § 1.404(a)-3(b)]

For example, a contribution calculated on the basis of an assumption that plan assets would earn interest at a rate of 5 percent was unreasonable in view of the availability of investments with a significantly higher interest rate. Further, the calculation under the normal cost method in a plan's first year of existence unreasonably failed to allocate costs between the normal cost of benefits accrued for service during the year of the contribution and the cost of benefits accrued during the year for past service, which must be amortized over ten years. [Jerome Mirza & Assocs, Ltd v United States, 882 F 2d 229 (7th Cir 1989); Custom Builders, Inc, 58 TCM 696 (1989); Ltr Ruls 9119007, 9031001]

An assumption that employees will retire at the normal retirement age specified in the plan, ignoring the fact that employees normally retire later, may be unreasonable and result in a nondeductible contribution (see Q 2:17). [Rev Rul 78-331, 1978-2 CB 158]

In a number of recent cases, however, courts have concluded that, since the assumptions used were not "substantially unreasonable" and represented the actuary's best estimate of anticipated experience under the plans based on actuarial assumptions used by similar plans, IRS was precluded from requiring a retroactive change of assumptions. [Rhoades, McKee and Boer v United States, No. 1:91:CV:540 (WD Mich 1993); Vinson & Elkins, 99 TC 9 (1992); Citrus Valley

Estates, Inc, 99 TC No. 21 (1992); Wachtell, Lipton, Rosen & Katz, 64 TCM 128 (1992)] For a discussion of these cases, see Question 8:8.

Q 12:19   Are excess amounts contributed to a defined benefit plan deductible in later years?

The excess contributions may be carried over and deducted in later years. For example, suppose that for 1992 the maximum deduction is $20,000 and the employer contributes $25,000 to the plan. There is a $5,000 carryover that is tax deductible only in a later year in which a full contribution is not made. So, if in 1993 the maximum deduction is $22,000 and the employer contributes $20,000 to the plan, $2,000 of the $5,000 carryover can be deducted for that year. [IRC § 404(a)(1)(E)]

Excess amounts contributed to a defined benefit plan (or any other qualified retirement plan) are subject to an excise tax equal to 10 percent of the nondeductible contributions (see Qs 12:8–12:10). [IRC § 4972]

Q 12:20   Are there any special limits on tax-deductible contributions if an employer maintains both a defined contribution plan and a defined benefit plan?

If no employee is covered by both plans, the regular deduction limitations apply with respect to each plan. However, if at least one employee is covered by any combination of defined contribution and defined benefit plans (see Qs 2:2, 2:3) maintained by the same employer, a special deduction limitation applies: the greater of (1) 25 percent of the aggregate compensation of all participants, or (2) the amount necessary to meet the minimum funding standard for the defined benefit plan (see Q 8:1). This limitation is applied after the regular limitations have been determined for each plan. [IRC § 404(a)(7)]

Example. Beth Corporation maintains a defined benefit plan and a money purchase pension plan on a calendar-year basis. Beth's employees participate in both plans. In 1993, Beth must make a contribution equal to 30 percent of the participants' aggregate compensation to fund both plans. The contribution to the defined benefit plan is an amount equal to 20 percent of the participants' aggregate compensation. Beth will not be able to deduct the full amount of both contributions on its 1993 income tax return, and the portion that is not deductible (5 percent of aggregate compensation) is subject to an excise tax (see Qs 12:8–12:10).

To alleviate the impact of the paired plan deduction limitation and the excise tax on nondeductible contributions, the defined contribution plan may provide that required contributions will be limited to amounts that are deductible.

Aggregate compensation includes the total compensation paid or accrued during the taxable year of all employees who are participants in either the defined benefit plan or the defined contribution plan, or both (see Q 12:14). [Treas Reg § 1.404(a)-13(a)]

If an employee is covered by both a defined contribution plan and a defined benefit plan, a special rule governs the overall benefits of the employee (see Q 6:15).

See Question 12:26 for a discussion of the family aggregation rule.

Q 12:21 Are there any other limitations on the deductibility of employer contributions?

Yes. For certain employers engaged in the production of property or the acquisition of property for resale, the uniform capitalization rules require the capitalization of a portion of contributions to various employee benefits plans, including qualified retirement plans. [IRC § 263A]

Essentially, an employer covered by the uniform capitalization rules that maintains a qualified retirement plan must first calculate its otherwise allowable deductible contribution under the generally applicable limits under Section 404 and then allocate that amount between production or inventory costs, which must be capitalized, and other costs, which are deductible. OBRA '87 repealed an exception that had exempted past service costs from the capitalization requirements. The effective date of this change generally requires that past service costs incurred after December 31, 1987, be capitalized. [IRC § 263A(a); General Explanation of TRA '86, Title VIII, D, p 513; Notice 88-86, 1988-2 CB 401; Ann 88-55, 1988-13 IRB 35]

Q 12:22   Will excess assets of an employer's overfunded defined benefit plan that are transferred to a defined contribution plan be considered taxable income to the employer?

Yes. However, the employer may deduct the amount transferred as a contribution to the defined contribution plan, subject to applicable deduction limits (see Qs 12:7, 12:16). [GCM 39744 (1988)]

Example. JCS Corporation maintains two qualified retirement plans: a defined benefit plan that is overfunded and a profit sharing plan. JCS terminates its defined benefit plan; and, after all benefits are paid to plan participants, it transfers the defined benefit plan's excess assets to the profit sharing plan. JCS deducted all of its contributions to the defined benefit plan when made. JCS must recognize income upon the transfer from the defined benefit plan to the profit sharing plan. JCS will be entitled to a deduction for the transferred funds if its contribution to the profit sharing plan during the year of the transfer and the amount of transferred funds are less than or equal to 15 percent of the compensation of plan participants.

A different result will occur if the profit sharing plan is a qualified replacement plan and the transfer from the defined benefit plan is limited to 25 percent of the excess assets. See Chapter 21 for details on plan terminations and the excise tax on reversions.

Q 12:23   Are excess amounts contributed to a combination of plans deductible?

If an amount is contributed by the employer to both a defined benefit plan and a defined contribution plan in excess of the deduction limitation (see Q 12:20), the excess contribution may be deducted in the succeeding taxable years. However, the total deduction in any succeeding year, including the contributions for that year, is limited to 25 percent of the compensation of the participants during that year. [IRC § 404(a)(7)(B); Treas Reg § 1.404(a)-13(c); Ltr Rul 9107033]

Example. Assume that in the example in Question 12:20, Beth Corporation makes its contribution to both plans on February 28, 1994. The contributions are timely for 1993 minimum funding standard purposes (see Q 8:1). The amount deductible in 1993 is only 25 percent of aggregate 1993 compensation, but the portion of the contributions not deductible in 1993 may be deductible in 1994.

Excess amounts contributed to any qualified retirement plan (or combination of plans) are subject to an excise tax equal to 10 percent of the nondeductible contributions (see Qs 12:8–12:10). [IRC § 4972]

Q 12:24   May an employer deduct contributions to provide benefits to a participant in excess of Section 415 limits?

No. The deductible limit for a contribution to a defined contribution plan (see Q 2:2) is reduced to the extent the contribution produces an annual addition in excess of the Section 415 limit for the year. Similarly, no deduction is allowed for the portion of a contribution to a defined benefit plan (see Q 2:3) to fund a benefit for any participant in excess of the annual benefit limitation for the year. For details on contribution and benefit limits, see Chapter 6. [IRC § 404(j)(1)]

In calculating the contribution to a defined benefit plan, anticipated cost-of-living increases in the allowable annual retirement benefit (see Q 6:8) cannot be taken into account before the year in which the increase first becomes effective. [IRC § 404(j)(2); Feichtinger, 80 TC 239 (1983)]

Example. SS Corporation sponsors a defined benefit plan for its only employee, Steve Smith, who is currently age 58 and has average annual compensation for plan purposes of $120,000. The plan provides an annual retirement benefit of 100 percent of compensation in the form of a straight life annuity at the normal retirement age of 65. Any portion of the company's contribution for the 1993 year that funds the excess benefit of $4,359 ($120,000 – $115,641) will not be deductible and will be subject to a 10 percent excise tax. That result is not changed by the fact that it is reasonable to project that Steve will be entitled to receive an annual benefit of $120,000 at retirement due to cost-of-living increases in the allowable annual retirement benefit.

Q 12:25   Is the employer's payment of plan expenses deductible?

Many qualified retirement plans provide that general administrative expenses may be paid from plan assets unless paid by the employer. If the employer pays the administrative fees (e.g., the fees of trustees and actuaries) directly, or indirectly by reimbursing the trust, the amounts paid are deductible under Section 162 or Section 212 to the extent that they satisfy the requirements of those sections and are not considered plan contributions. [Rev Rul 84-146, 1984-2 CB 61; Ltr Ruls 9001002, 8941010, 8941009, 8940014, 8940013]

However, brokers' commissions incurred in connection with non-recurring transactions such as the purchase and sale of plan assets, investment manager fees, and wrap fees are not separately deductible under Section 162 or Section 212. Instead, amounts paid by the employer directly to the broker or investment manager, or indirectly by payment to the trust as reimbursement for the brokers' commissions or the investment managers' fees, are treated as plan contributions and used to provide benefits. Consequently, such contributions are deductible, subject to the limits of Section 404. [Rev Rul 86-142, 1986-2 CB 60; Ltr Ruls 9124034 (modifying Ltr Rul 8941010), 9124035 (modifying Ltr Rul 8941009), 9124036 (modifying Ltr Rul 8940013), 9124037 (modifying Ltr Rul 8940014)]

Q 12:26 How does the family aggregation rule affect the employer's tax deduction?

No more than $200,000 of compensation (adjusted for inflation) for each participant may be taken into account in determining the limit on deductible contributions (see Q 12:14). In addition, the compensation of an employee who is either a 5 percent owner (see Q 3:4) or one of the ten most highly compensated employees of the employer is aggregated with the compensation of the family members of such employee, and the $200,000 limit (adjusted for inflation) is applied to the total compensation of all family members. For this purpose, the employee's family includes the employee's spouse and lineal descendants who have not attained age 19 before the end of the year. [IRC §§ 404(l), 414(q)(6)]

Example. The Mulligan Corporation of San Mateo, Inc. adopts a profit sharing plan for calendar year 1993. There are five participants—husband Kirk ($200,000), wife Cathy ($200,000), 18-year-old daughter Muffin ($30,000), 17-year-old son Sport ($20,000), and 16-year-old daughter Biscuit ($10,000). The maximum tax-deductible contribution is limited to $35,376 ($235,840 × 15%) (see Qs 12:7, 12:14), which will be allocated among the family members as follows:

Kirk	$15,381
Cathy	15,381
Muffin	2,307
Sport	1,538
Biscuit	769
Total	$35,376

If the family aggregation rule did not apply, the total contribution would be $69,000 [15% × $460,000 ($200,000 + $200,000 + $30,000 + $20,000 + $10,000)] The family aggregation rule does not apply to the annual addition limitation (see Qs 6:1, 6:27), so the total family contribution can exceed $30,000.

The reduction in the annual compensation limitation to $150,000 in 1994 (see Q 12:14) will reduce the Mulligan family's total contribution to $22,500 (15% × $150,000). However, TSB '93 (see Q 1:13) contains a provision repealing the family aggregation rule and, if enacted, will increase the Mulligan family's total contribution in 1994 to $54,000 [15% × $360,000 ($150,000 + $150,000 + $30,000 + $20,000 + $10,000)]. [TSB '93, Act § 221(c)]

Chapter 13

Taxation of Distributions

The form and time of payment of distributions from a qualified retirement plan depend primarily on the type of plan. Defined benefit plans generally pay benefits in the form of an annuity on the participant's early or normal retirement date. Defined contribution plans generally pay benefits in a single lump-sum payment upon the participant's termination of employment. Some retirement plans also permit participants to receive distributions prior to their retirement or termination of employment as in-service withdrawals or loans. This chapter discusses the tax treatment of the various forms of distribution.

Q 13:1 In general, how are distributions from qualified retirement plans taxed?

Generally, all distributions from qualified retirement plans are includible in the recipient's gross income when received. The taxation of certain types of distributions may be postponed through a tax-free rollover to an individual retirement account (IRA) or another qualified retirement plan; see Chapter 28 for more details. In some cases, favorable tax treatment may be available for a lump-sum distribution (see Q 13:4). A distribution received from a qualified retirement plan in the form of a loan will not be taxable if certain requirements are met (see Qs 13:44–13:48). [IRC §§ 72, 402]

A transfer of funds from a qualified retirement plan to the temporary administrator of a deceased participant's estate is a distribution includible in the estate's gross income in the year of receipt. [Ltr Rul 9320006]

Where an employee received a lump-sum distribution from a qualified retirement plan and, pursuant to a divorce decree, paid a portion of the distribution to the employee's former spouse, it has been ruled that the mere fact that the employee was required to pay over a portion of the distribution to the former spouse did not entitle the employee to exclude those funds from income. [Karem, 100 TC No. 34 (1993); Darby, 97 TC 51 (1991)] In another case, the court concluded that a transfer of funds from a qualified retirement plan to a holding company was a distribution to the participant who directed the transfer because the participant could not prove that the plan was a partner with the holding company or that the funds were invested on behalf of the plan. [Federated Graphics Companies, Inc, 63 TCM 3153 (1992)]

In certain instances, penalty taxes are imposed on distributions that exceed certain amounts (see Q 13:27) and on distributions that commence too early (see Qs 13:39–13:42) or too late (see Q 11:20).

Distributions to beneficiaries generally are also included in the deceased participant's estate for federal estate tax purposes. Such distributions may also be subject to penalty taxes if they exceed certain amounts (see Q 13:43).

Q 13:2 Are any distributions from qualified retirement plans income tax-free?

Yes, if the participant has an investment in the contract (also known as basis). [IRC §§ 72(b), 72(c); Guilzon, No. 92-4229 (5th Cir 1993); Shimota v United States, 21 Cls Ct 510 (1990), aff'd, 943 F 2d 1312 (Fed Cir 1991); Simmons, TCM 1993-50; Twombly, 62 TCM 597 (1991); Rev Proc 92-86, 1992-42 IRB 37]

A participant's investment in the contract or basis includes:

1. The participant's after-tax contributions to the qualified retirement plan (i.e., voluntary or mandatory contributions). [Ltr Rul 9310035]
2. PS-58 costs (see Qs 14:7, 14:13).

3. Loans from the qualified retirement plan to the participant that were treated as taxable distributions (see Qs 13:44–13:48). [Ltr Rul 9122059]

In one case, the beneficiary of a friend's qualified retirement plan death benefits had made an oral agreement to pay the friend's debts in return for being named beneficiary. The beneficiary could not deduct the friend's debts from the amount of the taxable distribution; the assumption of the debts did not constitute basis. [Ballard, 63 TCM 2748 (1992)]

Q 13:3 How are annuity payments from a qualified retirement plan taxed?

Annuity payments from a qualified retirement plan under which the participant has no investment in the contract or basis (see Q 13:2) are taxed as ordinary income in the year received by the participant or beneficiary. [IRC § 72(m)]

If a participant has basis, a portion of each distribution is considered a return of the participant's investment in the contract and is therefore not taxable. The following formula applies to determine the part of each payment that is excluded from taxable income:

$$\frac{\text{Investment in the contract}}{\text{Expected return under the annuity}} \times \text{Annual annuity payment}$$

The expected return is determined at the time the payments commence on the basis of unisex life expectancy tables. The ratio of the participant's investment in the contract to the expected return under the contract is then applied to each annuity payment to derive the nontaxable portion. [IRC §§ 72(b)(1), 72(e)(8); Treas Reg § 1.72-9; Guilzon, No. 92-4229 (5th Cir 1993); Shimota v United States, 21 Cls Ct 510 (1990), aff'd, 943 F 2d 1312 (Fed Cir 1991); Simmons, TCM 1993-50; Twombly, 62 TCM 597 (1991)]

The participant may not exclude from income an amount greater than the participant's investment in the contract. Thus, once the participant recovers the entire basis, all remaining payments are fully taxable. If the participant dies before recovering the entire investment in the contract, the unrecovered basis can be deducted on the participant's last income tax return. [IRC §§ 72(b)(2), 72(b)(3)]

Example 1. Able, an individual age 65, has a 20-year life expectancy. Able's monthly pension is $1,000, and he has basis of $24,000. The expected return is $240,000 ($1,000 × 12 × 20). The exclusion ratio is 10 percent ($24,000 ÷ $240,000), and $100 of the monthly payment (10% × $1,000) represents recovery of basis and is nontaxable. After 240 payments, 100 percent of each payment will be taxable. If Able died after 15 years, the unrecovered basis of $6,000 ($24,000 – $18,000) will be deductible on Able's last income tax return.

Instead of using the unisex life expectancy tables, a simplified safe harbor method may be used. [Notice 88-118, 1988-2 CB 450] Under the simplified method, the following table is used:

Age at annuity starting date	Number of payments
55 and under	300
56 – 60	260
61 – 65	240
66 – 70	170
71 and over	120

Example 2. If Able elected to use the simplified method, he would have the same total payments projection of $240,000 (240 × $1,000), and his exclusion ratio would still be 10 percent ($24,000 ÷ $240,000). However, if Able were 63, his exclusion ratio under the regular method would have only been 9.3 percent (expected return multiple of 21.6 × $12,000 = $259,200; $24,000 ÷ $259,200 = 9.3%).

TSB '93 (see Q 1:13) adopts the simplified method and repeals the regular method, except for an individual who has reached age 75 on the annuity starting date and has five or more years of guaranteed annuity payments. If enacted, this change will be effective if the annuity starting date is *after* 1993. [TSB '93, Act § 203]

Q 13:4   What is a lump-sum distribution?

A lump-sum distribution is a distribution from a qualified retirement plan of the balance to the credit of an employee (see Q 13:5) made within one taxable year of the recipient. The distribution must be made on account of the employee's death, attainment of age 59½, separation from service (except for self-employed individuals; see Q 29:8), or disability (self-employed individuals only). [IRC § 402(d)(4)(A); Acquisto, 62 TCM 44 (1991); Baskovich, 61 TCM 2628 (1991); Ltr Rul 9248047]

A distribution will not qualify as a lump-sum distribution unless the employee was a plan participant for at least five of the employee's taxable years prior to the year of distribution. IRS has ruled that plan participants who have their entire account balances transferred directly from an old plan to a new plan may include years of participation in both plans to satisfy the five-year participation requirement. This requirement does not apply to a beneficiary receiving a distribution after the participant's death. [IRC § 402(d)(4)(F); Prop Reg § 1.402(e)-2(e)(3); Deisenroth, 58 TCM 838 (1989); Ltr Ruls 9221045, 9114059, 9114058, 8805025]

Lump-sum distributions may qualify for favorable income tax treatment (see Q 13:13). Further, the participant (or surviving spouse) may elect to defer payment of taxes by rolling over the distribution into an IRA or another qualified retirement plan. See Chapter 28 for details.

Q 13:5 What does the term balance to the credit of an employee mean?

Balance to the credit of an employee means either the vested (nonforfeitable) account balance (see Q 9:2) that will be distributed from a defined contribution plan (see Q 2:2) or the vested (nonforfeitable) accrued benefit (see Q 9:2) that will be distributed from a defined benefit plan (see Q 2:3).

In determining whether a distribution is the balance to the credit of the employee, all qualified profit sharing plans must be aggregated, all qualified stock bonus plans must be aggregated, and all qualified pension plans (defined benefit, money purchase, and target benefit plans) must be aggregated. Because only similar plans of the employer are required to be aggregated, a distribution to the employee from a profit sharing plan may qualify as a lump-sum distribution even though the employee still has an interest in a pension plan maintained by the employer. [IRC § 402(d)(4)(C)]

Only the vested portion of an employee's account balance or accrued benefit is taken into account in determining the balance to the credit. For this purpose, amounts attributable to deductible employee contributions (see Q 13:26) are ignored. Accordingly, a partially vested employee who receives a distribution of the entire vested balance may qualify for lump-sum distribution tax treatment. However, if the employee is reemployed and is credited with additional vesting with respect to the employee's preseparation benefits, the tax benefits the employee received earlier will be recaptured. [IRC §§ 402(d)(4)(A), 402(d)(6)(B)]

The balance to the credit does not include amounts payable to an alternate payee under a qualified domestic relations order (QDRO). See Chapter 30. [IRC § 402(d)(4)(H)]

To qualify as a lump-sum distribution, the balance to the credit of the employee must be paid within one taxable year of the recipient. Thus, if more than one payment is planned, all the payments must be made within the same calendar year (most individuals are calendar-year taxpayers). However, if an individual receives lump-sum distributions from both a pension plan and a profit sharing plan of the same employer in the same taxable year, the individual must elect forward averaging treatment for both distributions or neither will qualify for forward averaging. The same rule applies if an individual receives lump-sum distributions from qualified retirement plans of different employers in the same taxable year. [IRC §§ 402(d)(4)(A), 402(d)(4)(B); Middleton v United States, Civ 91-1011-RV-M (SD Ala 1993); Fowler, 98 TC No. 34 (1992); Blyler, 67 TC 878 (1977); Ltr Rul 9003061]

If a portion of a participant's benefits in an existing qualified retirement plan (Plan A) is transferred to a new plan (Plan B) and Plan A is terminated soon thereafter, IRS has ruled that the distribution of the remaining benefits in Plan A does not constitute the balance to the credit of the employee and, therefore, is not a lump-sum distribution. [Rev Rul 72-242, 1972-1 CB 116; Ltr Rul 9139031]

Q 13:6   How are frozen plan assets treated for the balance to the credit requirement?

In order to determine whether a qualified retirement plan distribution is a lump-sum distribution (see Q 13:4), the employee's balance to the credit (see Q 13:5) in the plan must be determined.

When the distribution of plan assets invested in group annuity contracts was contingent upon their release pursuant to court authorized proceedings, IRS ruled that a plan participant's balance to the credit may be determined by excluding the portion of the participant's benefit that was attributable to amounts that were not being paid to the plan by the insurance company because of the court authorized proceedings. [IRS Special Ruling (Oct 3, 1991); Rev Rul 83-57, 1983-1 CB 92; Ltr Rul 9219042]

However, when complete distribution of plan assets could not be made within one taxable year because a portion of the plan assets was in a frozen real estate fund, IRS ruled that the distribution of all other plan assets would not be a lump-sum distribution. [Ltr Ruls 9316047, 9137046] But if a qualified retirement plan holds illiquid, nonmarketable assets, IRS has ruled that a distribution of both liquid assets and an interest in the illiquid assets can constitute a lump-sum distribution. An independent, nonqualified trust is established, and the illiquid assets are transferred to the nonqualified trust. Each participant, in addition to receiving a distribution of liquid assets, receives a transferable certificate representing the participant's interest in the nonqualified trust. This total distribution may qualify for favorable income tax treatment (see Q 13:13). [Ltr Ruls 9226066, 9108049, 9104038, 9046029, 9041075] Even though the final distribution may be a lump-sum distribution, it will not qualify for favorable income tax treatment (see Q 13:13) if the employee rolled over any prior distribution from the plan or from any plan required to be aggregated with the distributing plan (see Qs 13:5, 28:8–28:29). [IRC § 402(c)(10)]

Q 13:7 Can an employee who received installment payments later receive a lump-sum distribution from the same qualified retirement plan?

No. If an employee separates from service, receives benefits in installment payments, and then takes the balance to the employee's credit under the qualified retirement plan in a subsequent taxable year in lieu of the remaining installment payments, the payout will not qualify as a lump-sum distribution. [Prop Reg § 1.402(e)-2(d)(1)(ii)(C); Ltr Ruls 9137037, 8917020]

However, if an employee commences receiving distributions while still employed and subsequently terminates employment and receives the balance to the employee's credit under the plan within a single taxable year, IRS has ruled that the final distribution will qualify as a lump-sum distribution. [Ltr Ruls 9143078, 9052058]

Q 13:8 Are the tax benefits of a lump-sum distribution lost when an additional distribution is made in a subsequent taxable year?

Not necessarily. If a distribution constituted the balance to the credit of the employee at the time it was made and all other requirements are satisfied (see Qs 13:4, 13:5), it is treated as a lump-sum distribution even if additional amounts are credited and distributed to the employee in a later taxable year. The additional distribution, however, is not a lump-sum distribution. [Campbell, 64 TCM 1117 (1992); Prop Reg § 1.402(e)-2(d)(1)(ii)(B); Rev Rul 69-190, 1969-1 CB 131; Rev Rul 56-558, 1956-2 CB 290; Ltr Ruls 9009055, 8952010; but see Ltr Rul 9252034]

Q 13:9 What does separation from service mean?

Separation from service and termination of employment are synonymous. Separation from service does not occur when the employee continues on the same job for a different employer as a result of a corporate transaction (e.g., merger or sale) or continues on the same job for the same employer after the sale of a shareholder's shares, or when the individual's status changes from an employee and sole shareholder of a professional corporation to a sole proprietor (see Q 2:19). [GCM 39824; Burton, 99 TC No. 32 (1992); Dickson, 59 TCM 314 (1990); Edwards v Comm'r, 906 F 2d 114 (4th Cir 1990); Rev Rul 80-129, 1980-1 CB 86; Rev Rul 79-336, 1979-2 CB 187; Rev Rul 81-141, 1981-1 CB 204; Rev Rul 81-26, 1981-1 CB 200; Ltr Ruls 9243048, 8441071] However, IRS has ruled that separation from service did occur notwithstanding continued employment with another employer which had assumed certain functions performed previously by the first employer. Both employers were unrelated, ownership of both employers did not change, and the transfer of functions was not incident to an asset transfer, exchange of stock, merger, or consolidation. [Ltr Rul 9325045]

Distribution need not be made in the year of the employee's termination of employment to be considered made "on account of" the employee's separation from service. Thus, distributions from qualified retirement plans that permit distributions to be deferred until a specified age or time may qualify as lump-sum distributions. [Ltr Ruls 8949102, 8541094, 8541116]

A distribution to a self-employed individual (see Q 29:8) cannot qualify as a lump-sum distribution solely by reason of separation from service. [IRC § 402(d)(4)(A); Ltr Rul 8945053]

Q 13:10   Can a distribution from a qualified retirement plan to a disabled employee qualify as a lump-sum distribution?

No, unless the employee terminates employment at that time (see Q 13:9). On the other hand, a distribution from a qualified retirement plan to a disabled (see Q 26:39) self-employed individual (see Q 29:8) can be a lump-sum distribution. [IRC §§ 72(m)(7), 402(d)(4)(A)]

Although two courts [Wood, 590 F 2d 321 (9th Cir 1979); Masterson v United States, 478 F Supp 454 (DC Ill 1979)] have ruled that amounts paid to a disabled employee under the disability retirement provisions of a qualified retirement plan are tax-free disability payments, IRS and other courts have ruled that such amounts are taxable. [IRC § 105(c); Rev Rul 85-105, 1985-2 CB 53; Berman v Comm'r, 925 F 2d 936 (6th Cir 1991); Beisler v Comm'r, 787 F 2d 1325 (9th Cir 1986); Mabry, 50 TCM 336 (1985); Caplin v United States, 718 F 2d 544 (2d Cir 1983); Christensen v United States, 7 EBC 1110 (D Minn 1986); Gibson v United States, 643 F Supp 181 (WD Tenn 1986)]

Q 13:11   How is a lump-sum distribution from a qualified retirement plan to the beneficiary of a deceased participant taxed?

If the beneficiary is the surviving spouse of the deceased participant, the same options that would have been available to the participant (see Q 13:13) are available to the spouse. Other beneficiaries have the same options, except they cannot take advantage of a tax-free rollover to an IRA (see Q 28:6). [IRC §§ 402(c)(9), 402(d)(4)]

The five-year participation requirement (see Qs 13:4, 13:13) for electing forward averaging does not apply to distributions due to death. [IRC § 402(d)(4)(F)]

Q 13:12   Can the beneficiary of a deceased participant who received annuity payments from a qualified retirement plan receive a lump-sum distribution?

Yes. A distribution to an employee before the employee's death, in the form of annuity payments after retirement, will not prevent the employee's beneficiary from receiving a lump-sum distribution. [Prop Reg § 1.402(e)-2(d)(1)(ii)(B); Rev Rul 69-495, 1969-2 CB 100]

Q 13:13   How is a lump-sum distribution from a qualified retirement plan to an employee taxed?

An employee who has attained age 59½ and who has completed at least five years of plan participation prior to the year of distribution (see Q 13:4) has four income tax options:

1. The ordinary income portion of the distribution (amount attributable to post-1973 plan participation) might qualify for five-year forward averaging, and the rest of the distribution (amount attributable to pre-1974 plan participation) might qualify as long-term capital gain (see Qs 13:18, 13:21).

2. The entire distribution may be reported as ordinary income and might qualify for five-year forward averaging (see Q 13:18).

3. The entire distribution may be reported as ordinary income without electing five-year forward averaging. [IRC § 402(a)]

4. All or part of the distribution may be rolled over to an IRA or to another qualified retirement plan; no tax is paid on the amount rolled over; and the rest is taxed as ordinary income without the availability of electing five-year forward averaging. [IRC § 402(d)(4)(K); Barrett, 64 TCM 1080 (1992)]

For options available when the participant has not satisfied the five-year participation requirement, see Question 13:15.

An individual who receives a lump-sum distribution and who attained age 50 before January 1, 1986 is eligible to elect special tax treatment (see Q 13:14).

If more than one lump-sum distribution is received in a single taxable year, all such distributions received that year must be aggregated, and the election to use forward averaging will apply to the aggregate amount. Only one election to use forward averaging treatment is permitted after the employee has attained age 59½. If the employer maintains more than one qualified retirement plan, special rules apply (see Q 13:5). [IRC §§ 402(d)(4)(A), 402(d)(4)(B), 402(d)(4)(C); Hegarty, 63 TCM 2335 (1992)]

If enacted, TSB '93 (see Q 1:13) will repeal five-year forward averaging for taxable years beginning *after* 1993. [TSB '93, Act § 201]

Q 13:14 What special rules apply to a lump-sum distribution with regard to an individual who had attained age 50 before January 1, 1986?

If an individual who had attained age 50 before January 1, 1986 receives a lump-sum distribution, the requirement that an individual be at least age 59½ (see Q 13:13) to use forward averaging tax treatment will not apply, and the individual may elect capital gains treatment for the pre-1974 portion of the distribution (see Q 13:21). [Ltr Rul 9221045]

Forward averaging can be either five-year averaging at the rates in effect at the time of distribution or ten-year averaging at the rates in effect during 1986 (see Q 13:20). Under either alternative, capital gains will be taxed at a flat 20 percent rate.

Only one election to use forward averaging (and capital gains treatment) is permitted. Thus, an individual who makes an election under the special rule for individuals who attained age 50 before January 1, 1986 will be unable to make another election under the general rule after attaining age 59½. [TRA '86

§§ 1122(h)(5), 1122(h)(3)(A)(ii), 1122(h)(3)(B)(ii); Ltr Rul 9226076]

Even if TSB '93 is enacted (see Q 13:13), ten-year forward averaging and capital gains treatment will remain available to those individuals eligible to elect the special rules.

Q 13:15 What tax options are available when a participant does not satisfy the five-year participation requirement?

Forward averaging is not an option (see Q 13:4), so only two tax choices are available:

1. A tax-free rollover into an IRA or another qualified retirement plan (see Q 28:8), or
2. Inclusion of the distribution in gross income for the year of receipt.

Q 13:16 What portion of a lump-sum distribution is taxable?

Several adjustments that reduce the taxable amount of a lump-sum distribution are made before any tax is computed. The amount of the employee's investment in the contract (see Q 13:2) is subtracted from the distribution in computing the taxable amount. If any part of the distribution is made in employer securities, special rules apply (see Q 13:17).

If the recipient elects to use forward averaging, a minimum distribution allowance reduces the tax on relatively small distributions. The allowance, which is subtracted in computing the taxable amount of the payout, is the lesser of $10,000 or one-half of the total taxable amount of the payout, reduced by 20 percent of the excess of the total amount over $20,000. In effect, there is no minimum distribution allowance if the total taxable amount is $70,000 or more. [IRC § 402(d)(1)(C)]

> **Example.** Assume that Sallie receives a lump-sum distribution of $50,000 in cash from a qualified retirement plan, has no basis, and the entire payment is ordinary income (i.e., at-

tributable to post-1973 plan participation). The minimum distribution allowance is the lesser of $10,000 or one-half the total taxable amount. Because it is less than $25,000 (i.e., one-half of $50,000), the $10,000 figure applies. The $10,000 figure is then reduced by 20 percent of the excess of the taxable amount of the payment over $20,000, or $6,000 (20 percent of $30,000). This makes the minimum distribution allowance $4,000 and the taxable amount of the distribution $46,000.

Q 13:17   What is the tax treatment of a lump-sum distribution made in the form of employer securities?

Special rules apply to appreciated stock or other securities of the employer that are included in a lump-sum distribution. These rules apply to employer securities distributed from an employee stock ownership plan (ESOP; see Q 24:1) or from any other type of qualified retirement plan. The gain on the securities while they were held by the qualified retirement plan (the net unrealized appreciation) is not subject to tax until the securities are sold by the recipient, at which time the gain is eligible for capital gains treatment. The basis of the securities (the value when contributed to the plan) is includible in income upon distribution. If the value of the securities at the time of distribution is less than basis, the total value of the securities is taxable in accordance with the general rules applicable to lump-sum distributions. [IRC §§ 402(d)(4)(D), 402(e)(4), 402(j); Prop Reg § 1.402(a)-1(b)(1); Treas Reg § 1.402(a)-1(b)(2); Ltr Ruls 9233052, 9222055, 9222048, 9147053]

The recipient of a distribution that includes employer securities may elect to have the net unrealized appreciation included in income at the time the distribution is received rather than taxed as a capital gain at the time the securities are sold. This election is made on the recipient's tax return for the year in which the distribution is received. [IRC § 402(e)(4)(B); Notice 89-25 (Q&A 1), 1989-1 CB 662]

Q 13:18   How is the tax on a lump-sum distribution computed using the five-year averaging method?

The tax computed using the five-year averaging method is separate from and in addition to the regular income tax. To avoid double taxation, the ordinary income portion is deducted from the recipient's gross income. The tax on lump-sum distributions for which five-year averaging is elected is computed using IRS Form 4972.

There are three basic steps in computing the tax on ordinary income using five-year averaging.

Step One: Subtract the minimum distribution allowance (see Q 13:16) from the ordinary income portion of the distribution.

Step Two: Divide the net amount determined in Step One by five and compute the initial separate tax on this figure using the rate table for single individuals (regardless of the recipient's marital status).

Step Three: Multiply the initial separate tax determined in Step Two by five.

Multiple lump-sum distributions received during the taxable year are added together in computing the tax using the five-year averaging method. Only one election to use forward averaging may be made after 1986. [IRC §§ 402(d)(1)(B), 402(d)(3), 402(d)(4)(B); Ltr Rul 9231046]

If enacted, TSB '93 will repeal five-year forward averaging for taxable years beginning *after* 1993 (see Q 13:13). [TSB '93, Act § 201]

Q 13:19　How is the tax on a lump-sum distribution computed using the ten-year averaging method?

Ten-year forward averaging is available only if the participant had attained age 50 before January 1, 1986 (see Q 13:14). Since ten-year forward averaging remains keyed to the 1986 income tax rates, the following schedule (which takes into account the minimum distribution allowance; see Q 13:16) may be used to calculate the tax on a lump-sum distribution for which this averaging method is elected:

If the adjusted total taxable amount is:		The ten-year averaging tax is:		
At least	But not over	This amount	Plus this %	Of the excess over
. . . . . .	$ 20,000	Zero	5.5	Zero
$ 20,000	21,583	$ 1,100	13.2	$ 20,000
21,583	30,583	1,309	14.4	21,583
30,583	49,417	2,605	16.8	30,583
49,417	67,417	5,769	18.0	49,417
67,417	70,000	9,009	19.2	67,417
70,000	91,700	9,505	16.0	70,000
91,700	114,400	12,977	18.0	91,700
114,400	137,100	17,063	20.0	114,400
137,100	171,600	21,603	23.0	137,100
171,600	228,800	29,538	26.0	171,600
228,800	286,000	44,410	30.0	228,800
286,000	343,200	61,570	34.0	286,000
343,200	423,000	81,018	38.0	343,200
423,000	571,900	111,342	42.0	423,000
571,900	857,900	173,880	48.0	571,900
857,900	. . . . . .	311,160	50.0	857,900

Even if TSB '93 is enacted (see Q 13:13), ten-year forward averaging will remain available to those individuals eligible to elect the special rule.

Q 13:20 Is ten-year averaging always more favorable than five-year averaging?

No, because ten-year forward averaging remains keyed to the 1986 income tax rates. For a lump-sum distribution received during calendar year 1993, the ten-year averaging method is more favorable than five-year forward averaging *only if* the adjusted total taxable amount is $383,000 or less. Above $383,000, the ten-year averaging method results in a greater income tax than the five-year averaging method. This remains true even though RRA '93 (see Q 1:12), increasing top marginal rates and imposing a surtax on high-income taxpayers, has been enacted. [RRA '93 Act §§ 13201, 13202]

If the individual is not eligible to elect ten-year forward averaging (see Qs 13:13, 13:14), the five-year averaging method is always more favorable than regular ordinary income treatment, unless the individual has tax-deductible expenses to offset the income.

Q 13:21 What portion of a lump-sum distribution from a qualified retirement plan may be eligible for capital gains treatment?

Generally, no portion of a lump-sum distribution from a qualified retirement plan is eligible to be taxed under separate tax rates applicable to capital gains. [IRC § 402(a)(2) before repeal by TRA '86 § 1122(b)(1)(A)]

However, an individual who attained age 50 before January 1, 1986 may elect to treat the capital gain portion of a lump-sum distribution under the 1986 tax provisions. This means that the capital gain portion will be taxed at a flat 20 percent rate (see Q 13:14). [Ltr Rul 9221045]

An employee (or the employee's beneficiaries) who is able to treat the portion attributable to pre-1974 participation as long-term capital gain may also irrevocably elect to use forward averaging on the entire distribution. This election is significant because, as a capital gain, part of a lump-sum distribution might otherwise be subject to the alternative minimum tax. [IRC § 402(e)(4)(L) before repeal by TAMRA § 1011(A)(b)(8)(G); Brown, 93 TC 736 (1989)]

The allocation between the capital gain portion and the ordinary income portion is made on the basis of the number of months of active participation before 1974 as compared with the total number of months of plan participation. The portion of the taxable amount of a distribution that is taxed as long-term capital gain is determined as follows:

$$\text{Taxable amount} \times \frac{\text{Number of months of plan participation before 1974}}{\text{Number of months of plan participation}}$$

[IRC § 402(a)(2) before repeal by TRA '86 § 1122(b)(1)(A)]

If the qualified retirement plan from which the distribution is made had assets transferred to it from another qualified retirement plan, or if the distributee plan was merged into the plan making the distribution, the period of active participation includes both participation in the distributing plan and participation in the distributee plan. IRS has ruled that plan participants who have their entire account balances transferred directly from one plan to another may treat pre-1974 participation in the distributee plan as pre-1974 participation in the distributing plan for purposes of determining the capital gain portion of the distribution. [Ltr Ruls 9114059, 8934051, 8535116]

Q 13:22 How is the number of months of plan participation computed?

To compute an employee's number of months of participation, any part of a calendar year prior to 1974 in which the employee participated in the qualified retirement plan is counted as 12 months and any part of a calendar month after 1973 in which the employee participated in the plan is counted as one month. [Prop Reg § 1.402(e)-2(d)(3)(ii)]

Example. If an employee commenced participation in a plan on December 22, 1970 and terminated employment on May 2, 1993, the employee would have 48 (12 × 4) months of pre-1974 participation and 233 [(12 × 19) + 5] months of post-1973 participation, for a total of 281 months of participation. If the total taxable amount of the distribution received by the employee is $562,000, the capital gain portion is $96,000 (48/281 × $562,000) and the ordinary income portion is $466,000 (233/281 × $562,000).

Q 13:23 How is the distribution taxed if the retirement plan loses its qualified status?

If IRS revokes the favorable determination letter (see 15:1) previously issued to the retirement plan, the plan is no longer qualified and a distribution from the retirement plan will not be treated as a lump-sum distribution. [Treas Reg §§ 1.402(a)-1(a)(1)(ii), 1.402(a)-1(a)(1)(v), 1.402(b)-1(b); Cass v Comm'r, 774 F 2d 740 (7th Cir 1985); Baetens v Comm'r, 777 F 2d 1160 (6th Cir 1985); Woodson v Comm'r,

651 F 2d 1094 (5th Cir 1981); but see Greenwald v Comm'r, 366 F 2d 538 (2d Cir 1966)]

Q 13:24 How does a recipient elect special forward averaging for a lump-sum distribution?

Form 4972, Tax on Lump-Sum Distributions, is used for electing five-year and ten-year averaging and computing the tax. The form must be attached to the individual's tax return for the year in which the distribution is received. [Prop Reg § 1.402(e)-3(c)(2)]

Plan administrators must issue Form 1099-R (Distributions from Pensions, Annuities, Retirement or Profit-Sharing Plans, IRAs, Insurance Contracts, etc.) to let the recipient know the amount of the distribution and the breakdown between ordinary income and capital gain. This statement must be issued to the recipient by January 31 of the year following the distribution, and a copy must be sent to IRS by the end of February.

Q 13:25 Must all recipients of a single lump-sum distribution elect to use forward averaging?

No. When more than one person receives a payment qualifying as a lump-sum distribution (for example, if the payments are made to several beneficiaries on the participant's death), any eligible recipient may elect to use forward averaging even if the others do not. Similarly, any recipient may decide to treat amounts attributable to pre-1974 participation as ordinary income instead of capital gain (see Q 13:21). [TIR-1426, Dec 15, 1975; Ann 76-51, 1976-15 IRB 30]

Form 4972 (see Q 13:24) is used to make the election and compute the tax.

Q 13:26 What is the income tax treatment of distributions of deductible employee contributions made by a participant?

Distributions of deductible employee contributions (see Q 6:20), including earnings, are taxed as ordinary income in the year received. They do not qualify for forward averaging tax treatment as a lump-sum distribution (see Q 13:4) or the $5,000 income tax exemption for death benefits (see Q 14:18). If a distribution is premature (i.e., made before the participant reaches age 59½, dies, or is disabled), a penalty tax equal to 10 percent of the amount distributed may be imposed (see Qs 13:39–13:42). [IRC §§ 72(o), 72(t)]

Distributions of deductible employee contributions may be rolled over to an IRA or another qualified retirement plan on a tax-free basis. See Chapter 28.

Q 13:27   May any additional taxes be imposed on the recipient of a distribution from a qualified retirement plan?

In addition to penalty taxes imposed on distributions that commence too early (see Qs 13:39–13:42) or too late (see Q 11:20), a 15 percent excise tax is imposed on excess distributions (see Q 13:28). The individual with respect to whom the excess distributions are made is liable for this additional tax. [IRC §§ 4980A(a), 4980A(b); Temp Reg § 54.4981A-1T, Q&A a-1; Ltr Rul 9041041]

Q 13:28   What are excess distributions?

The term excess distributions means the aggregate amount of retirement plan distributions (see Q 13:29) made with respect to any individual during any calendar year to the extent that such amount exceeds either (1) $112,500 (as adjusted for inflation), or (2) $150,000. This is known as the threshold amount. The $112,500 adjusted threshold amount is used by individuals who elected the special grandfather rule, and the $150,000 unadjusted threshold amount is used by individuals who did not elect or were ineligible to elect the special grandfather rule (see Q 13:31). For 1993, the $112,500 amount has increased to $144,551. [IRC § 4980A(c)(1); Temp Reg § 54.4981A-1T, Q&A a-2, a-9; IR 93-2 (Jan 15, 1993)] For prior years, the adjusted amount was:

Year	Adjusted Amount
1992	$140,276
1991	$136,204
1990	$128,228
1989	$122,580
1988	$117,529

Example. Stella commences receiving annual distributions from three retirement plans in 1993: $90,000 from a defined benefit plan; $55,000 from a profit sharing plan; and $30,000 from an IRA. Stella did not make a grandfather election (see Q 13:31). Since Stella's total retirement distributions ($175,000) in 1993 exceed the $150,000 threshold amount by $25,000, the excise tax will be $3,750 (15% × $25,000).

See Question 13:30 regarding special treatment of lump-sum distributions.

Q 13:29 What distributions are taken into account to compute the individual's excess distributions?

All distributions from qualified retirement plans, tax-sheltered annuities, and IRAs must be taken into account in determining the amount of excess distributions for the calendar year. [Temp Reg § 54.4981A-1T, Q&A a-3, a-6]

The following amounts, whether or not they are actually distributed during the year or currently includible in income, are also included:

1. Amounts payable to an alternate payee under a QDRO (see Q 30:1) if not taxable to the alternate payee (e.g., a child);

2. Payments received under an annuity contract previously distributed from a plan;

3. P.S. 58 costs (see Qs 14:7, 14:13);

4. Loans that are treated as taxable distributions (see Qs 13:44–13:48);

5. Amounts includible in income because of plan disqualification (see Q 4:23); and

6. Net unrealized appreciation in employer securities (see Q 13:17) when distributed.

[IRC § 4980A(e); Temp Reg § 54.4981A-1T, Q&A a-5, a-8]

The following amounts, however, are not included:

1. Amounts received by any person as a result of the participant's death;

2. Amounts payable to an alternate payee under a QDRO (see Q 30:1) if taxable to the alternate payee (e.g., spouse or former spouse);

3. Amounts attributable to the individual's investment in the contract (e.g., a distribution that is excluded from gross income because it is treated as a recovery of nondeductible contributions from an IRA) (see Q 13:2);

4. Any amount rolled over into an IRA or another qualified retirement plan (see Chapter 28);

5. The distribution of an annuity contract from a plan;

6. Certain inherited benefits;

7. Any health coverage or any distribution of medical benefits provided to retirees under a pension or certain other plans to the extent that the coverage or distribution is excludible from an individual's gross income; and

8. Distributions of excess deferrals, excess contributions, excess aggregate contributions, and excess IRA contributions, including any income attributable to such amounts.

[IRC §§ 401(k)(8), 401(m)(6), 402(g)(2), 408(d)(4), 408(d)(5), 4980A(c)(2); Temp Reg § 54.4981A-1T, Q&A a-4, a-5, a-7, a-8, d-10; Ltr Ruls 9303023, 9138004, 9013008, 9013020, 9013076, 8927070]

Q 13:30 Is there a special rule regarding excess distributions when the individual receives a lump-sum distribution?

Yes. If the retirement distributions with respect to any individual include a lump-sum distribution (see Q 13:4) for which the individual elects forward averaging or capital gains tax treatment (see Qs 13:13, 13:14), the lump-sum distribution is treated separately from the other distributions and is subject to a threshold amount that is five times the threshold amount ($112,500 indexed or $150,000 unindexed) that applies to nonlump-sum distributions (see Q 13:28). [IRC § 4980A(c)(4); Temp Reg § 54.4981A-1T, Q&A c-1]

> **Example 1.** In 1993, Stephanie, age 60, receives a lump-sum distribution of $750,000 from a qualified retirement plan and elects five-year income averaging. Stephanie did not make a grandfather election (see Q 13:31) so her threshold amount is $150,000. Stephanie's distribution consists solely of an amount in the lump-sum category. Stephanie's threshold amount equals $750,000 (5 × $150,000). Because Stephanie's threshold amount ($750,000) equals the amount of her distribution from the plan ($750,000), no part of her lump-sum distribution is treated as an excess distribution subject to the 15 percent excise tax.

> **Example 2.** Assume the same facts, except that Stephanie receives an additional distribution from an IRA of $150,000. Stephanie's distributions consist of two categories: the lump-sum category (qualified retirement plan–$750,000) and the nonlump-sum category (IRA–$150,000). A separate threshold amount is subtracted from Stephanie's IRA distribution. This threshold amount equals $150,000, the same initial threshold amount that is applied against the lump-sum distribution prior to the multiplication by five. Because Stephanie's threshold amount ($150,000) equals the amount of her distribution from the IRA ($150,000), no part of her distribution from the IRA is treated as an excess distribution subject to the 15 percent excise tax.

If five-year forward averaging is repealed (see Q 13:13), the increased threshold amount will still be available if the individual receives a lump-sum distribution and makes an election; such an election may only be made once. [TSB '93, Act § 201]

Q 13:31 What is the grandfather rule?

An individual whose total benefits in all retirement plans (see Q 13:29) on August 1, 1986 (the initial grandfather amount) had a value in excess of $562,500 was eligible to elect the special grandfather rule.

The special grandfather rule permits an individual to offset distributions by the portion of the initial grandfather amount recovered during the year of distribution. The election had to be made no later than the due date of the individual's timely filed 1988 income tax return.

The $112,500 indexed threshold amount is used by individuals who elected the special grandfather rule. The $150,000 unindexed threshold amount is used by individuals who did not elect or were ineligible to elect the special grandfather rule. When the indexed $112,500 amount exceeds the unindexed $150,000, the higher indexed amount will be available to all individuals, whether or not the grandfather election was made.

If an individual elected the special grandfather rule, the individual also had to elect one of two alternative grandfather recovery methods (see Qs 13:33, 13:34) to determine the rate at which the initial grandfather amount would be recovered.

The excess distribution tax does not apply to the portion of the distribution that represents the recovery of the initial grandfather amount. The initial grandfather amount is then reduced by the amount that is treated as a recovery thereof. When an individual's initial grandfather amount has been reduced to zero, the special rule no longer applies and the entire amount of any subsequent excess distributions will be subject to the 15 percent excise tax. [IRC § 4980A(f); Temp Reg § 54.4981A-1T, Q&A b-1 through b-14 and c-1]

Q 13:32   What portion of a distribution is treated as the recovery of an individual's initial grandfather amount?

The total amount of all retirement distributions received between August 1 and December 31, 1986 is treated as a recovery of the initial grandfather amount. The portion of retirement distributions received after December 31, 1986 that is treated as a recovery of the initial grandfather amount is calculated under the method of recovery elected (see Q 13:31).

The amount that is treated as a recovery of the initial grandfather amount is then applied, on a dollar-for-dollar basis, as a reduction from the remaining unrecovered grandfather amount. After the entire initial grandfather amount has been recovered, the excise tax rules apply to excess distributions without regard to any grandfather amount.

[IRC § 4980A(f); Temp Reg § 54.4981A-1T, Q&A b-1]

Q 13:33 What is the discretionary method?

Under the discretionary method, 10 percent of the total retirement distributions (see Q 13:29) received by an individual during a calendar year will be treated as a recovery of the initial grandfather amount. This method also allows an individual to elect to accelerate the rate of recovery to 100 percent of the distributions received.

> **Example.** Susan had, as of December 31, 1986, a grandfather amount of $800,000. She made the required election to use the special grandfather rule and chose the discretionary method of recovery. In 1992, Susan received total retirement distributions of $100,000. With regard to her 1992 distributions, 10 percent, or $10,000, was treated as a recovery of her initial grandfather amount. In 1993, Susan receives $200,000 of distributions. With her 1993 tax return, Susan files Form 5329 electing to accelerate her recovery rate to 100 percent. This election will cause the entire $200,000 of 1993 retirement distributions to be treated as a recovery of Susan's initial grandfather amount. By making this election, Susan avoids the excise tax on the excess portion of her 1993 distributions because the entire $200,000 represents a recovery of a portion of her initial grandfather amount.

The acceleration election will also be effective for all years subsequent to the election. The election may be made (or revoked retroactively) on an individual's (amended) tax return. However, with respect to deceased individuals, the acceleration election may *not* be made on an amended return filed after the individual's death for a year for which a return was filed before the individual's death, but may be made after the individual's death on either the final tax return or on a return for a prior year that was *not* filed prior to the individual's death. [IRC § 4980A(f); Temp Reg § 54.4981A-1T, Q&A b-12; Ltr Rul 9246027]

If an election is made by the surviving spouse (see Q 14:26), the surviving spouse is allowed to use the deceased spouse's unrecovered grandfather amount (see Q 13:32) and is also deemed to have elected the same method of recovery that had been elected by the deceased participant (see Q 13:31). [Ltr Ruls 9311039, 9246026]

Q 13:34   What is the attained age method?

Under the attained age method, the rate of recovery is calculated based on a formula that takes into account the individual's age both on August 1, 1986 and at the end of the year in which the retirement distributions are received. The recovery rate is derived from a fraction whose numerator is the difference between the individual's attained age in months on August 1, 1986, and the individual's age in months at age 35 (420 months). The denominator of this fraction is the difference between the individual's attained age in months on December 31 of the calendar year in which the retirement distributions are received and the individual's age in months at age 35 (420 months). As a result, the rate of recovery diminishes as the individual ages. [IRC § 4980A(f); Temp Reg § 54.4981A-1T, Q&A b-13]

> **Example.** Christopher had an unrecovered grandfather amount of $1 million as of December 31, 1992. Christopher elected the special grandfather rule and the attained age method of recovery. If Christopher was born on December 1, 1944, his attained age on August 1, 1986 was 500 months. In 1993, Christopher received total distributions of $300,000. His attained age on December 31, 1993 was 589 months. Therefore, of the $300,000 distributed in 1993, $142,012 [$300,000 × [(500-420)/(589-420)]] represents a recovery of Christopher's initial grandfather amount.

Q 13:35   How is the amount of the excess distribution tax calculated when the special grandfather rule applies?

The 15 percent excise tax is applied to the amount by which the total retirement distributions received during the calendar year exceed the greater of (1) the threshold amount (see Q 13:28) applicable for the year in which the distribution is made, or (2) the initial grandfather amount recovered in that year. This means there is no tax benefit for the recovered grandfather amount up to the threshold amount. [IRC § 4980A(f); Temp Reg § 54.4981A-1T, Q&A b-4]

Example. Peter's unrecovered initial grandfather amount on December 31, 1992, is $600,000. Peter elected the discretionary method (see Q 13:33) of recovery. In 1993, Peter receives IRA distributions totaling $744,551 and makes an acceleration election (see Q 13:33). Even though the grandfather amount recovered ($600,000) is exempt from the excise tax, the remaining $144,551 is subject to the tax. The amount exempt from the excise tax is the greater of (1) the grandfather amount recovered or (2) the threshold amount, not the total of both amounts.

Q 13:36   How is the special grandfather rule applied if an individual receives both a lump-sum distribution and a nonlump-sum distribution in the same year?

If, in any calendar year, an individual receives both a lump-sum distribution and a nonlump-sum distribution, the grandfather amount will be recovered ratably from each of the two categories of distributions. The ratable recovery is required even if the distribution in one category is less than that category's threshold amount while the distribution in the other category exceeds the applicable threshold amount. [Temp Reg § 54.4981A-1T, Q&A c-1(b)]

Q 13:37   Is the excess distribution tax reduced by the early distribution tax?

Yes, the 15 percent excess distribution tax is offset by the 10 percent early distribution tax (see Q 13:39), but only to the extent that the early distribution tax is applied to the excess distribution. The early distribution tax is still applicable to the amount of the distribution that is not an excess distribution. [IRC § 4980A(b); Temp Reg § 54.4981A-1T, Q&A c-4]

Example. In 1993, Sharon, age 35, receives total distributions of $200,000. She did not elect the special grandfather rule (see Q 13:31), and her threshold amount is therefore $150,000. The excess distribution tax is $7,500 (15% × $50,000). The entire distribution is subject to an early distribution tax of $20,000 (10% × $200,000). Of that amount, $5,000 (10% × $50,000) may be offset against the excess distribution tax because $5,000 represents the early distribution tax applicable to the excess portion of the distribution.

Therefore, Sharon will owe a total of $22,500 [$20,000 + ($7,500 – $5,000)] in additional taxes on her 1993 distribution.

Q 13:38 Can a qualified retirement plan be amended to avoid the excess distribution tax?

If a plan sponsor chooses, it can amend a qualified retirement plan to limit future benefit accruals provided certain notice requirements are satisfied (see Q 9:26). [Temp Reg § 54.4981A-1T, Q&A c-2; ERISA § 204(h)]

However, a qualified retirement plan may not be amended to reduce accrued benefits in order to avoid the excess distribution tax. An amendment reducing accrued benefits generally is a violation of plan qualification requirements (see Q 9:24). [Temp Reg § 54.4981A-1T, Q&A c-3]

Q 13:39 May participants be subject to a penalty for early distribution of benefits?

Yes. The tax of an employee who participates in a qualified retirement plan is increased by 10 percent of the amount that is distributed from the plan and includible in the employee's income, unless the distribution is:

1. Made on or after the date the employee attained age 59½;

2. Made to a beneficiary (or to the estate of the employee) after the death of the employee;

3. Attributable to the employee's disability (see Q 26:39);

4. Part of a series of substantially equal periodic payments (not less frequently than annually) made for the life (or life expectancy) of the employee, or the joint lives (or joint life expectancy) of such employee and the employee's beneficiary, and that begin after the employee separates from service (see Qs 13:40, 13:41);

5. Made to an employee after separation from service and after attainment of age 55 (see Q 13:42);

6. A dividend paid with respect to certain stock held by an employee stock ownership plan (ESOP) (see Q 24:14);

7. A payment to an alternate payee pursuant to a QDRO (see Q 30:1); or

8. An amount not in excess of the total expenses deductible for the year under Section 213 by the employee (determined without regard to whether the employee itemizes deductions for the relevant taxable year).

[IRC § 72(t)]

Exceptions 5, 7, and 8 above are not applicable to a distribution from an individual retirement plan; and, for exception 4 to apply to an individual retirement plan, separation from service is not required. (For rules governing early distributions from individual retirement plans, see Q 26:39.)

The penalty tax applies only to distributions from qualified retirement plans and individual retirement plans. In one ruling, excess plan assets from a terminated plan were returned to the employer (see Q 21:48). After former participants started an action against the employer claiming that some of the excess plan assets should have been allocated to them, the employer placed some of the assets in an escrow account. Distributions from the escrow account to the former participants following settlement of the suit were not distributions from a qualified retirement plan, so the 10 percent penalty tax was not imposed. [Ltr Rul 9006055]

The 10 percent penalty tax applies only to the portion of the distribution subject to income tax and is in addition to the income tax. Thus, the 10 percent penalty tax does not apply to the portion of the distribution that is income tax-free (see Q 13:2). The penalty tax applies to a participant who made an irrevocable election to defer receipt of the distribution prior to both the effective date and the date of enactment of the penalty tax, and then received the distribution thereafter. [Bullard, TCM 1993-39; Shimota v United States, 21 Cls Ct 510 (1990), *aff'd*, 943 F 2d 1312 (Fed Cir 1991); Panos, 64 TCM 542 (1992)]

The additional tax on early distributions is treated as a penalty, not a tax, for bankruptcy law purposes. Thus, IRS does not have priority status over other creditors. [In re Cassidy, Jr, Nos. 91-1180 and 91-1244 (10th Cir 1992); but see Q 8:18]

The 10 percent penalty tax can be avoided if the early distribution qualifies for rollover treatment, and it is rolled over into another qualified plan or an IRA. See Chapter 28 for more information on rollovers.

Q 13:40 What are substantially equal periodic payments?

One of the exceptions to the 10 percent penalty tax (see Q 13:39) is for a distribution from a qualified retirement plan that commences after the employee separates from service and is part of a series of substantially equal periodic payments (not less frequently than annually) made over the life (or life expectancy) of the employee or the joint lives (or joint life expectancy) of the employee and the employee's designated beneficiary. [IRC §§ 72(t)(2)(A)(iv), 72(t)(3)(B)]

According to IRS, payments will be considered to be substantially equal periodic payments if they are made according to one of the methods set forth below.

1. Payments will be treated as satisfying this requirement if the annual payment is determined using a method that would be acceptable for purposes of calculating required minimum distributions. See Chapter 11 for details.

2. Payments will also be treated as substantially equal periodic payments if the amount to be distributed annually is determined by amortizing the employee's account balance over a number of years equal to the employee's life expectancy (or the joint life and last survivor expectancy of the employee and the employee's beneficiary) at an interest rate that does not exceed a reasonable interest rate on the date that payments commence.

   Example 1. V & S Corporation established a profit sharing plan many years ago. Vicente, age 50, has an account balance in the plan of $1,000,000 and has terminated employment. If Vicente receives $86,790 a year from the plan, the annual payments will be considered substantially equal periodic payments and will not be subject to the 10 percent penalty tax. This is because Vicente has a life expectancy of 33.1 years and amortizing $1,000,000 over 33.1 years at an interest rate of 8 percent results in an annual payment of $86,790.

3. As a third permissible method, payments will be treated as substantially equal periodic payments if the amount to be distributed annually is determined by dividing the employee's account balance by an annuity factor (the present value of an annuity of $1 per year beginning at the employee's age attained in the first distribution year and continuing for the life of the employee), with such annuity factor derived using a reasonable mortality table and an interest rate that does not exceed a reasonable interest rate on the date that payments commence.

Example 2. S & V Corporation established a money purchase pension plan many years ago. Sabine, age 50, has an account balance in the plan of $900,000 and has terminated employment. If the annuity factor for a $1 per year annuity for Sabine is 11.109 (assuming an interest rate of 8 percent and using the UP-1984 mortality table), Sabine would receive an annual distribution of $81,015 ($900,000/11.109). As substantially equal periodic payments, no 10 percent penalty tax would apply.

[Notice 89-25, 1989-1 CB 662, Q&A 12; Ltr Ruls 9310054, 9223049, 9152045, 9152044, 9152041, 9046064]

Under the above examples, the annual payment remains constant (at least until Vicente and Sabine attain age 59½; see Q 13:41). However, IRS has approved a method whereby the annual payments may increase from year to year, as illustrated in the example below. [Ltr Rul 9047043]

Example 3. In Example 2, assume that the first year of distribution was 1992 when the dollar limitation for the annual benefit under a defined benefit plan was $112,221 (see Q 6:8). In 1993, the dollar limitation increased to $115,641. In 1993, Sabine can receive an annual distribution of $83,484 ($81,015 × $115,641/$112,221).

Q 13:41   What happens if the substantially equal periodic payments are modified?

There is a special recapture provision. If the amount of the periodic payments is modified (other than by reason of death or disability) before the *later* of (1) the end of the five-year period beginning with the date of the first payment, or (2) the employee's attainment of age 59½, the 10 percent penalty tax that would have been imposed on all payments, plus interest, is imposed. [IRC § 72(t)(4)]

Example. Harriet commences receiving substantially equal annual payments from her qualified retirement plan after retirement at age 40. Harriet ceases receiving payments at age 48 after eight annual payments. The recapture tax will apply because even though Harriet has received more than five annual payments, she is not age 59½. Harriet must pay the recapture tax in the year in which she reaches age 48. The recapture amount will be 10 percent of the total of the eight annual payments. Interest will also be imposed.

Q 13:42   How does the age 55 requirement work?

If an employee receives a distribution from a qualified retirement plan after separation from service after the attainment of age 55, the 10 percent penalty tax (see Q 13:39) will not apply. IRS has ruled that both separation from service and the distribution must occur after the attainment of age 55. [IRC § 72(t)(2)(A)(v); Notice 87-13, 1987-1 CB 432, Q&A 20; Ltr Rul 9224056; but see Ltr Rul 9135060 (the employee retired at age 50) and replaced by Ltr Rul 9241063 (based on different facts)]

Example. Monroe participated in a profit sharing plan until 1991 when he retired at age 56. In 1993, at age 58, Monroe received a lump-sum distribution of his plan benefits. Since Monroe separated from service after age 55, his receipt of benefits will not be subject to the 10 percent penalty tax.

Q 13:43   May an additional estate tax be imposed at the participant's death?

Amounts accumulated in a decedent's retirement plans as of the date of death may be subject to an additional 15 percent estate tax on excess retirement accumulations (see Qs 14:21–14:29 for details).

Q 13:44   Are there any limitations on loans from qualified retirement plans?

Yes. Loans from qualified retirement plans are subject to a number of limitations and requirements (see Qs 13:45–13:48).

Even if all of the requirements are satisfied, any loan in excess of a maximum specified amount is treated as a taxable distribution. In addition, a taxable plan loan may also be subject to the early distribution tax (see Q 13:39) and the excess distribution tax (see Q 13:27). A bankruptcy court has ruled that it did not have jurisdiction to determine if plan loans were taxable distributions. [In re Somma, 585-648 (Bankr ND Ohio 1992)]

A loan from a qualified retirement plan to a participant or beneficiary is not treated as a taxable distribution to the extent the loan (when added to the outstanding balance of all other loans from the plan) does not exceed the lesser of:

1. $50,000 reduced by the excess (if any) of:

   a. The highest outstanding balance of loans from the plan during the one-year period ending on the day before the date on which such loan was made, over

   b. The outstanding balance of loans from the plan on the date such loan was made; or

2. The greater of:

   a. 50 percent of the present value of the participant's vested benefit (see Q 9:1) under the plan (determined without regard to any deductible employee contributions; see Q 6:20), or

   b. $10,000.

[IRC § 72(p)(2)(A)]

For the purpose of applying the loan limits, all qualified retirement plans maintained by the same employer and all qualified retirement plans maintained by a member of a controlled group (see Q 5:32) or an affiliated service group (see Q 29:31) are treated as one plan. [IRC § 72(p)(2)(D)]

Any amount received as a loan made under an insurance contract purchased under a qualified retirement plan is treated as a loan made from the plan. [IRC § 72(p)(5)]

Example. On April 3, 1993, Dan borrowed $40,000 from his employer's qualified retirement plan, and he repaid $30,000 on December 3, 1993. On March 6, 1994, Dan's vested interest under the plan is $150,000, and he wishes to make another loan. Until December 4, 1994, Dan can borrow only $10,000 more. Here's why:

Highest outstanding loan balance	$40,000
Balance on March 6, 1994	−10,000
Reduction in maximum loan amount	$30,000
Maximum loan amount	$50,000
Reduction	−30,000
Reduced loan limit	$20,000
Balance on March 6, 1994	−10,000
Maximum loan not a distribution	$10,000

IRS has ruled that mortgages given to plan participants under a qualified retirement plan's residential mortgage investment program would be deemed loans to the plan participants and not plan investments because over 90 percent of the persons eligible for mortgages under the program were plan participants. [Ltr Rul 9110039] IRS has also ruled that when a plan participant's account balance is transferred directly from one plan to another and the transfer includes an outstanding loan of the participant, the participant will not be considered to have received a distribution or to have renegotiated or modified the loan. [Ltr Rul 9043018; Rev Rul 67-213, 1967-2 CB 149] The rules regarding plan loans apply to both direct and indirect loans to a participant. IRS has ruled that bank loans to participants that were contingent upon the plan making deposits of plan funds in the bank equal to the amounts of the loans were indirect participant loans and, consequently, would be treated as if the plan had made the loans directly to the participants. [IRS Special Ruling (Aug 12, 1992)]

Q 13:45   Is there a maximum repayment period for a loan from a qualified retirement plan?

A loan to a participant from a qualified retirement plan must be required to be repaid within five years or it is treated as a taxable distribution at the time the loan is made. However, the five-year repayment period does not apply to a loan used to acquire any dwelling unit that within a reasonable time is to be used (determined at the time the loan is made) as the principal residence of the participant. [IRC § 72(p)(2)(B)]

The loan repayment schedule must provide for level amortization. That is, repayment must be made in substantially equal installments consisting of principal and interest and must be made not less frequently than quarterly over the term of the loan. Accordingly, the participant cannot repay the loan in one balloon payment at the end of the loan term. [IRC § 72(p)(2)(C)]

Q 13:46   Is interest paid on loans from qualified retirement plans deductible?

The deductibility of interest on a loan from a qualified retirement plan is first determined under the general rules governing the deductibility of interest. Notwithstanding the general rules, interest on plan loans is never deductible if the loan is made to a key employee (see Q 22:24), whether or not the plan is top-heavy, or if the loan is secured by elective contributions made under a 401(k) plan (see Q 23:1). [IRC §§ 72(p)(3), 163; Ltr Rul 8933019]

Q 13:47   Is it necessary to obtain spousal consent for a loan from a qualified retirement plan?

A qualified retirement plan that is subject to the automatic survivor benefit requirements (see Q 10:1) must provide that no portion of a participant's accrued benefit (see Q 9:2) may be used as security for a plan loan unless the participant's spouse consents to the loan within the 90-day period ending on the date the security agreement becomes effective. The consent must satisfy the requirements applicable to the QPSA and QJSA election procedures (see Q 10:21). However, spousal consent is not required if the accrued benefit subject to the security is $3,500 or less. [IRC § 417(a)(4); Treas Reg § 1.401(a)-20, Q&A 24]

Q 13:48 Are there any other requirements applicable to loans from qualified retirement plans?

Yes. Another set of requirements must be met to avoid a plan loan from being subject to an excise tax. An excise tax is imposed on certain prohibited transactions (e.g., loans) between a plan and a disqualified person (see Chapter 20 for details). However, an exemption is provided for any loan by a qualified retirement plan to a participant or beneficiary who is a disqualified person if the following requirements are met:

1. The loan must be available to all participants and beneficiaries on a reasonably equivalent basis;

2. Loans must not be made available to highly compensated employees (see Q 3:2) in amounts greater than the amounts made available to other employees;

3. The loan must be made in accordance with specific provisions in the plan;

4. The loan must bear a reasonable rate of interest; and

5. The loan must be adequately secured.

[IRC §§ 4975(c), 4975(d); Rev Rul 89-14, 1989-1 CB 111]

A shareholder-employee of an S corporation may not borrow from the corporation's qualified retirement plan, and the law prohibits a qualified retirement plan from lending to an owner-employee (see Q 29:9). [IRC §§ 401(a)(13), 4975(d)]

The term shareholder-employee means an individual who owns, on any day during the S corporation's taxable year, more than 5 percent of the outstanding stock of the S corporation, and includes the individual's spouse, children, grandchildren, and parents. The term owner-employee includes the individual's spouse, lineal descendants, ancestors, brothers, and sisters. [IRC §§ 1379(d) (prior to repeal), 318(a)(1), 401(c)(3), 267(c)(4)]

According to IRS, the loan may be secured by the participant's vested accrued benefit (see Qs 9:1, 9:2); but, according to DOL, no more than one-half of the vested accrued benefit may be used to secure the loan. [IRC § 401(a)(13)(A); Treas Reg § 1.401(a)-13(d)(2); DOL Reg § 2550.408b-1; DOL Advisory Opinion 89-30A]

Chapter 14

Life Insurance and Death Benefits

Although the primary purpose of a qualified retirement plan is to pay retirement benefits, the plan may also provide life insurance coverage for participants. This chapter examines the limits on life insurance coverage and the tax consequences of including insurance in a qualified retirement plan. A discussion of how death benefit payments by qualified retirement plans are taxed is also included.

Q 14:1 Must a qualified retirement plan provide a death benefit to participants?

Generally, a qualified retirement plan is not required to provide a death benefit with respect to employer contributions if the employee dies while a participant in the plan. However, in the case of married participants, a qualified retirement plan is required to provide a death benefit to the participant's surviving spouse unless an election and consent to waive such benefits have been made. [IRC §§ 401(a)(11), 411(a)(3), 417(a)]

For details on preretirement survivor annuities and joint and survivor annuities, see Chapter 10.

Q 14:2 May a qualified retirement plan provide life insurance coverage for participants?

Yes, but the primary purpose of a company's qualified retirement plan must be to pay retirement benefits to participants. Any life insurance coverage provided under the qualified retirement plan must be incidental to the provision of retirement benefits (see Q 14:4).

Q 14:3   Is a company allowed a deduction for life insurance purchased under a qualified retirement plan?

The portion of employer contributions to its qualified retirement plan that is used to purchase life insurance on behalf of plan participants is deductible.

However, if life insurance is provided under a qualified retirement plan for a self-employed individual (see Q 29:8), the cost of current life insurance protection (see Qs 14:6–14:8) is not deductible. [IRC § 404(e); Treas Reg § 1.404(e)-1A(g)]

Q 14:4   What limits apply to the amount of life insurance that can be purchased for participants under a qualified retirement plan?

The basic restriction is that the amount of life insurance coverage must be incidental to the plan's retirement benefits. [Treas Reg § 1.401-1(b)(1)]

For a defined contribution plan (see Q 2:2), life insurance coverage is considered incidental if less than 50 percent of the company's contributions to the plan on behalf of the participant is used to purchase whole life insurance, or no more than 25 percent is used to purchase term life insurance. [Rev Rul 54-51, 1954-1 CB 147; Rev Rul 57-213, 1957-1 CB 157; Rev Rul 66-143, 1966-1 CB 79; Rev Rul 69-408, 1969-2 CB 58; Rev Rul 76-353, 1976-2 CB 112]

For a defined benefit plan (see Q 2:3), life insurance coverage is generally considered incidental if the amount of the insurance does not exceed 100 times the participant's projected monthly benefit. For example, if a participant can expect a $1,000 monthly benefit, life insurance coverage of up to $100,000 can be provided for the participant under the defined benefit plan. However, life insurance coverage may exceed the 100 times limit and still be considered incidental. [Rev Rul 60-83, 1960-1 CB 157; Rev Rul 61-121, 1961-2 CB 65; Rev Rul 68-31, 1968-1 CB 151; Rev Rul 68-453, 1968-2 CB 163; Rev Rul 74-307, 1974-2 CB 126]

Q 14:5 Does the purchase of life insurance affect retirement benefits?

If part of the company's contributions to its defined contribution plan (see Q 2:2) goes toward the purchase of life insurance coverage, there may be less available for participants at retirement. This will be so if the return on the investment in life insurance is less than the return on the trust fund investments. Although retirement benefits may be reduced, death benefits will be substantially increased.

Using company contributions to pay for life insurance under a defined benefit plan (see Q 2:3) does not affect the amount of a participant's retirement benefit. However, because participants are promised a fixed level of benefits at retirement, the company may have to increase its contributions to cover any shortfall in funding for those benefits resulting from the use of company contributions to pay insurance premiums.

Q 14:6 What are the tax consequences to participants when their employer's qualified retirement plan provides life insurance protection?

The tax law allows participants to postpone payment of income taxes on retirement benefits payable to them from a qualified retirement plan. Participants pay no tax until they receive those benefits. They do, however, incur some tax cost when their employer's qualified retirement plan provides life insurance protection. Because participants receive a present benefit—current life insurance protection—they must include the value of that benefit in their gross incomes for the year in which employer contributions or trust earnings are used to pay life insurance premiums.

A participant must pay tax on the term cost of insurance protection paid for with employer contributions or trust earnings if, upon death, the proceeds of the life insurance policy on the participant's life are payable to either (1) the participant's estate or beneficiary, or (2) the trustee of the plan if the trustee is required by the plan's provisions to pay such proceeds to the participant's estate or beneficiary. [IRC § 72(m)(3)(B); Treas Reg § 1.72-16(b)]

The amount included in a participant's gross income, which is determined under special IRS tables that contain the P.S. 58 costs (see Q 14:7), is often well below the premium paid by the plan for the insurance. [Rev Rul 55-747, 1955-2 CB 228; Rev Rul 66-110, 1966-1 CB 12]

If a self-employed individual is covered by a life insurance policy under a qualified retirement plan, the individual will not be taxed with P.S. 58 costs because the cost of the current life insurance protection is not deductible to the employer (see Q 14:3). [IRC §§ 72(m)(3)(B), 404(e); Treas Reg § 1.404(e)-1A(g)]

Q 14:7 What are P.S. 58 costs?

IRS rulings set forth the method of calculating the amount of a participant's current taxable income as a result of receiving life insurance protection under a company's qualified retirement plan (see Q 14:6). [Rev Rul 55-747, 1955-2 CB 228; Rev Rul 66-110, 1966-1 CB 12]

The participant's current taxable amount is determined by applying the one-year premium term rate (the P.S. 58 rates) at the participant's age to the difference between the face amount of the policy and its cash surrender value at the end of the year.

The P.S. 58 rates are shown in the chart on page 14-5.

Example. Keren, age 35, is a participant in her company's qualified retirement plan. The plan provides Keren with a life insurance policy in the face amount of $40,000. At year end, the policy had a cash surrender value of $2,000. Keren must include $121.98 in her current taxable income [($40,000 – $2,000) multiplied by $3.21, divided by 1,000].

Q 14:8 Must the P.S. 58 rates be used to determine the cost of pure life insurance included in a participant's gross income?

No. If the insurance company's rates for individual one-year term policies available to all standard risks on an initial issue insurance basis are lower, the lower rates may be utilized. [Rev Rul 66-110, 1966-1 CB 12; Rev Rul 67-154, 1967-1 CB 11; Ltr Rul 9023044]

One-Year Term Premiums for $1,000 of Life Insurance Protection

Age	Premium	Age	Premium	Age	Premium
15	$1.27	37	$ 3.63	59	$ 19.08
16	1.38	38	3.87	60	20.73
17	1.48	39	4.14	61	22.53
18	1.52	40	4.42	62	24.50
19	1.56	41	4.73	63	26.63
20	1.61	42	5.07	64	28.98
21	1.67	43	5.44	65	31.51
22	1.73	44	5.85	66	34.28
23	1.79	45	6.30	67	37.31
24	1.86	46	6.78	68	40.59
25	1.93	47	7.32	69	44.17
26	2.02	48	7.89	70	48.06
27	2.11	49	8.53	71	52.29
28	2.20	50	9.22	72	56.89
29	2.31	51	9.97	73	61.89
30	2.43	52	10.79	74	67.33
31	2.57	53	11.69	75	73.23
32	2.70	54	12.67	76	79.63
33	2.86	55	13.74	77	86.57
34	3.02	56	14.91	78	94.09
35	3.21	57	16.18	79	102.23
36	3.41	58	17.56	80	111.04
				81	120.57

Q 14:9   Are loans from insurance policies purchased under qualified retirement plans taxable?

If a participant receives a loan from an insurance policy purchased under a qualified retirement plan (as well as any assignment or pledge of the policy), it is treated as a loan made from the plan.

Generally, such loans are not taxable. However, if the policy loan exceeds the Code limitations on loans from qualified retirement plans, the loan is treated as a taxable distribution to the participant (see Qs 13:2, 13:44–13:48). [IRC § 72(p)(5)]

Q 14:10　Who receives the proceeds from life insurance purchased under a qualified retirement plan when a participant dies before retirement?

Generally, if a participant dies while working for the company, the proceeds from life insurance purchased under a qualified retirement plan will be paid to designated beneficiaries. If the participant fails to designate a beneficiary or if the sole designated beneficiary predeceases the participant, the life insurance proceeds generally will be paid to the participant's estate in accordance with the provisions of the policy. When a widow named her daughter as beneficiary of a life insurance policy under her employer's profit sharing plan and subsequently remarried, the court ruled that the surviving spouse, and not the daughter, was entitled to the insurance proceeds. [Howard v Branham & Baker Coal Co, No. 91-5913 (6th Cir 1992)] (See Questions 10:1 through 10:32 for a discussion of the automatic survivor annuity requirements and their effect on the participant's right to designate a beneficiary.)

If there is a death benefit under the plan (other than life insurance) and there is no designated beneficiary, the provisions of the plan will determine who will receive the death benefit. [Jensen v Estate of McGowan, 101 Nev 182, 697 P 2d 1380 (1985)] In a case in which a deceased participant had not removed the former spouse as the designated beneficiary, the court ruled that ERISA preempted a state statute that purported to nullify the former spouse's right to receive the death benefit, and the beneficiary designation remained effective. [Iron Workers Mid-South Pensions Fund v Stoll, No. 91-0513 (ED La 1991)]

Q 14:11　How are proceeds from life insurance purchased under a qualified retirement plan taxed for income tax purposes?

The amount of the proceeds that is equal to the cash surrender value of the policy is included in the beneficiary's gross income. Any proceeds in excess of the cash surrender value of the insurance policy are not subject to federal income tax. However, the beneficiary's taxable amount is subject to a $5,000 death benefit exclusion and is reduced further by the P.S. 58 costs that were included in the deceased participant's gross income during such participant's lifetime (see Qs 13:2, 14:6; they are treated as a tax-free return of the participant's investment). [IRC § 101; Treas Reg § 1.72-16(b)]

If the participant's surviving spouse receives the proceeds, payment of income tax may be postponed by rolling over the taxable amount of the proceeds to an individual retirement account (IRA). In that case, the surviving spouse will not incur income tax liability until withdrawals are made from the IRA. For details on rollovers, see Chapter 28.

If all of the benefits payable under the qualified retirement plan—including the life insurance proceeds—are distributed within one taxable year, the recipient may be able to elect forward averaging income tax treatment for the entire distribution. See Chapter 13 for more details.

TSB '93 (see Q 1:13), if enacted, will repeal the $5,000 death benefit exclusion for taxable years beginning *after* 1993. [TSB '93, Act § 202]

Q 14:12 Are proceeds from life insurance purchased under a qualified retirement plan included in the participant's estate for tax purposes?

Yes. Life insurance proceeds (and other death benefits) paid under a qualified retirement plan are included in the participant's gross estate. [IRC § 2039] (See Questions 14:21 through 14:28 regarding additional estate tax liability that may apply to a deceased participant.)

Q 14:13 Can a participant recover P.S. 58 costs tax-free when qualified retirement plan benefits are distributed?

Yes. When an insurance policy purchased under a qualified retirement plan is distributed to a participant who had reported P.S. 58 costs as income (see Q 14:6), the total P.S. 58 costs that were included in gross income can be recovered tax-free from the benefits received under the plan (see Q 13:2). However, these costs can be recovered only if the original insurance policy is distributed to the employee. If the life insurance is surrendered and the cash value and investment fund are used to purchase an annuity, the P.S. 58 costs are not part of the participant's cost for the annuity because the benefits will not be provided under the same contract. However, if the participant elects an annuity settlement option under the original policy, the P.S. 58 costs are recoverable. [IRC § 72; Treas Reg § 1.72-16(b); Rev Rul 67-336, 1967-2 CB 66]

In addition, if the policy is surrendered by the plan's trustee and the cash surrender value is distributed to the participant, the participant's P.S. 58 costs are not recoverable.

Q 14:14 Are P.S. 58 costs recovered tax-free by a deceased participant's beneficiary?

Yes. P.S. 58 costs can be recovered tax-free by the beneficiary of the life insurance proceeds in the event of the participant's death (see Q 14:11). [Treas Reg § 1.72-16(c); Rev Rul 63-76, 1963-1 CB 23]

Q 14:15 What advantage does a participant gain when the company's qualified retirement plan provides life insurance protection?

By purchasing life insurance protection through the company's qualified retirement plan, the participant is able to shift a personal expense (not tax-deductible) to the plan without adverse tax consequences (see Q 14:3).

The income tax advantage of buying life insurance through the company's qualified retirement plan is even greater for a participant who could otherwise buy insurance only by paying a very high premium because of ill health. Instead of making large out-of-pocket premium payments, the participant merely includes the P.S. 58 costs (see Q 14:6) in gross income.

Q 14:16 May a qualified retirement plan purchase a life insurance policy from a plan participant or from the employer?

Generally, a prohibited transaction (see Q 20:1) occurs if there is a sale of property between a qualified retirement plan and a party in interest (see Q 20:2). Thus, a purchase by a qualified retirement plan of a life insurance policy from a plan participant or from the participant's employer would constitute a prohibited transaction. However, DOL is authorized to grant a class exemption under which a party in interest or disqualified person (see Q 20:3) who meets the requirements of the class exemption will automatically be entitled to relief from the prohibited transaction rules.

DOL has granted a class exemption so that the prohibited transaction rules do not apply to the sale of a life insurance policy to a qualified retirement plan from a plan participant on whose life the policy was issued, or from an employer, any of whose employees are covered by the plan, if:

1. The plan pays no more than the lesser of:
   a. The cash surrender value of the policy;
   b. If the plan is a defined benefit plan (see Q 2:3), the value of the participant's accrued benefit (see Q 9:2) at the time of the sale (determined under any reasonable actuarial method); or
   c. If the plan is a defined contribution plan (see Q 2:2), the value of the participant's account balance (see Q 9:2);
2. The sale does not involve any policy that is subject to a loan that the plan assumes; and
3. The sale does not contravene any provision of the plan.

The exemption is also available for plan participants who are owner-employees (see Q 29:9) or shareholder-employees (i.e., a more-than-5 percent shareholder) of an S corporation.

[PTCE 92-5 (57 FR 5019)]

Q 14:17 May a qualified retirement plan sell a life insurance policy to a plan participant or to the employer?

Generally, a prohibited transaction (see Q 20:1) occurs if there is a sale of property between a qualified retirement plan and a party in interest (see Q 20:2). Thus, a sale by a qualified retirement plan of a life insurance policy to a plan participant or to the participant's employer would constitute a prohibited transaction. However, DOL is authorized to grant a class exemption under which a party in interest or disqualified person (see Q 20:3) who meets the requirements of the class exemption will automatically be entitled to relief from the prohibited transaction rules.

DOL has granted a class exemption so that the prohibited transaction rules do not apply to the sale of a life insurance policy by a qualified retirement plan to (1) a participant under the plan; (2) a relative of the participant; (3) an employer, any of whose employees are covered by the plan; or (4) another qualified retirement plan, if:

1. The participant is the insured under the policy;

2. The relative is the beneficiary under the policy;

3. The policy would, but for the sale, be surrendered by the plan;

4. With respect to a sale of the policy to the employer, a relative, or another plan, the insured participant is first informed of the proposed sale and is given the opportunity to purchase the policy from the plan but delivers to the plan a written election not to purchase the policy and a written consent to the sale by the plan; and

5. The amount received by the plan as consideration for the sale is at least equal to the amount necessary to put the plan in the same cash position as it would have been in had it retained the policy, surrendered it, and made a distribution to the participant of the participant's vested (see Q 9:1) interest under the plan.

The exemption is also available for plan participants who are owner-employees (see Q 29:9) or shareholder-employees (i.e., a more-than-5-percent shareholder) of an S corporation.

[PTCE 92-6 (57 FR 5189)]

Q 14:18 How are death benefit payments under a qualified retirement plan taxed?

Death benefits payable under a qualified retirement plan are generally included in the deceased participant's gross estate. For the exceptions, see Question 14:19. [IRC § 2039]

The participant's beneficiary is subject to income tax on death benefit payments. The income tax treatment depends on how the beneficiary receives the death benefit payments. Forward averaging treatment may be available for a lump-sum distribution (see Q 13:11). If an annuity is purchased, ordinary income tax rates apply to amounts received under the annuity contract. A transfer of funds from a qualified retirement plan to the temporary administrator of a deceased participant's estate is a distribution includible in the estate's gross income in the year of receipt. [Ltr Rul 9320006]

Death benefit payments up to $5,000 are exempt from income tax. The $5,000 exemption is not available if the participant had a nonforfeitable right to receive the payment while the participant was alive. However, the exemption is available in any event for a lump-sum distribution. If there are two or more beneficiaries, the exemption is still $5,000 and must be apportioned between or among them. [IRC § 101(b)(2); Treas Reg §§ 1.101-2(a), 1.101-2(c); Rev Rul 71-146, 1971-1 CB 34]

TSB '93 (see Q 1:13), if enacted, will repeal the $5,000 death benefit exclusion for taxable years beginning *after* 1993. [TSB '93, Act § 202]

For rules on the taxation of life insurance proceeds, see Questions 14:11 and 14:14.

Q 14:19   Are any deceased participants entitled to an estate tax exclusion with respect to death benefit payments received from a qualified retirement plan?

Yes. The repeal of the $100,000 estate tax exclusion by TRA '84 does not apply to a participant who was receiving benefit payments under the plan prior to 1985 and who, prior to July 18, 1984, irrevocably elected the form of the benefit that the beneficiary would receive.

Furthermore, the total estate tax exclusion previously available if the participant had died before 1983 continues to apply if the participant was receiving benefit payments (i.e., was in pay status) under the plan prior to 1983, and had already irrevocably elected the form of benefit that the beneficiary would receive.

The estate tax exclusion remains available if the participant terminated employment before 1985 (in the case of the $100,000 exclusion) or 1983 (in the case of the total exclusion), irrevocably elected the form of benefit to be paid in the future, and was not in pay status as of the applicable date. [IRC § 2039; TEFRA § 245(c) as amended by TRA '84 § 525; Temp Reg § 20.2039-1T, Q&A-1; Ltr Rul 8630028] This exclusion applies only to qualified retirement plans and *not* to IRAs. [Rev Rul 92-22, 1992-1 CB 313; Ltr Ruls 9221030, 9144046; Senate Report, 1986-3 (Vol 3) CB 1019]

A participant was in pay status on the applicable date with respect to an interest in the plan if the participant irrevocably elected the form of benefit and received at least one payment under such form of benefit. [Temp Reg § 20.2039-1T, Q&A-2]

As of the applicable date, an election of the form of benefit is irrevocable if, as of such date, a written election had been made specifying the form of distribution (e.g., lump sum, annuity) and the period over which the distribution would be made (e.g., life annuity, term certain). An election is considered revocable if the form or period of the distribution could be determined or altered after the applicable date, but it will not be considered revocable just because the beneficiaries were not designated as of such date or could be changed thereafter. [Temp Reg § 20.2039-1T, Q&A-3]

Q 14:20   Is a deceased participant's estate entitled to a marital deduction for death benefit payments received by the surviving spouse from a qualified retirement plan?

A marital deduction is allowed for any property included in the deceased participant's estate that passes from the decedent to the surviving spouse. [IRC § 2056]

Death benefit payments from a qualified retirement plan to a deceased participant's surviving spouse will qualify for the marital deduction and will be deducted from the deceased participant's gross estate for estate tax purposes. This deduction will also be available if the surviving spouse receives the death benefit payments in the form of a qualified preretirement survivor annuity (see Q 10:9) and the deceased participant's executor does not elect to forgo the deduction. [IRC §§ 2039, 2056(b)(7)(C); Treas Reg § 301.9100-8; Ltr

Ruls 9245033, 9232036, 9204017, 9008003; see also Rev Rul 89-89, 1989-2 CB 231; Ltr Ruls 9052015, 9038015; but see Ltr Rul 9220007]

Q 14:21 May any additional taxes be imposed on the estate of a decedent?

The estate of a participant may be subject to an additional estate tax equal to 15 percent of the deceased participant's excess retirement accumulation (see Q 14:22). Neither the unified credit nor the credit for state death taxes allowable in the computation of the estate tax may be used to offset this additional estate tax. Further, neither the marital deduction (see Q 14:20) nor the charitable deduction for estate tax purposes is available. [IRC §§ 4980A(d)(1), 4980A(d)(2); Temp Reg § 54.4981A-1T, Q&A d-1, d-8]

Q 14:22 What is an excess retirement accumulation?

For purposes of determining the additional estate tax (see Q 14:21), an excess retirement accumulation generally means the excess (if any) of:

1. The value of the deceased participant's aggregate interests (see Q 14:23) in qualified retirement plans, tax-sheltered annuities, and IRAs as of the date of death (or, in the case of any alternate valuation election, the applicable valuation date), over
2. The present value of a single life annuity (see Q 14:24) with annual payments equal to the excess distribution threshold amount (see Q 13:28). [IRC §§ 4980A(c)(1), 4980A(d)(3); Temp Reg § 54.4981A-1T, Q&A d-2]

Q 14:23 How are the deceased participant's aggregate interests calculated?

Generally, the aggregate interests include all amounts payable to beneficiaries under any qualified retirement plan (including payments under a joint and survivor annuity or preretirement survivor annuity), tax-sheltered annuity, or IRA. [IRC § 4980A(d)(3)(A); Temp Reg § 54.4981A-1T, Q&A d-5]

However, the deceased participant's aggregate interests do *not* include (1) benefits that represent the participant's investment in the contract (e.g., P.S. 58 costs, nondeductible employee contributions, nondeductible IRA contributions); (2) amounts payable to an alternate payee spouse or former spouse pursuant to a qualified domestic relations order (QDRO) (see Qs 30:1, 30:3); (3) life insurance proceeds reduced by the cash surrender value of the policy immediately before the deceased participant's death; and (4) amounts inherited from other deceased individuals (see Q 14:29). [IRC §§ 4980A(d)(3)(A), 4980(A)(d)(4); Temp Reg § 54.4981A-1T, Q&A d-6]

Q 14:24 How is the present value of the single life annuity calculated for purposes of determining the amount of the participant's excess retirement accumulation?

The present value of the single life annuity is calculated using the applicable interest rate and mortality assumptions in effect on the date of the participant's death. [IRC §§ 4980A(d)(3)(B), 7520; Temp Reg §§ 54.4981A-1T, Q&A d-7, Treas Reg § 20.2031-7; Notice 89-60, 1989-1 CB 700; Notice 89-24, 1989-1 CB 660]

For purposes of this calculation, the amount of each annual payment under the single life annuity is equal to the greater of $150,000 (unindexed) or $112,500 (indexed). If the special grandfather rule (see Q 13:31) is applicable, each annual payment is $112,500 (indexed) even if no grandfather amount remains. For 1993, the indexed amount is $144,551. [IR 93-2 (Jan 15, 1993)] For prior years, the indexed amount was:

Year	Indexed Amount
1992	$140,276
1991	$136,204
1990	$128,228
1989	$122,580
1988	$117,529

The applicable interest rate is equal to 120 percent of the federal midterm rate rounded to the nearest .2 percent for the month in which the participant's death occurs. The applicable interest rate used to calculate present value may change each month; the mortality assumption will change at least once every ten years. [IRC § 7520]

Below is the present value of a single life annuity for ages 40 to 85 based upon an applicable 10 percent assumed interest rate (Table R(1)—single life remainder factors) and using the most current mortality table (Table 80CNSMT—mortality table based on the 1980 census):

Age at Death	Present Value Multiplier	PV/SLA at $150,000	PV/SLA at $144,551
40	9.2945	1,394,175	1,343,529
41	9.2465	1,386,975	1,336,591
42	9.1959	1,379,385	1,329,277
43	9.1424	1,371,360	1,321,543
44	9.0859	1,362,885	1,313,376
45	9.0264	1,353,960	1,304,775
46	8.9637	1,344,555	1,295,712
47	8.8978	1,334,670	1,286,186
48	8.8287	1,324,305	1,276,197
49	8.7567	1,313,505	1,265,790
50	8.6818	1,302,270	1,254,963
51	8.6037	1,290,555	1,243,673
52	8.5220	1,278,300	1,231,864
53	8.4365	1,265,475	1,219,505
54	8.3476	1,252,140	1,206,654
55	8.2550	1,238,250	1,193,269
56	8.1586	1,223,790	1,179,334
57	8.0581	1,208,715	1,164,806
58	7.9536	1,193,040	1,149,701
59	7.8449	1,176,735	1,133,988
60	7.7326	1,159,890	1,117,755
61	7.6169	1,142,535	1,101,031
62	7.4980	1,124,700	1,083,843
63	7.3760	1,106,400	1,066,208
64	7.2507	1,087,605	1,048,096
65	7.1213	1,068,195	1,029,391
66	6.9876	1,048,140	1,010,065
67	6.8492	1,027,380	990,059

Age at Death	Present Value Multiplier	PV/SLA at $150,000	PV/SLA at $144,551
68	6.7063	1,005,945	969,402
69	6.5595	983,925	948,182
70	6.4093	961,395	926,471
71	6.2564	938,460	904,369
72	6.1009	915,135	881,891
73	5.9425	891,375	858,994
74	5.7805	867,075	835,577
75	5.6144	842,160	811,567
76	5.4437	816,555	786,892
77	5.2689	790,335	761,625
78	5.0906	763,590	735,851
79	4.9103	736,545	709,789
80	4.7295	709,425	683,654
81	4.5501	682,515	657,722
82	4.3730	655,950	632,122
83	4.1993	629,895	607,013
84	4.0287	604,305	582,353
85	3.8608	579,120	558,083

To calculate the present value of a single life annuity at a different applicable interest rate, use the applicable remainder factor from Table R(1). For example, if the applicable interest rate is 9 percent, the present value multiplier for a decedent age 65 is 7.5989 [(1.0 − .31610) ÷ .09]. At a 9 percent applicable interest rate, the present value of a single life annuity for the age 65 decedent is $1,139,835 (7.5989 × $150,000) if the special grandfather rule is not applicable, or $1,098,429 (7.5989 × $144,551) if the special grandfather rule is applicable. An upward adjustment of the present value multiplier may be appropriate since the single life annuity is deemed to commence on the date of the decedent's death.

The decedent's age as of the date of death is the decedent's attained age (in whole years) as of the date of death. For example, if the decedent was born on December 23, 1927, and died on December 21, 1993, the decedent's age for purposes of valuing the single life annuity is 65. [Temp Reg § 54.4981A-1T, Q&A d-7]

Q 14:25   Is the special grandfather rule applicable in determining the amount of a deceased participant's excess retirement accumulation?

Yes. If the grandfather election (see Q 13:31) was made, the excess retirement accumulation is equal to the deceased participant's aggregate interests (see Q 14:23) minus the *greater* of (1) the unrecovered grandfather amount on the date of death or (2) the present value of a single life annuity (see Q 14:24). [IRC § 4980A(f)(2)(B); Temp Reg § 54.4981A-1T, Q&A d-3, d-4]

The unrecovered grandfather amount is the portion of the grandfather amount not previously recovered by the participant as of the date of death (see Q 13:32). [Temp Reg § 54.4981A-1T, Q&A b-11–b-14]

Q 14:26   Is there a special rule if the surviving spouse is the beneficiary of the deceased participant's aggregate interests?

Yes. If the surviving spouse is the beneficiary of at least 99 percent of the deceased participant's aggregate interests (see Q 14:23), the surviving spouse may elect to have such interests and any retirement distribution attributable to such interests treated as belonging to the surviving spouse. [IRC § 4980A(d)(5)]

If the surviving spouse makes the election, no additional estate tax will be imposed on the deceased participant's estate. However, the surviving spouse may, upon receipt of such interests, be subject to the excess distribution tax (see Q 13:27) unless the distribution is rolled over to an IRA (see Qs 28:6, 28:32). Even if the distribution is rolled over, distributions from the IRA to the surviving spouse may be subject to the excess distribution tax during the surviving spouse's lifetime and/or the excess retirement accumulation tax upon the surviving spouse's death. [Temp Reg § 54.4981A-1T, Q&A d-10]

If the election is made by the surviving spouse, the surviving spouse is allowed to use the deceased participant's unrecovered grandfather amount (see Q 13:32) and is also deemed to have elected the same method of recovery that had been elected by the deceased participant (see Qs 13:31, 13:33, 13:34). [Ltr Ruls 9311039, 9246026]

Q 14:27 Is the excess retirement accumulation tax deductible?

The additional estate tax is an administrative expense deductible either for estate tax purposes or for income tax purposes on a fiduciary income tax return if the estate or a trust is the beneficiary of the excess retirement accumulation. If the beneficiary is other than the deceased participant's estate or a trust, the tax is deductible only for estate tax purposes. [IRC §§ 642(g), 2053(c)(1)(B)]

Q 14:28 Who is liable for the excess retirement accumulation tax?

The deceased participant's estate is liable for the excise tax. [IRC § 4980(A)(d)(1)]

Additionally, the rules generally applicable for purposes of determining the apportionment of the estate tax apply to the apportionment of the excess retirement accumulation tax. The deceased participant's will or the applicable state apportionment law may provide that the estate is entitled to recover the tax. However, absent such a provision either in the will or under applicable state law, the estate is not entitled to recover the tax from the beneficiary. [Temp Reg § 54.4981A-1T, Q&A d-8A]

At least three states have estate tax apportionment laws that specifically refer to the excess retirement accumulation tax. [Cal Probate Code § 20114.5(b); NY EPTL §§ 2-1.8(a), 2-1.8(c), 2-1.8(d-1); Wash RCW § 83.110.020(2)]

Q 14:29 Whether or not the estate tax on an excess retirement accumulation is imposed, are postdeath distributions subject to the taxes on excess distributions or excess retirement accumulations?

Whether or not the additional estate tax is imposed (see Q 14:21), postdeath distributions may be disregarded for purposes of the taxes on both excess distributions and excess retirement accumulations. Thus, a beneficiary who is receiving distributions with respect to a participant after the participant's death is not required to aggregate those amounts with any other retirement distributions or accumulations except for a surviving spouse who made a spousal election (see Q 14:26). If the surviving spouse did not make a spousal election and rolled over the distribution, then postdeath distributions will be disregarded only if the surviving spouse did not commingle the rollover with any other IRA funds. [IRC § 4980A(d)(3)(A); Temp Reg § 54.4981A-1T, Q&A d-10; Ltr Ruls 9013076, 9013020, 9013008]

Chapter 15

Determination Letters

Before a company commits itself to making substantial contributions to a retirement plan, it must be certain that the plan qualifies for favorable tax treatment. This chapter discusses the procedure for submitting the retirement plan to IRS for an advance ruling on the plan's tax status.

Q 15:1   What is an IRS determination letter?

Although it is not required, an employer has the option of seeking an advance determination as to the qualified status of its retirement plan by IRS, rather than waiting for IRS to review the plan in connection with an audit. This written advance determination is called a determination letter. A favorable determination letter indicates that, in the opinion of IRS, the terms of the plan conform to the requirements of the Code. For more details, see Chapter 4. [Rev Proc 93-6, 1993-1 IRB 135; Rev Proc 91-66, 1991-2 CB 870; Rev Proc 80-30, 1980-1 CB 685]

A determination letter may also be requested when the retirement plan is amended or terminated.

Q 15:2   Is a fee charged for a request for a determination letter?

Yes. IRS charges a user fee for each request for a determination letter (as well as for letter rulings, opinion letters, and other similar rulings or determinations). The user fee program, which was to end September 30, 1990, has been extended for five years.

Each request must be accompanied by payment of the user fee (check or money order) attached to IRS Form 8717, User Fee for Employee Plan Determination Letter Request. Any determination letter request not accompanied by full payment will be returned to the applicant for resubmission. The fee is refundable only in certain situations (e.g., if IRS refuses to rule on an issue properly requested, or issues an erroneous ruling, or if the ruling issued is not responsive).

The amount of the user fee depends on the type of request and the number of plan participants. Some examples are listed below:

Determination of Qualification

Individually designed plans (Form 5300):

100 or more participants	$825
Fewer than 100 participants	$700
Adopters of master and prototype plans, volume submitter plans (Form 5307)	$125
Short amendments (Form 6406)	$125

Determination on Termination (Form 5310)

100 or more participants	$375
Fewer than 100 participants	$225

[OBRA '90 § 11319; Rev Proc 93-23, 1993-19 IRB 6; Ann 90-125, 1990-48 IRB 8]

Generally, Form 5303, Application for Determination for Collectively Bargained Plan, requires a user fee of $800 and is filed for all collectively bargained plans. However, IRS will accept requests for determination letters on Form 5307, Application for Determination for Adopters of Master or Prototype, Regional Prototype or Volume Submitter Plans, by adopters of pre-approved plans that are single-employer, collectively bargained plans and that automatically satisfy the minimum coverage requirements (see Q 5:15). The user fee in this case is $125. [Rev Proc 93-6, 1993-1 IRB 135]

Q 15:3 Must an employer apply for a determination letter?

No. However, the advantage of obtaining a favorable determination letter is that the employer is afforded some assurance that its retirement plan is qualified and will remain so if it qualifies in operation (see Q 15:4), if it is not amended (other than as may be required by IRS), and if there is no change in law. Receipt of a favorable determination letter allows the employer to make contributions to the retirement plan with the knowledge that its deductions for those contributions will most likely be allowed should IRS audit its tax returns.

See Question 4:6 for a discussion of timely filed determination letter requests and an employer's ability to recover its contributions to a disqualified retirement plan.

Q 15:4 What does the term qualifies in operation mean?

Generally, a retirement plan qualifies in operation if it is maintained according to the terms on which the favorable determination letter was issued. However, conditions may develop in operation that may jeopardize the qualification of the retirement plan. Examples of common operational features that arise after issuance of a favorable determination letter and that may adversely affect the favorable determination include the following:

- Failure to meet nondiscrimination requirements (see Q 4:9)
- Rapid turnover of lower paid employees (see Q 9:5)
- Contributions or benefits in excess of the limitations under Section 415 (see Chapter 6)
- Not providing top-heavy minimums (see Chapter 22)

Q 15:5 What are the limitations of a favorable determination letter?

A determination letter applies only to qualification requirements regarding the form of the retirement plan. For example, a determination letter does not consider whether actuarial assumptions are reasonable for funding purposes (see Qs 2:18, 8:8) or whether a specific contribution is deductible. The determination as to whether a retirement plan qualifies is made from the information in the written plan document and the supporting information submitted by the employer. Therefore, the determination letter may not be relied upon if:

1. There has been a misstatement or omission of material facts;
2. The facts subsequently developed are materially different from the facts on which the determination was made; or
3. There is a change in applicable law.

Also, the determination letter applies only to the employer and its participants on whose behalf the determination letter was issued. A determination letter may include one or more caveats that affect the scope of reliance represented by the letter (see Q 15:13).

Q 15:6   When should a retirement plan be submitted for IRS approval?

A retirement plan should be submitted for IRS approval as early as possible. Amendments needed to qualify a retirement plan can be made retroactively until the company's federal income tax return for the year is due (including extensions) or at a later time if allowed by IRS. If the retirement plan is submitted to IRS before the tax return is due, IRS will extend the time limit for amending the plan. If the retirement plan is submitted after the company's tax return is due, IRS may not allow the company to amend its plan retroactively, particularly if the changes that need to be made are significant. [IRC § 401(b); Treas Reg § 1.401(b)-1]

Qualified retirement plans must be amended to comply with the requirements of TRA '86 (and other laws) by the last day of the plan year beginning in 1994. However, the plan must comply in operation with the new rules as of each rule's effective date; and plan amendments, when made, must be retroactive to the applicable effective date (see Qs 4:6, 4:7). [Notice 92-36, 1992-2 CB 364; Ann 92-29, 1992-9 IRB 37; IRS Field Office Directive on Good-Faith Compliance (June 12, 1992); Notice 90-73, 1990-2 CB 353; Ltr Rul 9018062]

The IRS has made available an extended reliance period for certain defined contribution plans (see Q 2:2). Sponsors of individually designed (see Q 2:23) defined contribution plans, including volume submitter plans, who request a determination letter on or before

December 31, 1993 will not be required to amend their plans until the earlier of (1) the last day of the last plan year commencing prior to January 1, 1999, or (2) the date for plan amendment as set by legislation. A similar rule is applicable to employers who adopt master, prototype, or regional prototype plans submitted and approved before April 1, 1991. [Rev Proc 93-9, 1993-2 IRB]

Q 15:7 What are the filing requirements for obtaining a favorable determination letter?

Before the actual application may be filed, notice of the filing must first be given to all interested parties (see Q 15:8). The application should then be sent to the District Director of the key district (see Q 15:9) that covers the employer's principal place of business. Documents that should accompany the request include the following:

- Copies of the plan and trust
- Executed power of attorney (if the application is made on behalf of the employer)
- Employee census (Form 5302)
- IRS application Form 5300 or 5307 (for both defined benefit and defined contribution plans)
- Form 8717 and applicable user fee (see Q 15:2)
- Copy of latest favorable determination letter, if any
- Certification and demonstrations that the plan meets the requirements of TRA '86

[Rev Proc 93-6, 1993-1 IRB 135; Rev Proc 91-66, 1991-2 CB 870]

In the case of certain amendments to a retirement plan, Form 6406 may be filed as an alternative to Form 5300. The instructions to Form 6406 require that only the actual amendments, along with various explanatory information, and not the entire plan document, be included with Form 6406. Form 6406 cannot be used to request determination letters for restated plans or plans initially amended to comply with TRA '86. [Rev Proc 93-23, 1993-19 IRB 6; Rev Proc 93-6, 1993-1 IRB 135]

If an employer has adopted an interim amendment before the execution of a volume submitter, regional prototype, master, or prototype plan, Form 5300 must be submitted instead of Form 5307, *except* where:

1. The interim amendment was a simple amendment that could have been submitted on Form 6406; or

2. The interim amendment consists of an adoption agreement of an earlier version of a subsequently approved and adopted master, prototype, or regional prototype plan. [EP/EO Dallas Key District Newsletter, Winter 1992]

Form 5309, Application for Determination of Employee Stock Ownership Plan, should be filed together with Form 5300, Application for Determination for Employee Benefit Plan, (or Form 5303, if applicable) if the application relates to an employee stock ownership plan (ESOP; see Chapter 24). [Rev Proc 93-6, 1993-1 IRB 135; Rev Proc 92-60, 1992-2 CB 413]

Form 5310, Application for Determination Upon Termination, should be used when the employer intends to terminate a retirement plan. Form 6088, Distributable Benefits From Employee Pension Benefit Plans, should be included with the filing of Form 5310. Generally, IRS will not issue a determination letter with respect to the termination unless the retirement plan has been amended to meet the requirements of TRA '86 that are in effect at the time of termination. [Rev Proc 93-6, 1993-1 IRB 135; Notice 87-57, 1987-2 CB 368] However, IRS has provided some relief with respect to terminating retirement plans (see Q 21:60).

For details with regard to requesting a determination letter for an affiliated service group, see Question 29:32.

Q 15:8   What are the requirements regarding notice to employees?

All interested parties must be given notice that an application for a determination letter will be made. Generally, this means all current employees eligible to participate in the retirement plan must be notified. If that notice is given by posting or in person, it must be given not less than seven days, and not more than 21 days, before the application is filed. If notice is given by mail, it must be given not less than ten days, and not more than 24 days, before the application is filed. (The postmark date is what counts.) [IRC § 7476(b); Treas Reg §§ 1.7476-1, 1.7476-2, 601.201(o)(3)(xv); Rev Proc 93-6, 1993-1 IRB 135; Rev Proc 80-30 (§ 7.02), 1980-1 CB 685] An employer that mailed notice of an impending determination letter request to the last known address of each interested party fulfilled the notice requirement. [Halliburton Company, 64 TCM 713 (1992)]

The notice must contain the following information:

1. Brief description of the class of interested parties to whom the notice is addressed;
2. Name of plan, plan identification number, and name of plan administrator;
3. Name and identification number of the applicant;
4. Description of class of employees eligible to participate;
5. Description of the procedures for employees to submit comments to IRS or to request DOL to do so;
6. That an application for a determination letter will be sent to IRS, the address of the IRS office, and the purpose of the application (e.g., initial qualification);
7. Statement of whether IRS has ever issued a determination letter as to the qualified status of the plan; and
8. The procedure whereby certain additional information may be obtained by the interested parties. This additional information consists of:
   a. An updated copy of the plan and related trust agreement;
   b. A copy of the application;
   c. Other documents, whether sent to or from IRS in connection with this application; and
   d. Any other information that affects the rights of the interested parties.

An employer that fails to give proper notice to interested parties is barred from appealing IRS's refusal to issue a determination letter to the Tax Court. [IRC § 7476(b); Treas Reg §§ 601.201(o)(3)(xviii)–

601.201(o)(3)(xx); Rev Proc 93-6, 1993-1 IRB 135; Rev Proc 80-30, 1980-1 CB 685]

Q 15:9   Where is an application for a determination letter sent?

Seven IRS districts are designated as key districts. Each key district has a division known as the Employee Plans/Exempt Organization (EP/EO) Division. The other districts are associate districts.

The application for a determination letter with all supporting documents and forms (see Q 15:7) should be sent to the IRS key district that has jurisdiction over the employer. For example, an Albany-based employer files its application with the Brooklyn (New York) district because the Brooklyn district is the key district for Albany.

If employer is in IRS district covering:	*Send application to this key district address:*
Albany, Augusta, Boston, Brooklyn, Buffalo, Burlington, Hartford, Manhattan, Portsmouth, Providence	Internal Revenue Service EP/EO Division P.O. Box 1680, GPO Brooklyn, New York 11202
Baltimore, District of Columbia, Newark, Philadelphia, Pittsburgh, Richmond, Wilmington, any U.S. possession or foreign country	Internal Revenue Service EP/EO Division P.O. Box 17288 Baltimore, Maryland 21203
Atlanta, Birmingham, Columbia, Fort Lauderdale, Greensboro, Jackson, Jacksonville, Little Rock, Nashville, New Orleans	Internal Revenue Service EP/EO Division P.O. Box 941 Atlanta, Georgia 30370
Cincinnati, Cleveland, Detroit, Indianapolis, Louisville, Parkersburg	Internal Revenue Service EP/EO Division P.O. Box 3159 Cincinnati, Ohio 45201

Albuquerque, Austin, Cheyenne, Dallas, Denver, Houston, Oklahoma City, Phoenix, Salt Lake City, Wichita	Internal Revenue Service EP/EO Division Mail Code 4950 DAL 1100 Commerce Street Dallas, Texas 75242
Aberdeen, Chicago, Des Moines, Fargo, Helena, Milwaukee, Omaha, St. Louis, St. Paul, Springfield	Internal Revenue Service EP/EO Division 230 South Dearborn DPN 20-6 Chicago, Illinois 60604
Anchorage, Boise, Honolulu, Laguna Niguel, Las Vegas, Los Angeles, Portland, Sacramento, San Francisco, San Jose, Seattle	Internal Revenue Service EP Application EP/EO Division McCaslin Industrial Park 2 Cupania Circle Monterey Park, California 91754-7406

[Rev Proc 93-6, 1993-1 IRB 135; Instructions IRS Form 5300 revised Dec 1992; Instructions IRS Form 8717 revised May 1993]

Q 15:10 What happens to an application for a determination letter after it is sent to IRS?

After the application is stamped "received," it is reviewed by an individual known as a perfecter. The perfecter reviews the application and related documents for completeness and to ensure that it has been sent to the proper district. If the application is incomplete, it may be returned to the employer.

Once the perfecter is satisfied that the application is complete, case and file folder numbers are assigned to the application. The file folder number has nine digits; the case number has nine digits followed by the letters EP. In each instance, the first two digits reflect the district code; thus, for example, an application of a Brooklyn employer bears case and file folder numbers beginning with 11, the Brooklyn district code.

Data are then fed from the application through a computer terminal to one of the IRS Service Centers. The Service Center, in turn, performs the following two functions with those data:

1. The Service Center issues Form 4646, Deferred Compensation Plan, which is an acknowledgment to the applicant of IRS's receipt of the application. In addition to identifying data regarding the applicant, this acknowledgment contains the case and file folder numbers and the IRS control date, which starts the 270-day review period (see Q 15:11).

2. The Service Center generates preaddressed labels that are affixed to the annual reporting forms that are sent to the applicant.

The application is then either screened out for the early issuance of a favorable determination letter or winds its way through clerical functions and is assigned to a group. The group manager assigns the application to an employee plans specialist, depending on the degree of difficulty, the size of the applicant, and the workload of the specialists in the group. The application is assigned about 60 to 90 days after the control date.

The specialist reviews the application and contacts the applicant or authorized representative if additional information is needed. If everything is in order, the specialist recommends the issuance of a favorable determination letter. If the group manager agrees with the recommendation, the file is sent to the Review Staff. Not all applications receive this second level of review. Although some applications are subject to mandatory review, most are subjected to a random sampling review.

Assuming again that everything is in order and the reviewer agrees with the specialist, the district apprises the Service Center of its recommendation and a computer-generated favorable determination letter is issued to the applicant. The applicant's authorized representative receives a copy of the determination letter.

Q 15:11   How long does it take to obtain a determination letter?

Generally, a determination letter is issued within 180 days after the application is filed. Form 4646 (see Q 15:10) generally provides an estimate of the time period required to process the application (typically, 145 days.)

IRS has a maximum of 270 days to rule after it receives an application for a determination. If IRS fails to act within this period, the employer can ask the Tax Court for a favorable ruling (technically, a declaratory judgment) notwithstanding IRS's inaction (see Q 15:12).

On the other hand, IRS must wait at least 60 days after it receives the application before it can issue a determination letter. This gives IRS a chance to review any comments made by interested parties (see Q 15:8). [IRC § 7476; Rev Proc 93-6, 1993-1 IRB 135; Rev Proc 80-30, 1980-1 CB 685]

Q 15:12   What alternatives are available to an applicant if IRS proposes to issue an adverse determination letter?

Generally, IRS is inclined to issue a favorable determination letter to an applicant even if this means accepting amendments in proposed form as a basis for closing a case. There are circumstances, however, in which the applicant cannot satisfy the employee plans specialist (by amendment or otherwise) that a favorable determination letter should be issued. Three courses of action are then available to the applicant. The applicant can:

1. Request the employee plans specialist to seek technical advice from IRS's National Office;

2. Withdraw the application; or

3. Appeal the proposed adverse determination letter.

Requests for technical advice are made only when the issue involved satisfies certain criteria established by IRS. Chances of going this route are remote.

Withdrawal of an application at best restores the status quo. On occasion, withdrawal might even lead the employee plans specialist to issue an information report to the Examination Division (formerly the Audit Division) to consider selecting the employer's tax return for examination to see whether a tax deduction was claimed for the employer's contribution to the plan.

Appeal is the usual course of action. An appeal may be taken to an IRS Regional Office within time limits established by IRS. If the Appeals Officer sustains the district's position, the next appeal is to the IRS National Office. Finally, if that office sustains the district's position, the applicant must petition the Tax Court for a declaratory judgment that its retirement plan is qualified on or before the 91st day after the date of issuance of the final adverse determination. [Hamlin Development Co, TCM 1993-89] Failure to exhaust all IRS administrative remedies bars an applicant from proceeding in the Tax Court. [Joseph P Clawson, MD, Inc, PS, Profit and Pension Trusts, TCM 1993-174] However, an employer whose plan qualification request is unduly delayed by IRS is deemed to have exhausted administrative remedies. [IRC § 7476; Tipton and Kalmbach, Inc, 43 TCM 1345 (1982)]

Q 15:13 Once a favorable determination letter is issued, may IRS subsequently revoke such qualification?

Courts have generally held that in order for IRS to revoke a prior favorable determination letter, a material change of fact must have occurred since the time of the initial IRS review of the employer's retirement plan. However, the failure to amend a retirement plan on a timely basis after initial IRS approval may cause the plan to lose its qualified status (see Q 4:7). [Boggs v Comm'r, 784 F 2d 1166 (4th Cir 1986); Lansons, Inc, 622 F 2d 774 (5th Cir 1980); Mills, Mitchell & Turner, TCM 1993-99; Hamlin Development Co, TCM 1993-89; Kollipara Rajsheker, MD, Inc, 64 TCM 1153 (1992); Attardo, 62 TCM 313 (1991); Stark Truss Co, Inc, 62 TCM 169 (1991); Basch Eng'g, Inc, 59 TCM 482 (1990); Halligan, 51 TCM 1203 (1986)]

In one case, a favorable determination letter was conditioned on limiting the deduction for contributions to the retirement plan and requiring the participant to include a corresponding amount in his income; the participant, however, refused to include the amount in his income. The court found that the plan was not qualified because the participant did not comply with the conditions of the determination letter. [TCS Mfg, Inc Employees Pension Trust, 60 TCM 1312 (1990)]

Q 15:14 Will a retirement plan with disqualifying defects be disqualified?

In order to qualify, a retirement plan must meet certain requirements (see Q 4:1). A plan that does not meet these requirements both in form and operation has a disqualifying defect and may be disqualified. However, IRS has implemented three programs—the Employee Plans Closing Agreements Pilot Program (see Q 15:15), the Administrative Policy Regarding Sanctions (see Q 15:16), and the Voluntary Compliance Resolution Program (see Q 15:17)—to resolve disqualifying plan defects without the sanction of plan disqualification. [Rev Proc 92-89, 1992-2 CB 498; IRS Memoranda, Dec 21, 1990 and Mar 26, 1991]

Q 15:15 What is the Employee Plans Closing Agreements Pilot Program (CAP)?

The CAP program provides a mechanism for resolution of issues in dispute between IRS and plan sponsors where the issues would normally result in plan disqualification. The CAP program applies to both form and operational plan defects. Closing agreements will only be issued in those cases in which the plan sponsor will make (1) retroactive and prospective corrections of all plan defects, and (2) payment based on the outstanding tax liability as if the plan had been disqualified. The determination of whether to enter into a closing agreement and the amount of the tax sanction may be affected by the equities of the case. The CAP program, initiated in December, 1990, is now a permanent program.

Originally, the CAP program applied to the following four areas:

1. Failure to amend the plan timely for TEFRA, TRA '84, and REA;
2. Improper application of an integration formula;
3. Failure to apply full vesting on partial termination; and
4. Operational violation of top-heavy rules.

The CAP program has been expanded to include cases involving all qualification issues. However, the CAP program will not apply in cases where the exclusive benefit rule has been violated (see Q 4:1), where there is significant discrimination in favor of highly compensated employees (see Q 3:2), or where there are repeated, deliberate, or intentional violations. While the CAP program is designed to resolve matters at the key district office level, it is recommended that the key district consult with the National Office in cases involving 500 or more participants or more than $1,000,000 in potential tax liability. [IRS Memoranda, Oct 9, 1991 and Dec 21, 1990]

In one case, the Tax Court ruled that the taxpayer was not entitled to relief under the CAP program because the program was discretionary, may not have applied in the taxpayer's key district, and was not available as an alternative to disqualification at the time the taxpayer's plan was disqualified. [Mills, Mitchell & Turner, TCM 1993-99]

Q 15:16 What is the Administrative Policy Regarding Sanctions?

The Administrative Policy recognizes that even though a retirement plan may have an operational disqualifying defect, it may not need to be disqualified if the error is so minor that disqualification is not productive. The Administrative Policy applies only to operational defects, and no tax sanctions will be applied. An operational defect may not result in plan disqualification if the following six criteria are met:

1. The error is an isolated one;
2. There is a history of compliance;
3. Procedures to ensure compliance have been established;
4. The operational defect occurred through an oversight or mistake;
5. The dollar amount resulting from the defect is not substantial; and
6. The taxpayer makes an immediate and complete correction.

The Administrative Policy will not be available in cases involving exclusive benefit violations (see Q 4:1) and disqualification due to late statutory plan amendments (see Qs 15:13, 15:15).

[IRS Memorandum, March 26, 1991]

Q 15:17 What is the Voluntary Compliance Resolution Program (VCRP)?

VCRP permits plan sponsors to voluntarily correct operational defects in their retirement plans and to obtain a compliance statement that provides that the corrections are acceptable and that the IRS will not pursue plan disqualification.

A request for a compliance statement should be made to the National Office and contain a description of the defects, a description of the proposed method of correction, and other procedural items and supporting information. The plan sponsor must pay a fixed voluntary compliance fee that is based on the number of plan participants and amount of plan assets. The voluntary compliance fees are:

1. $500 for a plan with assets of less than $500,000, and no more than 1,000 participants.
2. $1,250 for a plan with assets of at least $500,000, and no more than 1,000 participants.
3. $5,000 for a plan with more than 1,000, but fewer than 10,000 participants.
4. $10,000 for a plan with 10,000 or more participants.

VCRP only applies to plans that have received a favorable determination letter for TEFRA, TRA '84, and REA. The program is not available in cases involving exclusive benefit violations (see Q 4:1), repeated, deliberate, or flagrant violations, or where the plan is under examination. VCRP, which was to end on December 31, 1993, has been extended until December 31, 1994.

[Rev Proc 93-36, 1993-29 IRB; Rev Proc 92-89, 1992-2 CB 498]

Chapter 16

Operating the Plan

By clearly placing the responsibility for administering a qualified retirement plan with the plan administrator, ERISA gave that role considerable significance. This chapter explains who the plan administrator is, what the plan administrator's responsibilities are, and which records must be maintained.

Q 16:1 Who is the plan administrator?

Generally, the plan administrator is a person specifically designated by the qualified retirement plan as the administrator (1) by name, (2) by reference to the person or group holding a named position, (3) by reference to a procedure for designating an administrator, or (4) by reference to the person or group charged with the specific responsibilities of plan administrator. If no person or group is designated, the employer is the administrator (in the case of a qualified retirement plan maintained by a single employer). The employer's board of directors (in the case of a corporation) may authorize a person or group to fulfill the responsibilities of administrator. In any case, if a plan administrator cannot be determined, the plan administrator is the person or persons actually responsible for control, disposition, or management of the property received by the qualified retirement plan. [ERISA § 3(16)(A); IRC § 414(g); Treas Reg § 1.414(g)]

The employer was held liable as plan administrator where the named administrator was inactive or was not solely responsible for plan administration, and where the employer retained some control over benefit decisions. [Rosen v TRW, Inc, 979 F 2d 191 (11th Cir 1992); Law v Ernst & Young, 956 F 2d 364 (1st Cir 1992)] However, where a retirement plan specifically designated an administrator, the employer, who was not the named administrator, could not be held liable for failure to provide requested information. [McKinsey v Sentry Ins, No. 92-3194 (10th Cir 1993)] (See Q 16:6.)

Q 16:2 Can officers or owners of the company function as plan administrator?

Yes. In small companies, a company officer or owner usually is designated as plan administrator. In large companies, three or more people (a committee) may be designated collectively as plan administrator.

Q 16:3 What are the basic responsibilities of the plan administrator?

The plan administrator is responsible for managing the day-to-day affairs of the qualified retirement plan. Specifically, these responsibilities include the following:

1. Hiring attorneys, accountants, consultants, and, for certain qualified retirement plans, actuaries;

2. Determining eligibility for plan participation, vesting, and accrual of benefits;

3. Advising participants or beneficiaries of their rights and settlement options;

4. Ruling on claims for benefits;

5. Directing distribution of benefits;

6. Preparing reports for IRS, DOL, and PBGC (see Chapter 17);

7. Preparing reports for participants and responding to information requests by participants (see Q 18:13); and

8. Keeping service records, benefit records, vesting records, and participant information.

Q 16:4   Which records should a plan administrator maintain?

The plan administrator is required to maintain records relating to the operation of the qualified retirement plan that will provide in sufficient detail the necessary information from which required reports (to IRS, DOL, and PBGC) may be verified, explained, or clarified. These records must be kept available for at least six years after the filing date of the reports. [ERISA § 107]

The plan administrator must also maintain records to determine the benefits due or that may become due in order to be able to report that information to any plan participant who:

1. Requests the information (but not more than once in any 12-month period);
2. Terminates service with the company; or
3. Has a break in service (see Q 5:10).

[ERISA § 209]

Thus, a plan administrator should maintain the following records:

Service: Precise records must be kept of time worked by all employees so that determinations of eligibility, vesting, or benefit accrual may be substantiated. These records have to be maintained for many years, even though a participant may have terminated employment and distributions may have been made.

Benefits: etailed records should be maintained to project benefits for highly paid participants to ensure that their benefits do not exceed the limitations provided by law. These records should also be maintained if a qualified retirement plan provides for deferred payment of benefits. For example, a participant who terminates employment at a young age might not receive benefits until a later age.

Vesting: The vesting alternatives under ERISA and the Code require calculations under specific formulas. In some cases, participants may be under different vesting schedules, requiring meticulous administrative records. For example, if a vesting schedule is changed by amendment, certain participants may elect to remain under the old vesting schedule (see Q 9:6). See also Questions 22:32 through Q 22:36 regarding vesting under top-heavy plans, which may require dual recordkeeping for vesting purposes.

Deductible employee contributions: Although no longer permitted, separate accounting for past contributions, if any, is still required (see Q 6:20).

Plan administrators are also required to retain all plan records necessary to support or validate PBGC premium payments. The records, which include actuarial calculations, must be kept for six years after the filing due date. For the consequences of a plan administrator's failure to maintain those records, see Question 16:6. [PBGC Reg § 2610.11]

Q 16:5 May the plan administrator rely on information gathered by those performing ministerial functions?

Yes, provided the plan administrator has exercised prudence in selecting and retaining these people. The plan administrator should consider whether those gathering information are competent, honest, and responsible. [DOL Reg § 2509.75-8, FR-11]

Q 16:6 What penalty is imposed for failure to comply with recordkeeping requirements?

If a plan administrator does not maintain records necessary to make required benefit status reports to participants (see Q 16:4), DOL may impose a penalty of $10 for each affected participant unless there is reasonable cause for the failure. [ERISA § 209(b)] Furthermore, a plan administrator who fails to comply with a request for information that is required to be furnished to a participant may be liable for up to $100 a day from the date of failure to comply (see Q 18:13). [ERISA § 502(c)(1)]

Also, PBGC may audit the records of a defined benefit plan covered by PBGC (see Qs 21:12, 21:13) regarding the calculation of the premium owed each year to the agency. If it is determined that the plan's records do not support the amount of unfunded vested benefits reported in the PBGC forms, PBGC will "deem" the variable-rate portion of the premium to be the maximum amount per participant ($53; see Q 21:14). [PBGC Reg § 2610.11]

Q 16:7   Is withholding required on the distribution of benefits from a retirement plan?

An eligible rollover distribution (see Q 28:8) is subject to automatic 20 percent withholding unless the distribution is transferred by a direct rollover (see Q 28:17) to an eligible retirement plan (see Q 28:16) that permits the acceptance of rollover distributions. [IRC §§ 401(a)(31), 3405(c); Temp Reg §§ 1.401(a)(31)-IT, Q&A 1(b)(1), 1.402(c)-2T, Q&A 1(b)(2), 31.3405(c)-IT, Q&A 1(a)]

Distributions other than eligible rollover distributions are subject to elective withholding provisions and are *not* subject to the mandatory 20 percent withholding. The elective withholding rules apply to both periodic payments (e.g., annuities) and nonperiodic payments (e.g., lump-sum distributions) that are not eligible rollover distributions. The option to elect out of withholding is not available if the payment is delivered outside the United States or its possessions, unless the payee certifies to the payor that the payee is not (1) a U.S. citizen or resident alien, or (2) a tax-avoiding expatriate under Section 877. [IRC §§ 3405(a), 3405(b), 3405(e); Temp Reg § 31.3405(c)-IT, Q&A 1(a); Notice 87-7, 1987-1 CB 420]

In addition to withholding, plan administrators are also subject to recordkeeping and reporting responsibilities (see Q 17:16).

Q 16:8   Is there any liability for failure to withhold income taxes?

Yes. Generally, the plan administrator (see Q 16:1) or payor will be liable for the tax that should have been withheld as well as any penalties if a taxable distribution is made from a retirement plan and the recipient of the distribution does not elect out of the withholding or if automatic withholding applies (see Q 16:7). [IRC §§ 3405(d), 6672(a); Temp Reg § 35.3405-1, G-2, G-20] With respect to an eligible rollover distribution (see Q 28:8), if the plan administrator reasonably relies on information provided by the participant, the plan administrator will not be liable for any taxes that should have been withheld solely because the distribution is paid to a plan that is not an eligible retirement plan (see Q 28:16). Although the plan administrator is not required to verify independently the accuracy of information provided by the distributee, the plan administrator's reliance on the information furnished must be reasonable. [Temp Reg § 31.3405(c)-IT Q&A 6]

Q 16:9   Which types of retirement plans are subject to the withholding rules on distributions?

All qualified and nonqualified retirement plans—including individual retirement accounts (IRAs) of any type—are subject to the general withholding rules. Only an eligible rollover distribution (see Q 28:8) is subject to automatic 20 percent withholding (see Q 16:7). [IRC § 3405]

Q 16:10   If property other than cash is distributed, how is withholding accomplished?

The plan administrator (or payor) must withhold on distributions of property even if this requires selling all or part of the property. However, the participant may remit to the administrator sufficient cash to satisfy the withholding obligation. [Temp Reg §§ 31.3405(c)-IT, Q&A 8, 35.3405-1, Q&A F-2, F-3]

Q 16:11   Is there an exception from withholding for distributions of employer securities?

Yes. The maximum amount withheld on any distribution (including any eligible rollover distribution; see Q 28:8) may not exceed the sum of the cash and the fair market value of other property (excluding employer securities) received in the distribution. If the distribution consists solely of employer securities or of employer securities and cash (not in excess of $200) in lieu of fractional shares, no amount is required to be withheld. [IRC §§ 402(e)(4)(E), 3405(e)(8); Temp Reg § 31.3405(c)-IT, Q&A 9]

Q 16:12   If the amount of an eligible rollover distribution is less than $200, must tax be withheld?

No. If the amount of the eligible rollover distribution (see Q 28:8) is less than $200, the plan administrator (see Q 16:1) need not withhold tax. However, all eligible rollover distributions received within one taxable year of the distributee under the same plan must be aggregated for purposes of determining whether the $200 floor is reached. If the plan administrator (or payor) does not know at the time of the first distribution (that is less than $200) whether there will be additional eligible rollover distributions during the year for which aggregation is required, the plan administrator need not withhold from the first distribution. If distributions are made within one taxable year under more than one plan of an employer, the plan administrator (or payor) may, but need not, aggregate distributions for purposes of determining whether the $200 floor is reached. [Temp Reg § 31.3405(c)-IT, Q&A 10]

Q 16:13 How are participant loans treated for the withholding rules?

With respect to a participant loan from a qualified retirement plan that is an offset amount (see Qs 28:12–28:14) and an eligible rollover distribution (see Q 28:8), the automatic withholding rules are applied in a manner similar to a distribution of employer securities (see Q 16:11). In other words, although the offset amount must be included in the aggregate amount that is subject to 20 percent withholding, the total amount required to be withheld from an eligible rollover distribution does not exceed the sum of the cash and the fair market value of property received by the participant, excluding any amount of the distribution that is an offset amount.

Example 1. In 1993, Julie, a participant in Kenneth Corporation's profit sharing plan, has an account balance of $10,000, of which $3,000 is represented by a plan loan secured by her account balance. Upon termination of employment in 1993, Julie elects a distribution of her entire account balance, and the outstanding loan is offset against the account balance on distribution. Julie elects a direct rollover of the distribution, and $7,000 is paid to an eligible retirement plan. When Julie's account balance was offset by the amount of the $3,000 unpaid loan balance, she received an offset amount (equivalent to $3,000) that is an eligible rollover distribution. No withholding is required on account of the distribution of the $3,000 offset amount because no cash or other property (other than the offset amount) is received by Julie from which to satisfy the withholding.

Example 2. The facts are the same as in Example 1, except that Julie elects to receive a distribution of her account balance that remains after the $3,000 offset. In this case, the amount of the distribution received by Julie is $10,000, not $3,000. Because the amount of the $3,000 offset attributable to the loan is included in determining the amount that equals 20 percent of the eligible rollover distribution received by Julie, withholding in the amount of $2,000 (20% × $10,000) is required. The $2,000 is required to be withheld from the $7,000 to be distributed to Julie in cash, so that Julie actually receives a check for $5,000.

[Notice 93-3, 1993-3 IRB 11]

Q 16:14 When are the new automatic withholding rules effective?

The new rules are applicable to eligible rollover distributions (see Q 28:8) made *after* December 31, 1992, even if the event giving rise to the distribution occurs *before* January 1, 1993 or even if the eligible rollover distribution is part of a series of payments that began *before* January 1, 1993. [Temp Reg §§ 1.401(a)(31)-1T, Q&A 1(c), 1.402(c)-2T, Q&A 1(c), 31.3405(c)-IT, Q&A 1(c)]

Example 1. Richie terminated employment with The Greatest Sandusky Corporation in 1991 but did not receive his pension plan benefits until 1993. Even though Richie's employment was terminated in 1991 (before the new rules became effective), the distribution of his benefits in 1993 is subject to the new automatic withholding rules.

Example 2. Helaine terminated employment with The Greatest Sandusky Corporation in 1989 and elected to receive her pension plan benefits in 60 equal monthly payments beginning January 1, 1990. Helaine's monthly payments, starting with the January 1, 1993 payment, are subject to the new automatic withholding rules even though the series of payments commenced before 1993.

Q 16:15 Must a recipient receive an explanation of the tax effects of a distribution from a qualified retirement plan?

The plan administrator (see Q 16:1) is required, within a reasonable time before making an eligible rollover distribution (see Q 28:8), to provide the distributee with a written explanation of the direct rollover provisions and other special tax rules. This explanation is known as the Section 402(f) Notice.

A participant's consent to a distribution is not valid unless the participant receives a notice of the participant's rights under the plan no more than 90 days and no less than 30 days prior to the annuity starting date (see Q 10:3). However, a participant may waive the 30-day requirement and, therefore, need not wait 30 days after receipt of the Section 402(f) Notice for a direct rollover (see Q 28:17) to be made if:

1. The participant is given the opportunity to consider the decision of whether or not to elect a direct rollover for at least 30 days after the notice is provided; and

2. The plan administrator provides information to the participant clearly indicating that the participant has a right to this period for making the decision.

[IRC 402(f); Temp Reg §§ 1.401(a)(31)-IT, Q&A 1(b)(2), 1.402(c)-2T, Q&A 11 through Q&A 15, 1.402(f)-2T; Notice 93-26, 1993-18 IRB]

There is a penalty of $10 for each recipient who is not given timely notice unless there is reasonable cause for the failure. [IRC § 6652(i)]

In one case, a participant could not recover money damages for failure of the plan's trustees to give notice of the rollover option upon distribution of the participant's benefits, even though the participant, because he failed to roll over the distribution, was taxed on the entire distribution. [Novak v Andersen Corp, No 91-1957MN (8th Cir 1992)]

IRS has announced that plan administrators can satisfy the notice requirement by providing each recipient of an eligible rollover distribution with a copy of the model IRS notice.

The complete model notice is lengthy, and the following is the summary portion of the notice:

SPECIAL TAX NOTICE REGARDING PLAN PAYMENTS

This notice contains information you will need before you decide how to receive your benefits from [INSERT NAME OF PLAN] (the "Plan").

SUMMARY

A payment from the Plan that is eligible for "rollover" can be taken in two ways. You can have *all or any portion* of your payment either (1) PAID IN A "DIRECT ROLLOVER" or (2) PAID TO YOU. A rollover is a payment of your Plan benefits to your individual retirement arrangement (IRA) or to another employer plan. This choice will affect the tax you owe.

If you choose a DIRECT ROLLOVER

- Your payment will not be taxed in the current year and no income tax will be withheld.

- Your payment will be made directly to your IRA or, if you choose, to another employer plan that accepts your rollover.

- Your payment will be taxed later when you take it out of the IRA or the employer plan.

If you choose to have your Plan benefits PAID TO YOU

- You will receive only 80% of the payment, because the Plan administrator is required to withhold 20% of the payment and send it to the IRS as income tax withholding to be credited against your taxes.

- Your payment will be taxed in the current year unless you roll it over. You may be able to use special tax rules that could reduce the tax you owe. However, if you receive the payment before age 59½, you also may have to pay an additional 10% tax.

- You can roll over the payment by paying it to your IRA or to another employer plan that accepts your rollover within 60 days of receiving the payment. The amount rolled over will not be taxed until you take it out of the IRA or employer plan.

- If you want to roll over 100% of the payment to an IRA or an employer plan, *you must find other money to replace the 20% that was withheld*. If you roll over only the 80% that you received, you will be taxed on the 20% that was withheld and that is not rolled over.

[Notice 92-48, 1992-2 CB 377]

Q 16:16   How should a plan administrator handle oral inquiries from participants?

Numerous questions by participants can be expected. The plan administrator can insist that inquiries be in writing unless the effect of that request is to make it difficult for participants to inquire about the plan (e.g., if the participants are not fluent in English).

The danger, of course, in responding orally to complex questions about the plan is that since there is no record of what was said, a participant may claim at a later date that the information provided by the plan administrator was misleading. Thus, the plan administrator should limit the number of individuals authorized by the plan to answer questions concerning the plan or its benefits. Such a policy should be strictly adhered to and conveyed to participants. Those authorized to answer questions should maintain a log for recording inquiries. They should also respond in writing to inquiries that they believe may affect an individual's benefits in order to have a record of what was said.

Q 16:17   May the plan administrator or trustee choose the form of distribution that will be made to a participant?

No. See Questions 10:42 through 10:51 regarding discretion with respect to distributions from a qualified retirement plan.

Q 16:18   Can innocent errors in the operation of a qualified retirement plan result in disqualification of the plan?

Yes. One qualified retirement plan, for example, was disqualified (i.e., lost its tax-favored status) after IRS determined that the plan was discriminatory because contributions had been allocated solely for the benefit of a shareholder-employee when, in fact, five additional employees were eligible for coverage. It did not matter that this situation resulted from an honest mistake. Furthermore, the company's offer to cure the discrimination retroactively was rejected. Although the Code authorizes retroactive corrections for defects in the retirement plan itself (see Q 15:6), there is no statutory authority for a retroactive correction of a mistake in the operation of the retirement plan. However, IRS has announced that it may not seek plan disqualification for operational errors under certain circumstances (see Qs 15:14–15:17). [IRC § 401(b); Myron v United States, 550 F 2d 1145 (9th Cir 1977); see also Buzzetta Constr Corp, 92 TC 641 (1989)]

Q 16:19 What is the actuary's role in administering a qualified retirement plan?

The actuary's primary function is to determine the amount needed by an employer's defined benefit plan (see Q 2:3) to pay promised retirement benefits to participants. Assumptions and methods used by the actuary are basic to the application of the minimum funding standards (see Q 8:1). The actuary is called upon to certify the amount of tax-deductible dollars the employer must contribute to its defined benefit plan.

If a defined benefit plan is not funded solely through insurance, the services of an enrolled actuary—that is, an actuary licensed to practice before the government agencies responsible for administering ERISA—are required. Some enrolled actuaries may work for insurance companies, and others may be employed by accounting firms or firms specializing in actuarial services. [ERISA §§ 3041, 3042, 3043; IRC § 7701(a)(35)]

Q 16:20 What is the trustee's role in administering a qualified retirement plan?

The trustee holds title to plan assets and is responsible for managing them unless this responsibility has been delegated to an investment manager. For details on the trustee's investment responsibilities, see Chapter 19.

Q 16:21 What is the accountant's role in administering a qualified retirement plan?

The accountant's role may entail preparing statements of plan assets, auditing the plan's books and records, and preparing reports to government agencies. A plan with 100 or more participants requires special reports by an independent qualified public accountant (see Q 17:13).

Q 16:22 Which plan officials must be bonded?

Generally, every fiduciary (anyone who has some discretionary authority or control over the plan or its assets; see Chapter 19), and anyone who handles funds or other property of the plan, must be bonded. The bond must cover at least 10 percent of the amount handled by the bonded individual; it may not be for less than $1,000 and need not be for more than $500,000. [ERISA §§ 3(21), 412]

Q 16:23 What are funds or other property for purposes of the bonding requirement?

The term funds or other property is intended to encompass all property that is or may be used as a source for the payment of benefits to plan participants. It includes property in the "nature of quick assets" (e.g., cash, checks, negotiable instruments) and property that is readily convertible into cash for distribution as benefits.

Although the term does not include permanent assets used in plan operation (land, buildings, furniture, and fixtures), land and buildings that are investments of a qualified retirement plan will be covered by the term other property. [DOL Reg § 2580.412-4]

Q 16:24 What is handling of funds?

A person handles funds or other property of a qualified retirement plan whenever that person's duties or activities are such that there is risk that the funds or other property could be lost if that person, acting alone or with others, engaged in dishonest or fraudulent conduct. Under this definition, handling is generally considered to include situations in which there is:

1. Physical contact with cash, checks, or property;
2. The power to secure physical possession of the cash, checks, or similar property;
3. The authority to cause a transfer of property such as mortgages or securities to oneself or another; or
4. Disbursement of funds or other property including the power to sign or endorse checks.

[DOL Reg § 2580.412-6]

Q 16:25   Are any fiduciaries exempt from the bonding requirements?

Yes. A bond generally is not required from:

1. A bank that is subject to federal regulation and federally insured;
2. A savings and loan association subject to federal regulation if it is the plan administrator; and
3. An insurance company that provides or underwrites, in accordance with state law, plan benefits for any plan other than one established or maintained for the insurance company's employees.

[ERISA § 412(a); DOL Reg §§ 2580.412-23 through 2580.412-32]

Q 16:26   May a party in interest provide a bond in satisfaction of the bonding requirements?

Generally, a bond may not be procured from a party in interest (see Q 20:2) or from any entity in which the qualified retirement plan or a party in interest, directly or indirectly, has any significant control or financial interest. However, a bond can be procured from a party in interest where the financial interest or control is not incompatible with an unbiased exercise of judgment. Thus, a bond may be obtained from a party in interest providing multiple services to plans. For example, if an insurance company providing life insurance for a plan is affiliated with a surety company, a bond may be obtained from the surety company. [ERISA § 412(c); DOL Reg §§ 2580.412-33 through 2580.412-36]

Q 16:27   Is bonding required for a plan with only one participant?

In the case of a qualified retirement plan covering only the owner (i.e., the shareholder or sole proprietor), or the owner and the owner's spouse, the qualified retirement plan is not subject to the bonding requirements. However, if the plan's only participant is not the owner, this exception does not apply. Furthermore, if a partnership's qualified retirement plan covers only partners (or partners and their spouses), the qualified retirement plan is not subject to the bonding requirements (see Q 19:5). [DOL Reg § 2510.3-3]

Chapter 17

Reporting to Government Agencies

Once a qualified retirement plan has been put into operation, the plan administrator has the responsibility of filing certain information returns, reports, and statements with the agencies that administer the federal pension laws: IRS, DOL, and PBGC. This chapter sets forth guidelines for the plan administrator to follow in meeting these reporting requirements.

Q 17:1 What are IRS's reporting requirements?

Each employer (subject to a limited exception—see Q 17:2) that maintains a qualified retirement plan is required to file an annual report. The annual report is commonly referred to as the Form 5500 series return/report.

The appropriate Form 5500 series return/report (Form 5500, 5500-C/R, or 5500EZ) must be filed for each qualified retirement plan (see Q 17:2) for each plan year in which the plan has assets. Therefore, the year of complete distribution of all plan assets is the last year for which a return/report must be filed (see Q 17:5). [IRC §§ 6058 and 6059]

Q 17:2   Which Form 5500 series return/report is required for a particular qualified retirement plan?

Qualified retirement plans with 100 or more participants must file Form 5500, Annual Return/Report of Employee Benefit Plan (With 100 or more participants), each year. Qualified retirement plans with less than 100 participants generally must file Form 5500-C/R, Return/Report of Employee Benefit Plan (With fewer than 100 participants). The Form 5500-C/R must be filed as Form 5500-C for the first plan year, at least once every three plan years thereafter, and for the final plan year. For the plan years that Form 5500-C is not required, Form 5500-C/R may be filed as Form 5500-R, a brief registration statement.

According to the instructions to Form 5500 and DOL regulations, if the plan has between 80 and 120 participants (inclusive) at the beginning of the plan year (year 2), the plan may file the same series of forms (Form 5500 or 5500-C/R) that it filed for the previous year (year 1). This rule appears to create an anomaly if the number of plan participants increases from below 100 in year 1 to between 100 and 120 in year 2 and subsequent years. For example, a qualified retirement plan with 95 participants in year 1 files Form 5500-C/R; and, in year 2, if the plan has 105 participants, it may again file Form 5500-C/R. Each year thereafter, if the plan has between 100 and 120 participants, it appears that the plan could file Form 5500-C/R for each such year. [DOL Reg § 2520.103-1(d); Instructions to 1992 IRS Forms 5500 and 5500-C/R]

Form 5500-C is enforcement-oriented and, according to IRS, PBGC, and DOL, "will provide the information necessary for each Agency to monitor compliance with ERISA. The 5500-R is designed to ensure that the Agencies receive annually certain minimal information to permit the continuous review of small plans." [Notice of Adoption of Revised Forms, filed with the Federal Register of July 31, 1980]

IRS has ruled that only the employer designated as plan sponsor or plan administrator (see Q 16:1) of a multiple employer plan adopted by other unrelated employers must annually file the complete Form 5500 or Form 5500-C/R, whichever is appropriate. The other unrelated employers must file Form 5500-C/R with only certain items completed. A plan is a multiple employer plan for this purpose only if the contributions of all employers are available to pay benefits to all participants. [Ltr Rul 8930050; Instructions to 1992 IRS Form 5500, § 2]

Form 5500EZ, Annual Return of One-Participant (Owners and Their Spouses) Pension Benefit Plan, may be used for certain qualified retirement plans. A one-participant plan is defined as a qualified retirement plan that covers only:

1. The owner of a business or both the owner and spouse; and the business, whether or not incorporated, is wholly owned by the owner, or both the owner and spouse; or

2. Partners (or the partners and their spouses) in a business partnership.

Form 5500EZ cannot be used if the plan sponsor is a member of an affiliated service group (see Q 29:32), controlled group of corporations (see Q 5:36), or group of businesses under common control (see Q 5:30), or if it leases employees (see Q 5:48). In addition, if the plan satisfies the coverage requirements (see Q 5:15) only when combined with another plan, Form 5500EZ cannot be used. A qualified retirement plan that cannot use Form 5500EZ must use Form 5500-C/R.

Employers with one or more one-participant plans that have total assets of $100,000 or less at the end of the plan year are not required to file any Form 5500 series return/report for the plan year. However, a one-participant plan should file Form 5500EZ for its final plan year even though the plan assets at the end of the year are less than $100,000. [Instructions to 1992 IRS Form 5500EZ]

Q 17:3   Does the plan administrator have the option of filing Form 5500-C/R as Form 5500-C annually instead of as Form 5500-R?

Yes. Plan administrators (see Q 16:1) and sponsors may file a Form 5500-C for any year in which a Form 5500-R registration statement could have been filed. If the Form 5500-C is filed, the three-year filing cycle starts again (see Q 17:2). [Instructions to 1992 IRS Form 5500-C/R]

Q 17:4 Must any special schedules accompany the employer's Form 5500 series return/report?

Yes. Schedule A (Form 5500), Insurance Information, must be attached to Forms 5500 and 5500-C/R if any benefits under the qualified retirement plan are provided by an insurance company. However, Schedule A is not needed if Form 5500EZ is filed, or if a Form 5500-C/R is filed, but the plan covers only a sole owner of a trade or business (or owner and owner's spouse) or partners (or partners and their spouses). [ERISA § 103(e); Instructions to 1992 IRS Form 5500-C/R]

Schedule B (Form 5500), Actuarial Information, must be attached to the Form 5500 series return/report of most defined benefit plans (see Q 2:3). [IRC § 6059]

Schedule C (Form 5500), Service Provider and Trustee Information, must be attached to Form 5500 to report the following:

1. Service providers receiving, directly or indirectly, $5,000 or more in compensation for services rendered to the plan during a plan year (see Instructions to IRS Form 5500 Schedule C for exceptions);
2. Trustee information; and
3. Information relating to the termination of all persons who acted as accountants, enrolled actuaries, insurance carriers, custodians, administrators, investment managers, and trustees of the plan during the plan year.

[Instructions to 1992 Schedule C to IRS Form 5500]

Schedule E (Form 5500), ESOP Annual Information, must be completed by an employer or plan administrator (see Q 16:1) of a qualified retirement plan that includes employee stock ownership plan (ESOP) benefits (see Q 24:1). If applicable, the completed Schedule E must be filed as an attachment to Form 5500, 5500-C/R, or 5500EZ . [Instructions to 1992 Schedule E to IRS Form 5500]

Schedule G (Form 5500), Financial Schedules, must be attached to Form 5500 for plan years beginning in 1993 to report certain investment information. Schedule G was optional for 1992. [Instructions to 1992 IRS Form 5500]

Schedule P (Form 5500), Annual Return of Fiduciary of Employee Benefit Trust, may be completed by a fiduciary (trustee or custodian) and filed as an attachment to Form 5500, 5500-C/R, or 5500EZ. It is strongly recommended that Schedule P be filed because it starts the running of the statute of limitations under Section 6501(a) for the trust (see Q 17:11). [Instructions to 1992 Schedule P to IRS Form 5500]

Schedule SSA (Form 5500), Annual Registration Statement Identifying Separated Participants With Deferred Vested Benefits, is used to inform IRS of plan participants who separated from service but were not paid retirement benefits. The Instructions to the 1992 IRS Form 5500 Schedule SSA describe when a separated participant must be reported on Schedule SSA. [IRC § 6057]

Q 17:5   When is a Form 5500 series return/report due?

Unless an extension is granted (see Qs 17:6, 17:7), the appropriate Form 5500 series return/report is due by the last day of the seventh month following the close of the plan year (July 31 for calendar-year plans). Note that the due date relates to the plan year and not to the employer's taxable year. [ERISA § 104]

Example. Just-In Corporation files its federal income tax return on a calendar-year basis. Just-In maintains a qualified retirement plan with a plan year end of January 31. For the plan year ending January 31, 1994, the Form 5500 series return/report is due August 31, 1994.

For a short plan year, the Form 5500 series return/report is due by the last day of the seventh month after the short plan year ends. A short plan year ends on the date of a change in a plan's accounting period or upon the complete distribution of assets with respect to a plan termination (see Chapter 21). If a current Form 5500 series return/report is not available before the due date for the short plan year return, the latest form available should be used and the date printed on the return should be changed to the current year. In addition, the dates the short plan year began and ended should be included on the return. [Instructions to 1992 IRS Forms 5500, 5500-C/R, 5500EZ; EP/EO Brooklyn Key District Newsletter, January 1993]

Q 17:6   May the due date for filing a Form 5500 series return/report be extended?

Yes. An extension of up to 2½ months may be granted for filing the Form 5500 series return/report. Form 5558, Application for Extension of Time to File Certain Employee Plan Returns, must be filed in sufficient time before the regular due date to permit IRS to consider and act on the application. A detailed statement of the reason for an extension must be attached to the application. (See Q 17:7.)

Q 17:7   Is the extension of time for filing the Form 5500 series return/report ever automatic?

Yes. An automatic extension of the due date for filing is available to an employer if all of the following conditions are met:

1. The plan year coincides with the employer's taxable year;
2. The employer has been granted an extension of time to file its federal income tax return to a date later than the due date for its Form 5500 series return/report; and
3. A copy of the income tax extension is attached to the Form 5500 series return/report.

Example. Just-In Corporation files its federal income tax return on a calendar-year basis. Just-In maintains a qualified retirement plan with a plan year end of January 31. Just-In receives extensions to file its federal income tax return through September 15, 1994. Is the August 31, 1994 due date for filing the Form 5500 series return/report automatically extended? No, because the plan year does not coincide with the tax year. However, if the plan year was a calendar year, the due date would have been extended from August 1, 1994 (July 31, 1994 is a Sunday) to September 15, 1994.

Q 17:8   What penalties may be imposed for late filing of the Form 5500 series return/report?

One or more of the following five penalties may be imposed or assessed for late or incomplete filings after the date they are due unless there was reasonable cause for the improper filing:

1. DOL may assess a civil penalty against a plan administrator (see Q 16:1) of up to $1,000 a day for the late filing of a Form 5500 series return/report. In addition, a Form 5500 series return/report rejected by DOL because it lacks material information will be treated as if it had not been filed. In other words, the plan administrator can be assessed a penalty for an incomplete as well as an untimely but complete filing.

2. A penalty of $25 a day (up to a maximum of $15,000) is imposed for each day a Form 5500 series return/report is overdue.

3. A plan administrator who fails to include all required separated participants in a timely filed annual registration statement (Schedule SSA; see Q 17:4) is subject to a penalty of $1 a day for each separated participant (the maximum penalty is $5,000).

4. A penalty of $1,000 is imposed if an actuarial report (Schedule B; see Q 17:4) is not filed for a defined benefit plan.

5. A penalty of $1 a day (up to a maximum of $1,000) is imposed if a notification of change of status of a plan is not filed on time.

[ERISA §§ 104(a)(4), 502(c)(2); IRC §§ 6652(e), 6652(d)(1), 6692, 6652(d)(2)]

DOL's assessment of a penalty for filing a deficient annual report was considered arbitrary and capricious because DOL failed to give the plan administrator sufficient opportunity to correct the report or to seek an administrative review of the penalty assessment. [Northwestern Institute of Psychiatry v Martin, No. 92-0321 (ED Pa 1993)]

Q 17:9 Are there any criminal penalties for violations of the reporting requirements?

Yes. Willful violations of the reporting and disclosure requirements of ERISA can result in penalties up to a maximum of $5,000 in the case of an individual ($100,000 for any other entity), one-year imprisonment, or both. [ERISA § 501]

In addition, it is a criminal offense to knowingly make a false statement, or conceal or fail to disclose any fact needed to prepare reports required by Title I of ERISA. The maximum penalties are a $10,000 fine, five-year imprisonment, or both. [18 USC § 1027] This provision has been applied to the following:

1. A service provider who provided the plan with false information regarding his profits, which the plan needed to complete its Form 5500. [United States v Martorano, 767 F 2d 63 (3d Cir 1985)]

2. A participant who submitted false information to his plan. [United States v Bartkus, 816 F 2d 255 (6th Cir 1987)]

Q 17:10 Does a plan administrator's reliance on a third party to timely file the Form 5500 series return/report constitute reasonable cause for late filing?

No. One court has upheld the imposition by IRS of a $5,000 penalty against an employer for the late filing of Form 5500-C, even though the employer relied on a bank to file the return on time, because the responsibility for timely filing remains with the employer or plan administrator (see Q 16:1). [IRC § 6058(a); Alton Ob-Gyn, Ltd v United States, 789 F 2d 515 (7th Cir 1986)]

Q 17:11 Does the statute of limitations apply to the Form 5500 series return/report?

The filing of Schedule P (Form 5500), Annual Return of Fiduciary of Employee Benefit Trust (see Q 17:4), with the Form 5500 series return/report starts the running of the statute of limitations for any tax-exempt trust that is part of a qualified retirement plan. [IRC § 6033(a), 6501(a)]

One court has held that the filing of Form 5500-C for 1980 without Schedule P attached started the running of the statute of limitations because the form disclosed the plan's trustees and was signed by a trustee under penalty of perjury. However, the 1979 Form 5500-C did not start the running of the statute of limitations because it did not disclose the plan's trustees. [Martin Fireproofing Profit Sharing Plan and Trust, 92 TC 1173 (1989)]

Q 17:12 Does the filing of the Form 5500 series return/report start the statute of limitations running with regard to a prohibited transaction?

Yes, if it discloses the transaction. Although Form 5330 is the appropriate form to report a prohibited transaction for the purpose of computing any excise taxes that may be owed (see Qs 17:15, 20:4), IRS conceded in one case that the filing of a Form 5500 series return/report that adequately discloses the facts of the transaction is sufficient to start the three-year statute of limitations running for prohibited transactions. [Rutland, 89 TC 1137 (1987)]

However, the six-year statute of limitations may be applicable if the Form 5500 series return/report does not disclose a prohibited transaction. [Thoburn, 95 TC 132 (1990)]

Q 17:13 Must a plan engage an independent accountant when it files its Form 5500 series return/report?

If a plan files Form 5500 (see Q 17:2), a certified public accountant or licensed public accountant (or an individual certified by DOL) must, in most cases, conduct an audit of the plan's books and records and issue an opinion, which is to be included in the annual report, covering:

1. The financial statements and schedules covered by the annual report;
2. The accounting principles and practices reflected in the report;
3. The consistency of the application of those principles and practices; and
4. Any changes in accounting principles having a material effect on the financial statements.

[ERISA §§ 103(a)(3), 109(b); DOL Reg § 2520.103-1(b)(5)]

If a plan does not file Form 5500 (see Q 17:2), an accountant's audit and opinion are not required. [DOL Reg § 2520.104-46]

[Instructions to 1992 Forms 5500, 5500-C/R, 5500EZ]

DOL has stated that both Form 5500 and Form 5500-C/R filers must use current value to determine realized and unrealized gains and losses, not the historical cost method. [DOL Notice (Jan 26, 1990); DOL News Release 91-2 (1991)]

Q 17:14   Where are the Form 5500 series returns/reports filed?

Returns should be filed at the IRS Service Center indicated below:

Location of the Principal Office of the Plan Sponsor or Plan Administrator	*Internal Revenue Service Center Address*
Connecticut, Delaware, District of Columbia, Maine, Maryland, Massachusetts, New Hampshire, New Jersey, New York, Pennsylvania, Puerto Rico, Rhode Island, Vermont, Virginia, and foreign addresses	Holtsville, NY 00501
Alabama, Alaska, Arkansas, California, Florida, Georgia, Hawaii, Idaho, Louisiana, Mississippi, Nevada, North Carolina, Oregon, South Carolina, Tennessee, and Washington	Atlanta, GA 39901
Arizona, Colorado, Illinois, Indiana, Iowa, Kansas, Kentucky, Michigan, Minnesota, Missouri, Montana, Nebraska, New Mexico, North Dakota, Ohio, Oklahoma, South Dakota, Texas, Utah, West Virginia, Wisconsin, and Wyoming	Memphis, TN 37501
All Form 5500EZ filers	Andover, MA 05501

[Instructions to 1992 IRS Forms 5500, 5500-C/R, 5500EZ]

Q 17:15   Which special returns must be filed with IRS?

Form 5310, Application for Determination Upon Termination, is filed as part of an application for a determination letter from IRS concerning the termination of a qualified retirement plan. Although there is no legal requirement to file for a determination letter regarding a plan's termination, it is strongly suggested that Form 5310 be filed with IRS (see Q 21:61).

Form 5310-A, Notice of Merger, Consolidation or Transfer of Plan Assets or Liabilities, is filed to notify IRS of a consolidation, merger, or transfer of plan assets and liabilities. Form 5310-A must be filed at least 30 days before the event. See Question 9:28 for details and Question 9:29 for filing exceptions.

Another special return is Form 5330, Return of Excise Taxes Related to Employee Benefit Plans. Form 5330 is used to report and pay the tax on the following:

- Prohibited transactions (see Q 17:12 and Chapter 20)
- Failure to meet minimum funding standards (see Q 8:1)
- Certain ESOP dispositions (see Chapter 24)
- Nondeductible contributions to qualified retirement plans (see Chapter 12)
- Excess contributions to 401(k) plans (see Qs 23:16, 23:18)
- Certain prohibited allocations of qualified securities by an ESOP (see Chapter 24)
- Reversions of qualified retirement plan assets to employers (see Q 21:51)

[IRC §§ 4971, 4972, 4975, 4978, 4978A, 4978B, 4979, 4979A, 4980; Instructions to IRS Form 5330 (revised May 1993)]

Form 5330 is generally due on or before the last day of the seventh month after the end of the taxable year of the employer or other person required to file Form 5330. An extension of up to six months may be requested by filing Form 5558 (see Q 17:6). However, Form 5558 does not extend the time to pay taxes. To report reversions, Form 5330 must be filed by the last day of the month following the month in which the reversion occurred. To report excess contributions to 401(k) plans, Form 5330 must be filed by the last day of the 15th month after the close of the plan year to which the excess contributions relate.

Another special return, Form 5329, Return for Additional Taxes Attributable to Qualified Retirement Plans (Including IRAs), Annuities, and Modified Endowment Contracts, is used to report any excise tax or additional tax owed in connection with a qualified retirement plan or IRA. Form 5329 is used to report and pay the tax on the following:

- Excess contributions to an IRA (see Q 26:6)
- Early distributions (see Qs 13:39, 26:39)
- Excess accumulations (failure to make a required minimum distribution; see Qs 11:20, 26:33)
- Excess distributions (see Qs 13:27–13:29)

Form 5329 should generally be attached to and filed by the same due date (including extensions) as the taxpayer's Form 1040, U.S. Individual Income Tax Return.

[IRC §§ 4973, 72(t), 4974, 4980A; Instructions to 1992 IRS Form 5329]

Q 17:16 Which form is used to report qualified retirement plan distributions?

Form 1099-R, Distributions From Pensions, Annuities, Retirement or Profit-Sharing Plans, IRAs, Insurance Contracts, etc., is used to report distributions from qualified retirement plans, including periodic payments, nonperiodic payments that are not total distributions, and total distributions. [Rev Proc 92-86, 1992-2 CB 495]

To implement the new requirements that payors report direct rollovers (see Q 28:17) from qualified retirement plans, two new distribution codes for use in box 7 of Form 1099-R have been created: "G" for a direct rollover to an IRA, and "H" for a direct rollover to a qualified retirement plan. [Ann 93-20, 1993-6 IRB; Ann 92-169, 1992-49 IRB]

Those receiving qualified retirement plan payments must receive Form 1099-R by January 31 of the year after the payment. Form 1099-R information is summarized on Form 1096, Annual Summary and Transmittal of U.S. Information Returns, which must be filed with IRS by the last day in February. Note: If magnetic media are used to transmit Forms 1099-R to IRS, Form 4804, Transmittal of Information Returns Reported Magnetically/Electronically (not Form 1096), must accompany such submission. [Instructions to 1993 IRS Form 1096]

The failure to timely file a required report can result in a $25 per day penalty up to a maximum of $15,000. [IRC § 6652(e)]

Form 1099-R is also used to report corrective distributions of excess deferrals and excess contributions to 401(k) plans (see Qs 23:28, 23:17). [Notice 89-32, 1989-1 CB 671, corrected by Ann 89-69, 1989-24 IRB 78]

Generally, the filing of Form 1099-R with respect to each payee satisfies information reporting requirements with respect to income tax withholding. For failing to report withholding taxes or to keep necessary records, IRS may impose a penalty of $50 for each affected individual, up to a maximum of $50,000 in a calendar year. [IRC §§ 6047(d), 6704; Treas Reg § 35.3405-1, Q&A E-9]

[Instructions to 1993 IRS Form 1099-R]

The IRS is considering simplifying Form 941, Employer's Quarterly Federal Tax Return, by removing from the form all nonpayroll items, including pension withholding. A new Form 945, Annual Return of Withheld Federal Income Tax, would then be used to report non-payroll items, including pension withholding, beginning in the first quarter of 1994. [Ann 93-51, 1993-14 IRB]

Q 17:17   What are DOL reporting requirements?

Unless a qualified retirement plan is exempt from the reporting and disclosure requirements of ERISA (see Q 17:18), the following reports are required:

1. Annual reports (Form 5500 series return/report);
2. Summary plan descriptions (SPDs);
3. Summary description of material modifications to the plan or SPD (sometimes referred to as SMMs); and

4. Supplementary or terminal reports. [ERISA §§ 101, 104]

To avoid duplicate reporting, annual reports are filed only with IRS. Copies of the reports are supplied to DOL by IRS.

Some of these reports must also be distributed to participants. See Chapter 18 for more details.

Q 17:18   Which types of plans are exempt from the reporting requirements of DOL?

There is a general exemption for individual retirement accounts (IRAs; see Chapter 26), governmental plans, church plans, and excess benefit plans (unfunded plans providing benefits above the limits on contributions and benefits for tax purposes). [ERISA § 4(b)]

There is also an exemption for "plans without employees;" that is, plans in which the only participants are either an individual and the individual's spouse if that individual is the only owner of the business (whether incorporated or not), or the partners in a partnership and the partners' spouses. In the case of any other family relationship, the exemption does not apply. For example, if the only plan participants are brothers, or father and son, the reporting requirements apply unless they are partners. This exemption does not apply to the requirement to file the Form 5500 series return/report with IRS (see Q 17:2). [DOL Reg § 2510.3-3]

Q 17:19   Which forms must be filed with PBGC?

PBGC Form 1, Annual Premium Payment (including Schedule A, Single-Employer Plan Variable Rate Portion of the Premium), and PBGC Form 1-ES, Estimated Premium Payment, are used to report premiums due to the PBGC. Qualified retirement plans with fewer than 500 participants file only PBGC Form 1, along with their total premium payment, by the final filing due date (see Q 17 :20).

The plan administrator of any qualified retirement plan (single-employer or multiemployer) that reported 500 or more participants on its PBGC Form 1 for the prior year must file a PBGC Form 1-ES to make its premium payment initially (the flat-rate portion of the premium for single-employer plans) on the basis of an estimated participant count. This filing and payment must be made by the first filing due date (see Q 17:20). Using the actual participant count, such single-employer and multiemployer plans must thereafter file PBGC Form 1 to make a reconciliation filing and pay the final fixed per-participant premium. In addition, all single-employer plans must file a Schedule A with PBGC Form 1 and pay the variable-rate portion of the premium (see Q 21:14). (It should be noted that if all the information needed to file PBGC Form 1 is known before the first filing due date, PBGC Form 1 should be filed instead of Form 1-ES. If Form 1-ES is filed, it will be necessary to file PBGC Form 1 by the final filing due date.) [Instructions to 1993 Annual Premium Payment Package]

A plan that was at the full funding limitation (see Q 8:16) for the preceding plan year is not liable for the variable-rate portion of the premium. [PBGC Reg § 2610.24(a)(5)]

Q 17:20   When are the PBGC premium forms due?

If the plan has 500 or more participants for the plan year, the plan sponsor must file a PBGC Form 1-ES by the last day of the second full calendar month following the close of the preceding plan year (first filing due date). For single-employer plans, only the flat-rate portion of the premium is due by the first filing due date; the variable-rate portion is due and PBGC Form 1 must be filed by the final filing due date (see below). For multiemployer plans, the entire premium is due by the first filing due date.

If the plan has fewer than 500 participants for the plan year, the plan sponsor must file Form 1 (single-employer plans must also file Schedule A to Form 1) and pay the entire premium by the fifteenth day of the eighth full calendar month following the month in which the plan year began (final filing due date). If the full amount due is not paid by the applicable date(s), the plan will be subject to late payment interest and penalty charges (see Q 17:23). [PBGC Reg §§ 2610.25, 2610.34]

Example 1. A single-employer plan has a plan year beginning July 1 and ending June 30. It had 950 participants as of the first day of its first plan year, July 1, 1992. For its second plan year beginning July 1, 1993, the plan must file a PBGC Form 1-ES on the first filing due date, August 31, 1993, using an estimated participant count to determine the flat-rate portion of the premium. The plan must file its PBGC Form 1 and pay any outstanding balance of the flat-rate portion of the premium plus the variable-rate portion by the final filing due date, March 15, 1994.

Example 2. A multiemployer plan has a July 15 to July 14 plan year. It had 1,500 participants as of the first day of the plan's first year, July 15, 1992. The first filing due date for the plan's second plan year beginning July 15, 1993 is September 30, 1993, and the plan must generally file a PBGC Form 1-ES on that date, using an estimated participant count to determine the amount of the premium. The plan must make a final reconciliation filing on PBGC Form 1 by the final filing due date, March 15, 1994.

New and newly covered single-employer and multiemployer plans, regardless of the number of plan participants, are not required to pay estimated premiums. Such plans are required to file and pay the applicable premium for the first time by the latest of the following dates:

1. The 15th day of the eighth full calendar month following the later of the month in which the plan year began or the month in which the plan first became effective for benefit accruals for future service;
2. The 90th day after the date of the plan's adoption; or
3. The 90th day after the date on which the plan became covered under Title IV of ERISA.

[PBGC Reg §§ 2610.25, 2610.34]

Example 1. A new plan has a plan year beginning January 1, 1994, and ending December 31, 1994. The plan was adopted on October 1, 1993, but became effective for benefit accruals on January 1, 1994. The filing due date is September 15, 1994.

Example 2. A professional service employer maintains a plan with a plan year beginning on January 1, 1993, and ending December 31, 1993. If this plan has always had no more than

25 participants, it is not a covered plan under ERISA Section 4021. On October 15, 1993, the plan has 26 participants for the first time. It is now a covered plan and will continue to be a covered plan regardless of the plan's future participant count. The filing due date is January 13, 1994, the date 90 days after the plan became covered under Title IV.

An extension of the due date granted by IRS for filing the Form 5500 series return/report does not extend the due date for filing PBGC Form 1.

PBGC Form 1-ES and Form 1 should be mailed with premium payments to:

> Pension Benefit Guaranty Corporation
> P.O. Box 105655
> Atlanta, GA 30348-5655

PBGC Form 1-ES and Form 1, along with premium payments, may be hand delivered to:

> NationsBank Retail Lockbox Processing Center
> PBGC Lockbox 105655
> 6000 Feldwood Rd.
> 5 Southside East
> College Park, GA 30349

[PBGC Reg § 2610.4; Instructions to 1993 Annual Premium Payment Package]

Q 17:21   How does a change in the plan year affect the due dates for filing the PBGC premium forms?

If the plan year is changed, two sets of PBGC forms must be filed: one for the old plan year and another for the new plan year. Each filing and premium payment must reflect a full 12-month plan year.

Plans that change their plan years as a result of a plan amendment must follow the due date rules for the short year as though it were a regular plan year (see Q 17:20).

For the plan year following the short year, the first filing due date is the later of (1) the last day of the second full calendar month following the close of the short plan year; or (2) 30 days after the date the amendment changing the plan year was adopted. The final filing due date is the later of (1) the 15th day of the eighth full calendar month following the month in which the plan year begins; or (2) 30 days after the date the amendment changing the plan year was adopted. [PBGC Reg § 2610.25(b)(3)]

Example 1. A plan amendment adopted on October 1, 1993, and made effective retroactively to February 1, 1993, changes a calendar-year plan to one with a plan year beginning February 1. The plan's 1992 Form 1 reported 350 plan participants. The final filing due date for the plan year that began on January 1, 1993, was September 15, 1993. The final filing due date for the new plan year, which began on February 1, 1993, was November 1, 1993 (October 31, 1993 was a Sunday).

Example 2. A plan changes its plan year from one that begins January 1 to one that begins June 1. The change is adopted on December 1, 1992. This results in a short plan year beginning January 1, 1993, and ending May 31, 1993. The plan's 1992 Form 1 reported 100 plan participants. The final filing due date was September 15, 1993, for the plan year that began January 1, 1993, and would have otherwise ended December 31, 1993. The final filing due date is February 15, 1994, for the new plan year beginning June 1, 1993, and ending May 31, 1994.

Refunds for duplicate premium payments for overlapping periods must be requested by writing to:

> Pension Benefit Guaranty Corporation
> FOD/Premium Operations Division (33700)
> 2020 K Street, N.W.
> Washington, DC 20006-1860

The employer must include copies of the relevant PBGC Forms 1, and the PBGC will calculate the amount of the refund and send it to the employer. [PBGC Reg § 2610.22(d)]

Q 17:22   Must PBGC Form 1 be filed after the plan is terminated?

The obligation to file PBGC Form 1 and make the required premium payment continues until the end of the plan year in which either the plan's assets are distributed or a trustee is appointed under ERISA. Any required premium payments will be for a full plan year and may not be prorated. However, a refund for premium payments applicable to the months after final distribution may be obtained by using the procedure for overlapping payments resulting from a change of plan year (see Q 17:21). [PBGC Reg §§ 2610.25(e), 2610.34(c)]

Q 17:23   What happens if the premium payment is late?

Late payment charges are assessed if PBGC receives a premium payment after the due date. The interest charge is based on the number of days the payment is late. The late filing penalty is the greater of 5 percent of the late payment for each late month (or part thereof), or $25, but not more than 100 percent of the unpaid premiums. [PBGC Reg § 2610.8]

Q 17:24   Can the late penalty charges be waived?

Generally, if the plan administrator (see Q 16:1) can show substantial hardship or otherwise demonstrate good cause, PBGC may waive the penalty (but not interest) charge. [PBGC Reg § 2610.8(b)]

Q 17:25   Are there any other notification requirements to PBGC?

Yes. PBGC must be notified by filing Form 200, Notice of Failure to Make Required Contributions, within ten days of the due date for a required plan contribution (see Q 8:18) if the aggregate unpaid balance, including interest, exceeds $1,000,000. [ERISA § 302(f)(4)]

Chapter 18

Summary Plan Descriptions

One of the major obligations of a plan administrator is the preparation of a summary of the plan for distribution to participants and beneficiaries. This chapter examines summary plan descriptions (SPDs)—what they are, the information they must contain, and how to avoid their legal pitfalls.

Q 18:1 What is a summary plan description?

An SPD is a booklet that describes the plan's provisions and the participants' benefits, rights, and obligations in simple language. Plan administrators (see Q 16:1) must supply an SPD to each plan participant and each beneficiary receiving benefits under the plan. [ERISA §§ 102(a)(1), 104(b)]

An SPD must contain certain information (see Q 18:4) and may be considered a legally binding document (see Q 18:5).

Q 18:2 When must an SPD be furnished to a participant?

An SPD must be furnished to each participant and beneficiary no later than (1) 90 days after becoming a participant or first receiving benefits, as the case may be, or (2) within 120 days after the plan first becomes subject to the reporting and disclosure requirements of ERISA. [ERISA § 104(b)]

In the case of a new plan that provides that it is effective only upon IRS approval, the 120-day period does not begin until the day after such condition is satisfied (i.e., the day after the IRS issues a favorable determination letter; see Q 15:1). [DOL Reg § 2520.104b-2(a)(3)] Conversely, if the plan is adopted retroactively, the 120-day period begins to run at the time of adoption.

In one case, penalties were assessed against a plan administrator (see Q 16:1) for failure to provide plan participants and beneficiaries with an SPD. [ERISA § 502(c); Sacks v Gross, Sklar & Metzger, PC, No. 88-5009 (ED Pa 1992)]

In another case, the court determined that the failure of an employer to provide an SPD did not negate the knowing waiver of ERISA claims by an employee who was aware of his potential eligibility for benefits at the time he signed the release. [Finz v Schlesinger, 957 F 2d 78 (2d Cir 1992)]

A plan administrator can refuse to provide an SPD to a deceased participant's son who was not a beneficiary. [Keys v Eastman Kodak Co, 739 F Supp 135 (WD NY 1990)]

Q 18:3   Where is the SPD filed?

The SPD must be filed with DOL no later than the time it is furnished to plan participants and beneficiaries. The SPD is filed at the following address:

> SPD, Pension and Welfare Benefits Administration
> Room N-5644
> U. S. Department of Labor
> 200 Constitution Avenue, N.W.
> Washington, DC 20210

[DOL Reg § 2520.104a-3]

Q 18:4   What information must an SPD contain?

An SPD must contain the following information:

1. Name of the plan;

2. Name and address of the employer whose employees are covered by the plan;

3. Employer identification number (EIN) assigned by IRS to the employer;

4. Plan number;

5. Type of plan (e.g., defined benefit plan, money purchase pension plan, profit sharing plan);

6. Type of administration of the plan (e.g., employer self-administration, contract administration, insurer administration);

7. Name, business address, and business telephone number of the plan administrator;

8. Name of the person designated as agent for the service of legal process, and the address at which the agent may be served (and a statement that a plan trustee or administrator may also be served);

9. Name, title, and business address of each trustee;

10. Plan's requirements regarding eligibility for participation and benefits, including the plan's normal retirement age;

11. Statement describing any joint and survivor benefits;

12. Description of the benefits and vesting provisions of the plan, including contingent top-heavy provisions, and circumstances that may result in disqualification, ineligibility, or denial, loss, forfeiture, or suspension of benefits;

13. Statement as to whether the plan is maintained pursuant to one or more collective bargaining agreements and, if so, a statement that copies of such agreement are available to participants and beneficiaries;

14. Statement as to whether the plan is covered by termination insurance from PBGC and, if so, a description of the guaranty provisions;

15. Plan's fiscal year end;

16. Source of contributions to the plan (employer and/or employee contributions) and the method used to calculate the amount of the contributions (a defined benefit plan need only state that the contribution is actuarially determined);

17. Plan's provisions governing termination of the plan, including the rights and benefits of participants and the disposition of assets;

18. Plan's procedures regarding claims for benefits and the remedies available for disputing denied claims; and

19. Statement of ERISA rights available to plan participants.

Bear in mind that technical jargon is out—the idea is simplicity and the goal is clarity. The SPD should be understood by the average plan participant. Clarifying examples and illustrations are recommended. The SPD must not mislead or misinform (see Q 18:5). Benefits should not be exaggerated, and restrictions and limitations should be described and not be minimized. [ERISA § 102(b); DOL Reg §§ 2520.102-2, 2520.102-3; DOL ERISA Tech Rel 84-1; DOL Opinion No. 85-05A]

Q 18:5   Is an SPD a legally binding document?

Although the status of an SPD is not entirely clear, the trend is to permit employees to rely on the SPD. Plan administrators (see Q 16:1) must make sure that they do not make any false or misleading representations in an SPD because the plan may be bound by a statement in the SPD that is inconsistent with the plan, even if the inconsistency is inadvertent (see Q 18:6). [Pierce v Security Trust Life Ins Co, 1992 US App Lexis 15562 (4th Cir 1992); Hansen v Continental Ins Co, 940 F 2d 971 (5th Cir 1991); Heidgerd v Olin Corp, No. 89-7869 (2d Cir 1990) ; Edwards v State Farm Mutual Automobile Ins Co, 851 F 2d 134 (6th Cir 1988); McKnight v Southern Life and Health Ins Co, 758 F 2d 1566 (11th Cir 1985); Gregory v Texasgulf, Inc, No. B-84-88 (WWE) (D Ct 1990)]

However, some courts have ruled that a participant must show reliance on a faulty SPD in order to recover denied benefits. [Maxa v John Alden Life Ins Co, No. 91-2203MN (8th Cir 1992); Bachelder v Communications Satellite Corp, 837 F 2d 519 (1st Cir 1988); Govoni v Bricklayers, Masons, and Plasterers Pension Fund, 732 F 2d 250 (1st Cir 1984); Thompson v Federal Express Corp, 1992 US Dist Lexis 19334 (MD Ga 1992); Freund v Gerson, 610 F Supp 69 (SD Fla 1985)]

An SPD gave adequate notice that a participant may receive only benefits guaranteed by PBGC (see Q 21:20) upon the termination of an underfunded defined benefit plan, and, therefore, the participant was not improperly denied benefits under the plan when reduced benefits were received. [Arnold v Arrow Transportation Co, No. 89-35280 (9th Cir 1991)]

One court ruled that an employer is not bound by an erroneous statement in a separate booklet distributed to employees with the SPD because the SPD was consistent with the plan. However, the court implied that an employer might be bound by an erroneous statement in the SPD. [Alday v Container Corp of America, No. 89-3476 (11th Cir 1990)] Another court held that a booklet describing plan benefits did not contain sufficient information to rise to the status of an SPD. Therefore, even though the booklet was in conflict with the actual plan document, the employee could not rely upon the booklet. [Hicks v Fleming Cos, Inc, 961 F 2d 537 (5th Cir 1992)]

Q 18:6   What is the purpose of a disclaimer clause?

Disclaimer language (see below) is a possible means of insulating plan assets and the plan administrator (see Q 16:1) from liability should the SPD prove to be misleading, incomplete, or contradictory to the provisions of the plan. Participants and their beneficiaries are placed on notice that the plan itself is the controlling document and that they should not rely solely upon the representations in the SPD. [Kolentus v Avco Corp, 798 F 2d 949 (7th Cir 1986)]

The following is a sample disclaimer clause:

> Please read this summary carefully. This summary is written in simple, nontechnical language, and it is intended to help you to understand how this plan will benefit you and your loved ones. The plan and trust documents are also available for you to read. Although these documents are written in technical language, they may be helpful to you.

> If it appears to you that any of the provisions of the plan or trust documents are not in agreement with the statements made in this summary, please bring this to the attention of the plan administrator. Keep in mind that, if there is any conflict between this summary and the provisions of the plan or trust documents, the terms of the plan or trust will govern.

You should rely solely on the provisions of the plan and trust documents.

However, it has been held that employees can rely on an SPD despite a disclaimer where the SPD favors the employees [Pierce v Security Trust Life Ins Co, 1992 US App Lexis 15562 (4th Cir 1992), and that an employer cannot disavow a disclaimer when the SPD favors the employer but the plan favors the employees. [Glocker v W R Grace & Co, No. 91-2262 (4th Cir 1992)]

Q 18:7   Will a disclaimer in an SPD be recognized in a lawsuit?

At present, there are no governmental prohibitions against the use of a disclaimer in an SPD. Nothing is risked, therefore, by including the disclaimer (see Q 18:6).

The courts have held that a participant or beneficiary cannot use an SPD to sue for relief under ERISA unless the lawsuit also asserts a claim arising under the plan itself. However, the courts have left the door open for a participant to sue on other than ERISA grounds on the basis of inaccurate or misleading statements in the SPD. In any event, it is reasonable to expect that a claim based on willful or negligent misrepresentations in an SPD would be upheld even when a disclaimer is included in the SPD. [O'Brien v Sperry Univac, 458 F Supp 1179 (D DC 1978); McKnight v Southern Life and Health Ins Co, 758 F 2d 1566 (11th Cir 1985)]

Q 18:8   What happens if the plan is changed?

Any change in the provisions of the plan or in the administration of the plan that constitutes a material modification (see Q 18:9) must be disclosed to participants and beneficiaries in the form of a summary description of material modifications (SMM) to the plan, which must be distributed within 210 days after the close of the plan year in which the material modification is adopted. [DOL Reg § 2520.104b-3]

The SMM must also be filed with DOL within the same 210-day period, at the following address:

SMM, Pension and Welfare Benefits Administration
Room N-5644
U. S. Department of Labor
200 Constitution Avenue, N.W.
Washington, DC 20210

[DOL Reg § 2520.104a-4]

Q 18:9   What constitutes a reportable material modification?

Basically, a material modification exists when there is a change or modification to any of the information required to be included in the SPD (see Q 18:4). [DOL Reg § 2520.104b-3]

For example, the elimination of a special retirement benefit that allowed participants not eligible for normal retirement benefits to qualify for reduced retirement benefits was held to be a material modification of a plan. [Baker v Lukens Steel Co, 793 F 2d 509 (3d Cir 1986)]

Q 18:10   How often is an updated SPD due?

Generally, every five years the plan administrator is required to furnish to each participant and each beneficiary receiving benefits under the plan an updated SPD that incorporates all plan amendments made within that five-year period. The updated SPD must be furnished no later than 210 days after the end of the fifth plan year after the previous SPD. This requirement for an updated SPD must be met even if SMMs have been issued (see Q 18:8). However, even if there have been no amendments to the plan, another copy of the original SPD must be distributed every ten years. [ERISA § 104(b); DOL Reg § 2520.104b-2]

Q 18:11   How is the five-year period for an updated SPD measured?

Each time an SPD is distributed and filed with DOL, the five-year period begins anew. If the plan distributes an updated SPD less than five years after the previous one was distributed, a new five-year period begins at that time. [DOL Reg § 2520.104b-2(b)]

Example. The plan administrator of the Justin Corporation profit sharing plan distributed the first SPD on March 1, 1990. On January 4, 1991, the vesting provisions of the calendar-year plan were amended and an SMM (see Q 18:8) was timely filed on July 29, 1992 (210 days after the end of the plan year of the amendment). An updated SPD will be due on July 29, 1996 (210 days after December 31, 1995, the end of the plan year of the fifth anniversary of the original SPD). If a new SPD (instead of the SMM) had been distributed on July 29, 1992, the next SPD would be due July 29, 1998.

Q 18:12 What happens if the plan is terminated?

If the plan terminates before the date by which an original or an updated SPD is required, the SPD requirement is waived if, and only if, all distributions to participants and beneficiaries have been completed. [DOL Reg § 2520.104a-3(c)]

Q 18:13 What documents other than an SPD can a participant obtain?

Other than an SPD, a participant is entitled to obtain, without charge and without request, a summary of material modifications (see Q 18:8) to the plan and a summary annual report.

Upon request, other documents must be furnished to a participant by the plan administrator (see Q 16:1). These include:

1. A statement of the participant's total accrued benefits;
2. The plan instrument;
3. The latest annual report (Form 5500 series return);
4. The trust agreement; and
5. The collective bargaining agreement or any other document under which the plan is established.

A reasonable charge (not to exceed $.25 a page) may be imposed for copies of these items (other than the annual benefit statement). [ERISA § 105(a); DOL Reg § 2520.104b-30] The plan administrator's failure to provide these documents within 30 days after the participant's request may subject the plan administrator to fines, attorney's fees, and costs (see Q 19:31). [ERISA §§ 502(c)(1), 502(g)(1); Lee v Benefit Plans Administrator of ARMCO, Inc, No. H-90-3642 (SD Tex 1992)] In addition, the failure may result in a participant's complaint to the local DOL field office, with the possibility of an ensuing investigation of the plan. [Thomas v Jeep-Eagle Corp, 746 F Supp 863 (ED Wis 1990)]

In one case, no penalty was imposed on the employer for a ten-month delay in providing plan information because the employee did not show that any damage resulted from the delay, or that bad faith or intentional delay existed on the part of the employer. [Plotkin v Bearings Ltd, No. CV 91-0472 (ED NY 1991)] Where an employee received inaccurate written benefit statements and oral communications, the employer was not bound by the inaccurate representations because the terms of the plan controlled. [Miller v Coastal Corp, No. 92-3030 (10th Cir 1992)]

Q 18:14   Is there any special requirement if many plan participants cannot read English?

Yes. If a sufficient number of plan participants (generally, 25 percent for plans with less than 100 participants, 10 percent for plans with 100 or more participants) are literate only in the same non-English language, then the plan administrator (see Qs 16:1, 18:1) must give these participants an SPD with a notice written in their own language. This notice must inform such participants of the availability of assistance sufficient to enable them to become informed as to their rights under the plan. [DOL Reg § 2520.102-2(c)]

Chapter 19

Fiduciary Responsibilities

Plan administrators, trustees, and fiduciaries must take special care to carry out their responsibilities properly. Carelessness in the investment of plan assets, for example, can mean financial ruin for these individuals. This chapter examines the meaning of fiduciary responsibility under ERISA, when a fiduciary can be held personally liable for losses sustained by the plan, how liability can be avoided, and guidelines for investing plan assets.

Q 19:1 Who is a fiduciary under ERISA?

A fiduciary under ERISA is any person who:

1. Exercises any discretionary authority or control over the plan's management;
2. Exercises any authority or control over the management or disposition of the plan's assets;
3. Renders investment advice for a fee or other compensation with respect to plan funds or property; or
4. Has any discretionary authority or responsibility in the plan's administration.

[ERISA § 3(21)(A)]

The test for determining fiduciary status is a functional one. In other words, if a person or entity has or exercises any of the functions described in ERISA Section 3(21)(A), the person or entity will be deemed to be a fiduciary. [Eaves v Penn, 587 F 2d 453 (10th Cir 1978); Blatt v Marshall and Lassman, 812 F 2d 810 (2d Cir 1987)] A person may be a fiduciary for a limited purpose and also perform other, nonfiduciary roles with regard to the same plan. [Harris Trust and Savings Bank v John Hancock Mutual Life Ins Co, 970 F 2d 1138 (2d Cir 1992)]

Those performing purely ministerial functions within guidelines established by others are not plan fiduciaries. DOL regulations list the following job categories as ministerial:

1. Application of rules to determine eligibility for participation or benefits;
2. Calculation of service and compensation for benefit purposes;
3. Preparing communications to employees;
4. Maintaining participants' service and employment records;
5. Preparing reports required by government agencies;
6. Calculating benefits;
7. Explaining the plan to new participants and advising participants of their rights and options under the plan;
8. Collecting contributions and applying them as specified in the plan;
9. Preparing reports covering participants' benefits;
10. Processing claims; and
11. Making recommendations to others for decisions with respect to plan administration.

[DOL Reg § 2509.75-8, D-2; Flacche v Sun Life Assurance Co of Canada, No. 91-3462 (6th Cir 1992); Reichling v Continental Bank, 813 F Supp 197 (ED NY 1993)]

Trustees were not fiduciaries to the extent they lacked discretion over the investment of plan assets, so they did not violate their fiduciary duties by investing all plan assets in group annuity contracts because the plan itself required such investment and the trustees had no discretion. [Arakelian v National Western Life Ins Co, No. 84-1953 SSH (D DC 1990)]

A broker or dealer registered under the Securities Exchange Act of 1934 is not deemed to be a fiduciary solely because the broker-dealer executes securities transactions on behalf of the plan in the ordinary course of its business, provided:

1. The broker-dealer is not affiliated with a plan fiduciary; and
2. The plan fiduciary specifies:
    a. The security to be purchased or sold;
    b. The price range within which the security may be purchased or sold;
    c. The time span, but not exceeding five days, during which the security may be purchased or sold; and
    d. The minimum or maximum quantity of the security that may be purchased or sold within such price range.

[DOL Reg § 2510.3-21(d)(1)]

Q 19:2 What is rendering investment advice for the purpose of determining fiduciary status?

A person is rendering investment advice to a plan only if such person (1) makes recommendations as to valuing, buying, holding, or selling securities or other property, and (2) has, directly or indirectly, (a) discretionary authority or control over buying or selling securities or other property for the plan, whether or not pursuant to an agreement, arrangement, or understanding, or (b) regularly renders advice to the plan pursuant to a mutual agreement, arrangement, or understanding that such advice will serve as a primary basis for plan investment decisions and that such advice will be based on the particular needs of the plan regarding such matters as investment policies or strategy, overall portfolio composition, or diversification of plan investments. [DOL Reg § 2510.3-21(c)(1)]

A broker's practice of recommending investments will not make that broker a fiduciary in the absence of any agreement, arrangement, or understanding referred to in item (2)(b) above. [Farm King Supply, Inc Integrated Profit Sharing Plan and Trust v Edward D Jones & Co, 884 F 2d 288 (7th Cir 1989)] However, a broker may be considered a fiduciary if the broker engages in unauthorized buying and selling of plan assets. [Olson v E F Hutton & Co, Inc, No. 91-1416MN (8th Cir 1992)]

Q 19:3 What is a named fiduciary?

Every plan is required to have at least one named fiduciary. A named fiduciary is one or more persons designated in the plan by name or title as responsible for operating the plan. The purpose of the requirement is to enable employees and other interested parties to ascertain the person responsible for plan operations. A plan covering employees of a corporation can designate the corporation as the named fiduciary. However, DOL regulations suggest that "a plan instrument which designates a corporation as 'named fiduciary' should provide for designation by the corporation of specified individuals or other persons to carry out specified fiduciary responsibilities under the plan . . . ." [ERISA § 402(a)(1); DOL Reg § 2509.75-5, FR-1, FR-3]

Officer-shareholders of the named fiduciary have been held not to be fiduciaries. [Confer v Custom Eng'g Co, No. 91-3259 (3d Cir 1991)]

Q 19:4 Are attorneys, accountants, actuaries, insurance agents, insurers, and consultants who provide services to a plan considered plan fiduciaries?

No. They are not considered plan fiduciaries solely because they render such services. However, they will be regarded as fiduciaries if they exercise discretionary authority or control over the management or administration of the plan or some authority or control over plan, assets even if such activities are unauthorized. [DOL Reg § 2509.75-5, D-1; Libby-Owens-Ford Co v Blue Cross & Blue Shield Mutual of Ohio, 982 F 2d 1061 (6th Cir 1993); Harris Trust and Savings Bank v John Hancock Mutual Life Ins Co, 970 F 2d 1138 (2d Cir 1992); Olson v E F Hutton & Co, Inc, No. 91-1416MN (8th Cir 1992); Bouton v Thompson 764 F Supp 20 (D Conn 1991); Procacci v Drexel Burnham Lambert, No. 89-0555 (ED Pa 1989); Brock v Self, 632 F Supp 1509 (WD La 1986)]

Recent cases have held that attorneys, accountants, actuaries, and consultants do not possess or exert the necessary discretionary authority or control respecting management of the plan to cause them to be fiduciaries under ERISA. [Kaniewski v Equitable Life Assurance Soc, No. 92-3604 (6th Cir 1993) (insurance company); Schloegel v Boswell, 1993 US App Lexis 16188 (5th Cir 1993) (insurance agent); Kyle Railways, Inc v Pacific Administration Svcs, Inc, 1993 US App Lexis (9th Cir 1993) (third-party administrator); Useden v Acker, No. 90-5445 (11th Cir 1991) (attorneys and bank); Mertens v Hewitt Assocs, 948 F 2d 607 (9th Cir 1991), aff'd, No. 91-1671 (S Ct 1993) (actuaries); Consolidated Beef Indus, Inc v New York Life Ins Co, Nos. 90-5131 and 90-5164 (8th Cir 1991) (insurance company and agent); Pappas v Buck Consultants, Inc, 923 F 2d 531 (7th Cir 1991) (actuaries); Anoka Orthopaedic Assocs, PA v Lechner, 910 F 2d 514 (8th Cir 1990) (attorneys and consultants); Pension Plan of Public Svc Co of NH v KPMG Peat Marwick, 1993 US Dist Lexis 2254 (D NH 1993) (accountants); Painters of Philadelphia District Council No. 21 Welfare Fund v Price Waterhouse, 879 F 2d 1146 (3d Cir 1989) (accountants); Nieto v Ecker, 845 F 2d 868 (9th Cir 1988) (attorneys)]

Although not fiduciaries, they may be liable to the plan based upon traditional theories of malpractice. [Horton v Cigna Individual Financial Svcs Co, 1993 US Dist Lexis 8639 (ND Ill 1993); Mazur v Gaudet, No. 89-2723 (ED La 1992)]

Q 19:5 Do the fiduciary responsibility rules of ERISA apply to a Keogh plan?

Generally, if the plan covers self-employed individuals as well as common-law employees, the fiduciary responsibility provisions of ERISA are applicable. However, the fiduciary responsibility provisions of ERISA do not apply to plans that cover only self-employed individuals. A plan covering only the owner-employee (see Q 29:9) and the owner-employee's spouse is not a plan providing retirement income to employees. Plans in which only sole proprietors or partners participate are not considered employee benefit plans, and sole proprietors, partners, and their spouses are not considered employees for ERISA's fiduciary responsibility rules. [ERISA § 3(3); DOL Reg §§ 2510.3-3(b), 2510.3-3(c); Robertson v Alexander Grant & Co, 798 F 2d 868 (5th Cir 1986); Schwartz v Gordon, 761 F 2d 864 (2d Cir 1985); Olsavsky v Casey, 1992 US Dist Lexis 18495 (D Conn 1992)]

Q 19:6   What is a self-directed account plan?

A self-directed account plan is an individual account plan described in ERISA Section 3(34) that permits a participant to make an independent choice, from a broad range of investment alternatives, regarding the manner in which any portion of the assets in the participant's individual account is invested. [ERISA § 404(c); DOL Reg § 2550.404c-1(b)(1)]

According to DOL, a self-directed account plan must:

1. Include at least three investment options with materially different risk and return characteristics;
2. Provide enough information to allow the participant to make informed investment decisions for every investment alternative offered;
3. Enable diversification of investments; and
4. Allow participants independent control to change investments at least quarterly, and more frequently if volatile investments are offered.

A participant will not be considered to have sufficient information to make informed investment decisions unless provided with an explanation that the plan is intended to constitute an ERISA Section 404(c) plan and a description of the investment alternatives available under the plan, including their investment objectives and risks and return characteristics. A participant must be provided, either directly or on request, with the following information (based on the latest information available to the plan):

- A description of the annual operating expenses of each investment alternative, and the aggregate amount of these expenses expressed as a percentage of average net assets
- Copies of any prospectuses, financial statements, and reports available to the plan
- List of the assets in the portfolio of each alternative, and, for any asset that is a fixed rate investment contract, the name of the issuer, the term, and the rate of return.

- Information on the value of shares of the alternatives available under the plan, as well as the past and current investment performance determined (net of expenses) on a reasonable and consistent basis

A plan offers a broad range of investment alternatives only if the available investment alternatives are sufficient to provide the participant with a reasonable opportunity to materially affect both the potential return on amounts in the account and the degree of risk to which these amounts are subject, and to permit the participant to choose from at least three investment alternatives, each of which is diversified; each of which has materially different risk and return characteristics, which, in the aggregate, enable the participant to achieve a portfolio with aggregate risk and return characteristics within the range normally appropriate for the participant; and each of which, when combined with the other, tends to minimize the overall risk of a portfolio through diversification.

Participants must also be advised that, if DOL requirements are satisfied, the plan's fiduciaries may be protected against liability for investment losses incurred as a result of the investment instructions given by participants to the fiduciaries.

[DOL Reg § 2550.404c-1(d)(2)]

The final ERISA Section 404(c) regulations are effective as of the first day of the first plan year beginning on or after October 13, 1993. For a calendar year plan year, the effective date is January 1, 1994.

Q 19:7 Is a participant or beneficiary who self-directs an individual account considered a fiduciary?

No. If the plan permits self-directed accounts (see Q 19:6), participants will not be considered fiduciaries solely because they exercise control over assets in their individual accounts. The consequences are twofold. First, other plan fiduciaries generally would have no co-fiduciary liability on account of participants' investment decisions. Second, because the participants are not fiduciaries, no prohibited transaction under ERISA would result if their exercise of control over the assets in their accounts caused the trust to engage in transactions with parties in interest (see Q 20:2). [ERISA § 404(c); DOL Reg §§ 2550.404c-1(a), 2550.404c-1(d)]

Q 19:8   Are any individuals prohibited from serving as fiduciaries?

Yes. A person who has been convicted of any of a wide range of crimes, including robbery, bribery, extortion, and fraud, cannot serve as a plan fiduciary for a period of 13 years after the conviction or after the end of imprisonment, whichever is later. A person who knowingly violates the rule is subject to a maximum fine of $10,000 or five years' imprisonment, or both. [ERISA § 411]

One court has gone further and permanently barred former plan fiduciaries from acting as fiduciaries or providing services to plans in the future. [Beck v Levering, No. 91-6174 (2d Cir 1991)]

Q 19:9   Can a trustee be appointed for life?

No. DOL has ruled that the appointment of a trustee for life, or the ability to remove a trustee only upon misfeasance or incapacity to perform the duties of the position, is inconsistent with ERISA's fiduciary responsibility provisions. [DOL Advisory Opinion No 85-41A]

Trustees did not breach their fiduciary duty by approving a trust amendment that transferred the power to appoint and remove trustees from a single joint council of local unions to three joint councils. The amendment only affected the distribution of power among the various unions and did not entrench current trustees. [International Brotherhood of Teamsters v The New York State Teamsters Council Health and Hospital Fund, 1990 US App Lexis 8409 (2nd Cir 1990)]

Q 19:10   What is a fiduciary's basic duty?

The basic duty of a fiduciary is to act solely in the interest of the plan's participants and beneficiaries and for the exclusive purpose of providing benefits for participants and their beneficiaries (and defraying reasonable administrative costs of the plan). A fiduciary must also act prudently, diversify the investment of the plan's assets, and act in a manner consistent with the plan's documents. A trustee did not breach its fiduciary duty when it invested all plan funds in employer stock because the plan itself required such investment upon the direction of the plan administrator (see Q 16:1) and the trustee had no discretion; and an employer did not breach its fiduciary duty when former ESOP (see Q 24:1) participants who elected cash distributions, rather than employer stock, were not advised by the employer that it had commenced preliminary discussions to sell the company at a price substantially in excess of the current market price. [ERISA § 404(a); Ershick v United Missouri Bank of Kansas City, NA, No. 90-3283 (10th Cir 1991); Sweeney v The Kroger Co, 773 F Supp 1266 (ED Mo 1991)] However, misleading communications or misrepresentations to participants may constitute a breach of fiduciary duty. [Fischer v The Philadelphia Electric Co, No. 92-1684 (3d Cir 1993); Kurz v The Philadelphia Electric Co, No. 92-1685 (3d Cir 1993); Drennan v General Motors Corp, Nos. 90-3659 and 90-3660 (6th Cir 1992)]

A trustee's transfer of excess plan assets to the employer before participants received all their benefits violated the trustee's fiduciary duty to the participants (see Q 21:48). [PBGC v Fletcher, No. MO-89-CA-179 (WD Tex 1990)] Trustees breached their fiduciary duty to a participant's widow by failing to distribute plan benefits to her as soon as the amount payable was determined as required by the plan, and a company breached its fiduciary duty when it unreasonably delayed implementing a plan participant's request to transfer his plan account from a common stock fund to a fixed income investment fund. [Sherwood Group, Inc v Meselsohn, No. 88 Civ 3650 (JSM) (SD NY 1990); Carich v James River Corp, No. 90-35567 (9th Cir 1992)]

Q 19:11 What is the applicable standard of care for a fiduciary ?

A fiduciary is subject to the prudent man standard of care; that is, the fiduciary must act "with the care, skill, prudence, and diligence under the circumstances then prevailing that a prudent man acting in a like capacity and familiar with such matters would use in the conduct of an enterprise of a like character and with like aims." [ERISA § 404(a)(1)(B); Kowalewski v Detweiler, 770 F Supp 290 (D Md 1991)]

Q 19:12 How does the prudent man standard apply to trustees or investment managers?

A trustee or other fiduciary responsible for investing the plan's assets must, in order to satisfy the prudent man standard, consider the following factors:

1. The composition of the portfolio with regard to diversification;
2. The liquidity and current return of the portfolio relative to the anticipated cash flow requirements of the plan; and
3. The projected return of the portfolio relative to the funding objectives of the plan.

In addition, the trustee or other fiduciary must determine that the particular investment or investment strategy is reasonably designed to further the purposes of the plan, taking into consideration the risk of loss and the opportunity for gain (or other return) associated with the investment or the investment strategy. [DOL Reg § 2550.404a-1]

Q 19:13 Would a transaction involving the plan that benefits the employer result in a breach of fiduciary duty?

Not necessarily. A transaction that incidentally benefits the employer will not violate the rule that a fiduciary act solely in the interest of the plan's participants and beneficiaries as long as the fiduciary correctly concludes, on the basis of a careful, thorough, and impartial inquiry, that the transaction is in the interests of participants and beneficiaries. [Donovan v Bierwirth, 680 F 2d 263 (2d Cir 1982); Andrade v The Parsons Corp, No. 90-56202 (9th Cir 1992); see also Phillips v Amoco Oil Co, 799 F 2d 1464 (11th Cir 1986)]

However, management trustees of an ESOP (see Q 24:1) breached their fiduciary duty by not voting the ESOP shares at a shareholder meeting. If their conflicting loyalties to the company and the participants prevented them from properly representing the participants, they should have sought advice from a competent, independent advisor (see Q 24:41). [Newton v Van Otterloo, No. S89-610 (ND Ind 1991)

Q 19:14   Must the assets of the plan be segregated?

Yes. The plan's assets must be segregated from the employer's property and held in trust. [ERISA § 403(a)]

Q 19:15   What are plan assets when a plan invests in another entity?

Generally, the plan's assets will include its investment in an entity but not any of the underlying assets of such entity. However, if the plan's equity interest in an entity is neither a publicly offered security nor a security issued by an investment company registered under the Investment Company Act of 1940, the plan's assets will include both the equity interest and an undivided interest in each of the underlying assets (the look-through rule; see Q 19:16). In that event, any person who has any authority or control over the management of the underlying assets or provides investment advice for a fee with respect to such assets is a fiduciary of the investing plan (see Q 19:1). [DOL Reg § 2510.3-101(a)]

Q 19:16   Are there any exceptions to the look-through rule?

The look-through rule (see Q 19:15) will not apply if:

1. The equity interest (see Q 19:17) is in an operating company (see Q 19:18); or
2. The amount of equity participation in the entity by benefit plan investors is not significant (see Qs 19:19, 19:20).

[DOL Reg. § 2510.3-101(a)(2)]

Q 19:17   What is an equity interest and a publicly offered security?

An equity interest is any interest in an entity other than an instrument that is treated as indebtedness under applicable local law and that does not have substantial equity features. Examples include a profits interest in a partnership, an undivided interest in property, and a beneficial interest in a trust.

A publicly offered security is a security that is freely transferable, is part of a widely held class of securities, and covered under certain federal securities registration rules.

Example 1. A plan acquires debentures issued by the Jaykay Corporation pursuant to a private offering. All of Jaykay's shareholders are benefit plan investors. Jaykay is engaged primarily in investing and reinvesting in precious metals on behalf of its shareholders, so it is not an operating company. By their terms, the plan's debentures are convertible into common stock of Jaykay at the plan's option. At the time of the plan's acquisition of the debentures, the conversion feature is incidental to Jaykay's obligation to pay interest and principal. The plan's assets do not include an interest in the underlying assets of Jaykay because the plan has not acquired an equity interest in Jaykay.

Example 2. Assume the same facts in Example 1, except the plan exercises its option to convert the debentures into common stock, thereby acquiring an equity interest in Jaykay. Assuming that the common stock is not a publicly offered security and that there has been no change in the composition of the other equity investors in Jaykay, the plan's assets would then include an undivided interest in the underlying assets of Jaykay. As a result, employees of Jaykay with authority or control over the assets of Jaykay would be fiduciaries of the plan.

[DOL Reg §§ 2510.3-101(b), 2510.3-101(j)(1)]

Q 19:18   What is an operating company?

An operating company is generally an entity that is primarily engaged, directly or through subsidiaries, in the production or sale of a product or services other than the investment of capital. Also, a venture capital operating company or a real estate operating company will be treated as an operating company. [DOL Reg § 2510.3-101(c)]

An entity is a venture capital operating company if at least 50 percent of its assets (other than short-term investments made pending long-term commitments) are invested in an operating company (other than a venture capital operating company) as to which the investing entity has and exercises the right to participate substantially in or influence the management of the operating company. [DOL Reg § 2510.3-101(d)]

An entity is a real estate operating company if at least 50 percent of its assets are invested in managed or developed real estate and the investing entity has the right to participate substantially and directly in the management or development activities. In addition, the investing entity, in the ordinary course of its business, must actually engage in real estate management or development activities. [DOL Reg § 2510.3-101(e)]

Q 19:19 What level of participation of benefit plan investors is considered "significant"?

Equity participation in an entity is significant on any date if, immediately after the most recent acquisition or redemption of any equity interest (see Q 19:17) in the entity, 25 percent or more of the value of any class of equity interest in the entity is held by benefit plan investors (see Q 19:20). [DOL Reg § 2510.3-101(f)(1); DOL Advisory Opinion No 89-05A]

Q 19:20 What is a benefit plan investor?

The term "benefit plan investor" includes:

1. An employee benefit plan as defined by ERISA;
2. A qualified retirement plan, individual retirement account, or individual retirement annuity; or
3. Any entity whose underlying assets include plan assets as a result of a plan's investment in that entity.

[DOL Reg § 2510.3-101(f)(2)]

Q 19:21 Are there any investments by a plan that may never satisfy the exceptions to the look-through rule?

Yes. If a plan acquires or holds an interest in any entity (other than a licensed insurance company) established or maintained to provide any pension or welfare benefit to participants or beneficiaries of the investing plan, none of the exceptions may apply (see Qs 19:15, 19:16). As a result, the assets of the plan will include its investment and an undivided interest in the underlying assets of that entity.

> **Example.** A qualified retirement plan acquires a beneficial interest in a trust that is not an insurance company licensed to do business in a state. Under this arrangement, the trust will provide the plan benefits that are promised to the participants and beneficiaries under the terms of the plan. The plan's assets include its beneficial interest in the trust and an undivided interest in each of the trust's underlying assets. Thus, persons with authority or control over trust assets would be fiduciaries of the qualified retirement plan.

[DOL Reg §§ 2510.3-101(h)(2), 2510.3-101(j)(12)]

Q 19:22   When are participant contributions considered plan assets?

Amounts paid by participants, or withheld by the employer from participants' wages, as contributions to a plan will be considered plan assets as of the earliest date on which the contributions can reasonably be segregated from the general assets of the employer. That date can be no later than 90 days after the date on which the contributions are received by the employer or would have been paid to the employee in cash if not withheld from wages. [DOL Reg § 2510.3-102(a)]

> **Example.** Cee & Ess Company employs a small number of people at a single payroll location. Cee & Ess maintains a contributory profit sharing plan in which there is 100 percent participation. Because the small number of participants are all in a single location, the company could reasonably be expected to transmit participant contributions to the trust within ten days of the close of each pay period. Therefore, the assets of the plan would include the participants' contributions as of that date. [DOL Reg § 2510.3-102(b)(2)]

Q 19:23   What expenses relating to the plan may be paid out of plan assets?

Generally, plan assets are held exclusively to provide benefits to participants or beneficiaries and to defray reasonable expenses of administering the plan (see Q 19:10). Plan assets may therefore be used to pay plan expenses that are reasonably related to plan administration and authorized by the plan.

Services provided in conjunction with establishing the plan, terminating the plan, and other plan design functions would not properly be paid out of the plan. Payment of PBGC premiums is proper if the plan is silent or explicitly states that the plan may pay the premiums. However, the payment would be improper if the document indicates that the plan sponsor will pay them. [ERISA §§ 403(c)(1), 404(a)(1); DOL Information Letter, Mar 2, 1987]

Q 19:24   What are the consequences if plan assets are used improperly?

An improper payment of plan assets for expenses other than reasonable plan administration expenses would be a breach of fiduciary duty and would subject the fiduciary to personal liability for the breach (see Q 19:25). In addition, the payment may be a prohibited transaction if the payment is made to, on behalf of, or for the benefit of, a party in interest (see Qs 20:2, 20:4) and does not qualify for a statutory or administrative exemption under ERISA or the Code (see Qs 20:7–20:9). Finally, the payment may be considered a violation of the exclusive benefit provision of the Code and result in plan disqualification (see Q 4:1).

Q 19:25   Can a fiduciary be held liable for a breach of duty?

Yes. ERISA permits a civil action to be brought by a participant, beneficiary, or other fiduciary against a fiduciary for a breach of duty. The fiduciary is personally liable for any losses to the plan resulting from the breach of duty, and any profits obtained by the fiduciary through the use of plan assets must be turned over to the plan. The court may require other appropriate relief, including removal of the fiduciary. [ERISA §§ 409, 502(a)(2); Oscar A Samos, MD, Inc v Dean Witter Reynolds, Inc, No. 91-0209 P (D RI 1991)]

Courts have generally determined that a jury trial is not available in an action alleging breach of fiduciary duty. [Chilton v Savannah Foods & Industries, Inc, 814 F 2d 620 (11th Cir 1986); Henley v Lokey

Oldsmobile-Countryside, Inc, 1993 US Dist Lexis 3742 (MD Fla 1993); Landry v Air Line Pilots Assoc, International, AFL-CIO, No. 86-3196 (ED La 1991); but see McDonald v Artcraft Electric Supply Co, 774 F Supp 29 (D DC 1991), upholding a right to a jury trial]

An agreement between a trustee and investment advisor to arbitrate an ERISA claim of breach of fiduciary duty may be enforced. ERISA does not require that ERISA claims be decided only by courts. [Bird v Shearson Lehman/American Express, Inc, 926 F 2d 116 (2d Cir 1991); Witkowski v Welch, No. 90-0924 (ED Pa 1993); Fabian Financial Services v The Kurt H Volk Inc Profit Sharing Plan, 768 F Supp 728 (CD Cal 1991); but see Pritzker v Merrill Lynch Pierce Fenner & Smith, Inc, No. 92-5800 (ED Pa 1993), refusing to follow the Bird case without guidance from the Third Circuit Court of Appeals, and Johnson v St Francis Xavier Cabrini Hospital of Seattle, 910 F 2d 594 (9th Cir 1990)] In certain circumstances, arbitration may be ordered with respect to a claim against a party to an arbitration agreement, while the court stays the action with regard to other defendants who are not parties to the arbitration agreement. [Schorr v GB Resources, No. 91-5155 (SD NY 1992)]

A fiduciary, however, cannot be held liable for a breach of fiduciary duty that was committed prior to the fiduciary becoming a fiduciary. Although the fiduciary may not be liable for the original breach, if the fiduciary knows about the breach, the fiduciary should take steps to remedy the situation. Failure to do so may constitute a subsequent independent breach of fiduciary duty by the successor fiduciary.

Example. Esther has no existing relationship with the plan. She negotiates an agreement to provide investment advice to the plan, which will render her a fiduciary. She will not be liable for any investment decisions made prior to her becoming a fiduciary that are held to have been imprudent and, consequently, a fiduciary breach. [ERISA § 409(b); Barker v American Mobile Power Corp, 1993 US Dist Lexis 2987 (ND Cal 1993); Baeten v Van Ess, 446 F Supp 868 (ED Wis 1977); DOL Opinion Letter 76-95]

A breach of fiduciary duty can occur by reason of omission as well as commission. A plan administrator was held to have breached his fiduciary duty by not investing plan assets, liquidating assets only to pay benefits, not making an effort to collect obligations owed to the plan, and holding an unspecified sum of plan funds in cash at his home. [Newport v Elms, 1992 US Dist Lexis 9130 (ED La 1992)]

A qualified retirement plan can set off a fiduciary's liability to a plan for breach of fiduciary duty against the fiduciary's benefits from the plan, notwithstanding ERISA's anti-alienation provision (see Qs 4:24, 29:40). [Coar v Kazimir, 1993 US App Lexis 7817 (3d Cir 1993); United States v Gaudet, No. 91-3647 (5th Cir 1992); but see Guidry v Sheet Metal Workers National Pension Fund, 493 US 365 (1990) and Herberger v Shanbaum, 897 F 2d 801 (5th Cir 1990)]

For breaches of fiduciary duties (or knowing participation therein) on or after December 19, 1989, DOL imposes a penalty of 20 percent of the amount payable pursuant to a court order or settlement agreement with DOL. DOL may waive or reduce the penalty if the fiduciary or other person (1) acted responsibly and in good faith, or (2) will not otherwise be able to restore all plan losses without severe financial hardship. [ERISA § 502(l)]

Q 19:26   Can a nonfiduciary be held liable for a breach of duty?

No. ERISA does not authorize suits by plan participants for money damages against nonfiduciaries who knowingly participate in a fiduciary's breach of fiduciary duty. [Mertens v Hewitt Associates, No. 91-1671 (S Ct 1993)] Certain earlier cases imposed liability on nonfiduciaries who:

1. Had actual knowledge that a breach was occurring; and

2. Participated or took action that furthered or completed the breach.

[Diduck v Kaszycki & Sons Contractors, Inc, 974 F 2d 270 (2d Cir 1992); Brock v Hendershott, 840 F 2d 339 (6th Cir 1988); Thornton v Evans, 692 F 2d 1064 (7th Cir 1982); Bouton v Thompson, 764 F Supp 20 (D Conn 1991); Weir v Northwestern National Life Ins Co, 1992 US Dist Lexis 9653 (ED Pa 1992); PBGC v Ross, 733 F Supp 1005 (MD NC 1990); Mid-Jersey Trucking Industry-Local 701 v Omni Funding Group, 731 F Supp 161 (D NJ 1990); Brock v Gerace, 635 F Supp 563 (D NJ 1986); Freund v Marshall & Isley Bank, 485 F Supp 629 (WD Wis 1979)]

Individuals controlling a fiduciary, however, can be jointly and severally liable for a fiduciary's breach of duty. [Lowen v Tower Asset Mgmt, Inc, 829 F 2d 1209 (2d Cir 1987); but see Confer v Custom Eng'g Co, No. 91-3259 (3d Cir 1991)]

The DOL 20 percent penalty tax (see Q 19:25) may be imposed against nonfiduciaries.

Q 19:27 May a fiduciary be held liable for breaches committed by a co-fiduciary?

Yes, if the fiduciary:

1. Knowingly participates in or tries to conceal a co-fiduciary's breach;
2. Enables a co-fiduciary to commit a breach by failing to meet the fiduciary's specific responsibilities; or
3. Knowing of a co-fiduciary's breach, fails to make a reasonable effort to remedy it. [ERISA § 405(a)]

Example. Anna and Amy are co-trustees. The trust specifies that they cannot invest in commodity futures. If Anna suggests to Amy that she invest part of the plan assets in commodity futures and Amy does so, both Anna and Amy may be held personally liable for any losses sustained by the plan. Similarly, if Amy invests in commodity futures and tells Anna about it, Anna could be held personally liable for any losses if she conceals the investment or fails to make a reasonable effort to correct it.

The co-fiduciary may be liable by virtue of failing to perform the co-fiduciary's fiduciary duties, even if the co-fiduciary is not aware of the other fiduciary's breach of duty. [Russo v Unger, No. 86 Civ 9741 (SD NY 1991)] Fiduciaries may also be liable where, by not following the procedures set forth in the plan, they enable a co-fiduciary to embezzle plan assets. [Mazur v Gaudet, No. 89-2723 (ED La 1992)]

Q 19:28   What should a fiduciary do if a co-fiduciary commits a breach of duty?

The fiduciary must try to remedy the breach. For example, if an improper investment was made, the fiduciary might consider disposing of the asset. Alternatively, the fiduciary might notify the company of the breach, institute a lawsuit against the co-fiduciary, or bring the matter before DOL. The fiduciary's resignation as a protest against the breach, without making reasonable efforts to prevent it, will not relieve the fiduciary of liability. [ERISA § 405(a)(3); DOL Reg § 2509.75-5, FR-10]

Q 19:29   Can a breaching fiduciary obtain contribution or indemnity from other breaching co-fiduciaries?

Although certain early decisions expressed a right of contribution or indemnity among fiduciaries in plans governed by ERISA so that a passive trustee could seek indemnification from an active trustee, later decisions held no such right exists under ERISA, under a rationale that remedies not explicitly provided under ERISA should not be implied. [Free v Briody, 732 F 2d 1331 (7th Cir 1984) permitting contribution; Call v Sumitomo Bank of California, 881 F 2d 626 (9th Cir 1989), Kim v Fujikawa, 871 F 2d 1427 (9th Cir 1989), and Physicians Healthchoice, Inc v Trustees of the Automotive Employee Benefit Trust, 764 F Supp 1360 (D Minn 1991) denying contribution]

Recent cases, however, have held that a fiduciary's right to seek contribution and indemnity is a fundamental principle of the law governing trusts and that those remedies should be incorporated into a federal common law of ERISA. [Maher v Strachan Shipping Co, 817 F Supp 43 (ED La 1993); Chemung Canal Trust Co v Sovran Bank/Maryland, 939 F 2d 12 (2d Cir 1991)] Such federal common law would include a system of proportional fault among fiduciaries. [In re Masters, Mates & Pilots Pension Plan and IRAP Litigation, Nos. 91-6276, 91-6288 (SD NY 1992)]

A right of contribution under ERISA may also have been endorsed by implication in a decision that resolved a conflict among the circuits by holding that defendants in an action under Section 10(b) of the Securities Exchange Act of 1934 have a right to seek contribution as a matter of federal law. [Musick, Peeler & Garrett v Employers Ins of Wausau, No. 92-34 (S Ct 1993)]

Q 19:30 Does ERISA authorize punitive damages for breach of fiduciary duty?

The Supreme Court has held that punitive damages are not available to a beneficiary in an action against the plan fiduciary for an alleged breach of fiduciary duty when the alleged breach was the untimely processing of the beneficiary's claim for benefits. Remedies available to the beneficiary in such instances would include only recovery of the benefits owed, clarification of the beneficiary's right to present or future benefits, or removal of the breaching fiduciary. [Mass Mutual Life Ins Co v Russell, 473 US 134 (1985)]

However, the Supreme Court expressly left open certain issues— for instance, whether a plan, as opposed to a participant or beneficiary, could recover punitive damages, and whether a participant or beneficiary could recover such damages when the injurious conduct was not a breach of fiduciary duty but a violation of other sections of ERISA or of the terms of the plan. Most courts since the Russell decision have concluded that punitive damages under such circumstances are likewise unavailable under ERISA. [Medina v Anthem Life Ins Co, 1993 US App Lexis 1317 (5th Cir 1993); Lafoy v HMO Colorado, 988 F 2d 97 (10th Cir 1993); Novak v Andersen Corp, 962 F 2d 757 (8th Cir 1992); Harsch v Eisenberg, 956 F 2d 651 (7th Cir 1992); McRae v Seafarers' Welfare Plan, 920 F 2d 819 (11th Cir 1991); Reinking v Philadelphia American Life Ins Co, 910 F 2d 1210 (4th Cir 1990); Drinkwater v Metropolitan Life Ins Co, 846 F 2d 821 (1st Cir 1988); Varhola v Doe, 820 F 2d 809 (6th Cir 1987); Kleinhans v Lisle Savings Profit Sharing Trust, 810 F 2d 618 (7th Cir 1987); Sommers Drug Stores Co Employee Profit Sharing Trust v Corrigan Enters, Inc, 793 F 2d 1456 (5th Cir 1986); Powell v Chesapeake and Potomac Tel Co of Va, 780 F 2d 419 (4th Cir 1985); Diduck v Kaszycki & Sons Contractors, 974 F 2d 270 (2d Cir 1992); Bone v Association Management Servs, Inc, 632 F Supp 493 (SD Miss 1986); but see Warren v Society National Bank, 905 F 2d 975 (6th Cir 1990); California Digital Defined Benefit Pension Plan v Union Bank, 705 F Supp 489 (CD Cal 1989)] However, one court concluded that a fiduciary could recover punitive damages from another fiduciary who was guilty of malicious conduct. [Ampere Automotive Corp v Employee Benefit Plans, Inc, No. 92 C 2580 (ND Ill 1993)]

Q 19:31 Does ERISA authorize the recovery of attorney's fees and costs?

Yes. A court may, in its discretion, award reasonable attorney's fees and costs to either party. [ERISA § 502(g)]

Courts have examined the following factors in deciding whether to award fees and costs:

- Opponent's bad faith
- Opponent's ability to pay
- Deterrent effect on others in similar circumstances
- Whether action benefited all plan participants
- Relative merits of parties' positions

[Rodriguez v MEBA Pension Trust, Nos. 91-2336, 91-2358 (4th Cir 1992); Chisholm v Daniel, No. 89-16430 (9th Cir 1992); Miles v New York State Teamster Fund, 698 F 2d 593 (2d Cir 1983); Hummell v S E Rykoff & Co, 634 F 2d 446 (9th Cir 1980); Eaves v Penn, 587 F 2d 453 (10th Cir 1978); Maryland Electric Industry Health Fund v Triangle Sign & Service Div of Lok-Tite Ind, Inc, 1993 US Dist Lexis 2606 (D Md 1993); Plotkin v Bearings Ltd, 1992 US Dist Lexis 7787 (ED NY 1992); Lanning v Maxwell, 1992 US Dist Lexis 14089 (D Kan 1992)]

The "lodestar/multiplier" method has been used to determine reasonable attorney's fees. The lodestar is a reasonable hourly rate multiplied by the number of hours reasonably spent on the case. The multiplier is then applied to increase or decrease the lodestar amount on the basis of other relevant factors. [D'Emanuele v Montgomery Ward & Co, 904 F 2d 1379 (9th Cir 1990)]

Attorney's fees have been awarded even though all substantive issues were settled out of court. [Cefali v Buffalo Brass Co, Inc, No. 87-102L (WD NY 1990)] However, one court ruled that attorney's fees were not recoverable for administrative proceedings; fees could be awarded only for formal court proceedings. [Cann v Carpenters'

Pension Trust Fund of Northern California, No. 91-15628 (9th Cir 1993)]

Q 19:32 Can the plan contain a provision relieving a fiduciary of personal liability?

No. [Martin v NationsBank of Georgia, NA, 1993 US Dist Lexis 6322 (ND Ga 1993)] The plan may, however, buy insurance to cover liability or losses due to acts or omissions of fiduciaries if the insurance company is given a right to sue the breaching fiduciary. [ERISA § 410] If misrepresentations are made in the insurance application by one fiduciary, the policy may be voided as against all fiduciaries, some of whom may be without coverage through no fault of their own; otherwise, the insurance company would suffer hardship by providing coverage for a risk it never meant to insure. A fiduciary may buy insurance to cover the fiduciary's own liability. [Mazur v Gaudet, No. 89-2723 (ED La 1992)] The fiduciary may also be indemnified from a non-plan source, such as the plan sponsor. [DOL Reg § 2509.75-4]

A plan may provide for indemnification of expenses of a fiduciary who successfully defends against a claim of breach of fiduciary duty. [Packer Eng'g, Inc v Kratville, No. 91-2976 (7th Cir 1992)]

Q 19:33 Is a release executed by a plan beneficiary freeing plan fiduciaries from past liability under ERISA valid?

Yes. A release that is part of a settlement of a bona fide dispute over past fiduciary breaches is valid, but not one relating to the performance of future fiduciary duties. [Blessing v Struthers-Dunn, Inc, No. 85-1362 (ED Pa 1985)]

Q 19:34 Can fiduciary responsibility be delegated?

Yes. For example, the trust instrument can provide that one trustee has responsibility for one-half of the plan assets and a second trustee has responsibility for the other half of the plan assets. Neither trustee would be liable for the acts of the other except under the co-fiduciary liability rule of ERISA Section 405(a) (see Q 19:27). [ERISA § 405(b)]

If the plan expressly so provides, the named fiduciaries can allocate among themselves or delegate to others their fiduciary duties, other than the management or control of the plan's assets. The management or control of the plan's assets can be delegated only to an investment manager. [ERISA §§ 405(c)(1), 402(c)(3)]

An effective allocation or delegation will generally relieve the named fiduciary from liability for the acts of the person to whom such duties are allocated or delegated. The named fiduciary, however, is not relieved of liability under the co-fiduciary rules of ERISA Section 405(a). [ERISA § 405(c)(2)]

Q 19:35   What is the liability of an investment manager for its decisions regarding investment of plan assets?

An investment manager is a bank, insurance company, or registered investment advisor that acknowledges in writing that it is a fiduciary with respect to the plan (see Q 19:1). Therefore, any failure to comply with fiduciary standards may result in a breach of fiduciary duty, and the investment manager will be liable for any losses to the plan resulting from the breach. In addition, the investment manager may be required to disgorge any profits derived from the breach.

Example. An investment manager who bought and sold on behalf of a plan was found to have engaged in churning the plan's portfolio. Over 17 months, there were approximately 94 transactions. The churning transactions resulted in a loss of $47,000, while the broker received commissions of $9,700 in one three-month period. The investment manager was held liable for the losses to the plan and was ordered to return the commissions to the plan. [Dasler v E F Hutton and Co, Inc, 694 F Supp 624 (D Minn 1988)]

Q 19:36   Are there any limits on the investments a qualified retirement plan can make?

There are no specific dollar or percentage limits placed on the amount a qualified retirement plan can invest in any particular type of asset (other than qualifying employer securities or qualifying employer real property; see Q 19:41). Nor are there any limits on the types of investments that can be made. Investments in such tangible assets as real estate, gold, art, or diamonds are permitted, even though these investments may not generate current income for the plan and generally lack liquidity. However, see the discussion regarding a fiduciary's standard of care at Questions 19:11 and 19:12.

Limits on investments in qualifying employer securities or qualifying employer real property are discussed at Question 19:41. The consequences of investments by self-directed accounts in collectibles are discussed at Question 19:44.

Q 19:37　May a qualified retirement plan borrow to make investments?

Yes. There is no prohibition against any particular method by which a qualified retirement plan invests its assets. However, securities purchased on margin are considered acquisition indebtedness, subject to the unrelated business income tax on the income—both dividends and gains—resulting from its acquisition indebtedness. [IRC §§ 511, 514; Ocean Cove Corp Retirement Plan and Trust v United States, 657 F Supp 776 (SD Fla 1987); Elliot Knitwear Profit Sharing Plan v Comm'r, 614 F 2d 347 (3d Cir 1980), aff'g, 71 TC 765 (1979)]

However, when a plan borrows money to acquire or improve real estate, the debt generally is not considered acquisition indebtedness, so the income or gain from the real estate is not treated as unrelated business taxable income. [IRC § 514(c)(9)]

Q 19:38　What is the diversification requirement?

A trustee (or any other fiduciary responsible for investing plan assets) is required to discharge the trustee's duties "by diversifying the investments of the plan so as to minimize the risk of large losses, unless under the circumstances it is clearly not prudent to do so." [ERISA § 404(a)(1)(C)]

The degree of investment concentration that would violate the diversification rule cannot be stated as a fixed percentage but depends on the facts and circumstances of each case. However, factors that should be considered include:

- The purposes of the plan
- The amount of plan assets
- Financial and industrial conditions
- The type of investment made
- Diversification along geographic lines
- Diversification along industry lines
- The date the investment matures

So, for example, if the trustee is investing in real estate mortgages, the trustee should not invest a disproportionate amount in mortgages within a particular area or on a particular type of property even if that investment would result in social gains to a particular community. [H Conf Rep No. 1280, 93d Cong, 2d Sess, reprinted in 1974 US Code Cong & Admin News 5038, 5084, 5085]

One court held that trustees violated the diversification rule when over 65 percent of the plan's assets were invested in commercial first mortgages secured by property located in one area. The lack of diversification caused too much risk that the value of the assets would decline in the event of a severe economic downturn in the area where the property securing the mortgages was located. As a result, the investments in the aggregate were held to be imprudent. [Brock v Citizens Bank of Clovis, 841 F 2d 344 (10th Cir)]

Another court held that an investment company that invested over 70 percent of a plan's assets in long-term government bonds did not properly diversify plan assets because the investment company failed to determine the plan's particular cash flow needs and was forced to sell some bonds at a loss to meet the plan's need for cash. [GIW Inds, Inc v Trevor, Stewart, Burton & Jacobsen, Inc, 845 F 2d 729 (11th Cir 1990)] However, other courts have found that no violation occurred with an investment of almost 90 percent of a plan's assets in one profitable investment or that the failure to diversify was not an imprudent act. [Etter v J Pease Const Co, Inc, 963 F 2d 1005 (7th Cir 1992); Lanka v O'Higgins, No. 88-CV-922 (ND NY 1992)]

It is possible to meet the diversification requirement by investing plan assets in a bank's pooled investment fund (see Q 19:45), a mutual fund (see Q 19:46), or insurance or annuity contracts if the bank, mutual fund, or insurance company diversifies its investments.

The diversification requirement does not apply to an investment in employer securities by an ESOP (see Q 24:1). [Ershick v United Missouri Bank of Kansas City, NA, No. 90-3283 (10th Cir 1991)] However, an ESOP must offer certain participants the right to elect to diversify the stock acquired after 1986 and allocated to their accounts (see Qs 24:42–24:52).

Q 19:39   Must a plan make only blue chip investments?

No. DOL says "although securities issued by a small or new company may be a riskier investment than securities issued by a blue chip company, the investment in the former company may be entirely proper under . . . [the] prudence rule." [Preamble to DOL Reg § 2550.404a-1]

The degree of risk that the trustee takes in making investments depends in part on the type of plan the employer maintains. In a defined contribution plan (see Q 2:2), benefits received by a plan participant are based on the employer's contributions, increased or decreased by the return on plan investments. Thus, it may be appropriate to consider some speculative investments in a defined contribution plan.

In a defined benefit plan (see Q 2:3), a rate of return on investments above that assumed by the actuary reduces required contributions, and a rate of return below the assumed rate increases required contributions. Thus, investments will normally be of a nature that will return at least as much as the actuary has assumed. It is likely, therefore, that speculative investments in a defined benefit plan will have less appeal than in a defined contribution plan.

Q 19:40   How can a trustee or other plan fiduciary be protected from lawsuits for failure to meet the prudent man rule?

In acting prudently, trustees or other fiduciaries should also act defensively, building a record to defend their actions. Fiduciaries should, for example:

1. Keep detailed records of the actions taken and the factors that went into the decisions;

2. Make sure these records describe in detail the relevant circumstances prevailing at the time—that is, outline the conditions under which the action was taken; and

3. Make sure all reasonable steps have been taken to acquire the information needed to make informed decisions.

Q 19:41 May a qualified retirement plan invest in employer securities or employer real property?

A plan subject to ERISA generally may not acquire or hold qualifying employer securities (see Q 19:43) or qualifying employer real property (see Q 19:42) if the total fair market value of such assets exceeds 10 percent of the fair market value of the plan's assets at the time of acquisition. The 10 percent limitation does not apply to an eligible individual account plan that specifically authorizes such investments. An eligible individual account plan is defined as:

1. A profit sharing, stock bonus, thrift, or savings plan;

2. An ESOP; or

3. A money purchase pension plan in existence on the date of ERISA's enactment that invested primarily in qualifying employer securities at that time. [ERISA § 407]

Individual account plans that are part of a floor offset arrangement—an arrangement under which the plan's benefits are taken into account in determining a participant's benefits under a defined benefit plan—established after December 17, 1987, do not fall within this exception. [ERISA § 407(d)(3)(C)]

In addition, the two plans that constitute the floor offset arrangement will be treated as a single plan for purposes of the 10 percent limit.

Example. Samsin Corporation and Tasha Corporation each have floor offset arrangements with assets of $200,000 divided equally between their defined benefit and profit sharing plans. Samsin Corporation established its floor offset arrangement in 1985; Tasha Corporation's was established in 1988. Up to $10,000 of the assets of Samsin Corporation's defined benefit plan and up to $100,000 (which is 100 percent of the assets) of Samsin Corporation's profit sharing plan can be invested in qualifying employer securities—for a total of $110,000. In contrast, the amount of Tasha Corporation's qualifying employer securities held by the floor offset arrangement may not exceed $20,000 (10 percent of its assets in the aggregate). [ERISA § 407(d)(9)]

Q 19:42   What is qualifying employer real property?

Employer real property is real property leased to an employer of employees covered by the plan or an affiliate of the employer. Such real property is qualifying only if it is dispersed geographically, suitable for more than one use, and held without violation of the other ERISA fiduciary rules (except the diversification and prohibited transaction rules, which do not apply). [ERISA §§ 406(d)(2), 406(d)(4)]

Q 19:43   What are qualifying employer securities?

Employer securities are stock, marketable obligations, or certain publicly traded partnership interests issued by an employer of employees covered by the plan or an affiliate of the employer. Stock or partnership interests acquired by a plan other than an eligible individual account plan after December 17, 1987 will be qualifying employer securities only if (1) not more than 25 percent of the aggregate amount of stock of the same class issued and outstanding at the time of acquisition is held by the plan, and (2) at least 50 percent of such aggregate amount is held by persons independent of the issuer. For stock acquired on or before December 17, 1989, plans had until December 31, 1992 to comply with the new rules. [ERISA §§ 407(d)(5), 407(f)]

Q 19:44   What does earmarking investments mean?

Earmarking in a defined contribution plan (see Q 2:2) allows each participant, on a nondiscriminatory basis, an opportunity to invest funds contributed to the plan on the participant's behalf as the participant sees fit in any investment vehicle that the trustees are willing to administer. Traditional retirement plan investments—blue chip stocks, bonds, and real estate—can be passed over in favor of more speculative investments such as new stock issues, diamonds, gold, art, and antiques. However, amounts invested in collectibles under an earmarked plan will be treated as distributions for tax purposes. Collectibles are defined as works of art, rugs, antiques, precious metals, stamps, coins, and any other tangible property specified as a collectible by IRS. [IRC § 408(m)]

There is no place for earmarking of employer contributions in a defined benefit plan (see Q 2:3) since there are no individual accounts and investment gains or losses affect the amount the employer must contribute to the plan rather than the level of benefits payable to participants. However, earmarking of voluntary or rollover contributions by participants may be appropriate. Earmarking in a self-directed account plan (see Q 19:6) has the added advantage of possibly relieving the plan's trustees of liability for poor investment decisions made by the participant.

Q 19:45   What are pooled investment funds?

Pooled investment funds are commingled funds maintained by a bank on behalf of many qualified retirement plans. When a bank is appointed as trustee and the qualified retirement plan's assets are invested by the bank, the company retains only a limited choice in directing the investment of the plan's assets.

Generally, the bank has a dual fund arrangement—a fixed-income fund and a common stock fund—that permits the company to direct the proportion of its contributions invested in each fund.

The pooling of funds makes it possible to offer small plans the economies and security of a large plan. This investment vehicle may be particularly attractive to small and medium-sized plans, such as plans in which the annual contribution is below $100,000.

To participate in a pooled investment fund, the company maintaining the plan must adopt the bank's collective trust as part of its own trust and authorize investments in the bank's trust.

A trustee must, of course, be prudent in selecting and retaining the bank that directs the plan's investments.

Q 19:46 Can plan assets be invested in a mutual fund?

Yes. Mutual funds are a common investment vehicle, especially for small plans desiring professional investment management but not wishing to retain a bank's trusteeship or for plans that are too small to participate in a bank's pooled investment fund. A trustee must, of course, be prudent in selecting and retaining the mutual fund in which plan assets are invested, taking into account the wide variety of funds available with different investment goals.

Chapter 20

Prohibited Transactions

Both ERISA and the Code prohibit certain classes of transactions between a retirement plan and parties in interest to the plan, regardless of the fairness of the particular transaction involved or the benefit to the plan. In addition, fiduciaries are prohibited from engaging in certain conduct that would affect their duty of loyalty to the plan. This chapter examines the nature of prohibited transactions, the penalties that apply when a prohibited transaction occurs, and the statutory, administrative, and class exemptions to the prohibited-transaction rules.

Q 20:1   What is a prohibited transaction?

A prohibited transaction occurs under ERISA if a plan fiduciary (see Q 19:1) causes the retirement plan (see Q 20:3) to engage in a transaction that the fiduciary knows or should know constitutes a direct or indirect:

1. Sale, exchange, or lease of any property between the plan and a party in interest (see Q 20:2);
2. Loan or other extension of credit between the plan and a party in interest (Ltr Rul 9238003);
3. Furnishing of goods, services, or facilities between the plan and a party in interest;
4. Transfer of plan assets to a party in interest or the use of plan assets by or for the benefit of a party in interest; or

   5. Acquisition of employer securities or employer real property in excess of the limits set by law (see Q 19:41). [ERISA § 406(a)(1)]

In addition, ERISA prohibits a fiduciary from:

   1. Dealing with plan assets (see Q 19:15) in the fiduciary's own interest or for the fiduciary's own account;

   2. Acting in any transaction involving the plan on behalf of a party whose interests are adverse to the interests of the plan or its participants or beneficiaries; or

   3. Receiving any consideration for the fiduciary's own personal account from any person dealing with the plan in connection with any transaction involving plan assets. [ERISA § 406(b)]

For example, receipt of commissions by a fiduciary's wholly owned subsidiary on loans from a plan to unrelated borrowers is a prohibited transaction. [Murphy v Dawson, No. 88-2992 (4th Cir 1989)] A plan's payment of legal fees to the attorneys defending a trustee in a criminal prosecution is a prohibited transaction between the plan and the trustee. [O'Malley v Comm'r, No. 91-3470 (7th Cir 1992), *aff'g* 96 TC 644 (1991)]

Loans from a law firm's qualified retirement plan to clients of the law firm pending settlement of their lawsuits are prohibited transactions because the loans benefit the law firm's business. [Ltr Ruls 9118001, 9238001] Similarly, a loan from a plan to a partnership in which a trustee had a 39 percent interest was a prohibited transaction between the plan and the trustee because of the loan's benefit to the partnership in which the trustee had a significant interest. [Ltr Rul 9119002]

An investment by a qualified retirement plan in a participating mortgage loan made to a limited partnership in which the plan investment advisor held a 7.5 percent interest was a prohibited transaction because the ownership interest created a conflict of interest resulting in the advisor having divided loyalties. [Ltr Rul 9208001] The mere retention of an investment management company—a party in interest because it was half-owned by a corporation that also wholly owned a company sponsoring the qualified retirement plan—to manage the plan's assets did not result in a prohibited transaction because the sponsoring company, not the plan, paid the investment management fees. [DOL Opinion 91-44A]

For a discussion of statutory, administrative, and class exemptions, see Qs 20:7, 20:9, 20:12.

Q 20:2   Who is a party in interest?

Under ERISA, the following are parties in interest with respect to a plan:

1. Any fiduciary, counsel, or employee of the plan;
2. A person providing services to the plan;
3. An employer any of whose employees are covered by the plan, and any direct or indirect owner of 50 percent or more of such employer;
4. A relative—that is, spouse, ancestor, lineal descendant, or spouse of a lineal descendant—of any of the persons described in (1), (2), or (3) above;
5. An employee organization, any of whose members are covered by the plan;
6. A corporation, partnership, estate, or trust of which at least 50 percent is owned by any person or organization described in (1), (2), (3), (4), or (5) above;
7. Officers, directors, 10-percent-or-more shareholders, and employees of any person or organization described in (2), (3), (5), or (6) above; and
8. A 10-percent-or-more partner of or joint venturer with any person or organization described in (2), (3), (5), or (6) above. [ERISA § 3(14)]

Q 20:3   How do the prohibited-transaction provisions under the Code differ from the prohibited-transaction provisions under ERISA?

The prohibited-transaction provisions under the Code are in many respects the same as those under ERISA. However, the Code uses the term disqualified person rather than party in interest (see Q 20:2) and does not require knowledge on the part of a fiduciary that the transaction or conduct is prohibited. The definition of the terms party in interest under ERISA and disqualified person under the Code are nearly identical, but the term party in interest is slightly more inclusive (i.e., the ERISA, but not the Code, definition includes counsel to and employees of the plan, and all employees—not only highly compensated employees (see Q 3:3)—of the employer). [IRC § 4975(e)(2)]

Plans that cover only a sole shareholder and/or the shareholder's spouse and plans that cover only partners are not subject to ERISA and, therefore, are not subject to ERISA's prohibited-transaction provisions. However, such plans are subject to the prohibited-transaction provisions of the Code. [DOL Reg § 2510.3-3(b) and (c)]

In addition, the prohibited-transaction provisions under the Code apply to individual retirement accounts (IRAs) while ERISA's prohibited-transaction provisions do not. [IRC § 4975(c)]

Q 20:4　What penalties may be imposed on a party in interest or disqualified person for engaging in a prohibited transaction?

Under the Code, a penalty tax equal to 5 percent of the amount involved in the transaction is imposed on the disqualified person (other than a fiduciary acting solely in that capacity) for each year or part thereof that the transaction remains uncorrected. An additional tax equal to 100 percent of the amount involved is imposed if the prohibited transaction is not timely corrected (see Q 20:5). [IRC §§ 4975(a), 4975(b)]

Under ERISA, any fiduciary (see Q 19:1) who engages in a prohibited transaction is personally liable for any losses to the plan and must restore to the plan any profit made by the fiduciary through the use of the plan's assets. Also, the civil penalty imposed by DOL for certain breaches of fiduciary duty applies to prohibited transactions (see Q 19:25), but the penalty is reduced by any penalty tax imposed under Section 4975. [ERISA §§ 409(a), 502(l)]

Q 20:5　How is a prohibited transaction corrected?

A prohibited transaction is corrected by undoing the transaction to the extent possible, but in any event placing the plan in a financial position no worse than the position it would have been in had the party in interest (see Q 20:2) acted under the highest fiduciary standards. [IRC § 4975(f)(5)]

A subsidiary that sold customer loans to its parent corporation's profit sharing plan was not entitled to an exemption from the 5 percent tax on prohibited transactions (see Q 20:4) because no class exemption (see Q 20:12) was available since the plan trustee was also the sole shareholder and president of the parent corporation and president of the subsidiary. The plan could not cure the prohibited transaction by retroactively appointing an unrelated co-trustee (see Q 20:10). However, the subsidiary was not assessed the 100 percent tax because the plan timely sold the loans. [Westoak Realty and Investment Co, Inc, 63 TCM 2502 (1992)]

A sole shareholder's transfer of assets from the employer's two retirement plans to the employer's checking account constituted a prohibited transaction. Furthermore, the sole shareholder's payments to former participants from the employer's assets and from his own funds did not correct the prohibited transaction because the plans were not restored to the same financial position they would have been in had the prohibited transaction not occurred. The employer and the shareholder were found jointly and severally liable for both the 5 percent and the additional 100 percent penalty taxes (see Q 20:4). [Ltr Rul 9316001]

Q 20:6 May a plan purchase insurance to cover any losses to the plan resulting from a prohibited transaction?

Yes, a plan may carry insurance to protect itself from loss due to the conduct of a fiduciary (see Q 19:1). However, a plan cannot contain a provision relieving a fiduciary from liability for actions taken with respect to a prohibited transaction. [ERISA § 410]

Q 20:7 Are there any statutory exceptions to the prohibited-transaction provisions?

There are numerous statutory exceptions to the prohibited-transaction provisions. Some of the most common are as follows:

1. Loans made by a plan to a party in interest (see Q 20:2) who is a plan participant or beneficiary if such loans (1) are available to all participants and beneficiaries on a reasonably equivalent basis, (2) are not made available to highly compensated employees (see Q 3:2) in an amount greater than the amount made available to other employees, (3) are made in accordance with specific provisions regarding such loans set forth in the plan, (4) bear a reasonable rate of interest, and (5) are adequately secured. For more details on plan loans, see Questions 13:44 through Q 13:48.

2. Services rendered by a party in interest to a plan that are necessary for the establishment or operation of the plan if no more than reasonable compensation is paid. DOL has found no violation when a fiduciary received investment management fees from a plan. [DOL Opinions 93-06A and 92-08A]

3. A loan to an employee stock ownership plan (ESOP), provided the interest rate is not in excess of a reasonable interest rate (see Q 24:4).

4. Ancillary services provided by a federal or state supervised bank or similar financial institution that is a fiduciary (see Q 19:1) to the plan, provided (1) the bank or similar financial institution has adopted adequate internal safeguards to ensure that provision of the ancillary service is consistent with sound banking and financial practice, and (2) no more than reasonable compensation is paid for such services.

5. The acquisition or sale by a plan of qualifying employer securities (see Q 19:43) or the acquisition, sale, or lease by a plan of qualifying employer real property (see Q 19:42) if (1) the acquisition, sale, or lease is for adequate consideration, (2) no commission is charged, and (3) the restrictions and limitations of ERISA Section 407 are satisfied. In one case, disqualified persons sold their interest in land including mineral rights to an ESOP (see Q 24:1). Because the mineral rights were not leased to the employer and, with respect to the land leased, such properties were not dispersed geographically, the land did not constitute qualifying employer real property and the exemption did not apply. [Zabolotny, 97 TC 385 (1991)] In another case, a real estate transaction between a disqualified person and a profit sharing plan did not satisfy the requirements for

an exemption because the property was never leased to the corporation sponsoring the plan or to an affiliate and was not composed of a substantial number of land parcels dispersed geographically. [Pearland Investment Co., 62 TCM 1221 (1991)]

[ERISA §§ 408(b), 408(e); IRC § 4975(d); DOL Opinion 90-04A]

Q 20:8 Can an employer's contribution of property to a qualified retirement plan be a prohibited transaction?

According to DOL and IRS, the contribution of property to a pension plan (e.g., defined benefit or money purchase pension plan; see Qs 2:3, 2:4) is a prohibited transaction because the contribution discharges the employer's legal obligation to contribute cash to the plan. On the other hand, if the plan is not a pension plan (e.g., profit sharing plan; see Q 2:6), the contribution of property is not a prohibited transaction because it is purely voluntary and does not relieve the employer of an obligation to make cash contributions to the plan. However, a transfer of encumbered property would be treated as a sale or exchange (i.e., prohibited transaction) no matter what type of plan is involved. [DOL Opinions 81-69A and 90-05A; also see Ltr Rul 9145006]

The U.S. Supreme Court, agreeing with both DOL and IRS, ruled that the transfer of unencumbered property to a defined benefit plan is a prohibited transaction because it constitutes a sale or exchange within the meaning of the Code. [Comm'r v Keystone Consolidated Ind, Inc, No. 91-1677 (S Ct 1993)]

Q 20:9 Can a party in interest obtain an exemption from the prohibited-transaction restrictions?

DOL may grant an exemption from the prohibited-transaction rules if the exemption is (1) administratively feasible, (2) in the interests of the plan and of its participants and beneficiaries, and (3) protective of the rights of the plan's participants and beneficiaries. [ERISA § 408(a); IRC § 4975(c)(2)]

IRS has granted DOL primary authority to issue rulings and regulations on, and grant exemptions from, the prohibited-transaction restrictions. A specific statement explaining how the proposed exemption satisfies the requirements listed above and detailed information concerning the proposed transaction are required. [DOL Reg §§ 2570.30–2570.52]

Q 20:10 Can a prohibited-transaction exemption be granted retroactively?

Yes, but only under very limited circumstances. DOL generally will grant a retroactive exemption only if the applicant acted in good faith and the safeguards necessary for the grant of a prospective exemption were in place when the prohibited transaction occurred. DOL generally will not grant a retroactive exemption if the transaction resulted in a loss to the plan or was inconsistent with the general fiduciary responsibility provisions of ERISA Sections 403 and 404. [DOL Tech Rel 85-1]

Q 20:11 Can a prohibited-transaction exemption be used to benefit the owner of a closely held corporation?

Yes. Although the continued well-being of the plan is the prime consideration in qualifying for an exemption from the prohibited-transaction restrictions, the fact that the corporation or a shareholder also benefits from the transaction will not preclude the granting of an exemption. For example, it may be possible for the corporation to borrow from its cash-rich qualified retirement plan or to sell assets to the plan to improve the business's cash flow without incurring a penalty. As the following case histories illustrate, DOL is willing to approve an exemption even if the corporation or shareholder will reap a substantial benefit from the transaction with the qualified retirement plan.

Business financing: Leep Homes, a corporation engaged in building homes in California, received approval from DOL to enter into a sale-leaseback arrangement for its model homes with its profit sharing and defined benefit plans. Investments in the corporation's model homes were estimated to yield the plans a net return of 10 percent and would be limited to 25 percent of each plan's assets. Leep would buy the land and incur all development expenses. The purchase price was set at Leep's costs for building the homes.

An independent real estate investment advisor was to check out the model homes and have the power to reject any home offered to the plans. Leep was to pay all maintenance expenses and taxes. The plan's trustee was to have an option to sell the homes back to Leep at cost or fair market value, whichever was greater. Any offers to buy from third parties would be reviewed by the real estate advisor; Leep, however, would have a right of first refusal. Elwood J. Leep, sole stockholder of Leep Homes, was to personally guarantee the corporation's lease payments. [PT Exemption 80-61]

Loan to corporation: DOL granted a New York law firm an exemption that permitted the corporation's defined benefit plan to make loans to the law firm on a recurring basis over a five-year period. The proceeds of the loans were to be used by the corporation to buy automobiles. [PT Exemption 82-125]

Selling an unwanted asset: A doctor's professional corporation had a profit sharing plan that permitted him (as well as all other participants) to direct the investment of funds for his own account. Several years ago, he had the plan invest in residential farmland. The land cost the plan $55,000 plus $30,000 spent on improvements. Since the land supported only subsistence agricultural activities and yielded little or no income, the land was not helping to build much of a nest egg for the doctor's retirement.

The plan received approval from DOL to sell the land to the doctor for $88,000, its then current value. After selling the land, which represented a substantial part of the assets in the doctor's account, the plan was able to invest in other assets yielding a much higher return. [PT Exemption 80-38]

Sale by parties in interest to plan: DOL granted an exemption to participants in a medical corporation's profit sharing plan that enabled the participants to sell promissory notes to their respective individual plan accounts. The promissory notes, which were issued by an unrelated third party, were held by the participants and sold for cash to their respective fully vested individual plan accounts at fair market value. [PT Exemption 82-143]

Lease of facilities: A professional corporation's profit sharing and money purchase pension plans acquired medical facilities and then sought to lease them to the plans' sponsor. Based on evidence that the terms of the lease were at least as favorable to the plans as those they could obtain from an unrelated party, the transaction was exempted. [PT Exemption 83-124]

Loan to plan: DOL granted an exemption, on both a retroactive and a prospective basis, to loans by an insurance company to a qualified retirement plan of the maximum loan values of life insurance policies held by the plan on the lives of the plan participants. [PT Exemption 86-13]

Q 20:12   What is a prohibited-transaction class exemption?

In addition to the statutory and administrative exemptions from the prohibited-transaction rules, DOL can grant a class exemption under which a party in interest or disqualified person (see Qs 20:2, 20:3) who meets the requirements of the class exemption will automatically be entitled to relief from the prohibited-transaction rules.

The following is a brief summary of some of the transactions for which prohibited-transaction class exemptions (PTCEs) have been issued. Many of these exemptions have detailed requirements that are not summarized here.

PTCE 86-128: PTCE 86-128 allows broker-dealers who are plan fiduciaries to effect or execute securities transactions for a fee paid by the plan, if certain requirements are satisfied. The exemption also allows sponsors of pooled separate accounts and other pooled investment funds to use their affiliates to effect or execute securities transactions for such accounts if certain conditions are met. [51 FR 41686]

PTCE 75-1: PTCE 75-1 permits certain transactions among employee benefit plans, broker-dealers, reporting dealers, and banks. Under this exemption, the prohibited-transaction provisions of ERISA will not apply to the purchase or sale of securities between a broker-dealer registered under the Securities and Exchange Act of 1934 and an employee benefit plan during the existence of an underwriting or selling syndicate with respect to such securities or a reporting dealer who is a market maker. The exemption also allows the extension of credit between a broker-dealer and a plan. [40 FR 50845]

PTCE 84-14: PTCE 84-14 permits parties in interest to engage in various transactions involving plan assets that would otherwise be prohibited transactions if, among other conditions, the plan assets are managed by persons defined in the exemption as qualified professional asset managers (QPAMs). QPAMs can be banks, savings and loans, insurance companies, and investment managers that are regulated by applicable state or federal law and meet certain financial standards. A major condition of the exemption is the requirement that the QPAM maintain independence from the entities in which the plan invests by retaining full authority over the terms of transactions and investment decisions. [49 FR 9494, as amended by 50 FR 41430]

PTCE 81-6: Securities lending arrangements between a security owner and a broker-dealer may enable the owner to increase its return on its assets. PTCE 81-6 permits such arrangements provided neither the borrower nor any affiliate of the borrower has any discretionary authority with respect to the investment of plan assets involved in the transaction. [46 FR 7527, as amended by 52 FR 18754]

PTCE 77-3: PTCE 77-3 permits the acquisition and sale of shares of an open-end mutual fund registered under the Investment Company Act of 1940 by an employee benefit plan covering only employees of the mutual fund, the investment advisor, or principal underwriter of the mutual fund, or any affiliate thereof (whether or not such mutual fund, investment advisor, principal underwriter, or affiliate is a fiduciary of the plan). [42 FR 18734]

PTCE 79-13: PTCE 79-13 permits the acquisition and sale of shares of a closed-end mutual fund that is registered under the Investment Company Act of 1940 by an employee benefit plan covering only employees of the mutual fund, the investment advisor of the fund, or any affiliate thereof (whether or not the mutual fund, investment advisor, or affiliate is a fiduciary of the plan). [44 FR 25533]

PTCE 93-1: PTCE 93-1 permits banks, credit unions, and other financial institutions to give cash or other premiums as an incentive to open, or make contributions to, an IRA or Keogh plan (see Q 26:23).

PTCE 93-33: PTCE 93-33 allows banks to offer services at reduced or no cost to persons who maintain IRAs, SEPs, and Keogh plans, provided that the services offered are the same as those offered by the bank in the ordinary course of business to customers who do not maintain such plans or IRAs (see Q 26:23).

A proposed class exemption would permit an employee benefit plan and a bank or any affiliate that is a party in interest to enter into a foreign currency exchange transaction if the transaction is directed by an independent fiduciary. [56 FR 11757]

See Questions 14:16 and 14:17 for PTCEs regarding the purchase and sale of life insurance policies, and Question 26:22 regarding application of the prohibited transaction rules to IRAs.

Chapter 21

Termination of the Plan

To qualify for tax-favored status, an employer's qualified retirement plan must be permanent. Nevertheless, an employer may amend the plan, terminate the plan, or stop contributing to the plan. This chapter examines how these actions may affect plan participants and the plan status, and discusses the rules regarding the termination of qualified retirement plans.

Q 21:1 Once a qualified retirement plan is established, may the employer terminate it?

Yes. Although the employer must have intended the plan to be permanent, it may be terminated if the plan permits it. In addition, in the case of a defined benefit plan (see Q 2:3) covered by Title IV of ERISA (see Qs 21:9, 21:12, 21:13), the applicable termination rules must be satisfied.

Defined contribution plans (see Q 2:2) and defined benefit plans not covered by Title IV of ERISA are not subject to these rules. However, not less than 15 days before the effective date of termination, the plan administrator must provide a written notice to each participant and beneficiary in a terminating pension plan (see Q 21:57). [ERISA § 204(h)]

Q 21:2 May a qualified retirement plan be terminated by a formal declaration of the plan sponsor's board of directors?

Although the plan sponsor's board of directors should adopt a resolution authorizing the termination of a qualified retirement plan, certain substantive and/or notice requirements must also be met to implement a plan termination (see Qs 21:17, 21:19, 21:57).

The date that a plan subject to PBGC jurisdiction is deemed to terminate can be no earlier than the date determined under applicable PBGC provisions (see Q 21:32). Where a plan sponsor never notified PBGC of its intention to terminate its defined benefit plan, PBGC properly established the date on which the sponsor ceased operations as the plan's involuntary termination date, not the date ten years earlier when the plan sponsor informed its employees that the plan was being terminated. [PBGC v Mize Company, Inc, No. 92-1351 (4th Cir 1993)] In the case of any other qualified retirement plan, the date of termination is generally established by the terms of the plan and by the actions of the company officials (e.g., a meeting of the board of directors). [ERISA § 4041(a)(1); Treas Reg § 1.411(d)-2; Phillips v Bebber, Nos. 89-2184 and 89-2189 (4th Cir 1990); Rev Rul 89-87, 1989-2 CB 81, Rev Rul 79-237, 1979-2 CB 190]

An independent plan administrator may terminate a pension plan despite the plan sponsor's desire to continue the plan. [Delgrosso v Spang and Co, No. 82-2672 (WD Pa 1991); ERISA § 4041(a)] Pension plan trustees who terminated a plan after a plan sponsor changed the plan's funding method acted in good faith and did not breach their fiduciary duties (see Qs 19:10, 19:11). [Morgan v Independent Drivers Assn Pension Plan, Nos. 91-1029, 91-1310 (10th Cir 1992)]

However, IRS has declared that a termination will not occur if plan assets are not distributed as soon as administratively feasible, even if the plan has been terminated in accordance with Title IV of ERISA (see Q 21:61).

Q 21:3 Which factors may cause a qualified retirement plan to be terminated?

A defined benefit plan covered by the Title IV program (see Qs 21:12, 21:13) will be considered to be terminated only if the conditions and procedures prescribed by PBGC are satisfied (see Qs 21:2, 21:17, 21:19).

Whether a defined contribution plan (see Q 2:2) is terminated is generally a question to be determined with regard to all the facts and circumstances in a particular case. For example, a plan may be terminated when, in connection with the winding up of the company's trade or business, the company begins to discharge its employees (see Q 21:5). However, a plan is not terminated merely because a company consolidates or replaces that plan with a comparable plan (see Q 21:6). [Treas Reg § 1.401-6(b)] Similarly, a plan is not terminated merely because the company sells or otherwise disposes of its trade or business if the acquiring company continues the plan as a separate and distinct plan of its own or consolidates or replaces that plan with a comparable plan.

Q 21:4 What is the effect of a plan termination on a participant's accrued benefit?

A qualified retirement plan must provide that (1) upon its full or partial termination or (2) in the case of a profit sharing plan upon complete discontinuance of contributions under the plan "the rights of all affected employees to benefits accrued to the date of such termination, partial termination, or discontinuance, to the extent funded as of such date, or the amounts credited to the employees' accounts, are nonforfeitable" (see Q 9:12). [IRC § 411(d)(3)]

The practical effect of a plan termination, therefore, is that each affected participant becomes 100 percent vested in the participant's accrued benefit (see Q 9:2) as of the date of termination if the plan has sufficient assets to cover the benefit. In one case, where there was a partial termination (see Q 21:5) of an ESOP (see Q 24:1), the court held that the terminated participants were not required to be vested in unallocated assets held in a suspense account because these assets were not accrued benefits. [Rummel v Consolidated Freightways, Inc, 1992 US Dist Lexis 15144 (ND Cal 1992)]

Generally, a participant who is partially vested need not become 100 percent vested upon termination of the plan if the participant separates from service and is paid the vested accrued benefit prior to the date of termination. However, a partially vested participant who terminates service, is not paid the vested accrued benefit, and does not incur a one-year break in service (see Q 5:10) prior to the date of termination must become 100 percent vested upon termination of the plan. Some IRS district offices have interpreted the above rule to require that all nonvested former participants with breaks in service of less than five years who have not been paid their vested accrued benefits be fully vested (see Q 9:16). [IRC §§ 411(a)(6)(B), 411(a)(6)(C); Penn v Howe-Baker Eng'rs, Inc, No. 89-2257 (5th Cir 1990); GCM 39310 (Nov 29, 1984)]

In one case, the court upheld a plan administrator's decision to deny full credit to employees who were laid off prior to a plan's termination. The court reasoned that "a person is unaffected by a plan's termination unless either he or she was employed by the plan-sponsoring employer at the time of the plan's termination or his or her discharge was directly linked to the plan's termination." (See Q 21:5.) [Bayer v Holcroft/Loftus, Inc, 769 F Supp 225 (ED Mich 1991)]

Q 21:5   What is a partial termination?

Generally, whether or not a partial termination of a qualified retirement plan has occurred will be determined on the basis of all the facts and circumstances. Under applicable regulations, a partial termination may be found to have occurred when a significant group of employees covered by the plan is excluded from coverage, as a result of either an amendment to the plan or their discharge by the employer. Similarly, a partial termination may be held to have occurred when benefits or employer contributions are reduced or the eligibility or vesting requirements under the plan are made less liberal. However, if a partial termination of a qualified retirement plan occurs, the provisions of the Code and regulations apply only to the part of the plan that is terminated. [Treas Reg §§ 1.401-6(b)(2), 1.411(d)-2(b)(3)]

> **Example 1.** A profit sharing plan was not partially terminated where layoffs due to a sharp decline in the company's business resulted in a 19.85 percent reduction in the number of plan participants. The facts did not show employer abuse, bad faith, or misconduct (i.e., no reversion was created, the financial health of the plan was not adversely affected, and there was no discrimina-

tion in favor of highly compensated participants). Furthermore, the employer rehired a significant number of terminated employees in succeeding years. [Halliburton Co, 100 TC No. 15 (1993)] However, a partial termination did occur when a company sold most of its operating assets and did not make continued employment available to 83 percent of its employees. [Collingnon v Reporting Services Co, 1992 US Dist Lexis 10070 (CD Ill 1992)]

Example 2. Where between 40 and 70 percent of employees were laid off after completion of a project, and the union pension plan defined "partial termination" as a layoff of more than 20 percent of employees, the terminated employees became 100 percent vested. [Duncan v Northern Alaska Carpenters Retirement Fund, No. 90-133-DA (DC Ore 1992)] Similarly, a partial termination occurred when a multiemployer plan experienced two reductions of over 50 percent in participation. [Thayer v Alaska Teamster-Employer Pension Trust, No. A90-147 (DC Alas 1992)]

Example 3. An employer discharged 132 of the 395 employees participating in its qualified retirement plan. Of the discharged employees, 65 were not fully vested. The court originally held that no partial termination occurred because the 65 nonvested discharged participants represented only 16.4 percent of all 395 participants. Upon reconsideration, the court held that all discharged plan participants must be taken into account, including vested participants. Thus, a partial termination occurred because 33.4 percent of all plan participants, a significant group, were discharged. [Weil v Retirement Plan Administrative Committee of the Terson Co, Inc, 913 F 2d 1045 (2nd Cir 1991)]

Example 4. Two major oil companies (Gulf and Chevron) merged their operations in 1984 and merged their pension plans in 1986. The merger of operations resulted in a partial termination with respect to the significant number of Gulf plan participants (almost 10,000) who were discharged (prior to the merger of the plans) because of the merger of operations. A second partial termination occurred with respect to Gulf plan participants who were still employed by Chevron at the time of the merger of the plans. That merger resulted in a substantial reduction in future benefit accruals to those employees, thereby increasing the potential reversion to Chevron upon termination of the plan. [In re Gulf Pension Litigation, No. 86-4365 (SD Tex 1991)]

Example 5. A partial termination of a qualified retirement plan occurred when the employer's business was closed and 12 of the 15 participating employees were discharged upon refusing the opportunity to transfer to the employer's new business location. [Rev Rul 73-284, 1973-1 CB 139; see also Rev Rul 81-27, 1981-1 CB 228]

Example 6. In two successive years, an employer experienced reductions in its workforce of 34 percent and 51 percent, respectively, as a result of adverse economic conditions. The Tax Court ruled that, based on all the facts and circumstances, a partial termination occurred in each year. [Tipton & Kalmbach, Inc, 83 TC 154 (1984)]

Example 7. A corporation maintaining pension and profit sharing plans operated two divisions: one manufactured paint, and the other produced other types of wallcoverings. As a result of a split-off of one of the divisions to a new corporation, 16 employees (representing 14.7 percent of the participating employees) were transferred and were no longer eligible to participate in the original corporation's plans. In reviewing these facts, a court held that there was not a "significant percentage" of participants affected by the corporation's actions and that a partial termination of the plans did not occur. [Babb v Olney Paint Co, 764 F 2d 240 (4th Cir 1985); see also Kreis v Charles O. Townley, MD & Assocs, PC, 833 F 2d 74 (6th Cir 1987)]

If a determination letter on the continued qualification of the plan after a possible partial termination is desired, Form 5300 (see Q 15:7) should be filed with IRS.

Q 21:6 Does the adoption of a new qualified retirement plan to replace another plan result in a termination of the original plan?

Not necessarily. A qualified retirement plan is not considered to be terminated if it is either replaced by or converted into a comparable plan. For this purpose, a comparable plan is defined as a qualified retirement plan covered by the same limitations on deductions as the original plan. Since stock bonus plans, employee stock ownership plans (ESOPs), and profit sharing plans are generally covered by the same limitations on deductions, these plans are considered to be comparable. [Treas Reg §§ 1.381(c)(11)-1(d)(4), 1.401-6(b)(1)]

On the other hand, a defined benefit plan covered by Title IV is considered to be terminated if an amendment is adopted to convert the plan to a defined contribution plan, such as a profit sharing plan, an ESOP, or a stock bonus plan. However, the amendment will not take effect unless and until the requirements for a standard or distress termination under Title IV are satisfied (see Qs 21:17, 21:19). [ERISA § 4041(e)]

Furthermore, a transfer of assets in excess of those necessary to satisfy liabilities on a termination basis from a defined benefit plan to a defined contribution plan results in taxable income to the employer (see Qs 21:48, 21:51, 21:52). [GCM 39744 (Jul 14, 1988)]

Q 21:7 Can termination of a qualified retirement plan affect its tax-favored status for earlier years?

Yes. The termination of a plan, or the complete discontinuance of contributions to a profit sharing plan, can result in the retroactive disqualification of the plan, causing the disallowance of tax deductions for the employer. This will depend on whether the plan was intended as a permanent program for the exclusive benefit of employees or a temporary device to set aside funds for the benefit of highly compensated employees, and whether the plan was discriminatory in operation.

Generally, IRS will not treat the termination as a device to benefit highly compensated employees (see Qs 3:2, 4:19) if the termination is caused by a change in circumstances that would make it financially impractical to continue the plan. When termination of the plan occurs within a few years of its adoption, the reasons for termination will be examined closely. IRS will assume the plan was not temporary if the termination is for a "valid business reason" or on account of "business necessity."

Form 5310, Application for Determination Upon Termination, provides some insight into IRS's views as to what reasons for plan termination it considers valid, notwithstanding the presumed permanence of the plan. The listed reasons include:

- A change in ownership by merger
- The liquidation or dissolution of the employer
- A change in ownership by sale or transfer
- The existence of adverse business conditions
- The adoption of a new plan

If the plan termination is due to adverse business conditions, IRS requires an explanation of why such adverse conditions require the plan's termination.

When the termination occurs after ten years of active operation, IRS will usually not challenge the plan on these grounds even though a valid business reason for the termination is lacking. [Rev Rul 72-239, 1972-1 CB 107]

Q 21:8 Is there a limit on the amount that a pension plan may pay to participants in the first ten years of operation?

Prior to the issuance of regulations under Section 401(a)(4), a plan that substantially funded benefits for older, higher-paid employees at a more rapid pace than for younger, lower-paid employees (e.g., a defined benefit plan) was limited in the amount that it could pay out. The restriction applied to the 25 highest paid employees if:

1. The plan terminated within ten years of its establishment;
2. Benefits became payable within ten years of the plan's establishment or before the full current costs for the first ten years had been funded; or
3. The plan was amended before the end of the ten-year period and the amendment substantially increased benefits. In this situation, a new ten-year limitation period would begin.

Treas Reg § 1.401-4(c)]

However, the full benefit was allowed to be paid if there was adequate provision for repayment of any part of the distribution representing the restricted portion. A participant, part of the restricted group, who was to receive a large distribution, agreed to provide the plan trustee with a security agreement and letter of credit to fund his obligation to repay the plan if necessary. The agreement did not violate the restriction. [Rev Rul 81-135, 1981-1 CB 203; Ltr Rul 9210037]

The regulations under Section 401(a)(4) change the above rules and, with respect to plan terminations, place different restrictions on distributions commencing in a plan year beginning on or after January 1, 1994. A qualified retirement plan will not satisfy Section 401(a)(4) if the plan's termination discriminates significantly in favor of highly compensated employees (see Qs 3:2, 4:19). The determination of discrimination is based on all relevant facts and circumstances. [Treas Reg § 1.401(a)(4)-5(a)]

Also, a defined benefit plan (and a money purchase pension plan with an accumulated funding deficiency) must provide that the annual payments to an employee are restricted to an amount equal to a straight life annuity that is the actuarial equivalent of the accrued benefit and other benefits to which the employee is entitled under the plan (other than a Social Security supplement) plus the amount an employee would be entitled to receive under a Social Security supplement. The restrictions apply to distributions to all highly compensated employees and highly compensated former employees. However, in any given year, the plan may limit the preceding restricted group to those 25 highly compensated employees whose compensation was the highest.

The above restrictions are not applicable to a qualified retirement plan if:

1. The distribution to a restricted highly compensated employee is less than 1 percent of plan assets after the payment of the benefit;

2. The value of the plan assets is at least 110 percent of the plan's current liabilities; or

3. The value of the benefit payable to the restricted highly compensated employee does not exceed $3,500 (the amount described in Section 411(a)(11)(A)).

[Treas Reg § 1.401(a)(4)-5(b); Rev Rul 92-76, 1992-2 CB 76]

Q 21:9   What is Title IV of ERISA?

Title IV of ERISA established the rules regarding the termination of many defined benefit plans (see Q 2:3). In addition, it established an insurance program to guarantee that participants and beneficiaries will receive certain pension benefits promised under an employer's defined benefit plan if the plan does not have sufficient assets to cover certain benefits in the event of the plan's termination. The program was designed to be self-financed, funded with premiums paid by sponsors of covered plans.

Q 21:10   What is the Pension Benefit Guaranty Corporation?

ERISA established PBGC as a wholly owned government corporation to administer the termination rules and to establish the mechanism for insuring benefits under Title IV. [ERISA § 4002]

Q 21:11   What are the Single Employer Pension Plan Amendments Act and the Pension Protection Act?

SEPPAA was enacted as a sweeping reform of the single-employer defined benefit plan termination rules of Title IV. It was designed to bolster an increasingly overburdened plan termination insurance program and to correct a system that, in some instances, encouraged employers to terminate a plan, avoid their obligations to pay benefits, and shift unfunded pension liabilities to PBGC. PPA was designed to protect the fiscal integrity of the Title IV program, for example, by increasing premium rates and limiting the circumstances in which an employer may terminate its defined benefit plan (see Q 2:3).

As a result of SEPPAA and PPA, a defined benefit plan may be voluntarily terminated (i.e., terminated by the plan administrator) only if the conditions for either a standard or a distress termination are satisfied (see Qs 21:17, 21:19). In addition, these laws expanded the employer's liability upon termination if the plan is underfunded (see Q 21:47).

Q 21:12   What pension plans are insured by PBGC?

To be entitled to coverage, the plan must be a defined benefit plan (see Q 2:3). In addition, the plan must:

1. Have been in effect for at least one year;
2. Be maintained by an employer engaged in commerce or in an industry or activity that affects commerce, or by a labor organization that represents employees who are engaged in commerce or in activities affecting commerce; and
3. Be a qualified pension plan, or have been operated in practice as a qualified pension plan for the five plan years prior to the termination.

[ERISA § 4021(a)]

In one case, the court ruled that an employer was not liable to the PBGC for its terminated pension plan's underfunding because the plan was not qualified and, thus, was not insured by PBGC. [PBGC v Artra Group Inc, No. 90 C 5358 (ND Ill 1991)]

PBGC has stated that with respect to defined benefit plans that terminated prior to September 26, 1980 and were not amended to comply with the minimum vesting schedules, benefits are guaranteed only to the extent that they were vested under the express terms of the plan. [Policy Submission of Board of Directors of PBGC, Jan 14, 1993; also see, Page v PBGC, 968 F 2d 1310 (DC Cir 1992)]

Q 21:13   Are any qualified defined benefit plans exempt from PBGC coverage?

Excluded from plan termination insurance coverage are defined benefit plans (see Q 2:3) that are established and maintained:

1. For government employees (or to which the Railroad Retirement Acts apply);
2. For church employees, unless the plan elects under Section 410(d) to be covered and has notified PBGC that it wishes to have this section of the law apply to it;
3. Outside the United States for nonresident aliens;

4. Exclusively for one or more substantial owners (i.e., the sole owner of the trade or business, a more-than-10 percent partner, or a more-than-10 percent shareholder); or

5. By professional service employers that at no time have had more than 25 active participants.

In addition to the aforementioned plans, all defined contribution plans (e.g., profit sharing, money purchase pension, ESOPs, stock bonus) as well as certain nonqualified plans are excluded from Title IV coverage. [ERISA § 4021(b)]

A defined benefit plan becomes exempt as exclusively for the benefit of the substantial owner when (1) all nonowner employees have retired and received their plan benefits and (2) the owner remains as the only plan participant. [PBGC Opinion Letter No 90-6]

Q 21:14 What must plan sponsors pay as an insurance premium to PBGC?

The basic annual premium rate is $19 for each participant in a single-employer pension plan during the plan year. [ERISA § 4006(a)(3)(A)(i)] In addition, each plan year, a variable-rate component must be paid for underfunded plans equal to $9 for every $1,000 of unfunded vested benefits, divided by the number of participants for whom premiums are being paid as of the close of the preceding plan year. Because this variable premium may not exceed $53 per participant, the total premium amount for each participant cannot exceed $72. The variable-rate component does not apply to a plan if, for the prior plan year, contributions were made in an amount not less than the full funding limitation (see Q 8:16). [ERISA § 4006(a)(3)(E); PBGC Reg §§ 2610.22(a)(3), 2610.24(a)(5)]

For multiemployer plans—that is, plans maintained under a collective bargaining agreement to which two or more employers contribute—the annual PBGC premium is $2.60 per participant (see Q 25:2). [ERISA § 4006(a)(3)(A)(iii)]

The total amount of premiums is determined on the basis of the number of plan participants (see Q 21:15).

Q 21:15 How is the number of participants determined for insurance premium purposes?

The participant count is made as of the last day of the prior plan year, except that, for a new plan, the count is made as of the date on which the plan becomes subject to PBGC jurisdiction. [PBGC Reg § 2610.22]

The following categories of individuals are considered participants:

- All individuals accruing benefits or retaining or earning credited service under the plan
- Former employees with vested rights to either immediate or deferred benefits
- Retirees receiving or eligible to receive benefits
- Deceased participants whose beneficiaries are receiving benefits, and
- Any other "participants" as defined under the plan

Certain individuals to whom an insurance company has made an irrevocable commitment to pay benefits are not considered participants. The number of participants in the above categories should equal the total number reported on the Form 5500 series return/report (see Q 17:1) for the plan for the prior plan year. [PBGC Reg § 2610.2]

Q 21:16 Must a plan administrator notify PBGC when certain significant events affecting a single-employer defined benefit plan occur?

Yes. The plan administrator (see Q 16:1) may be required to notify PBGC within 30 days after the plan administrator knows or has reason to know of a reportable event.

The 30-day notice is always required for the following:

- Inability to pay benefits when due
- Failure to meet minimum funding standards (see Q 8:1) if the present value of unfunded vested benefits equals or exceeds $250,000 (unless PBGC Form 200 is filed; see Q 17:25)

- Bankruptcy, liquidation, or dissolution of a plan sponsor, and
- Certain transactions involving a change of employer

PBGC has waived the notice requirement for those reportable events that would have minimal impact on the plan, the employer, or PBGC, and for those reportable events about which IRS or DOL is required by ERISA to notify PBGC. Examples of these events include:

- Plan disqualification
- Decrease in benefits
- DOL finding of an ERISA violation
- Plan merger, consolidation, or transfer
- Certain corporate reorganizations
- A determination by IRS that there has been a complete or partial termination

[ERISA §§ 4043(a), 4043(b); PBGC Reg § 2615]

Q 21:17 What is a standard termination?

A single-employer defined benefit plan may be voluntarily terminated under Title IV's standard termination procedures only if it is determined that when the final distributions are made, the assets of the plan will be sufficient to cover all benefit liabilities (see Q 21:18) as of the termination date. In addition:

1. The plan administrator (see Q 16:1) must provide a 60-day advance notice of termination to affected parties (see Qs 21:29, 21:33);
2. A notice containing specified information (completed by the plan administrator), together with an enrolled actuary's certification, must be filed with PBGC (see Q 21:34);
3. A notice containing required information must be provided to participants and beneficiaries regarding benefits to be paid (see Q 21:35); and
4. PBGC must not have issued a notice of noncompliance stating that it has reason to believe that the standard termination

requirements have not been met or that the plan does not have sufficient assets for benefit liabilities (see Q 21:37).

[ERISA § 4041(b)]

Q 21:18   What are benefit liabilities?

Benefit liabilities under a single-employer defined benefit plan are defined as "the benefits of employees and their beneficiaries under the plan (within the meaning of § 401(a)(2) of the Internal Revenue Code of 1986)." [ERISA § 4001(a)(16)]

If a plan does not have sufficient assets for benefit liabilities, the plan sponsor may consider making a contribution to the plan. Also, a contributing sponsor, or a member of a controlled group (see Q 5:30) of a contributing sponsor, may make a commitment to contribute any additional sums necessary to make the plan sufficient. [PBGC Reg § 2617.7(a)] However, because of the rules relating to deductibility of contributions and funding requirements, the contribution may not be deductible. In this circumstance, some limited relief is offered whereby contributions made to a plan under a standard termination are deductible, but only to the extent that they are guaranteed by PBGC. [IRC § 404(g), clarified by OBRA '89 § 11841]

Alternatively, in order to facilitate the termination of a plan in a standard termination, a majority owner (i.e., an individual who owns 50 percent or more of the company) may agree to forgo receipt of all or part of the majority owner's benefit. To be valid:

1. The agreement must be in writing;

2. If the benefit is greater than $3,500, the spouse, if any, must consent in writing; and

3. The agreement must not be inconsistent with a QDRO (see Q 30:1).

[PBGC Reg § 2617.7(b)]

Q 21:19   What is a distress termination?

If a defined benefit plan (see Q 2:3) cannot satisfy the conditions for a standard termination (see Q 21:17), it can be voluntarily terminated only if the conditions for a distress termination of a single-employer plan are satisfied. This type of termination may occur if the employer contributing to the plan and each member of its controlled group (see Q 5:30) meet at least one of the following conditions:

1. Liquidation in bankruptcy or insolvency proceeding.

2. Reorganization in bankruptcy or insolvency proceeding. In addition, the bankruptcy petition must be filed prior to the proposed date of plan termination, and the bankruptcy or other appropriate court must determine that, unless the plan is terminated, the employer and all the members of the controlled group will be unable to pay their debts under a reorganization plan and unable to continue without a reorganization.

3. Termination of the plan is required to enable payment of debts while staying in business or to avoid unreasonably burdensome pension costs caused by a decline of the employer's covered workforce.

If PBGC determines that the requirements of a distress termination have been met, additional information may be required of the plan administrator and the enrolled actuary in order to determine the sufficiency of plan assets. PBGC must then notify the plan administrator as soon as possible after reaching its determination. [ERISA § 4041(c)]

Q 21:20   What benefits under a single-employer defined benefit plan are guaranteed by PBGC?

When a single-employer defined benefit plan terminates under the distress termination procedures, PBGC will guarantee the payment of "certain benefits." The characteristics of this type of benefit are that:

1. It is a pension benefit;

2. It is nonforfeitable (see Q 21:21) on the date of plan termination; and

3. A participant must be entitled to the benefit. The benefit will be guaranteed to the extent that it does not exceed the limitations set forth in ERISA and its regulations (see Qs 21:22–21:25). [ERISA §§ 4022(a), 4022(b); PBGC Reg § 2613.3]

Under a special rule, a qualified preretirement survivor annuity is not treated as forfeitable solely because the participant has not died as of the termination date. [ERISA § 4022(e)]

Q 21:21 Does PBGC guarantee a benefit that becomes nonforfeitable solely as a result of the plan's termination?

No. Although the plan must provide for 100 percent vesting upon termination (see Q 21:4), a benefit that vests because of this rule is not a guaranteed benefit. [ERISA § 4022(a)]

Q 21:22 Are there any limitations on the amount of the benefit PBGC will guarantee?

Yes. PBGC's guarantee may be subject to one or more statutorily prescribed benefit limitations (see Qs 21:23–21:25). For example, the guarantee may not exceed the maximum monthly benefit limitation amount, which is expressed in terms of an annuity that is payable for the life of the participant commencing at age 65. The maximum guaranteed benefit is adjusted annually to reflect inflation and cost-of-living increases (see Q 21:23).

Furthermore, the guaranteed benefit may not exceed the actuarial equivalent of a monthly benefit in the form of a life annuity commencing at age 65. Accordingly, if a benefit is payable at an earlier age, the maximum guaranteed benefit is actuarially reduced to reflect the earlier commencement of the receipt of the benefit. [ERISA § 4022(b); PBGC Reg § 2621.4]

Q 21:23 What is the maximum guaranteed monthly benefit?

The maximum guaranteed monthly benefit for plans terminating in 1993 is $2,437.50. This amount applies even though a participant may not retire and receive the benefit until years after the termination of the plan. [ERISA § 4022(b)(3); PBGC News Release No. 93-05, Dec 8, 1992; Appendix A to 29 CFR Part 2621]

The maximum guaranteed benefit has been adjusted for inflation and was initially $750.00 in 1974. For the prior five years, the adjusted amount was:

Year	Adjusted Amount
1992	$2,352.27
1991	$2,250.00
1990	$2,164.77
1989	$2,028.41
1988	$1,909.09

Q 21:24 What is the effect on PBGC's guarantees of a plan amendment prior to the plan's termination?

If an amendment is adopted within five years of the termination and adds a new benefit or increases the value of a benefit for any participant who is not a substantial owner (see Q 21:13), PBGC's guarantee will be subject to a phase-in rule. Such increases include any changes that advance a participant's entitlement (such as liberalization of the participation or vesting requirement), a reduction in the normal or early retirement ages, or a change in the form of benefit. Increases due to salary increases or additional years of service are not subject to this rule. Under this five-year phase-in rule, a benefit increase will be subject to the following formula: multiply the number of years a benefit increase has been in effect by the greater of 20 percent of the monthly increase or $20 per month (but not in excess of the actual increase). [ERISA § 4022(b)(7); PBGC Reg §§ 2621.2, 2621.6]

Any benefits provided under a plan to a participant who is a substantial owner, and thereafter any amendment benefiting a substantial owner, will be subject to a 30-year phase-in rule. [ERISA § 4022(b)(5); PBGC Reg § 2621.7] In one case, a substantial owner was precluded from receiving PBGC benefits after amendment and termination of the plan, because, under the original plan, the substantial owner would not have received any benefits. [Brown v PBGC (DC DC 1993)]

Q 21:25 What is the effect of the plan's disqualification on the guaranteed benefit?

PBGC will not guarantee any benefits that accrue after IRS has disqualified a plan or an amendment. [ERISA § 4022(b)(6); PBGC Reg § 2621.8]

Q 21:26 Can PBGC initiate the termination of a plan?

Yes. PBGC may institute termination proceedings in federal court if it finds that:

1. Minimum funding standards (see Q 8:1) have not been satisfied;
2. The plan will be unable to pay benefits when due;
3. A distribution of more than $10,000 was made to a substantial owner in any 24-month period for reasons other than death and, after the distribution, there are unfunded vested liabilities; or
4. The possible long-run liability of the employer to PBGC is expected to increase unreasonably if the plan is not terminated.

[ERISA § 4042(a)]

Where PBGC determined that its liability would increase unreasonably if a company's defined benefit plans were terminated after bankruptcy reorganization, PBGC was allowed to terminate the plans prior to reorganization. [PBGC v Fel, 798 F Supp 239 (DC NJ 1992)] In another case, the court upheld the decision of PBGC to terminate defined benefit plans where the record included reports that the plans were underfunded and there was no prospect that the plans would be properly funded in the future. [Pan American World Airways, Inc Cooperative Retirement Income Plan v The Pension Committee of Pan American World Airways, Inc, Nos. 91 Civ 5016 (MBM) and 91 Civ 5017 (MBM) (SD NY 1991)]

However, PBGC must institute termination proceedings whenever it determines that a single-employer defined benefit plan does not have enough assets to pay benefits that are currently due. [ERISA § 4042(a)]

Furthermore, PBGC may cease the termination of a plan and restore the plan to its status prior to termination if circumstances change. In a much publicized case, the Supreme Court allowed PBGC to restore terminated defined benefit plans. LTV Corporation (LTV) filed for bankruptcy. At that time, LTV maintained three underfunded defined benefit plans all covered by PBGC. PBGC instituted proceedings to involuntarily terminate the plans. Subsequently, LTV established new plans that provided benefits lost by the termination. In effect, the new "follow-on" plans provided benefits equal to the difference between the promised benefits under the terminated plans and PBGC guaranteed benefits. PBGC objected and determined to restore the plans. The Supreme Court upheld PBGC's authority to return responsibility for funding the terminated plans to the plan sponsor. [PBGC v LTV Corp, No. 89-390 (S Ct 1990)] The PBGC restoration order was held enforceable because PBGC was not required to consider whether restoration would lead to the retermination of the plans or whether the bankruptcy court would approve contributions to the restored plans. [PBGC v LTV Corp, No. 87 Civ 7261 (RJS)(SD NY 1990)] Employers may now be discouraged from using "follow-on" plans to shift the burden of paying benefits from the plan sponsor to PBGC. [ERISA § 4047]

Since the minimum funding standards (see Q 8:1) do not apply between the dates of termination and restoration and the plan will be underfunded, or become more underfunded, during this period, PBGC will issue a restoration payment schedule that provides for the amortization of the restored plan's unfunded liabilities over a period of up to 30 years after the PBGC restoration order. The restoration payment schedule is used to determine the minimum funding standards for the unfunded pre-restoration plan liabilities. Restored plans must reimburse PBGC for any guaranteed benefit payments (see Q 21:20) made by PBGC while the plan was terminated, and PBGC insurance premiums (see Q 21:14) must be paid on behalf of restored plans. [PBGC Reg § 2625; Temp Reg § 1.412(c)(1)-3T]

Q 21:27 Can a plan covered by Title IV be terminated if the termination would violate an existing collective bargaining agreement?

The authority of PBGC to terminate a plan under these circumstances will depend on whether the termination is initiated by the plan administrator (see Q 16:1) or PBGC. If the plan administrator attempts to terminate the plan under the standard or distress termination provisions (see Qs 21:17, 21:19), PBGC may not proceed with the termination. However, PBGC's authority to institute involuntary termination proceedings for such a plan is not limited by the fact that the termination would violate the collective bargaining agreement. [ERISA § 4041(a)(3); PBGC Opinion Letter No 87-4]

Q 21:28 Is there any restriction on the form of a benefit paid by a terminating defined benefit plan?

Yes. The general rule is that a benefit be paid in annuity form, unless the participant elects an optional form of benefit under the terms of the plan. [ERISA § 4041(b)(3)(A)(i); PBGC Reg § 2617.4] However, an exception exists for small amounts of benefits. PBGC and any other plan administrator of a terminating plan may choose to pay a benefit in a single payment without the consent of the participant if the present value of the benefit is $3,500 or less. [PBGC Reg §§ 2613.8, 2617.6; PBGC Opinion Letter No 90-5]

Q 21:29 Who must be notified of the company's intention to terminate a defined benefit plan covered by Title IV—and when must this notice be given?

The plan administrator (see Q 16:1) must provide to all affected parties (see Q 21:33) written notice of the company's intention to terminate a defined benefit plan covered by Title IV (Notice of Intent to Terminate—NOIT) at least 60 days and no more than 90 days before the proposed date of termination. [ERISA § 4041(a)(2); PBGC Reg §§ 2617.3(b)(1), 2617.22(a)]

Q 21:30 What information must be included in the NOIT?

According to regulations issued by PBGC, the plan administrator (see Q 16:1) must issue the NOIT (see Q 21:29) to each affected party (see Q 21:33) individually. Each notice must be either hand delivered or delivered by first-class mail or courier service to the affected party's last known address.

The plan administrator must include in the NOIT the following information:

1. The name of the plan and sponsor;

2. The sponsor's employer identification number and the plan number;

3. The name, address, and telephone number of the person who may be contacted with questions concerning the plan's termination;

4. A statement that the plan administrator expects to terminate the plan in a standard termination on a proposed termination date;

5. If the proposed termination date is dependent on the occurrence of a future event, a description of the nature of the event, when the event is expected to occur, and when the termination will occur in relation to the event;

6. A statement that benefit and service accruals will continue until the date of termination or, if applicable, that benefit accruals were or will be frozen as of a specific date;

7. A statement that, in order to terminate in a standard termination, plan assets must be sufficient to provide all benefit liabilities under the plan;

8. A statement that, after plan assets have been distributed to provide all benefit liabilities, either by the purchase of irrevocable commitments from an insurer or by an alternative form of distribution provided for under the plan, the PBGC's guarantee ends;

9. If distribution of benefits under the plan may be wholly or partially provided by the purchase of irrevocable commitments from an insurer:

a. The name and address of the insurer or insurers from whom the plan administrator intends to purchase the irrevocable commitments; or

b. If the plan administrator has not identified an insurer or insurers at the time the NOIT is issued, a statement that (i) irrevocable commitments may be purchased from an insurer to provide some or all of the benefits under the plan, (ii) the insurer or insurers have not yet been identified, and (iii) affected parties will be notified of the name and address of the insurer or insurers at a later date (but no later than 45 days before the date of distribution);

10. A statement that if the termination does not occur, the plan administrator will notify the affected parties in writing of that fact;

11. A statement that each affected party, other than an employee organization, will be receiving a written notification of the benefits that the party will receive; and

12. For retirees only, a statement that their monthly (or other periodic) benefit amounts will not be affected by the plan's termination.

[PBGC Reg § 2617.22]

Q 21:31   What is the relevance of the date of plan termination?

The termination date is critical for determining the rights of the participants and beneficiaries to the benefits under the plan that are guaranteed by PBGC, the employer's liability to PBGC for any under-funding, and PBGC's exposure for guaranteed benefits. [ERISA § 4048; Audio Fidelity Corp v PBGC, 624 F 2d 513 (4th Cir 1980)]

Q 21:32   What factors are considered by PBGC in establishing a defined benefit plan's termination date?

The date of termination will depend on whether the termination is filed by the plan administrator (see Q 16:1) under the standard or distress termination procedures (see Qs 21:17, 21:19) or whether

PBGC has initiated the termination (see Q 21:26). However, in a termination other than one initiated by PBGC, the date must be prospective and at least 60 days after the NOIT is issued to affected parties (see Qs 21:2, 21:29, 21:33). [ERISA § 4041(a)(2); Phillips v Bebber, Nos. 89-2184 and 89-2189 (4th Cir 1990)]

Q 21:33 Who is an affected party?

An affected party, for purposes of a termination subject to PBGC's jurisdiction, is:

- A participant
- A beneficiary of a deceased participant
- A beneficiary who is an alternate payee under a qualified domestic relations order (see Chapter 30)
- Any employee organization that represents plan participants or that represented plan participants within five years prior to the issuance of the NOIT (see Q 21:29)
- PBGC (in the case of a distress termination; see Q 21:19), or
- Any person designated in writing to receive notice on behalf of an affected party

[ERISA §§ 4001(a)(21), 4041(a)(2), 4041(c)(1)(A); PBGC Reg §§ 2616.2, 2617.2]

Q 21:34 Are there any other notice requirements if the company intends to terminate a defined benefit plan?

Yes. Notice must be provided to PBGC by filing PBGC Form 500, Standard Termination Notice Single-Employer Plan Termination. Schedule EA-S, Standard Termination Certification of Sufficiency, attached to Form 500, must be used by the enrolled actuary to certify that the plan is projected to have sufficient assets to provide all benefit liabilities. [ERISA § 4041(b)(2)(A)]

Form 500 should be filed no later than 120 days after the proposed termination date. [PBGC Reg § 2617.25(a)]

In addition, no later than the date on which the notice is filed with PBGC, the plan administrator (see Q 16:1) must provide each participant and beneficiary with a Notice of Plan Benefits (see Q 21:35). [ERISA § 4041(b)(2)(B)]

Q 21:35 What information must be included in the Notice of Plan Benefits?

The plan administrator (see Q 16:1) must issue a notice to each affected party (other than an employee organization; see Q 21:33) that (1) specifies the amount of the individual's benefits as of the proposed termination date and the form of benefit on the basis of which the amount was determined; and (2) includes the following information used in determining the individual's benefits:

- Length of service
- Age of the participant or beneficiary
- Wages
- Assumptions (including the interest rate)
- Such other information as PBGC may require

[ERISA § 4041(b)(2)(B); PBGC Reg §§ 2617.23, 2617.24]

Q 21:36 Are there any special rules regarding the purchase of annuity contracts?

Yes. PBGC has issued regulations requiring plan administrators (see Q 16:1) to inform both participants and PBGC of the identity of the insurer or insurers from whom irrevocable commitments (i.e., annuity contracts) may be purchased prior to the distribution of plan assets. This information must be included in the NOIT (see Q 21:29) and must be included with the filing of the standard termination with PBGC (see Q 21:34). If the identity of the insurer is not known, the information must be provided to participants and PBGC no later than 45 days prior to the date of distribution. [PBGC Reg §§ 2617.22(e), 2617.25(b)]

Q 21:37   After the notice is filed with PBGC, does PBGC have to act within designated time limits?

Yes. Within 60 days after the plan administrator (see Q 16:1) notifies PBGC (see Q 21:34), PBGC must issue to the plan administrator a notice of noncompliance if it (1) has reason to believe that any of the notice requirements have not been met or (2) otherwise determines, on the basis of information provided by affected parties (see Q 21:33) or otherwise obtained by PBGC, that there is reason to believe that the plan assets are not sufficient for benefit liabilities (see Q 21:18). [ERISA § 4041(b)(2)(C); PBGC Reg §§ 2617.26, 2617.27]

Q 21:38   May the 60-day period for PBGC to issue a notice of noncompliance be extended?

Yes. PBGC and the plan administrator (see Q 16:1) may extend the 60-day period (see Q 21:37) for the noncompliance notice by jointly signing a written agreement before expiration of the initial 60-day period. Additional extensions are also permitted. [ERISA § 4041(b)(2)(C); PBGC Reg § 2617.26(a)(2)]

Q 21:39   Assuming that PBGC does not issue a notice of noncompliance, when should final distribution of assets occur?

The plan administrator (see Q 16:1) must complete the distribution of assets, pursuant to a standard termination, no later than 180 days after expiration of the 60-day (or extended) period (see Qs 21:37, 21:38), assuming that plan assets are sufficient to meet benefit liabilities (see Q 21:18), determined as of the termination date, when the final distribution occurs. [ERISA § 4041(b)(2)(D); PBGC Reg § 2617.28(a)]

The distribution deadline will automatically be extended until the 60th day after the plan's receipt of a favorable IRS determination letter (see Q 15:1), if:

1. On or before the date that the plan administrator files Form 500, the plan administrator submitted to IRS a request for a determination letter with respect to the plan's termination;

2. The plan administrator does not receive the IRS's determination letter at least 60 days before the expiration of the 180-day period for distribution; and

3. On or before the expiration of the 180-day period, the plan administrator notifies PBGC in writing that an extension of the distribution deadline is required and certifies that the conditions in 1 and 2 above have been met.

[PBGC Reg § 2617.28(e)]

If the plan administrator will be unable to complete the distribution of plan assets within the 180-day period, PBGC may grant a discretionary extension only if PBGC is satisfied that the delay in making the distribution is not due to the action or inaction of the plan administrator or the contributing sponsor, and that distribution can in fact be completed by the date requested. The request must be filed no later than 30 days before the expiration of the 180-day period, must explain the reason for the request, and must provide a date certain by which the distribution will be made. PBGC will not grant any request based on:

1. Insufficient plan assets to provide all benefit liabilities;

2. Failure to meet the requirements for an automatic extension; or

3. Failure to locate all participants and beneficiaries.

[PBGC Reg § 2617.28(f)]

Q 21:40   What is the method for the final distribution of assets?

The plan administrator (see Q 16:1) must distribute the plan's assets in accordance with the required allocation of assets (see Q 21:42). In distributing the assets, the plan administrator must:

1. Purchase irrevocable commitments from an insurer to provide for all benefit liabilities (and any other benefits to which assets are required to be allocated) (see Q 21:41); or

2. Otherwise fully provide the benefit liabilities (and any other benefits to which assets are required to be allocated) in accord-

ance with the plan's provisions and any applicable PBGC regulations.

[ERISA § 4041(b)(3)]

In order to have a valid termination, the benefits of all participants must be distributed. Before a reversion of excess assets occurs (see Q 21:48), all plan liabilities must first be satisfied. [IRC § 401(a)(2); ERISA § 4044(d)]

If a participant cannot be located, a request can be sent to the Social Security Administration or IRS. If the participant still cannot be located, PBGC has advised that unclaimed *de minimis* benefits in a terminating plan should be placed in a separate bank account opened in the missing participant's name. According to the instructions to Form 501 (see Q 21:45) and the preamble to PBGC Regulations Section 2617, if the benefit of a participant who cannot be located is $3,500 or less, the amount may be deposited into an interest-bearing bank account opened in the participant's name or a pooled interest-bearing account where appropriate. If the amount is greater than $3,500, the plan administrator should purchase an irrevocable commitment (e.g., annuity contract) to provide benefits for the participant. [PBGC Opinion Letter No 89-4 (July 26, 1989)]

Q 21:41 Is PBGC or the employer liable to participants if an insurer fails to make payments under annuity contracts?

No. When irrevocable commitments (i.e., annuity contracts) have been purchased to pay all benefit liabilities, the plan termination process is completed and the PBGC guarantee obligation ends. [PBGC Opinion Letter No 91-1] Similarly, employers are not liable to participants if an insurer fails to meet its obligations under the annuity contracts. The purchase of annuity contracts that irrevocably provide for the payment of all benefit liabilities satisfies the employer's obligation with respect to the termination. [PBGC Opinion Letter No 91-4]

However, the trustees must select the insurer that issues the annuity contracts in a way that satisfies their fiduciary duty to plan participants (see Q 19:10). Fiduciaries of defined benefit plans may be liable for purchasing annuities without adequately evaluating the insurer's financial condition. [DOL News Release 91-281]

See Question 21:36 regarding notice requirements with respect to insurers providing annuity benefits for terminating plans.

Q 21:42 How are plan assets allocated when a defined benefit plan is terminated?

There are six categories into which plan assets must be divided upon termination of a single-employer defined benefit plan. The assets are assigned to these categories, starting with the first category, until the value of the assets has been exhausted. On termination of a defined benefit plan, the assets are allocated in the following order:

1. Employee voluntary contributions;
2. Employee mandatory contributions;
3. Annuity payments in pay status at least three years before the termination of the plan (including annuity payments that would have been in pay status for at least three years if the employee had retired then) based on the provisions of the plan in effect during the five years before termination of the plan under which the benefit would be the least;
4. All other guaranteed insured benefits, determined without regard to the aggregate limit on benefits guaranteed with respect to a participant under all multiemployer and single-employer plans;
5. All other vested benefits; and
6. All other benefits under the plan (see Q 21:43).

[ERISA § 4044(a)]

Q 21:43 What does the phrase "all other benefits under the plan" cover?

According to PBGC and IRS, the statutory language in ERISA Section 4044(a)(6) encompasses only those benefits that participants have accrued as of the date of termination (or in the case of benefit subsidies protected by REA, benefits to which participants may become entitled in the future). [PBGC Opinion Letter No 87-11; GCM 39665]

The Supreme Court has agreed with the PBGC and IRS positions and held that the "all other accrued benefits" category under ERISA Section 4044(a)(6) covers participants' accrued forfeitable benefits, but not unaccrued benefits. [Mead Corp v Tilley, 109 S Ct 2156 (1989); see also May v The Houston Post Pension Plan, No 89-2249 (5th Cir 1990) and Blessitt v Retirement Plan for Employees of Dixie Engine Co, 848 F 2d 1164 (11th Cir 1988)] After remand by the Supreme Court, the Fourth Circuit ruled that the unaccrued subsidized early retirement benefits of participants who satisfied the service requirement but not the age requirement to be eligible for the subsidized benefits at the time of plan termination constituted contingent liabilities that the plan required to be satisfied before excess assets could be returned to the employer (see Q 21:48). [Tilley v Mead Corp, No. 86-3858 (4th Cir 1991)]

One court held that unaccrued early retirement subsidies did not automatically vest upon plan termination where the participants did not meet the age and service eligibility requirements for early retirement subsidies. [Berard v Royal Electric, Inc, 795 F Supp 519 (DC RI 1992)]

Another court held that a plan sponsor was not required to place additional funds in the pension plan upon the plan's termination in 1986 in order to satisfy the "participants' contingent, forfeitable right to subsidized early retirement benefits." However, the court noted that, for terminations initiated after October 16, 1987, the law changed, and a plan sponsor would be prevented from limiting its liability upon its own failure to fund. [Aldridge v Lily-Tulip, Inc Salary Retirement Plan Benefits Committee, No. 90-8686 (11th Cir 1992)]

Q 21:44   Can a distribution of plan assets be reallocated?

Yes. The traditional rules provide that if the asset allocation discriminates in favor of highly compensated employees (see Q 3:2), the allocation (see Q 21:42) may be changed to the extent necessary to avoid the prohibited discrimination (see Q 21:8).

A qualified retirement plan will be considered discriminatory if a plan amendment or series of plan amendments discriminates significantly in favor of highly compensated employees. For this purpose, a plan amendment includes the termination of a plan and any change in the benefits, rights, or features under a plan (see Qs 4:18, 4:19). [Treas Reg § 1.401(a)(4)-5(a)(1)]

However, the law also provides that a defined benefit plan cannot terminate in a standard termination (see Q 21:17) unless it has sufficient assets to cover all benefit liabilities of the plan, which would obviate any such reallocation. [ERISA § 4041(b)(1)(D)]

One court upheld a reallocation of excess plan assets solely to 13 management employee-participants upon a plan termination that occurred after 102 plan participants terminated employment and received annuity contracts in satisfaction of their entire plan benefits. Those 102 former employees were not entitled to share in the reallocation because they were not plan participants when the plan was terminated. [Teagardener v Republic-Franklin, Inc, No. 89-3865 (6th Cir 1990)]

Q 21:45   Must PBGC be notified once final distribution of assets is completed?

Yes. Within 30 days after the final distribution of assets is completed, the plan administrator (see Q 16:1) must file with PBGC a notice certifying that the assets have been distributed in accordance with the required order of allocation of assets and that all benefits have been distributed in accordance with either method of distribution described in Question 21:40. PBGC Form 501, Post-Distribution Certification for Standard Terminations, has been designed for this purpose. [ERISA § 4041(b)(3)(B); PBGC Reg § 2617.28(h)]

Q 21:46   Does PBGC perform post-termination audits for compliance with the Title IV requirements?

Yes. PBGC selectively conducts post-termination compliance audits. The data request may include copies of the following:

- The plan and trust documents

- Applicable labor contracts
- Applicable insurance contracts to fund the plan
- Actuarial reports and enrolled actuary's worksheets
- The plan's financial statement as of the termination date
- Benefit data for each participant
- Election and spousal consent forms

The plan administrator (see Q 16:1) or sponsor should maintain records relating to the plan's termination for six years after Form 501 (see Q 21:45) is filed with PBGC. [PBGC Reg § 2617.10]

Q 21:47 Does an employer incur any liability to PBGC for the payment of benefits to plan participants of an underfunded terminated plan?

Yes. When PBGC incurs liabilities for benefits in the case of a distress termination (see Q 21:19) or a termination instituted by the PBGC (see Q 21:26), it can obtain reimbursement from the contributing employer or a member of its controlled group (see Q 5:30). If more than one employer jointly sponsors a plan, the liability to PBGC is separately applicable to each such entity.

Any trade or business, whether or not incorporated, can be a member of the contributing employer's controlled group if a prescribed control or ownership test is satisfied. In that case, it will be jointly and severally liable to reimburse PBGC. [ERISA §§ 4062(b), 4001(b)]

The liability of a contributing employer or member of its controlled group generally is the total amount of the unfunded benefit liabilities to all participants and beneficiaries as of the termination date, plus interest at a reasonable rate calculated from the termination date. [ERISA § 4062(b)]

If the liability to PBGC is not paid, a lien in favor of PBGC arises in an amount equal to the lesser of (1) the unfunded benefit liabilities or (2) 30 percent of the collective net worth of the contributing employers of a plan and members of the controlled group (but treating as zero any negative net worth). [ERISA §§ 4062(d)(1), 4068(a)]

Q 21:48   May excess assets remaining after the standard termination of a defined benefit plan be returned to the employer after payment of all plan benefit liabilities?

Yes, provided that the distribution does not contravene any other provision of law, the excess was the result of an "erroneous actuarial computation," and the plan specifically permits the distribution of excess assets in this situation (see Qs 21:40, 21:49–21:51). [ERISA § 4044(d); Treas Reg § 1.401-2; International Union of Elec Workers v Murata Erie No Amer, Inc, No. 89-255 (WD Pa 1991)]

In one case, the employer received $3.5 million of excess funds as a result of actuarial error. The section of the plan containing a general prohibition against reversion of funds had to be read in conjunction with another section that contained a specific exception allowing for a reversion after the satisfaction of all liabilities. [Parrett v American Ship Building Co, 990 F 2d 854 (6th Cir 1993)] In another case, an employer recovered $275 million to use in expanding and improving its ongoing business [Walsh v The Great Atlantic & Pacific Tea Co, 4 EBC 2577 (3d Cir 1983)]; and, in another, the court held that a reversion of $600,000 of excess assets to the receiver of the insolvent employer did not violate ERISA's "exclusive benefit" rule [Outzen v Federal Deposit Insurance Corp, No. 90-8077 (10th Cir 1991)].

In another case, the court held that a 1959 plan provision that "in no event and under no circumstances" could plan assets be returned to the employer precluded any subsequent amendment to the plan to allow such a reversion upon termination of the plan [Bryant v International Fruit Products, Inc, 793 F 2d 118 (6th Cir 1986)]; and another court held that plan participants were entitled to excess assets upon plan termination because an amendment providing for a reversion of excess assets to the employer was not properly executed according to plan procedures [Albedyll v Wisconsin Porcelain Company Revised Retirement Plan, Nos. 89-3067, 89-3453 and 89-3622 (7th Cir 1991)]. Similarly, the employer was not entitled to the excess assets upon plan termination where the plan did not specifically provide for a reversion even though the reversion provision had existed in an earlier version of the plan and was provided for in the trust agreement. [Rinard v Eastern Co, 978 F 2d 265 (6th Cir 1992)] (See Q 21:49.)

In yet another case, a board resolution required that all assets be distributed to participants although the plan permitted reversions. The court determined that this resolution informally amended the plan to require that excess assets be distributed to plan participants. [Horn v Berdon, Inc Defined Benefit Pension Plan, No. 89-55391 (9th Cir 1991)]

Further, if an overfunded plan with mandatory employee contributions is terminated, certain assets attributable to such contributions must be distributed to participants and beneficiaries. [ERISA § 4044(d)(3)(B)]

Q 21:49 May a defined benefit plan that did not originally provide for distribution of excess assets to the employer be amended to authorize such a distribution?

Yes. However, for defined benefit plans covered by PBGC (see Qs 21:12, 21:13), any amendment providing for a reversion, or increasing the amount that may revert to the employer, is not effective before the fifth calendar year following the date of the adoption of such an amendment. A special rule provides that a distribution to the employer will not be treated as failing to satisfy this rule if the plan has been in effect for fewer than five years.

For plans that, as of December 17, 1987, had no provision relating to the distribution of plan assets to the employer, the new rule applies to such amendments that were adopted more than one year after the effective date of the new law. For plans that, as of December 17, 1987, provided for the distribution of plan assets to the employer, the new law applies to any amendment made after December 17, 1987. [ERISA § 4044(d)(2)]

In one case, participants in one plan that was merged into a plan of another employer were not entitled to any portion of the surplus assets of the merged plan at the time of the merger because the merged plan reserved the employer's right to amend the plan to allow for the reversion of surplus assets on plan termination. The fact that the merger resulted in a partial termination (see Q 21:5) of the merged plan did not prevent amendment of the surviving plan to allow for the reversion of the surplus assets at the time of the merger. However, two other plans that were simultaneously merged into the surviving plan did provide an irrevocable provision for the reallocation of excess assets to plan participants upon plan termination. Thus, the surviving plan could not be amended to allow reversion of the surplus assets of those plans at the time of the merger. Although the surplus assets were not required to be distributed until complete termination, the court considered the two merged plans as terminated as of the day prior to the merger and ordered the distribution of the surplus assets to the participants. [In re Gulf Pension Litigation, No. 86-4365 (SD Tex 1991)]

Q 21:50   May an employer terminate a defined benefit plan to recover any excess assets and adopt a new defined benefit plan covering the same employees?

Yes, if the plan specifically permits the recovery of excess assets and:

1. All employees covered by the original plan are given notice of the termination and adoption;
2. All accrued benefits are vested as of the termination date and annuities are purchased to cover those benefits;
3. The plan's funding method is changed to take into consideration the termination and adoption, and IRS approves the change in funding method;
4. No other termination and adoption will be made in the next 15 years; and
5. The new plan is intended to be permanent.

[PBGC News Release 84-23, on the Joint Implementation Guidelines for Termination of Defined Benefit Plans]

Recent legislation has sought to deter employers from terminating plans in order to recover excess assets (see Q 21:51).

Q 21:51   Is the employer liable for any taxes on the reversion?

Yes. The amount of the reversion is taxable to the employer as ordinary income. Furthermore, a nondeductible excise tax equal to 50 percent of the amount of the reversion is imposed upon the employer; however, the excise tax is reduced from 50 percent to 20 percent if the employer either establishes a qualified replacement plan (see Q 21:52) or amends the plan to provide pro rata benefit increases (see Q 21:53). For an exception to the excise tax, see Question 21:54. [IRC §§ 4980(a), 4980(d)(l)]

The excise tax applies to direct and indirect reversions. An indirect reversion includes the use of plan assets for the benefit of the employer on plan termination and, therefore, would include the use of plan assets to satisfy an obligation of the employer. [IRC § 4980(c)(2)(A); Ltr Rul 9136017]

A reversion received by a tax-exempt organization from its terminated defined benefit plan is generally not subject to the excise tax on reversions [IRC § 4980(c)(1)(A); Ltr Ruls 9320050, 9120029], and an exception to the excise tax exists for certain reversions transferred to an ESOP (see Chapter 24). [IRC § 4980(c)(3); Ltr Rul 9138065]

An employer's transfer of liabilities from an underfunded defined benefit plan to an overfunded defined benefit plan did not constitute a reversion of plan assets to the employer [Ltr Rul 9318035], and the merger of three overfunded defined benefit plans sponsored by a parent company's subsidiaries into the parent company's underfunded defined benefit plan did not constitute a reversion of plan assets. [Ltr Rul 9224032] Furthermore, an employer's transfer of a portion of the assets and liabilities of its defined benefit plan to a new defined benefit plan for certain former employees was not a termination of the original defined benefit plan, and the transfer of plan assets was not considered a reversion of plan assets. [Ltr Rul 9046046]

The excise tax imposed on a reversion was not considered a penalty for bankruptcy purposes and, therefore, had priority status over the claims of unsecured creditors. [In re C-T of Virginia, Inc, No. 91-2397 (4th Cir 1992)]

Form 5330 (see Q 17:15) is used to report the reversion and pay the excise tax. If the 20 percent rate is used, the employer must explain why it qualifies for the lower rate.

Q 21:52 What is a qualified replacement plan?

The 50 percent excise tax on reversions is reduced to 20 percent if the employer, in connection with the termination of its defined benefit plan, establishes or maintains a qualified replacement plan (see Q 21:51). [IRC § 4980(d)(2)]

Qualified replacement plans must satisfy the following requirements:

1. At least 95 percent of the active participants in the terminated plan who remain as employees of the employer after the termination must be active participants in the replacement plan.

2. The replacement plan must receive a transfer from the terminated plan of an amount equal to 25 percent (no more and no less) of the maximum amount of the reversion (less the present value of any benefit increases due to plan amendments within the 60-day period prior to plan termination). The amount that is transferred to the replacement plan is not includible in the employer's income and is not subject to the excise tax on reversions; and, concomitantly, the employer is not permitted a tax deduction for the transfer.

Example. Lauren, Inc. maintains a defined benefit plan that has excess assets of $200,000. As part of the termination of this plan, it establishes a qualified replacement plan funded with $50,000. Lauren's excise tax on the reversion is $30,000 (20% × $150,000) and also reports $150,000 of income. Assuming that Lauren is taxed at 34 percent on its income, it will owe $51,000 in income tax on the reversion and end up with $69,000 [$200,000 − ($50,000 + $30,000 + $51,000)] after paying both taxes and funding the replacement plan.

3. If the replacement plan is a defined contribution plan, the amount transferred to it must be allocated to the accounts of participants in the plan year in which the transfer occurs or be credited to a suspense account and allocated from the account to the participant accounts no less rapidly than ratably over seven plan years beginning with the year of the transfer. If the limitation on annual additions to defined contribution plans (see Q 6:1) prevents any amount in the suspense account from being allocated to a participant by the end of the seven-year period, that amount will be allocated to the accounts of other participants. If any amount credited to the suspense account is not allocated as of the termination date of a replacement plan, it must be allocated to the accounts of participants as of such date. Any amount that cannot be so allocated will be treated

as an employer reversion subject to the excise tax. [Ltr Rul 9224033]

Because certain employees elected out of the predecessor defined benefit plan and were not accruing benefits on the plan's termination date, they were not considered active participants as of the termination date and, therefore, were not considered in determining whether the plan satisfied the 95 percent requirement in 1 above. [Ltr Rul 9252035] Amounts transferred to a qualified replacement plan can be used as matching contributions (see Q 23:50) if the requirements of 3 above are satisfied. [Ltr Rul 9302027]

In order to qualify, the asset transfer must be a "direct transfer from the terminated plan to the replacement plan . . . before any employer reversion." [IRC § 4980(d)(2)(B)(i)] In one case, the employer deposited funds from the terminated plan into its own account and subsequently transferred those funds into a replacement profit sharing plan. The court ruled that the new plan did not satisfy the requirements of a qualified replacement plan because the transfer was an "indirect transfer." [Southern Aluminum Castings Co v United States, Civ 90-0235-P-C (SD Ala 1991)]

Q 21:53   What is a pro rata benefit increase?

If, in connection with the termination of its defined benefit plan, the employer amends the plan, effective as of the date of termination, to provide pro rata benefit increases in the accrued benefits (see Q 9:2) of qualified participants equal to at least 20 percent of the amount of the reversion, the 50 percent excise tax on the reversion will be reduced to 20 percent (see Q 21:51). [IRC § 4980(d)(3); Ltr Rul 9236043]

The pro rata increase must benefit all qualified participants. Qualified participants include active participants, participants in pay status, certain beneficiaries, and individuals who have a nonforfeitable right to an accrued benefit under the terminated plan as of the termination date and whose service terminated during the period beginning three years before the termination date.

Q 21:54   Are there any exceptions to the imposition of the excise tax on defined benefit plan reversions?

If a defined benefit plan (see Q 2:3) is overfunded and the plan termination would expose the employer to the excise tax on reversions (see Q 21:51), the amount of the excess assets can be reduced by a qualified transfer of assets to a postretirement health benefits account that is part of the plan. The amount transferred is not considered a reversion subject to either income or excise taxes. One qualified transfer can be made during each tax year beginning after 1990 and before 1996 of the amount reasonably estimated to be required to pay qualified current retiree health liabilities for the year. The amount of a qualified transfer, however, cannot exceed the amount of excess plan assets as of the last valuation date before the transfer. All accrued benefits (see Q 9:2) of all plan participants must become fully vested (see Q 21:4) as if the plan terminated at the time of a qualified transfer. [IRC §§ 401(h), 420; ERISA Technical Release No 91-1]

The IRS has issued procedures for requesting determination letters regarding the effect on the qualified plan status of a transfer of excess pension assets to a retiree health benefit account. [Rev Proc 92-24, 1992-1 CB 739]

Q 21:55   If an employer wants to withdraw from a plan maintained by two or more unrelated employers, would the withdrawal be considered a plan termination?

No. The general rule is that such a withdrawal would not constitute a plan termination. However, the withdrawal of one or more employers may result in a partial termination of the plan (see Q 21:5). [Treas Reg § 1.411(d)-2(b)]

Q 21:56   What is a complete discontinuance of contributions under a profit sharing plan?

Instead of directly defining a complete discontinuance, IRS describes what it is and what it is not.

First, IRS regulations distinguish a complete discontinuance from a suspension of contributions under a plan that is "merely a temporary cessation of contributions by the employer." The regulations provide that "a complete discontinuance of contributions may occur although some amounts are contributed by the employer under the plan if such amounts are not substantial enough to reflect the intent on the part of the employer to continue to maintain the plan. The determination of whether a complete discontinuance of contributions under the plan has occurred will be made with regard to all the facts and circumstances in the particular case, and without regard to the amount of any contributions made under the plan by employees." [Treas Reg § 1.411(d)-2(d)]

Second, the regulations state that, in any case in which a suspension of a profit sharing plan is considered a discontinuance, the discontinuance becomes effective no later than the last day of the taxable year that follows the last taxable year for which a substantial contribution was made under the profit sharing plan. [Treas Reg § 1.411(d)-2(d)(2)]

Example. SOS Corporation maintains a calendar-year profit sharing plan. The last "substantial" contribution made by the corporation was on November 12, 1992. If a discontinuance of contributions was deemed to have occurred, it would become effective no later than December 31, 1993.

Employees who become eligible to enter a plan subsequent to its discontinuance receive no benefits, nor do any additional benefits accrue to any of the participants unless employer contributions are resumed. IRS, therefore, takes the position that discontinuance of contributions is equivalent to a plan termination.

What if an employer has no profits? IRS says that the failure of an employer to make contributions to its profit sharing plan for five consecutive years due solely to the absence of current or accumulated earnings and profits is not a discontinuance of contributions if the plan requires the employer to resume contributions as soon as it has profits. [Rev Rul 80-146, 1980-1 CB 90] Since current or accumulated profits are no longer required for the employer to make tax deductible contributions to a profit sharing plan, such failure to make contributions may ripen into a discontinuance. [IRC § 401(a)(27)]

Q 21:57 Must a profit sharing plan provide for full vesting of benefits upon a complete discontinuance of contributions?

Yes. A Tax Court decision upheld IRS's position that a profit sharing plan did not qualify merely because it did not provide for full vesting of participants' accrued benefits on complete discontinuance of contributions. Even though IRS conceded that there never was a discontinuance of contributions, and that no employee's rights to benefits were ever adversely affected, the absence of such a provision from a plan was, according to the court, a sufficient defect in the instrument to disqualify the plan, resulting in the disallowance of the employer deduction. [Tionesta Sand and Gravel, Inc, 73 TC 758 (1980), *aff'd,* 3d Cir in unpublished opinion (Feb 27, 1981)]

Q 21:58 Can a plan amendment result in the termination of the plan?

Yes. If benefits or employer contributions to the plan are reduced, or vesting or eligibility requirements are made less liberal, the plan is considered to be curtailed. Full vesting of a portion of the benefits may be required if IRS decides that the curtailment is a partial termination of the plan (see Q 21:5).

If an employer seeks to amend a defined benefit plan covered by Title IV to convert it to a defined contribution plan, the termination rules of Title IV must be satisfied first before the former plan is treated as terminated (see Q 21:6). [ERISA § 4041(e)]

Q 21:59 Can a plan be amended to reduce or stop benefit accruals?

Yes, but if the amendment provides for a significant reduction in the rate of future benefit accrual, certain notice requirements must be satisfied. After adoption of the amendment and no less than 15 days before the effective date of a plan amendment that significantly reduces future accruals, each participant, beneficiary who is an alternate payee under a QDRO (see Chapter 30), and labor organization representing plan participants must be provided with written notice of the amendment and its effective date. This rule applies to amendments to defined benefit plans and to defined contribution plans subject to the funding standards of ERISA Section 302, namely, money purchase pension plans and target benefit plans. [ERISA § 204(h)]

In one case, the court ruled that a company's notice violated ERISA Section 204(h) when the notice came before the plan amendment was adopted and after the amendment's effective date—exactly the opposite of what ERISA requires. By posting the notice, the company also failed to provide individual written notice to each plan participant (see Q 21:30). [Production and Maintenance Employees' Local 504 v Roadmaster Corp, Nos. 89-1464 and 90-2698 (7th Cir 1992)]

Q 21:60   Must terminating plans be amended to conform to TRA '86 qualification requirements?

Yes. Generally, all plans must be amended to comply with the qualification requirements (and other rules) effective at the time of termination. [Rev Proc 93-6, 1993-1 IRB 135; Ann 93-9, 1993-3 IRB 62; Notice 90-73, 1990-2 CB 353; Rev Proc 88-9, 1988-1 CB 634; Notice 87-57, 1987-2 CB 368]

IRS has provided some temporary relief for employers faced with making their plans comply with TRA '86 requirements. Employers that adopted Model Amendment 4 by December 31, 1989 were not required to amend their plans to comply with the TRA '86 post-1988 requirements (although they were still required to comply with the TRA '86 pre-1989 requirements, as well as those of OBRA '86 and OBRA '87). [Notice 88-131, 1988-2 CB 546; Notice 89-92, 1989-2 CB 410]

Q 21:61   Must IRS be notified when a plan terminates?

Just as there is no legal requirement to file a request for a favorable determination letter (see Q 15:1) with IRS with regard to a new or amended plan, there is no requirement regarding a plan's termination. However, a plan administrator (see Q 16:1) must notify IRS on the Form 5500 series return/report (see Q 17:1) for the year in which the plan terminates. In addition, a Form 5500 series return/report must be filed every year (even after a plan terminates) until all assets are distributed from the trust.

It is strongly suggested that plan administrators file Form 5310 (see Q 15:7) with IRS requesting a favorable determination letter with regard to a plan's termination. IRS has developed guidelines when examining plans for compliance with qualification requirements (see Q 4:1) where a plan was terminated and a determination letter request was not submitted to IRS. [Ann 93-9, 1993-3 IRB 62]

IRS has issued a revenue ruling explaining that a termination of a qualified retirement plan is not complete until the final distribution of plan assets. However, if the "terminated" retirement plan fails to distribute its assets as soon as administratively feasible following the established plan termination date, IRS will not treat the plan as being terminated. [Rev Rul 89-87, 1989-2 CB 81]

The ruling provides that whether a distribution is made as soon as administratively feasible will be determined under all the facts and circumstances of the given case; but, generally, a distribution that is not completed within one year following the date of plan termination specified by the employer will be presumed not to have been completed as soon as administratively feasible. If a plan's assets are not distributed as soon as administratively feasible, the plan is considered to be an ongoing plan and must meet the requirements of Section 401(a) in order to maintain its qualified status. For example, such a plan remains subject to the minimum funding requirements under Section 412 (see Q 8:1) and the information reporting requirements of Sections 6057 and 6058 (and, in the case of a defined benefit plan, the actuarial reporting requirements of Section 6059). It is not clear under the ruling whether a pending determination letter request on the plan's termination or a delay caused by the termination procedures of Title IV of ERISA (applicable to certain defined benefit plans) will excuse a distribution delay of more than one year. However, one IRS key district (see Q 15:9) has advised that, if the determination letter request is submitted timely, distributions completed within six months after the issuance of the determination letter will be treated as having been made as soon as administratively feasible. [EP/EO Baltimore Key District Newsletter, April 1991]

Chapter 22

Top-Heavy Plans

A qualified retirement plan that primarily benefits key employees—a top-heavy plan—can qualify for tax-favored status only if, in addition to the regular qualification requirements, it meets several special requirements. This chapter examines what top-heavy plans are and the special requirements these plans must satisfy.

Q 22:1   What is a top-heavy defined benefit plan?

A defined benefit plan (see Q 2:3) is top-heavy if, as of the determination date (see Q 22:21), the present value of the accrued benefits of all key employees (see Q 22:24) exceeds 60 percent of the present value of the accrued benefits of all employees. [IRC § 416(g)(1)(A)(i); Treas Reg § 1.416-1, Question T-1(c)]

Q 22:2   How are accrued benefits calculated for purposes of determining whether a qualified retirement plan is top-heavy?

Solely for determining whether the present value of cumulative accrued benefits for key employees (see Q 22:24) exceeds 60 percent of the present value of cumulative accrued benefits for all employees (90 percent for purposes of the super-top-heavy plan rules, see Q 22:57), the accrued benefit of an employee (other than a key employee) is determined by the method that is used for benefit accrual purposes under all qualified retirement plans maintained by the employer or, if there is no such single method used under all the plans, as if the benefit accrues no more rapidly than the slowest permitted rate under the fractional accrual rule. [IRC § 416(g)(4)(F)]

Q 22:3 What is a top-heavy defined contribution plan?

A defined contribution plan (see Q 2:2) is top-heavy if, as of the determination date (see Q 22:21), the total of the accounts of all key employees (see Q 22:24) exceeds 60 percent of the total of the accounts of all employees. [IRC § 416(g)(1)(A)(ii); Treas Reg § 1.416-1, Questions T-1(c) and M-16]

Q 22:4 Which qualified retirement plans are subject to the top-heavy rules?

Generally, all defined benefit plans (see Q 2:3) and defined contribution plans (see Q 2:2) are subject to the top-heavy rules. A simplified employee pension (SEP) is also subject to the top-heavy rules (see Qs 22:7, 27:1). [Treas Reg § 1.416-1, Question G-1]

Q 22:5 Is a multiple employer plan subject to the top-heavy rules?

Yes. A multiple employer plan is subject to the top-heavy rules. A multiple employer plan is a qualified retirement plan to which more than one employer contributes and that is not the subject of a collective bargaining agreement.

If five employers contribute to a multiple employer plan and the accrued benefits of the key employees (see Q 22:24) of one employer exceed 60 percent of the accrued benefits of all employees of that employer, the plan is top-heavy with respect to that employer. If the retirement plan fails to satisfy the top-heavy rules for the employees of that employer, all five employers will be maintaining a retirement plan that is not qualified. [IRC § 413(c); Treas Reg § 1.416-1, Questions G-2, T-2]

Q 22:6 Are qualified nonelective contributions under a 401(k) plan taken into account for top-heavy purposes?

Yes. Qualified nonelective contributions to a 401(k) plan (see Q 23:14) may be taken into account for the purpose of satisfying the minimum top-heavy contribution requirement. Also, matching contributions to a 401(k) plan may not be treated as elective contributions in order to satisfy the actual deferral percentage (ADP) test (see Q 23:12) if they are allocated to non-key employees in order to satisfy the minimum top-heavy contribution requirement (see Qs 22:43, 22:46, 22:48). [Treas Reg §§ 1.401(k)-1(e)(7), 1.416-1, Questions M-18, M-19]

Q 22:7 What is a top-heavy simplified employee pension?

A SEP (see Q 27:1) is top-heavy if, as of the determination date (see Q 22:21), the total of the accounts of all key employees (see Q 22:24) exceeds 60 percent of the total of the accounts of all employees. However, at the employer's election, top-heavy status may be determined by taking into account only the total employer contributions (rather than account balances) to the SEP. [IRC §§ 408(k)(1), 416(i)(6)]

Q 22:8 Which factors must be considered in determining whether a qualified retirement plan is top-heavy?

To determine whether a qualified retirement plan is top-heavy, it is necessary to consider:

1. Which employers must be treated as a single employer (see Q 22:13);

2. What the determination date is for the plan year (see Q 22:21);

3. Which employees are or formerly were key employees (see Q 22:24);

4. Which former employees have not performed any services for the employer during the five-year period ending on the determination date;

5. Which plans of such employers are required or permitted to be aggregated in determining top-heavy status (see Qs 22:9, 22:10); and

6. The present value of the accrued benefits (under a defined benefit plan) or the account balances (under a defined contribution plan) of key employees, former key employees, and non-key employees (see Qs 22:1, 22:3).

[Treas Reg § 1.416-1, Question T-1(a)]

Q 22:9   What is a required aggregation group?

A required aggregation group consists of each retirement plan of the employer in which a key employee (see Q 22:24) is a participant in the plan year containing the determination date (see Q 22:21) or any of the four preceding plan years, and any other retirement plan of the employer that enables a retirement plan covering a key employee to satisfy the coverage and nondiscriminatory benefit requirements (see Qs 5:15, 4:9). [IRC § 416(g)(2)(A); Treas Reg § 1.416-1, Question T-6]

Example 1. Elaine Corporation maintains a defined benefit plan covering key employees and other salaried employees and also maintains a second defined benefit plan covering hourly employees. The first defined benefit plan by itself does not satisfy the coverage or nondiscriminatory benefit requirements but does so when the two plans are considered together. The two defined benefit plans constitute a required aggregation group. If the first plan by itself satisfies the coverage and nondiscriminatory benefit requirements, the second plan would not be part of the required aggregation group.

Example 2. Jamie, a sole proprietor, terminated her qualified retirement plan in 1992. In 1993, Jamie incorporated and established a corporate qualified retirement plan. In determining whether the corporate plan is top-heavy, Jamie's terminated retirement plan and the corporate retirement plan are part of a required aggregation group.

Q 22:10   What is a permissive aggregation group?

A permissive aggregation group consists of each retirement plan of the employer that is required to be aggregated (see Q 22:9) and any other retirement plan of the employer that is not part of the required aggregation group but that satisfies the coverage and non-discriminatory benefit requirements (see Qs 5:15, 4:9) when considered together with the required aggregation group. [IRC § 416(g)(2)(A)(ii); Treas Reg § 1.416-1, Question T-7]

In Example 1 in Question 22:9, suppose that the second defined benefit plan was not part of the required aggregation group. If so, the second plan could be permissively aggregated with the first retirement plan only if the benefits or contributions under the second retirement plan were comparable to those under the first plan.

Q 22:11   Must collectively bargained retirement plans be aggregated with other retirement plans of the employer?

Collectively bargained retirement plans that include a key employee (see Q 22:24) must be included in the required aggregation group for the employer (see Q 22:9). Collectively bargained retirement plans that do not include a key employee may be included in a permissive aggregation group (see Q 22:10). However, the special qualification requirements applicable to top-heavy plans (see Q 22:23) generally do not apply to collectively bargained retirement plans, whether or not they include a key employee. [IRC §§ 416(i)(4), 7701(a)(46); Treas Reg § 1.416-1, Questions T-3, T-7, T-8]

Q 22:12   What is a top-heavy group?

If a required aggregation group (see Q 22:9) is a top-heavy group, each retirement plan that is required to be included in the aggregation group is treated as a top-heavy plan. If, however, the group is not top-heavy, no retirement plan in the required aggregation group is treated as a top-heavy plan.

If a permissive aggregation group (see Q 22:10) is top-heavy, only those retirement plans that are part of the required aggregation group are subject to the special qualification requirements (see Q 22:23) placed on top-heavy plans. Retirement plans that are not part of the required aggregation group are not subject to these added requirements. If a permissive aggregation group is not top-heavy, on the other hand, the top-heavy requirements do not apply to any retirement plan in the group.

An aggregation group is a top-heavy group if, as of the determination date (see Q 22:21), the sum of:

1. The present value of the accumulated accrued benefits for key employees (see Q 22:24) under all defined benefit plans included in the group, and

2. The account balances of key employees under all defined contribution plans included in the group

exceeds 60 percent of the same amount determined for all employees under all retirement plans included in the group. [IRC § 416(g)(2)(B); Treas Reg § 1.416-1, Questions T-9, T-10, T-11]

Example. Nat Corporation maintains a defined benefit plan covering key employees and other salaried employees and also maintains a second defined benefit plan covering hourly employees that enables the first plan to satisfy the coverage and nondiscriminatory benefit requirements. If the present value of the total accrued benefits for all key employees exceeds 60 percent of the present value of the total accrued benefits for all employees under both plans, both plans are considered top-heavy plans. If, however, the first plan satisfied the coverage and nondiscriminatory benefit requirements by itself, the two plans would not constitute an aggregation group and only the first plan would be a top-heavy plan.

Q 22:13 How are separate retirement plans of related employers treated for purposes of the top-heavy rules?

The aggregation group rules (see Qs 22:9, 22:10) and the top-heavy group rules (see Q 22:12) apply to all retirement plans of related employers if the related employers are treated as a single employer for retirement plan purposes. [IRC §§ 414(b), 414(c), 414(m); Treas Reg § 1.416-1, Question T-1(b)]

Q 22:14 **How is a terminated retirement plan treated for purposes of the top-heavy rules?**

A terminated retirement plan must be aggregated with the employer's other retirement plans if it (1) was maintained within the five-year period ending on the determination date (see Q 22:21) for the plan year in question and (2) would be part of a required aggregation group (see Q 22:9) for that plan year had it not been terminated. (A terminated retirement plan is a retirement plan that has formally terminated, has ceased crediting service for benefit accruals and vesting, and has been or is distributing plan assets to the participants.)

No additional vesting, benefit accruals, or contributions must be provided for participants in a terminated retirement plan. [IRC § 416(g)(3); Treas Reg § 1.416-1, Question T-4]

Q 22:15 **How is a frozen retirement plan treated for purposes of the top-heavy rules?**

A frozen retirement plan must provide minimum benefits or contributions (see Qs 22:37, 22:43) and provide top-heavy vesting (see Q 22:32). (A frozen retirement plan is a retirement plan that has ceased crediting service for benefit accruals, but has not distributed all assets to the participants.) [Treas Reg § 1.416-1, Question T-5]

Q 22:16 **What happens if an employee ceases to be a key employee?**

If an employee ceases to be a key employee (see Q 22:24) and continues to work for the employer, that employee is treated as a non-key employee and the employee's accrued benefit under the defined benefit plan and account balance under the defined contribution plan are disregarded for purposes of determining whether the retirement plan is top-heavy for each plan year following the last plan year for which the employee was a key employee. [IRC § 416 (g)(4)(B); Treas Reg § 1.416-1, Questions T-1(d), T-12]

Q 22:17   How are plan distributions to employees treated for purposes of determining whether the qualified retirement plan is top-heavy?

The present value of the accrued benefit of an employee in a defined benefit plan, or the account balance of an employee in a defined contribution plan, includes any amount distributed with respect to the employee under the plan within the five-year period ending on the determination date (see Q 22:21). This rule applies whether or not the employee is a key employee (see Q 22:24) and applies to distributions made to a beneficiary of an employee (see Q 22:31). [IRC § 416(g)(3); Treas Reg § 1.416-1, Question T-30]

If the employee does not render any services to the employer at any time during the five-year period ending on the determination date (see Q 22:21), the present value of the employee's accrued benefit or account balance is not taken into account for purposes of top-heavy plan testing. [IRC § 416(g)(4)(E); Treas Reg § 1.416-1, Question T-1(d)]

Q 22:18   Are death benefits treated as distributions for purposes of determining whether a qualified retirement plan is top-heavy?

Death benefits up to the present value of the deceased participant's accrued benefit immediately prior to death are treated as distributions for top-heavy testing purposes, but any death benefits in excess of this amount are not taken into account. For example, the distribution from a defined contribution plan, including the cash value of life insurance policies, of a participant's account balance on account of the participant's death is treated as a distribution for top-heavy testing purposes. [Treas Reg § 1.416-1, Question T-31]

Q 22:19   How are rollovers and transfers treated for purposes of determining whether a retirement plan is top-heavy?

The rules for handling rollovers and plan-to-plan transfers depend on whether the rollovers and transfers are unrelated (both initiated by the employee and made from a qualified retirement plan maintained by one employer to a qualified retirement plan maintained by another employer) or related (either not initiated by the employee or made to a qualified retirement plan maintained by the same or a related employer).

In the case of unrelated rollovers or transfers, (1) the qualified retirement plan making the distribution always counts the distribution (see Q 22:17), and (2) the qualified retirement plan accepting the rollover or transfer does not consider it if it was accepted after 1983, but considers it if it was accepted prior to 1984.

In the case of related rollovers or transfers, the qualified retirement plan making the rollover or transfer does not count it as a distribution, but the qualified retirement plan accepting the rollover or transfer counts it. The rules for related rollovers do not depend on whether the rollover or transfer was accepted prior to 1984. [IRC § 416(g)(4)(A); Treas Reg § 1.416-1, Question T-32]

Q 22:20 How are employee contributions treated for purposes of determining whether a qualified retirement plan is top-heavy?

For purposes of determining the present value of accumulated accrued benefits under a defined benefit plan and the sum of the account balances under a defined contribution plan, benefits derived from both employer contributions and employee contributions (whether mandatory or voluntary) are taken into account. However, accumulated deductible employee contributions (see Q 6:20) under a qualified retirement plan are disregarded. [Treas Reg § 1.416-1, Question T-28]

Q 22:21 When is the determination date?

The date on which a qualified retirement plan is determined to be top-heavy is called the determination date. The determination date for a new retirement plan is the last day of the first plan year; for an existing plan, it is the last day of the preceding plan year. [IRC § 416(g)(4)(C); Treas Reg § 1.416-1, Question T-22]

Example. Charles Corporation established a calendar-year defined contribution plan on January 1, 1993. On December 31, 1993 (the last day of the first plan year), the accounts of the key employees exceed 60 percent of all employees' accounts under the plan. For 1993, the plan is top-heavy. The plan will also be top-heavy for the 1994 plan year because the determination date for the 1994 plan year is the last day of the 1993 plan year.

Q 22:22 If the employer has more than one qualified retirement plan, when is the top-heavy determination made?

When two or more retirement plans are aggregated (see Qs 22:9, 22:10), the present value of the accrued benefits or account balances is determined separately for each plan as of each plan's determination date (see Q 22:21). The retirement plans are then aggregated by adding the results of each plan as of the determination dates that fall within the same calendar year. The combined results indicate whether or not the retirement plans are top-heavy. [Treas Reg § 1.416-1, Question T-23]

Example. David Corporation maintains two qualified retirement plans, Plan A and Plan B, each covering a key employee. Plan A's plan year commences July 1 and ends June 30. Plan B's plan year is the calendar year. For Plan A's plan year commencing July 1, 1993, the determination date is June 30, 1993. For Plan B's 1994 plan year, the determination date is December 31, 1993. These plans must be aggregated.

On the respective determination dates of each plan, separate calculations of the present value of the accrued benefits of all employees are made. The determination dates, June 30, 1993, and December 31, 1993, fall within the same calendar year. Accordingly, the present values of accrued benefits or account balances with respect to each of these determination dates are combined for purposes of determining whether the plans are top-heavy. If, after combining the two, the total results show that the plans are top-heavy, Plan A will be top-heavy for the plan year commencing July 1, 1993, and Plan B will be top-heavy for the 1994 calendar plan year.

Q 22:23 Are there special qualification requirements that apply to top-heavy plans?

Yes. In addition to the qualification requirements that apply to all retirement plans, a top-heavy plan must satisfy the following requirements:

1. Minimum vesting (see Q 22:32); and
2. Minimum benefits or contributions (see Qs 22:37, 22:43).

[IRC § 416(a); Treas Reg § 1.416-1, Questions T-35, T-36, T-37]

Q 22:24 Who is a key employee?

A key employee is an employee who, at any time during the plan year containing the determination date (see Q 22:21) or any of the four preceding plan years, is (or was):

1. An officer having annual compensation in excess of 50 percent of the annual dollar limitation for defined benefit plans in effect for such plan year (see Qs 22:25, 6:8);
2. One of the ten largest owners of the employer having annual compensation in excess of the annual addition limitation in effect for such plan year (see Qs 22:27, 6:1);
3. A 5 percent owner (see Q 22:28); or
4. A 1 percent owner whose annual compensation exceeds $150,000 (see Q 22:28).

[IRC § 416(i)(1)(A); Treas Reg § 1.416-1, Question T-12]

Q 22:25 Who is an officer of the employer for top-heavy plan purposes?

The determination as to whether an employee is an officer is made on the basis of all the facts and circumstances—including, for example, the source of the employee's authority, the term for which the employee was elected or appointed, and the nature and extent of the employee's duties. As generally accepted in connection with corporations, the term "officer" means an administrative executive who is in regular and continued service. It implies continuity of service and excludes those employed for a special and single transaction, or those with only nominal administrative duties. So, for example, all the employees of a bank who have the title of vice-president or assistant vice-president are not automatically considered officers. An employee who does not have the title of an officer but has the authority of an officer is an officer for purposes of the key employee test. [Rev Rul 80-314, 1980-2 CB 152; Treas Reg § 1.416-1, Question T-13]

The number of employees that can be considered officers is equal to 10 percent of all employees, or three, whichever is greater. In no case, however, can the total number of officers exceed 50. Thus, if the employer has fewer than 30 employees, no more than three can be considered officers. [IRC § 416(i)(1)(A); Treas Reg § 1.416-1, Question T-14]

Q 22:26   Do any organizations other than corporations have officers?

Sole proprietorships, partnerships, unincorporated associations, trusts, and labor organizations may have officers. [Treas Reg § 1.416-1, Question T-15]

Q 22:27   Who is one of the ten largest owners of the employer?

The ten largest owners are the ten employees owning the largest interest in the employer. An employee who has some ownership interest is considered to be one of the top ten owners unless at least ten other employees own a greater interest than the employee owns.

In determining the ten employees owning the largest interests in the employer, only employees with annual compensation in excess of the annual addition limitation for such plan year (see Q 6:1) and having more than a ½ percent ownership interest are taken into account as key employees. If two employees have the same interest in the employer, the employee with the greater annual compensation is treated as having a larger interest. [IRC § 416(i)(1); Treas Reg § 1.416-1, Question T-19]

Example. Twenty-five employees at Allyson Corporation have a 4 percent interest in the employer. Compensation for 15 of these employees ranges from $25,000 to $45,000. Compensation for the other ten employees ranges from $60,000 to $75,000. Only the latter ten employees are considered key employees for top-heavy plan testing purposes.

Q 22:28   Who is a 5 percent owner or a 1 percent owner for top-heavy plan purposes?

A 5 percent owner is a person who owns, directly or indirectly, more than 5 percent of the stock of the corporation. A 1 percent owner is a person who owns, directly or indirectly, more than 1 percent of the stock of the corporation. A 1 percent owner is a key employee (see Q 22:24) only if such owner's annual compensation from the employer is more than $150,000.

If the employer is not a corporation, the ownership test is applied to the person's capital or profits interest in the employer. In determining ownership percentages, each employer, whether related or unrelated (see Q 5:32), is treated as a separate entity. But for purposes of determining whether an employee has compensation of more than $150,000, compensation from each related entity is aggregated. [IRC §§ 416(i)(1)(B), 416(i)(1)(C); Treas Reg § 1.416-1, Questions T-16, T-17, T-18, T-20, T-21]

Q 22:29   Who is a non-key employee?

Any employee who is not a key employee (see Q 22:24) is a non-key employee. [IRC § 416(i)(2)]

Q 22:30   Who is a former key employee?

A former key employee is an individual who, when employed by the employer, was once a key employee (see Q 22:24).

Example. Melanie, who was a 5 percent owner of Whitney Corp. in 1993, sold all of her interest in the corporation before the end of the year and retired. Even though Melanie is no longer an employee or owner, she will be treated as a key employee for each plan year through the 1998 plan year. For the 1999 plan year and subsequent plan years, Melanie will be treated as a former key employee.

Former key employees are non-key employees and are excluded entirely from the calculation in determining top-heaviness. [Treas Reg § 1.416-1, Questions T-1(d), T-12]

Q 22:31 How is a beneficiary treated under the top-heavy plan rules?

For purposes of the top-heavy plan rules, the terms key employee, former key employee, and non-key employee include their beneficiaries. [IRC § 416(i)(5); Treas Reg § 1.416-1, Question T-12]

Q 22:32 What is the minimum vesting requirement for a top-heavy plan?

A top-heavy plan must contain either a three-year vesting provision or a six-year graded vesting provision. [IRC § 416(b)(1); Treas Reg § 1.416-1, Question V-1]

Under three-year vesting, an employee who completes at least three years of service (see Q 22:33) must be 100 percent vested. Under six-year graded vesting, an employee must become vested as determined under the following table:

Completed Years of Service	Vested Percentage
2	20
3	40
4	60
5	80
6 or more	100

Q 22:33 Which years of service must be taken into account for minimum vesting purposes?

The rules for determining an employee's years of service for vesting under non-top-heavy plans (see Chapter 9) also apply for the minimum vesting requirements under top-heavy plans. Thus, years of service completed before 1984 (the year the top-heavy rules went into effect) and years of service completed after 1983 (including years when the plan is not top-heavy) are counted for minimum vesting purposes. [IRC § 416(b)(2); Treas Reg § 1.416-1, Question V-2]

Q 22:34   Which benefits must be subject to the minimum top-heavy vesting requirement?

All benefits must be subject to the minimum top-heavy vesting requirement. These benefits include benefits accrued before a retirement plan becomes top-heavy. However, when a retirement plan becomes top-heavy, the accrued benefit of an employee who does not have an hour of service after the plan becomes top-heavy is not required to be subject to the minimum vesting requirement. [Treas Reg § 1.416-1, Question V-3]

Q 22:35   When a top-heavy plan ceases to be top-heavy, may the vesting schedule be changed?

Yes. When a top-heavy plan ceases to be top-heavy, the vesting schedule may be changed to one that would otherwise be permitted. However, in changing the vesting schedule, any portion of the benefit that was nonforfeitable before the plan ceases to be top-heavy must remain nonforfeitable, and any employee with three or more years of service must be given the option of remaining under the prior (i.e., top-heavy) vesting schedule (see Q 9:6). [IRC § 411(a)(10); Treas Reg § 1.416-1, Question V-7]

Q 22:36   Which top-heavy vesting schedule is more favorable to the employer?

It depends on how long the employees usually stay with the employer.

Example. Rena Corporation adopted a 10-percent-of-compensation money purchase pension plan on January 1, 1992. Bob completes a year of service on January 1, 1993, and enters the plan. Bob earns $10,000 a year. Set forth below is a calculation of

Bob's benefits under the six-year graded and three-year cliff vesting schedules (see Q 22:32):

Plan Year	6-Year		3-Year	
	Contribution/ Account Balance	Vesting Percentage/ Vested Benefits	Contribution/ Account Balance	Vesting Percentage/ Vested Benefits
1	0 _____ 0		0 _____ 0	
2	$1,000 _____ $1,000	20% _____ $200	$1,000 _____ $1,000	0% _____ $0
3	$1,000 _____ $2,000	40% _____ $800	$1,000 _____ $2,000	100% _____ $2,000
4	$1,000 _____ $3,000	60% _____ $1,800	$1,000 _____ $3,000	100% _____ $3,000
5	$1,000 _____ $4,000	80% _____ $3,200	$1,000 _____ $4,000	100% _____ $4,000
6	$1,000 _____ $5,000	100% _____ $5,000	$1,000 _____ $5,000	100% _____ $5,000

In plan year 2, less vested benefits are provided under the three-year cliff vesting schedule; in plan years 3, 4, and 5, less vested benefits are provided under the six-year graded vesting schedule. Thus, if employees customarily leave before completing three years of service, three-year cliff vesting is more favorable to the employer; if they leave after completing three years of service, the six-year graded schedule is more favorable to the employer. After six years of service, both schedules provide equal benefits.

As an alternative, Rena Corporation could require employees to complete two years of service to become eligible, but then employees must be 100 percent vested immediately (see Q 9:12). With a two-year service requirement and 100 percent immediate vesting, Bob's benefits would be as follows:

Plan Year	Contribution/ Account Balance	Vesting Percentage/ Vested Benefits
1	0 / 0	
2	0 / 0	
3	$1,000 / $1,000	100% / $1,000
4	$1,000 / $2,000	100% / $2,000
5	$1,000 / $3,000	100% / $3,000
6	$1,000 / $4,000	100% / $4,000

In plan year 2, the least vested benefits occur under three-year cliff or with the two-year service requirement; in plan years 3 and 4, the least vested benefits occur under six-year graded; in plan years 5 and 6, and in all subsequent plan years, the least vested benefits occur with the two-year service requirement. Therefore, if employees customarily leave after completing five or more years of service, the two-year service requirement will be most favorable to the employer maintaining a top-heavy plan.

Q 22:37 What is the minimum benefit requirement for a top-heavy defined benefit plan?

Under a top-heavy defined benefit plan, the annual retirement benefit (see Q 22:38) of a non-key employee (see Q 22:29) must not be less than the employee's average compensation (see Q 22:40) multiplied by the lesser of:

1. 2 percent times the number of years of service (see Q 22:41); or

2. 20 percent.

Benefits attributable to employer contributions are considered, but benefits attributable to employee contributions must be ignored.

[IRC §§ 416(c)(1)(A), 416(c)(1)(B); Treas Reg § 1.416-1, Questions M-1, M-2, M-5, M-6]

Q 22:38   What does annual retirement benefit mean for the minimum benefit requirement?

Annual retirement benefit means a benefit attributable to employer contributions payable annually in the form of a single life annuity (with no ancillary benefits) beginning at the retirement plan's normal retirement age (see Q 10:55). [IRC § 416(c)(1)(E); Treas Reg § 1.416-1, Question M-2(d)]

If benefits under the defined benefit plan are payable in a form other than a straight life annuity (under a straight life annuity, payments terminate upon the death of the annuitant), the minimum benefit is adjusted downward to a benefit that is equivalent to a straight life annuity. For example, if the annuity payments under the defined benefit plan are guaranteed for a period of ten years (that is, if the participant dies within the ten-year period, payments will be made to the participant's beneficiary for the rest of the period), the minimum annual retirement benefit (see Q 22:37) is reduced by 10 percent. [Treas Reg § 1.416-1, Question M-3]

Q 22:39   What is the minimum benefit required if the employee receives benefits other than at normal retirement age?

If the benefit commences at a date other than at normal retirement age (see Q 10:55), the employee must receive an amount that is at least the actuarial equivalent of the minimum single life annuity benefit (see Qs 22:37, 22:38) commencing at normal retirement age. The employee may receive a lower benefit if the benefit commences before normal retirement age and must receive a higher benefit if the benefit commences after normal retirement age. [Treas Reg § 1.416-1, Question M-3]

Q 22:40 What does the term participant's average compensation mean for the minimum benefit requirement?

A participant's average compensation means the participant's compensation averaged over a period of no more than five consecutive years (the testing period) during which the participant had the greatest aggregate compensation from the employer. [IRC § 416(c)(1)(D)(i); Treas Reg § 1.416-1, Questions M-2(c), T-21]

A year need not be taken into account during the testing period if it ends in a plan year beginning before 1984 or begins after the close of the last plan year in which the plan was a top-heavy plan. [IRC § 416(c)(1)(D)(iii); Treas Reg § 1.416-1, Question M-2(c)]

Q 22:41 Which years of service are taken into account in determining the minimum annual benefit under a top-heavy defined benefit plan?

A year of service generally means a year during which the employee completes 1,000 hours of service. The rules for determining years of service parallel those for calculating vesting (see Qs 9:3, 9:9–9:11). However, the following years of service are not taken into account for determining the minimum annual retirement benefit:

1. A year of service within which ends a plan year for which the defined benefit plan is not top-heavy; and

2. A year of service completed in a plan year beginning before 1984.

[IRC § 416(c)(1)(C); Treas Reg § 1.416-1, Question M-2(b)]

The minimum annual benefit under a top-heavy defined benefit plan (see Q 22:37) is the lesser of (1) 2 percent of the employee's compensation multiplied by the employee's years of service, or (2) 20 percent of the employee's compensation. This determination of the employee's total years of service is important only if the total is less than ten, because if years of service equal or exceed ten, the 20 percent minimum can be used.

In one circumstance, IRS allowed the top-heavy minimum accrued benefit to start to accrue when the employee became a participant.

According to the facts, a non-key employee was hired January 1, 1985, and became eligible to participate in the company's defined benefit plan on January 1, 1988. For purposes of the top-heavy rules, IRS stated that the minimum accrued benefit starts to accrue when an employee becomes a participant, so that in the circumstances of the above case, the accrued benefit as of January 1, 1988, was zero. *The foregoing was offered as general information and was not to be construed as a ruling relating to any actual case.*

Q 22:42   Which employees must receive a minimum benefit in a top-heavy defined benefit plan?

Each non-key employee (see Q 22:29) who is a participant and who has at least 1,000 hours of service during the year must receive a minimum benefit in a top-heavy defined benefit plan for that period. A non-key employee may not fail to receive a minimum benefit merely because the employee was not employed on a specified date (e.g., the last day of the plan year). Similarly, a non-key employee who is excluded from participation (or who accrues no benefit) because either (1) the employee's compensation is below a stated amount or (2) the employee fails to make mandatory employee contributions must nevertheless accrue a minimum benefit. [Treas Reg § 1.416-1, Questions M-1, M-4]

Q 22:43   What is the minimum contribution requirement for a top-heavy defined contribution plan?

Under a top-heavy defined contribution plan, the employer's contribution for each non-key employee (see Q 22:29) must not be less than 3 percent of compensation (see Q 22:45). However, if the highest contribution percentage rate for a key employee (see Q 22:24) is less than 3 percent of compensation, the 3 percent minimum contribution rate is reduced to the rate that applies to the key employee. [IRC §§ 416(c)(2)(A), 416(c)(2)(B); Treas Reg § 1.416-1, Questions M-1, M-7, M-8, M-9]

Example. Aviva Corporation established a calendar-year defined contribution plan (see Q 2:2) on January 1, 1993. The plan is top-heavy and contains a contribution formula of 2 percent of compensation below the taxable wage base and 4 percent of compensation in excess of the taxable wage base. Andrea, the highest paid key employee, earns $70,000, and the contribution on her behalf is $1,648 [(2% × $57,600) + 4% × ($70,000 – $57,600)]. Because her contribution rate is 2.35 percent ($1,648/$70,000), Aviva Corporation has to contribute only 2.35 percent of compensation for each non-key employee.

Q 22:44   Do forfeitures affect the minimum contribution requirement?

Under the minimum contribution rules (see Q 22:43), reallocated forfeitures are considered as employer contributions. For example, if no amount is contributed by the employer under a profit sharing plan for any key employee but forfeitures are allocated to key employees, contributions may be required under the minimum contribution rules for non-key employees. [Treas Reg § 1.416-1, Question M-7]

Q 22:45   What does participant's compensation mean for purposes of the minimum contribution requirement?

The term participant's compensation means the participant's total compensation from the employer during the year (see Q 6:3)—even though compensation, as defined in the plan, may exclude certain forms of compensation (e.g., bonuses). [IRC §§ 415(c)(3), 416(c)(2)(A); Treas Reg § 1.416-1, Questions M-7, T-21]

Q 22:46   Which employees must receive the top-heavy defined contribution plan minimum contribution?

Those non-key employees (see Q 22:29) who are participants and have not separated from service at the end of the plan year, whether or not they have completed 1,000 hours of service, must receive the top-heavy defined contribution plan minimum contribution. A non-key employee who is excluded from participation (or who accrues no benefit) because (1) the employee declines to make mandatory contributions to the plan or (2) the employee declines to make elective contributions under a 401(k) plan (see Qs 22:48, 23:13) is considered an employee covered by the plan for purposes of the minimum contribution requirement. [Treas Reg § 1.416-1, Question M-10]

Q 22:47   Can Social Security benefits or contributions be used to satisfy the minimum benefit and contribution requirements?

No. A top-heavy plan cannot take benefits or contributions under Social Security into account to satisfy the minimum benefit requirement (see Q 22:37) or the minimum contribution requirement (see Q 22:43). Thus, the required minimum benefit or contribution for a non-key employee may not be eliminated or reduced by providing for permitted disparity in the plan. [IRC § 416(e); Treas Reg § 1.416-1, Question M-11]

Q 22:48   Can elective contributions under a 401(k) plan be used to satisfy the top-heavy minimum contribution rules?

No. Elective contributions to a 401(k) plan (see Q 23:13) on behalf of non-key employees may not be treated as employer contributions for the purpose of satisfying the top-heavy minimum contribution requirement. However, in determining the percentage at which contributions are made for the key employee with the highest percentage, elective contributions on behalf of key employees are taken into account (see Qs 22:6, 22:43, 22:46). [Treas Reg §§ 1.401(k)-1(e)(7), 1.416-1, Question M-20]

Q 22:49   Must an employer that has both a top-heavy defined benefit plan and a top-heavy defined contribution plan provide both a minimum benefit and a minimum contribution for non-key employees?

No. If a non-key employee (see Q 22:29) participates in both a top-heavy defined benefit plan and a top-heavy defined contribution plan maintained by an employer, the employer is not required to provide the non-key employee with both the minimum benefit and the minimum contribution.

There are four safe-harbor rules a top-heavy plan may use in determining which minimum an employee must receive. Because the defined benefit minimums are generally more valuable, if each employee covered under both a top-heavy defined benefit plan and a top-heavy defined contribution plan receives the defined benefit minimum, receipt of that minimum will satisfy the standards. A safe-harbor defined contribution minimum is provided by IRS. If the contributions and forfeitures under the defined contribution plan equal 5 percent of compensation in each year the plan is top-heavy, that minimum will also satisfy the standards.

The other two safe-harbor rules are:

1. Using a floor offset under which the defined benefit minimum is provided in the defined benefit plan and is offset by the benefits provided under the defined contribution plan; and

2. Proving by use of a comparability analysis that the plans provide aggregate benefits at least equal to the defined benefit minimum.

[IRC § 416(f); Treas Reg § 1.416-1, Questions M-12, M-13, M-15; Rev Rul 76-259, 1976-2 CB 111]

Example. Alicia, a non-key employee, participates in a top-heavy money purchase pension plan that provides an annual contribution rate of 5 percent of compensation and a top-heavy defined benefit plan that provides a retirement benefit equal to 8 percent of compensation. The employer is not required to provide an additional retirement benefit for Alicia under the defined benefit plan.

Q 22:50   What is the limitation on compensation that may be taken into account under a top-heavy plan?

Only the first $200,000 (adjusted for cost-of-living increases) of an employee's compensation (see Qs 6:21, 6:22) may be taken into account, regardless of whether the plan is top-heavy. For 1993, this amount has increased to $235,840. [IRC § 401(a)(17); IRB 93-2 (Jan 15, 1993)]

The $200,000 limitation is reduced to $150,000 for the plan year beginning in 1994 (see Qs 6:21, 6:22). Although the first cost-of-living adjustment could occur in the plan year beginning in 1995, it probably will not because an adjustment will be made only if it is $10,000 or greater and then will be made in multiples of $10,000 (i.e., rounded down to the next lowest multiple of $10,000). For example, an increase in the cost-of-living of $9,999 will result in no adjustment, and an increase of $19,999 will create an upward adjustment of $10,000. Therefore, the cost-of-living must increase by 6⅔ percent before the first adjustment to the annual compensation limit will occur [(6⅔% × $150,000 = $10,000)]. [RRA '93, Act § 13212]

Q 22:51 What happens if a key employee participates in both a defined benefit plan and a defined contribution plan?

If a key employee (see Q 22:24) participates in both a defined benefit plan and a defined contribution plan that are included in a top-heavy group (see Q 22:12), the overall maximum limitation for the key employee is computed under a more restrictive formula unless certain requirements are met (see Q 22:56).

For combined plans in a top-heavy group, the sum of the defined benefit plan fraction and the defined contribution plan fraction cannot exceed 1.0 (the same rule that applies in a non-top-heavy situation; see Q 6:15). However, the denominator of each fraction is calculated differently.

To arrive at the overall maximum limitation, take the following steps:

1. Compute a defined benefit plan fraction. The numerator of this fraction is the projected annual retirement benefit determined at year end. The denominator is the lesser of 1.0 (instead of 1.25) times the dollar limitation for the current year or 1.4 times the percentage limitation for the current year (see Q 6:8). [IRC §§ 415(e)(2), 416(h)(1)]

2. Compute a defined contribution plan fraction. The numerator of this fraction is the total of the annual additions to the participant's account for all years determined at year end. The denominator is the lesser of 1.0 (instead of 1.25) times the dollar limitation or 1.4 times the percentage limitation for the current year and all years of prior service (see Q 6:1). [IRC §§ 415(e)(3), 416(h)(1); Treas Reg § 1.416-1, Question T-33]

3. Add the two fractions. The total may not exceed 1.0.

[IRC § 415(e)(1)]

Each plan may contain a fail-safe provision (see Q 6:15).

Example. Mr. James incorporates his business in January 1993. The corporation adopts a 100 percent defined benefit plan and a 10-percent-of-compensation money purchase pension plan that are included in a top-heavy group. Mr. James earns $102,804 in 1993. Here is how the top-heavy 1.0 rule works:

1. The defined benefit plan fraction is .889 [$102,804/$115,641 (i.e., the lesser of 1.0 × $115,641 or 1.4 × $102,804)].

2. The defined contribution plan fraction is .343 [$10,280/ $30,000 (i.e., the lesser of 1.0 × $30,000 or 1.4 × $25,701)].

3. The two fractions total 1.232.

At this point, the top-heavy 1.0 rule comes into play so that one of the fractions must be reduced. If the 10-percent-of-compensation contribution formula under the defined contribution plan is reduced to 3.24 percent, the defined contribution plan fraction will be .111 [$3,331 (i.e., 3.24% × $102,804)/$30,000]. Then, the total of the fractions will be 1.0.

Q 22:52   At what level of compensation is a key employee excluded from participating in a second plan?

If either the defined benefit plan fraction or the defined contribution plan fraction is 1.0, the key employee is excluded from participating in a second plan.

If the key employee's annual compensation is $115,641 or more and the key employee's annual retirement benefit under the defined benefit plan is $115,641 (the current maximum; see Q 6:8), the defined benefit plan fraction is 1.0 [$115,641/$115,641 (i.e., the lesser of 1.0 × $115,641 or 1.4 × $115,641)].

If the key employee's annual compensation is $120,000 or more and the annual addition (see Q 6:1) under the defined contribution plan is $30,000 (the current maximum; see Q 6:1), the defined contribution plan fraction is 1.0 [$30,000/$30,000 (i.e., the lesser of 1.0 × $30,000 or 1.4 × $30,000)].

If the maximum dollar limits increase (see Qs 6:2, 6:8), the level of compensation at which a key employee is excluded from a second plan will also increase.

Q 22:53 At what level of compensation will the top-heavy 1.0 rule have an effect on a key employee?

If the employee's annual compensation exceeds $82,601, the top-heavy 1.0 rule requires a reduction in one of the plans (see Q 22:51). At $82,601 or less, the 1.0 rule as applied to combined plans in a non-top-heavy group will be equivalent to the top-heavy 1.0 rule.

Under the non-top-heavy rule, at $82,601 of compensation, the total of the fractions of a 100 percent defined benefit plan ($82,601/$115,641 = .714) plus a 10 percent defined contribution plan ($8,260/$28,910 = .286) equals 1.0. Under the top-heavy rule, at $82,601 of compensation, the total of the fractions of the same 100 percent defined benefit plan ($82,601/$115,641 = .714) plus the same 10 percent defined contribution plan ($8,260/$28,910 = .286) also equals 1.0.

If the maximum dollar limits increase (see Qs 6:2, 6:8), the threshold level of compensation for equivalency will also increase, but not necessarily in proportion to the percentage increase in the dollar limits.

Q 22:54 What is the special rule if two qualified retirement plans were adopted prior to 1984?

If the employer adopted both a defined benefit plan and a defined contribution plan prior to 1984 (the defined contribution plan must have been in existence on or before July 1, 1982), the plan administrator may make a special election to calculate the denominator of the defined contribution plan fraction for each participant for all limitation years (see Q 6:14) ending before 1983.

This calculation is made in two steps. First, the denominator of the fraction for the 1982 limitation year is determined. Then, the denominator is multiplied by a transition fraction.

The numerator of the transition fraction is the lesser of:

1. $41,500 (instead of $51,875—the amount used in a non-top-heavy situation); or

2. 1.4 times 25 percent of the participant's compensation for the 1981 limitation year.

The denominator of the fraction is the lesser of:

1. $41,500; or

2. 25 percent of the participant's compensation for the 1981 limitation year.

[IRC §§ 415(e)(6), 416(h)(4)]

Example. Dr. Saul incorporated his medical practice in January 1975. His compensation for each of the years 1975 through 1982 was $185,000. The corporation adopted a 25-percent-of-compensation money purchase pension plan (a defined contribution plan) in 1977 and a defined benefit plan in 1982.

The denominator of the defined contribution plan fraction for 1982 was $266,600, and Dr. Saul earned $185,000 in 1981. The numerator of the transition fraction is $41,500 [the lesser of $41,500 or $64,750 (i.e., 1.4 × 25% × $185,000)]; the denominator is also $41,500 [the lesser of $41,500 or $46,250 (i.e., 25% × $185,000)]. The transition fraction is 1.0 (i.e., $41,500/$41,500), and the adjusted denominator of the defined contribution plan fraction remains $266,600 (i.e., 1.0 × $266,600). In this example, electing the transition rule is of no value.

If Dr. Saul earned less than $166,000 in 1981, the transition fraction would exceed 1.0 and Dr. Saul would therefore benefit by electing to use the transition fraction.

Q 22:55 What happens if a key employee's combined fractions exceed 1.0?

In some cases, the total of a key employee's defined benefit plan fraction and defined contribution plan fraction may exceed 1.0 at the time the key employee becomes subject to this rule. In that event, the key employee is permitted no further benefit accruals under the defined benefit plan and no additional employer contributions (including forfeitures and voluntary nondeductible contributions) under the defined contribution plan until the total of these fractions becomes less than 1.0. [IRC § 416(h)(3)]

Q 22:56   If a key employee participates in both a defined benefit plan and a defined contribution plan, can the overall maximum limitation be computed under the regular 1.0 rule?

Yes. The 1.0 rule (see Q 6:15), which applies to an employee covered by two qualified retirement plans that are not top-heavy, also applies to a key employee covered by two qualified retirement plans in a top-heavy group (rather than the more restrictive rule that is usually applied; see Q 22:51) if these additional requirements are met:

1. A concentration test is satisfied (see Q 22:57); and
2. An extra minimum benefit or extra minimum contribution is given to non-key employees (see Q 22:58).

[IRC § 416(h)(2); Treas Reg § 1.416-1, Questions T-33, M-14]

Q 22:57   What is the concentration test for purposes of the 1.0 rule?

One of the two requirements (see Q 22:56) that must be satisfied before a key employee is subject to the less restrictive 1.0 rule (see Q 6:15) is the concentration test. This test is generally satisfied with respect to a key employee for a year if, as of the last determination date (see Q 22:21):

1. The present value of the accumulated accrued benefits for key employees under the defined benefit plan, plus
2. The sum of the account balances of key employees under the defined contribution plan

is not greater than 90 percent of the same amount determined for all participants under the retirement plans.

[IRC § 416(h)(2)(B); Treas Reg § 1.416-1, Question T-33]

Qualified retirement plans may be permissively aggregated to avoid exceeding the 90 percent amount (see Q 22:10). [Treas Reg § 1.416-1, Question T-34]

Q 22:58 What is an extra minimum benefit or extra minimum contribution for purposes of the 1.0 rule?

The second requirement (see Q 22:56) that must be satisfied before a key employee is subject to the less restrictive 1.0 rule (see Q 6:15) is that non-key employees must be given an extra minimum benefit or an extra minimum contribution.

To satisfy this requirement, any one of the four safe-harbor rules (see Q 22:49) may be used with the following modifications. Each non-key employee in the defined benefit plan accrues an extra benefit, which is not less than:

1. One percent of the employee's average annual compensation multiplied by years of service with the employer, or
2. Ten percent of the employee's average annual compensation, whichever is less.

This extra minimum benefit generally is determined in the same manner as the minimum benefit required for a top-heavy defined benefit plan (see Q 22:37).

The defined contribution minimum is increased to 7½ percent of compensation. If the floor offset or comparability analysis approach is used, each non-key employee in the defined benefit plan will accrue the extra 1 percent benefit discussed above. [IRC § 416(h)(2)(A)(ii); Treas Reg § 1.416-1, Questions T-33, M-14, M-15]

Q 22:59 Must every qualified retirement plan be amended to incorporate the top-heavy plan requirements?

The additional rules for top-heavy plans are tax-qualification requirements. A top-heavy plan will be a qualified retirement plan, and a trust forming part of a top-heavy plan will be a qualified trust, only if the additional requirements are met. Other than governmental plans and collectively bargained plans that are not top-heavy, any retirement plan qualifies for tax-favored status only if the plan includes provisions that will automatically take effect if the plan becomes a top-heavy plan and also has provisions that will meet the additional qualification requirements for top-heavy plans. [IRC § 401(a)(10)(B); Treas Reg § 1.416-1, Questions G-1, T-38]

Chapter 23

401(k) Plans

Qualified plans containing cash-or-deferred arrangements, commonly known as 401(k) plans, are one of the most popular and widely offered employee benefit plans. This chapter describes how a 401(k) plan operates and the special qualification requirements that must be satisfied. This chapter also describes the special qualification requirements applicable to qualified retirement plans that provide for employer matching contributions and/or employee voluntary contributions.

Q 23:1 What is a 401(k) plan?

A 401(k) plan is a qualified profit sharing or stock bonus plan that contains a cash-or-deferred arrangement (CODA). Under a CODA, an eligible employee may make a cash-or-deferred election (see Q 23:2) to have the employer make a contribution to the plan on the employee's behalf or pay an equivalent amount to the employee in cash. The amount contributed to the plan under the CODA on behalf of the employee is called an elective contribution (see Q 23:13). Subject to certain limitations (see Qs 23:8, 23:26), elective contributions are excluded from the employee's gross income for the year in which they are made and are not subject to taxation until distributed. For purposes of many of the rules applicable to 401(k) plans, elective contributions are considered employer contributions.

A 401(k) plan may be a stand-alone plan (permitting elective contributions only) or may also permit other types of employer contributions and/or employee voluntary contributions. However, a 401(k) plan is the only method available under which employees may defer compensation on an elective, pretax basis to a qualified retirement plan. [IRC § 401(k); Treas Reg §§ 1.401(k)-1(a), 1.401(k)-1(e), 1.401(k)-1(g)(3)]

A CODA is not a qualified CODA (see Q 23:5) if it is part of a plan maintained by a state or local government (other than a rural cooperative plan; see Q 23:6) or a tax-exempt organization. If TSB '93 (see Q 1:13) is enacted, 401(k) plans will be available to tax-exempt organizations. [IRC § 401(k)(4)(B); TSB '93, Act § 212]

Q 23:2   What is a cash-or-deferred election?

Under a 401(k) plan, an employee can elect either to have the employer make an elective contribution to the plan on the employee's behalf or to receive an equivalent amount in cash. This is known as a cash-or-deferred election. The election may take the form of a compensation reduction agreement between the employee and the employer, under which the employee elects to reduce cash compensation or to forgo an increase in cash compensation and to have the employer contribute such amount to the plan on the employee's behalf. A cash-or-deferred election may be made at any time permitted under the plan, but may be made only with respect to amounts that are not currently available (see Q 23:3) to the electing employee as of the date of the election. [IRC § 401(k)(2)(A); Treas Reg §§ 1.401(k)-1(a)(2), 1.401(k)-1(a)(3)(i)1.401(k)-1(a)(3)(iii)]

Example 1. Adam Corporation gives each employee an annual bonus of 10 percent of compensation payable on January 30 each year with respect to the previous calendar year. Under Adam Corporation's profit sharing plan, each eligible employee may elect prior to January 30 to receive all or part of the bonus in cash or to have Adam Corporation contribute such amount to the plan on the employee's behalf. This constitutes a cash-or-deferred election under a CODA.

Example 2. Dana Corporation maintains a profit sharing plan under which each eligible employee may elect to have Dana Corporation contribute up to 10 percent of the employee's compensation for each payroll period during the plan year or to receive an equivalent amount in cash. The election must be made prior to the date on which such compensation will be paid to the employee. This constitutes a cash-or-deferred election under a CODA.

Q 23:3 When is an employee's election a cash-or-deferred election?

A qualified cash-or-deferred election does not occur if amounts contributed to a plan at the employee's election are either currently available to the employee or designated as after-tax employee voluntary contributions. Compensation is currently available if it has been paid to the employee or if the employee is able currently to receive the cash at his or her discretion. An amount is not currently available if there is a significant restriction on the employee's right to receive the amount currently, or if the employee may under no circumstances receive the amount before a particular time in the future. Contributions of amounts that were currently available to the employee at the time of the election are treated as employee voluntary contributions and are included in the employee's gross income at the time they are contributed to the plan. [Treas Reg §§ 1.401(k)-1(a)(2)(ii), 1.401(k)-1(a)(3)(i)1.401(k)-1(a)(3)(iii), 1.401(k)-1(a)(5)(ii), 1.402(a)-1(d)(2)]

In addition, an employee's elective contributions are treated as not having been made pursuant to a cash-or-deferred election if they are made pursuant to a one-time irrevocable election by the employee to have a specified amount or percentage of his or her compensation (including no amount of compensation) contributed by the employer to the plan for the duration of his or her employment or, in the case of a defined benefit plan (see Q 2:3), to receive accruals or other benefits (including no benefits) under the plan. The election must be available either at the employee's inception of employment or when the employee first becomes eligible under any plan of the employer and must relate to all plans of the employer, including those not in existence at the time the election is made (see Q 23:7). [Treas Reg § 1.401(k)-1(a)(3)(iv)]

Q 23:4   Does a 401(k) plan qualify for favorable tax treatment?

Yes, provided certain special qualification requirements are met in addition to the regular plan qualification requirements (see Chapter 4 for details). The special qualification requirements are the following:

1. The plan must permit the employee to elect either to have the employer make a contribution to the plan on the employee's behalf or to receive an equivalent amount in cash (see Q 23:1).

2. The plan must not allow distributions to employees with respect to amounts attributable to elective contributions merely because of the completion of a stated period of plan participation or the passage of a fixed number of years (see Q 23:33).

3. Employees' rights to their benefits derived from elective contributions must be nonforfeitable (i.e., 100 percent vested) (see Q 23:31).

4. The employer must not condition the availability of any other benefit (except for employer matching contributions) on the employee's electing, or not electing, to make elective contributions under a CODA in lieu of receiving cash. [IRC § 401(k)(4)(A); Treas Reg § 1.401(k)-1(e)(6)]

5. The plan meets the special nondiscrimination test with respect to the amount of elective contributions made to the plan each plan year (see Q 23:8). [IRC § 401(k)(3); Treas Reg § 1.401(k)-1(b)(2)(i)]

6. The plan does not condition participation on completion of more than one year of service with the employer. [IRC § 401(k)(2)(D); Treas Reg § 1.401(k)-1(e)(5)]

7. The amount of elective contributions made to the plan on behalf of each employee does not exceed the applicable limit (see Q 23:26). [IRC §§ 401(a)(30), 402(g)(1); Treas Reg §§ 1.401(a)-30, 1.402(g)-1(d)]

Q 23:5   Are elective contributions to a 401(k) plan taxable to the employee?

Elective contributions made to a plan under a qualified CODA are not includible in the employee's gross income. Income taxes are postponed until the employee receives a distribution from the plan. In addition, earnings on elective contributions are accumulated tax-free until distributed. [IRC § 402(e)(3); Treas Reg §§ 1.401(k)-1(a)(4), 1.402(a)-1(d)(2)]

A plan that includes a CODA that is not qualified (the arrangement does not satisfy the special requirements; see Q 23:4) may, nevertheless, be a qualified plan under the regular plan qualification requirements (see Chapter 4). However, if the plan satisfies only the regular requirements, contributions to the plan made at the election of the employee for the plan year are considered employee voluntary contributions and are includible in the employee's gross income. [Treas Reg §§ 1.401(k)-1(a)(5), 1.402(a)-1(d)(1)]

Q 23:6   Must a cash-or-deferred plan be a profit sharing plan?

Generally, a CODA must be part of a profit sharing or stock bonus plan and cannot be part of a pension plan. There is a limited exception for preERISA money purchase pension plans and rural cooperative plans. [IRC §§ 401(k)(1), 401(k)(2), 401(k)(6), 401(k)(7); Treas Reg §§ 1.401(k)-1(a)(1), 1.401(k)-1(g)(12), 1.401(k)-1(g)(14), 1.401(k)-1(h)(3)]

Elective contributions to profit sharing plans may be made without regard to whether or not the employer has current or accumulated profits. [IRC § 401(a)(27)]

Q 23:7   May a self-employed individual, including a partner, participate in a 401(k) plan?

Yes. The term "employee" for purposes of 401(k) plans includes a self-employed individual (see Q 29:8). If the self-employed individual is a sole proprietor, the individual is treated as the individual's own employee. If the self-employed individual is a partner, the individual is treated as an employee of the partnership. The compensation of a self-employed individual is earned income (see Q 29:10). [IRC § 401(c)(1); Treas Reg § 1.401(k)-1(g)(5)]

Special rules apply to a profit sharing plan of a partnership that includes a CODA (see Q 23:1). A partnership may maintain a CODA, and individual partners may make cash-or-deferred elections (see Q

23:2) with respect to compensation attributable to services rendered to the partnership. Generally, the same qualification rules apply to a partnership CODA as apply to any other CODA (see Q 23:4). [Treas Reg § 1.401(k)-1(a)(6)(i)]

A CODA includes any arrangement that directly or indirectly permits individual partners to vary the amount of contributions made on their behalf. However, a partnership, like any other employer, may allow each of its employees (including partners, who are treated as employees) to make a one-time irrevocable election (see Q 23:3), upon commencement of employment or initial eligibility under any plan of the employer, to have a specified amount or percentage of compensation (including no amount) contributed by the employer throughout the employee's employment or, in the case of a defined benefit plan (see Q 2:3), to receive accruals or other benefits (including no benefits) under the plan. This permits partners to elect different rates of employer contributions; however, since this arrangement is not treated as a CODA, these employer contributions must satisfy Section 401(a)(4) (see Qs 4:9–4:23) without relying on the ADP test (see Q 23:8). [Treas Reg §§ 1.401(k)-1(a)(3)(iv), 1.401(k)-1(a)(6)(ii)(A)]

A partnership plan had until the later of March 31, 1989, or the first day of the first plan year beginning after December 31, 1988, either to be amended to become a qualified CODA or to require employees and partners to make one-time irrevocable elections. The latter approach permitted then-current employees and partners, as well as new ones, to make one-time irrevocable elections without causing the plan to become a CODA. Because many partnerships may have missed the deadline, thereby jeopardizing the qualification of their plans, IRS gave limited relief and did not disqualify the plans if certain steps were taken by the last day of the first plan year beginning on or after January 1, 1992. [Treas Reg § 1.401(k)-1(a)(6)(ii)(C); Rev Proc 91-47, 1991-2 CB 757]

A partner's compensation is deemed currently available on the last day of the partnership taxable year (see Q 23:3). Accordingly, an individual partner may not make a cash-or-deferred election with respect to compensation for a partnership taxable year after the last day of that year. However, a partner's compensation for a partnership taxable year that ended with or within a plan year beginning before

January 1, 1992, was deemed not to be currently available until the due date, including extensions, for filing the partnership's federal income tax return for its taxable year that ended with or within the plan year. [Treas Reg §§ 1.401(k)-1(a)(6)(ii)(B), 1.401(k)-1(b)(4)(iii)]

If a partnership makes matching contributions (see Q 23:14) with respect to an individual partner's elective contributions (see Q 23:13) or employee contributions, then the matching contributions are treated as elective contributions made on behalf of the partner. [Treas Reg § 1.401(k)-1(a)(6)(iii)]

Q 23:8   What are the special nondiscrimination tests for a 401(k) plan?

A qualified 401(k) plan must meet a special actual deferral percentage (ADP) test, which is designed to limit the extent to which elective contributions made on behalf of highly compensated employees (see Q 3:3) may exceed the elective contributions made on behalf of nonhighly compensated employees (see Q 3:13). [IRC § 401(k)(3)(C)]

The ADP test for the plan year will be satisfied if:

1. The ADP for the plan year for highly compensated employees does not exceed the ADP for such plan year for nonhighly compensated employees multiplied by 1.25; or

2. The ADP for the plan year for highly compensated employees does not exceed the ADP for such plan year for nonhighly compensated employees multiplied by 2.0, provided that the ADP for the highly compensated employees does not exceed the ADP for the nonhighly compensated employees by more than two percentage points. [IRC § 401(k)(3); Treas Reg § 1.401(k)-1(b)(2)(i)]

Example. Ellen of New City Corporation's 401(k) plan has a 12 percent ADP for highly compensated employees and an 8 percent ADP for nonhighly compensated employees for the 1993 plan year. The plan does not meet the ADP test because (1) 12 percent exceeds 8 percent multiplied by 1.25 and (2) the ADP of highly compensated employees exceeds the ADP of nonhighly compensated employees by more than two percentage points.

A 401(k) plan will not fail the ADP test if all of the eligible employees are highly compensated employees.

If TSB '93 (see Q 1:13) is enacted, satisfaction of the ADP test will be simplified in three ways:

1. For the *first* plan year of a 401(k) plan, the ADP for the nonhighly compensated employees can be the *greater* of (1) 3 percent or (2) the actual ADP for the first plan year;

2. After the first plan year, the ADP of the highly compensated employees for the *current* plan year is tested against the ADP of the nonhighly compensated employees for the *preceding* plan year; and

3. The ADP test will automatically be satisfied if the employer *either:*

   a. makes a matching contribution (see Q 23:14) of 100 percent of the employee's elective contributions (see Q 23:13) up to 3 percent of the employee's compensation (see Q 23:11) *and* 50 percent of the elective contributions between 3 and 5 percent of compensation, or

   b. makes a contribution to a defined contribution plan of at least 3 percent of each nonhighly compensated employee's compensation.

   To qualify under this alternative, the matching or nonelective contributions must satisfy the vesting (see Q 23:31) and distribution (see Q 23:33) requirements applicable to elective contributions, and the employer must give written notice to each eligible employee prior to the plan year of the employee's rights and obligations under the CODA.

The first two changes effectively give the employer advance notice of what the ADP of the highly compensated employees can be for the current plan year, and the third change provides a safe harbor. These changes will be effective for years beginning *after* 1993.

[TSB '93, Act § 223]

Q 23:9 How is the ADP calculated for purposes of applying the ADP test?

The ADP is calculated by first determining the actual deferral ratio (ADR) (expressed as a percentage) of each eligible employee's elective contributions (including qualified nonelective contributions and qualified matching contributions that are treated as elective contributions; see Q 23:14) for the plan year to the employee's compensation (see Q 23:11) for the plan year. For example, if Gerri's compensation is $50,000 and she made elective contributions of $3,000, her ADR is 6 percent ($3,000 ÷ $50,000).

The ADP for the highly compensated employees (see Q 3:3) is then determined by taking the average of the ADRs (expressed as a percentage) for all eligible highly compensated employees. For example, if there are three highly compensated employees with ADRs of 5, 7, and 3 percent, respectively, the ADP is 5 percent [(5% + 7% + 3%) ÷ 3]. This procedure is then performed for the group of eligible nonhighly compensated employees (see Q 3:13). The ADP test (see Q 23:8), comparing the ADP of the highly compensated employees to the ADP of the nonhighly compensated employees, is then applied. The ADRs and ADP for each group are calculated to the nearest one-hundredth of 1 percent. [IRC § 401(k)(3)(B); Treas Reg § 1.401(k)-1(g)(1)]

Example. Lenny of Lido Corp., with six eligible employees, maintains a 401(k) plan. Each employee may elect to receive up to 15 percent of compensation (or $7,000, adjusted for inflation, if less) in cash or to have part or all of this amount contributed to the plan as an elective contribution. The employees make the following elections:

Highly Compensated	Compensation	Elective Contribution	Percentage of Compensation
A	$70,000	$7,000	10
B	65,000	4,875	7.5
			17.5

Nonhighly Compensated	Compensation	Elective Contribution	Percentage of Compensation
C	$20,000	$1,000	5
D	15,000	0	0
E	10,000	350	3.5
F	10,000	350	3.5
			12.0

The ADP for the highly compensated employees is 8.75 percent (17.5% ÷ 2); the ADP for the nonhighly compensated employees is 3 percent (12% ÷ 4). The plan fails the ADP test (see Q 23:8) because the ADP of the highly compensated employees is more than the ADP of the nonhighly compensated employees multiplied by 1.25 and the ADP of the highly compensated employees exceeds the ADP of the nonhighly compensated employees by more than two percentage points.

See Question 23:11 concerning RRA '93 and Questions 23:56 and 23:57 for discussions of the multiple use limitation and the family aggregation rules.

Q 23:10   How is the ADR of an employee calculated if an employer maintains more than one 401(k) plan?

For purposes of the ADP test, if a highly compensated employee (see Q 3:3) is eligible to participate in more than one 401(k) plan of the employer, the ADR is generally calculated by treating all such plans in which the highly compensated employee may participate as one plan. If the plans have different plan years, all plans having plan years ending with or within the same calendar year are combined. [IRC § 401(k)(3)(A); Treas Reg § 1.401(k)-1(g)(1)(ii)(B)]

Example. Steve, who earns $100,000, may make elective contributions under two of Dolly Corporation's 401(k) plans. If Steve makes elective contributions of $5,000 to one and $1,000 to the other, Steve's ADR is 6 percent ($5,000 + $1,000 ÷ $100,000).

Q 23:11   What does compensation mean for purposes of the ADP test?

For purposes of determining the availability of making elective contributions (see Q 23:13) by an employee, the term "compensation" must satisfy a general nondiscriminatory definition—that is, the definition cannot discriminate in favor of highly compensated employees (see Q 3:3). An employer may elect to include or exclude elective contributions in the definition of compensation (see Qs 6:28–6:32). [IRC §§ 401(k)(9), 414(s); Treas Reg §§ 1.401(k)-1(g)(2)(i), 1.414(s)-1]

The period used to determine an employee's compensation for a plan year must be either the plan year or the calendar year ending within the plan year. Whichever period is selected must be applied uniformly to determine the compensation of every eligible employee under the plan for that plan year. An employer may, however, limit the period taken into account under either method to that portion of the plan year or calendar year in which the employee was an eligible employee, provided that this limit is applied uniformly to all eligible employees under the plan for that plan year. [Treas Reg § 1.401(k)-1(g)(2)(i)]

The amount of compensation used for purposes of the ADP test may not exceed $200,000. This amount is adjusted annually to reflect increases in cost-of-living. For 1993, the annual compensation limit is $235,840. [IRC § 401(a)(17); IR 93-2 (Jan 15, 1993)] For prior years, the annual compensation limit was:

Year	Annual Compensation Limit
1992	$228,860
1991	$222,220
1990	$209,200

The adjustment applies to plan years *beginning* in the calendar year in which the adjustment is effective.

The $200,000 limitation is reduced to $150,000 for the plan year beginning in 1994. Although the first cost-of-living adjustment could occur in the plan year beginning in 1995, it probably will not because an adjustment will be made only if it is $10,000 or greater and then will be made in multiples of $10,000 (i.e., rounded down to the next lowest multiple of $10,000). For example, an increase in the cost-of-living of $9,999 will result in no adjustment, and an increase of $19,999 will create an upward adjustment of $10,000. Therefore, the cost-of-living must increase by 6⅔ percent before the first adjustment to the annual compensation limit will occur [6⅔% × $150,000 = $10,000]. Additionally, this reduction will affect the ADP calculation (see Q 23:9). If a highly compensated employee (see Q 3:3) earning $200,000 defers $6,000, the ADR is 3 percent; with the reduction to $150,000, the ADR becomes 4 percent. [RRA '93, Act § 13212]

Q 23:12 What contributions are counted for purposes of the ADP test?

In applying the ADP test, a participant's elective contributions (see Q 23:13) are taken into account, but only if the following two requirements are satisfied:

1. The elective contribution is allocated to the employee as of a date within the plan year; and

2. The elective contribution relates to compensation that either (a) would have been received by the employee in the plan year but for the employee's cash-or-deferred election (see Q 23:2), or (b) is attributable to services performed by the employee in the plan year and, but for the employee's cash-or-deferred election, would have been received by the employee within 2½ months after the close of the plan year.

For purposes of the first requirement, an elective contribution is considered to be allocated to the employee as of a date within the plan year if the allocation is not contingent upon the employee's participation in the plan or performance of services on any later date, and the elective contribution is actually paid to the plan no later than the end of the 12-month period immediately following the plan year to which it relates (see Q 19:22). [Treas Reg § 1.401(k)-1(b)(4)(i); Ltr Rul 9317037]

Elective contributions that do not meet these requirements may not be taken into account in applying the ADP test for the plan year for which they are made or for any other plan year. Instead, they must satisfy the nondiscrimination requirements of Section 401(a)(4) (without the application of the ADP test; see Qs 4:9–4:23) for the plan year for which they are allocated as if they were the only employer contributions for that plan year. [Treas Reg § 1.401(k)-1(b)(4)(iv)]

In addition, for purposes of applying the ADP test, all or any part of qualified nonelective contributions and qualified matching contributions (see Q 23:14) made to any plan of the employer with respect to those employees who are eligible under the 401(k) plan being tested may, if the plan so provides, be treated as elective contributions. [IRC § 401(k)(3)(D); Treas Reg § 1.401(k)-1(b)(5)]

Qualified nonelective contributions may be used to satisfy the ADP test even though they are also used to satisfy the actual contribution percentage (ACP) test (see Q 23:48). However, if qualified matching contributions are used to satisfy the ADP test, they may not also be used to satisfy the ACP test, nor are they subject to that test. Qualified matching contributions made on behalf of non-key employees (see Q 22:29) may be used to satisfy the top-heavy minimum contribution requirement (see Qs 22:6, 22:48); but, if applied for this purpose, the matching contributions cannot be used to satisfy the ADP or ACP test. [Treas Reg §§ 1.401(m)-1(b)(5), 1.416-1, Question M-10]

Q 23:13   What are elective contributions?

Elective contributions are those contributions made to a plan by the employer on an employee's behalf pursuant to the employee's cash-or-deferred election (see Q 23:2). Any amount that is contributed to the plan pursuant to a special one-time irrevocable election, that is designated as an employee voluntary contribution, or that is currently available to the employee at the time of the employee's election is not treated as an elective contribution (see Qs 23:3, 23:7). [Treas Reg §§ 1.401(k)-1(a)(2), 1.401(k)-1(a)(3), 1.401(k)-1(g)(3)]

Elective contributions cannot be used to satisfy the top-heavy minimum contribution requirement (see Q 22:48).

Q 23:14   What are qualified nonelective contributions and qualified matching contributions?

A nonelective contribution is an employer contribution made to the plan (other than a matching contribution) that the employee could not have elected to receive in cash. [Treas Reg § 1.401(k)-1(g)(10)]

A matching contribution is an employer contribution made to the plan on behalf of an employee because of an after-tax voluntary contribution or an elective contribution made by or on behalf of such employee. [Treas Reg §§ 1.401(k)-1(g)(9), 1.401(m)-1(f)(12)]

To be qualified, nonelective contributions and matching contributions must satisfy the vesting (see Q 23:31) and distribution (see Q 23:33) requirements as though they were elective contributions. [Treas Reg §§ 1.401(k)-1(g)(13)(i)–1.401(k)-1(g)(13)(iii)]

To be qualified, the following requirements must also be satisfied to the extent applicable:

1. The nonelective contributions, including those qualified nonelective contributions treated as elective contributions for purposes of the ADP test, must satisfy the nondiscrimination requirements of Section 401(a)(4) (see Qs 4:9–4:23).

2. The nonelective contributions, excluding those qualified nonelective contributions treated as elective contributions for purposes of the ADP test and those qualified nonelective contributions treated as matching contributions for purposes of the ACP test, must satisfy the nondiscrimination requirements of Section 401(a)(4).

3. The qualified nonelective contributions and qualified matching contributions must satisfy the allocation rules (see Q 23:12).

4. The plan year of the plan that includes the CODA and takes qualified nonelective contributions and qualified matching contributions into account in determining whether elective contributions satisfy the ADP test must be the same as the plan year of the plan or plans to which the qualified nonelective contributions and qualified matching contributions are made. [Treas Reg § 1.401(k)-1(b)(5)]

Q 23:15   Is there a simple rule to follow in determining whether the ADP test is satisfied?

Yes. If the ADP (see Qs 23:8, 23:9) for the nonhighly compensated employees (see Q 3:13) is less than 2 percent, the ADP for the highly compensated employees (see Q 3:3) can be up to two times higher. If the ADP for the nonhighly compensated employees is between 2 percent and 8 percent, the ADP for the highly compensated employees can be two percentage points higher. If the ADP for the nonhighly compensated employees is more than 8 percent, the ADP for the highly compensated employees can be up to 1.25 times higher.

For example, a 4 percent ADP for the nonhighly compensated employees means that an ADP of 6 percent (4% + two percentage points) for the highly compensated employees is not discriminatory. Likewise, an ADP of 10 percent for the nonhighly compensated employees permits an ADP of 12.5 percent (10% × 1.25) for the highly compensated group. [IRC § 401(k)(3); Treas Reg § 1.401(k)-1(b)(2)(i)]

Q 23:16   What are excess contributions?

An excess contribution for a plan year is the excess of the elective contributions (including qualified nonelective and matching contributions that are treated as elective contributions) made on behalf of highly compensated employees (see Q 3:3) for the plan year over the maximum amount of such contributions permitted under the ADP test (see Q 23:8) for such plan year. [IRC § 401(k)(8)(B); Treas Reg § 1.401(k)-1(g)(7)(i)]

The ADP test compares the elective contribution percentage for highly compensated employees with the elective contribution percentage for nonhighly compensated employees (see Q 3:13). If the ADP test is failed, there is an excess contribution made to the plan. However, correction of the excess contribution (see Q 23:17) is done on an individual employee basis. [IRC § 401(k)(8)(C)]

The amount of the excess contribution allocated to a highly compensated employee for a plan year is determined by the following leveling method, under which the ADR of the highly compensated employee with the highest ADR is reduced to the extent required to:

1. Enable the plan to satisfy the ADP test; or
2. Cause such highly compensated employee's ADR to equal the ratio of the highly compensated employee with the next highest ADR.

This process is repeated until the plan satisfies the ADP test. For each highly compensated employee, the amount of excess contributions is equal to (1) the total elective contributions made on behalf of the employee (determined without regard to the above described reduction) minus (2) the amount determined by multiplying the employee's ADR (as reduced under the above described procedure) by the employee's compensation used in determining the ADR.

The total elective contributions in (1) above ordinarily include qualified nonelective contributions and qualified matching contributions that are treated as elective contributions. However, if a highly compensated employee's share of excess contributions is recharacterized for a plan year in order to correct the excess contribution (see Q 23:17), that share may not exceed the actual amount of elective contributions made on the employee's behalf for that plan year. [Treas Reg § 1.401(k)-1(f)(2)]

If TSB '93 (see Q 23:8) is enacted, for years beginning *after* 1993, the leveling method will change so that the highly compensated employee with the greatest elective contribution amount will incur a reduction even if that employee does not have the highest ADR. For example, if a highly compensated employee earning $200,000 makes an elective contribution of $7,000 [3.5% ($7,000/$200,000)] and another highly compensated employee earning $100,000 makes an elective contribution of $5,000 [5% ($5,000/$100,000)], the $7,000 elective contribution of that highly compensated employee will be reduced first. [TSB '93, Act § 223]

See Questions 23:56 and 23:57 for discussions of the multiple use limitation and the family aggregation rules.

Q 23:17 How are excess contributions corrected?

A 401(k) plan will not be considered as failing the ADP test (see Q 23:8) for any plan year (and, therefore, will maintain its qualification) if:

1. The amount of the excess contributions for such plan year (plus any income allocable to such contributions) is distributed to the appropriate highly compensated employees (see Q 3:3) within 12 months after the close of the applicable plan year; or

2. The highly compensated employee elects to treat the amount of the excess contributions as an amount distributed to the employee and then contributed by the employee to the plan as an after-tax employee voluntary contribution. This is known as recharacterization. [IRC § 401(k)(8)(A); Treas Reg §§ 1.401(k)-1(f)(3), 1.401(k)-1(f)(4)]

A plan may use qualified nonelective contributions, qualified matching contributions, the recharacterization method, the corrective distribution method, or a combination of these methods, to avoid or correct excess contributions (see Qs 23:14, 23:16, 23:19, 23:24). [Treas Reg § 1.401(k)-1(f)(1)]

Q 23:18 What happens if a 401(k) plan fails to correct excess contributions?

If a 401(k) plan does not correct excess contributions (see Q 23:17) within 2½ months after the end of the plan year for which they were made, the employer is subject to a 10 percent penalty tax on the amount of the excess contributions. Qualified nonelective contributions and qualified matching contributions (see Q 23:14) properly taken into account for a plan year may permit a plan to avoid having excess contributions even if such contributions are made after the close of the 2½-month period. [IRC § 4979(f); Treas Reg §§ 1.401(k)-1(f)(6)(i), 54.4979-1; Ann 91-50, 1991-13 IRB 50]

If excess contributions are not corrected before the end of the plan year following the plan year for which the excess contributions were made, the 401(k) plan will fail to qualify for the plan year for which the excess contributions were made and for all subsequent plan years during which the excess contributions remain in the plan. [IRC § 401(k)(8); Treas Reg § 1.401(k)-1(f)(6)(ii)]

Q 23:19   How are excess contributions recharacterized?

The recharacterization (see Q 23:17) of all or a portion of a highly compensated employee's (see Q 3:3) share of excess contributions is done in the following manner:

1. The payor or plan administrator (see Q 16:1) must report the recharacterized excess contribution as an employee voluntary contribution to IRS and the employee. This is done by timely providing the employer and the employee whose contribution is recharacterized with such forms as IRS may designate for this purpose and taking such other action as IRS may prescribe.

2. The plan administrator must account for the recharacterized amounts as an employee voluntary contribution for purposes of Section 72 (relating to rules under which distributions from qualified retirement plans are taxed) and Section 6047 (relating to information returns with respect to owner-employees). [Notice 89-32, 1989-1 CB 671; Treas Reg § 1.401(k)-1(f)(3)(ii)]

For plan years beginning before January 1, 1992, excess contributions may not be recharacterized unless they are recharacterized under the plan with respect to which the excess contributions were made or under a plan with the same plan year as that plan. For plan years beginning after December 31, 1991, excess contributions may not be recharacterized unless they are recharacterized under the plan with respect to which the excess contributions were made or under a plan that may be combined with that plan for minimum coverage purposes (see Q 5:15). [Treas Reg § 1.401(k)-1(f)(3)(iii)(C)]

Q 23:20   What are the tax consequences of the recharacterization of excess contributions?

A recharacterized excess contribution (see Q 23:17) is included in the employee's gross income on the earliest date it would have been received by the employee if the employee had originally elected to receive the elective contribution in cash (see Q 23:1). [Treas Reg § 1.401(k)-1(f)(3)(ii)]

A recharacterized amount is treated as an employee voluntary contribution for purposes of Sections 72 and 6047 (see Q 23:19),

the ACP test (see Q 23:51), and the nondiscrimination requirements of Section 401(a)(4) (see Qs 4:9–4:23). For all other purposes under the Code, a recharacterized excess contribution is
treated as an employer contribution that is an elective contribution. Thus, for example, they are so treated for purposes of the
vesting (see Q 23:31) and distribution (see Q 23:33) requirements
applicable to elective contributions (see Q 23:13). [Treas Reg
§ 1.401(k)-1(f)(3)(ii)]

Q 23:21 When must the recharacterization of excess contributions occur?

Recharacterization must be accomplished no later than 2½
months after the close of the plan year to which the excess
contribution relates. For purposes of this rule, recharacterization
occurs on the date on which the last of the highly compensated
employees (see Q 3:3) with excess contributions to be recharacterized is notified (see Q 23:19). [Treas Reg § 1.401(k)-
1(f)(3)(iii)(A)]

Q 23:22 Does the recharacterization of excess contributions result in a penalty tax to the employee?

No. If a timely recharacterization of excess contributions is made,
no penalty tax is imposed on the employee. [IRC §§ 72(t),
401(k)(8)(A), 401(k)(8)(D), 4980A(c)(2)(F); Treas Reg § 1.401(k)-
1(f)(4)(v)]

Q 23:23 Is there an excise tax on recharacterized excess contributions?

A 10 percent excise tax is imposed on the employer for excess
contributions made to a plan. If excess contributions are recharacterized within 2½ months after the end of the plan year for which
they were made, they are not treated as excess contributions for
purposes of the excise tax. [IRC §§ 4979(a), 4979(f); Treas Reg
§§ 1.401(k)-1(f)(6)(i), 54.4979-1]

Q 23:24　How is an excess contribution corrected by distribution?

In addition to recharacterization, another method of correcting a highly compensated employee's (see Q 3:3) share of excess contributions for a plan year is for the plan to distribute such amount plus any allocable income to the highly compensated employee.

For a distribution to effectively correct an excess contribution, it must be designated as a distribution of an excess contribution, and allocable income and the distribution must be made to the appropriate highly compensated employee within 12 months after the close of the plan year in which the excess contribution arose. [Treas Reg § 1.401(k)-1(f)(4)(i)]

The plan may use any reasonable method for computing the income allocable to the excess contribution, provided that the method is nondiscriminatory, is used consistently for all participants and for all corrective distributions under the plan for the plan year, and is used by the plan for allocating income to participants' accounts. [Treas Reg § 1.401(k)-1(f)(4)(ii)]

Q 23:25　How is a distribution of an excess contribution taxed?

If the distribution is made within 2½ months following the close of the plan year to which the excess contribution relates, it is included in the highly compensated employee's (see Q 3:3) gross income on the earliest date any elective contribution (see Q 23:13) made by the employee during that plan year would have been received had the employee originally elected to receive it in cash. If the distribution is made after the 2½-month period, it is included in the employee's gross income for the taxable year of the employee in which it is distributed. A corrective distribution of less than $100, however, is includible in gross income in the year of distribution rather than in the year deferred even if it occurs within the 2½-month period. [IRC § 4979(f)(2)(B); Treas Reg § 1.401(k)-1(f)(4)(v)]

A corrective distribution of excess contributions is not subject to the 10 percent excise tax on early distributions imposed by Section 72(t) (see Q 13:39), the 15 percent excise tax on excess distributions imposed by Section 4980A (see Q 13:27), or the spousal consent requirements (see Q 10:21). [IRC §§ 401(k)(8)(A), 401(k)(8)(D); Treas Reg §§ 1.401(k)-1(f)(4)(iii), 1.401(k)-1(f)(4)(v)]

In addition, if the distribution is made to the employee within 2½ months following the close of the plan year to which the excess contribution relates, the 10 percent excise tax on excess contributions imposed on the employer does not apply. [IRC § 4979(f); Treas Reg §§ 1.401(k)-1(f)(6)(i), 54.4979-1]

A corrective distribution is not considered a distribution for purposes of the minimum distribution requirements of Section 401(a)(9) (see Chapter 11). Therefore, any distribution that must be made to the employee to satisfy the minimum distribution requirements is not satisfied by the corrective distribution. [Treas Reg § 1.401(k)-1(f)(4)(vi)]

Q 23:26 Is there a dollar limitation on the amount of elective contributions?

An employee's elective contributions (see Q 23:13) under all plans in which the employee participates (even if not maintained by the same employer) during any taxable year (including SEPs that offer salary reduction arrangements; see Q 27:9) are limited to $7,000, and the amount of the elective contributions in excess of $7,000 (excess deferrals) is included in such individual's gross income. [IRC § 402(g)(1); Treas Reg §§ 1.402(g)-1(a), 1.402(g)-1(d)(1)]

The $7,000 limit on elective contributions is adjusted annually at the same time and in the same manner as the dollar limit on benefits payable under a defined benefit plan (see Q 6:8). [IRC § 402(g)(5); Treas Reg § 1.402(g)-1(d)(1)]

The $7,000 limitation on the amount of a participant's elective contributions has been increased to $8,994 for 1993. [IR 93-2 (Jan 15, 1993)] For prior years, the elective contribution limit was:

Year	Elective Contribution Limit
1992	$8,728
1991	$8,475
1990	$7,979
1989	$7,627
1988	$7,313

Since a CODA is part of a defined contribution plan, the amount of a participant's elective contributions is also subject to the limitation on annual additions (see Q 6:1). For example, a participant with compensation of $30,000 could not make an elective contribution of $8,994 in 1993, because the 25-percent-of-compensation limitation would be violated [25% × ($30,000 – $8,994) = $5,252]. The maximum deferral would be $6,000 [25% × ($30,000 – $6,000)]. [Treas Reg § 1.415-6(b)(6)(iv); Rev Proc 92-93, 1992-2 CB 505]

A 401(k) plan is not qualified unless the plan provides that the elective contributions on behalf of an employee under the plan and all other plans of the employer may not exceed the applicable limit for the employee's taxable year *beginning* in the calendar year. The plan may incorporate the applicable limit by reference. [IRC § 401(a)(30); Treas Reg § 1.401(a)-30(a)]

Q 23:27   To what time period does the dollar limitation on elective contributions apply?

The limitation on elective contributions applies on the basis of the participant's tax year. In most cases, this is the calendar year. The limitation applies without regard to:

1. The plan year of the plan under which the elective contributions are made;

2. When the participant elects to make the contributions; and

3. When the elective contributions are made to the plan.

[IRC §§ 401(a)(30), 402(g)(1); Treas Reg §§ 1.401(a)-30(a), 1.402(g)-1(a)]

Q 23:28   How are excess deferrals corrected?

If an excess deferral is included in a participant's gross income for any taxable year, then, not later than March 1 following the close of the taxable year, the participant may allocate the amount of the excess deferral among the plans under which it arose (assuming more than one plan) and may notify each such plan of the portion allocated to it. Regulations issued by IRS extend the March 1 date to April 15. A plan may provide that the participant is deemed to have notified the plan of excess deferrals to the extent the participant has excess deferrals for the taxable year calculated by taking into account only elective deferrals under the plan and other plans of the same employer. A plan may instead provide that the employer may notify the plan on behalf of the individual under these circumstances. [IRC § 402(g)(2)(A)(i); Treas Reg § 1.402(g)-1(e)(2)(i)]

Not later than April 15 following the close of the taxable year in which the excess deferral arose, the plan may distribute to the participant the amount allocated to it by the participant plus any income allocable to that amount. This distribution may be made notwithstanding any other provision of law. [IRC § 402(g)(2)(A)(ii); Treas Reg § 1.402(g)-1(e)(2)(ii)]

A corrective distribution of an excess deferral may also be made during the same year in which the excess deferral arose. Such a distribution may be made only if the following conditions are satisfied:

1. The participant designates the distribution as an excess deferral;
2. The corrective distribution is made after the date on which the plan received the excess deferral; and
3. The plan designates the distribution as a distribution of an excess deferral.

[Treas Reg § 1.402(g)-1(e)(3)]

Corrective distributions must be provided for under the terms of the plan. A plan may require that the notification and designations referred to above must be in writing, and may also require that the participant certify or otherwise establish that the specified amount is an excess deferral. [Treas Reg § 1.402(g)-1(e)(4)]

Q 23:29 What are the tax consequences of making excess deferrals?

Excess deferrals for a taxable year are included in the employee's gross income for the taxable year in which they were made. However, the income allocable to excess deferrals is included in the employee's gross income for the taxable year in which it is distributed. [IRC § 402(g)(1), 402(g)(2)(C)(ii); Treas Reg § 1.402(g)-1(a)]

> **Example.** In 1993, Susan defers $9,300 under a 401(k) plan. Earnings attributable to the excess deferral [$306 ($9,300 – $8,994)] are $20. If Susan withdraws $326 [$306 + $20] by April 15, 1994, $306 is taxable in 1993 and $20 in 1994.

The 10 percent penalty tax on early distributions (see Q 13:39) does not apply to a corrective distribution of an excess deferral. Similarly, it is not treated as a distribution for purposes of the 15 percent excise tax on excess distributions, nor is it subject to the spousal consent requirements (see Qs 13:27, 10:21). [Treas Reg §§ 1.402(g)-1(e)(7), 1.402(g)-1(e)(8)(i)]

If excess deferrals are not timely distributed, the amount of the excess deferrals is included in the employee's gross income for the taxable year in which the excess deferrals arose *and* will again be included in the employee's gross income in the year when they are actually distributed. Accordingly, failure to make a corrective distribution of excess deferrals within the specified period causes double taxation on such deferrals. [Treas Reg § 1.402(g)-1(e)(8)(iii)]

A plan may use any reasonable method for computing the income allocable to excess deferrals, provided that the method is nondiscriminatory, is used consistently for all participants and for all corrective distributions under the plan for the plan year, and is used by the plan for allocating income to participants' accounts. [Treas Reg § 1.402(g)-1(e)(5)]

Q 23:30 Are excess deferrals distributed after year-end to an employee nevertheless counted for purposes of the ADP test?

Whether or not excess deferrals are timely distributed to an employee after the end of the employee's taxable year, any excess deferrals of highly compensated employees (see Q 3:3) are still counted for purposes of the ADP test (see Q 23:8); excess deferrals of nonhighly compensated employees (see Q 3:13) are not taken into account. [IRC § 402(g)(2)(B); Treas Reg § 1.402(g)-1(e)(1)(ii)]

Q 23:31   Must all contributions under a 401(k) plan be nonforfeitable?

A 401(k) plan is not qualified unless the employee's rights to benefits derived from elective contributions, as well as from qualified matching and qualified nonelective contributions (see Q 23:12) used to satisfy the ADP test (see Q 23:8), are nonforfeitable—i.e., 100 percent vested immediately. [IRC §§ 401(k)(2)(C), 401(k)(3)(D); Treas Reg § 1.401(k)-1(c)]

Nonelective contributions and/or matching contributions not used to satisfy the ADP test may be forfeitable, i.e., subject to a vesting schedule. See Chapter 9.

Q 23:32   What is a combined 401(k) plan?

A combined 401(k) plan is a plan that permits both elective contributions (those contributions that are made pursuant to a cash-or-deferred arrangement; see Qs 23:2, 23:13) and other types of employer contributions. By establishing a combined plan, the employer can fail safe the 401(k) plan so that it will always satisfy the ADP test (see Q 23:8). [Treas Reg § 1.401(k)-1(b)(6)]

Example. Cindy-Joe Corporation has a profit sharing plan with a CODA. Each employee may elect to receive up to 2 percent of compensation in cash or to have that amount contributed to the plan as an elective contribution. In 1993, all highly compensated employees (see Q 3:3) elect to have 2 percent of their compensation contributed to the plan, and all other employees elect to receive cash. Cindy-Joe Corporation also makes a nonelective contribution to the plan equal to 2 percent of each employee's compensation. The nonelective contribution is qualified because it is subject to the same nonforfeitability and distribution provisions as the elective contributions (see Q 23:14).

The elective contributions, taken alone, do not satisfy the ADP test. Nevertheless, the 2 percent nonelective contributions may be taken into account in applying the ADP test because such contributions satisfy the nonforfeitability and distribution requirements. When these contributions are considered, the ADP for the highly compensated employees is 4 percent (2% + 2%) and the ADP for the nonhighly compensated employees (see Q 3:13) is 2 percent (0% + 2%). Because 4 percent is not more than two percentage points greater than 2 percent and not more than 2 percent multiplied by 2.0, the ADP test is now satisfied. Because the ADP for the nonhighly compensated employees will never be less than 2 percent, this enables the plan to pass the ADP test in a year when it would otherwise fail—when the difference between the ADP for the highly compensated employees and the ADP for the nonhighly compensated employees exceeds the permissible spread.

See Question 23:8 for a discussion of the effect of TSB '93.

Q 23:33 When may distributions be made under a 401(k) plan?

Contrary to the usual rule for a profit sharing or stock bonus plan, a qualified 401(k) plan may not permit a distribution from the plan of amounts attributable to elective contributions (see Q 23:13) merely because of the completion of a stated period of participation or the lapse of a fixed number of years. [IRC § 401(k)(2)(B)(ii); Treas Reg § 1.401(k)-1(d)(6)(i)]

A qualified 401(k) plan must provide that amounts attributable to elective contributions (including qualified nonelective contributions and qualified matching contributions that are treated as elective contributions; see Q 23:14) may not be distributed to a participant or beneficiary before the occurrence of one of the following events:

1. The participant's retirement, death, disability, or other termination of service;

2. The termination of the plan without the establishment of a successor defined contribution plan (other than an ESOP (see Q 24:1) or a SEP (see Q 27:1);

3. The date of the sale by a transferor corporation to an unrelated transferee corporation of substantially all of the assets used by the transferor corporation in a trade or business of the trans-

feror corporation with respect to an employee who continues employment with the transferee corporation acquiring such assets;

4. The date of the sale or other disposition by a corporation of such corporation's interest in a subsidiary to an unrelated entity with respect to an employee who continues employment with such subsidiary;

5. The participant's attainment of age 59½ if the CODA is part of a profit sharing or stock bonus plan; or

6. The participant's hardship (see Q 23:34) if the CODA is part of a profit sharing or stock bonus plan.

[IRC §§ 401(k)(2)(B), 401(k)(10); Treas Reg § 1.401(k)-1(d)(1)]

Where the transferee entity was a partnership and not a corporation, IRS ruled that the requirements of item (3) were not satisfied. [IRC § 401(k)(10)(A)(ii); Ltr Rul 9102044]

If the amounts attributable to elective contributions (including qualified nonelective and qualified matching contributions) are transferred to another qualified retirement plan of any employer, the distribution limitations continue to apply to the transferred amounts. Thus, such other plan will not be qualified if the transferred amounts are distributed before the occurrence of one of the events specified above. [Treas Reg § 1.401(k)-1(d)(6)(iv)]

Q 23:34 What amounts may be distributed in the case of a participant's hardship?

Prior to attaining age 59½, participants in a 401(k) plan are permitted to make in-service withdrawals only in the case of a hardship (see Qs 23:35–23:39).

A distribution on account of hardship must be limited to the distributable amount. The distributable amount is equal to the employee's total elective contributions (see Q 23:13) as of the date of distribution, reduced by the amount of previous distributions on account of hardship. If the plan so provides, the employee's total elective contributions used in determining the distributable amount may be increased by earnings thereon, and by qualified matching contributions and qualified nonelective contributions (see Q 23:14) used to satisfy the ADP test (see Q 23:8) and earnings thereon. The distributable amount may only include amounts that were credited to the employee's account as of a date specified in the plan that is no later than December 31, 1988, or, if later, the end of the last plan year ending before July 1, 1989. Thus, the maximum amount available to a participant for a hardship withdrawal consists of the amount of all such contributions and earnings thereon as of the applicable date, plus elective contributions made thereafter. [IRC § 401(k)(2)(B)(i)(IV); Treas Reg §§ 1.401(k)-1(d)(1)(ii), 1.401(k)-1(d)(2)(ii)]

If the participant does not qualify for a hardship withdrawal, the participant may be permitted to make a loan from the plan (see Qs 13:44–13:48).

A hardship distribution made *after* 1992 is an eligible rollover distribution (see Q 28:8) and is, therefore, subject to the new 20 percent income tax withholding rules (see Qs 16:7, 23:38, 23:39).

Q 23:35 What constitutes hardship?

For a withdrawal to qualify as having been made on account of hardship, it must satisfy the following two-part test:

Part 1—The withdrawal must be made on account of the participant's immediate and heavy financial need, and

Part 2—The withdrawal must be necessary to satisfy such need.

Under the regulations, two methods are available for granting hardship withdrawals from qualified 401(k) plans. Under the first method, a determination of whether a participant qualifies for a hardship withdrawal under the two-part test specified above is based on a review of all the relevant facts and circumstances in each individual situation. This is known as the facts-and-circumstances test.

Under the second method, if the plan uses certain types of expenditures and specific requirements as set forth in the regulations as a basis for granting hardship withdrawals, the withdrawal will be conclusively considered to have satisfied the two-part test specified above. This is known as the safe-harbor test.

A 401(k) plan may use the safe-harbor test for Part 1 and the facts-and-circumstances test for Part 2 and *vice versa,* or it may use the same test for both parts. [Treas Reg §§ 1.401(k)-1(d)(2)(iii), 1.401(k)-1(d)(2)(iv)]

Q 23:36 How is an immediate and heavy financial need (Part 1) determined under the facts-and-circumstances test?

The determination of whether a participant has an immediate and heavy financial need is made on the basis of all relevant facts and circumstances. Thus, a plan that uses the facts-and-circumstances test for Part 1 will have to establish rules regarding the purposes for which hardship withdrawals will be permitted. The plan can allow hardship withdrawals for any reason, provided the surrounding facts and circumstances create an immediate and heavy financial need. In this regard, the regulations note that, generally, the need to pay funeral expenses for a family member would constitute an immediate and heavy financial need, but that the need to purchase a boat or television would not. Additionally, the regulations provide that a financial need will not fail to qualify as immediate and heavy merely because such need was reasonably foreseeable or voluntarily incurred by the participant—for example, the need to purchase a home or send a child to college. [Treas Reg § 1.401(k)-1(d)(2)(iii)(A)]

Q 23:37 How is an immediate and heavy financial need (Part 1) determined under the safe-harbor test?

Under the safe-harbor test, a hardship withdrawal will be deemed to be made on account of an immediate and heavy financial need of the participant if the withdrawal is made for any of the following reasons:

1. Payment of medical fees incurred by the participant, the participant's spouse, or any dependents of the participant; or obtainment of medical care if the withdrawal is necessary for these persons to obtain medical care;

2. Purchase of the participant's principal residence (excluding mortgage payments);

3. Payment of tuition and related educational fees for the next 12 months of post-secondary education for the participant or the participant's spouse, children, or dependents;

4. Payment of amounts necessary to prevent the eviction of the participant from the participant's principal residence or foreclosure on the mortgage of the participant's principal residence; or

5. Any additional events that may be prescribed by IRS in the future.

[Treas Reg §§ 1.401(k)-1(d)(2)(iv)(A), 1.401(k)-1(d)(2)(iv)(C)]

Q 23:38 How is a hardship withdrawal determined to be necessary (Part 2) under the facts-and-circumstances test?

A withdrawal will be treated as necessary to satisfy an immediate and heavy need of the participant if the amount of the withdrawal does not exceed the amount necessary to relieve the financial need and such need cannot be satisfied from other sources that are reasonably available to the participant. This determination is made on the basis of all relevant facts and circumstances. For these purposes, a participant's resources are deemed to include assets of the participant's spouse and minor children that are reasonably available to the participant. For example, a vacation home owned by the participant and the participant's spouse as community property, joint tenants, tenants by the entirety, or tenants in common is deemed a resource of the participant, whereas property held for a participant's child under the Uniform Gifts to Minors Act is not treated as a resource of the participant. The amount of an immediate and heavy financial need may include any amounts necessary to pay any federal, state, or local income taxes or penalties reasonably anticipated to result from the distribution and may also include mandatory income tax withholding (see Q 23:34).

A withdrawal generally may be treated as necessary to satisfy an immediate and heavy financial need if the employer relies on the participant's written representation, unless the employer has actual knowledge to the contrary, that the need cannot reasonably be relieved:

1. Through reimbursement or compensation by insurance or otherwise;

2. By liquidation of the participant's assets;

3. By the participant's cessation of elective and voluntary contributions under the plan; or

4. By the participant's making other withdrawals or nontaxable loans from all plans in which the participant participates or by borrowing from commercial sources on reasonable commercial terms in an amount sufficient to satisfy such need.

A need cannot reasonably be relieved by one of the actions listed above if the effect would be to increase the amount of the need. For example, the need for funds to purchase a principal residence cannot reasonably be relieved by a plan loan if the loan would disqualify the employee from obtaining other necessary financing.

[Treas Reg § 1.401(k)-1(d)(2)(iii)(B)]

Q 23:39   How is a hardship withdrawal determined to be necessary (Part 2) under the safe-harbor test?

Under the safe-harbor test, a withdrawal will be deemed to be necessary to satisfy an immediate and heavy financial need if the employer relies on the participant's representation that the amount of the withdrawal does not exceed the amount necessary to satisfy the participant's financial need (including any amounts necessary to pay any federal, state, or local income taxes or penalties reasonably anticipated to result from the distribution and possibly including mandatory income tax withholding; see Q 23:34) and all of the following requirements are satisfied:

1. The participant has made all withdrawals (other than hardship withdrawals) and all nontaxable loans currently available under all plans maintained by the employer.

2. The plan and all other plans maintained by the employer provide that the maximum elective contribution that a participant may make in the next taxable year is reduced by the amount of the elective contribution the participant made in the year in which the participant received a hardship withdrawal.

3. The plan and all other plans maintained by the employer provide that the participant will not be permitted to make any contributions (elective and voluntary) to the plan for at least 12 months after receipt of the hardship withdrawal. However, the participant is still counted as an eligible employee for purposes of the ADP test. All other plans maintained by the employer means all qualified and nonqualified plans of deferred compensation maintained by the employer, including a stock option, stock purchase, or similar plan, or a cash or deferred arrangement that is part of a cafeteria plan within the meaning of Section 125.

4. Any additional methods of distribution that may be prescribed by IRS in the future.

[Treas Reg §§ 1.401(k)-1(d)(2)(iv)(B), 1.401(k)-1(d)(2)(iv)(C), 1.401(k)-1(g)(4)(i)]

Q 23:40 Are matching contributions and nonelective contributions subject to the nonforfeitability and distribution requirements applicable to elective contributions?

Employer matching contributions and nonelective contributions under a 401(k) plan need not be subject to the special nonforfeitability and distribution requirements (see Qs 23:31, 23:33) applicable to elective contributions unless they are needed to satisfy the ADP test (see Q 23:12). However, if elective contributions are not accounted for separately (see Q 23:41), the nonforfeitability and distribution requirements will also apply to all matching contributions and nonelective contributions, whether or not they are used to satisfy the ADP test. [Treas Reg § 1.401(k)-1(e)(3)]

A matching contribution is not forfeitable for minimum vesting purposes (see Q 9:3) merely because it is forfeitable if the related contribution is treated as an excess contribution (see Q 23:16), excess deferral (see Q 23:26), or excess aggregate contribution (see Q 23:53). [IRC § 411(a)(3)(G)]

Q 23:41   What is a separate accounting under a 401(k) plan?

The portion of an employee's benefit that is attributable to elective contributions (see Q 23:13) (including qualified matching and qualified nonelective contributions used to satisfy the ADP test; see Q 23:12) must be determined by an acceptable separate accounting between such portion and any other benefits of the employee under the plan by allocating investment gains and losses on a reasonable and consistent basis, and by adjusting account balances for withdrawals and contributions. [Treas Reg § 1.401(k)-1(e)(3)]

Q 23:42   Can an employer maintain two or more 401(k) plans?

Yes. But an employer that maintains two or more plans with CODAs and aggregates the plans for purposes of meeting the minimum coverage requirements (see Q 5:15) must also aggregate the plans for purposes of the ADP test (see Q 23:8). [Treas Reg §§ 1.401(k)-1(b)(3)(i), 1.401(k)-1(b)(3)(ii)(A)] For purposes of the ADP test, a highly compensated employee's elective contributions are aggregated (see Q 23:10).

Contributions and allocations under an ESOP (see Q 24:1) may not be combined with contributions or allocations under any plan that is not an ESOP for purposes of determining whether either the ESOP or the non-ESOP satisfies the minimum coverage requirements and the ADP test. This rule applies even if the ESOP and CODA are part of the same plan. [Treas Reg § 1.401(k)-1(b)(3)(ii)(B); see also Treas Reg §§ 54.4975-11(a)(5), 54.4975-11(e)]

Q 23:43   Can a CODA be part of a thrift or savings plan?

Yes. A thrift or savings plan (see Q 2:10) is a plan in which employee or elective contributions and employer contributions are made on a matching basis. The matching contributions by the employer encourage greater participation by the nonhighly compensated employees (see Q 3:13) and may be important in satisfying the ADP test (see Qs 23:8, 23:48).

For example, if the employer makes a $.50 matching contribution for every $1.00 of elective contributions made by the employee, the employee receives an immediate 50 percent return on the investment and has a greater incentive to participate in the plan.

See Question 23:8 for a discussion of the effect of TSB '93.

Q 23:44 How does a CODA affect the employer's tax-deductible contributions?

Since a CODA must be part of a profit sharing or stock bonus plan (see Q 23:6), the limitation on an employer's tax-deductible contributions to such type of plan applies—15 percent of total compensation paid to all participants (see Qs 12:7, 12:14). [IRC § 404(a)(3)(A); Ltr Rul 9225038]

If any employee of the employer is covered by both a defined contribution plan and a defined benefit plan, a special tax-deduction limitation applies (see Q 12:20). [IRC § 404(a)(7)]

The deduction for contributions to a 401(k) plan that are attributable to services rendered by participants after the end of the employer's taxable year will not be allowed because compensation must be earned before it can be deferred and contributed to the plan. [Treas Reg § 1.404(a)-1(b); Rev Rul 90-105, 1990-2 CB 69]

Example. JMK Corporation files its federal income tax return on a June 30 fiscal-year basis and maintains a 401(k) plan with a plan year end of December 31. By December 31, 1993, JMK contributes to the plan elective deferrals attributable to participants' compensation earned both before and after the end of its June 30, 1993, taxable year. The plan contributions attributable to compensation earned after June 30, 1993, cannot be deducted on JMK's tax return for its taxable year ended June 30, 1993.

Q 23:45 How does a CODA affect the annual addition limitation?

Since a CODA must be part of a profit sharing or stock bonus plan (see Q 23:6), the limitation on annual additions to defined contribution plans applies (see Qs 6:1, 23:26). In computing the annual addition, elective contributions made under a qualified CODA are considered employer contributions. [IRC § 415(c); Treas Reg § 1.401(k)-1(a)(4)(ii)]

If the employee also participates in a defined benefit plan of the employer, a combined plan contribution limit applies (see Q 6:15). [IRC § 415(e)]

Q 23:46 Are elective contributions subject to payroll taxes?

Yes. Elective contributions (see Q 23:13) made under a CODA are included in the Social Security taxable wage base for both employer and employee withholding purposes. Elective contributions are also subject to the Federal Unemployment Taxes Act (FUTA). [Social Security Act Amendments of 1983 § 324(d)]

Elective contributions are also included for purposes of measuring the annual increases in Social Security average wages, which will affect the calculation of both the taxable earnings base and benefit computations. [Social Security Act § 209]

Q 23:47 Does a 401(k) plan require registration with the Securities and Exchange Commission?

The Securities and Exchange Commission (SEC) has expressed its opinion that CODAs do not require registration of plan interests or employer stock purchased by the plan, but that a salary reduction plan under which an employee accepts a reduction in salary to obtain a contribution of a like amount by the employer to a qualified profit sharing plan may create plan interests that are securities. (SEC Rel No. 33-6281; Diasonics, Inc, SEC, Div of Corp Fin, Dec 23, 1982)

In a case in which the employer adopted a wage reduction program that consisted of eligibility to participate in an ESOP (see Q 24:1) and profit sharing plan in return for a reduction in wages, the court held that, in order to be considered an investment contract subject to protection under the Securities Acts of 1933 and 1934, there must be (1) an investment of money (2) in a common enterprise (3) with profits derived from the efforts of other persons. Since the wage reduction program constituted an investment of money, the ESOP is a common enterprise, and profits (i.e., dividends and appreciation in value) would result primarily from efforts of management and employees, each employee's interest in the ESOP was an investment contract. [Uselton v Commercial Lovelace Motor Freight, Inc, Nos.

88-1253 and 88-1750 (10th Cir 1991); also see International Brotherhood of Teamsters v Daniel, 439 US 551 (1979); SEC v W J Howey Co, 328 US 293 (1946)]

In another case, the court ruled that the Securities Acts applied to employee claims involving an ESOP because (1) the plan, as an ESOP, lacked the primary indicia of a pension plan (i.e., payment of benefits only upon retirement), (2) participation was voluntary, (3) the ESOP was contributory because participants gave up a percentage of income, and (4) participants acquired common stock, a security specifically enumerated in the Security Act of 1933. [Hood v Smith's Transfer Corp, 762 F Supp 1274 (1991)]

Q 23:48   What is the special nondiscrimination test for qualified plans with employer matching contributions and/or employee contributions?

A special nondiscrimination test, the actual contribution percentage (ACP) test, applies to employer matching contributions and employee contributions under all qualified defined contribution plans (see Q 2:2). The ACP test also applies to employee contributions under a defined benefit plan to the extent they are allocated to a separate account for each individual participant. The ACP test is essentially the same as the ADP test that is applied to elective contributions (see Q 23:8).

A plan will be treated as meeting the nondiscrimination requirements of Section 401(a)(4) (see Qs 4:9–4:23) as to the amount of matching contributions and/or employee contributions only if the plan satisfies the ACP test. Satisfaction of the ACP test is the exclusive method of satisfying Section 401(a)(4) with respect to matching and employee contributions. [IRC § 401(m); Treas Reg §§ 1.401(m)-1(a)(1), 1.401(m)-1(a)(2)]

The ACP test for the plan year will be satisfied if:

1. The ACP (see Q 23:49) for the plan year for highly compensated employees (see Q 3:3) does not exceed the ACP for such plan year for nonhighly compensated employees (see Q 3:13) multiplied by 1.25; or

2. The ACP for the plan year for highly compensated employees does not exceed the ACP for such plan year for nonhighly compensated employees multiplied by 2.0, provided that the ACP for highly compensated employees does not exceed the ACP for nonhighly compensated employees by more than two percentage points. [IRC § 401(m)(2)(A); Treas Reg § 1.401(m)-1(b)(1)]

A plan that permits employee or matching contributions does not satisfy the general qualification requirements (see Q 4:1) unless it provides that the ACP test will be met.

See Questions 23:56 and 23:57 for discussions of the multiple use limitation and the family aggregation rules.

If TSB '93 is enacted, satisfaction of the ACP test will be simplified in the same ways as the ADP test (see Q 23:8). However, the matching or nonelective contributions need not satisfy the vesting and distribution requirements (see Qs 23:31, 23:33); but, to satisfy the safe-harbor, matching contributions on behalf of an employee may not be made with respect to the employee's contributions or elective deferrals (see Q 23:26) in excess of 6 percent of the employee's compensation, and the level of the matching contributions cannot increase as the employee's contributions or elective deferrals increase. [TSB '93, Act § 223]

Q 23:49   How is the ACP calculated for purposes of applying the ACP test?

The ACP is calculated by first determining the actual contribution ratio (ACR) (expressed as a percentage) for each employee. This is the ratio of the sum of the employee's employee contributions and matching contributions to the employee's compensation for the year. [IRC § 401(m)(3); Treas Reg § 1.401(m)-1(f)(1)]

For example, an employee whose compensation is $60,000 and who makes employee contributions of $5,000, which are matched by $1,000 of employer contributions, has an ACR of 10 percent ($5,000 plus $1,000 divided by $60,000). The ACP of the highly compensated employees (see Q 3:3) is determined by taking the average of the ACRs for all highly compensated employees. If there are three highly compensated employees with ACRs of 5, 7, and 3 percent, respectively, the ACP is 5 percent [(5% + 7% + 3%) ÷ 3]. The same procedure is followed for the group of nonhighly compensated employees (see Q 3:13). The ACP test is applied by comparing the ACP of the highly compensated employees to the ACP of the nonhighly compensated employees. ACRs and ACPs are calculated to the nearest one-hundredth of 1 percent. [Treas Reg § 1.401(m)-1(f)(1)(i)]

Q 23:50 What contributions may be included for purposes of the ACP test?

A plan is generally required to apply the ACP test with respect to matching contributions and employee contributions. However, if qualified matching contributions are treated as elective contributions for purposes of satisfying the ADP test (see Q 23:12), then they do not have to satisfy the ACP test (see Q 23:48) and may not be used to help employee contributions and other matching contributions satisfy the ACP test. The matching contributions that are eliminated from the ACP test under this rule are only those contributions used to satisfy the ADP test. [Treas Reg § 1.401(m)-1(b)(4)(ii)(B)]

If the ACP test cannot be met with respect to matching and employee contributions, the plan has the option of treating as matching contributions all or any part of any qualified nonelective contributions (see Q 23:14) and elective contributions (see Q 23:13) made to any plan of the employer with respect to those employees who are eligible employees under the plan being tested. The plan year of the plan that uses qualified nonelective contributions and/or elective contributions to meet the ACP test must be the same as the plan year of the plans to which the qualified elective and nonelective contributions are made. [IRC § 401(m)(3); Treas Reg §§ 1.401(m)-1(b)(3)(ii), 1.401(m)-1(b)(5)(v), 1.401(m)-1(d)]

> **Example.** Judi-Michael Corporation maintains a profit sharing plan that permits elective and employee contributions. The plan permits elective contributions made by nonhighly compensated employees to be treated as employee contributions if required to

meet the ACP test. The following contributions, as a percentage of compensation, are made to the plan.

	Elective Contributions	*Employee Contributions*
Highly compensated employees	10%	10%
Nonhighly compensated employees	10%	6%

The plan does not satisfy the ACP test with respect to employee contributions because the 10 percent ACP for the highly compensated employees is both more than two percentage points greater than the ACP for the nonhighly compensated employees and more than such ACP multiplied by 1.25. If one-fifth of the nonhighly compensated employees' elective contributions are treated as employee contributions, the elective contributions and employee contributions for the nonhighly compensated employees each becomes 8 percent. The plan can then meet the ACP test because the 10 percent ACP for the highly compensated employees is not more than the 8 percent ACP for the nonhighly compensated employees multiplied by 1.25.

Matching contributions made on behalf of non-key employees (see Q 22:29) may be used to satisfy the top-heavy minimum contribution requirement (see Qs 22:6, 22:48); but, if applied for this purpose, the matching contributions cannot be used to satisfy the ADP or ACP test. [Treas Reg §§ 1.401(m)-1(b)(5); 1.416-1, Question M-10]

If an overfunded defined benefit plan (see Q 2:3) is terminated and a portion of the overfunding is transferred to a qualified replacement plan (see Qs 21:51, 21:52), the amount transferred may be used as matching contributions. [Ltr Rul 9302027]

Q 23:51   When are contributions counted for purposes of applying the ACP test?

For purposes of the ACP test (see Q 23:48), an employee contribution is taken into account for the plan year in which it is made. Payment to an agent of the plan is treated as a contribution if the funds are transmitted to the plan within a reasonable time.

If an excess contribution under a 401(k) plan is recharacterized as an employee contribution, then such recharacterized contribution is taken into account for the plan year in which it is included in the employee's gross income (see Q 23:17).

A matching contribution is taken into account for the plan year in which it is allocated to the participant's account under the terms of the plan, provided that:

1. It is actually paid to the plan no later than the end of the 12-month period beginning after the close of that plan year (see Q 19:22); and

2. It is made on account of the employee's voluntary or elective contributions for that plan year.

If a matching contribution does not satisfy these conditions, it may not be taken into account for purposes of the ACP test for the plan year in which it is made or any other plan year. Instead, it must satisfy the nondiscrimination requirements of Section 401(a)(4) (see Q 4:9–4:23) (without application of the ACP test) for the plan year for which it is allocated as if it were the only employer contribution for that year. [Treas Reg § 1.401(m)-1(b)(4)(ii)(A)]

Q 23:52 What other requirements must a plan subject to the ACP test meet?

To satisfy the nondiscrimination requirements of Section 401(m), a plan must maintain the records necessary to demonstrate compliance with those requirements. Among other things, the records must be adequate to show that the ACP test (see Q 23:48) has been met and must include information regarding the extent to which elective and nonelective contributions were taken into account to satisfy the ACP test. [Treas Reg § 1.401(m)-1(c)(2)]

To be a qualified retirement plan, it is not sufficient that a plan to which employee and/or matching contributions are made satisfy the ACP test. In addition, the plan must not discriminate in favor of highly compensated employees (see Q 3:2) with respect to other benefits or rights of the plan, including the availability (as opposed to the amount) of voluntary and matching contributions. The determination of whether a rate of matching contributions discriminates in favor of highly compensated employees is made after correction of excess deferrals, excess contributions, and excess aggregate contributions. [Treas Reg § 1.401(m)-1(a)(2)]

Q 23:53 What are excess aggregate contributions under the ACP test?

Excess aggregate contributions are the excess of the aggregate amount of employee contributions and matching contributions made on behalf of highly compensated employees (see Q 3:3) for a plan year over the maximum amount of such contributions that are permitted under the ACP test (see Q 23:48). Any qualified nonelective contributions and elective contributions treated as matching contributions for purposes of the ACP test are treated as matching contributions under this definition. However, qualified matching contributions that are treated as elective contributions for purposes of meeting the ADP test (see Q 23:8) are not treated as matching contributions under this definition. [IRC § 401(m)(6)(B); Treas Reg § 1.401(m)-1(f)(8)]

If the ACP test is failed, there are excess aggregate contributions in the plan. However, correction of the excess aggregate contributions must be done on an individual employee basis. Allocation of the excess aggregate contributions among the highly compensated employees is done under the same leveling method that is used in allocating excess contributions under a 401(k) plan to individual highly compensated employees (see Q 23:16). [IRC § 401(m)(6)(C); Treas Reg §§ 1.401(m)-1(e)(1)(i), 1.401(m)-1(e)(2)(i)]

If TSB '93 is enacted, the same leveling method that will be used to allocate excess contributions will be used to allocate excess aggregate contributions (see Q 23:16).

Q 23:54 How are excess aggregate contributions corrected?

The principal method of correcting a highly compensated employee's (see Q 3:3) share of excess aggregate contributions for a plan year is for the plan to distribute the share plus any allocable income to the employee. However, to the extent that excess aggregate contributions are forfeitable (i.e., not vested) under the terms of the plan, they may be forfeited rather than distributed. [IRC § 401(m)(6)(A); Treas Reg §§ 1.401(m)-1(e)(1)(i), 1.401(m)-1(e)(3), 1.415-6(b)(6)(iv); Rev Proc 92-93, 1992-2 CB 505]

The following are *not* permissible methods of correcting an excess aggregate contribution:

1. Recharacterization (see Q 23:17);
2. Failing to make matching contributions for highly compensated employees that are required under the terms of the plan; and
3. Forfeiting vested matching contributions made on behalf of highly compensated employees. [Treas Reg §§ 1.401(m)-1(e)(3)(iii), 1.411(a)-4(b)(7)]

For a distribution to effectively correct an employee's share of excess aggregate contributions and allocable income, it must be designated as a distribution of an excess aggregate contribution and must be made within 12 months after the close of the plan year in which the excess contribution arose. However, if the excess aggregate contributions are not distributed within 2½ months following the close of the plan year in which they arose, a 10 percent penalty tax will be imposed on the employer. [IRC §§ 401(m)(6)(A), 4979(f); Treas Reg §§ 1.401(m)-1(e)(3)(i), 1.401(m)-1(e)(5), 54.4979-1; Ann 91-50, 1991-13 IRB 50]

Q 23:55 What is the tax treatment of excess aggregate contributions?

Amounts attributable to excess aggregate contributions are generally included in the gross income of a highly compensated employee (see Q 3:3). However, amounts attributable to employee contributions are includible only to the extent of the income on such contributions. [IRC § 401(m)(7)(B)]

If the distribution is made within the first 2½ months after the close of the plan year for which the excess aggregate contributions were made, the year of inclusion is the taxable year of the employee ending with or within that plan year. If the distribution is made at a later date, the year of inclusion is the taxable year of the employee in which the distribution occurs. A corrective distribution of less than $100, however, is includible in gross income in the year of distribution even if it occurs within the 2½-month period. [IRC § 4979(f)(2)(B); Treas Reg § 1.401(m)-1(e)(3)(v)]

A corrective distribution of excess aggregate contributions is not subject to the 10 percent excise tax on early distributions imposed by Section 72(t) (see Q 13:39), nor is it treated as a distribution for purposes of the 15 percent excise tax on excess distributions imposed by Section 4980A (see Q 13:27). [IRC § 401(m)(7)(A); Treas Reg § 1.401(m)-1(e)(3)(v)(A)]

A corrective distribution may be made without regard to the spousal consent requirements of Sections 401(a)(11) and 417 (see Q 10:21) and is not regarded as a distribution for purposes of the minimum distribution requirements of Section 401(a)(9) (see Chapter 11). Therefore, any distribution required under Section 401(a)(9) is not satisfied by a corrective distribution. [Treas Reg §§ 1.401(m)-1(e)(3)(iii), 1.401(m)-1(e)(3)(vi)]

Q 23:56   What is the multiple use limitation?

The multiple use of the alternative limitation with respect to any highly compensated employee (see Q 3:3) is prohibited. The alternative limitation is the 2.0/two percentage point limitation (see Qs 23:8, 23:48). [IRC § 401(m)(9)(B); Treas Reg §§ 1.401(m)-2(a), 1.401(m)-2(b)(2)]

Multiple use of the alternative limitation does not occur unless the ADP and ACP of the highly compensated employees each exceeds 1.25 times the corresponding percentage of the nonhighly compensated employees (see Q 3:13). Furthermore, multiple use of the alternative limitation does not occur unless (1) one or more highly compensated employees are eligible to participate in both a CODA and a plan to which employee contributions or matching contributions are made, and (2) the percentage obtained by adding the ADP and the ACP of the highly compensated employees exceeds an aggregate limit. The aggregate limit is the greater of:

1. The sum of (a) 1.25 times the greater of the ADP or the ACP of the nonhighly compensated employees and (b) two percentage points plus the lesser of the ADP or the ACP of the nonhighly compensated employees, but this latter amount cannot exceed 2.0 times the lesser of the ADP or the ACP of the nonhighly compensated employees; or

2. The sum of (a) 1.25 times the lesser of the ADP or the ACP of the nonhighly compensated employees and (b) two percentage points plus the greater of the ADP or the ACP of the nonhighly compensated employees, but this latter amount cannot exceed 2.0 times the greater of the ADP or the ACP of the nonhighly compensated employees.

If the sum of the ADP and ACP of the highly compensated employees exceeds this aggregate limit, there is prohibited multiple use. [Treas Reg §§ 1.401(m)-2(b)(1), 1.401(m)-2(b)(3)]

Example. Under SBK Corporation's 401(k) plan, which provides for matching contributions, the ADPs for highly compensated employees and nonhighly compensated employees are 3.9 percent and 2.0 percent, respectively, while the ACPs for the two groups are 1.3 percent and 1.0 percent, respectively. The sum of the ADP and ACP for the highly compensated employees is 5.2 percent, and the prohibited multiple use does not occur because the limitation is 5.25 percent, as follows:

1. Greater of ADP or ACP of nonhighly compensated employees	2.0
2. 1.25 × 2.0	2.5
3. Lesser of ADP or ACP of nonhighly compensated employees	1.0
4. 2.0 × 1.0	2.0
5. First limit (2.5 + 2.0)	4.5
6. Lesser of ADP or ACP of nonhighly compensated employees	1.0
7. 1.25 × 1.0	1.25
8. Greater of ADP or ACP of nonhighly compensated employees	2.0

9.	2.0 × 2.0	4.0
10.	Second limit (1.25 + 4.0)	5.25
11.	Aggregate limit: greater of first or second limit	5.25

When prohibited multiple use of the alternative limitation occurs, the ADP and/or ACP of the highly compensated employees is reduced by use of the leveling method (see Qs 23:16, 23:53) so that the combined ADP and ACP does not exceed the aggregate limit. The amount of the reduction must be distributed to the highly compensated employees according to the allocation produced by the leveling method; or, at the employer's election, the reduction may be allocated among all highly compensated employees under the plan or CODA that is being reduced or among only those highly compensated employees who are eligible under both the CODA and the plan for which employee contributions or employee and matching contributions are made. [Treas Reg § 1.401(m)-2(c)(3)]

Q 23:57   What are the family aggregation rules?

If an individual is a member of the family of a 5 percent owner (see Q 3:4) or one of the ten most highly compensated employees, that individual is not treated as a separate employee and his or her compensation (and any applicable contribution or benefit on his or her behalf) is treated as if paid to (or on behalf of) a single 5 percent owner or highly compensated employee. Family members include the employee's spouse, lineal descendants or ascendants, and spouses of such lineal descendants or ascendants. [IRC §§ 401(k)(5), 414(q)(6), 416(i)(1)(B)(i); Treas Reg § 1.401(k)-1(g)(1)(ii)(C)]

For such a family group, which is treated as one highly compensated employee, the combined ADR (see Q 23:9) is the ADR determined by combining the elective contributions, compensation, and amounts treated as elective contributions of all the eligible family members. Generally, the elective contributions, compensation, and amounts treated as elective contributions of all family members are disregarded in determining the ADP (see Q 23:9) of the nonhighly compensated employees. [Treas Reg § 1.401(k)-1(g)(1)(ii)(C)(2)]

Example. Shirley has a child, Ellen. Both participate in a 401(k) plan maintained by EMK Corporation. Shirley is one of the ten most highly compensated employees, and Ellen is a nonhighly compensated employee. Shirley has compensation of $100,000 and defers $7,000 under the 401(k) arrangement; Ellen has compensation of $40,000 and defers $4,000 under the arrangement. The ADR of the family unit is 7.86 percent, calculated by aggregating the contributions and compensation of Shirley and Ellen ($7,000 + $4,000)/($100,000 + $40,000).

If the ADR of the family unit creates an excess contribution (see Q 23:16), the reduction is applied in proportion to both Shirley's and Ellen's contributions. [Treas Reg §§ 1.401(k)-1(f)(5)(ii), 1.401(k)-1(f)(7), Example 3]

The family aggregation rules also apply for purposes of the ACP test (see Q 23:48) and correcting excess aggregate contributions (see Q 23:54). [Treas Reg §§ 1.401(m)-1(e)(2)(iii), 1.401(m)-1(f)(1)(i)(C)]

If TSB '93 (see Q 1:13) is enacted, the family aggregation rule will be repealed for years beginning *after* 1993. [TSB '93, Act § 221(c)]

Q 23:58 Are 401(k) plan benefits exempt from the participants' creditors?

In 1992, the United States Supreme Court held that a participant's interest in a qualified retirement plan is exempt from the claims of creditors in a bankruptcy proceeding, thereby resolving the conflict among the Courts of Appeals. [Patterson v Shumate, 112 S Ct 2242 (1992)]

See Question 29:40 for more details.

Chapter 24

Employee Stock Ownership Plans

An employee stock ownership plan (ESOP) is a special breed of qualified retirement plan. In addition to providing retirement benefits for employees, an ESOP can be used as a market for company stock, as a method of increasing the company's cash flow, and as a means of financing the company's growth. This chapter examines the requirements for establishing and maintaining an ESOP and explains how an ESOP works.

Q 24:1   What is an employee stock ownership plan?

An ESOP is essentially a defined contribution plan (see Q 2:2) whose funds must be invested primarily in employer securities (see Q 24:10). Generally, the funds may come from any or all of the following sources: (1) company contributions of cash or employer securities, (2) an exempt loan to the ESOP (see Q 24:4), or (3) a defined contribution plan converted to an ESOP (see Q 24:20). The amount of tax deductible contributions to an ESOP is generally determined in the same manner as for other defined contribution plans (see Qs 12:1–12:16), although there is a special rule increasing the deductible amount of employer contributions used to repay exempt loans to the ESOP (see Q 24:11). [IRC §§ 404(a)(3), 404(a)(9), 409, 4975(e)(7)]

The funds are held in trust for the benefit of employees and their beneficiaries and are used to buy employer securities from shareholders or from the company itself. When a participant retires or leaves, the participant receives the vested interest in the ESOP in the form of cash or employer securities. However, an ESOP may preclude a participant from obtaining a distribution of employer securities if the company's corporate charter or bylaws restrict the ownership of substantially all employer securities to employees or the ESOP. [IRC § 409(h)(2)]

Participants can exercise a put option and put the employer securities back to the company for their fair market value if the securities are not readily tradable on an established market (see Q 24:2). To keep the employer securities from falling into the hands of competitors, either the ESOP or the company may be given the right of first refusal if the participant attempts to sell the securities. However, a participant generally can demand a distribution of benefits in the form of employer securities and cannot be required to sell the securities back to the company. [IRC § 409(h)(1); Treas Reg § 54.4975-7(b)(9)]

The basic purpose of an ESOP is the investment of plan assets in employer securities. One court has ruled that an ESOP trustee did not breach its fiduciary duty (see Q 19:10) to plan participants by investing plan assets in employer securities even though the employer was in serious financial decline. [Ershick v United Missouri Bank of Kansas City, NA, No. 90-3283 (10th Cir 1991)]

Q 24:2   When can participants exercise their put option?

The put option must last for a period of at least 60 days following the date of distribution of employer securities (see Q 24:10). If the option is not exercised, the participant must be given the opportunity to sell the stock to the employer during an additional 60-day period in the following plan year. [IRC § 409(h)(4)]

If a put option is exercised with respect to stock distributed in a total distribution, the employer must pay for the stock in substantially equal periodic payments (not less frequently than annually) over a period beginning no later than 30 days after the exercise of the put option and ending no later than five years thereafter. Reasonable interest and adequate security must be provided for unpaid amounts. For this purpose, a total distribution is a distribution of the balance of the recipient's account within one calendar year. [IRC § 409(h)(5); Treas Reg § 54.4975-7(b)(12)(iv)]

If the stock is distributed in installments, the employer must pay for the stock no later than 30 days after the put option is exercised. [IRC § 409(h)(6)]

Q 24:3 How is an ESOP different from a stock bonus plan?

A stock bonus plan (see Q 2:12) permits, but does not require, current investments in employer securities (see Q 24:10). An ESOP must invest primarily in employer securities. Further, an ESOP, but not a stock bonus plan, may borrow from the employer or use the employer's credit to acquire employer securities. [ERISA § 407(d)(6); IRC § 4975(d)(3)]

Q 24:4 What is an exempt loan?

Generally, the lending of money by the employer to a qualified retirement plan is a prohibited transaction (see Q 20:1). However, an employer's loan or guarantee of a loan to an ESOP will not be a prohibited transaction if the loan satisfies the requirements for being an exempt loan. The exempt loan requirements include the following:

1. The loan must be primarily for the benefit of participants and beneficiaries of the ESOP;
2. The proceeds of the loan must be used to acquire qualifying employer securities (see Q 24:10) or to repay an exempt loan;
3. The interest rate of the loan must be reasonable;
4. The loan must be without recourse against the ESOP and without collateral other than qualifying employer securities acquired (or refinanced) with the proceeds of the exempt loan; and
5. The loan must provide for the release from encumbrance of employer securities used as collateral as the loan is repaid.

[IRC § 4975(d)(3); Treas Reg § 54.4975-7(b)]

The amendment of an ESOP and the write-down of loans to the ESOP because of the decline in value of the employer securities did not cause the remaining ESOP loan to fail to qualify as an exempt loan. [Ltr Rul 9237037]

Q 24:5   Do commercial lenders have a tax incentive to make loans to ESOPs?

Yes. If a commercial lender (see Q 24:7) makes a securities acquisition loan (see Q 24:6) that enables the ESOP to acquire employer securities (see Q 24:10), then 50 percent of the interest received by the commercial lender during the excludible period (see Q 24:9) is not subject to income tax. The commercial lender may make the loan directly to the ESOP or to the employer (which in turn lends the money to the ESOP). Loans between related persons do not qualify for the exclusion. [IRC §§ 133(a), 133(b); Rev Rul 89-76, 1989-1 CB 24; Ltr Rul 8941071]

Q 24:6   What is a securities acquisition loan?

A securities acquisition loan is:

1. Any loan to an ESOP that qualifies as an exempt loan (see Q 24:4) to the extent the proceeds are used to acquire employer securities (see Q 24:10) for the ESOP or are used to refinance an exempt loan that was used to acquire employer securities [Ltr Rul 9314007]; or

2. An immediate allocation loan to an employer that, within 30 days, transfers employer securities to the ESOP in an amount equal to the proceeds of the loan and such securities are allocable to accounts of participants within one year of the date of the loan.

A loan made to an employer sponsoring an ESOP may also qualify as a securities acquisition loan if the employer then, in turn, uses the proceeds to make an exempt loan to the ESOP with substantially similar repayment terms as the loan from the lender to the employer. If the repayment terms of the two loans are not substantially similar, the loan to the sponsoring employer will still qualify as a securities acquisition loan if (1) the loan to the ESOP provides for more rapid payment of principal or interest than the loan to the sponsoring employer and (2) the allocations of employer securities within the ESOP attributable to the difference in payment schedules do not result in discrimination in favor of highly compensated employees (see Q 5:28).

A loan made after July 10, 1989 will be treated as a securities acquisition loan only if the ESOP owns more than 50 percent of the issuing corporation's stock immediately after the ESOP receives the employer securities acquired with the loan proceeds. For purposes of the 50 percent test, certain nonvoting, nonconvertible preferred stock is disregarded, and IRS may provide that warrants, options, and convertible debt interests may be treated as stock. Also, the commercial lender's 50 percent exclusion does not apply to interest income received during a period in which the ESOP's stock ownership percentage falls to 50 percent or less. The 50 percent ESOP stock ownership requirement is reduced to 30 percent for loans made after July 10, 1989 but before November 18, 1989.

The term of a securities acquisition loan made after July 10, 1989 cannot exceed 15 years. Also, the ESOP must permit participants to vote stock allocated to their accounts that was acquired with a post-July 10, 1989 securities acquisition loan on a "one share/one vote" basis on all issues put to a shareholder vote.

A 10 percent nondeductible excise tax is imposed on the employer with respect to the amount realized on dispositions of employer securities acquired with a securities acquisition loan made after July 10, 1989 in a transaction to which Section 133 applied if:

1. Within three years, the total amount of employer securities held by the ESOP decreases;

2. Within three years, the value of the ESOP's employer securities drops below 50 percent of the value of all employer securities; or

3. The ESOP disposes of employer securities not allocated to participants and does not allocate the proceeds to participants.

Certain distributions to participants, including distributions pursuant to a diversification election (see Q 24:42), exchanges in corporate reorganizations, and dispositions required by state law, are not treated as dispositions for purposes of the excise tax. [IRC §§ 133, 4978B; Treas Reg §§ 54.4975-7, 54.4975-11; Temp Reg § 1.133-1T, Q&A 1; Ltr Rul 8821021]

Q 24:7 Which commercial lenders are eligible for the 50 percent interest exclusion?

A bank, an insurance company, a regulated investment company, or a corporation actively engaged in the business of lending money is eligible to exclude from gross income 50 percent of the interest received with respect to a securities acquisition loan (see Q 24:6). Entities eligible for the 50 percent interest exclusion are often referred to as qualified lenders. [IRC § 133(a)]

A corporation is actively engaged in the business of lending money if:

1. It is not an S corporation;
2. It lends money to the public on a regular and continuing basis (other than in connection with the purchase by the public of goods and services from the lender or a related party); and
3. A predominant share of such loans is not securities acquisition loans.

[Temp Reg § 1.133-1T, Q&A 2; Ltr Ruls 9119065, 8951027]

Q 24:8 May loans that qualify for the 50 percent interest exclusion be transferred to other lending institutions?

Yes. A holder of a securities acquisition loan (see Q 24:6) may sell or transfer such loan to another lending institution. A subsequent holder of the debt instrument may qualify for the interest exclusion if the holder is a qualified lender (see Q 24:7). Further, a qualified lender will be eligible for the 50 percent interest exclusion even if a previous holder of the debt instrument was not a qualified lender. [IRC § 133; Rev Rul 89-76, 1989-1 CB 24]

Q 24:9 Is there a limit on the time period for which the 50 percent interest exclusion applies?

Yes. The interest exclusion is allowable for the excludible period measured with respect to the date of the original securities acquisition loan. The excludible period generally is seven years or the term of the original securities acquisition loan, if longer. However, the excludible period is only seven years for immediate allocation loans and back-to-back loans with more rapid repayment provisions for the ESOP than the employer (see Q 24:6). Also, the refinancing of an original securities acquisition loan does not extend the excludible period with respect to the original securities acquisition loan. [IRC § 133(e)]

Q 24:10   What are employer securities?

Employer securities include common stock issued by the employer that is readily tradable on an established securities market. If the employer has no readily tradable common stock, employer securities include employer-issued common stock that has a combination of voting power and dividend rights at least the equal of the class of common stock with the greatest voting power and the class of common stock with the greatest dividend rights. Noncallable preferred stock that is convertible into common stock that meets the requirements of employer securities also qualifies if the conversion price is reasonable.

Employer securities also include stock issued by a member of a controlled group of corporations (see Q 5:32) that includes the employer if the stock meets the same requirements as qualifying employer-issued stock. If a U.S. corporation is a wholly owned subsidiary of a foreign corporation whose stock is not tradable on an established U.S. securities market, the U.S. subsidiary is deemed to have no readily tradable common stock and employer securities may include both stock of the foreign parent and stock of the U.S. subsidiary. [IRC § 409(l); Ltr Ruls 9219038, 9135059, 8610082] Common stock of a parent corporation does not constitute employer securities with respect to the employees of a partnership partially owned by the parent's subsidiary because a partnership cannot be a member of a controlled group of *corporations*. Consequently, the employees of the partnership could not participate in the ESOP maintained by the parent corporation. [GCM 39880; Ltr Rul 9236042]

Q 24:11   What is the limitation on tax-deductible contributions to an ESOP?

Generally, the limitation on deductions for employer contributions to an ESOP is 15 percent of covered compensation. However, money purchase pension ESOPs have a 25 percent limitation. In addition, the overall limitation on deductible contributions to all defined contribution plans in combination is 25 percent of covered compensation (see Qs 12:7, 12:16, 12:20). [IRC §§ 404(a)(3), 404(a)(7)]

The employer may deduct up to 25 percent of covered compensation for contributions to a leveraged ESOP (an ESOP that borrows to acquire employer securities) used to repay loan principal, and an unlimited amount for contributions used to pay interest on the loan. [IRC § 404(a)(9)]

Q 24:12 Are dividends paid on employer securities held by an ESOP ever deductible by the employer?

Yes. The employer may be allowed to deduct dividends it pays on employer securities (see Q 24:10) held by an ESOP that it maintains, or by an ESOP maintained by another member of a controlled group (see Q 5:32) that includes the employer.

To be deductible, the dividend must be:

1. Paid in cash to the ESOP participants or their beneficiaries;
2. Paid to the ESOP and distributed to the participants or beneficiaries not later than 90 days after the close of the plan year in which paid; or
3. Used to make payments on an exempt loan. (For employer securities acquired by the ESOP after August 4, 1989, the deduction for dividends used for loan repayment is applicable only if the dividends are on employer securities acquired with the proceeds of the loan being repaid.)

The deduction is allowed for the taxable year of the employer during which the dividend is paid, distributed, or used to repay an exempt loan. [IRC §§ 404(k), 409(l)(4); Ltr Ruls 9321065, 9219038, 9124038]

If dividends on employer securities allocated to a participant are used to repay an exempt loan, the ESOP must provide that employer securities with a fair market value equal to the dividends be allocated to such participant in lieu of the dividends. [IRC § 404(k)(2)(B); Ltr Rul 9132024]

An employer's cash distribution to an ESOP in redemption of a portion of the ESOP's stock may be considered a dividend and deductible by the employer. [IRC §§ 301, 302, 316; Ltr Rul 9211006]

It is important to note that IRS has authority to disallow the deduction if the dividends constitute an evasion of taxation or are unreasonably excessive in amount. [IRC § 404(k)(5)(A); Ltr Rul 9304003]

Q 24:13 Are dividends paid to participants deductible even if participants can elect whether or not to receive them in a current cash payment?

Yes. Dividends actually paid in cash to plan participants are deductible despite a plan provision that permits participants to elect to receive or not to receive payment of dividends. [IRC § 404(k); Temp Reg § 1.404(k)-1T, Q&A 2]

Q 24:14 How are dividends paid to ESOP participants taxed?

Dividends paid in cash directly to ESOP participants by the employer and dividends paid to the ESOP and then distributed in cash to participants are treated as paid separately from any other payments from the ESOP. Thus, a deductible dividend is treated as a plan distribution and as paid under a separate contract providing only for payment of deductible dividends. A deductible dividend is a taxable distribution even though an employee has basis (see Q 13:2), but the distribution is not subject to the 10 percent tax on early distributions (see Q 13:39). [IRC §§ 72(e)(5)(D), 72(t)(2)(A)(vi), 402; Temp Reg § 1.404(k)-1T, Q&A 3]

A distribution of a participant's entire account balance from an ESOP is eligible for treatment as a lump-sum distribution (see Q 13:4) even if the participant received dividend distributions with respect to employer securities held by the ESOP in earlier years. [Ltr Ruls 9045048, 9024083]

Employers must report deductible dividends on Form 1099-DIV; but, if the dividend is paid in the same year that a total distribution is made to the participant, the entire amount should be reported on Form 1099-R. Participants must report the dividend distribution on their tax returns as a plan distribution and not as investment income. IRS is directed to establish procedures for information returns and reports with respect to deductible dividend payments. [IRC § 6047(e); Ann 85-168, 1985-48 IRB 40; Ann 85-180, 1985-51 IRB 24]

Q 24:15　What is the limit on the amount that may be added to an ESOP participant's account each year?

The amount that can be added to a participant's account (the annual addition) is limited to the lesser of $30,000 (or, if greater, 25 percent of the maximum dollar limit payable under a defined benefit plan) or 25 percent of the participant's compensation. (see Q 6:1). [IRC §§ 415(c)(1), 415(c)(2)]

If no more than one-third of the employer's contributions for the year are allocated to highly compensated employees (see Q 3:3), contributions applied to pay interest on a loan, as well as forfeitures of ESOP stock acquired through a loan, are disregarded for purposes of computing the annual addition. [IRC § 415(c)(6)]

It appears that dividends on employer securities (see Q 24:10) held by an ESOP are not considered to be part of the annual addition, so contributions to an ESOP may be effectively increased. [IRC § 404(k)]

Q 24:16　Can a company obtain a tax deduction for stock contributions to its ESOP?

Yes. One of the basic advantages of using an ESOP is the ability to use either cash or employer securities (see Q 24:10) for the company's contributions. A company strapped for cash can make its contributions in authorized but unissued securities and still get a tax deduction for the full amount of the contribution. Thus, for example, a company with an annual payroll of $500,000 that contributes $75,000 (15 percent of $500,000) to its ESOP in the form of employer securities is allowed a tax deduction of $75,000. The contribution in the form of employer securities not only keeps cash in the company but also provides a cash flow from the tax savings realized by the deduction.

The amount of the contribution is the fair market value of the employer securities even though there is no cost to the company.

Note, however, that a contribution of employer securities to a money purchase pension ESOP *could* be a prohibited transaction (see Q 20:8).

Q 24:17 Can an ESOP provide for permitted disparity?

A qualified retirement plan designated as an ESOP after November 1, 1977 may not provide for permitted disparity (i.e., integration with Social Security; see Chapter 7). An ESOP providing for permitted disparity before that date can continue to do so, but the plan cannot be amended to increase the integration level or the integration percentage. [Treas Reg § 54.4975-11(a)(7)(ii)]

Q 24:18 How can a company use an ESOP to help finance the acquisition of another company?

A purchasing company that needs cash to acquire another company (the target) may obtain the necessary cash by arranging a bank loan to its ESOP. The ESOP gets the borrowed cash to the purchasing company by buying employer securities (see Q 24:10) of the purchasing company. The purchasing company then buys the target's assets or stock with the cash. The bank loan is paid off through tax-deductible cash contributions by the purchasing company to the ESOP.

Another approach is to have the ESOP itself buy the stock of the target with the borrowed funds, and then exchange the target stock for newly issued stock of its own company. This approach is riskier, however, because the exchange of stock may be considered a prohibited transaction under ERISA (see Q 20:1). Before proceeding in this way, a DOL exemption request should be considered (see Q 20:9).

A third approach is for the company itself to borrow the cash and buy the target directly, using the cash flow created by a tax deduction for the stock contributions to the ESOP to help finance the purchase. This approach has the advantages of avoiding prohibited transaction problems and producing less dilution of the purchasing company's stock.

Q 24:19   Are ESOPs used by publicly traded companies to defend against unwanted takeovers?

Yes. By establishing an ESOP that purchases stock on the open market, management hopes to place a block of stock in the presumably friendly hands of its employees. However, to the extent that publicly traded stock (i.e., a registration-type class of securities) is allocated to participants, each participant must be given the opportunity to direct the ESOP as to the voting of the allocated shares. With respect to unallocated stock, the trustees and other fiduciaries must take special care to be sure they are acting solely in the interest of ESOP participants and beneficiaries (see Q 24:41). [IRC § 409(e)]

Shareholders of the target company and the potential acquiring company may challenge the voting of the ESOP's stock. In one case, an ESOP that acquired 14 percent of the stock of a publicly traded company in response to a takeover threat was upheld as fundamentally fair to the shareholders of the public company. The ESOP required that unallocated stock be voted in the same proportion as allocated stock. [Shamrock Holdings v Polaroid, 559 A 2d 257 (Del Ch 1989)]

However, the trustees of NCR's leveraged ESOP established in the midst of AT&T's takeover threat were enjoined from voting the ESOP's convertible preferred NCR stock in a special shareholders' meeting at which AT&T was expected to try to replace NCR's board of directors. Even though the ESOP required the trustees to vote unallocated stock in the same proportion as allocated stock, NCR's directors approved the establishment of the ESOP without adequate information about its fairness to NCR shareholders. The ESOP's purpose was to entrench management and prevent AT&T's takeover. [NCR v AT&T, No. C-3-91-78 (SD Ohio 1991); Menowitz v NCR, No. C-3-91-12 (SD Ohio 1991)]

Q 24:20   Can a profit sharing plan be converted to an ESOP?

Yes. If the company currently has a profit sharing plan and wants to replace it with an ESOP, the company has three alternatives. It can:

1. Continue the profit sharing plan and make future contributions to both the profit sharing plan and the ESOP.

2. Terminate the profit sharing plan. This results in the immediate 100 percent vesting of all the accounts of plan participants (see Q 21:4). The assets under the profit sharing plan can be either distributed currently or maintained in the plan for distribution as employees retire or separate from service.

3. Adopt the ESOP as a continuation of the profit sharing plan. Replacement of the profit sharing plan will not be considered a termination of the plan for vesting purposes. Employer securities must be purchased with plan assets because an ESOP must invest primarily in employer securities (see Q 24:1 and Q 24:10).

Plan fiduciaries must beware that the conversion of a profit sharing plan into an ESOP may, depending on the purpose and financial consequences of the conversion, be a violation of the prudent man rule. In other words, if the business goes sour after the conversion, it is likely that participants will bring a claim against the fiduciaries for making an imprudent investment. The courts have been sympathetic to such claims. [Eaves v Penn, 587 F 2d 453 (10th Cir 1978); Bradshaw v Jenkins, No. C83-771R (DC Wash 1984); Baker and Goss v Smith, 2 EBC 1380 (DC Pa 1981); but see Andrade v The Parsons Corp, No. CV 85-3344-RJK (CD Cal 1990)]

Q 24:21   How can an ESOP be used as an estate planning tool for the owner of a closely held corporation?

The bulk of an owner's estate frequently consists of the value of the stock in the owner's corporation. If the value of that stock is not established before the owner's death, an arbitrary figure—one based on a compromise between an IRS valuation expert and the estate's expert—may be used to determine the amount of estate taxes due. The establishment of an ESOP before the owner's death may ease this burden on the estate because the fair market value of the stock acquired by the ESOP would be determined by an independent appraiser beforehand, reducing the chances of a dispute with IRS. [IRC § 401(a)(28)]

The ESOP can also provide cash to pay the estate taxes and administration expenses of a deceased majority shareholder. The tax law provides various solutions to the liquidity problems of an estate that consists mostly of the stock of a closely held corporation. If the estate fails to qualify for this special treatment, it may be able to raise the cash through the sale of stock to the ESOP.

For example, assume that the estate of a deceased shareholder fails to meet the requirements that permit it to pay the estate tax in installments over a period of up to 15 years. The estate tax is then due within nine months of the shareholder's death. By selling the deceased shareholder's stock to the ESOP, the estate can raise the cash it needs. However, one court has indicated that a premium price paid by the ESOP to purchase a majority of a corporation's stock from the estates of two shareholders may be unreasonable corporate waste. [RCM Securities Fund v Stanton, No. 90-7047 (2d Cir 1991)]

The ESOP can also rescue an estate of a deceased shareholder that cannot avail itself of the benefits of a Section 303 redemption. This provision of the Code permits the redemption of a portion of a deceased shareholder's stock for the express purpose of paying estate taxes and administration expenses. If an estate fails to qualify, the proceeds of a redemption of the deceased shareholder's stock are likely to be subject to income tax as a dividend. This result can be avoided by having the ESOP buy the stock from the estate. The sale to the ESOP does not have the danger of being treated as a dividend.

Generally, a sale to the corporation or to the ESOP will result in no gain at all because the estate's basis for the stock it sells will equal the fair market value of the stock on the deceased shareholder's date of death, and the purchase price paid by the corporation or the ESOP will likely be this amount. [IRC §§ 302, 303, 1014, 6166]

Q 24:22   How can an ESOP be used to provide a market for the stock of controlling shareholders in a closely held corporation?

An ESOP is a mechanism that enables controlling shareholders to sell all or a portion of their shares to the employees, who would be the logical buyers if they could obtain the financing.

The transaction clearly benefits the shareholders by allowing them to cash out their interests in the corporation. It also benefits the corporation because the shares may be purchased with pretax dollars (i.e., annual cash contributions to the ESOP), resulting in a substantial reduction in the cash required to finance the transaction. Further, a commercial lender may be eligible to exclude from its taxable income 50 percent of the interest received on the loan to purchase the shares of a selling shareholder, so the lender may charge a reduced rate of interest (see Qs 24:5, 24:9).

Another advantage of this type of transaction is that it provides for the continuity of management by enabling new employees to acquire stock as older employees and shareholders retire without diluting the equity of the remaining shareholders. That is, the ESOP, by purchasing outstanding shares from existing shareholders, avoids the diluting effect that would be involved if the ESOP purchased newly issued shares from the corporation.

There may, however, be some dilution of earnings to the extent that the ESOP creates expenses that the corporation would not otherwise have. Even this may not be the case if the corporation previously had a profit sharing plan and the ESOP is installed simply as a replacement for the profit sharing plan (see Q 24:20).

An existing buy-sell agreement between two controlling shareholders, a father and son, giving each the option to buy the other's shares at a below-market price, may pose a problem. IRS ruled that the father's sale of some of his shares to an ESOP at market value (after the son's waiver of his rights under the agreement) would be a taxable gift by the son to his father to the extent the ESOP's purchase price exceeds the option price under the buy-sell agreement. [Ltr Rul 9117035]

Q 24:23   May gain on the sale of securities to an ESOP be deferred?

Yes. A shareholder who sells qualified securities (see Q 24:25) to an ESOP may elect to defer recognition of all or part of the gain, which would otherwise be recognized as long-term capital gain, by purchasing qualified replacement property (see Q 24:26) within the replacement period (see Q 24:27). If the shareholder makes an election (see Q 24:29), gain is immediately taxable only to the extent that the amount realized on the sale exceeds the cost of the replacement property. If the sale to the ESOP is an installment sale, any taxable gain (that is, the gain relating to the portion of the proceeds not invested in qualified replacement property within the replacement period) must be reported on the installment basis, unless the seller elects otherwise. [IRC §§ 453, 1042; Temp Reg § 1.1042-1T, Q&A 1; Ltr Ruls 9102021, 9102017]

Note: If the selling shareholders' interests in the ESOP are in excess of 20 percent of the total account balances for all employees, IRS may consider the sale to the ESOP to be a distribution under Section 301 and not a sale. [Rev Proc 87-22, 1987-1 CB 718]

Q 24:24   Are all taxpayers eligible to elect deferral of gain upon the sale of securities to an ESOP?

All taxpayers (including grantor trusts) other than C corporations (see the Glossary) can make the election (see Q 24:29). [IRC § 1042(c)(7); Ltr Ruls 9141046, 9041027]

However, only the taxpayer who sells the qualified securities (see Q 24:25) is eligible to make the election. A trust with eight individual beneficiaries sold its stock to an ESOP, elected to defer recognition of the gain, and purchased qualified replacement property (see Q 24:26) with a portion of the proceeds. Soon thereafter, the trust was divided into eight equal separate trusts, one for each beneficiary. The separate trusts are not eligible to defer gain by acquiring replacement property with the remaining proceeds because the original trust and the resulting eight separate trusts are not the same taxpayer. [Ltr Rul 9143013]

Q 24:25   What are qualified securities?

Qualified securities are employer securities (see Q 24:10) that (1) are issued by a domestic corporation that for one year before and immediately after the sale has no readily tradable stock outstanding, and (2) have not been received by the seller as a distribution from a qualified retirement plan or pursuant to an option or other right to acquire stock granted by the employer. Shares of common stock are not qualified securities if the employer's stock had been traded over the counter on NASDAQ within one year of the sale to the ESOP. [IRC

§ 1042(c)(1); Temp Reg § 1.1042-1T, Q&A 1(b); Ltr Ruls 9215026, 9036039]

Q 24:26 What is qualified replacement property?

Qualified replacement property is any security issued by a domestic operating corporation that did not have passive investment income (e.g., rents, royalties, dividends, or interest) that exceeded 25 percent of its gross receipts in its taxable year preceding the purchase. Securities of the corporation that issued the employer securities (see Q 24:10), and of any corporation that is a member of a controlled group of corporations with such corporation (see Q 5:32), cannot be qualified replacement property. An operating corporation is a corporation that uses more than 50 percent of its assets in the active conduct of a trade or business. Banks and insurance companies are considered operating corporations. [IRC §§ 409(l), 1042(c)(4)]

A sale of employer securities to an ESOP in exchange for a promissory note, followed by a transfer of the note to an unrelated corporation in exchange for shares of its stock, qualifies for deferral treatment (see Q 24:23) because the stock of the unrelated corporation constitutes qualified replacement property. [Ltr Rul 9321067]

Q 24:27 What is the replacement period?

The replacement period is the period beginning three months before the date of sale to the ESOP and ending 12 months after the sale. The qualified replacement property (see Q 24:26) must be purchased during this period. [IRC § 1042(c)(3); Temp Reg § 1.1042-1T, Q&A 3(c)]

Q 24:28 What other conditions apply before the deferral of gain is permitted?

After the sale, the ESOP must own at least 30 percent of either (1) each class of outstanding stock of the corporation or (2) the total value of all outstanding stock of the corporation. Also, for sales after July 10, 1989, the selling shareholder must have held the stock for at least three years. As part of the election (see Q 24:29), the selling shareholder must file with IRS a verified written statement of the corporation sponsoring the ESOP consenting to the application of the excise taxes on early dispositions and prohibited allocations of the qualified securities (see Qs 24:34–24:36). [IRC § 1042(b); Temp Reg § 1.1042-1T, Q&A 2(a)]

Q 24:29 How does the selling shareholder elect not to recognize gain?

The election not to recognize the gain realized upon the sale of qualified securities (see Q 24:25) is made in a statement of election attached to the selling shareholder's income tax return filed on or before the due date (including extensions) for the taxable year in which the sale occurs. The election is irrevocable. If the selling shareholder does not make a timely election, the shareholder may not subsequently make an election on an amended return or otherwise. [Ltr Rul 8932048]

The statement of election must provide that the selling shareholder elects to treat the sale of securities as a sale of qualified securities and must contain the following information:

- Description of the qualified securities sold, including the type and number of shares
- Date of the sale of the qualified securities
- Adjusted basis of the qualified securities
- Amount realized upon the sale of the qualified securities
- Identity of the ESOP to which the qualified securities were sold, and
- Names and taxpayer identification numbers of the others involved if the sale was part of a single interrelated transaction including other sales of qualified securities, and the number of shares sold by the other sellers.

If the selling shareholder has purchased qualified replacement property (see Q 24:26) at the time of the election, a statement of purchase must be attached to the statement of election. The statement of purchase must describe the qualified replacement property, give the date of the purchase and the cost of the property, declare such property to be the qualified replacement property, and be notarized within 30 days after the purchase of the qualified replacement property.

If the selling shareholder has not purchased qualified replacement property at the time of the filing of the statement of election, the notarized statement of purchase described above must be attached to the shareholder's income tax return filed for the following taxable year. The statement of purchase must be filed with the IRS district where the election was originally filed if the return is not filed with such district. [IRC § 1042(a)(1); Temp Reg § 1.1042-1T, Q&A 3]

IRS ruled that an election that substantially complied with the rules was valid even though the notarized statement did not declare that the property purchased with the sales proceeds was intended to be qualified replacement property. [Ltr Rul 9028082]

Q 24:30   What is the basis of qualified replacement property?

If the selling shareholder makes an election not to recognize the gain (see Q 24:29), the basis of the qualified replacement property (see Q 24:26) purchased during the replacement period (see Q 24:27) is reduced by an amount equal to the amount of gain that was not recognized. If more than one item of qualified replacement property is purchased, the basis of each item is reduced by an amount determined by multiplying the total gain not recognized by a fraction whose numerator is the cost of such item of property and whose denominator is the total cost of all such items of property. [IRC § 1042(d); Temp Reg § 1.1042-1T, Q&A 4; Ltr Ruls 9102021, 9102017]

Q 24:31   What happens if the taxpayer who elects nonrecognition treatment later disposes of the qualified replacement property?

If the taxpayer disposes of any qualified replacement property (see Q 24:26), gain must be recognized unless exempted (see Q 24:32) to the extent not previously recognized in connection with the acquisition of the qualified replacement property, notwithstanding any other provision of the law that might defer recognition. A special recapture rule applies if the taxpayer controls the corporation that issued the qualified replacement property and the corporation disposes of a substantial portion of its assets other than in the ordinary course of its trade or business. [IRC § 1042(e)]

A taxpayer's transfer of qualified replacement property to a revocable trust created by the taxpayer is not a disposition, and the division of a trust that acquired qualified replacement property into eight separate trusts is not a disposition (see Q 24:24). Furthermore, the distribution of qualified replacement property by a trust to its beneficiary is not a disposition. [Ltr Ruls 9327080, 9226027, 9143013, 9141046]

Contributions of qualified replacement property to a charitable remainder trust constitute a disposition of such property but do not result in a recapture of the deferred gain because of the nature of the trust. [Ltr Rul 9234023]

Q 24:32   Do all dispositions of qualified replacement property result in the recapture of gain?

No. The following dispositions are exempted from the recapture provisions:

- Dispositions upon death
- Dispositions by gift
- Subsequent sales of the qualified replacement property to an ESOP pursuant to Section 1042, and
- Transfers in a corporate reorganization, provided no corporation involved in the reorganization is controlled by the taxpayer holding the qualified replacement property

[IRC § 1042(e)(3)]

Q 24:33   What is the statute of limitations when a selling shareholder elects nonrecognition of the gain on the sale of qualified securities?

If any gain is realized, but not recognized, by the selling shareholder on the sale of any qualified securities (see Q 24:25), the statute of limitations with respect to such nonrecognized gain will not expire until three years from the date of IRS receipt of:

1. A notarized statement of purchase that includes the cost of the qualified replacement property (see Q 24:29);
2. A written statement of the selling shareholder's intent not to purchase qualified replacement property (see Q 24:26) within the replacement period (see Q 24:27); or
3. A written statement of the selling shareholder's failure to purchase qualified replacement property within the replacement period.

If the selling shareholder files a statement of intent not to purchase or failure to purchase qualified replacement property, the statement must be accompanied, if appropriate, by an amended return for the taxable year in which the gain from the sale of the qualified securities was realized. The amended return must report any gain from the sale of qualified securities that is required to be recognized in the taxable year in which the gain was realized due to a failure to meet the nonrecognition requirements. [IRC § 1042(f); Temp Reg § 1.1042-1T, Q&A 5]

Q 24:34   What happens if the ESOP disposes of qualified securities within three years of their acquisition?

An excise tax is imposed on the amount realized on the disposition (see Q 24:35) of qualified securities (see Q 24:25) if:

1. The ESOP acquires any qualified securities in a sale for which nonrecognition treatment was elected (see Q 24:29);
2. The ESOP disposes of any of such qualified securities during the three-year period after the date on which any qualified securities were acquired; and
3. Either (a) the total number of shares of employer securities (see Q 24:10) held by the ESOP after such disposition is less than the total number of shares of employer securities held immediately after the sale for which nonrecognition treatment was elected, or (b) the value of the employer securities held by the

ESOP immediately after such disposition is less than 30 percent of the total value of all employer securities outstanding at that time.

[IRC § 4978(a); Temp Reg § 54.4978-1T, Q&A 1]

Q 24:35 What is the amount of the excise tax on the disposition of qualified securities?

The tax is 10 percent of the amount realized on the disposition that is allocable to qualified securities acquired within the three-year period following their acquisition. [IRC § 4978(b); Temp Reg § 54.4978-1T, Q&A 2]

A disposition is any sale, exchange, or distribution. However, the excise tax will not apply to any disposition of qualified securities that is made by reason of:

- Death of the employee
- Retirement of the employee after the employee has attained age 59½
- Disability of the employee (see Q 26:39) or
- Separation from service by the employee for any period that results in a one-year break in service (see Q 5:10)

In addition, dispositions necessary to comply with the diversification requirements (see Q 24:42) and exchanges pursuant to corporate reorganizations will not trigger the excise tax. [IRC § 4978(d); Temp Reg § 54.4978-1T, Q&A 3]

The excise tax is imposed on the corporation or corporations that made the verified written statement of consent to the application of such excise tax on the disposition of employer securities (see Q 24:29). [IRC § 4978(c); Temp Reg § 54.4978-1T, Q&A 4]

Q 24:36 Are there any restrictions on the allocation of qualified securities acquired by the ESOP in a transaction in which the seller elected nonrecognition of gain?

Yes. None of the employer securities (see Q 24:10) acquired by the ESOP in a nonrecognition transaction may be directly or indirectly allocated to or accrue to the benefit of the selling shareholder or a member of the shareholder's family during the nonallocation period (see Q 24:37), or to an owner of more than 25 percent of any class of employer stock at any time. The family-member restriction does not apply if the family member is a lineal descendant of the shareholder and the total amount allocated to all such lineal descendants does not exceed more than 5 percent of the employer securities held by the plan that are attributable to the sale to the plan by a person related to such descendants. In addition, a person will not be treated as a 25 percent shareholder if such person was not a 25 percent shareholder at any time during the one-year period ending on the date of sale of the employer securities to the plan or on the date the employer securities are allocated to participants. [IRC §§ 409(n)(1), 409(n)(3)]

For purposes of determining whether the prohibition against an accrual of qualified securities (see Q 24:25) is satisfied, the allocation of any contributions or other assets that are not attributable to qualified securities sold to the ESOP must be made without regard to the allocation of the qualified securities. In effect, this allocation restriction operates to prohibit any direct or indirect accrual of benefits under all qualified retirement plans of an employer. [IRC § 409(n)(1); Temp Reg § 1.1042-1T, Q&A 2(c); Ltr Rul 9041071]

Example. Bill, Rodelle, and Evan own 50, 25, and 25 shares, respectively, of the 100 outstanding shares of common stock of Pal-O-Mo Corporation. The corporation establishes an ESOP that obtains a loan, and the loan proceeds are used to purchase the 100 shares of qualified securities from Bill, Rodelle, and Evan, all of whom elect nonrecognition treatment with respect to the gain realized on their sale of such securities. No part of the assets of the ESOP attributable to the 100 shares of qualified securities may accrue under the ESOP for the benefit of Rodelle or Evan during the nonallocation period or to Bill at any time. These restrictions also generally apply to any person who is a member of any of their families. Furthermore, no other assets of the ESOP may accrue to the benefit of such individuals in lieu of the receipt of assets attributable to such qualified securities.

The prohibited allocation is treated as a distribution to the person receiving such allocation. Also, there is an excise tax imposed on the employer equal to 50 percent of the amount involved in a prohibited allocation of qualified securities acquired by an ESOP after October 23, 1986. [IRC §§ 409(n)(2), 4979A]

Q 24:37   What is the nonallocation period?

The nonallocation period, for purposes of the nonrecognition provisions regarding sales of stock to an ESOP (see Qs 24:23–24:36), is the period beginning on the date of sale and ending on the later of (1) the date that is ten years after the date of sale, or (2) the date of the plan allocation attributable to the final payment of acquisition indebtedness incurred in connection with the sale. [IRC § 409(n)(3)(C)]

Q 24:38   How can an ESOP be used to facilitate a buyout of shareholders in a closely held corporation?

An ESOP can be used to purchase all or a portion of the stock of minority shareholders, inactive shareholders, and outside shareholders. In these instances, the primary advantage is that the corporation purchases the shares with pretax dollars. From the minority shareholder's point of view, it is generally irrelevant whether the shares are purchased by the corporation or by the ESOP, since the shareholder would generally be entitled to the same tax treatment in either case. However, the sale of the stock to the ESOP is more likely to be treated as a sale (and not a distribution of property) than a sale of stock to the corporation. [Ltr Rul 8931040]

The purchase of stock from existing shareholders can be financed in a number of ways, depending on the size of the payroll, the assets of the ESOP, and the needs and objectives of the selling shareholder. If the selling shareholder needs immediate liquidity, the ESOP may use any cash on hand and borrow funds either from the corporation or from an outside lender to purchase the shareholder's stock for cash.

If the selling shareholder does not need immediate liquidity, the shareholder may prefer to receive interest by selling the stock to the ESOP on an installment-sale basis in return for an interest-bearing note. An installment sale has the advantages of spreading out the tax over a number of years and fixing the price of the shares at the time of the sale.

Finally, the shareholder may simply sell a portion of the shares each year on a serial-sale basis. This is the approach usually taken when the shareholder is not yet ready to sell a block of stock at one time.

Note: In order to meet qualification requirements and avoid a prohibited transaction (see Q 20:1), an independent appraiser (see Q 24:57) must determine the purchase price in each transaction on the basis of the stock's fair market value at the time of sale. [IRC §§ 401(a)(28)(C), 4975(d)(13); ERISA § 408(e)]

Q 24:39   How can an ESOP be used to finance a business?

Under conventional financing, a corporation that needs to raise $1 million for working capital or expansion purposes borrows the funds from a bank or other lender and repays the loan with after-tax dollars. Although the interest component of each debt payment is a deductible expense to the corporation, the principal repayment is not deductible and is, therefore, considered an after-tax payment.

By use of an ESOP, it is possible to arrange the financing so that both the interest and principal repayments are tax deductible. This is accomplished either by having the ESOP rather than the corporation borrow the $1 million or by having the corporation reloan the proceeds to the ESOP. The ESOP uses the loan proceeds to purchase $1 million worth of newly issued stock from the corporation. The corporation has the $1 million needed for working capital or expansion purposes, and the ESOP owns $1 million worth of the corporation's stock. Thereafter, the corporation may make an annual tax-deductible contribution to the plan consisting of (1) an amount of up to 25 percent of covered payroll for the purpose of repaying the loan principal, plus (2) an unlimited amount used to pay interest on the loan. [IRC § 404(a)(9)]

In the case of a typical private corporation, the lender may demand both a pledge agreement, pledging the shares of stock as collateral for the loan, and a guarantee agreement from the corporation. Under the guarantee agreement, the corporation agrees to make annual contributions to the ESOP sufficient to amortize the loan and, in the event that the corporation fails to make such contributions, to pay the loan directly.

See Questions 24:5 through 24:9 for a discussion of the 50 percent interest exclusion available to certain lenders.

Q 24:40　May an ESOP enter into an agreement obligating itself to purchase stock when a shareholder dies?

No. An ESOP may, however, be given an option to buy stock when the shareholder dies. [Treas Reg § 54.4975-11(a)(7)(i)]

Q 24:41　Must plan participants be given voting rights with respect to their stock?

If the employer securities (see Q 24:10) are registered with the Securities and Exchange Commission (SEC), participants must be given full voting rights with respect to stock allocated to their accounts.

An ESOP maintained by an employer that does not have registration-type securities (e.g., a closely held corporation) is required to pass through voting rights to participants with stock allocated to their accounts only with respect to any corporate merger or consolidation, recapitalization, reclassification, liquidation, dissolution, sale of substantially all assets of a trade or business, or other similar transaction prescribed by regulations. The plan may authorize the trustees of an ESOP maintained by such an employer to vote such allocated stock on a one vote per participant basis. [IRC §§ 133(b)(7), 409(e)]

These voting requirements do not apply to stock held by the ESOP in a suspense account, i.e., stock not yet allocated to participants. The trustees have discretion in voting unallocated stock and allocated stock not subject to the pass-through rule, but they must vote such stock in accordance with their fiduciary duty to plan participants and beneficiaries (see Q 19:10). [The Central Trust Company, NA v American Advents Corp, 771 F Supp 871 (SD Ohio 1991)]

Q 24:42   What is diversification of investments in an ESOP?

A qualified participant (see Q 24:43) in an ESOP must be permitted to direct the ESOP as to the investment of up to 25 percent of the participant's account during the 90-day period following each plan year in the qualified election period (see Q 24:44). With the final diversification election during the qualified election period, the participant may elect to diversify up to 50 percent of the participant's account. [IRC § 401(a)(28)(B)]

Q 24:43   Who is a qualified participant?

A qualified participant is any employee who has completed at least ten years of participation in the ESOP and has attained age 55. [IRC § 401(a)(28)(B)(iii)]

When an ESOP was terminated and a successor ESOP adopted, a participant's years of participation in both ESOPs can be aggregated for purposes of the ten-year requirement. [Ltr Rul 9213006]

Q 24:44   What is the qualified election period?

The qualified election period is the six-plan-year period beginning with the plan year after the first plan year beginning after 1986 in which the employee is a qualified participant (see Q 24:43). [IRC § 401(a)(28)(B)(iv)]

Example. IRV of Kings Point Ltd. maintains an ESOP with a calendar-year plan year. Iris completes ten years of participation in the ESOP in 1993 when she is age 56. Thus, Iris becomes a qualified participant in the plan year beginning January 1, 1993. Iris will be eligible to make diversification elections during the election periods in 1994, 1995, 1996, 1997, 1998, and 1999.

Q 24:45   What must an ESOP do to satisfy the diversification requirements?

A qualified participant (see Q 24:43) must be given the opportunity to make a diversification election within 90 days after the close of each plan year within the qualified election period (see Q 24:44) with respect to a cumulative amount of at least 25 percent of the participant's account (50 percent for the last election period). The ESOP can satisfy this requirement by offering any of the following:

1. To distribute all or part of the amount subject to the diversification election;
2. At least three other distinct investment options; or
3. To transfer the portion of the account balance subject to the diversification election to another qualified defined contribution plan (see Q 2:2) of the employer that offers at least three investment options.

The ESOP must complete diversification in accordance with a diversification election within 90 days after the end of the period during which the election could be made for the plan year. [IRC § 401(a)(28)(B)(ii); Notice 88-56, 1988-1 CB 540, Q 13]

If this requirement is satisfied by the distribution of all or part of the amount subject to the diversification election, the distribution will be an eligible rollover distribution (see Q 28:8) subject to the new 20 percent income tax withholding rules (see Q 16:7).

Q 24:46   What is the effect of the diversification or distribution of a participant's employer securities?

Amounts diversified pursuant to a diversification election are generally treated as amounts not held by an ESOP and are no longer subject to the statutory provisions governing amounts held by an ESOP. Thus, for example, a qualified participant (see Q 24:43) cannot demand that the distribution of diversified amounts be made in the form of employer securities (see Q 24:10). [Notice 88-56, 1988-1 CB 540, Q 16]

Amounts distributed in satisfaction of the diversification requirements that consist of employer securities are subject to a participant's put option (see Qs 24:1, 24:2). Distributions in satisfaction of the diversification requirements do not violate the restrictions regarding distributions before a participant's termination of employment or certain other events. [Notice 88-56, 1988-1 CB 540, Q 14; IRC § 409(h)]

Q 24:47 Are all employer securities held by an ESOP subject to diversification?

No. Only employer securities (see Q 24:10) acquired by or contributed to an ESOP after December 31, 1986 are subject to the diversification requirements. Therefore, employer securities allocated to participant accounts after December 31, 1986 will not be subject to diversification if they were acquired or contributed before that date. [Notice 88-56, 1988-1 CB 540, Q 1]

Also, if an ESOP received cash contributions prior to January 1, 1987, and thereafter—but within certain time limits—used the contributions to acquire employer securities, those securities will be deemed to have been acquired before January 1, 1987 and will not be subject to the diversification rules. [Notice 88-56, 1988-1 CB 540, Q 3]

Q 24:48 Are dividends paid to an ESOP subject to the diversification rules?

Yes. Dividends paid after December 31, 1986 in the form of employer securities (see Q 24:10), or in cash or other property used to acquire employer securities, are subject to the diversification rules. This is true even though the dividends are paid with respect to employer securities acquired by the ESOP before January 1, 1987. [Notice 88-56, 1988-1 CB 540, Q 1]

However, the diversification rules will not apply to securities acquired with cash dividends paid before January 1, 1987 if the acquisition occurred within 60 days of the date of payment of the dividend. [Notice 88-56, 1988-1 CB 540, Q 1 and Q 3]

Q 24:49 How is the determination made as to which employer securities are subject to diversification?

An ESOP may separately account for employer securities (see Q 24:10) contributed or acquired after December 31, 1986 and those contributed before January 1, 1987. If the ESOP does not maintain separate accounts for securities based on the date of acquisition, any securities allocated after 1986 will be presumed to consist, first, of securities acquired or contributed after 1986 and, second, of securities acquired or contributed before 1987. [Notice 88-56, 1988-1 CB 540, Q 4]

An ESOP may, under certain circumstances, use an alternative formula to determine the portion of a qualified participant's (see Q 24:43) account attributable to employer securities acquired or contributed after December 31, 1986. Under this formula, the number of securities in a qualified participant's account deemed acquired or contributed after December 31, 1986 is determined by multiplying the number of shares allocated to a qualified participant's account by a fraction representing, as of the plan valuation date closest to the date on which the individual becomes a qualified participant, the portion of the total shares that were acquired by or contributed to the ESOP after December 31, 1986. This formula is available only if the IRS model plan amendments to conform to the TRA '86 changes were adopted by the ESOP sponsor on or before January 1, 1989. [Notice 88-56, 1988-1 CB 540, Q 5; Notice 87-2, 1987-1 CB 396]

> **Example.** WAP Corporation adopted the model plan amendments with respect to its ESOP. On January 1, 1993—the plan's valuation date—the ESOP holds 100,000 shares of WAP Corporation's stock. Of those 100,000 shares, 75,000 were acquired by the ESOP after December 31, 1986. Rodelle, a participant in the ESOP with 40 shares allocated to her account, becomes a qualified participant on January 15, 1993. The number of shares allocated to Rodelle's account that are subject to the diversification requirements is 30 (75,000/100,000 × 40). If Rodelle does not elect to diversify within 90 days after the close of the 1993 plan year, and eight more shares are allocated to her account on January 1, 1994, the number of shares in her account subject to diversification increases to 36 [(75,000/100,000) × (40 + 8)]. [Notice 88-56, 1988-1 CB 540, Q 9]

Q 24:50   May any qualified participants in ESOPs that hold employer securities acquired after December 31, 1986 be excluded from making the diversification election?

Yes. If an ESOP holds and allocates to a qualified participant's (see Q 24:43) account a *de minimis* amount of employer securities (see Q 24:10) acquired after December 31, 1986 (see Qs 24:47, 24:49), it will not be required to offer diversification to that participant. A fair market value of $500 or less will be considered to be a *de minimis* amount for this purpose, although an ESOP may elect to use a lower threshold. If the *de minimis* level is exceeded later in the qualified election period (see Q 24:44), then all employer securities allocated to the qualified participant that were acquired or contributed after December 31, 1986, are subject to diversification. [Notice 88-56, 1988-1 CB 540, Q 7 and Q 8]

Q 24:51   May employer securities acquired before 1987 be diversified?

Yes. The shares diversified need not be those actually acquired after 1986 (see Q 24:47 and Q 24:49). The number of shares that must be available for diversification is nevertheless determined by the number of shares acquired or contributed after December 31, 1986. The diversified shares, however, must be employer securities (see Q 24:10) that, immediately prior to diversification, were subject to the put option and right to demand requirements of Section 409(h) (see Q 24:1). [Notice 88-56, 1988-1 CB 540, Q 10]

Q 24:52   May an ESOP permit a qualified participant to elect diversification of amounts in excess of that required by statute?

Yes, an ESOP may permit diversification of amounts in excess of the minimum requirements (see Q 24:42). However, such amounts are not treated as available for diversification or as diversified in accordance with Section 401(a)(28)(B). Amounts in excess of the minimum diversification requirements remain subject to the participant's right under Section 409(h) to demand distribution in the form of employer securities (see Q 24:10). [Notice 88-56, 1988-1 CB 540, Q 11]

Q 24:53   Is a loan from a shareholder to an ESOP a prohibited transaction?

Not necessarily. Although ERISA generally prohibits loans (or loan guarantees) between a qualified retirement plan and a disqualified person (a 10 percent or more shareholder, for example), a loan (or a loan guarantee) by a disqualified person to an ESOP is not a prohibited transaction (see Q 20:1) if the loan qualifies as an exempt loan (see Q 24:4). [ERISA § 408(b)(3); IRC § 4975(d)(3)]

Q 24:54   Must distributions under an ESOP commence by specified dates?

Yes. As a qualification requirement, with regard to distributions attributable to stock acquired after December 31, 1986, an ESOP must provide that, if a participant elects (and, if applicable, the participant's spouse consents), the distribution of the participant's account balance will begin not later than one year after the end of the plan year:

1. In which the individual terminates employment by reason of reaching retirement age, disability (see Q 26:39), or death; or
2. That is the fifth plan year following the plan year in which the individual otherwise terminates employment (unless the individual is reemployed by the employer before such time).

For purposes of this rule, the individual's account balance is deemed not to include any employer securities (see Q 24:10) acquired with the proceeds of an exempt loan (see Q 24:4) until the end of the plan year in which such loan is repaid in full. In addition to these requirements, the ESOP must comply with the minimum distribution requirements (see Chapter 11). [IRC §§ 401(a)(9), 409(o)(1)(A), 409(o)(1)(B)]

Q 24:55   Must distributions under an ESOP be made at certain intervals?

With regard to distributions attributable to stock acquired after December 31, 1986, an ESOP must provide that (unless the participant elects otherwise) the distribution of the participant's account balance will be in substantially equal periodic payments (not less frequently than annually) over a period not longer than five years. If the participant's account balance exceeds $500,000, the distribution period may be extended one year for each $100,000 (or part thereof) by which the account balance exceeds $500,000. However, the distribution period cannot exceed ten years. [IRC § 409(o)(1)(C)]

Both of the dollar amounts are adjusted for inflation. For 1993, the respective amounts have increased to $642,450 and $128,490. [IR 93-2 (Jan 15, 1993)]

Q 24:56 How are distributions from an ESOP taxed?

Distributions from an ESOP are generally taxed like any other distribution from a qualified retirement plan (see Chapter 13). If appreciated employer securities (see Q 24:10) are included in a lump-sum distribution, the recipient may defer tax on the net unrealized appreciation until the securities are sold (see Q 13:17). [Ltr Rul 9147053]

Distributions from ESOPs are subject to the 10 percent additional tax on early distributions (see Q 13:39). However, distributions before January 1, 1990 were exempt from the additional tax if the distributions were attributable to assets that had been invested in employer securities (see Q 24:10) for the five-plan-year period preceding the plan year in which the distributions were made. [IRC § 72(t)(2)(C)].

ESOP assets will be considered invested in employer securities in a variety of circumstances. If an ESOP receives cash or other assets for employer securities as part of a reorganization, the assets will satisfy the requirement if they are invested in employer securities within 90 days (or an extended period if granted by IRS) of the acquisition of cash or other assets. Cash received by an ESOP as the result of an exempt loan, earnings, dividends, or other cash contributions will satisfy the requirement if invested in employer securities within 60 days of the contribution. Cash or cash equivalents allocated to a participant's account will be deemed to be invested in employer securities if the value of those benefits does not exceed 2 percent of the value of the allocated securities. Also, amounts transferred to an ESOP following a reversion from a terminated defined benefit plan will meet the investment requirement if the amounts are invested in employer securities within 90 days of the transfer. [Notice 88-56, 1988-1 CB 540, Q 18; IRC § 4980(c)(3)]

Q 24:57   Which factors are used to value employer securities that are not readily tradable?

Employer securities (see Q 24:10) that are not readily tradable must be valued by an independent appraiser. [IRC § 401(a)(28)(C)]

The valuation of employer securities must be reasonable, written, made in good faith, and based on all relevant factors used to determine fair market value. Relevant factors include:

- Nature of the business and history of the enterprise
- Economic outlook in general and condition of specific industry
- Book value of the securities
- Earning capacity of the company
- Dividend-paying capacity of the company
- Existence of goodwill
- Market price of similar stocks
- Marketability of securities, including an assessment of the company's ability to meet its put obligations, and
- Existence of a control premium, which means a block of security that provides actual control of the company (control must be actual control that is not dissipated within a short period of time)

[DOL Prop Reg § 510.3-18]

Q 24:58   Can employees' interests in an ESOP be investment contracts under the Securities Acts of 1933 and 1934?

Yes, says one court. The company solicited new employees to participate in its wage reduction program, which constituted eligibility to participate in the company's ESOP and profit sharing plan in return for a reduction in wages. The court held that, in order to be considered an investment contract subject to protection under the Securities Acts of 1933 and 1934, there must be (1) an investment of money (2) in a common enterprise (3) with profit derived from the efforts of other persons. Since the wage reduction program constituted an investment of money, the ESOP is a common enterprise, and profits (i.e., dividends and appreciation in value) would result primarily from efforts of management and employees, each employee's interest in the ESOP was an investment contract. [Uselton v Commercial Lovelace Motor Freight, Inc, Nos 88-1253 and 88-1750 (10th Cir 1991); also see International Brotherhood of Teamsters v Daniel, 439 US 551 (1979); SEC v WJ Howey Co, 328 US 293 (1946)]

Another court has ruled that the Securities Acts applied to employee claims involving an ESOP because (1) the plan, as an ESOP, lacked the primary indicia of a pension plan (i.e., payment of benefits only upon retirement), (2) participation was voluntary, (3) the ESOP was contributory because participants gave up a percentage of income, and (4) participants acquired common stock, a security specifically enumerated in the Security Act of 1933. [Hood v Smith's Transfer Corp, 762 F Supp 1274 (1991)]

Q 24:59 Is a participant's interest in an ESOP exempt from bankruptcy?

In 1992, the United States Supreme Court held that a participant's interest in a qualified retirement plan is exempt from the claims of creditors in a bankruptcy proceeding, thereby resolving the conflict among the Courts of Appeals. [Patterson v Shumate, 112 S Ct 2242 (1992)]

See Question 29:40 for more details.

Chapter 25

Multiemployer Plans

Many companies maintain qualified retirement plans established under collective bargaining agreements. Frequently, more than one employer is required to contribute to the plan. How these multiemployer plans work, their basic advantages, and the system for guaranteeing benefits are examined in this chapter.

Q 25:1   What kind of retirement plan is used to provide retirement benefits for union workers?

Retirement plans are subject to collective bargaining. Often a retirement plan negotiated by a union is set up on an industrywide (sometimes regional) basis. An employer, out of necessity or voluntarily, will negotiate to join this industrywide retirement plan. In other cases, the employer may find it possible or desirable to have a separate (individual) retirement plan for its own employees as a result of negotiations with the union.

If the employer decides to go with an individual retirement plan, the plan is virtually identical to those plans adopted in nonunion situations. The only differences are that the retirement plan covers union workers and that the benefits result from the collective bargaining process. All of the requirements for qualification as a tax-favored retirement plan that apply to retirement plans that do not cover union employees apply to the individual collectively bargained retirement plan.

If, on the other hand, the employer decides to provide benefits under an industrywide or areawide retirement plan, commonly referred to as a multiemployer plan, an entirely different set of rules applies (in addition to some of the basic requirements). [IRC §§ 413(a), 413(b); see also ERISA §§ 4201–4225] For example, hours of service that are credited to a participant for purposes of eligibility, vesting, and accrual of benefits are determined under different rules. [IRC § 413(b)] The minimum funding requirements applicable to qualified retirement plans are modified. [IRC § 412(b)(7)] Also, the provisions governing plan termination differ greatly from the rules for single-employer plans. [Compare ERISA §§ 4041, 4041A]

Q 25:2   What is a multiemployer plan?

Generally, a multiemployer plan is a plan established under a collective bargaining agreement that is maintained by two or more unrelated employers. From a technical or legal standpoint, however, the multiemployer plan is defined as a plan:

1. To which more than one employer is required to contribute;

2. That is maintained under a collective bargaining agreement between an employee organization and more than one employer; and

3. That meets any additional requirements that may be issued by DOL.

[ERISA §§ 3(37); IRC § 414(f)]

The multiemployer plan should be distinguished from the single-employer plan. Although the multiemployer plan is established through negotiations between employers, an association of employers, or a trade association and the union representing the plan participants, the single-employer plan is established or maintained by only one employer, either unilaterally or through a collective bargaining agreement. Generally, the sponsoring single employer has the ultimate responsibility for the administration of the plan. In contrast, responsibility for a multiemployer plan lies with a board of trustees composed of both union and employer representatives. [ERISA § 3(37)(A); Labor-Management Relations Act § 302(c)(5)]

Q 25:3 What are the basic advantages of a multiemployer plan?

The multiemployer plan has been developed to meet the needs of industries (e.g., construction, transportation, or mining) that usually use craftsmen and draw their employees from a limited pool of workers within a specific geographical area. A multiemployer plan can benefit a particular industry because it:

1. Permits mobile employees to take their pension benefits with them when they move from one participating employer to another within the same industry;

2. Stabilizes pension costs among participating employers, reducing competitive wrangling for select employees;

3. Makes possible economies of scale because of the pooling of pension resources, either increasing benefits or reducing employer costs; and

4. Reduces administrative costs through use of experienced and knowledgeable administrators and trustees.

Q 25:4 How are hours of service credited to an employee under a multiemployer plan?

For purposes of participation and vesting, a multiemployer plan is treated as if all participating employers constitute a single employer. Thus, with certain exceptions, all covered service with an employer participating in the plan as well as all contiguous noncovered service with that same employer are taken into account. For purposes of the accrual of benefits, only covered service is counted. [DOL Reg § 2530.210; IRC §§ 413(a), 413(b); Gauer v Connors, 953 F 2d 97 (4th Cir 1991); Rev Rul 85-130, 1985-2 CB 137]

The determination of covered service is functional. Full-time employees performed covered service even though their employers claimed they were casual employees under the collective bargaining agreement. [Central States, Southeast & Southwest Areas Pension Fund v Independent Fruit & Produce Co, No. 89-1927 (8th Cir 1990)]

Q 25:5   Is a retirement plan maintained by two or more affiliated companies considered a multiemployer plan?

No. In considering whether more than one employer is required to contribute to the plan, employers that are under common control (see Q 5:32) are considered as only one employer. Thus, a plan that requires contributions from two or more companies that are controlled by the same interests is not a multiemployer plan because only one employer is required to contribute to the plan; multiemployer plans require more than one unrelated employer (see Q 25:2). [ERISA § 3(37)(B)]

Q 25:6   Are benefits under a multiemployer plan guaranteed?

Yes. PBGC has the authority to insure the benefits of a defined benefit multiemployer plan. Although a multiemployer plan usually combines the features of a defined benefit plan (see Q 2:3) and a defined contribution plan (see Q 2:2)—i.e., both benefits and contributions are fixed—the courts have said that a multiemployer plan is a defined benefit plan. Therefore, the benefits under a multiemployer plan are guaranteed by PBGC. [Connolly v PBGC, 581 F 2d 729 (9th Cir 1978); PBGC v Defoe Shipbuilding Co, 639 F 2d 311 (6th Cir 1981)]

Note, however, that the benefits under a multiemployer plan are guaranteed only if the plan becomes insolvent (see Q 25:7). [ERISA § 4022A(a)(2)]

Q 25:7   When is a multiemployer plan insolvent?

A multiemployer plan is considered insolvent when its available resources are insufficient to pay benefits when due for the plan year or when the plan is determined by the plan sponsor to be insolvent while the plan is in reorganization. The plan's available resources include cash, marketable securities, earnings, payments due from withdrawn employers, and employer contributions, minus reasonable administration expenses and amounts owed to PBGC for financial assistance. [ERISA § 4245]

Q 25:8 What level of benefits is guaranteed?

The level of guaranteed benefits is generally lower than the guarantees provided under single-employer defined benefit plans. However, benefits accrued through July 29, 1980 that are payable to retirees or beneficiaries as of that date or to vested participants who were within three years of normal retirement age as of that date are guaranteed in accordance with the higher ERISA single-employer rules. [ERISA §§ 4022A(a), 4022A(c), 4022A(h)]

PBGC now guarantees 100 percent of the first $5 of monthly benefits per year of service. The next $15 of monthly benefits or, if less, the accrual rate over $5 per month per year of service is guaranteed at 75 percent for strong plans and 65 percent for weaker plans. [ERISA § 4022A(c)]

Q 25:9 What benefits are not guaranteed by PBGC?

PBGC will not guarantee benefits that have been in effect under the multiemployer plan for less than 60 months. Also, benefit improvements that have not been in effect for at least 60 months are not guaranteed.

This differs from coverage provided for single-employer plans, which phases in benefit guarantees of 20 percent a year, with a minimum phase-in of $20 each month, during the five-year period following the implementation of a benefit improvement (see Q 21:24). [ERISA §§ 4022(b), 4022A(b)]

Q 25:10 What is the financial liability of an employer that withdraws from a multiemployer plan?

An employer that withdraws from a multiemployer plan is liable for its proportionate share of unfunded vested benefits (UVBs), determined as of the date of withdrawal. The liability is imposed upon withdrawal without reference to the plan's termination.

The employer's withdrawal liability is based on the plan's total unfunded liability for vested benefits, not the lesser guaranteed benefits that apply to single-employer terminations. The method used to determine the employer's share can vary from plan to plan (see Q 25:22).

The result is that an employer that withdraws from an under-funded multiemployer plan may have to continue to contribute to the plan at approximately the same dollar level after withdrawal as before withdrawal until the liability is fully paid. In some cases, the withdrawing employer can make payments over a 20-year period (see Q 25:33).

Q 25:11 Can withdrawal liability be assessed against any employer that withdraws from a multiemployer plan?

Withdrawal liability applies only to withdrawals that occur on or after September 26, 1980. The U.S. Supreme Court has ruled that the withdrawal liability provisions of ERISA are constitutional. [Connolly v PBGC, 475 US 211 (1986)]

When an employer temporarily ceased contributions to a multi-employer plan prior to September 26, 1980, but a complete withdrawal (see Q 25:13) did not occur until thereafter, the employer was assessed withdrawal liability, and the U.S. Supreme Court ruled that the assessment did not violate the employer's right to due process of law and did not constitute an unconstitutional taking of property without just compensation. [Concrete Pipe and Products of California, Inc v Construction Laborers Pension Trust for Southern California, No. 91-904 (S Ct 1993)] However, an employer who, prior to September 26, 1980, entered into a binding agreement to withdraw and ceased business operations before the end of 1980 was not assessed withdrawal liability. [Crown Cork & Seal Co, Inc v Central States, Southeast and Southwest Areas Pension Fund, 1992 US App Lexis 33426 (3d Cir 1992)]

Q 25:12 What steps are involved in determining multiemployer plan withdrawal liability?

The withdrawal liability process consists of five phases:

1. Determining whether the employer has withdrawn;
2. Computing the withdrawn employer's share of the plan's UVBs;

3. Determining whether any reductions apply to the withdrawal liability;

4. Notifying the employer of the amount of the withdrawal liability; and

5. Collecting the liability.

[ERISA §§ 4201, 4202]

Q 25:13 When is a participating employer considered to have withdrawn from a multiemployer plan?

An employer is considered to have withdrawn, and therefore is subject to withdrawal liability, when it (1) permanently ceases to have an obligation to contribute to the multiemployer plan or (2) permanently ceases all covered operations under the plan.

Special rules apply for determining whether there is a complete or partial withdrawal (see Q 25:15) of employers in the following industries:

- Building and construction
- Trucking
- Household goods moving
- Public warehousing
- Retail food
- Certain segments of the entertainment industry

[ERISA § 4203]

The key issue is whether the employer's obligation to contribute has ceased. [Connors v Barrick Gold Exploration, Inc, No. 91-7073 (DC Cir 1992)] If the employer is no longer obligated to make contributions to the multiemployer plan, it cannot escape withdrawal by either continuing to make payments or getting another company to agree to make contributions on its behalf. [Connors v B&W Coal Co, 646 F Supp 164 (D DC 1986)] However, the result may be different if another company signs an agreement undertaking the obligation on behalf of the original employer. [ILGWU Nat'l Retirement Fund v Distinctive Coat Co, 6 EBC 2631 (SD NY 1985)]

In an arbitration, it was held that although the passage of some time may be necessary for a determination of whether a cessation of covered operations is permanent, once it is determined to be permanent, the date of withdrawal will relate back to the date when contributions ceased. [E H Hatfield Enters, Inc v UMW 1950 and 1974 Pension Plans, 9 EBC 1980 (1988) (Jaffe, Arb)] In another case, a general contractor was not required to continue making contributions after it subcontracted the covered employees' work to a nonunion employer. [Board of Trustees of the Chicago Plastering Inst Pension Trust Fund v William A Duguid Co, No. 87 C 10768 (ND Ill 1991)]

Q 25:14 Can an employer be held liable for withdrawal liability as a result of circumstances such as decertification of the union or a plant closing?

Yes. The issue is whether the employer's obligation to contribute to the multiemployer plan has ceased or whether all covered operations under the plan have ceased. If the answer is yes to either, then the circumstances that led to the cessation of the obligation to contribute or to the cessation of all covered operations are irrelevant. For example, an employer may be subject to withdrawal liability if the employer's employees vote to decertify the union representing them. Similarly, withdrawal liability may be triggered by a plant closing or merger of a facility. [ERISA §§ 4203, 4205, 4212]

Q 25:15 Does a participating employer have any liability if there is a partial withdrawal from the multiemployer plan?

Yes. Withdrawal liability applies when a participating employer partially withdraws from the multiemployer plan. Generally, a partial withdrawal occurs when:

1. There is at least a 70 percent decline in the employer's contribution base units (for example, hours worked);

2. The employer ceases to have an obligation to contribute to the plan under at least one, but not all, of its collective bargaining agreements and continues the same type of work in the geographical area covered by the agreement; or

3. The employer ceases to have an obligation to contribute to the plan for work performed at one or more, but fewer than all, of its facilities (see Q 25:16) covered under the agreement.

[ERISA § 4205]

Q 25:16   What is a facility for purposes of a partial withdrawal?

The term facility has been determined by PBGC to be a discrete economic unit of an employer. For example, the term will ordinarily apply to a single retail store rather than to a group of stores in a metropolitan area. [PBGC Opinion Letter Nos. 86-2, 82-33, 82-22; May Stern & Co v Western Pennsylvania Teamsters and Employers Pension Fund, 8 EBC 2202 (1987) (Nagle, Arb)]

Q 25:17   Is withdrawal liability affected if employers are under common control?

Employers under common control (see Qs 5:30, 5:32) are considered as only one employer. Withdrawal liability can be assessed against all members of the commonly controlled group, even if only one member of the commonly controlled group is required to contribute to the multiemployer plan. [ERISA § 4001(b); Central States, Southeast and Southwest Areas Pension Fund v Slotky, No. 90-3546 (7th Cir 1992); Central States, Southeast and Southwest Areas Pension Fund v Newbury Transport Corp, No. 91 C 803 (ND Ill 1992); Central States, Southeast and Southwest Areas Pension Fund v Chatham Properties, No. 89-1451 (6th Cir 1991); IUE AFL-CIO Pension Fund v Barker & Williamson, Inc, 788 F 2d 118 (3d Cir 1986); O'Connor v DeBolt Transfer, Inc, 737 F Supp 1430 (WD Pa 1990); Board of Trustees of the W Conference of Teamsters Pension Trust Fund v Salt Creek Terminals, Inc, No. C85-2270R (WD Wash 1986); Connors v Calvert Dev Co, 622 F Supp 877 (D DC 1985)] In one case, an acquiring corporation was liable for the withdrawal liability payments of the acquired corporation even after the acquired corporation was discharged in bankruptcy because of the acquiring corporation's control both before and after the bankruptcy reorganization. [Teamsters Joint Council No. 83 v Centra, Inc, No. 90-1815 (4th Cir 1991)] However, a public entity that hired a private company to manage a marine terminal was not considered the employer of the private company's employees. [Seaway Port Auth of Duluth v Duluth-Superior ILA Marine Assoc Restated Pension Plan, No. 89-5601MN (8th Cir 1990)]

The employer of leased employees for withdrawal liability purposes is not necessarily the same as under the Code (see Qs 5:48–5:53). In one case, a company leased truck drivers to another company and made interim withdrawal liability payments (see Q 25:38) after the lease ended. Although both companies may be considered employers, the issue of each company's withdrawal liability to the plan is subject to arbitration (see Q 25:37). [Global Leasing, Inc v Henkel Corp, No. 89-2674(JCL) (D NJ 1990)]

Where the shareholders of a bankrupt company also operated a real estate business that leased property to the company and the leasing of property was considered a trade or business, the shareholders were liable for the withdrawal liability of the company as members of a commonly controlled group. [Central States, Southeast and Southwest Areas Pension Fund v Ditello, No. 91-2072 (7th Cir 1992)] In other cases, sole proprietors were found personally liable for the withdrawal liability of their failed companies because their real estate investments constituted a business and the individuals had common control over both the failed company and the sole proprietorship. [Central States, Southeast and Southwest Areas Pension Fund v Personnel, Inc, No. 91-2392 (7th Cir 1992); Central States, Southeast and Southwest Areas Pension Fund v Koder, No. 91-2441 (7th Cir 1992); Central States, Southeast and Southwest Areas Pension Fund v Landvatter, 1993 US Dist Lexis (ND Ill 1993)]

One court ruled that an individual's estate planning trust was jointly and severally liable for the withdrawal liability of a company owned by the individual who established the trust. The trust had leased property to the company and another entity under the individual's control and was thus a trade or business under common control. [Vaughn v Sexton, No. 91-3145 (8th Cir 1992)]

Q 25:18   Does a withdrawal occur if there is a change in business structure?

No, provided the change in corporate structure does not cause an interruption in the employer's contributions or obligations under the multiemployer plan. [ERISA § 4218]

Changes in corporate structure include the following:

- Reorganization involving a mere change in identity, form, or place of organization
- Liquidation into a parent corporation
- Merger, consolidation, or division, and
- Change to an unincorporated form of business enterprise

[ERISA § 4069(b)]

The incorporation of a sole proprietorship or partnership does not constitute a withdrawal if the successor corporation continues to have an obligation to contribute and does so. [PBGC Opinion Letter No. 83-18]

Similarly, changes in the composition of an employer-partnership (e.g., sale of partnership interests to new partners) do not result in a withdrawal if the partnership continues to have an obligation to contribute and continues to honor that obligation. [Park S Hotel Corp v New York Hotel Trades Council, 851 F 2d 578 (2d Cir 1988); Connors v B&W Coal Co, Inc, 646 F Supp 164 (D DC 1986); but see E H Hatfield Enters, Inc v UMW 1950 and 1974 Pension Plans, 9 EBC 1980 (1988) (Jaffe, Arb)] Assignees of a partnership interest were not subject to withdrawal liability because they were assignees and not partners. [Connors v Middle Fork Corp, No. 89-0698(GHR) (D DC 1992)]

Q 25:19 Does a withdrawal occur if there is a suspension of contributions during a labor dispute?

No withdrawal occurs as a result of the temporary suspension of contributions during a labor dispute. However, a withdrawal may occur if the cessation of contributions is permanent even though the cessation occurred during a labor dispute. [ERISA § 4218; PBGC Opinion Letter Nos. 82-2 and 82-21; Combs v Adkins Coal Co, Inc, 597 F Supp 122 (D DC 1984)]

Q 25:20 Who determines when a withdrawal from a multiemployer plan occurs?

The plan sponsor determines whether and when an employer has withdrawn from the multiemployer plan. [ERISA §§ 3(16)(B), 4202]

Q 25:21 Is a sale of employer assets considered a withdrawal from a multiemployer plan?

If the assets sold by the employer represent all of its covered operations, there may be a complete withdrawal. However, if only part of the employer's operation is sold, a partial withdrawal (see Q 25:15) may result. The withdrawal liability of the selling employer is limited to a maximum amount. [ERISA § 4225]

The selling employer is relieved of primary withdrawal liability only if the following conditions are satisfied:

1. The purchasing company is an unrelated party that assumes substantially the same contribution obligation;
2. The purchasing company posts a bond; and
3. The contract of sale provides that the selling employer is secondarily liable if the purchasing company completely or partially withdraws during the following five plan years and fails to pay its withdrawal liability.

If the above conditions are not satisfied, the purchasing company is not responsible for any of the seller's withdrawal liability. However, PBGC is authorized to grant individual or class exemptions or variances from the requirement that the purchasing company post a bond if it determines that the request for exemption or variance would more effectively or equitably carry out the purposes of Title IV of ERISA and would not significantly increase the risk of financial loss to the plan. [ERISA § 4204(c); PBGC Reg § 2643.3(b); PBGC Notice of Exemption, 57 FR 7408 (Mar 2, 1992)] Also, if the purchaser withdraws after the sale, the determination of the purchaser's withdrawal liability takes into account the seller's required contribution for the year of the sale and the four preceding years. [ERISA § 4204]

In one case, the purchasing company continued to contribute on behalf of the selling company's employees pursuant to its own collective bargaining agreement, which was essentially identical to that of the selling employer. The court held that no withdrawal had occurred. [Dorns Transp, Inc v Teamsters Pension Trust Fund of Philadelphia and Vicinity, 787 F 2d 897 (3d Cir 1986)] In another case, the court ruled that when the purchasing company assumed substantially the same contribution obligation as the seller and subsequent events caused a reduction in work force and contributions, withdrawal liability could not be assessed against the selling employer because the sale of assets did not cause the reduction in contributions and the reduction was neither abusive nor significantly harmful to the plan. [IAM Nat'l Pension Fund Benefit Plan A v Dravo Corp, 7 EBC 1892 (D DC 1986)]

A parent company sold one of its subsidiaries to an unrelated entity, relieving the parent of primary withdrawal liability. Subsequently, the parent closed facilities owned by two other subsidiaries. In calculating the parent's withdrawal liability, the contribution history of the previously sold subsidiary could not be considered. [Borden, Inc v Bakery & Confectionery Union & Industry International Pension, Nos. 91-1787, 91-1788 (4th Cir 1992)]

Also, at least one court has held that a company that purchased a selling company's assets for cash may still be liable for the selling company's delinquent contributions in some circumstances. [Upholsterer's Int'l Union Pension Fund v Artistic Furniture of Pontiac, No. 89-3058 (7th Cir 1990)] Moreover, where a pension fund agreement provided that participants' service with a withdrawing employer would include service with a predecessor employer, the withdrawing employer was required to pay the withdrawal liability of the predecessor employer from whom it had purchased assets. [Artistic Carton Co v Paper Industry Union-Management Pension Fund, No 91-1801 (7th Cir 1992)]

Q 25:22 How is a withdrawing employer's share of the multiemployer plan's UVBs computed?

The withdrawing employer's share of the multiemployer plan's UVBs (see Q 25:10) may be computed under a statutory method or a PBGC-approved alternative method. The four statutory methods are:

1. The presumptive method;

2. The modified presumptive method;

3. The rolling-five method;

4. The direct attribution method.

The presumptive method is generally used to determine withdrawal liability unless the plan is amended to permit the use of an alternative method. [ERISA § 4211; PBGC Reg § 2642.1]

The plan may adopt a statutory alternative method, but such an alternative may not be applied to an employer without its consent if it withdrew before the adoption of the alternative method. An assessment of withdrawal liability was found to be erroneous and unenforceable where the fund used a calculation method adopted after the employer had withdrawn. [ERISA § 4214(a); Sigmund Cohn Corp v District No. 15 Machinists Pension Fund, No. CV 91-2691 (RJD) (ED NY 1992)]

PBGC has issued a final regulation modifying the presumptive and modified presumptive methods of allocating UVBs, and plans may adopt these modifications without prior PBGC approval. [PBGC Reg § 2642.5(a)] In addition, final PBGC regulations contain rules for determining the allocation of UVBs for an employer that withdraws from a multiemployer plan after the plan has merged with another multiemployer plan and rules concerning the partial withdrawal of an employer from a multiemployer plan and its subsequent reentry into the plan. [PBGC Reg §§ 2640.4, 2642.1, 2642.21–2642.27]

One court ruled that death, disability, and early retirement benefits provided in a defined benefit multiemployer plan are nonforfeitable under ERISA and are therefore properly included in calculations used to determine an employer's withdrawal liability. [United Foods, Inc v The Western Conference of Teamsters Pension Trust Fund, Nos. C-92-2725 MHP and C-92-2748 MHP (ND Ca 1993)]

Q 25:23   Can withdrawal liability be imposed if the multiemployer plan has no UVBs?

Yes. Even if a multiemployer plan as a whole has no UVBs (see Q 25:10), each of the statutory methods of calculating withdrawal liability except the rolling-five method (see Q 25:22) may result in liability for a withdrawing employer. Under the statutory methods, the withdrawing employer is deemed responsible for the vested benefits of its employees. Accordingly, withdrawal liability may be imposed even if plan assets would be sufficient to fund this liability. [RXDC, Inc v Oil, Chemical and Atomic Workers Union-Industry

Pension Fund, No. 90-S-438 (D Col 1992); Wise v Ruffin, 914 F 2d 570 (4th Cir 1990); Ben Hur Constr Co v Goodwin, 784 F 2d 876 (8th Cir 1986); PBGC Withdrawal of Notice of Interpretation, 56 FR 12288 (Mar 22, 1991); but see Berkshire Hathaway, Inc v Textile Workers Pension Fund, 874 F 2d 53 (1st Cir 1989)]

Q 25:24 May multiemployer plan withdrawal liability be waived or reduced?

There are numerous circumstances under which multiemployer plan withdrawal liability can be either waived or reduced. These waivers are designed to protect small employers and employers in certain industries.

For example, an employer's liability is waived in full if its share is less than the lesser of $50,000 or .75 percent of the total unfunded liability of the plan. If the employer's share is between $50,000 and $150,000, it is reduced but not eliminated. The plan may increase the $50,000 and $150,000 limits to $100,000 and $250,000, respectively. [ERISA § 4209]

Also, waivers of withdrawal liabilities are provided in the construction industry on a mandatory basis when the employer leaves the area. A similar waiver is provided in certain cases for plans covering the entertainment industry. In both cases, there is no withdrawal liability unless the employer either continues to perform the same work in the same jurisdiction or resumes the same work in the same jurisdiction within five years and does not renew its obligation to contribute to the plan. PBGC may exclude certain employers in the entertainment industry from the waiver provision if PBGC determines that it is necessary to protect the plan's participants. [ERISA §§ 4203(b), 4203(c)]

Plans in industries other than construction or entertainment may be amended to provide for special withdrawal liability rules if PBGC finds that the rules apply to an industry in which the characteristics that make use of the special rules appropriate are clearly shown and that the rule would not pose a significant risk to PBGC. [PBGC Notice of Approval, 56 FR 49804 (Oct 1, 1991)]

Employers that withdraw from a plan that receives substantially all its contributions from employers in the trucking, public warehousing, or household goods moving industries may post a five-year bond instead of making withdrawal liability payments. If the withdrawal of an employer that posted a bond substantially damages the plan, PBGC may require that the bond be paid to the plan. A bond could not be posted by an employer that withdrew from a plan that received approximately 62 percent of its contributions from employers primarily involved in the trucking business; the plan does not receive substantially all its contributions from truckers. [ERISA § 4203(d); Continental Can Co v Chicago Truck Drivers, Helpers and Warehouse Workers Union Pension Fund, 916 F 2d 1154 (7th Cir 1990)]

Q 25:25 What happens if an employer reenters a plan after a prior withdrawal?

PBGC has issued regulations providing for the reduction or abatement of withdrawal liability under certain circumstances. A reentering employer that seeks an abatement of its complete withdrawal liability must formally apply for the waiver by the date of the first scheduled withdrawal liability payment falling due after the employer resumes covered operations or, if later, at least 15 days from the date the employer resumes covered operations under the multiemployer plan. The application must:

1. Identify the withdrawn employer and the date it withdrew;
2. Identify the reentered employer and all trades and businesses under common control with the employer as of both the date of withdrawal and the date of resumption of covered operations;
3. Set forth the list of operations for which the employer is obligated to contribute to the plan; and
4. Include the date the employer resumes covered operations.

[ERISA § 4207(a); PBGC Reg § 2647.2]

PBGC has issued proposed regulations that allow multiemployer plans to adopt alternative rules for reduction or waiver of complete withdrawal liability. A plan sponsor is required to submit a written request for PBGC approval of a plan amendment adopting the alternative rules. The request must contain the following information:

1. The name and address of the plan and the telephone number of the plan sponsor or its duly authorized representative.

2. The sponsor's nine-digit employer identification number (EIN) and the three-digit plan identification number (PIN).

3. A copy of the executed amendment, including the date on which the amendment was adopted, its proposed effective date, and the full text of the alternative rules.

4. A certification that notice of the adoption of the amendment and of the request for PBGC approval has been given to all employers with an obligation to contribute to the plan and to all employee organizations representing employees covered by the plan.

5. In addition, the plan may submit any other information that it believes is pertinent to its request. The PBGC may require the plan sponsor to submit any other information that it may need to review the request.

PBGC will approve a plan amendment if it determines that the alternative rules contained therein are consistent with the purposes of ERISA. However, PBGC will not approve an abatement rule if its implementation would be adverse to the interest of plan participants and beneficiaries or the rule would increase PBGC's risk of loss with respect to the plan.

[ERISA § 4207(b); PBGC Proposed Reg § 2647.9]

Q 25:26 What withdrawal liability payments must the employer make while the abatement determination is made?

The reentering employer may post a bond or establish an escrow account equal to 70 percent of the required withdrawal liability payments, in which case, pending the abatement determination, no withdrawal liability payments need be made. [PBGC Reg § 2647.3]

Q 25:27   What is required for abatement of an employer's withdrawal liability upon reentry to the multiemployer plan?

An employer that completely withdraws from a multiemployer plan and subsequently reenters the plan will have its liability abated if it resumes covered operations under the plan and assumes a post-entry level of contribution base units (see Q 25:15) that exceeds 30 percent of the employer's prewithdrawal amount. [PBGC Reg § 2647.4]

Q 25:28   What are the effects of an abatement?

If the plan sponsor determines that the reentering employer is eligible for abatement:

1. The employer has no obligation to make future withdrawal liability payments to the multiemployer plan with respect to its complete withdrawal;

2. The employer's liability for a subsequent withdrawal will be calculated under modified rules;

3. The bond will be canceled or amounts held in the escrow account (see Q 25:26) will be returned to the employer; and

4. Any withdrawal liability payments made by the employer will be refunded by the plan.

[PBGC Reg § 2647.2]

Q 25:29   What are the effects of a nonabatement?

If the plan sponsor determines that the employer is not eligible for abatement:

1. The sponsor notifies the employer of its determination;

2. Within 30 days of the sponsor's notice, the bond posted or the escrow account established by the employer (see Q 25:26) must be paid to the multiemployer plan;

3. Within 30 days of the sponsor's notice, the employer must make the balance of the withdrawal liability payment not covered by the bond or escrow account;

4. The employer must resume its withdrawal liability payments under the plan schedule; and

5. The employer will be treated as a new employer for purposes of any future application rules.

[PBGC Reg § 2647.2]

Q 25:30 How can a reentering employer elect nonabatement?

A reentering employer can elect nonabatement by not filing the application for a waiver of its withdrawal liability (see Q 25:25) upon its reentry to the multiemployer plan. [PBGC Reg § 2647.2]

Q 25:31 Does the value of the employer affect the amount of its withdrawal liability?

Yes. If all, or substantially all, of the employer's assets are sold in an arm's-length transaction to an unrelated party and the purchasing company does not assume the withdrawal liability (see Q 25:21), the employer's withdrawal liability is limited to the greater of (1) the UVBs (see Qs 25:10, 25:22) attributable to its employees or (2) a percentage of the employer's liquidation or dissolution value, as determined under the following table:

Liquidation or dissolution value of employer after sale	*Percentage*
Not more than $2,000,000	30% of the amount
More than $2,000,000, but not more than $4,000,000	$600,000, plus 35% of the amount in excess of $2,000,000
More than $4,000,000, but not more than $6,000,000	$1,300,000, plus 40% of the amount in excess of $4,000,000

Liquidation or dissolution value of employer after sale	Percentage
More than $6,000,000, but not more than $7,000,000	$2,100,000, plus 45% of the amount in excess of $6,000,000
More than $7,000,000, but not more than $8,000,000	$2,550,000, plus 50% of the amount in excess of $7,000,000
More than $8,000,000, but not more than $9,000,000	$3,050,000, plus 60% of the amount in excess of $8,000,000
More than $9,000,000, but not more than $10,000,000	$3,650,000, plus 70% of the amount in excess of $9,000,000
More than $10,000,000	$4,350,000, plus 80% of the amount in excess of $10,000,000

However, the withdrawal liability is not included in determining the liquidation or dissolution value of the employer. [ERISA § 4225]

Q 25:32   Does an insolvent employer have withdrawal liability?

Yes, but that liability may be limited. An insolvent employer in liquidation or dissolution is liable for the first 50 percent of its normal withdrawal liability, and the remainder of its liability is limited to the employer's value, as of the commencement of liquidation or dissolution, reduced by the first 50 percent. [ERISA § 4225(b)]

An employer is insolvent if its liabilities, including withdrawal liability, exceed its assets as of the commencement of liquidation or dissolution. However, the employer's liquidation or dissolution value is determined without regard to withdrawal liability. [ERISA § 4225(d); Trustees of Amalgamated Ins Fund v Geltman Indus, Inc, 784 F 2d 926 (9th Cir 1986)] An employer in Chapter 11 reorganization, however, is not said to be in liquidation or dissolution and so may not have its withdrawal liability cut in half. [Granada Wines, Inc v New England Teamsters & Trucking Indus Pension Fund, 748 F 2d 42 (1st Cir 1984)]

Q 25:33   What is the 20-year cap on a withdrawing employer's liability?

The withdrawing employer's liability is paid over the number of years required to amortize the liability in level annual installments. The annual liability payments are basically equal to the annual payments of the employer's plan contributions before withdrawal. If the annual payments will not amortize the withdrawal liability in 20 years, the withdrawal liability is reduced to the amount that can be paid off in the 20-year period. [ERISA § 4219(c)]

Q 25:34   When is the employer notified of its liability for withdrawal from a multiemployer plan?

The plan sponsor must notify the employer of the amount of its liability "as soon as practicable" after the employer's withdrawal. At the same time, the plan sponsor will demand payment in accordance with a schedule of payments. In one case, a notice given to an employer two years after the withdrawal liability arose was considered timely. [ERISA § 4219(b); Brentwood Financial Corp v Western Conference of Teamsters Pension Fund, 902 F 2d 1456 (9th Cir 1990)] In another case, notice given five and one-half years after the withdrawal liability arose was not considered timely. [Teamsters Pension Trust Fund of Philadelphia and Vicinity v Custom Cartage, Co, No. 89-0626 (ED Pa 1991)]

Notice of, and demand for, withdrawal liability made to one member of a commonly controlled group is sufficient to constitute notice and demand to all members of the group. Thus, courts have held an entity within a commonly controlled group liable for the withdrawal liability of another group member even though only the withdrawing employer received actual notice of the withdrawal liability. The rationale for this is that all trades or businesses under common control are treated as a single employer and, thus, notice to one is notice to all (see Q 25:17). [IAM Nat'l Fund v Slyman Indus, Inc, 901 F 2d 127 (DC Cir 1990); Teamsters Pension Trust Fund-Board of the W Conference v Allyn Transp Co, 832 F 2d 502 (9th Cir 1987); IUE AFL-CIO Pension Fund v Barker & Williamson, Inc, 788 F 2d 118 (3d Cir 1986); Central States, Southeast & Southwest Areas Pension Fund v Bay, 684 F Supp 483 (ED Mich 1988); Board of Trustees of the W Conference of Teamsters Pension Trust Fund v Salt Creek Terminals, Inc, No. C85-2270R (WD Wash 1986); Connors v Calvert Dev Co, 622 F Supp 877 (D DC 1985)]

The date when one employer in a commonly controlled group receives notice of withdrawal liability is used to determine the timeliness of any group member's request to arbitrate disputes concerning the withdrawal liability (see Q 25:36). [McDonald v Centra, No. S 89-1734 (D Md 1990); Teamster Pension Trust Fund of Philadelphia v Laidlaw Indus, Inc, 745 F Supp 1016 (D Del 1990)] However, one court permitted a husband and wife who jointly owned an unincorporated farm to arbitrate the amount of withdrawal liability assessed against the husband's manufacturing company. The plan sponsor's notice of withdrawal liability demanded payment only from the husband's corporation and other commonly controlled corporations. [ILGWU Nat'l Retirement Fund v Minotola Indus, Inc, 88 Civ 9131 (RJW) (SD NY 1991)]

ERISA Section 4301 imposes a three- or six-year statute of limitations on civil actions with respect to multiemployer plans, including issues of withdrawal liability. Because the statute of limitations begins to run when notice and demand for payment of withdrawal liability is not met by the withdrawing employer, an action brought more than six years thereafter is not timely. [Central States, Southeast and Southwest Areas Pension Fund v Van Vorst Industries, Inc, No. 91 C 2624 (ND Ill 1992)]

Q 25:35   Is the initial determination of a withdrawing employer's liability presumptively correct?

When an employer withdraws from a multiemployer plan, the plan sponsor determines the amount of the withdrawing employer's liability (see Q 25:10 and Q 25:12). The initial determination is presumed to be correct. To overcome this presumption, the employer must demonstrate, by a preponderance of evidence, that the actuarial assumptions and methods used by the plan's actuary are unreasonable or that a significant error has been made in applying the assumptions or methods. In one case, a plan's actuarial calculations were not unreasonable in the aggregate even though the interest rate assumption may have been unreasonably low. [ERISA § 4221(a); Combs v Classic Coal Corp, No. 90-7066 (DC Cir 1991)]

A number of employers have raised unsuccessful constitutional challenges to the presumption of correctness accorded plan sponsors' determinations of withdrawal liability. [Keith Fulton & Sons, Inc v New England Teamsters and Trucking Indus Pension Fund, 762 F 2d 1137 (1st Cir 1985); Board of Trustees of the W Conference of Teamsters Pension Trust Fund v Thompson Bldg Materials, Inc, 749 F 2d 1396 (9th Cir 1984); Washington Star Co v International Typographical Union Negotiated Pension Plan, 729 F 2d 1502 (DC Cir 1984); Textile Workers Pension Fund v Standard Dye & Finishing Co, 725 F 2d 843 (2d Cir 1984); Republic Indus, Inc v Teamsters Joint Council No. 83 of Virginia Pension Fund, 718 F 2d 628 (4th Cir 1983); Centennial State Carpenters Pension Trust Fund v Woodworkers of Denver, Inc, 615 F Supp 1063 (D Col 1985)]

However, two courts have held that the presumption of correctness of the determination of the amount of the withdrawing employer's liability by plan sponsors who owe a fiduciary duty to the plan and who are therefore biased in favor of the plan is unconstitutional. [United Retail & Wholesale Employees Teamsters Union Local No. 115 Pension Plan v Yahn & McDonnell, Inc, 787 F 2d 128 (3d Cir 1986), *aff'd per curiam sub nom*, PBGC v Yahn & McDonnell, Inc, 481 US 735 (1987); Robbins v Pepsi-Cola Metropolitan Bottling Co, 636 F Supp 641 (ND Ill 1986)] In affirming the Third Circuit's decision that the presumption in favor of the correctness of a plan sponsor's initial determination regarding withdrawal liability is unconstitutional, the Supreme Court split four to four. Thus, the decision is binding only with respect to the parties in the case. As a result, the conflict among the circuits continues.

Q 25:36   May an employer contest the determination of its liability for withdrawing from a multiemployer plan?

Yes. When the employer receives notice of its withdrawal liability (see Q 25:34) from the plan sponsor, it may, within 90 days of its receipt of such notice, ask the plan sponsor to review any specific matter relating to its determination, point out any inaccuracy in their determination, or provide additional information to the trustees bearing on their determination. The plan sponsor must also comply with an employer's request for an explanation of its calculation of the employer's withdrawal liability even if the employer has not yet requested arbitration. [ERISA §§ 4219(b)(2), 4221(e); John J Nissen Baking Co, Inc v New England Teamsters and Trucking Indus Pension Fund, 737 F Supp 679 (D Me 1990)]

The plan sponsor has 120 days to respond to an employer's request that it reconsider its earlier determination of withdrawal liability. If it takes no action, then the employer must request arbitration within 60 days after the expiration of the 120-day period or it may be estopped from disputing the amounts owed in a later court action to collect the withdrawal liability (see Q 25:37). The plan sponsor, however, is required to undertake a "reasonable review" of the employer's contentions and notify the employer of its decision, setting forth the basis for its decision and the reasons behind any change in its liability determination. The employer must request arbitration within 60 days of its receipt of this second notice even though 120 days may not have lapsed since the employer requested a review of its withdrawal liability. [ERISA § 4221(a)(1)]

The plan sponsor, too, may request arbitration within 60 days of either (1) notification to the employer of its decision after review of the employer's dispute of the liability determination or (2) the expiration of 120 days after the employer requests review of the plan sponsor's initial determination. Alternatively, both the plan sponsor and the employer may jointly request arbitration within 180 days of the initial demand for payment of withdrawal liability. [ERISA §§ 4219(b), 4221(a); PBGC Reg § 2641.2]

The time limits set forth above are strictly enforced. In one case, an employer erroneously mailed its timely arbitration request to the plan sponsor, not to the arbitration association as required under the plan. The court refused to order arbitration, even though the arbitration request was hand-delivered to the arbitration association immediately upon discovery of the error two days after the deadline. [Central States, Southeast and Southwest Areas Pension Fund v TW Servs, No. 89 C 7415 (ND Ill 1989)]

Q 25:37 Does the employer run any risk if it does not demand arbitration of the plan sponsor's claim for withdrawal liability?

Yes. An employer that fails to initiate arbitration within the statutory periods (see Q 25:36) risks being barred from disputing the plan's determination of withdrawal liability in a subsequent court action by the plan sponsor to recover that liability. [Chicago Truck Drivers, Helpers, and Warehouse Workers Union (Independent) Pension Fund v R Sumner Trucking Co, Inc, No. 91 C 3967 (ND Ill 1992); Trustees of the Colorado Pipe Indus Pension Trust v Howard Elec & Mechanical, Inc, 909 F 2d 1379 (10th Cir 1990); New York State Teamsters Conference Pension & Retirement Fund v McNicholas Transp Co, 848 F 2d 20 (2d Cir 1988); ILGWU Nat'l Retirement Fund v Levy Bros Frocks, Inc, 846 F 2d 879 (2d Cir 1988); Robbins v Admiral Merchants Motor Freight, Inc, 846 F 2d 1054 (7th Cir 1988); Teamsters Pension Trust Fund-Board of Trustees v Allyn Transp Co, 832 F 2d 502 (9th Cir 1987); IAM Nat'l Pension Fund v Clinton Engines Corp, 825 F 2d 415 (DC Cir 1987)]

Additionally, courts will generally dismiss an employer's action to challenge a determination of withdrawal liability when arbitration has been bypassed. [McDonald v Centra, Inc, No. 90-2483 (4th Cir 1991); Caleb v Smith & Son of Ohio, Inc, 946 F 2d 1059 (SD NY 1991); Mason and Dixon Tank Lines, Inc v Central States, Southeast and Southwest Areas Pension Fund, 852 F 2d 156 (6th Cir 1988); Flying Tiger Line v Teamsters Pension Trust Fund, 830 F 2d 1241 (3d Cir 1987); Central States, Southeast and Southwest Areas Pension Fund v Conaway, No. 91 C 485 (ND Ill 1991)] However, an employer has been permitted to proceed in court in the absence of arbitration when only statutory or constitutional issues, not factual issues, were raised. [IAM Nat'l Pension Fund Benefit Plan C v Stockton Tri Indus, 727 F 2d 1204 (DC Cir 1984); Central States, Southeast and Southwest Areas Pension Fund v Skyland Leasing Co, 691 F Supp 6 (WD Mich 1987)] There is no right to a jury trial in a suit contesting the enforcement of withdrawal liability because the arbitrator is the fact-finder. [Connors v Ryan's Coal Co, Inc, No. 89-7046 (11th Cir 1991)]

Even if the employer attempts to initiate arbitration but does not do so properly—i.e., in accordance with the rules of the plan—it may be held to have waived its right to contest the claim. For example, merely expressing a desire for arbitration and requesting information on how to proceed is not the equivalent of initiation of arbitration within the meaning of the plan's rules. [Robbins v Braver Lumber and Supply Co, No. 85 C 08332 (ND Ill 1987)]

Q 25:38   When are withdrawal liability payments due?

The plan sponsor sets the schedule of payments. The first payment is due 60 days after demand (see Q 25:34), and subsequent payments are usually made quarterly.

Even if the employer contests the determination of liability either with the plan sponsor or through arbitration, the employer is not relieved of its obligation to begin payment of the withdrawal liability. [ERISA §§ 4219(c)(2), 4219(c)(3), 4221(d); Central States, Southeast and Southwest Areas Pension Fund v Ten D, Inc, No. 91 C 05061 (ND Ill 1992); DeBreceni v Merchants Terminal Corp, 889 F 2d 1 (1st Cir 1989)] Further, one court ordered an employer that refused to make withdrawal liability payments pending arbitration to pay the plan's attorney's fees and costs. [Retirement Fund of the Fur Mfg Indus v Getto & Getto, Inc, 714 F Supp 651 (SD NY 1989)] In addition, one court ordered an employer that was not subject to withdrawal liability to pay liquidated damages for its failure to make interim payments while challenging the withdrawal liability assessment. [Central States, Southeast and Southwest Areas Pension Fund v Lady Baltimore Foods, Inc, Nos. 91-2414, and 91-2617 (7th Cir 1992)]

In limited situations, an employer may be relieved from making withdrawal liability payments pending arbitration upon a showing of the employer's likelihood of success in arbitration and irreparable harm to be suffered due to payment. [Robbins v McNicholas Transportation Co, 819 F 2d 682 (7th Cir 1987)] The employer must provide evidence of irreparable harm after first demonstrating that the pension fund lacks a "colorable claim" for the assessment of withdrawal liability. [Trustees of the Chicago Truck Drivers, Helpers, and Warehouse Workers Union (Independent) Pension Fund v Rentar Indus, Inc, Nos. 90-3214 and 90-3473 (7th Cir 1991)]

The bankruptcy or insolvency of the parent member of a controlled group does not relieve the subsidiary controlled group members of their obligation to make withdrawal liability payments (see Q 25:17) even if the liquidation or dissolution of the insolvent parent may reduce the amount of the withdrawal liability (see Q 25:32). [Central States Southeast and Southwest Areas Pension Fund v Chatham Properties, No 89-1451 (6th Cir 1991)]

A default will not occur, however, until 60 days after a demand for payment is made (see Q 25:39).

If, after review, the plan sponsor or arbitrator determines that the employer has overpaid, the employer is entitled to a lump-sum refund with interest. [PBGC Reg § 2644.2(d); Huber v Casablanca Indus, Inc, Nos. 89-3776, 89-3780 (3d Cir 1990)]

Q 25:39   What happens if a withdrawal liability payment is missed?

If a payment is not made by the due date, interest is charged from that date until the payment is actually made. [ERISA § 4219(c)(3); Carriers Container Council, Inc, v Mobile Steamship Assoc, Inc, No. 90-7825 (11th Cir 1991)] A default generally occurs 60 days after the employer gets written notice from the plan sponsor of failure to make a payment when due. If the payment is not made within the 60 days, the entire amount of the withdrawal liability plus interest becomes due immediately. [ERISA § 4219(c)(5); PBGC Reg §§ 2644.2, 2644.3; Huber v Casablanca Indus, Inc, Nos. 89-3776 and 89-3780 (3d Cir 1990); Local 807 Labor-Management Pension Fund v ABC Fast Freight Forwarding Corp, No. 82 C 3356 (ED NY 1984)]

A plan's action to collect withdrawal liability from an employer that stopped making payments in 1982 was not barred by the statute of limitations. The statute did not start running until the plan demanded payment in 1987. [ERISA § 4301(f); ILGWU Nat'l Retirement Fund v Smart Modes of California, Inc, 735 F Supp 103 (SD NY 1990)]

An employer must make withdrawal liability payments even if the National Labor Relations Board has exclusive jurisdiction to determine whether the employer must continue to make plan contributions after the expiration of the collective bargaining agreement. [Trustees of the Colorado Pipe Indus Pension Trust v Howard Electrical & Mechanical, Inc, 909 F 2d 1379 (10th Cir 1990)]

Q 25:40 Are owners of the employer personally liable for withdrawal liability?

Generally, shareholders of corporations are not personally liable for amounts the employer cannot pay. [Operating Eng'r Pension Trust v Reed, 726 F 2d 513 (9th Cir 1984); but see, Laborers Clean-Up Contract Admin Trust Fund v Uriarte Clean-Up Serv, Inc, 736 F 2d 516 (9th Cir 1984)] Controlling or dominant shareholders are not considered employers for withdrawal liability purposes. [DeBreceni v Graf Bros Leasing, Inc, 828 F 2d 877 (1st Cir 1987); Connors v P & M Coal Co, 801 F 2d 1373 (DC Cir 1986)] However, shareholders were held personally liable when they did not observe corporate formalities and removed assets from the corporation. [Plumbers' Pension Fund, Local 130, UA v A-Best Plumbing & Sewer, Inc, No. 88 C 3087 (ND Ill 1992); see also Schaffer, Jr v Charles Benjamin, Inc, No. 92-1312 (3rd Cir 1992)]

However, a shareholder of a dissolved corporation may be personally liable to the extent of corporate assets distributed to the shareholder upon dissolution. [Retirement Fund of the Fur Manufacturing Indus v Robert Goldberg Furs, Inc, 88 Civ 6033 (JES) (SD NY 1991); Central States, Southeast and Southwest Areas Pension Fund v Minneapolis Van & Warehouse Co, No. 90 C 0531 (ND Ill 1991); Retirement Fund of the Fur Manufacturing Indus v Strassberg and Tama, Inc, 88 Civ 6034 (MBM) (SD NY 1989)] Also, a state law under which the ten largest shareholders of a closely held corporation can be held liable for unpaid plan contributions was held not to be preempted by ERISA. [Sasso v Vachris, 66 NY 2d 28 (1985)]

A corporate officer is not personally liable for withdrawal liability payments solely by virtue of the individual's capacity as an officer of the withdrawing employer. [Connors v BMC Coal Co, 634 F Supp 74 (D DC 1986); Connors v Darryll Waggle Constr, Inc, 631 F Supp 1188 (D DC 1986)]

Partners or sole proprietors are personally liable, but assets that would be exempt under bankruptcy law are also exempt from satisfaction of the withdrawal liability obligation. Furthermore, a husband and wife who jointly operated a farm were personally liable for the unpaid withdrawal liability of a corporation controlled by the husband because the farm and corporation were under common control (see Q 25:17). [ERISA § 4225(c); Connors v Ryan's Coal Co,

Inc, No. 89-7046 (11th Cir 1991); Board of Trustees of the W Conference of Teamsters Pension Trust Fund v H F Johnson, Inc, 830 F 2d 1009 (9th Cir 1987)] However, the spouse of an unincorporated business owner is not personally liable for the business owner's withdrawal liability unless it can be shown that she intended to form a partnership with her husband with respect to the business. [Central States, Southeast and Southwest Areas Pension Fund v Johnson, 1993 US App Lexis 7706 (7th Cir 1993)]

Q 25:41 Are withdrawal liability claims entitled to priority in bankruptcy proceedings?

It has been held that withdrawal liability is considered a general unsecured claim and is not entitled to priority in bankruptcy proceedings because it is not an administrative expense claim. [Trustees of the Amalgamated Ins Fund v McFarlin's, Inc, 789 F 2d 98 (2d Cir 1986)]

Q 25:42 What is a mass withdrawal from a multiemployer plan?

A mass withdrawal is one form of multiemployer plan termination (see Q 25:43). A mass withdrawal occurs if:

1. Every employer withdraws from the plan; or
2. The obligation of all employers to contribute to the plan ceases.

[ERISA § 4041A(a)(2)]

If a mass withdrawal occurs, all withdrawing employers lose the benefit of the waiver or reduction of small liabilities (see Q 25:24) and the 20-year cap (see Q 25:33), and the plan's unfunded vested benefits are fully allocated among all of the withdrawing employers. For this purpose, the withdrawal of substantially all employers by agreement or arrangement is considered a mass withdrawal. [ERISA §§ 4209, 4219(c); PBGC Reg §§ 2640.7, 2648.1–2648.5]

PBGC has given guidance as to the administration of multiemployer plans that have terminated by mass withdrawal. Generally, the plan sponsor must periodically determine whether the value of nonforfeitable benefits exceeds the value of plan assets. If so, the plan sponsor must reduce benefits other than accrued benefits guaranteed by PBGC (see Q 25:8), suspend certain benefit payments, or seek financial assistance in the form of a PBGC loan (see Q 25:43) to the extent necessary to ensure the plan's sufficiency. Under these circumstances, the reduction of accrued benefits does not cause plan disqualification (see Q 9:24). [ERISA § 4281; IRC § 411(a)(3)(F); PBGC Reg §§ 2675.1–2675.44]

Generally, the plan sponsor of a plan that terminates by mass withdrawal can only pay benefits that were nonforfeitable at plan termination without first obtaining PBGC approval. Thus, PBGC approval is not needed to pay a qualified preretirement survivor annuity (QPSA; see Q 10:9) to the surviving spouse of a participant who died before the plan termination date. Further, the plan sponsor does not need PBGC approval to pay the QPSA for a participant who died after the plan termination date unless the plan sponsor has determined that plan assets are not sufficient to pay all nonforfeitable plan benefits. [ERISA § 4041A(c); PBGC Opinion Letter No. 91-2]

Q 25:43 What is the liability of an employer upon termination of a multiemployer defined benefit plan?

For multiemployer plans, plan termination does not mean dissolution of the plan, nor does it result in PBGC involvement as the provider of benefits. Instead, termination means mass withdrawal (see Q 25:42), the amendment of the plan to freeze vested benefits and to give no credit for further service, or the conversion of the plan into a defined contribution plan. Employers must continue to contribute to the frozen plan in order to fund the plan's unfunded liabilities. The plan administrator must notify PBGC after the effective date of termination and follow PBGC reporting requirements and rules regarding administration of terminated multiemployer plans. [ERISA § 4041A; PBGC Reg §§ 2673.2, 2675.1, 2675.2]

PBGC funds are available only if a plan becomes insolvent (see Q 25:7). These PBGC funds are only loans and must be repaid. [ERISA §§ 4022A(a), 4261]

Q 25:44 May a multiemployer plan exclude some newly adopting employers from withdrawal liability?

Yes. A multiemployer plan may adopt a rule under which an employer may withdraw from the plan without liability within six years after joining the plan or, if less, the number of years required for vesting under the plan. This free-look rule is applicable to the employer only if it (1) contributes less than 2 percent of all employer contributions to the plan each year, and (2) has not previously used this rule with respect to the plan.

In addition, for the free-look rule to be enforceable, the plan must (1) be amended to permit the rule, (2) have an eight-to-one assets-to-benefits payable ratio in the year before the employer joins the plan, and (3) provide that an employee's service before the employer joined the plan will not be counted in determining benefits. Plans primarily covering employees in the building and construction industry are not permitted to adopt the free-look rule. [ERISA § 4210]

One court held that the free-look rule did not apply to an employer after it was acquired by another employer because both employers were then under common control and the acquiring employer was ineligible to use the free-look rule (see Q 25:17). [Central States, Southeast and Southwest Areas Pension Fund v Hoosier Dairy, Inc, No. 90 C 3795 (ND Ill 1991)]

Chapter 26

Individual Retirement Plans

Anyone who receives compensation may set aside a modest amount of money each year for retirement in a tax-deferred account known as an individual retirement plan (IRA). However, not all IRA contributions are deductible. This chapter examines how IRAs work.

Q 26:1   What is an individual retirement plan?

An individual retirement plan is a personal retirement plan. This type of plan allows employees, self-employed individuals (see Q 29:8), and certain other individuals, whether or not they participate in qualified retirement plans (including Keogh plans, simplified employee pensions (SEPs), tax-sheltered annuities, and government plans), to establish IRAs and make annual contributions to them. For active plan participants, however, these contributions might not be deductible (see Q 26:7). [IRC §§ 219, 408]

There are two types of individual retirement plans: (1) individual retirement accounts (see Q 26:2) and (2) individual retirement annuities (see Q 26:3). Both types are commonly referred to as IRAs.

A working spouse may set up an IRA for the nonworking spouse (see Q 26:18). In addition, certain divorced or separated persons may make deductible contributions to IRAs even though they receive no wages or salary (see Q 26:5).

Deductible contributions to an IRA are tax deductible whether or not the individual itemizes deductions. [IRC § 62(a)(7)]

Earnings on all amounts contributed to any IRA accumulate on a tax-deferred basis. [IRC § 408(e)]

Q 26:2 What are the basic characteristics of an individual retirement account?

An IRA is a trust or custodial account established for the exclusive benefit of an individual and the individual's beneficiaries. The trustee (or custodian) must be a bank, thrift institution, insurance company, brokerage firm, or other person who demonstrates to IRS that such person will administer the account in a manner consistent with the requirements of the law. No part of the account funds can be invested in life insurance contracts. Assets of the account cannot be commingled with other property except if there is a common trust fund or common investment fund. [IRC § 408(a); Nichola, 63 TCM 2150 (1992)]

An IRA cannot be a shareholder of an S corporation, and IRA assets should not be invested in collectibles (works of art, rugs, antiques, metals, gems, stamps, coins, or other items of tangible personal property specified by IRS). Amounts invested in collectibles are treated as distributions for tax purposes (that is, taxed as current income; if the individual is under age 59½, a 10 percent penalty tax for a premature withdrawal also applies). However, gold or silver coins issued by the U.S. government or any type of coin issued under the laws of any state will not be considered collectibles. An interest in a portion of a gold coin portfolio is not considered a collectible. [IRC §§ 408(m), 1361; Rev Rul 92-73, 1992-2 CB 224; Ltr Rul 8940067]

The individual's interest in the IRA must be nonforfeitable. Distributions must satisfy the minimum distribution requirements in order to avoid penalties for insufficient distributions (see Qs 26:32, 26:33). [IRC §§ 408(a)(4), 408(a)(6)]

An account that is identified as an IRA and meets the statutory requirements is treated as an IRA, even if the owner later claims it is not an IRA because the owner made an untimely rollover contribution that is an excess contribution (see Q 26:6). [Michel, 58 TCM 1019 (1989)]

Q 26:3   What are the basic characteristics of an individual retirement annuity?

An individual retirement annuity is an annuity contract or endowment contract issued by an insurance company. However, an endowment contract issued after November 6, 1978 cannot qualify. The contract must be nontransferable and nonforfeitable. Premiums may not be fixed, nor may they exceed $2,000 a year. Distributions must satisfy the minimum distribution requirements and must be made by specified dates in order to avoid penalties for insufficient distributions (see Qs 26:32, 26:33). [IRC § 408(b); Treas Reg § 1.408-3(e)(ix)]

Participation in a group annuity may be used instead of an individual annuity contract. Only part of the premium for an endowment contract builds an annuity; the rest buys current life insurance protection. The part of the premium that pays for current life insurance protection is not tax deductible. [IRC §§ 219(d)(3), 408(a)(3), 408(b); Ltr Rul 8439026]

If an individual borrows any money from or against an individual retirement annuity, the annuity contract ceases to be a qualified individual retirement annuity as of the first day of the year. Because of the borrowing, the individual must include in gross income for the year the fair market value of the annuity as of the first day of such year. [IRC § 408(e)(3); Griswold, 85 TC 869 (1985)]

Q 26:4   Who is eligible to set up an IRA?

Any individual under age 70½ receiving compensation may establish an IRA (also see Q 26:5). [IRC § 219(d)(1)]

An IRA may also be established as a vehicle for deferring taxes on eligible rollover distributions from qualified retirement plans, including distributions received after attainment of age 70½ and distributions to surviving spouses of plan participants. For details, see Chapter 28.

Q 26:5   How much can be contributed to an IRA?

Each year an individual may contribute 100 percent of compensation up to a maximum of $2,000 to an IRA. [IRC §§ 219(b), 408(a),

408(b)] The contribution limit is $2,250 if a spousal IRA is also established (see Q 26:18). [IRC § 219(c)(2)] However, there is no dollar limit with respect to a rollover contribution (see Q 28:2).

IRS has provided a safe harbor definition of compensation for the purpose of determining eligibility to make an IRA contribution. Under the safe harbor, compensation is the amount properly shown on Form W-2, Box 10 (wages, tips, and other compensation) less the amount properly shown in Box 16 (nonqualified plans). [IRC § 219(f)(1); Rev Proc 91-18, 1991-1 CB 522]

Compensation includes taxable alimony and separate maintenance payments. A divorced or separated spouse who receives taxable alimony, but no other compensation, is able to make contributions to an IRA. Deferred compensation and amounts received as a pension or annuity are not treated as compensation and cannot be used as a basis for contributions to an IRA even if the safe harbor definition of compensation is used. A separation pay allowance received by an employee is considered deferred compensation for this purpose. Also, a fee paid by a husband to his wife for services rendered in connection with their jointly held investments is not compensation to her, nor is a payment by a husband to his wife where, in fact, the wife did not render any services to the husband's business. [IRC § 219(f)(1); Treas Reg § 1.219-1(c); Bingo, 61 TCM 2782 (1991); Ltr Ruls 8535001, 8519051]

In a novel ruling, a farmer transferred hogs to his wife, who was a *bona fide* employee, as compensation for her services to his farming business. IRS ruled that the hogs constituted compensation and could be used as a basis for contributions to an IRA. [Ltr Rul 9202003]

A contribution made to an IRA for the year in which an individual attains age 70½, or any year thereafter, is a nondeductible excess contribution (see Q 26:6) that cannot be treated as a designated nondeductible IRA contribution (see Q 26:14). [IRC §§ 219(d)(1), 408(o)]

An estate cannot make an IRA contribution on behalf of the decedent or to the spousal IRA of the decedent's spouse for the year in which the decedent died. [Ltr Rul 8439066]

Q 26:6   What penalty is imposed on an excess contribution to an IRA?

If an individual contributes more to an IRA than the amount allowable (see Q 26:5), the excess contribution is subject to a 6 percent excise tax. Further, the penalty will be charged each year the excess contribution remains in the IRA. [IRC § 4973]

The individual can avoid the penalty by withdrawing the excess contribution, along with the net income allocable to the excess, before the due date (including extensions) of the individual's federal income tax return for the year of the excess contribution. The net income on the excess contribution is treated as gross income for the taxable year in which the excess contribution was made. [IRC §§ 408(d)(4), 4973(b)]

If the individual does not withdraw the excess contribution before such filing deadline, the 6 percent excise tax must be paid for the year of the excess contribution. To avoid the 6 percent excise tax for the following year, the remaining excess contribution can be eliminated by either withdrawing such amount from the IRA or making a contribution for such year equal to the maximum allowable amount (see Q 26:5) reduced by the remaining excess contribution. [IRC § 4973(b)]

Q 26:7   Can active participants in qualified retirement plans also make deductible IRA contributions?

Not necessarily. If an individual is an active participant (see Q 26:9) in a qualified retirement plan for any part of a plan year ending with or within the individual's taxable year, IRA contributions cannot be deducted if the individual's adjusted gross income exceeds certain specified amounts (see Qs 26:10, 26:11). For married couples (see Q 26:10), if either spouse is an active participant, both are treated as active participants. [IRC § 219(g)]

Q 26:8   What is active participation?

Generally, active participation refers to participation in a qualified retirement plan, SEP (see Chapter 27), tax-sheltered annuity, or governmental plan. An individual's status as an active participant must be reported on Form W-2.

Q 26:9   Who is an active participant?

An active participant in a defined benefit plan (see Q 2:3) is an individual who participates or meets the eligibility requirements for participation at any time during the plan year ending with or within the individual's taxable year. Thus, an individual is an active participant if the individual is eligible but declines to participate or fails to complete the minimum period of service or to make an employee contribution necessary to accrue a benefit. [Wartes, TCM 1993-84]

An individual is an active participant in a money purchase pension or target benefit plan (see Qs 2:4, 2:5) if an employer contribution or forfeiture is required to be allocated to the individual's account for the plan year ending with or within the individual's taxable year. Thus, an individual who separates from service before the beginning of a calendar year may still be an active participant for such calendar year if, under the terms of the plan, the individual is eligible to receive an allocation for the plan year ending in such calendar year.

An individual is treated as an active participant under a profit sharing or stock bonus plan (see Qs 2:6, 2:12) if any employer contribution is added or any forfeiture is allocated to the individual's account during the individual's taxable year. A contribution is added to the individual's account on the later of the date the contribution is made or allocated.

An individual is not an active participant in a defined contribution plan (see Q 2:2) if only earnings (rather than contributions or forfeitures) are allocated to the individual's account.

An individual is treated as an active participant for any taxable year in which the individual makes a voluntary or mandatory employee contribution or an elective contribution under a 401(k) plan (see Q 23:1). However, an individual is not an active participant merely because the individual is eligible but chooses not to make such elective contribution.

The determination of whether an individual is an active participant is made without regard as to whether the individual's rights are nonforfeitable. [Wartes, TCM 1993-84] An individual is not an active participant if the employer has frozen benefit accruals (unless pre-freeze benefit accruals increase as compensation increases). [Ltr Rul 8948008] However, an individual who is an active participant will remain an active participant even if an employer temporarily suspends benefit accruals by adopting Model Amendment 2 or 3, pending restatement of the qualified retirement plan to meet the requirements of TRA '86 (see Q 4:7). [IRC § 219(g); Ann 91-11, 1991-4 IRB 80; Notice 88-131, 1988-2 CB 546; Notice 87-16, 1987-1 CB 446]

For married couples filing jointly, if either spouse is an active participant under the rules described above, both spouses are treated as active participants for purposes of determining the amount that each may contribute to an IRA. However, in the case of a married couple filing separate tax returns and who do not live together at any time during the taxable year, the active participant status of one spouse will not affect the status of the other spouse. [IRC § 219(g)(4); Wartes, TCM 1993-84; Felber, 64 TCM 261 (1992)]

Q 26:10   What level of income affects an active participant's deduction limitation?

Adjusted gross income over the applicable dollar amount results in a limit on the IRA deduction for active participants (see Q 26:9). The applicable dollar amounts are:

1. $40,000 for taxpayers filing a joint return;
2. $25,000 for any unmarried taxpayer; and
3. Zero for married individuals filing separate returns.

However, married individuals filing separately who live apart during the entire year are treated as not married for this purpose. [IRC § 219(g); Notice 87-16, 1987-1 CB 446]

For purposes of the IRA deduction limit, adjusted gross income is calculated without taking into account any deductible IRA contributions made for the taxable year or certain exclusions for foreign earned income and U.S. savings bond redemptions, but taking into account any taxable Social Security benefits and passive loss limitations applicable to the taxpayer (see Q 26:12). [IRC § 219(g)(3)]

Q 26:11   If an individual is an active participant in a qualified retirement plan, what are the applicable IRA deduction limits?

The amount that may be deducted will be the contribution limitation (see Q 26:5) reduced by an amount that bears the same ratio to the contribution limitation as the amount by which the taxpayer's adjusted gross income exceeds the applicable dollar amount (see Q 26:10) bears to $10,000. Thus, a married couple with at least one active participant spouse and adjusted gross income of at least $50,000 cannot make a deductible IRA contribution. [Wartes, TCM 1993-84; Felber, 64 TCM 261 (1992)]

Example. Ed, an active participant in his employer's qualified retirement plan, is married to Lois, and they file a joint return. Their adjusted gross income for 1993 is $47,500, and each earns over $2,000. Both Ed and Lois may make a deductible IRA contribution of up to $500, computed as follows:

Adjusted gross income	$47,500
Less: Applicable dollar amount	40,000
Difference	$ 7,500
Reduction in $2,000 limitation	
($2,000 multiplied by $7,500/$10,000)	$ 1,500
Maximum deductible IRA contribution	
($2,000 less $1,500)	$ 500

[IRC § 219(g)(2); Notice 87-16, 1987-1 CB 446]

The reduction in the $2,000 limitation is rounded to the next lowest $10 in the case of a reduction that is not a multiple of $10. [IRC § 219(g)(2)(C)]

For individuals whose adjusted gross income is not above the level that would totally eliminate a deductible IRA contribution, there is a $200 minimum IRA deduction allowable.

Example. Norman, an unmarried individual who is an active participant in his employer's qualified retirement plan, has adjusted gross income of $34,900. He may make a deductible IRA contribution of $200.

[IRC § 219(g)(2)(B)]

Q 26:12 Does the receipt of Social Security benefits affect deductible IRA contributions?

If an individual is an active participant (see Q 26:9) in a qualified retirement plan, the deduction for IRA contributions is subject to a phase-out if adjusted gross income exceeds certain specified amounts (see Qs 26:10, 26:11). An individual's adjusted gross income includes the taxable portion of Social Security benefits. [IRC §§ 219(g)(3)(A)(i), 219(g)(3)(B)]

The determination of the taxable portion of Social Security benefits depends in part upon the individual's modified adjusted gross income. In determining modified adjusted gross income, the individual may subtract deductible IRA contributions. Therefore, a deductible IRA contribution may cause a reduction in the taxable portion of Social Security benefits, and the individual must compute taxable Social Security benefits twice. The first computation is for the purpose of determining the tentative amount of Social Security benefits that must be included in gross income if the individual did not make any IRA contribution. This first computation determines the amount of hypothetical adjusted gross income for purposes of the IRA phase-out provision. The second computation actually determines the amount of taxable Social Security benefits by taking into account the deductible IRA contribution that was determined under the first computation. [IRC § 86(b)(2); Ann 88-38, 1988-10 IRB 60; Conf Rpt No. 99-841, 1986-3 (Vol 4) CB 377; IRS Publication 590 (For use in preparing 1992 returns)]

Q 26:13 May an individual who is ineligible to make a fully deductible IRA contribution make a nondeductible IRA contribution?

Yes. An individual who is ineligible to make a deductible IRA contribution to the full extent of the contribution limitation (see Q 26:5) may make a designated nondeductible IRA contribution (see Q 26:14). [IRC § 408(o)]

Q 26:14 What is a designated nondeductible IRA contribution?

A designated nondeductible IRA contribution is a nondeductible IRA contribution to the extent of the excess of (1) the lesser of $2,000 (or $2,250 when a spousal IRA is also involved) or 100 percent of compensation over (2) the IRA deduction limit with respect to the individual (but see Q 26:15). [IRC § 408(o)]

Q 26:15 May an individual who is eligible to make a deductible IRA contribution elect to treat such a contribution as nondeductible?

Yes. An individual is permitted to make such an election and might do so if, for example, the individual had no taxable income for the year after taking into account other deductions. [IRC § 408(o)(2)(B)(ii)]

Q 26:16 Is an individual required to report a designated nondeductible contribution on the tax return?

Yes. An individual who makes a designated nondeductible contribution (see Q 26:14) to an IRA (or who receives any amount from an IRA) must include the following information on the income tax return for the applicable taxable year:

1. The amount of designated nondeductible contributions for the year;
2. The amount of distributions from IRAs for the year;
3. The excess (if any) of (a) the aggregate amount of designated nondeductible contributions for all preceding taxable years, over (b) the aggregate amount of distributions from IRAs that were excludible from gross income for such taxable years;
4. The aggregate balance of all IRAs of the individual as of the end of the taxable year; and
5. Such other information as IRS may prescribe.

[IRC § 408(o)(4)]

If the required information is not provided on the individual's tax return for a taxable year, all IRA contributions are considered to have been deductible and, therefore, are taxable upon withdrawal from the IRA. However, an individual may change a designation of a contribution from deductible to nondeductible (or *vice versa*) by filing an amended return before the expiration of the statute of limitations on assessment of tax for such year. [Notice 87-16, 1987-1 CB 446]

There is a $50 penalty for failure to report the required information, and a $100 penalty for overstating the amount of designated nondeductible contributions—unless the taxpayer can demonstrate that the error was due to reasonable cause. [IRC §§ 408(o)(4), 6693(b)]

Q 26:17   What is the tax treatment of IRA withdrawals by an individual who has previously made both deductible and nondeductible contributions?

The amount includible in an individual's income is determined by subtracting from the amount of the IRA withdrawal an amount that bears the same ratio to the amount withdrawn as the individual's aggregate nondeductible IRA contributions bear to the aggregate balance of all IRAs of the individual (including rollover IRAs and SEPs).

The formula for determining the nontaxable portion of an IRA distribution is:

$$\frac{\text{Total nondeductible contributions}}{\substack{\text{Aggregate IRA} \\ \text{year-end account} \\ \text{balances plus} \\ \text{amount of IRA} \\ \text{distributions}}} \times \text{IRA distribution} = \substack{\text{Nontaxable portion} \\ \text{of distribution}}$$

[Notice 87-16, 1987-1 CB 446]

Example. Assume that Anne has made aggregate deductible IRA contributions into two IRAs for 1991 and 1992 of $1,800 and aggregate nondeductible IRA contributions of $2,200 during those two years. In January 1993, Anne withdrew $1,000 from one IRA. At the end of 1993, the account balance of both IRAs is $4,500. Of the $1,000 withdrawn during 1993, $400 is treated as a partial return of nondeductible contributions, calculated as follows:

$$\frac{\text{Total nondeductible contributions (\$2,200)}}{\begin{array}{c}\text{Aggregate IRA year-end}\\\text{account balances (\$4,500)}\\\text{plus amount of IRA}\\\text{distributions during year}\\\text{(\$1,000)}\end{array}} = \frac{\$2,200}{\$5,500} \times \$1,000 = \$400$$

The balance of the withdrawn amount ($1,000 – $400 = $600) is includible in income on Anne's 1993 tax return.

For further discussion of the taxability of withdrawals from IRAs, see Q 26:34.

Q 26:18   What is a spousal IRA?

If only one spouse is working, the working spouse may make an additional contribution to an IRA (a spousal IRA) on behalf of the nonworking spouse (provided a joint income tax return is filed). A spousal IRA is available even if both spouses work if the spouse for whom the spousal IRA is set up consents to being treated as having no compensation, for IRA purposes, for the taxable year. The total amount of allowable annual contributions to the working spouse's IRA and to the spousal IRA is $2,250 (or 100 percent of the working spouse's earnings if less). The contributions to both IRAs need not be split equally between the spouses. However, the maximum IRA contribution on behalf of either spouse is $2,000. [IRC § 219(c); Bingo, 61 TCM 2782 (1991); Harris, 51 TCM 1154 (1986)]

If either spouse is an active participant in a qualified retirement plan, the allowable contributions are not fully deductible if the couple's adjusted gross income is more than $40,000 (see Q 26:10). If the couple's adjusted gross income is between $40,000 and $50,000, the deductible portion of the allowable contributions ($2,250) is proportionately reduced (see Q 26:11). None of the contribution is deductible if the couple's adjusted gross income is $50,000 or more. [IRC § 219(g); Wartes, TCM 1993-84; Felber, 64 TCM 261 (1992)]

What happens if the working spouse has reached age 70½? As long as the working spouse continues to receive compensation, the working spouse can make deductible contributions to the nonworking spouse's IRA. The nonworking spouse must, however, be less than age 70½, and the maximum contribution on behalf of the nonworking spouse is $2,000. [IRC § 219(d)(1)]

What happens if the working spouse dies? A contribution may be made to a spousal IRA by the surviving spouse if a joint income tax return is filed for the year for which the contribution was made. [Ltr Rul 8527083]

Q 26:19 When must IRA contributions be made?

A deductible or nondeductible contribution to an IRA must be made by the due date, not including extensions, for filing the return. [IRC § 219(f)(3)]

Example. Betty wants to make a contribution to her IRA for 1993. Betty can do so any time in 1993, or she can wait until her 1993 tax return is due, April 15, 1994. Even if Betty obtains an extension to file her return to August 15, 1994, Betty's IRA contribution is due by April 15, 1994.

An IRA contribution is timely if it is received by the IRA sponsor in an envelope bearing a post office cancellation date no later than the due date of the individual's federal income tax return, not including extensions. [Ltr Ruls 8628047, 8611090, 8551065, 8536085]

Q 26:20 Can an IRA deduction be claimed before the contribution is actually made?

Yes, as long as the contribution is made by the due date, not including extensions, for filing the return. [Rev Rul 84-18, 1984-1 CB 88]

Example. Danielle files her 1993 return on February 4, 1994, and claims a deduction of $2,000 for an IRA contribution that she has not made. If she makes the contribution by the due date of the return, April 15, 1994, the deduction is allowed.

Q 26:21   Does the payment of a fee to the trustee of an IRA reduce the amount otherwise allowable as a contribution to the IRA?

No. The payment of a fee to the trustee for the establishment and maintenance of an IRA, or for various other administrative services performed, is not considered a contribution to an IRA for purposes of the annual contribution limit (see Q 26:5) or the excess contribution penalty (see Q 26:6). Moreover, the trustee fees may be deductible as expenses incurred for the production of income. [Rev Rul 84-146, 1984-2 CB 61; Ltr Ruls 8329049, 8432109; IRC § 212]

However, the payment of brokerage commissions incurred for the purchase or sale of IRA assets is considered a contribution to the IRA subject to the annual contribution limit. [Ltr Rul 8711095; Rev Rul 86-142, 1986-2 CB 60] This rule also applies to commissions paid to insurance agents attributable to the purchase of individual retirement annuities. [Ltr Rul 8747072]

Q 26:22   What happens if an individual engages in a prohibited transaction with regard to the IRA?

A retirement account is not treated as an IRA if an individual engages in a prohibited transaction (see Q 20:1) with respect to the retirement account. The account is treated as having distributed all its assets to the individual on the first day of the taxable year in which the prohibited transaction occurs. [IRC § 408(e)(2)]

An individual is a disqualified person (see Q 20:3) with respect to the individual's IRA, so the individual's guarantee of a loan to the IRA is a prohibited transaction. [IRC §§ 4975(c)(1), 4975(e)(2); DOL Advisory Opinion No. 90-23A]

DOL has granted a class exemption permitting purchases and sales by IRAs of American Eagle bullion coins from or to authorized purchasers even if the authorized purchasers are disqualified persons (see Qs 20:2, 20:3). [PTCE 91-55 (56 FR 49209)]

Q 26:23 Will the receipt of reduced or no-cost services by a customer who directs the IRA to invest in a bank's financial products constitute a prohibited transaction?

Effective May 11, 1993, banks are permitted to provide IRA holders or their family members with institutional services either at reduced costs or at no cost, such as free checking. The services offered must be the same as those offered by the bank in the ordinary course of its business to customers who do not maintain IRAs at the bank. Therefore, a prohibited transaction (see Q 20:1) will not occur when an IRA holder, who is a fiduciary with respect to the IRA, uses IRA assets to obtain services from the bank. [IRC § 4975(c)(1); PTCE 93-33 (58 FR 31053)]

Retroactively effective to 1975, banks and other financial institutions can offer cash or other premiums as incentives for opening IRAs or for making additional IRA contributions. The value of the premium on deposits up to $5,000 is limited to $10 and to $20 on deposits in excess of $5,000. Free group-term life insurance can be offered to IRA holders annually if the face amount of the insurance does not exceed the lesser of $5,000 or the value of the account. [PTCE 93-1 (58 FR 3567)]

Q 26:24 May an individual borrow money to fund an IRA?

Yes. The deductibility of the interest paid on the loan is determined under the general rules applicable to interest payments. The interest payments are not subject to the rule prohibiting interest deductions on loans incurred to purchase or carry tax-exempt assets because the income earned on the IRA is tax-deferred, not tax-exempt. [IRC § 163; Ltr Rul 8527082]

Q 26:25 May an individual make a contribution to an IRA with a credit card?

Yes, according to IRS. An individual established an IRA at a bank and funded the IRA with a cash advance drawn on his bank credit card. The bank executed the transaction pursuant to written instructions of the individual. IRS ruled that if, by April 15, a cash advance was drawn on the individual's credit card, credited to the IRA, and designated as a contribution for the previous year, the individual could deduct the contribution for the previous year, provided the bank honored its obligation to make payment on the credit card cash advance. [Ltr Rul 8622051]

Q 26:26 What is an employer-sponsored IRA?

An employer may establish IRAs for its employees (and for the nonworking spouses of these employees). The contributions are deductible by the employer and includible as compensation income by the employee, subject to Social Security and unemployment taxes. Whether the employee can deduct the contribution is determined under the rules generally applicable to IRA contributions (see Qs 26:7–26:11). The assets of the employer-sponsored IRAs may be held in a common trust fund. [IRC §§ 219(f)(5), 408(c)]

If the employer contributes less than the maximum allowed (100 percent of compensation up to $2,000; increased to $2,250 in the case of a spousal IRA), the employee can contribute the difference.

Example. Jason's employer contributes $1,500 to an IRA on his behalf. Because Jason earns more than $2,000 a year, the maximum allowable contribution is $2,000. Jason can contribute an additional $500 to the IRA.

There is no requirement that an employer-sponsored IRA cover a certain number or group of employees. In fact, the employer may discriminate in favor of highly compensated employees (see Q 3:3). [IRC § 408(c)]

An IRA is not considered employer sponsored merely because the employer acts as trustee or custodian of its employees' IRAs. However, the employer is a disqualified person (see Qs 20:2, 20:3) with respect to the IRA, so the employer must be careful to avoid engaging in a prohibited transaction (see Q 20:1) that would disqualify the IRA (see Q 26:22). For example, the purchase of stock of the employer's parent company by the employer as IRA custodian may be considered a prohibited transaction. [DOL Advisory Opinion No. 90-20A]

Q 26:27 Can employer-sponsored IRAs help an employer that has a qualified retirement plan satisfy coverage requirements?

No. An employer maintaining a qualified retirement plan cannot satisfy the coverage requirements that must be met by taking into consideration the fact that employees not covered under the plan are covered by an employer-sponsored IRA.

For details on coverage requirements, see Chapter 5.

Q 26:28 What is a payroll-deduction IRA?

An employer may choose to play a limited role in promoting retirement savings (IRAs) for its employees by establishing a payroll-deduction program in conjunction with a financial institution (e.g., a bank, insurance company, mutual fund, or brokerage firm). Each employee is allowed to set up an IRA with the sponsoring institution, and the amount the employee wishes to contribute to the IRA each pay period is deducted from the employee's paycheck by the employer.

Q 26:29 Does a payroll-deduction IRA expose the employer to ERISA liabilities and compliance requirements?

A payroll-deduction IRA is not considered a pension plan subject to ERISA as long as the employer does not endorse the program. The employer will not be considered to have endorsed the program and will be free of ERISA responsibilities if all of the following conditions are met:

1. Materials distributed to the employees, either by the employer or by the IRA sponsor, clearly say that:
   a. The program is completely voluntary;
   b. The employer is not endorsing the sponsor or its investment program;
   c. There are other IRA investments available to employees outside the payroll-deduction program;
   d. An IRA may not be appropriate for everyone; and

    e. The tax consequences are the same whether or not payroll deductions are used to make the IRA contributions;

2. The employer is not the IRA sponsor or an affiliate of the sponsor;

3. No significant investments will be made in securities of the employer; and

4. If the payroll-deduction IRA is the result of a collective bargaining agreement, no investments designed to provide more jobs, loans, or similar direct benefits to union members are permitted.

In addition, the employer must promptly transfer the funds it deducts from its employees' paychecks to the IRA sponsor or it risks the imposition of some ERISA responsibilities. [DOL Advisory Opinion No. 81-80A]

Q 26:30 How does a simplified employee pension differ from an employer-sponsored IRA?

A SEP allows a company to contribute the lesser of $30,000 or 15 percent of an eligible employee's compensation to an IRA established by the employee. The employer-sponsored IRA limit is the lesser of $2,000 ($2,250 for a spousal IRA) or 100 percent of compensation (see Q 26:5). SEPs must comply with coverage and nondiscrimination requirements, while an employer-sponsored IRA may discriminate in favor of highly compensated employees (see Q 3:3).

For details on how a SEP works, see Chapter 27.

Q 26:31 Are there restrictions on IRA distributions?

No. Unlike qualified retirement plans, an individual may withdraw all or any part of an IRA at any time. Also, spousal consent to a withdrawal is not necessary, and there are no limitations as to the form of distribution.

However, minimum annual distributions must start by April 1 of the year after the year in which the individual reaches age 70½ (see

Q 26:32), and a penalty tax is imposed for insufficient distributions (see Q 26:33). [IRC §§ 408(a)(6), 408(b)(3); see also IRC § 401(a)(9)]

Also, additional taxes may apply to distributions before an individual reaches age 59½ (see Q 26:39) and to distributions in excess of certain limits (see Q 13:27).

Q 26:32   What is the minimum distribution requirement?

Once distributions from an IRA are required to begin (see Q 26:31), the owner must withdraw a certain amount during each year or be subject to a penalty for insufficient distributions (see Q 26:33).

IRS has issued proposed regulations detailing the methods for satisfying the minimum distribution requirement. The proposed regulations indicate that distributions from an IRA are subject to requirements similar to those governing minimum distributions from qualified retirement plans, including the minimum distribution incidental benefit requirement. [Prop Reg § 1.408-8, Q&A A-1, B-13] See Chapter 11 for details.

Generally, the minimum required distribution for a year is calculated by dividing the account balance of the IRA as of December 31 of the previous year by the owner's life expectancy (or by the joint life expectancy of the owner and the owner's designated beneficiary). [Prop Reg § 1.401(a)(9)-1, Q&A F-1]

An individual who is the owner or beneficiary of more than one IRA must calculate the required minimum distribution with respect to each IRA. However, the amounts required to be distributed may then be aggregated and the distribution taken from any one or more of the IRAs. [Notice 88-38, 1988-1 CB 524]

The minimum distribution for a year is not reduced even if a portion of the IRA assets is transferred to a former spouse pursuant to a divorce decree during the year. The minimum distribution is still based on the IRA balance on December 31 of the year before the transfer. [Ltr Rul 9011031]

See Question 26:38 for the minimum distribution requirements after the death of the IRA owner.

Q 26:33　What is the penalty imposed for insufficient distributions from an IRA?

An annual nondeductible 50 percent excise tax is imposed on the difference between the minimum required distribution from an IRA (see Q 26:32) and the amount distributed. [IRC § 4974]

IRS can waive the penalty tax if the shortfall resulted from a reasonable error and the individual is taking steps to correct the situation. [IRC § 4974(d)]

Q 26:34　How are distributions from an IRA taxed?

Generally, a recipient of a payment or distribution from an IRA must include the amount received in gross income for the year of receipt. The naming of a trust as the beneficiary of an individual's IRA does not constitute a distribution from the IRA even though the individual is the creator, trustee, and sole beneficiary of the trust because no amount was actually distributed from the IRA to either the individual or the trust. Amounts embezzled from an IRA by an officer of the IRA trustee and then restored to the IRA by the trustee are not taxable distributions. [GCM 39858; Ltr Ruls 9253054, 9234016]

IRA distributions are taxed as ordinary income. IRA distributions are not eligible for capital gains treatment or the forward averaging method that may apply to lump-sum distributions from qualified retirement plans (see Q 13:13). [IRC § 408(d)(1); Costanza, 50 TCM 280 (1985)]

If the IRA is paid out all in one year, the individual pays income tax on the entire amount in one year. If distributions are received as an annuity or over a period of years, tax payments are spread over several years. If the individual has made only deductible IRA contributions, the entire amount of each IRA distribution is fully taxable. If, however, the individual has made nondeductible contributions to any IRA, a portion of all IRA distributions, even distributions made from an IRA to which only deductible contributions have been made, will be considered a tax-free return of the individual's nondeductible contributions (see Q 26:17). For purposes of determining what portion of an IRA distribution is taxable, the following special rules apply:

1. All IRAs and SEPs maintained by the individual are aggregated;

2. All distributions during the year are treated as one distribution;

3. The aggregate account balance is determined as of the end of the year, and includes distributions made during the year; and

4. The individual's overall nondeductible contributions are determined as of the end of the year.

[IRC § 408(d)(2)]

A distribution from a rollover IRA (see Q 28:2) established by a surviving spouse with a distribution from the deceased spouse's tax-sheltered annuity is fully taxable. The surviving spouse does not receive a basis (see Q 13:2) equal to the fair market value of the amount rolled over. [Ltr Rul 9031046] However, when an individual rolled over the entire distribution to an IRA and was informed the following year by the trustee of the qualified retirement plan that the individual's benefits had been erroneously overvalued, IRS ruled that the amount distributed to the individual to repay the employer would not be includible in the individual's income. [Ltr Rul 9118020]

If a distribution from an IRA is premature, the amount distributed is taxed as ordinary income and a penalty tax may be imposed (see Q 26:39). [IRC § 72(t)] IRA distributions are also subject to the penalty tax on excess distributions (see Q 13:27). A distribution from an IRA is not taxable if there is a valid rollover of the distribution to another IRA, or to the same IRA (see Qs 28:3, 28:4).

The payment of a fee directly from the IRA to a company for services in connection with transferring IRA assets between mutual funds is not a taxable distribution to the IRA owner. [Ltr Rul 8747072]

A disclaimer of IRA benefits by the beneficiary of a deceased IRA owner that satisfies the requirements of state law and the Code is not an assignment of income, does not violate the nonforfeitability requirement (see Q 26:2) or the nontransferability requirement (see Q 26:3), and will be taxable to the actual recipient and not to the disclaiming beneficiary. [GCM 39858; IRC §§ 408(a)(4), 408(b)(1), 2518(b)]

Q 26:35   Are amounts remaining in an IRA at death subject to federal estate taxes?

The entire amount in the IRA is included in the decedent's gross estate. [IRC § 2039] Amounts accumulated in a decedent's IRA as of the date of death may be subject to the 15 percent excise tax on excess retirement accumulations (see Q 14:21).

An IRA may constitute qualified terminable interest property (QTIP) for which an estate tax marital deduction may be elected (see Q 14:20). IRS has allowed a QTIP election when all IRA income is paid to a QTIP trust that, in turn, pays out all such income received from the IRA, plus all trust income, to the surviving spouse annually during her lifetime. IRS also allowed a QTIP election for an IRA that pays the greater of all IRA income or the required minimum distribution (see Q 26:38) to a QTIP trust that then pays an amount equal to the IRA income and all trust income to the surviving spouse. [IRC § 2056(b)(7); Rev Rul 89-89, 1989-2 CB 231; Ltr Ruls 9322005, 9321035, 9321032, 9204017, 9038015]

Q 26:36   What is an inherited IRA?

An IRA becomes an inherited IRA after the death of the IRA owner unless the beneficiary is the IRA owner's surviving spouse. The non-spouse beneficiary cannot make a tax-deductible contribution to an inherited IRA, and distributions from an inherited IRA do not qualify for rollover treatment. If a trust is named as beneficiary of an IRA, the IRA will be an inherited IRA even if the surviving spouse is the sole trust beneficiary; and, since an inherited IRA cannot be rolled over, distributions from the IRA will be taxable to the beneficiary. (See Q 26:38 for the applicable minimum distribution requirements.) [IRC §§ 219(d)(4), 408(d)(3)(C); Ltr Ruls 9322005, 9321032; Rev Rul 92-47, 1992-1 CB 198]

Q 26:37   Do special rules apply if the beneficiary is the IRA owner's surviving spouse?

Yes. A surviving spouse who inherits an IRA from a deceased spouse can elect to treat the IRA as that of the surviving spouse. In that event, the surviving spouse can make contributions to the IRA, and the minimum distribution requirements during the surviving spouse's lifetime (see Q 26:32) and after the surviving spouse's death (see Q 26:38) apply exactly as if the surviving spouse were the original owner of the IRA. The surviving spouse may make such election even if the deceased spouse had started taking distributions from the IRA. However, if the surviving spouse dies before the election is made, the surviving spouse's estate cannot make the election. [IRC § 408(d)(3); Prop Reg § 1.408-8, Q&A A-4; Ltr Rul 9237038]

Alternatively, a surviving spouse who is the beneficiary of a deceased spouse's IRA may roll the IRA distribution into the surviving spouse's own IRA. Such rollover was allowed when the deceased spouse named his estate as beneficiary of his IRA, and his surviving spouse was the sole beneficiary of the estate. [IRC § 402(c)(9); Ltr Ruls 9010084, 9006050, 8842058]

Q 26:38 What minimum distribution requirements apply after the IRA owner's death?

Generally, the minimum distribution rules applicable to qualified retirement plans apply to distributions from IRAs (see Qs 11:5, 11:7). [IRC §§ 408(a)(6), 408(b)(3)]

Thus, if a decedent who died after the required beginning date (see Q 11:3) had been receiving lifetime distributions, post-death distributions must be made at least as rapidly as under the lifetime distribution method. [IRC § 401(a)(9)(B)(i); Ltr Rul 9119067] If distributions had not begun or had begun but before the required beginning date, the IRA must be distributed in one of two methods:

1. The entire IRA must be distributed by December 31 of the year that includes the fifth anniversary of the decedent's death; or

2. Distributions may be made over a period not extending beyond the life expectancy of the designated beneficiary if distributions begin by December 31 of the year that includes the first anniversary of the decedent's death.

[IRC §§ 401(a)(9)(B)(ii), 401(a)(9)(B)(iii); Ltr Ruls 9322005, 9253052, 9106044]

If the designated beneficiary is the surviving spouse, distribution may be deferred until the decedent would have reached age 70½. Alternatively, the surviving spouse may choose to treat the IRA as that of the surviving spouse (see Q 26:37). [IRC § 401(a)(9)(B)(iv)]

For details on minimum distribution requirements, see Chapter 11.

Q 26:39 What is the penalty imposed on a premature distribution from an IRA?

A distribution from an IRA before the individual for whose benefit the IRA was established reaches age 59½ is subject to a 10 percent penalty tax (i.e., the tax is increased by an amount equal to 10 percent of the amount includible in gross income). The penalty tax does not apply, however, if an early distribution is made because of the IRA owner's death or disability. [IRC § 72(t); Ltr Ruls 9106044, 9043063]

To come within the exception for disability:

1. The individual must be unable to engage in any substantial gainful activity due to a medically determinable physical or mental impairment;
2. The disability must be expected to result in death or be of a long-continued and indefinite duration; and
3. The individual must furnish proof of the disability in the form and manner required by IRS.

[IRC § 72(m)(7); Treas Reg § 1.72-17A(f); Kovacevic, 64 TCM 1076 (1992); Kane, 63 TCM 2753 (1992); Ltr Ruls 9318043, 9249034]

In addition, the penalty tax does not apply if the payment is part of a series of substantially equal periodic payments (not less frequently than annually) made over the life (or life expectancy) of the IRA owner or the joint lives (or joint life expectancy) of the IRA owner and the owner's designated beneficiary (see Qs 13:39, 13:40). However, if the amount of the periodic payments is modified (other than by reason of death or disability) before the later of (1) the end of the five-year period beginning with the date of the first payment, or (2) the owner's attainment of age 59½, the penalty tax that would have been imposed on all payments, plus interest, is imposed (see Q 13:41). IRS has provided acceptable methods of calculating substantially equal periodic payments. [Notice 89-25, 1989-1 CB 662, Q&A 12; Ltr Ruls 9312035, 9253053, 9241063, 9240042, 9231048, 9217048, 9152045, 9152044, 9152041, 9104020]

An individual with more than one IRA can take periodic payments from one IRA without taking periodic payments from the others. Also, the account balances of the other IRAs are not considered in calculating the amount of the periodic payment from the distributing IRA. [Ltr Ruls 9243054, 9050030, 8946045]

Q 26:40   May an IRA be transferred incident to divorce?

Yes. A transfer of an individual's interest in an IRA to the individual's spouse or former spouse under a divorce decree or a written instrument incident to the divorce is not a taxable distribution or transfer (see Q 30:5). After the transfer, the transferred interest is treated as the IRA of the transferee spouse or former spouse. [IRC § 408(d)(6); Ltr Rul 9006066] However, if funds are withdrawn from an IRA and paid over to the former spouse by the IRA owner to satisfy a divorce decree, the withdrawal will be taxable to the IRA owner. [Harris, 62 TCM 406 (1991)]

When a decedent had designated his wife as the beneficiary of his IRA and failed to change the beneficiary after their divorce, the court ruled that the ex-spouse released her interest in the IRA when she executed a divorce settlement agreement stating that any IRAs were the sole and exclusive property of the depositor. [Kruse v Todd, Nos. S89A0554 and S89A0555 (Ga Sup Ct 1990)] However, another court ruled otherwise because the settlement agreement contained only a general waiver provision and did not express a specific intention to surrender any rights as the beneficiary of the IRA. [Maccabees Mutual Life Ins Co v Morton, No. 90-8618 (11th Cir 1991)]

Q 26:41   Can an IRA be reached by judgment creditors?

It depends on state law because ERISA does not apply to IRAs. Some courts have ruled that an IRA can be reached by all judgment creditors because the money deposited in the IRA is (1) contributed voluntarily, (2) set aside for the depositor's own benefit, (3) subject to the depositor's control, and (4) the IRA is revocable at will. Additionally, some courts will consider the special needs of the depositor. [In re Brewer, No. 92-25198-BM (Bankr WD Pa 1993); In re Huebner, No. C 91-3067 (ND Ia 1992); Velis v Kardanis, 949 F 2d 78 (3rd Cir 1991); In re Swenson, No. 90A-04222 (Bankr D Utah 1991); In re Damast, No. 90-1815 (Bankr D NH 1991); In re Kramer, No. 190-12067-260 (ED NY 1991); In re Iacono, 120 BR 691 (ED NY 1990); In re Ree, No. 89-00723-W (ND Okla 1990); In re Lownsberry, No. 89-B-07144-J (DC Col 1989); Schoneman v Schoneman, No. 62-852 (Kans Ct of App 1989); In re Gillett, 46 BR 642 (SD Fla 1985); In re Montavon, 52 BR 99 (D Minn 1985)]

Conversely, other courts have ruled that an IRA is exempt property under state law. [In re Walker, No. 90-5171 (10th Cir 1992); In re Templeton, Jr, No. 92 B04870 (Bankr ND Ill 1992); In re Kulp, No. 90-1190 (10th Cir 1991); Reliance Ins Co v Ziegler, Nos. 90-1628, 90-1799, and 90-2068 (7th Cir 1991); In the Matter of Volpe, No. 90-8496 (5th Cir 1991); In re Suarez, No. 90-18947 BKC-AJC (Bankr SD Fla 1991); In re Shumaker, 124 BR 820 (Bankr D Mont 1991); In re Volpe, 120 BR 843 (Bankr WD Tex 1990); In re Galvin, No. 89-21638-7 (D Kan 1990); In re Herrscher, No. B-88-07650-PHX-RGM (D Ariz 1990); In re Ewell, No. 89-1736-8P7 (BR MD Fla 1989); In re Maitin, No. 3-88-02890 (BR ED Tenn 1989); In re Laxson, 102 BR 85 (ND Tex 1989)]

One court ruled that a rollover IRA (see Q 28:33) was exempt from execution by judgment creditors under state law because ERISA does not apply to IRAs and the state elected to opt out of the federal scheme. [In re Mann, No. 889-92426 (ED NY 1992); NY CPLR § 5205(c)] At least one court ruled that even though an IRA is not exempt from bankruptcy, the portion of the IRA attributable to a rollover from a qualified retirement plan retained its exempt status. [In the Matter of Woods, 59 Bankr 221 (WD Wis 1986)]

Another court has held that an IRA, upon the depositor's death, passed directly to the named beneficiary and did not become part of the deceased depositor's estate subject to the claims of creditors. [Estate of Davis, 6 EBC 2491, No. A024159 (Cal Apps Ct 1985)]

Q 26:42 What are the IRA reporting requirements?

The reporting requirements by IRA trustees apply to contributions to and distributions from IRAs, even if the IRA is revoked. Thus, Form 5498 (Individual Retirement Arrangement Information) must be filed to report a contribution to an IRA even if the IRA is later revoked. An exception is made for amounts transferred from one IRA to another IRA. In this case, the transferor IRA trustee will generally have reported an IRA contribution on Form 5498 when the IRA was established (and when additional contributions were made). Therefore, the transferee IRA trustee should not file a Form 5498 upon the establishment of the transferred IRA.

In addition, Form 1099-R (Distribution From Pensions, Annuities, Retirement or Profit Sharing Plans, IRAs, Insurance Contracts, etc.) must be filed for all distributions even on account of revocation. Distributions should be reported as taxable in the year distributed.

Form 5498 is used both to report any contributions made to an IRA and to report the fair market value of any IRA balance as of December 31 of the tax year. In addition, the IRA trustee is required to report the fair market value of the IRA as of December 31 to the IRA owner by the following January 31. Generally, if the fair market value of the IRA is zero on December 31, no reporting of the fair market value is required. However, the IRA trustee may still be required to file a Form 5498 to report any contribution made for the year.

If both an IRA contribution and revocation of the IRA occur in the same calendar year, the contribution must be reported. The fair market value on December 31 need not be reported because the account balance is zero on that day. However, if the IRA is revoked in the year after it is established, both the contribution and the fair market value must be reported. [Rev Proc 91-70, 1991-2 CB 899; IRC §§ 408(i), 6047(d)]

Chapter 27

Simplified Employee Pensions

Complex and burdensome rules may cause the owner of a small business to think twice before adopting a qualified retirement plan. But then both the company and the owner forgo significant tax benefits. The simplified employee pension (SEP) offers a practical alternative with respect to the institution of a retirement program. Requirements for establishing and maintaining a SEP are explained in this chapter.

Q 27:1   What is a simplified employee pension?

A SEP is an individual retirement account or individual retirement annuity (IRA) established for an employee to which the employer makes direct tax-deductible contributions. [IRC § 408(k)]

For a discussion on IRAs, see Chapter 26.

Q 27:2   Who is eligible to participate in a SEP?

Each employee age 21 or over who, for 1993, earns at least $385 during the year (adjusted for cost-of-living increases) and has performed services for the employer in at least three of the immediately preceding five calendar years must participate in the SEP. Employees covered by a collective bargaining agreement in which retirement benefits were the subject of good-faith bargaining and employees who are nonresident aliens may be excluded from participation. All employees, including part-time employees, not excluded under one of the above statutory exclusions must participate in the SEP. [IRC § 408(k)(2); Prop § 1.408-7(d); IR 93-2 (Jan 15, 1993)]

> **Example.** JTS Corporation, a calendar year corporation, maintains a SEP. Mindy commenced employment on October 1, 1990. Mindy worked 250 hours in 1990 and 900 hours each year in 1991, 1992, and 1993. If Mindy is at least age 21 and earns $385 or more, she must participate in the SEP in 1993.

The compensation requirement amount of $385 for 1993 has been adjusted for inflation and was initially $300. [IRC § 408(k)(2)(C)] For prior years, the adjusted amount was:

Year	Adjusted Amount
1992	$374
1991	$363
1990	$342
1989	$327
1988	$313

Contributions must be made on behalf of all employees who meet the participation requirements during the calendar year, whether or not they are employed as of a particular date. [Prop Reg § 1.408-7(d)(3)]

Contributions must also be made on behalf of eligible employees over age 70½, even though the employees may already have started to receive required distributions from the SEP and may not make contributions to their own IRAs (see Chapter 11 and Q 26:4). [IRC § 219(b)(2)]

For purposes of participation in a SEP, the rules regarding controlled businesses, affiliated service groups, and leased employees are applicable (see Qs 5:30, 5:48, 29:31). [IRC §§ 414(b), 414(c), 414(m)(4), 414(n)(3); Ltr Rul 9026056]

Q 27:3   Does the prohibition against discrimination in favor of highly compensated employees apply to a SEP?

Yes. A SEP may not discriminate in favor of highly compensated employees (see Q 3:2). Contributions must bear a uniform relationship to the compensation of each employee. However, the amount of employee compensation that may be taken into account in computing the employer's annual contribution in 1993 may not exceed $235,840 (adjusted for cost-of-living increases; see Q 6:3 regarding the compensation limit for prior years). [IRC § 408(k)(3); IR 93-2 (Jan 15, 1993)]

> **Example.** In 1993, Jill Corporation has three employees: the business owner earning $300,000 and two other employees earning $20,000 each. Since all three employees meet the eligibility requirements and the SEP may take into account only the first $235,840 of compensation paid to an employee, only $275,840 ($235,840 plus $40,000) would be counted for purposes of determining the amount of the contribution to the SEP. Assuming Jill Corporation wants to contribute the maximum amount allowed on behalf of the owner (see Q 27:6), it must use a 12.72 percent formula for its contribution. The contribution on behalf of the owner would be $30,000 (12.72% × $235,840), and the contribution for the other two employees would be $2,544 each (12.72% × $20,000).

If the SEP is top-heavy, the employer contributions on behalf of each eligible non-key employee must generally be at least 3 percent of compensation. [IRC §§ 408(k)(1)(B), 416(c)(2), 416(e)] For details on top-heavy plans, see Chapter 22.

For benefits accruing in plan years beginning *after* December 31, 1993, the amount of employee compensation on which SEP contributions may be based will be reduced from $200,000 to $150,000 (see Qs 6:21, 6:22). In addition, the cost-of-living adjustment will be made only if the adjustment is $10,000 or greater, and then will be made in multiples of $10,000 (i.e., rounded down, to the next lowest multiple of $10,000). For example, an increase in the cost of living of $9,999 will result in no adjustment and an increase of $19,999 will create an upward adjustment of $10,000. [RRA '93, Act § 13212]

Q 27:4 May a SEP provide for permitted disparity?

Yes. The permitted disparity (or integration) rules applicable to defined contribution plans also apply to employer contributions to SEPs. These rules permit a limited disparity between the contribution percentages applicable to compensation below and above the Social Security taxable wage base. [IRC §§ 401(l)(2), 408(k)(3)(D)] For details on permitted disparity, see Chapter 7.

A SEP will not be considered discriminatory if the contribution percentage for compensation in excess of the Social Security taxable wage base does not exceed the contribution percentage for compensation below the taxable wage base by more than the lesser of (1) the contribution percentage for compensation below the wage base or (2) the greater of (a) 5.7 percentage points or (b) the percentage equal to the rate of tax attributable to the old age insurance portion of the Old-Age, Survivors, and Disability Insurance (OASDI) as of the beginning of the plan year (see Question 7:7 regarding the taxable wage base for prior years).

Example. Sharon Corporation establishes a SEP for the 1993 calendar year. The SEP provides that each participant will receive an allocation of 5 percent of compensation up to the taxable wage base ($57,600 in 1993) and 10.7 percent of compensation in excess of the taxable wage base. The SEP does not meet the permitted disparity requirements because the contribution percentage for compensation in excess of the taxable wage base (10.7 percent) exceeds the contribution percentage for compensation below the taxable wage base by more than 5 percentage points. However, if the excess contribution percentage was reduced to 10 percent, the plan would meet the permitted disparity requirements.

Q 27:5 Are contributions made to a SEP on an employee's behalf forfeitable?

No. Employer contributions under a SEP must fully vest when made and are nonforfeitable. Employers may not condition any contribution to a SEP on the employee's retaining any portion of the contribution in the account and may not prohibit withdrawals from a SEP. The employee may take a distribution from the SEP at any time and at the employee's discretion, but the distribution must then be included in income (see Q 27:18). [IRC § 408(k)(4)]

Q 27:6   How much may be contributed to an employee's IRA through a SEP?

The employer's annual contribution to a SEP on behalf of each employee is limited to the lesser of (1) 15 percent of the employee's compensation (not including the SEP contribution) or (2) $30,000 (or, if greater, one-quarter of the dollar limitation in effect for defined benefit plans; see Q 6:2). If the employer's contribution exceeds the above limitation, the excess contribution is includible in the employee's income and regarded as having been contributed by the employee to the IRA under the SEP. [IRC § 402(h)(2)]

A 6 percent excise tax is imposed on an excess contribution to an IRA, and this tax is applicable to SEPs. [IRC § 4973]

The employee may contribute an additional $2,000 to a personal IRA even though the employee is a participant in a SEP. However, for the purpose of determining the deductibility of the IRA contribution, the employee will be considered an active participant because of the employee's participation in the SEP (see Q 26:9). [IRC §§ 219(g)(5)(A)(v), 408(j); Notice 87-16, 1987-1 CB 446]

The maximum contribution to a SEP on behalf of an employee will be reduced, for 1994 (see Q 27:3), to $22,500 (15% × $150,000).

Q 27:7   How much can an employer deduct for contributions to a SEP?

Subject to the $30,000 annual addition limitation for each employee (see Q 27:6), the employer may deduct no more than 15 percent of the total compensation (see Q 12:14) paid to all participating employees during the calendar year ending with or within the employer's taxable year (or during the taxable year in the case of a SEP maintained on the basis of the employer's taxable year). [IRC § 404(h)(1)(C)]

An excess contribution is deductible in succeeding taxable years in order of time, subject to the 15 percent limitation. If the employer maintains both a SEP and a profit sharing plan, the deduction limitation for the profit sharing plan contribution is reduced by the amount of the allowable deduction for the SEP contribution with respect to the participants in such plan. [IRC § 404(h)(2)]

Q 27:8   When are contributions to a SEP deductible?

Contributions to a SEP are deductible:

1. In the case of a SEP maintained on a calendar-year basis, for the taxable year within which the calendar year ends; or
2. In the case of a SEP maintained on the basis of the taxable year of the employer (that is not a calendar year), for such taxable year.

[IRC § 404(h)(1)(A)]

The contribution must be made no later than the due date of the employer's return for the taxable year (including extensions). [IRC § 404(h)(1)(B)]

Q 27:9   Which employers may adopt salary reduction SEPs?

An employer that has fewer than 26 employees who were eligible to participate at any time during the preceding calendar year may establish a SEP whereby each employee is permitted to elect to have contributions made to the SEP or to receive the contributions in cash under procedures similar to a 401(k) plan. At least 50 percent of the eligible employees of the employer must elect to defer part of their compensation to the SEP. [IRC § 408(k)(6)] For details on 401(k) plans, see Chapter 23.

A state or local government or a tax-exempt organization may not maintain a salary reduction SEP. [IRC § 408(k)(6)(E); Ltr Rul 9030014]

If TSB '93 is enacted (see Q 1:13), employers with less than 101 eligible employees will be permitted to establish a salary reduction SEP and the requirement that 50 percent of eligible employees elect to defer part of their compensation will be eliminated. These changes will be effective for years beginning *after* December 31, 1993. [TSB '93, Act § 211]

Q 27:10   What are the limits on elective deferrals to a SEP?

Elective deferrals under a SEP are treated like elective deferrals under a 401(k) plan and are subject to an annual $7,000 limitation for an employee. The $7,000 amount is adjusted for cost-of-living increases; and, for 1993, the maximum deferral amount has been increased to $8,994 (see Q 23:26 regarding the adjusted amount for prior years). [IRC §§ 401(a)(30), 402(g), 408(k)(6)(A)(iv); IR 93-2 (Jan 15, 1993)]

Q 27:11   Is there a special nondiscrimination test for salary reduction SEPs?

Yes. Under a salary reduction SEP, the deferral percentage for each highly compensated employee (see Q 3:3) cannot exceed 125 percent of the average deferral percentage for all eligible nonhighly compensated employees (see Q 3:13). The deferral percentage for an employee for a year is the ratio of: (1) the amount of elective employer contributions actually paid over to the SEP on behalf of the employee for the year to (2) the employee's compensation for the year. [IRC §§ 408(k)(6)(A)(iii), 408(k)(6)(D)]

The above calculation is different from the calculation applicable to a 401(k) plan (see Qs 23:8, 23:9). Under a 401(k) plan, after the actual deferral percentage (ADP) is calculated separately for each employee, the *average* of the ADP for all highly compensated employees cannot exceed 125 percent of the average of the ADP for all nonhighly compensated employees. Also, an alternative test is available under a 401(k) plan. If the average ADP for highly compensated employees does not exceed the average ADP for nonhighly compensated employees multiplied by 2, and the average ADP for highly compensated employees does not exceed the average ADP for the nonhighly compensated employees by more than two percentage points, then the ADP test will be satisfied even if the first test is not satisfied.

Example. L&S Corporation establishes a salary reduction SEP. The deferral percentage for each highly compensated employee equals 5.5 percent. The average deferral percentage for the non-highly compensated employees equals 4 percent. The special nondiscrimination test is not satisfied because 5.5 percent is greater than 5 percent (125% x 4%). If the salary reduction SEP was a 401(k) plan, the requirement would be met because 5.5 percent does not exceed 4 percent by more than two percentage points and 5.5 percent is less than 4 percent multiplied by 2.

Q 27:12   How is a SEP established?

Generally, any employer may establish a SEP. SEPs are available to both C and S corporations, partnerships, and sole proprietorships. In order to establish a SEP, the employer must execute a written instrument within the time prescribed for making deductible contributions. This instrument must include the name of the employer, the participation requirements, the allocation formula, and the signature of a responsible official. [IRC § 408(k)(5); Prop Reg § 1.408-7(b)]

The SEP may be set up in one of three ways:

1. By executing Form 5305-SEP or Form 5305A-SEP in the case of a salary reduction SEP (see Q 27:9);
2. By a master or prototype plan for which a favorable opinion letter has been issued; or
3. By an individually designed plan.

Q 27:13   When may an employer use a model SEP?

IRS has designed a model SEP agreement to be used by employers wishing to implement SEPs with relatively little paperwork. This is done by completing Form 5305-SEP or 5305A-SEP for salary reduction SEPs. The form is not filed with IRS but is retained by the employer and distributed to all participating employees. This fulfills the employer's reporting and disclosure obligations relating to the adoption of the agreement and also satisfies the notification requirements. However, a model SEP may not be used:

1. By an employer currently maintaining another qualified retirement plan.
2. By an employer that has ever maintained a defined benefit plan (even if it has been subsequently terminated).
3. By members of an affiliated service group, a controlled group of corporations, or trades or businesses under common control, unless all eligible employees of all members participate in the SEP.
4. By an employer that uses the services of leased employees.

5. If any eligible employee has not established an IRA.
6. If the contribution formula considers permitted disparity.
7. By an employer with no nonhighly compensated employees (this applies only to a salary reduction SEP).

To adopt a model SEP or model salary reduction SEP, the plan must be maintained on a calendar-year basis. [See Instructions to Forms 5305-SEP and 5305A-SEP]

Use of a nonmodel SEP requires the employer to distribute certain other summaries regarding the SEP. Once an employee becomes eligible to participate in the SEP, the employer must furnish certain specific information to the employee including an explanation of participation requirements, the formula allocating employer contributions, the name of the person designated to supply any additional SEP information, and an explanation of the terms of the IRA accepting the SEP contribution.

Q 27:14   Can a dissolved partnership's SEP be continued by its successor sole proprietors?

No. A SEP adopted by a partnership is not considered a plan covering its employees after the partnership is dissolved, even though the former partners continue to operate the same business as sole proprietors. A sole proprietor must adopt a new SEP in order to continue making deductible contributions for the employees. [Ltr Rul 8450051]

Q 27:15   What are the annual reporting requirements of a SEP?

Once a SEP is established, there is limited annual reporting to both IRS and participants. There is no requirement that the employer file the Form 5500 series for the SEP (see Q 17:1). The trustee or issuer of the IRA is required to furnish annual information regarding contributions to the SEP and the fair market value of assets in the SEP. For this purpose, Form 5498 must be filed with IRS by May 31. [Prop Reg § 1.408-5]

The information on Form 5498 must also be supplied to the participants. The employer maintaining the SEP must notify each participant of the SEP contribution made on the employee's behalf on Form W-2 by the later of January 31 following the contribution year or 30 days after the contribution. [IRC § 408(l); Prop Reg § 1.408-9]

Q 27:16 Are SEP contributions taxable to the employee?

No. Both employer contributions and employee elective deferrals under the SEP are excludable from the employee's gross income. [IRC § 402(h)]

Notwithstanding the exclusion from gross income, SEP contributions made under a salary reduction agreement are subject to the Federal Insurance Contributions Act (FICA) and the Federal Unemployment Taxes Act (FUTA) taxes, but SEP contributions under a nonsalary reduction arrangement are not subject to such taxes. [IRC §§ 3121(a)(5)(C), 3306(b)(5)(C)]

Q 27:17 How are SEP assets managed?

The assets of a SEP are managed by a financial institution and not by individual trustees, although the employee may be permitted to direct the investment of the employee's account. The SEP must be established with a bank, thrift institution, insurance company, brokerage firm, or other entity that is eligible to be an IRA custodian. Each individual who participates in the SEP may set up or use a personal IRA for investment purposes. If the participant does not have an IRA, the employer *must* establish one for the participant.

Similar to an individual's personal IRA, the participant may make trustee-to-trustee transfers and change the investment manager of the SEP. Since IRA rules govern the types of investments in a SEP, SEP assets cannot be loaned to participants or invested in life insurance contracts, collectibles, or any other assets in which IRAs may not invest (see Qs 26:2, 26:23). [IRC §§ 408(a)(3), 408(e)(4), 408(m)]

Q 27:18 How are distributions from a SEP taxed?

Generally, the same rules that apply to IRA distributions apply to distributions from a SEP. Distributions from a SEP are includible in ordinary income in the year received; and, as with an IRA, favorable tax elections (e.g., special averaging) are not available for distributions from a SEP.

If a withdrawal from a SEP is premature (that is, a distribution is made before the individual reaches age 59½, becomes disabled, or dies) the amount withdrawn, in addition to ordinary income tax, is subject to a 10 percent penalty tax. Similar to distributions from an IRA, an exception to the 10 percent penalty tax exists if the individual receives a distribution from the SEP in substantially equal periodic payments (see Q 26:39). [IRC §§ 72(t)(1), 72(t)(2)(A)(iv)]

Distributions from a SEP must begin no later than the April 1st of the calendar year following the year in which the participant reaches age 70½. If the required minimum distribution is not made, a penalty tax is imposed equal to 50 percent of the amount by which such minimum required distribution exceeds the actual amount distributed during the taxable year (see Q 26:32). [IRC §§ 401(a)(9), 4974(a)]

If the employee has at any time made nondeductible IRA contributions, the amount includible in income upon a distribution from a SEP is determined in accordance with an allocation formula (see Q 26:17). [IRC §§ 402(h)(3), 408(d)]

The assets of a decedent's SEP are included in the decedent's gross estate. [IRC § 2039]

The 15 percent excise tax on excess distributions from qualified retirement plans and excess accumulations upon the employee's death is also applicable to SEPs (see Qs 13:27, 13:43). [IRC § 4980A]

Q 27:19 How may assets be moved from a SEP without penalty?

An employee may wish to move funds from an IRA under the SEP to another IRA for higher interest rates, different investment alternatives, or more favorable withdrawal and transfer terms. Similar to IRAs, there are two ways to move assets from the SEP without penalty. One method is through a rollover, whereby the employee withdraws all or part of the amount from the SEP account and rolls over that amount to another IRA, or even the same IRA, within 60 days. Assets withdrawn, but not timely rolled over, will be included in the employee's income and may be subject to penalty taxes. Also, such rollovers may not be made more frequently than once every 12 months; otherwise, the subsequent rollover will be included in the employee's income and may be subject to penalty taxes. [IRC § 408(d)(3)]

The second, and more advisable, way to move funds from an IRA under a SEP to another IRA is through a trustee-to-trustee transfer of funds. Under this method, the employee directs the trustee of the IRA to transfer the IRA funds directly to the trustee of a second IRA. There are no restrictions on the number of trustee-to-trustee transfers that may be made to or from a SEP.

For more details, see Chapter 28.

Q 27:20   May a distribution from a qualified retirement plan be rolled over into a SEP?

Yes. If, within 60 days after receipt, a participant rolls over an eligible rollover distribution (see Q 28:8) from a qualified retirement plan to an IRA funded as a SEP, the rollover amount will not be includible in income. [IRC § 402(c); Ltr Rul 8630068]

However, if a participant wishes to retain the ability to roll the distribution back into another qualified retirement plan, a conduit IRA must be used (see Q 28:36).

Q 27:21   What advantages does a SEP offer to the business owner?

The greatest advantage a SEP offers over qualified retirement plans is the minimal amount of paperwork and bookkeeping necessary to start and maintain the plan. Costs for consultants (lawyers, accountants, or actuaries) are sharply reduced, possibly even eliminated. Another advantage of a SEP is the flexibility it affords with respect to contributions. The employer can contribute any amount it wishes, up to a maximum set by law (see Q 27:6), or it can choose not to make any contribution at all. Although this is generally true for profit sharing plans also, it is not true for pension plans. Furthermore, a SEP may be established after the end of the employer's taxable year.

Q 27:22   What are the drawbacks to the adoption of a SEP?

Eligibility rules for a SEP tend to be less restrictive than the rules for qualified retirement plans, and this can increase the employer's costs. Many of the employees who need not be covered under a qualified retirement plan must be covered under a SEP. For example, a SEP must include part-time and seasonal workers, regardless of how few hours they worked during the year (assuming they satisfy the compensation requirement and have worked for the employer in at least three of the previous five years; see Q 27:2).

Another drawback to a SEP is that employees must be fully vested at all times (see Q 27:5). A qualified retirement plan does not operate this way; vesting can be gradually phased in to favor longer-term employees (see Chapter 9).

Also, although SEPs are subject to fewer reporting requirements, employers may not be aware of many of the rules applicable to SEPs. For example, the employer must determine which employees are eligible, who are highly compensated employees, and who are key employees. In addition, ADP and top-heavy tests may need to be performed. (See Qs 27:2, 27:3, 27:11.)

Furthermore, the extent to which assets in a SEP are protected from creditors may not be as great as under a qualified retirement plan (see Qs 26:41, 29:40, 29:41). In one case, the court allowed the assets in a SEP to be attached. Although, under state law, exemptions existed for qualified retirement plans and IRA rollover accounts, SEPs were not included in the list of exemptions. [European American Bank v H Frenkel, Ltd, 555 NYS 2d 1016 (1990)]

Chapter 28

Rollovers

It is possible to postpone payment of taxes on certain distributions from a qualified retirement plan by transferring (rolling over) all or part of the distribution to an individual retirement account (IRA) or to another qualified retirement plan. In addition, money contributed to one IRA can be withdrawn and transferred to another IRA without tax or penalty. This chapter examines how rollovers work and describes the tax advantages and drawbacks involved.

Q 28:1   What is a rollover?

A rollover is a tax-free transfer of cash or other property from a qualified retirement plan to an individual and then from the individual to another qualified retirement plan. There are two types of rollovers to an IRA. First, amounts may be transferred from one IRA to another. Second, amounts may be transferred from a qualified retirement plan to an IRA. A rollover from one qualified retirement plan to another is also possible, as is a rollover to a qualified retirement plan from an IRA if all amounts in the IRA are attributable to an earlier rollover contribution from a qualified retirement plan (see Q 28:36). However, an individual cannot roll over a distribution from a qualified retirement plan to an IRA of the individual's spouse. [IRC §§ 402(c), 408(d); Ltr Rul 9315031]

Q 28:2   What are IRA rollover accounts?

An IRA rollover account is an individual retirement plan to which certain distributions from a qualified retirement plan or from another individual retirement plan have been transferred. The transfer is on a tax-free basis. There is no dollar limit on the amount that may be transferred into an IRA rollover account. [IRC §§ 402(c)(2), 408(d)(3)]

A distribution from a qualified retirement plan may be rolled over to any type of individual retirement plan except an endowment contract (see Q 26:3). [IRC §§ 402(c)(8)(B)(i), 402(c)(8)(B)(ii)]

Nondeductible employee contributions to a qualified retirement plan that are included in the distribution may not be rolled over to an IRA. Instead, they are returned to the employee tax-free. Any distribution that represents a participant's investment in the contract or basis (see Q 13:2) may not be rolled over and is received tax-free. See Question 28:36 for details of a conduit IRA.

Q 28:3   How does a rollover from one IRA to another work?

All or part of the money contributed to a particular IRA may be withdrawn and transferred (rolled over) to another IRA without tax or penalty. This gives the IRA participant flexibility by enabling the participant to shift investments. For example, the participant may shift from one annuity IRA to another or, seeking higher interest or dividends, from one trusteed IRA to another.

To make the switch, certain requirements must be met. To qualify for a tax-free rollover:

1. The amount distributed to the individual from the old account must be transferred to the new account not later than 60 days after receipt.
2. If property, other than cash, is received from the old account, that same property must be transferred to the new account (although provision is made for a sale of the property and a rollover of the proceeds).
3. If a tax-free rollover of a particular IRA has been made during the preceding 12-month period, a second (tax-free) rollover

from that IRA is not permitted (see Q 28:5). [IRC § 408(d)(3)(B); Martin, 63 TCM 3122 (1992); Ltr Rul 8502044]

Example 1. On January 10, 1993, Paul received a first distribution from IRA X and, on January 21, 1993, deposited the distribution in IRA Y. Since Paul did not receive any distributions from IRA X during the preceding 12-month period, the rollover from IRA X to IRA Y is permitted.

Example 2. On January 28, 1993, Paul received a second distribution from IRA X and, on March 4, 1993, deposited this distribution in IRA Y. Even though the distribution was rolled over within the 60-day period, this rollover is *not* permitted because Paul received the *first* rollover distribution from IRA X within the preceding 12-month period. [Ltr Rul 9308050]

To avoid the adverse consequences resulting to Paul in Example 2, Paul could have had the funds in IRA X transferred directly to IRA Y (see Q 28:5).

Involuntary distributions made by the Resolution Trust Corporation from an IRA held in an insolvent financial institution may be rolled over to another IRA even if the amount had been rolled over to the IRA within the preceding 12-month period. [IRS Special Ruling, Feb 5, 1991]

Q 28:4 May an individual borrow from an IRA?

No, but IRS has ruled that the requirements for a valid rollover are met when an individual receives a distribution from an IRA and the distribution is redeposited in the same IRA within 60 days. Such a transaction will constitute a tax-free rollover and not be subject to the excess contribution limits (see Q 26:6). [IRC §§ 408(e), 4975(d); Ltr Ruls 9010007, 8826009]

Example. Susan has a $10,000 certificate of deposit (CD) maturing in 45 days. Susan has a $4,000 tuition payment due now and does not want to cash in the CD early. Susan withdraws $4,000 from her IRA and makes the tuition payment. When the CD matures, Susan immediately repays the $4,000 to her IRA. The withdrawal and redeposit are tax-free.

Q 28:5   May more than one tax-free transfer between IRAs be made during a 12-month period?

Yes, but only if the individual has the funds in an IRA transferred from the IRA *directly* to another IRA. Because this type of transfer is not considered a rollover, the 12-month waiting period (see Q 28:3) does not apply. [Ltr Ruls 9106044, 9034068; IRS Publication 590 (For use in preparing 1992 returns); see Martin, 63 TCM 3122 (1992); Ltr Rul 9308050]

Further, if the individual has more than one IRA, a separate 12-month waiting period applies for each IRA. [Prop Reg § 1.408-4(b)(4)(ii)]

Q 28:6   May a beneficiary of an IRA roll over the proceeds at the death of the owner of the IRA?

Yes, but only if the beneficiary is the surviving spouse of the IRA's owner. [IRC § 408(d)(3); Ltr Rul 9011035]

IRS has ruled that a surviving spouse may roll over funds received from the deceased spouse's IRA if the funds were paid to the surviving spouse under the laws of intestacy (i.e., the decedent died without a will) or as a beneficiary of the decedent's estate, rather than as the designated beneficiary of the IRA. [Ltr Ruls 9047065, 9034046, 9010084, 8842058]

IRS has also ruled that, if the deceased spouse's IRA is paid to a trust and the trust distributes the IRA funds to the surviving spouse, the surviving spouse may roll over the distribution. [Ltr Ruls 9302022, 9235058, 9234032, 9047060, 9016067, 8920045]

An IRA acquired by a beneficiary upon the death of a nonspouse is an inherited IRA and does not qualify for rollover treatment (see Q 26:36). [IRC § 408(d)(3)(C); Ltr Ruls 9305025, 9250040, 9014071, 8623054] IRS has ruled that a surviving spouse could *not* roll over an IRA distribution from a trust created by the deceased spouse. Because the surviving spouse had no discretionary control over the trust, the IRA was considered an inherited IRA, ineligible for rollover treatment. [Ltr Rul 9303031]

Q 28:7 What types of distributions from a qualified retirement plan may be rolled over?

For qualified retirement plan distributions made after 1992, only an eligible rollover distribution (see Q 28:8) may be rolled over. [IRC § 402(c)]

For qualified retirement plan distributions made before 1993, only a qualified total distribution or a partial distribution could be rolled over. For a discussion of qualified total distributions and partial distributions, see the *Pension Answer Book,* Eighth Edition, Chapter 27.

Q 28:8 What is an eligible rollover distribution?

An eligible rollover distribution is any distribution to an employee of all or any portion of the employee's qualified retirement plan benefit *except:*

1. A required minimum distribution (see Q 28:11);
2. A distribution which is one of a series of substantially equal periodic payments (at least annually) made (a) over the life or life expectancy of the employee or over the joint lives or joint life expectancy of the employee and the employee's beneficiary or (b) over a specified period of *ten* or more years;
3. The portion of any distribution that is not includible in gross income (determined without regard to the exclusion for net unrealized appreciation) (see Qs 13:2, 13:17);
4. Elective contributions (see Q 23:13) that are returned as a result of Section 415 limitations (see Q 23:26);
5. Corrective distributions of excess contributions (see Q 23:17) and excess deferrals (see Q 23:28) and corrective distributions of excess aggregate contributions (see Q 23:54), together with the income allocable to these corrective distributions;
6. Loans treated as taxable distributions (see Qs 28:12–28:14)
7. Loans in default that are deemed distributions (see Qs 28:12–28:14);
8. Dividends paid on ESOP employer securities (see Q 24:14); and

9. The costs of life insurance coverage (P.S. 58 costs; see Q 14:7).

[IRC § 402(c)(4); Temp Reg § 1.402(c)-2T, Q&A 3, Q&A 4]

An eligible rollover distribution is subject to automatic 20 percent withholding unless the distribution is transferred by a direct rollover (see Q 28:17) to an eligible retirement plan (see Q 28:16) that permits the acceptance of rollover distributions (see Q 16:7). To be a qualified retirement plan, the plan *must* provide that if the distributee of an eligible rollover distribution elects to have the distribution paid directly to an eligible retirement plan, and specifies the eligible retirement plan to which the distribution will be paid, then the distribution will be paid to that eligible retirement plan in a direct rollover. Thus, the plan *must* give the distributee the option of having the distribution paid in a direct rollover to an eligible retirement plan specified by the distributee. [IRC §§ 401(a)(31), 3405(c); Temp Reg §§ 1.401(a)(31)-1T, Q&A 1(a), 1.402(c)-2T, Q&A 1(a)]

Q 28:9   What is a series of substantially equal periodic payments?

One of the exceptions to the 10 percent penalty tax (see Q 13:39) is for a distribution that is part of a series of substantially equal periodic payments. To determine whether a series of payments is a series of substantially equal periodic payments, and therefore not an eligible rollover distribution (see Q 28:8), generally the same principles are followed (see Q 13:40). Whether the series is one of substantially equal periodic payments over a specified period of *ten* or more years is generally determined at the time payments begin without regard to contingencies or modifications that have not yet occurred. For example, a joint and survivor annuity with a 50 percent survivor annuity to the participant's spouse will be treated as a series of substantially equal payments at the time payments commence, as will a joint and survivor annuity that provides for increased payments to the participant if the participant's spouse dies before the participant. [IRC §§ 72(t)(2)(A)(iv); 402(c)(4)(A); Temp Reg § 1.402(c)-2T, Q&A 5(a)]

For purposes of determining whether a distribution is one of a series of payments that are substantially equal, Social Security supplements are disregarded. Similarly, a series of payments that is not substantially equal but that generally produces a series of substantially equal payments when expected Social Security payments are taken into account, is treated as substantially equal for purposes of determining whether a distribution is an eligible rollover distribution.

Example. Judy will receive a life annuity from the PJK Corp. pension plan of $500 per month, plus a Social Security supplement consisting of payments of $200 per month until Judy reaches the age at which Social Security benefits begin. The $200 supplemental payments are disregarded so that each monthly payment of $700 made before the Social Security age and each monthly payment of $500 made after the Social Security age will be treated as one of a series of substantially equal periodic payments for life. Therefore, each monthly payment to Judy will not be an eligible rollover distribution. [Temp Reg § 1.402(c)-2T, Q&A 5(b)]

If a series of periodic payments began before January 1, 1993, the determination of whether the post-December 31, 1992 payments are a series of substantially equal periodic payments over a specified period of *ten* or more years is made by taking into account all payments made, including payments made before January 1, 1993.

Example 1. Paul commenced receiving a series of substantially equal periodic payments on January 1, 1983, which were scheduled to be paid over a period of 15 years. Payments in the series that are made after December 31, 1992 will not be eligible rollover distributions even though they will continue for only five years after December 31, 1992, because the pre-January 1, 1993 payments are taken into account in determining the specified period. [Temp Reg § 1.402(c)-2T, Q&A 5(d)]

Example 2. If the series commenced on January 1, 1989 and were scheduled to be paid over six years, each payment made in the series after December 31, 1992 will be an eligible rollover distribution because the total specified period is less than ten years.

Q 28:10   If a payment is independent of a series of substantially equal periodic payments that are not eligible rollover distributions, can that payment be an eligible rollover distribution?

Yes. A payment is treated as independent of the payments in a series if the payment is substantially larger or smaller than the other payments in the series (see Q 28:9). An independent payment is an eligible rollover distribution (see Q 28:8) if it is not otherwise excepted from the definition of eligible rollover distributions. This is the case regardless of whether the payment is made before, with, or after payments in the series. [Temp Reg § 1.402(c)-2T, Q&A 6]

> **Example 1.** Bob elects a single payment of half of his account balance under The Gordons of Chappaqua, Inc. profit sharing plan, with the remainder of his account balance to be paid over his life expectancy. The single payment is treated as independent of the payments in the series and is an eligible rollover distribution unless otherwise excepted.

> **Example 2.** If a participant's surviving spouse receives a survivor life annuity of $1,000 per month plus a single payment of $5,000, the single payment is treated as independent of the annuity payments and is an eligible rollover distribution unless otherwise excepted.

If an annuity contract is purchased for a participant and distributed to the participant by a qualified retirement plan, amounts paid under the annuity contract may be eligible rollover distributions. For example, if the participant surrenders the contract for a single sum payment of its cash surrender value, the payment would be an eligible rollover distribution to the extent it is includible in gross income and not a required minimum distribution (see Q 28:11). This is true even if the annuity contract is distributed in connection with the termination of a qualified retirement plan (see Q 28:30). [Notice 93-26, 1993-18 IRB]

Q 28:11   When is a distribution from a plan a required minimum distribution?

A required minimum distribution is not an eligible rollover distribution (see Q 28:8). If a minimum distribution is required for a calendar year, all amounts distributed during that calendar year are treated as required minimum distributions as long as the total required minimum distribution for that calendar year has not been made. [Temp Reg § 1.402(c)-2T, Q&A 7(a)]

> **Example.** Linda is required to receive a minimum distribution from The Gordons of Chappaqua, Inc. profit sharing plan in 1993

of $21,000. During 1993, Linda receives four quarterly distributions of $7,500 each. The first two distributions and $6,000 of the third distribution are required minimum distributions. However, the remaining $1,500 of the third distribution and all of the fourth distribution are not required minimum distributions because these are the amounts by which the total of the distributions exceeds the required minimum distribution. [Notice 93-3, 1993-3 IRB 11]

If the total amount that is required to be distributed for a calendar year in order to satisfy the minimum distribution requirements is not distributed in that calendar year, the amount that was required but not distributed is added to the amount required to be distributed for the next calendar year in determining the portion of any distribution in the next calendar year that is a required distribution.

Example. Bob should have received, but did not receive, a minimum distribution in 1993 of $8,000. For 1994, Bob should receive a minimum distribution of $6,000. Bob's required minimum distribution for 1994 is $14,000.

For purposes of determining whether a distribution is an eligible rollover distribution, the plan administrator (see Q 16:1) is permitted to determine the amount of the required minimum distribution for a calendar year by assuming that there is no designated beneficiary (see Q 11:8). If the employee determines that the amount required to be distributed is less than the amount determined by the plan administrator (for example, by taking into account the beneficiary's life expectancy), the employee may roll over the difference to an eligible retirement plan (see Q 28:16). [Temp Reg § 1.402(c)-2T, Q&A 7(b)]

Proposed regulations issued by IRS in 1987 imply that annuity payments from a defined benefit plan (see Q 2:3) may be required minimum distributions even if annuity payments are made before the employee attains age 70½ and for a period of less than ten years (see Qs 11:4, 11:6). To clarify this issue, IRS has provided two rules:

1. Annuity payments made in or after the year in which the employee is (or would have been) 70½ are required minimum distributions and, hence, not eligible rollover distributions.

2. Annuity payments, as well as distributions from individual accounts, made before the year in which the employee is (or

would have been) 70½ are not required minimum distributions and, hence, are eligible rollover distributions.

[Notice 93-3, 1993-3 IRB 11]

For a detailed discussion of the minimum distribution requirements, see Chapter 11.

Q 28:12 How are participant loans treated?

Loans to a participant from a qualified retirement plan can give rise to two types of distributions:

1. A deemed distribution (see Qs 13:44–13:48), and

2. A distribution of an offset amount.

A deemed distribution occurs when certain requirements are not satisfied, either when the loan is made or at a later time, such as when the loan is in default. A deemed distribution is treated as a distribution to the participant only for income tax purposes and is not a distribution of the participant's accrued benefit (see Q 9:2).

A distribution of an offset amount occurs when the participant's accrued benefit is reduced (offset) in order to repay the loan. A distribution of an offset amount can occur in a variety of circumstances, such as where the plan requires that, in the event of the participant's termination of employment, a loan be repaid immediately or treated as in default. [Temp Reg § 1.402(c)-2T, Q&A 4, Q&A 8; Notice 93-3, 1993-3 IRB 11]

Q 28:13 When is a distribution attributable to a plan loan an eligible rollover distribution?

The only type of distribution related to a plan loan that cannot be an eligible rollover distribution (see Q 28:8) is a deemed distribution (see Q 28:12). In contrast, when a participant terminates employment and the participant's accrued benefit (see Q 9:2) is offset by the amount of an unpaid plan loan balance, the offset amount (see Q 28:12) can be an eligible rollover distribution (see Q 28:14).

An offset amount to repay a plan loan can be an eligible rollover distribution whether or not the offset occurs after the participant's employment has terminated. Similarly, an offset amount can be an eligible rollover distribution even if the offset occurs because the loan is accelerated or is treated as if it were in default (e.g., where the plan treats a loan as in default upon termination of employment or within a specified period thereafter). [Temp Reg § 1.402(c)-2T, Q&A 4, Q&A 8; Notice 93-3, 1993-3 IRB 11]

Q 28:14 Must a direct rollover option be provided for an offset amount that is an eligible rollover distribution?

A plan will *not* fail to satisfy the direct rollover requirement (see Q 28:8) merely because the plan does not permit a participant to elect a direct rollover (see Q 28:17) of an offset amount (see Q 28:12) that is an eligible rollover distribution (see Q 28:8). Nevertheless, the amount by which a participant's accrued benefit (see Q 9:2) is offset to repay a plan loan can be an eligible rollover distribution (see Q 28:13). Thus, an amount equal to the offset amount can be rolled over by the participant to an eligible retirement plan (see Q 28:16) within 60 days (see Q 28:33) unless the offset amount fails to be an eligible rollover distribution for another reason. [Notice 93-3, 1993-3 IRB 11]

Example 1. In 1993, Dale has an account balance of $10,000 in Stu 'N Dale Corporation's profit sharing plan, of which $3,000 is represented by a plan loan secured by her account balance. The plan does not provide any direct rollover option with respect to plan loans. Upon termination of employment in 1993, Dale, who is under age 70½, elects a distribution of her entire account balance, and her outstanding loan is offset against the account balance on distribution. Dale elects a direct rollover of $7,000. When Dale's account balance was offset by the amount of the $3,000 unpaid loan balance, she received an offset amount (equivalent to $3,000) that is an eligible rollover distribution. Dale may roll over $3,000 to an eligible retirement plan within 60 days.

Example 2. The facts are the same as in Example 1, except that the plan provides that, upon termination of employment, Dale's account balance is automatically offset by the amount of the unpaid loan balance. Dale terminates employment but does not request a distribution from the plan. The $3,000 offset amount attributable to the plan loan in this example is treated in the same manner as the $3,000 offset amount in Example 1.

Example 3. The facts are the same as in Example 2, except that, instead of providing for an automatic offset upon termination of employment, the plan requires full repayment of the loan by Dale within 30 days of termination. Dale terminates employment, does not elect a distribution from the plan, and also fails to repay the plan loan within 30 days. The plan declares the plan loan in default and executes on the loan by offsetting Dale's account balance by $3,000. The $3,000 offset amount in this example is treated in the same manner as the $3,000 offset amount in Examples 1 and 2. The result in this example is the same, even though the plan treats the loan as in default before offsetting Dale's accrued benefit by the amount of the unpaid loan.

Example 4. Stuart, who is age 50, has an account balance in the Lori–Dana Corp. 401(k) plan. In 1990, Stuart made a plan loan, which is secured by elective contributions; and, in 1993, Stuart stops repayment. In 1993, Stuart is taxed on a deemed distribution equal to the amount of the unpaid loan balance. The deemed distribution is *not* an eligible rollover distribution. Because Stuart has not separated from service or experienced any other event that permits the distribution of his elective contributions that secure the loan, the plan is prohibited from executing on the loan. Accordingly, Stuart's account balance is not offset by the amount of the unpaid loan balance at the time he stops repayment on the loan. Thus, there is no distribution of an offset amount that is an eligible rollover distribution in 1993. However, Stuart has basis (see Q 13:2) in his account balance to the extent of the deemed distribution. In 1994, Stuart separates from service and is eligible, and elects, to receive a total distribution of his account balance. As part of the distribution to Stuart, his account balance is offset by the amount of the unpaid loan balance. Although an offset amount can generally be part of an eligible rollover distribution, the portion of the distribution to Stuart that equals the amount of the prior deemed distribution will not be eligible for rollover because it is not includible in his gross income.

Q 28:15 Can a person other than an employee receive an eligible rollover distribution?

If a distribution attributable to an employee is paid to the employee's surviving spouse, the rollover rules apply to the distribution in the same manner as if the spouse were the employee. The same rules apply if a distribution is paid to a spouse or former spouse as an alternate payee (see Q 30:3) under a qualified domestic relations order (QDRO; see Q 30:1). Therefore, a distribution to the surviving spouse of an employee (or to a spouse or former spouse as an alternate payee under a QDRO) can be an eligible rollover distribution (see Q 28:8). However, a qualified retirement plan is *not* treated as an eligible retirement plan (see Q 28:16) with respect to the distribution to a surviving spouse; only an IRA is treated as an eligible retirement plan for the surviving spouse's eligible rollover distribution. [Temp Reg § 1.402(a)-2T, Q&A 10(a)]

Distributions from a qualified retirement plan to a distributee other than the employee or the employee's surviving spouse (or spouse or former spouse as an alternate payee under a QDRO) cannot be rolled over and, therefore, do not constitute eligible rollover distributions. [Temp Reg § 1.402(c)-2T, Q&A 10(b)]

Q 28:16 What is an eligible retirement plan?

For *regular* rollover purposes (see Q 28:1), an eligible retirement plan means an IRA or a qualified retirement plan. [IRC § 402(c)(8)(B); Temp Reg § 1.402(c)-2T, Q&A 2]

For *direct* rollover purposes (see Q 28:17), an eligible retirement plan means an IRA or a qualified defined contribution plan (see Q 2:2) but *not* a defined benefit plan (see Q 2:3). [IRC §§ 401(a)(31)(D), 402(c)(8)(B)] However, IRS has informally advised that a qualified retirement plan *must* permit direct rollovers to defined contribution plans and *may* permit direct rollovers to defined benefit plans that have employee contribution accounts. IRS noted that neither the model amendment (see Q 28:29) nor the Section 402(f) Notice (see Q 28:27) distinguishes between transfers to defined contribution or defined benefit plans.

An individual cannot roll over a distribution from a qualified retirement plan to an IRA of the individual's spouse because the spouse's IRA is not an eligible retirement plan. [Ltr Rul 9315031]

Q 28:17   What is a direct rollover?

A direct rollover is an eligible rollover distribution (see Q 28:8) that is paid directly to an eligible retirement plan (see Q 28:16) for the benefit of the distributee; i.e., the distribution is made in the form of a direct trustee-to-trustee transfer from a qualified retirement plan to the eligible retirement plan. [IRC § 401(a)(31); Temp Reg § 1.401(a)(31)-1T, Q&A 3]

A direct rollover may be accomplished by any reasonable means of direct payment to an eligible retirement plan. Reasonable means include a wire transfer or the mailing of a check to the eligible retirement plan. If the payment is made by wire transfer, the wire transfer must be directed only to the trustee of the eligible retirement plan. If payment is made by check, the check must be negotiable only by the trustee of the eligible retirement plan (see Q 28:18). In the case of an eligible retirement plan that does not have a trustee (e.g., an individual retirement annuity), the custodian of the plan or issuer of the contract under the plan, as appropriate, should be substituted for the trustee. [Temp Reg § 1.401(a)(31)-1T, Q&A 3]

Q 28:18   Is providing a distributee with a check for delivery to an eligible retirement plan a reasonable means of accomplishing a direct rollover?

Providing the distributee with a check and instructing the distributee to deliver the check to the eligible retirement plan (see Q 28:16) is a reasonable means of direct payment (see Q 28:15), *provided* that the check is made payable as follows: [Name of the trustee] as trustee of [name of eligible retirement plan]. For example, if the name of the eligible retirement plan is "Individual Retirement Account of Jack N. Jill" and the name of the trustee is "ABC Bank," the payee line of the check should read "ABC Bank as trustee of Individual Retirement Account of Jack N. Jill."

Unless the name of the distributee is included in the name of the eligible retirement plan, the check also must indicate that it is for the benefit of the distributee. If the eligible retirement plan is not an IRA, the payee line of the check need not identify the trustee by name and may read "Trustee of the XYZ Corporation Savings Plan FBO Jane Plane." [Temp Reg § 1.401(a)(3)-1T, Q&A 4]

Q 28:19   Is an eligible rollover distribution that is paid to an eligible retirement plan in a direct rollover includible in gross income?

No. An eligible rollover distribution (see Q 28:8) that is paid to an eligible retirement plan (see Q 28:16) in a direct rollover (see Q 28:17) is excludible from the distributee's gross income. However, when any portion of the eligible rollover distribution is subsequently distributed from the eligible retirement plan, that portion will be includible in gross income. [IRC § 402(c)(1); Treas Reg § 1.401(a)(31)-1T, Q&A 5]

Q 28:20   What procedures may a plan administrator prescribe for electing a direct rollover?

The plan administrator (see Q 16:1) may prescribe any reasonable procedure for a distributee to elect a direct rollover (see Q 28:17). The procedure may include any reasonable requirement for information or documentation from the distributee. For example, it would be reasonable for the plan administrator to require the distributee to provide a statement from the plan designated by the distributee that it is, or is intended to be, an IRA or a qualified retirement plan, and that it will accept the direct rollover for the benefit of the distributee. It would not be reasonable, however, for the plan administrator to require information or documentation or to establish procedures that effectively eliminate the distributee's ability to elect a direct rollover. For example, it would not be reasonable for the plan administrator to require the distributee to obtain an opinion from the distributee's attorney that the eligible retirement plan (see Q 28:16) receiving the rollover is a qualified retirement plan or IRA. As another example, the plan administrator cannot require the trustee of an eligible retirement plan receiving a direct rollover to agree to return, upon demand, any portion of the distribution that the plan administrator subsequently claims was paid incorrectly. [Temp Reg § 1.401(a)(31)-1T, Q&A 6; IRS Special Ruling (June 3, 1993)]

The plan administrator may establish a default procedure whereby a distributee who fails to make an affirmative election is treated as having either made or not made a direct rollover election. However, the plan administrator may not make a distribution under any default procedure unless the distributee has received an explanation of the direct rollover option (see Q 28:27). [Temp Reg § 1.401(a)(31)-1T, Q&A 7]

The plan administrator may establish a deadline after which the distributee may not revoke an election to make or not to make a direct rollover, but the plan administrator is not permitted to prescribe any deadline or time period that is more restrictive for the distributee than that which otherwise applies under the plan to a revocation of the form of distribution elected by the distributee. [Temp Reg § 1.401(a)(31)-1T, Q&A 8]

Q 28:21 Can a distributee elect a partial direct rollover?

Yes. The plan administrator (see Q 16:1) must permit a distributee to elect to have a portion of an eligible rollover distribution (see Q 28:8) paid to an eligible retirement plan (see Q 28:16) in a direct rollover (see Q 28:17) and to have the remainder paid to the distributee. The plan administrator is permitted to require that, if the distributee elects to have only a portion of an eligible rollover distribution paid to an eligible retirement plan in a direct rollover, that portion be equal to at least $500. If the entire amount of the eligible rollover distribution is $500 or less, the plan administrator need not allow the distributee to divide the distribution. [Temp Reg § 1.401(a)(31)-1T, Q&A 9]

Q 28:22 Can a direct rollover be paid to two or more eligible retirement plans?

The plan administrator (see Q 16:1) is not required (but is permitted) to allow the distributee to divide an eligible rollover distribution (see Q 28:8) into separate distributions to be paid to two or more eligible retirement plans (see Q 28:16) in direct rollovers (see

Q 28:17). The plan administrator is permitted to limit the distributee to a single direct rollover for each eligible rollover distribution. [Temp Reg § 1.401(a)(31)-1T, Q&A 10]

Q 28:23 Can there be a dollar limitation on a direct rollover?

Yes. A qualified retirement plan will satisfy the direct rollover requirement (see Qs 28:8, 28:17) even though the plan does not permit a distributee to elect a direct rollover with respect to eligible rollover distributions during a year that are reasonably expected to total less than $200 or any lower minimum amount specified by the plan administrator. [Temp Reg § 1.401(a)(31)-1T, Q&A 11]

Q 28:24 How many elections are required for a series of periodic payments?

Each distribution in a series of substantially equal periodic payments may be an eligible rollover distribution (see Qs 28:8, 28:9).

Example. Joe participates in The Golfing Grace Corporation's money purchase pension plan. Joe retires and elects to receive payment of his account balance in 60 substantially equal monthly payments. Each of the 60 monthly payments is an eligible rollover distribution, and Joe may make a direct rollover election.

A qualified retirement plan is permitted to treat a distributee's election to make or not to make a direct rollover with respect to one payment in a series of periodic payments as applying to all subsequent payments in the series, provided that:

- The employee is permitted at any time to change, with respect to subsequent payments, a previous election to make or not to make a direct rollover; and

- The written explanation (see Q 28:27) explains that the election to make or not to make a direct rollover will apply to all future payments unless the employee subsequently changes the election. [Temp Reg § 1.401(a)(31)-1T, Q&A 12]

Q 28:25   Must a plan accept a direct rollover?

No. Although qualified retirement plans are required to provide distributees with the option to make a direct rollover (see Q 28:17) of their eligible rollover distributions (see Q 28:8) to an eligible retirement plan (see Q 28:16), there is no requirement that an eligible retirement plan accept rollovers. Thus, an eligible retirement plan can refuse to accept rollovers. Alternatively, a plan can limit the circumstances under which it will accept rollovers. For example, a plan can limit the types of plans from which it will accept a rollover or limit the types of assets it will accept in a rollover (such as only cash or its equivalent). [Temp Reg § 1.401(a)(31)-1T, Q&A 13]

Q 28:26   Is a direct rollover a distribution and rollover or a transfer of assets and liabilities?

A direct rollover (see Q 28:17) is a distribution and rollover of the eligible rollover distribution (see Q 28:8) and not a transfer of assets and liabilities. If the spousal consent requirements (see Q 10:21) apply to the distribution, the requirements must be satisfied before the eligible rollover distribution may be distributed in a direct rollover. Similarly, the direct rollover is not a transfer of assets and liabilities that must satisfy the merger or consolidation requirements (see Q 9:28). Finally, a direct rollover is not a transfer of benefits for purposes of applying the optional forms of benefits requirement (see Q 10:42). Therefore, the eligible retirement plan (see Q 28:16) is not required to provide, with respect to amounts paid to it in a direct rollover, the same optional forms of benefits that were provided under the qualified retirement plan that made the direct rollover. [Temp Reg § 1.401(a)(31)-1T, Q&A 14]

Q 28:27   Must distributees receive a written explanation of the rollover rules?

The plan administrator (see Q 16:1) is required, within a reasonable period of time (see Q 16:15) before making an eligible rollover distribution (see Q 28:8), to provide the distributee with a written explanation known as a Section 402(f) Notice. The Section 402(f) Notice must be designed to be easily understood and must explain the following:

1. The rules under which the distributee may have the distribution paid in a direct rollover (see Q 28:17) to an eligible retirement plan (see Q 28:16);

2. The rules that require the withholding of tax on the distribution if it is not paid in a direct rollover (see Qs 16:7–16:13);

3. The rules under which the distributee will not be subject to tax if the distribution is contributed in a rollover to an eligible retirement plan within 60 days of the distribution (see Q 28:33);

4. If applicable, certain special rules regarding the taxation of the distribution (see Chapter 13); and

5. If the plan administrator intends to treat a distributee's election to make or not to make a direct rollover with respect to one payment in a series of periodic payments as applicable to all subsequent payments in the series unless the distributee subsequently changes the election (see Q 28:24).

[IRC § 402(f); Temp Reg §§ 1.401(a)(31)-1T, Q&A 1(b)(2), 1.402(c)-2T, Q&A 11 through Q&A 15, 1.402(f)-2T; Notice 93-26, 1993-18 IRB]

IRS has issued a model Section 402(f) Notice (see Q 16:15). [Notice 92-48, 1992-2 CB 377]

Q 28:28   **When are the new eligible rollover distribution rules effective?**

The new rules are applicable to eligible rollover distributions (see Q 28:8) made after December 31, 1992, even if the event giving rise to the distribution occurs before January 1, 1993, or if the eligible rollover distribution is part of a series of payments that began before January 1, 1993. [Temp Reg §§ 1.401(a)(31)-1T, Q&A 1(c), 1.402(c)-2T, Q&A 1(c)]

Example 1. Phil terminated employment with The Rollin' Dolen Corporation in 1991 but did not receive his pension plan benefits until 1993. Even though Phil's employment was terminated in 1991 (before the new rules became effective), the distribution of his benefits in 1993 is subject to the new eligible rollover distribution rules.

Example 2. Linda terminated employment with The Rollin' Dolen Corporation in 1989 and elected to receive her pension plan benefits in 60 equal monthly payments beginning January 1, 1990. Linda's monthly payments, starting with the January 1, 1993 payment, are subject to the new eligible rollover distribution rules even though the series of payments commenced before 1993.

Q 28:29 When must qualified retirement plans be amended to incorporate the direct rollover provisions?

Even though the direct rollover provisions apply to distributions from qualified retirement plans made after December 31, 1992, a qualified retirement plan is not required to be amended before the last day of the first plan year beginning on or after January 1, 1994 (or, if later, the last day by which amendments must be made to comply with TRA '86 and related provisions, as permitted in other administrative guidance of general applicability), provided that:

- In the interim period between January 1, 1993, and the date on which the plan is amended, the plan is operated in compliance with the new requirements; and
- The amendment applies retroactively to January 1, 1993.

[Temp Reg § 1.401(a)(31)-1T, Q&A 15]

IRS has issued a model amendment, which may be adopted by plan sponsors. [Rev Proc 93-12, 1993-3 IRB]

Q 28:30 Is a rollover available for a distribution from a terminated retirement plan?

A participant who has not separated from service but who receives a distribution from a qualified retirement plan because of the plan's termination can roll over all or part of the distribution to postpone the payment of tax if it is an eligible rollover distribution (see Q 28:8). The distribution can be an eligible rollover distribution even if the participant continues to participate in another qualified retirement plan of the same employer (see Q 28:10). [IRC § 402(c)]

Q 28:31   May a person who is over age 70½ roll over a qualified retirement plan distribution?

An individual over age 70½ may roll over a distribution from a qualified retirement plan except to the extent that such distribution is a required minimum distribution (see Qs 11:2, 28:8). [IRC §§ 401(a)(9), 402(c)(4)(B); Rev Rul 82-153, 1982-2 CB 86; Ltr Rul 9143078]

Q 28:32   Is a rollover of qualified retirement plan benefits available to the spouse of a deceased employee?

Yes. The spouse of an employee who receives an eligible rollover distribution (see Qs 28:8, 28:15) from a qualified retirement plan on account of the employee's death is permitted to roll over all or part of the distribution to an IRA. This applies only to a surviving spouse and not to a nonspouse beneficiary. [IRC § 402(c)(9); Ltr Rul 9005071] IRS has also ruled that, if the deceased spouse's qualified retirement plan benefits are paid to a trust and the trust distributes the benefits to the surviving spouse, the surviving spouse may roll over the distribution. [Ltr Ruls 9234032, 9232041, 9047060; but see Ltr Rul 9145041]

If the deceased spouse's qualified retirement plan benefits are paid to the decedent's estate and the surviving spouse is the sole beneficiary of the decedent's residuary estate, IRS has ruled that the surviving spouse may roll over the distribution to an IRA [Ltr Ruls 9229022, 9138067]; but the surviving spouse cannot roll over any part of the distribution that represents a required minimum distribution (see Qs 11:2, 28:8, 28:11). [Ltr Rul 9211059]

The surviving spouse was permitted to roll over the benefit to an IRA when the deceased spouse named a trust as the beneficiary of the death benefit payable from a qualified retirement plan, the trust beneficiaries disclaimed the benefit, and, as a result of the disclaimer, the benefit was paid to the surviving spouse (see Q 4:24). [Ltr Rul 9247026]

The spouse may establish an IRA rollover account even if the spouse would not be eligible to establish a regular IRA. However, the surviving spouse may not roll over the distribution to another qualified retirement plan or from the rollover IRA to another qualified retirement plan in which the spouse is a participant. [IRC § 402(c)(9)]

Q 28:33   How does a rollover from a qualified retirement plan to an IRA work?

The payout must be transferred into one or more IRAs within 60 days after receipt (see Q 28:34). It is not necessary, however, to transfer the entire amount into the IRA; but the portion not rolled over is taxed as ordinary income in the year received. No special tax treatment (e.g., forward averaging) is available with respect to the portion of the distribution that is currently taxed. [IRC §§ 402(c)(3), 402(d)(4)(K); Barrett, 64 TCM 1080 (1992); Ltr Rul 9243054]

A distribution from a qualified retirement plan may be rolled over into an IRA that has previously been established by a participant for purposes of the participant's annual contributions; but, when the rollover is made into this type of IRA, the participant cannot later roll over the amount of the original distribution into a second qualified retirement plan maintained by the same or a new employer. The only way around this pitfall is to set up a separate IRA (a conduit IRA) to receive the rollover (see Q 28:36). [IRC § 408(d)(3)(A)]

Q 28:34   When does the 60-day rollover period begin?

IRS has held that if a distribution qualifying for rollover treatment is received by an individual in more than one payment, for purposes of the 60-day rollover period, that individual is deemed to have received all distributions on the day the last payment is received. [Ltr Ruls 9318044, 8434052] It is doubtful that this rule remains effective because, in the example in Question 28:24, Joe should not be permitted to roll over all 60 payments within the 60-day period following the last payment.

The distribution need not occur in any particular year. An individual who receives an eligible rollover distribution (see Q 28:8) a number of years after termination of employment may still roll over the distribution. [Ltr Ruls 9152041, 9049047]

Q 28:35   Can the 60-day rollover period be extended?

According to IRS, the 60-day rollover period may not be extended under any circumstances. IRS has held that transfers not completed within 60 days of the date of distribution are not valid rollovers, even though they were caused by clerical error and not the fault of the individual. IRS says that neither the statute nor the regulations grant IRS the authority to waive or extend the 60-day period. [Ltr Ruls 9211035, 9145036, 9013078, 8824047, 8819074]

But, when an individual received a distribution of cash and stock, delivered the distribution to a brokerage company with instructions to deposit the distribution into his IRA, and the brokerage company mistakenly credited the stock to the individual's personal account, the bookkeeping error was disregarded and the IRA rollover was ruled timely. [Wood, 93 TC 114 (1989)]

When a state agency, as receiver of an insolvent financial institution, distributed IRA proceeds and the individual failed to roll over the proceeds within 60 days of receipt of the funds, the distribution was includible in the individual's income. [Aronson, 98 TC 283 (1992)]

Q 28:36   Can amounts in a rollover IRA be transferred to a qualified retirement plan?

An IRA that contains only assets attributable to a rollover contribution from a qualified retirement plan may be rolled over to a second qualified retirement plan. This type of IRA is called a conduit IRA. Also, the second qualified retirement plan must provide for the acceptance of rollovers. [IRC §§ 402(c)(5), 408(d)(3)(A)(ii); Ltr Rul 9108057]

Transferring money from one qualified retirement plan to another through a conduit IRA may provide a big tax advantage. The amount rolled over might remain eligible for special tax treatment (e.g., electing forward averaging tax treatment for a lump-sum distribution received from the second qualified retirement plan), although generally a trust-to-trust transfer provides more assurance of retaining eligibility for favorable tax treatment (see Q 13:4). [Ltr Ruls 9226076, 9151024, 9146045]

Q 28:37 Can a distribution from a disqualified retirement plan be rolled over?

A distribution from a retirement plan that is retroactively disqualified is includible in income and is not eligible for a rollover to an IRA or a qualified retirement plan. Rollover treatment is permitted for a distribution from a retirement plan that is qualified at the time of distribution, not at the time when contributions by the employer were made. [Treas Reg §§ 1.402(a)-1(a)(1)(ii), 1.402(a)-1(a)(1)(v), 1.402(b)-1(b); Cass v Comm'r, 774 F 2d 740 (7th Cir 1985); Baetens v Comm'r, 777 F 2d 1160 (6th Cir 1985); Woodson v Comm'r, 651 F 2d 1094 (5th Cir 1981); but see Greenwald v Comm'r, 366 F 2d 538 (2d Cir 1966)]

A payment made to an employee in settlement of the employee's claim for benefits from a qualified retirement plan was not eligible for rollover treatment because the settlement payment was made from the employer's general assets and not from a qualified retirement plan. [Ltr Rul 9241008]

Q 28:38 What are the tax advantages and disadvantages of rolling over a qualified retirement plan distribution to an IRA?

A rollover of a qualified retirement plan distribution to an IRA provides three distinct tax advantages:

1. Postponement of tax payments;
2. Possible reduction of tax liability on the eventual payout; and
3. Continued tax-free buildup of retirement savings.

The rollover defers tax on the qualified retirement plan payout and on the income earned in the IRA. Subsequently, tax liability on amounts in the IRA can be spread out by making withdrawals over a period of years.

Nevertheless, an IRA rollover has drawbacks. First, amounts in the IRA generally cannot be withdrawn without penalty before age 59½ (see Q 26:39). Second, IRA withdrawals are taxed as ordinary income with no special tax-reducing rules available (e.g., forward averaging). [IRC §§ 72(t), 408(d); Costanza v Comm'r, 50 TCM 280 (1985)]

Whether the advantages of a rollover will outweigh the disadvantages depends on each individual situation.

Q 28:39 Can an IRA rollover be revoked?

Upon receipt of a lump-sum distribution from a qualified retirement plan, an individual has the option of electing to roll over the distribution to another eligible retirement plan or to have the tax on such distribution computed by using the forward averaging method (see Qs 13:13, 13:14). Once the individual elects to roll over the distribution into an IRA, those funds become part of the IRA and are then subject to the rules governing IRAs. The amount timely rolled over to an IRA cannot be considered an excess contribution and, therefore, cannot be withdrawn as such. [IRC §§ 402(c)(5), 4973(b)] An individual cannot recharacterize a rollover contribution made to an IRA once the rollover has been made. Once an individual has chosen the form of a transaction for tax purposes, the individual cannot later disavow the form of the transaction merely because the tax consequences of the form chosen have become disadvantageous. [Barrett, 64 TCM 1080 (1992); Hall, 61 TCM 2236 (1991); Ltr Ruls 8536098, 8536097]

For the IRA rollover to be tax-free, the individual must irrevocably elect to treat the IRA contribution as a rollover contribution. Once any portion of the lump-sum distribution is irrevocably designated as a rollover contribution, the amount rolled over is not taxable and no part of the distribution is eligible for special income tax treatment. An irrevocable election is made by a written designation to the IRA sponsor (at the time of contribution) that it is a rollover contribution. [Temp Reg § 1.402(a)(5)-1T, Q&A 3, Q&A 4; Ltr Rul 8815035]

However, when an individual rolled over the entire distribution to an IRA and was informed the following year by the trustee of the qualified retirement plan that the individual's benefits had been erroneously overvalued, IRS ruled that the amount distributed to the individual to repay the employer would not be includible in the individual's income. [Ltr Rul 9118020]

Chapter 29

Business Owners

One of the best tax shelters available—especially for the business owner—is a qualified retirement plan. This chapter examines how a qualified retirement plan benefits the business owner and reduces income tax liability. A self-employed business owner may also adopt a qualified retirement plan to accumulate funds on a tax-favored basis. How much the business owner can contribute to a plan, what type of plan is best suited for the business owner, and several strategies for reducing the cost of the retirement plan to the business owner are also examined.

Q 29:1 How do the working owners of a closely held corporation benefit from a qualified retirement plan?

There are two basic ways for a working owner to get money out of a closely held corporation: compensation and dividends.

If a working owner earns a salary or bonus from a closely held corporation, the corporation will get a deduction for the amounts paid to the owner. In turn, the owner is taxed on compensation at ordinary income tax rates. A dividend paid to the working owner is treated differently: it is not deductible by the corporation. The dividend is also taxable to the working owner at ordinary income tax rates. Payments of dividends, therefore, are subject to double taxation.

Adoption of a qualified retirement plan provides the corporation with a deduction for the amount it contributes to the plan. The working owner, as a participant in the plan, is not currently taxed on the amounts contributed for the owner's benefit. Further, earnings from investments made by the plan build up tax-free. When the owner eventually receives the plan benefits, the distribution may be eligible for special tax treatment if it is made in a lump sum (see Q 13:13). [IRC § 402(d)]

Therefore, adoption of a qualified retirement plan provides the corporation with the same tax benefits as does the payment of current compensation. But the working owner of a closely held corporation is able to defer payment of taxes until benefits are received, and these benefits may be eligible for special tax treatment.

Q 29:2   How can the adoption of a qualified retirement plan increase the wealth of the owner of a closely held corporation?

Dramatic results can be achieved by a qualified retirement plan.

Example. Neal, the owner of a closely held corporation, earns a $50,000 annual salary, and the corporation is able to pay a 15 percent bonus ($7,500) each year. From the additional $7,500 each year, Neal will keep about $5,400 after taxes (assuming a 28 percent bracket). If that $5,400 is invested at 8 percent per year, Neal will earn about 6 percent net after taxes. Over a 25-year period, he will be able to build up about $314,000 after taxes.

If the corporation has a qualified profit sharing plan (see Q 2:6) and, instead of giving Neal a $7,500 bonus, contributes that $7,500 to the plan each year on his behalf, the corporation gets the same $7,500 deduction that it would have received had it paid the bonus.

If the profit sharing trust earns the same 8 percent that Neal would have earned individually, then, because the profit sharing trust pays no income taxes, the total buildup of these annual investments in the trust on Neal's behalf, over the 25-year period, will come to $592,000. (Remember, the full $7,500 per year—not $5,400 after taxes—is accumulating in the trust. Furthermore, it is accumulating at the full 8 percent interest rate.)

If this $592,000 buildup in funds is paid out to Neal in one year upon his retirement, he may be eligible to elect special tax treatment (see Q 13:13).

The above example is oversimplified, especially in the case of a small or medium-sized corporation. To give this type of dramatic buildup to the business owner, other employees must also be covered. This, of course, boosts costs. But there are methods that can be used to reduce costs. These methods (e.g., permitted disparity; see Qs 7:1, 29:21) may be incorporated into the plan.

Q 29:3 How does the adoption of a qualified retirement plan reduce a corporation's tax liability?

To illustrate how a qualified retirement plan reduces a corporation's tax liability, assume the corporation had taxable income of $45,000 in 1993 and no qualified plan. Its income tax liability would be $6,750. If, however, the owners decided to adopt a qualified retirement plan and make a tax-deductible contribution of $21,000 to the plan, the corporation's taxable income would now be $24,000 ($45,000 minus $21,000). Its income tax liability would be reduced to $3,600. By adopting the plan and making the contribution, this corporation would cut its tax liability by almost 50 percent. [IRC § 11(b)]

Q 29:4 Can a self-employed individual set up a qualified retirement plan?

Yes. A plan covering a self-employed individual (see Q 29:8) must, however, satisfy certain requirements in addition to the normal corporate retirement plan qualification requirements (see Q 29:28). [IRC §§ 401(c), 401(d)]

A self-employed individual is an individual who has income (see Q 29:10) from self-employment for the taxable year (see Q 29:8).

Q 29:5 What tax advantage does a self-employed individual gain by adopting a qualified retirement plan?

The basic tax advantages of adopting a qualified retirement plan, which are similar to those received by the owner of a closely held corporation, are:

1. The self-employed individual (see Q 29:8) receives a federal income tax deduction, subject to the applicable limitations of the Code, for contributions made to the qualified retirement plan.

2. To the extent the contribution the self-employed individual makes to a qualified retirement plan is tax-deductible, the tax on this income is deferred (it will be taxable when it is ultimately received from the plan).

3. Income earned on contributions to the plan (whether or not tax-deductible when made) will escape tax while in the plan, thereby permitting a greater total compounding of earnings than would otherwise be possible.

4. Reduced tax rates may apply to lump-sum distributions (see Q 13:13) to the self-employed individual or the individual's beneficiary.

Q 29:6   Is it worthwhile for a self-employed individual to incorporate?

Although there generally is parity between qualified corporate retirement plans and qualified retirement plans for the self-employed, the incorporated business owner will still have advantages that will be unavailable to the unincorporated business owner. Among the advantages are the following:

1. The incorporated business owner may be permitted to borrow from the plan (see Q 29:25). [IRC §§ 401(a)(13), 4975(d)]

2. Plan contributions for the incorporated business owner allocable to life, accident, health, or other insurance are deductible (see Qs 1:23, 1:24). [IRC § 404(e)]

3. The incorporated business owner can terminate employment for lump-sum distribution purposes (see Q 13:9). [IRC § 402(d)(4)(A)]

4. Plan contributions on behalf of an incorporated business owner can create or increase a net operating loss. [IRC § 172(d)(4)(D)]

5. The incorporated business owner may receive tax-free group term life insurance benefits. [IRC § 79]

6. The incorporated business owner may receive tax-free benefits under a medical expense reimbursement plan. [IRC §§ 105(b), 105(g)]

Note: An individual who incorporates principally to obtain tax deductions not otherwise available to a self-employed individual (see Q 29:8) should review those circumstances in which IRS may allocate income and deductions of a personal service corporation to an employee-owner (see Q 29:34).

Q 29:7 How should an existing qualified retirement plan be handled if a self-employed individual incorporates the business?

The simplest and most practical arrangement may be to have the corporation adopt the qualified retirement plan. If the corporation establishes a new qualified retirement plan, the assets of the prior plan can be merged into the new plan or transferred directly to the trustees of the new plan.

If the qualified retirement plan that covered the self-employed individual is being terminated, IRS should be notified (see Q 21:61).

Another alternative is to freeze the plan. Since the individual is no longer self-employed, the individual can make no further contributions to the plan. However, amounts in the plan will continue to accumulate on a tax-free basis. Distributions can later be made from the plan in accordance with its provisions. However, if a qualified retirement plan covering a self-employed individual is frozen, the plan must still comply with the requirements of the Code. [Rev Rul 89-87, 1989-2 CB 81; IRC § 401(a); Treas Reg § 1.401(a)(26)-2(b)]

Q 29:8 Who is a self-employed individual?

Anyone who carries on a trade or business as a sole proprietor or who is a member of a partnership is self-employed. Although the individual need not carry on regular full-time business activities to be considered self-employed, an individual must have earned income (see Qs 29:10, 29:11). [IRC § 401(c); Treas Reg § 1.1402(c)-1]

Q 29:9   Who is an owner-employee?

An owner-employee is a self-employed individual (see Q 29:8) who is either a sole proprietor or, in the case of a partnership, a partner who owns more than 10 percent of either the capital interest or the profits interest in such partnership. [IRC § 401(c)(3); Treas Reg § 1.401-10(d)]

Q 29:10   What is earned income?

The criterion for contributions to a qualified retirement plan on behalf of a self-employed individual (see Q 29:8) is earned income. This means that contributions by or for a sole proprietor or partner may be made to a qualified retirement plan only if personal services are performed. Thus, for example, inactive owners who derive income solely from investments may not participate in a qualified retirement plan. [Treas Reg § 1.401-10(c)(3); Frick, 56 TCM 1368 (1989); Pugh, 49 TCM 748 (1985); Frick, 50 TCM 1334 (1985)] Earned income is defined as the net earnings from self-employment in a trade or business in which personal services of the taxpayer are a material income-producing factor. In effect, earned income is the net profit of the business. The fact that capital is an important aspect of the self-employed individual's business is not significant in determining earned income. [IRC § 401(c)(2); see also IRS Pub 560]

Distributions of income to a limited partner are not considered net earnings from self-employment. However, guaranteed payments made to a limited partner are considered net earnings from self-employment if paid for services rendered to or for the partnership. [IRC § 1402(a)(13); Treas Reg § 1.401-11(d)(2)(ii)]

Payments to a former employee under a deferred-compensation plan represent compensation for past services and are not considered earned income. [Ltr Rul 8522057]

For purposes of computing the limitations on deductions for contributions to a qualified retirement plan, earned income is computed after taking into account amounts contributed to the plan on behalf of the self-employed individual (i.e., the self-employed individual's earned income is reduced by the deductible contributions to the plan). Furthermore, earned income is computed after the deduction allowed to the self-employed individual for one-half of the individual's self-employment taxes (see Q 29:16). [IRC §§ 164(f), 401(c)(2)(A)(v), 401(c)(2)(A)(vi), 404(a)(8)(D), 1401]

Q 29:11 May an individual be both self-employed and an employee of another employer?

An individual may be an employee of one entity and still be self-employed with regard to another entity. With respect to the same employer, regardless of the form of entity (e.g., sole proprietorship, partnership, or corporation), the classifications as self-employed and employee are normally mutually exclusive; however, it is possible to be an employee of an entity and also be self-employed with regard to that entity. [Reese, 63 TCM 3129 (1992)]

Example. Alison is employed by Richard Corporation as an accountant and also has her own part-time accounting practice. Even though she may participate in Richard Corporation's qualified retirement plan, she is also able to establish a qualified retirement plan for her self-employment income. [Treas Reg § 1.401-10(b)(3)(ii)]

Q 29:12 Can the bulk of qualified retirement plan contributions and benefits be set aside for the business owner and other essential employees under the terms of the plan?

Generally, no. A qualified retirement plan may not discriminate in favor of employees who are considered highly compensated. Discrimination in favor of highly compensated employees (see Q 3:2) must be avoided in coverage, contributions, and benefits. [IRC §§ 401(a)(4), 410(b)]

An obvious example of discrimination would be a money purchase pension plan (see Q 2:4) that provides for a contribution equal to 25 percent of compensation for highly compensated employees, but only 10 percent of compensation on behalf of all other employees. Such a plan would not qualify for tax-favored status. An important exception applies if the plan takes permitted disparity into account (see Qs 7:1, 29:21).

For details on minimum contribution and benefit requirements that may apply to the plan, see Chapter 22.

Q 29:13   May a qualified retirement plan lose its tax-favored status if only the business owner and other essential employees will receive benefits?

Even if the plan is not discriminatory as it is written (see Q 4:1), the operation of the plan can result in discrimination, and the plan may lose its tax-favored status.

Example. A plan covers all employees and provides a schedule for the vesting of benefits that meets the requirements of the Code (see Q 9:3). If the only employees attaining vested benefits are the business's highly compensated employees (because rank-and-file workers leave before they have enough years of service to earn vested benefits, for example), the plan—in actual operation—may discriminate in favor of the highly compensated employees and may lose its tax-favored status (see Q 29:12). [Rev Rul 66-251, 1966-2 CB 121]

In one case, IRS denied tax-favored status to a profit sharing plan because the rapid rate of turnover among lower-paid employees caused the bulk of the benefits to go to the business owner and the essential employees. However, IRS was rebuffed by the court. The court found that, if there was any discrimination in the operation of the plan, it was in favor of permanent employees and against transient employees, not in favor of the highly compensated employees and against rank-and-file employees. This type of discrimination is not prohibited. [Lansons, Inc, 69 TC 773 (1978), *aff'd,* 622 F 2d 774 (5th Cir 1980)]

On the other hand, if discrimination in benefits results from a pattern of abuse by the business owner—for example, if rank-and-file employees are fired before their benefits become nonforfeitable—the plan is likely to lose its tax-favored status. [IRC § 411(d)(1)(A)]

Q 29:14 How much can a business owner contribute to the qualified retirement plan?

It depends on the type of retirement plan the business owner adopts. If either a single defined contribution plan or a combination of defined contribution plans is adopted, the annual addition (see Q 6:1) to the business owner's account during any year may not exceed the lesser of (1) $30,000 (or, if greater, 25 percent of the maximum dollar limitation permitted under a defined benefit plan) or (2) 25 percent of compensation. [IRC § 415(c)]

The maximum annual benefit that may be provided to a participating business owner under a defined benefit plan is the lesser of (1) $90,000 (with adjustments for inflation) or (2) 100 percent of the business owner's average compensation for the highest three consecutive years. [IRC § 415(b)]

Bear in mind that, under a defined benefit plan, the limitation is placed on the annual benefit payable, not the annual contribution necessary to fund the benefit. The annual contribution is determined actuarially, based on the business owner's age and anticipated annual benefit, the plan's normal retirement age, the form of benefit payable, and the actuarial assumptions used (see Q 29:20).

For a discussion of the limitations on contributions and benefits, see Chapter 6.

Q 29:15 Is there any limit on tax-deductible contributions to a qualified retirement plan by a corporation?

Yes. Compensation paid to any employee is tax-deductible by the corporation only if the amount paid is reasonable. In determining reasonableness, all forms of compensation are considered, including contributions to the corporation's qualified retirement plan. Whether a particular business owner's compensation is reasonable is a question of fact in each case. [IRC § 162; Treas Reg § 1.404(a)-1(b); Barton-Gillet Co, 442 F 2d 1343 (4th Cir 1971); Bianchi, 66 TC 324, aff'd, 553 F 2d 93 (2d Cir 1977)]

For a discussion on the limits of tax-deductible contributions, see Chapter 12 and Question 29:17.

Q 29:16   How much may be contributed to a qualified retirement plan on behalf of a self-employed individual?

The contribution limits that apply to corporate plans apply to plans covering self-employed individuals (see Q 29:8). Thus, the annual addition limit for defined contribution plans is the lesser of $30,000 or 25 percent of compensation (see Q 6:1). But because earned income is computed after taking into account amounts contributed to the plan on behalf of the self-employed individual and after the deduction for one-half of the individual's self-employment taxes (see Q 29:10), the effective percentage limit on the contribution is 20 percent of earned income computed after the self-employment tax deduction but before the contribution $[1 \div 1.25 = .80; 1.0 - .80 = .20]$.

If the self-employed individual adopts a profit sharing plan only, the effective percentage limit on the contribution is 13.0435 percent of earned income computed after the self-employment tax deduction but before the contribution $[1 \div 1.15 = .869565; 1.0 - .869565 = .130435]$.

For 1993, the self-employment tax rate is 15.3 percent (12.4 percent for Social Security and 2.9 percent for Medicare) and the Social Security base is $57,600, but the Medicare base is $135,000. Therefore, in 1993, the maximum self-employment tax is $11,057.40 $[(12.4\% \times \$57,600) + (2.9\% \times \$135,000)]$.

Example 1. James adopted a 10-percent-of-compensation money purchase pension plan for 1993. His earned income before the deductions for the plan contribution on his behalf and one-half of his self-employment taxes is $57,600. James's deductible contribution to the plan is $4,866, determined by completing the following steps:

Step 1	Enter the rate $[1.0 - (1 \div 1.10)]$	.090909
Step 2	Enter James's net earnings	$ 57,600
Step 3	Enter deduction for one-half of James's self-employment taxes	
	$\frac{15.3\%}{2} \times [\$57,600 - (\frac{15.3\% \times \$57,600}{2})]$	$ 4,069

Step 4	Step 2 less Step 3	$ 53,531
Step 5	Step 1 × Step 4	$ 4,866
Step 6	Maximum dollar limitation	$ 30,000
Step 7	Deductible contribution: lesser of Step 5 or Step 6	$ 4,866
Proof	(Step 2 − Step 3 − Step 7) × 10%	$ 4,866

Example 2. Caroline adopted a profit sharing plan for 1993. Her earned income before the deductions for the plan contribution on her behalf and one-half of her self-employment taxes is $135,000. Caroline's maximum deductible contribution to the plan is $16,920, determined by completing the following steps:

Step 1	Enter the maximum rate [1.0 − (1 ÷ 1.15)]	.130435
Step 2	Enter Caroline's net earnings	$135,000
Step 3	Enter deduction for one-half of Caroline's self-employment taxes	

$$\frac{12.4\%}{2} \times [\$57,600 - (\frac{12.4\% \times \$57,600}{2})]$$

$$+$$

$$\frac{2.9\%}{2} \times [\$135,000 - (\frac{2.9\% \times \$135,000}{2})] \qquad \$ \ 5,279$$

Step 4	Step 2 less Step 3	$129,721
Step 5	Step 1 × Step 4	$ 16,920
Step 6	Maximum dollar limitation	$ 30,000
Step 7	Deductible contribution: lesser of Step 5 or Step 6	$ 16,920
Proof	(Step 2 − Step 3 − Step 7) × 15%	$ 16,920

Example 3. Stephanie adopted a 25-percent-of-compensation money purchase pension plan for 1993. Her earned income before the deductions for the plan contribution on her behalf and one-half of her self-employment taxes is $235,840. Stephanie's deductible

contribution to the plan is $30,000, determined by completing the following steps:

Step 1	Enter the rate [1.0 – (1 ÷ 1.25)]	.20
Step 2	Enter Stephanie's net earnings	$235,840
Step 3	Enter deduction for one-half of Stephanie's self-employment taxes (maximum of $5,529)	$ 5,529
Step 4	Step 2 less Step 3	$230,311
Step 5	Step 1 × Step 4	$ 46,062
Step 6	Maximum dollar limitation	$ 30,000
Step 7	Deductible contribution: lesser of Step 5 or Step 6	$ 30,000
Proof	(Step 2 – Step 3 – Step 7) × 25% but not more than $30,000	$ 30,000

The contribution limit to a defined benefit plan is based upon a maximum annual retirement benefit equal to the lesser of $90,000 or 100 percent of compensation (see Qs 6:8, 29:17).

With the enactment of RRA '93 (see Q 1:12) is enacted, two changes will affect the amount that may be contributed on behalf of a self-employed individual. First, for 1994 and subsequent calendar years, there will be no dollar limitation on the Medicare base, so that the 2.9 percent tax rate for Medicare will apply to an unlimited amount of net earnings from self-employment. Second, for benefits accruing in plan years beginning after December 31, 1993, the amount of earnings on which contributions or benefits may be based will be reduced from $200,000 (see Qs 6:21, 6:22) to $150,000. In addition, the cost-of-living adjustment will be made only if the adjustment is $10,000 or greater and then will be made in multiples of $10,000 (i.e., rounded down to the next lowest multiple of $10,000). For example, an increase in the cost of living of $9,999 will result in no adjustment, and an increase of $19,999 will create an upward adjustment of $10,000. [RRA '93, Act §§ 13207, 13212]

Assuming that the Social Security base remains at $57, 600 for 1994, in Example 3, Stephanie's deductible contribution to the plan for 1994 may be reduced to below $30,000. This will depend upon whether the $150,000 limit applies at Step 2 or Step 4.

Example 3A. If the $150,000 limit is applied at Step 2, Stephanie's deductible contribution to the plan will be $28,656, determined by completing the following steps:

Step 1	Enter the maximum rate $[1.0 - (1 \div 1.25)]$	.20
Step 2	Enter Stephanie's net earnings	$150,000
Step 3	Enter deduction for one-half of Stephanie's self-employment taxes	

$$\frac{12.4\%}{2} \times [\$57,600 - (\frac{12.4\% \times \$57,600}{2})]$$

$$+$$

	$\frac{2.9\%}{2} \times [\$235,840 - (\frac{2.9\% \times \$235,840}{2})]$	$ 6,720
Step 4	Step 2 less Step 3	$143,280
Step 5	Step 1 × Step 4	$ 28,656
Step 6	Maximum dollar limitation	$ 30,000
Step 7	Deductible contribution: lesser of Step 5 or Step 6	$ 28,656
Proof	(Step 2 − Step 3 − Step 7) × 25%	$ 28,656

Example 3B. If the $150,000 limit is applied at Step 4, Stephanie's deductible contribution to the plan will remain at $30,000, determined by completing the following steps:

Step 1	Enter the rate $[1.0 - (1 \div 1.25)]$	.20
Step 2	Enter Stephanie's net earnings	$235,840

Step 3   Enter deduction for one-half of
            Stephanie's self-employment taxes

$$\frac{12.4\%}{2} \times [\$57,600 - (\frac{12.4\% \times \$57,600}{2})]$$

$$+$$

$$\frac{2.9\%}{2} \times [\$235,840 - (\frac{2.9\% \times \$235,840}{2})] \qquad \$ \ \ 6,720$$

Step 4   Step 2 less Step 3,
            but not more than $150,000 $150,000

Step 5   Step 1 × Step 4 $ 30,000

Step 6   Maximum dollar limitation $ 30,000

Step 7   Deductible contribution:
            lesser of Step 5 or Step 6 $ 30,000

Proof   (Step 2 − Step 3, but not more
            than $150,000 − Step 7) × 25% $ 30,000

Since the deduction for the plan contribution on behalf of a self-employed individual is based upon earned income, and not net earnings from self-employment, the $150,000 limit should be applied at Step 4 in Example 3B and not at Step 2 in Example 3A.

Q 29:17 Do any special limitations apply to the deduction for contributions made to a defined benefit plan on behalf of a self-employed individual?

Yes. Unlike a corporate defined benefit plan to which an employer can make deductible contributions in excess of an employee's compensation if such contributions are necessary to fund the employee's benefit, an employer's deductible contribution on behalf of a self-employed individual (see Q 29:8) is limited to the self-employed individual's earned income for the year (computed after the deduction for one-half of the individual's self-employment taxes, but without regard to the deduction for employer contributions made on the individual's behalf). [IRC §§ 162, 164(f), 212, 401(c)(2), 404(a)(8)(B), 404(a)(8)(C), 404(a)(8)(D); Temp Reg § 1.404(a)(8)-1T]

Example. Caroline, a sole proprietor, has net earnings (after the deduction for one-half of her self-employment taxes) of $50,000 from her business. The maximum deductible contribution she can make on her own behalf to her defined benefit plan is $50,000. (Caroline's earned income is $50,000 for deduction purposes.)

Q 29:18 What type of qualified retirement plan should the business owner install?

From a business viewpoint, it depends initially on the business owner's objectives. The plan may be used to achieve one or more of the following:

1. Building a tax-sheltered retirement fund for the business owner and essential employees;
2. Recruiting essential employees from competitors;
3. Reducing employee turnover; and
4. Establishing a market for the corporate business owner's stock in a closely held corporation.

Another consideration is the ability of the business to support the retirement plan. In choosing a plan, the business owner must decide what contributions the business can afford to make.

From a personal viewpoint, the business owner's objectives must be ascertained. These may include one or more of the following:

- Maximizing retirement benefits
- Maximizing contributions made on the owner's behalf
- Having flexibility with regard to annual contributions

If the business owner wants to maximize retirement benefits (the amount available at retirement), the owner's age may be the key factor in determining what type of plan to adopt. A younger business owner may accumulate the most dollars for retirement using a defined contribution plan; older business owners may do better using a defined benefit plan.

Similarly, if maximizing contributions is the goal, the older business owner can accomplish that by using a defined benefit plan; the younger business owner might do better using a defined contribution plan, although a defined benefit plan could also accomplish the objective.

If flexibility is the goal, a profit sharing plan should be considered. This type of defined contribution plan gives the business owner control over the amount of annual contributions. Although a profit sharing plan generally reduces the maximum amount that may be contributed on behalf of the business owner, it can be combined with a money purchase pension plan to afford the business owner the opportunity to make larger contributions.

Other factors, however, may influence the business owner's decision. For example, how much will it cost to cover the employees? This will depend on how many of them must be covered, their compensation, and their ages. If the business owner's goals would be achieved using a defined benefit plan, but the cost of funding benefits for employees who are older than the business owner is substantial, it may be necessary to modify the objectives and use a defined contribution plan. But, if the employees are younger than the business owner, a defined benefit plan may be better than a defined contribution plan. In either situation, taking permitted disparity into consideration in designing the plan (see Qs 7:1, 29:21) may cut the cost of covering the business owner's employees and enable the objectives to be accomplished.

The older business owner may both maximize contributions and retain flexibility over the amount of annual contributions by adopting an age-based profit sharing plan (see Q 2:7).

Q 29:19 What type of qualified retirement plan (or plans) should a business owner use to maximize retirement benefits?

There is no one answer. The age of the business owner and the expected rate of return on the plan's investments, however, are the key factors in determining what type of qualified retirement plan will provide the most at retirement.

In a defined benefit plan, the actuary first determines the amount needed at retirement to pay the business owner's annual benefit as set by a formula in the plan. The actuary then determines the amount that must be contributed to the plan each year to reach the amount needed at retirement. The actuary uses various factors to compute the annual contribution, including an interest factor (the rate of return on plan investments). This interest factor is usually conservative, even when market rates are greater (see Q 8:8).

Investment gains and losses affect the amount of each year's contribution. Thus, if the interest assumption is 6 percent and the investment return is 9 percent, the investment gain reduces the business owner's future contributions. If the investment return is only 4 percent, the investment loss increases the subsequent contributions. Whether or not the interest assumption holds true, the annual adjustment in required contributions does not affect the final result—the amount in the plan at retirement. If the business owner's compensation remained constant over the period of participation, the amount available at the end would be known at the beginning.

In a defined contribution plan (other than a target benefit plan), no actuarial calculations are made and no interest factor is assumed. The annual contribution is generally determined by multiplying the business owner's compensation for the year by the contribution percentage established in the plan. Gains from the investment of plan assets inure to the business owner's benefit, and losses are absorbed to the owner's detriment. Thus, if compensation stays constant, under a money purchase pension plan, the business owner will know the annual contribution, but not how much will be available at retirement. That will depend on the investment performance.

Example. Matthew, a business owner, aged 45, will retire at age 65 and has $30,000 a year to contribute to the qualified retirement plan. Under a defined contribution plan that provides for a $30,000 annual contribution, Matthew will have at retirement $600,000 plus the actual earnings or minus the actual losses on the plan's investments. Thus, if Matthew thinks the plan can realize a return on its investments greater than the interest assumption, the defined contribution plan may be preferable to the defined benefit plan.

In this example, the business owner's age had no bearing on the final result. If, under the defined contribution plan, the maximum contribution is $30,000 and, under the defined benefit plan, the amount that could be contributed is $50,000, the business owner would have more available at retirement under the defined benefit plan (unless the defined contribution plan's investment return was very high). If the business owner is age 35 at the time the plan is adopted, the extra ten years of compounded earnings—assuming a better-than-average return—may make the defined contribution plan a better choice.

Q 29:20   How can the use of a normal retirement age earlier than 65 benefit the business owner?

In a defined benefit plan, using a retirement age earlier than 65 may substantially increase the amount of contributions that must be made each year to fund the retirement benefits, which, in turn, increases the business owner's tax deduction. This is because there are fewer years in which to fund the retirement benefits.

There are several obstacles that must be overcome to take advantage of this planning opportunity. First, IRS says that a retirement age earlier than 65 can be used as a basis for computing required contributions only if the lower age approximates the age at which company employees customarily retire. [Rev Rul 78-331, 1978-2 CB 158; Rev Rul 78-120, 1978-1 CB 117; Ltr Ruls 8552001, 8610002]

Second, because the defined benefit plan will require larger contributions, the company will have to produce a higher cash flow to fund the plan. If it cannot meet the increased funding required, it may be subject to a penalty tax (see Q 8:16).

Finally, the business owner must be able to show that the total compensation package salary plus retirement plan contributions made on the business owner's behalf is reasonable (see Qs 12:1, 29:15).

The IRS position regarding the use of a normal retirement age earlier than 65 is that an actuarial assumption that employees retire at a normal retirement age that ignores the actual incidence of retirement in the work force could cause the assumptions to be unreasonable and the amounts to be not currently deductible. Assumptions should be monitored and adjusted accordingly to reflect current experience. The analysis for funding purposes is at what age is retirement most likely to take place, a determination of probability that is derived from the average retirement age of the group. [Ltr Rul 8808005; Rev Rul 78-331, 1978-2 CB 158; also see Jerome Mirza & Assocs, Ltd v United States, 882 F 2d 229 (7th Cir 1989)]

In more recent years, however, courts have concluded that, since the assumptions used were not "substantially unreasonable" and represented the actuary's best estimate of anticipated experience under the plans based on actuarial assumptions used by similar plans, IRS was precluded from requiring a retroactive change of assumptions. [Rhoades, McKee and Boer v United States, No. 1:91:CV:540 (WD Mich 1993); Vinson & Elkins, 99 TC 9 (1992); Citrus Valley Estates, Inc, 99 TC No. 21 (1992); Wachtell, Lipton, Rosen & Katz, 64 TCM 128 (1992)] For a discussion of these cases, see Question 8:8.

Q 29:21 How does permitted disparity benefit the business owner?

Taking permitted disparity into consideration can help business owners reach what may be their primary goal in setting up a retirement plan: rewarding themselves and their essential employees. By designing the retirement plan with permitted disparity, the business owners can give proportionately greater benefits or make proportionately greater contributions to the plan on their behalf than they do for rank-and-file workers. A qualified retirement plan that covers self-employed individuals (see Q 29:8) may consider permitted disparity in the same way that a corporate qualified retirement plan may.

For details on how permitted disparity works, see Chapter 7.

Q 29:22 Is a voluntary contribution feature attractive to the business owner?

A business owner can make voluntary nondeductible contributions to a qualified retirement plan, but such contributions are now subject to limitations and nondiscrimination tests. These nondiscrimination requirements reduce the attractiveness of allowing voluntary employee contributions. For details regarding the limitations on voluntary contributions, see Questions 23:48 through 23:55.

Q 29:23   Is it advantageous for the business owner to include life insurance protection in the qualified retirement plan?

By including life insurance in the plan, the corporate business owner is able to shift a personal expense (not tax-deductible) to the corporation. Just as the corporation's plan contributions are deductible, contributions (within limits) to pay for the life insurance are deductible. The corporate business owner will, however, have to include in gross income the cost of the current life insurance protection received under the plan.

There is a different rule for a self-employed individual (see Q 29:8). Plan contributions made on behalf of a self-employed individual that are allocable to the purchase of pure life insurance (the term element, not the entire premium) are not deductible (see Q 14:3). [IRC §§ 404(a)(8)(C), 404(e); Treas Reg § 1.404(e)-1A(g)] For further details, see Chapter 14.

Q 29:24   May the company borrow from its qualified retirement plan to acquire assets needed in its business?

Generally, no. A penalty tax (see below) is imposed on any prohibited transaction (see Q 20:1), which includes the lending of money between a plan and the company. Thus, a company may not borrow from its plan for any purpose. [IRC § 4975(c)(1)(B)]

DOL, however, may grant an exemption from the loan restrictions. Generally, an exemption is granted only if it is (1) administratively feasible; (2) in the interests of the plan, its participants, and beneficiaries; and (3) protective of the rights of participants and beneficiaries of the plan. [IRC § 4975(c)(2)]

Exemptions for loans from a qualified retirement plan to the company to buy business assets have been approved by DOL. The company must have a good credit rating, the interest rate must be comparable to what a bank would charge, and adequate security must be provided. For examples of when an exemption will be allowed, see Question 20:11.

The penalty tax on a prohibited transaction is imposed at the rate of 5 percent of the amount involved in the transaction for every year (or part of a year). If the 5 percent tax is imposed and the prohibited transaction is not corrected within the taxable period, an additional tax equal to 100 percent of the amount involved in the transaction is imposed.

Both the initial and additional taxes are payable by the individual who participated in the prohibited transaction. The taxable period begins when the prohibited transaction occurs; it ends, if it is not corrected, on the earlier of the date the notice of deficiency with respect to the 5 percent tax is mailed or the date the 5 percent tax is assessed. [IRC §§ 4975(a), 4975(b), 4975(f)]

Q 29:25   May a business owner borrow from the qualified retirement plan?

Yes, if the owner is a participant in the corporation's qualified retirement plan and the plan contains a provision authorizing loans to participants. However, a shareholder-employee (i.e., a more-than-5-percent shareholder) of an S corporation, and certain related individuals, may not borrow from the corporation's qualified retirement plan. [IRC §§ 401(a)(13), 4975(d)]

The general rules for loans apply to a self-employed individual (see Q 29:8) other than an owner-employee (see Q 29:9). However, the law prohibits a qualified retirement plan from lending to an owner-employee or to the owner-employee's spouse and certain other relatives. [IRC §§ 401(a)(13), 4975(d)]

See Questions 13:44 through 13:48 and Question 20:7 for further discussion.

Q 29:26   May a director of a corporation establish a qualified retirement plan based on the director's fees?

An outside director may establish a qualified retirement plan on the basis of such fee income. Since many outside directors are in high income tax brackets, the creation of a qualified retirement plan may be an especially attractive tax-saving device for these individuals. [Rev Rul 68-595, 1968-2 CB 378]

Special rules apply to an inside director. An inside director is an individual who is both an employee (or leased employee, owner, or manager) and a director of the same corporation. If the inside director maintains a qualified retirement plan apart from any plan maintained by the corporation, then, to the extent that contributions, forfeitures, and benefits under the inside director's individual plan are attributable to services performed for the corporation as a director, the individual is treated as an employee of the corporation and the inside director's interest in the individual plan is treated as though it was provided under both (1) a separate qualified retirement plan maintained by the corporation and covering only the inside director, and (2) any actual plan maintained by the corporation in which the director participates.

If either of these plans fails to meet the qualification requirements (see Chapter 4), any plan actually maintained by the corporation that covers the inside director and the plan maintained by the inside director may be disqualified.

Q 29:27 What happens if a business owner controls two corporations?

For purposes of determining whether a retirement plan is qualified, all employees of corporations that are members of a controlled group of corporations are treated as if they were employed by a single employer. If the business owner controls both Kenneth Corp. and Robert Corp. but establishes a retirement plan only for the employees of Kenneth Corp., the plan may not be approved by IRS (see Qs 5:30–5:32). [IRC § 414(b)]

Q 29:28 Does any special coverage requirement apply if an owner-employee controls another business?

Yes. If an individual is an owner-employee (see Q 29:9) of more than one business and participates in a qualified retirement plan maintained by one of the individual's businesses (Plan X), all employees of any other business controlled by the owner-employee must be covered by a plan that gives them benefits at least as favorable as those provided for the owner-employee under Plan X. [IRC §§ 401(d)(1), 401(d)(2); Treas Reg § 1.401-12(l); see also IRC § 414(c)]

Control means (1) ownership of the entire interest in an unincorporated trade or business or (2) ownership of more than 50 percent of either the capital interest or the profits interest in a partnership.

Example. Debi is the sole owner of a record store and is also a 51 percent partner in a hardware store. The hardware store maintains a qualified retirement plan. No contributions to the hardware store's qualified retirement plan can be made on Debi's behalf unless her record store gives its employees equal benefits under a qualified retirement plan.

This special coverage requirement is one of the few restrictions that apply to qualified retirement plans that cover owner-employees but not to corporate retirement plans. If TSB '93 (see Q 1:13) is enacted, Debi could participate in the hardware store's plan because the record store and the hardware store are not trades or businesses under common control (see Qs 5:30–5:32). However, the qualified retirement plan must provide that contributions on behalf of the owner-employee may be made only with respect to the owner-employee's earned income (see Q 29:10) derived from the trade or business adopting the plan. This change will be effective for years beginning after December 31, 1993. [TSB '93, Act § 233]

Q 29:29 What happens if the business owner sets up a management corporation?

If the business owner establishes a second corporation to perform management functions for the owner's other closely held corporation (e.g., a manufacturing corporation) and owns at least 80 percent of the stock of each corporation, both corporations will be considered to be members of a controlled group of corporations (see Qs 29:27, 5:30–5:32). [IRC §§ 414(b), 1563(a)]

If the management corporation establishes a qualified retirement plan for the business owner (its only employee) and the manufacturing corporation has no plan for its employees, the plan probably will not be qualified because of inadequate coverage and participation (see Q 5:1).

In addition, even if there is no common ownership, if an organization principally performs management functions for one other organization, both such organizations are considered to be an affiliated service group (see Qs 29:31, 29:32).

Q 29:30　Are there advantages gained by using a professional corporation together with a professional service partnership?

The answer may be yes, but all employees of members of an affiliated service group (see Q 29:31) will be treated as employed by a single employer for purposes of plan qualification. [IRC § 414(m)]

Q 29:31　What is an affiliated service group?

An affiliated service group consists of a service organization (FSO) and one or both of the following:

1. A service organization (A-ORG) that is a shareholder or partner in the FSO and that either regularly performs services for the FSO or is regularly associated with the FSO in performing services for third persons; and
2. Any other organization (B-ORG) if a significant portion of the business of the B-ORG is the performance of services for the FSO or the A-ORG (or for both) of a type historically performed in the service field of the FSO or the A-ORG by employees, and 10 percent or more of the interests in the B-ORG is held by individuals who are highly compensated employees of the FSO or A-ORG.

[IRC § 414(m); Rev Rul 81-105, 1981-1 CB 256]

Example. Medical partnership P consists of corporate partners A, B, and C. Each partner owns one-third of the partnership. The partnership employs nurses and clerical employees. Corporations A, B, and C have only one employee each, the respective shareholders. The partnership does not maintain a retirement plan. Corporations A, B, and C maintain separate retirement plans.

Partnership P may be designated as the FSO. Since Corporations A, B, and C are partners in the FSO and regularly perform services for the FSO, Corporations A, B, and C are A-ORGs. Because

Corporations A, B, and C are A-ORGs for the same FSO, Corporations A, B, and C and the FSO constitute an affiliated service group. Consequently, all the employees of Corporations A, B, and C and the employees of P are considered as employed by a single employer for purposes of testing the qualification of the three separate retirement plans maintained by Corporations A, B, and C.

IRS had issued proposed regulations directed at determining what types of organizational structures would be disregarded in order to prevent the avoidance of employee benefit requirements. These regulations covered affiliated service groups, leased employees (see Q 5:48), and other organizational arrangements. However, in 1993, as part of the Regulatory Burden Reduction Initiative, IRS withdrew those proposed regulations because IRS did not plan to finalize them. [TD 8474]

Q 29:32   Will IRS rule on the qualified status of the retirement plan of a member of an affiliated service group?

Yes. IRS has set out procedures for obtaining determination letters on the qualification of a retirement plan established by a member of an affiliated service group.

An employer (1) that has adopted a new retirement plan, (2) that has amended an existing retirement plan to satisfy the affiliated service group rules, or (3) whose affiliated service group status has changed may request a determination on whether the retirement plan is qualified, taking into consideration employees of any other organization who must be treated as employees of that employer. Generally, a determination letter issued with respect to the retirement plan will cover the affiliated service group rules only if the employer submits, with the determination letter application, certain information. If IRS considers whether the retirement plan of the employer (or group of employers) satisfies the requirements of the affiliated service group rules, the determination letter issued to the employer(s) will indicate that these questions have been considered and that the retirement plan satisfies qualification requirements relating to the affiliated service group rules. Without this statement, a determination letter does not apply to any qualification issue arising by reason of the affiliated service group rules.

The application for a determination letter must include the following:

1. A description of the business of the employer, specifically discussing whether it is a service organization or an organization whose principal business is the performance of management functions.

2. Identification of other members (or possible members) of the affiliated service group.

3. A description of the nature of the business of each member (or possible member) of the affiliated service group, specifically discussing whether the member is a service organization or management organization.

4. The ownership interests between the employer and the members (or possible members) of the affiliated service group.

5. A description of services performed for the employer by the members (or possible members) of the affiliated service group, or vice versa, including financial data as to whether the services are a significant portion of the member's business and are of a type historically performed in the employer's service field by employees.

6. A description of how the employer and the members (or possible members) of the affiliated service group associate in performing services for other parties.

7. A description of management functions, if any, performed by the employer for the members (or possible members) of the affiliated service group, or received by the employer from any other members (or possible members) of the group (including data as to whether such management functions are performed on a regular and continuing basis) and whether it is not unusual for such management functions to be performed by employees of organizations in the employer's business field.

8. If management functions are performed by the employer for the members (or possible members) of the affiliated service group, a description of what part of the employer's business constitutes the performance of management functions for the members (or possible members) of the group (including the

percentage of gross receipts derived from management activities as compared to the gross receipts from other activities).

9. A brief description of any other retirement plan(s) maintained by the members (or possible members) of the affiliated service group if such other retirement plan(s) is designated as a unit for qualification purposes.

10. A description of how the retirement plan(s) satisfies the coverage requirements if the members (or possible members) of the affiliated service group are considered part of an affiliated service group with the employer.

11. A copy of any ruling issued by the IRS National Office to the employer as to whether the employer is a member of an affiliated service group; a copy of any prior ruling that considered the effect of affiliated service group status on the employer's retirement plan; and, if known, a copy of any such ruling issued to any other member or possible member of the same affiliated service group, accompanied by a statement as to whether the facts upon which the ruling was based have changed.

[Rev Proc 85-43, 1985-2 CB 501; Rev Rul 83-36, 1983-1 CB 763; Rev Proc 80-30, 1980-1 CB 685]

Q 29:33 What is a personal service corporation?

A personal service corporation is a corporation that provides, as its principal activity, personal services substantially performed by the employee-owners (see Q 29:35). This definition is not limited to incorporated professionals but will also apply to incorporated salesmen, consultants, and other service-rendering individuals. [IRC § 269A(b)(1); Prop Reg § 1.269A-1(b)(1)]

Q 29:34 Can the income of a personal service corporation be allocated to the employee-owner?

If substantially all of the services of a personal service corporation (see Q 29:33) are performed for one other organization (see Q 29:36) and the principal purpose for forming the corporation is the avoidance of income tax by reducing the income of, or obtaining the benefit of any deduction for, any employee-owner (see Q 29:35) that would not otherwise be available, IRS may allocate income and deductions between the personal service corporation and its employee-owners. [IRC §§ 269A, 482; Prop Reg §§ 1.269A-1(a), 1.269A-1(f); Haag, 88 TC 604 (1987); Foglesong v Comm'r, 691 F 2d 848 (7th Cir 1982), *rev'g* 77 TC 1102 (1981); Achiro, 77 TC 881 (1981); Keller, 723 F 2d 58 (10th Cir 1983), *aff'g* 77 TC 1014 (1981)]

Since the personal service corporation must perform services for only one other organization and need not have any ownership interest in such organization, this provision both broadens the affiliated service group rules (see Q 29:31) and applies to other situations.

Now that parity between the amount of retirement benefits and contributions available to the employee-owner under qualified corporate retirement plans and qualified retirement plans covering self-employed individuals (see Q 29:8) has been achieved, IRS should not be able to allocate qualified retirement plan deductions to the incorporated employee-owner, since the employee-owner could then receive the same benefits without incorporating. However, if the incorporated employee-owner uses the corporation to obtain other tax benefits not available to an unincorporated employee-owner, those tax deductions may be lost (see Qs 29:6, 29:38).

Where the individual was *not* self-employed and was initially an employee of one other organization (see Q 29:36), IRS failed in its attempt to tax the individual on contributions made to the qualified retirement plan adopted by the individual's personal service corporation. The individual, a professional hockey player, entered into an employment contract with his personal service corporation, which, in turn, contracted with the hockey club to provide the individual's services. The court ruled that valid contractual relationships existed so IRS could not allocate the plan contributions to the individual as taxable income. [Sargent v Comm'r, 929 F 2d 1252 (8th Cir 1991)]

Q 29:35   Who is an employee-owner?

An employee-owner is an employee who, directly or indirectly, owns more than 10 percent of the stock of the personal service corporation. [IRC § 269A(b)(2); Prop Reg § 1.269A-1(b)(2)]

Q 29:36 What is one other organization for purposes of the personal service corporation rules?

For the potential reallocation of income and deductions between the personal service corporation and the employee-owner (see Q 29:35) to occur, substantially all of the services of the corporation must be performed for one other corporation, partnership, or other entity. [IRC § 269A(a)(1); Prop Reg § 1.269A-1(a)(1)]

All related persons are treated as one other entity. [IRC §§ 144(a)(3), 269A(b)(3); Prop Reg § 1.269A-1(b)(3)]

Q 29:37 Is there a safe harbor for a personal service corporation?

Yes. In general, a personal service corporation (see Q 29:33) will be deemed not to have been formed for the principal purpose of avoiding income tax if the federal income tax liability of no employee-owner (see Q 29:35) is reduced in a 12-month period by more than the lesser of (1) $2,500 or (2) 10 percent of the federal income tax liability of the employee-owner that would have resulted in that 12-month period had the employee-owner performed the personal services in an individual capacity. [Prop Reg § 1.269A-1(c)]

Q 29:38 Is a retirement plan considered in determining whether the principal purpose of a personal service corporation is the avoidance of income taxes?

Generally, the existence of a qualified retirement plan will not be taken into account in determining the presence or absence of a principal purpose of the personal service corporation (see Q 29:33) to avoid income tax for purposes of the safe-harbor rule (see Qs 29:34, 29:37). [Sargent v Comm'r, 929 F 2d 1252 (8th Cir 1991); Prop Reg § 1.269A-1(d)]

Q 29:39 Is there any type of tax-favored qualified retirement plan for the business owner that is simple to adopt and inexpensive to operate?

Yes, a simplified employee pension (SEP) requires only a minimal amount of paperwork and expense to adopt and administer. For details on SEPs, see Chapter 27.

Q 29:40   Are qualified retirement plan benefits exempt from participants' creditors?

In 1992, the United States Supreme Court held that a participant's interest in a qualified retirement plan is exempt from the claims of creditors in a bankruptcy proceeding, thereby resolving the conflict among the Courts of Appeals. [Patterson v Shumate, 112 S Ct 2242 (1992)]

ERISA and the Code require every qualified retirement plan to prohibit the assignment or alienation of benefits under the plan. [ERISA § 206(d)(1); IRC § 401(a)(13)] Federal Bankruptcy Code Section 541(c)(2) excludes from the bankruptcy estate property of the debtor that is subject to a restriction on transfer enforceable under applicable nonbankruptcy law. The Supreme Court ruled that the anti-alienation provision contained in a qualified retirement plan constitutes a restriction on transfer enforceable under applicable nonbankruptcy law and, accordingly, a debtor may exclude his interest in such a plan from the property of the bankruptcy estate.

After the Supreme Court decision, bankruptcy trustees developed a new strategy. Since ERISA protects only *qualified* retirement plan benefits, bankruptcy trustees are bringing into question the qualified status of the plan. What was once the domain of IRS (see Q 15:1) may now become a territorial dispute with the bankruptcy courts. [Pitrat v Garlikov, 1993 US App Lexis 10361 (9th Cir 1993); In re Lane, Jr, No. 91-17010-260 (Bankr ED NY 1993)]

Despite the Supreme Court decision, courts have tended to permit IRS to levy against a participant's benefits (see Q 4:24).

Chapter 30

Qualified Domestic Relations Orders

The rate of divorce in the United States continues to increase; and, in many cases, qualified retirement plan benefits represent the major marital asset. The Retirement Equity Act of 1984 established a new category of plan benefit recipients—alternate payees under qualified domestic relations orders (QDROs). This chapter analyzes the requirements for QDROs and their tax consequences.

Q 30:1   What is a qualified domestic relations order?

A QDRO is a domestic relations order (DRO; see Q 30:2) that creates or recognizes the existence of an alternate payee's (see Q 30:3) right to, or assigns to an alternate payee the right to, receive all or a portion of the benefits payable with respect to a participant under a qualified retirement plan, and that complies with certain special requirements (see Q 30:2). [IRC § 414(p)(1)(A); Treas Reg § 1.401(a)-13(g)(1); Brotman v Molitch, No. 88-9876 (ED Pa 1989)]

Federal courts and state courts have concurrent jurisdiction to rule on the validity of QDROs. [Board of Trustees of the Laborers Pension Trust Fund for Northern California v Levingston, 816 F Supp 1496 (ND Ca 1993); ERISA §§ 502(a)(1)(B), 502(e)(1)]

The rules relating to QDROs generally became effective on January 1, 1985. However, a plan administrator (see Q 16:1) may treat a DRO entered before 1985 as a QDRO, whether or not it meets the above definition, but must treat it as a QDRO if, on January 1, 1985, the plan administrator was paying benefits in compliance therewith. If a plan administrator chooses not to treat a pre-1985 order as a QDRO, the alternate payee should try to have the DRO amended to satisfy the requirements for a QDRO.

Q 30:2   What is a domestic relations order?

A DRO is a judgment, decree, or order (including approval of a property settlement agreement) made pursuant to a state domestic relations law (including a community property law) that relates to the provision of child support, alimony payments, or marital property rights to an alternate payee (see Q 30:3). [IRC § 414(p)(1)(B)]

A DRO must also satisfy certain special requirements. The DRO must clearly specify:

1. The name and last known mailing address (if any) of the participant and the name and mailing address of each alternate payee covered by the order;

2. The amount or percentage of the participant's benefits to be paid by the qualified retirement plan to each such alternate payee or the manner in which such amount or percentage is to be determined;

3. The number of payments or period to which the order applies; and

4. The qualified retirement plan to which the order applies.

[IRC § 414(p)(2)]

In addition, a DRO may not require:

1. The qualified retirement plan to provide any type or form of benefit, or any option, not otherwise provided under the plan (see Q 30:8);

2. The qualified retirement plan to provide increased benefits (determined on the basis of actuarial value); or

3. The payment of benefits to an alternate payee that are required to be paid to another alternate payee under another order previously determined to be a QDRO (see Q 30:1).

[IRC § 414(p)(3)]

An order will not be disqualified merely because it does not specify the current mailing address of the participant and each alternate payee as long as the plan administrator (see Q 16:1) has reason to know the addresses independently of the order (for example, the alternate payee is also a plan participant and the plan records include a current address for each participant). [REA Senate Comm Report]

An order will not be treated as providing increased benefits unless it provides for the payment of benefits in excess of those to which the participant would be entitled in the absence of the order. A DRO will remain qualified with respect to a successor qualified retirement plan of the same employer or a qualified retirement plan of a successor employer. [REA Senate Comm Report]

An order will not fail to be a QDRO even if the form of the benefit does not continue to be a form permitted under the qualified retire- ment plan because of a plan amendment or a change of law. In the case of a plan amendment, an alternative payee remains entitled to receive benefits in the form specified in the order. In the case of a law change that makes the benefit form specified in the order impermis- sible, the plan must permit the alternative payee to select a form of benefit specified in the plan. In either case, the elected form cannot affect, in any way, the amount or form of benefits payable to the participant. [TRA '86 Comm Reports]

If a DRO satisfies all of the above requirements, then the order will satisfy the special requirements of a QDRO (see Q 30:1).

Q 30:3   Who is an alternate payee?

An alternate payee is a spouse, former spouse, child, or other dependent of a participant who is recognized by a DRO (see Q 30:2) as having a right to receive all or a portion of the benefits payable under the qualified retirement plan with respect to the participant. [IRC § 414(p)(8)]

Whether the alternate payee is the spouse or a former spouse of the participant, as opposed to a child or other dependent of the participant, affects the tax consequences of a distribution from the qualified retirement plan pursuant to a QDRO (see Q 30:1). See Questions 30:17 through 30:19 for details.

Q 30:4   Does a QDRO violate the anti-assignment rule?

Generally, a retirement plan will not be a qualified retirement plan unless the plan provides that plan benefits may not be assigned or alienated. However, this prohibition against the assignment of plan benefits does not apply to the creation, assignment, or recognition of a right to any benefit payable with respect to a participant pursuant to a QDRO (see Qs 4:24, 30:1). [IRC § 401(a)(13); Temp Reg § 1.401(a)-13(g); Ltr Rul 9234014; but see Fox Valley & Vicinity Construction Workers Pension Fund v Brown, No. 88-2322 (7th Cir 1990)]

Q 30:5   Do the QDRO rules apply to all qualified retirement plans?

Yes. The QDRO (see Q 30:1) requirements apply to all qualified retirement plans and also apply to tax-sheltered annuities. [IRC §§ 401(a)(13), 414(p)(9)]

The QDRO rules have also been extended to governmental plans and church plans; however, distributions from such plans are treated as made pursuant to a QDRO without the necessity of satisfying the special QDRO requirements (see Qs 30:1, 30:2). If these types of plans provide that plan benefits may not be assigned or alienated (see Q 30:4) and such a provision is enforceable under state law, it is possible that plan benefits may not be reachable even with a QDRO. [IRC §§ 414(d), 414(e), 414(p)(11)]

Although the QDRO rules do not apply to IRAs (see Q 26:1), the transfer of an individual's interest in an IRA to the individual's spouse or former spouse under a divorce or separation agreement is not considered a taxable transfer made by such individual; and, thereafter, the IRA is treated as maintained for the benefit of the spouse or former spouse. It is also possible for a QDRO to require a distribution of benefits to the participant and then a transfer of a portion or all of the distribution to an IRA for the benefit of the former spouse. [IRC § 408(d)(6); Ltr Rul 9016077]

An IRA may also be used to implement a QDRO if a direct transfer of the participant's interest in a retirement plan to the participant's spouse is otherwise prohibited. When a QDRO required a participant-contract holder to transfer his interest in a tax-sheltered annuity to his spouse, but the terms of the annuity prevented a transfer to anyone other than the contract holder, the participant-contract holder could surrender the tax-sheltered annuity for its cash surrender value, roll over the distribution to an IRA, and then transfer the IRA to his spouse. [IRC § 408(d)(6); Ltr Rul 8916083]

Q 30:6 Does a QDRO affect the qualification of a retirement plan?

A qualified retirement plan will not be treated as failing to satisfy the general qualification requirements (see Q 4:1) and the restriction on distributions under a 401(k) plan (see Q 23:33) solely because of a payment to an alternate payee (see Q 30:3) pursuant to a QDRO (see Q 30:1). This is the case even if the plan provides for payments pursuant to a QDRO to an alternate payee prior to the time the plan may make payments to a participant. For example, a qualified retirement plan may pay an alternate payee even though the participant may not receive a distribution because the participant continues to be employed by the employer (see Q 30:8). [IRC § 414(p)(10); Treas Reg § 1.401(a)-13(g)(3)]

Q 30:7 Must a qualified retirement plan include provisions regarding QDROs?

No. A qualified retirement plan need not include provisions with regard to QDROs, and this exclusion will not cause the retirement plan to fail to satisfy the general qualification requirements. [Treas Reg § 1.401(a)-13(g)(2)]

Q 30:8   What is the earliest retirement age rule?

A DRO may not require a qualified retirement plan to provide any type or form of benefit, or any option, not otherwise provided under the plan (see Q 30:2). [IRC § 414(p)(3)(A)]

A DRO will not fail to satisfy the above requirement solely because the DRO requires that payment of benefits be made to an alternate payee (see Q 30:3):

1. In the case of any payment before the participant has separated from service, on or after the date on which the participant attains (or would have attained) the earliest retirement age (see Q 30:9);
2. As if the participant had retired on the date on which such payment is to begin under the DRO; and
3. In any form in which such benefits may be paid under the qualified retirement plan to the participant.

[IRC § 414(p)(4)(A)]

A DRO will be a QDRO (see Q 30:1) even though the order provides that payments to the alternate payee may begin on or after the date on which the participant attains the earliest retirement age under the qualified retirement plan, whether or not the participant actually retires on that date. Therefore, a participant cannot delay an alternate payee's receipt of benefits by failing to take advantage of an early retirement option provided by the plan. [IRC § 414(p)(4)(A)(i)] For an exception to the earliest retirement age rule, see Question 30:10.

Payments of benefits prior to a participant's separation from service, but after earliest retirement age, must be made as if the participant had actually retired on the date payments are to begin under the QDRO. Only benefits actually accrued on that date are taken into account, and any employer subsidy for early retirement is not taken into account. An employer subsidizes an early retirement benefit to the extent that the benefit provided is greater than the actuarial equivalent of a retirement benefit commencing at normal retirement age. For example, if a participant would be entitled to a monthly retirement benefit under a qualified retirement plan of $1,000 at age 65 and the plan permits the participant to retire at age 62 with the full $1,000 monthly retirement benefit, the employer is subsidizing the early retirement benefit. Actuarial equivalency is computed using the interest rate specified in the qualified retirement plan. If the plan does not specify an interest rate for determining actuarial equivalency (as would be the case if the employer were subsidizing the benefit), a 5 percent interest rate is used. [IRC § 414(p)(4)(A)(ii)]

Benefit payments to an alternate payee after the earliest retirement age generally may be in any form allowed under the qualified retirement plan; however, benefits may not be paid in the form of a joint and survivor annuity with respect to the alternate payee and the alternate payee's subsequent spouse. [IRC § 414(p)(4)(A)(iii); Treas Reg § 1.401(a)-13(g)(4)(iii)(B)]

The amount payable under a QDRO following the participant's earliest retirement age cannot exceed the amount that the participant would be entitled to receive at such time. For example, assume that a profit sharing plan provides that a participant may withdraw some, but not all, of the participant's account balance (see Q 9:2) before separation from service. A QDRO may provide for payment to an alternate payee up to the amount that the participant may withdraw. [REA Senate Comm Report]

Q 30:9   What does earliest retirement age mean?

Earliest retirement age means the earlier of:

1. The earliest date on which the participant is entitled to a distribution under the qualified retirement plan; or
2. The later of (a) the date on which the participant attains age 50, or (b) the earliest date on which the participant could begin receiving a distribution from the plan if the participant separated from service. [IRC § 414(p)(4)(B)]

If the plan permits distributions to be made to the employee while an active participant (in-service distributions), the QDRO (see Q 30:1) can require that payments be made to the alternate payee (see Q 30:3) at any time when the participant qualifies for an in-service distribution. If the plan does not permit in-service distributions but distributions may begin at any time after separation from service, the earliest retirement age will be the earlier of age 50 or the date of separation from service. If the plan does not permit in-service distributions and does not permit distributions until the attainment of a specified age (age 65, for example), the earliest retirement age will, in this case, be age 65.

Q 30:10 Can a distribution to an alternate payee be made before the earliest retirement age?

Yes. If the qualified retirement plan so permits, a QDRO (see Q 30:1) may require that payments be made to the alternate payee (see Q 30:3) prior to the participant's earliest retirement age (see Q 30:9). If the plan does not contain such a provision, the plan must be amended to permit a pre-earliest retirement age distribution. [TRA '86 Comm Reports; Ltr Ruls 8837013, 8744023]

Q 30:11 Must a qualified retirement plan establish a procedure to determine the qualified status of a DRO?

A qualified retirement plan must establish reasonable procedures to determine the qualified status of DROs (see Q 30:2) and to administer distributions made pursuant to QDROs (see Q 30:1). [IRC § 414(p)(6)(B)]

Although a qualified retirement plan need not include provisions regarding QDROs (see Q 30:7), the plan procedures must be in writing and the procedures must permit an alternate payee (see Q 30:3) to designate a representative to receive copies of the notices sent to the alternate payee with respect to a DRO. [REA Senate Comm Report]

Where a plan required that a "hold" be placed on a participant's account *after* receipt of a DRO, but the hold was placed *before* receipt because the plan administrator (see Q 16:1) had been informed that a DRO would be issued, the court ruled that the hold violated ERISA because it was contrary to the plan's written procedures. [Schoonmaker v The Employee Savings Plan of Amoco Corp and Participating Cos, No. 91-2944 (7th Cir 1993)]

Q 30:12   What happens when a qualified retirement plan receives a DRO?

If a DRO (see Q 30:2) is received by a qualified retirement plan, the plan administrator (see Q 16:1) must promptly notify the participant and each alternate payee (see Q 30:3) of the receipt of the DRO and the plan's procedures (see Q 30:11) for determining its qualified status. In addition, the plan administrator must determine whether the DRO is a QDRO (see Q 30:1) and notify the participant and each alternate payee of the determination. After the DRO is issued, it is not the responsibility of the plan administrator to determine if an individual is, in fact, the spouse, former spouse, child, or other dependent of the participant. [IRC § 414(p)(6)(A); Sippe v Sippe, 101 NC App 194 (1990); DOL Opinion 92-17A]

During the period in which the determination of whether a DRO is a QDRO is being made (by the plan administrator, by a court of competent jurisdiction, or otherwise), the plan administrator must separately account for the amounts (segregated amounts) that would have been payable to the alternate payee during such period if the DRO had been determined to be a QDRO. [IRC § 414(p)(7)(A); Board of Trustees of the Laborers Pension Trust Fund for Northern California v Levingston, No. 816 F Supp 1496 (ND Ca 1993)]

If, within the 18-month period beginning with the date on which the first payment under the DRO would be required, the DRO (or any modification thereof) is determined to be a QDRO, the plan administrator must pay the segregated amounts (including any interest thereon) to the alternate payee or payees. [IRC §§ 414(p)(7)(B), 414(p)(7)(E)]

If, within the 18-month period, it is determined that the DRO is not a QDRO or the determination is not made, then the plan administrator must pay the segregated amounts (including any interest thereon) to the person or persons who would have been entitled to such amounts if there had been no DRO. If a determination that a DRO is a QDRO is made after the 18-month period, it may be applied prospectively only. Therefore, the qualified retirement plan should not be liable to the alternate payee for payments for the period prior to the determination if the qualification is determined after the 18-month period. However, if a DRO is determined to be a QDRO after the 18-month period, the alternate payee may have a cause of action against the participant under state law for the amounts that were paid to the participant but that otherwise should have been paid to the alternate payee. [IRC §§ 414(p)(7)(C), 414(p)(7)(D); REA Senate Comm Report]

If the plan administrator fails to notify the participant and each alternate payee promptly of the procedures for determining the qualified status of the DRO, or fails to complete the determination process within a reasonable period after receipt, the plan administrator may be liable for breach of fiduciary duty.

Q 30:13 Can the amounts segregated for an alternate payee under a QDRO be forfeited?

If an alternate payee (see Q 30:3) cannot be located, the qualified retirement plan is not permitted to provide for the forfeiture of the alternate payee's segregated amounts (see Q 30:12) unless the plan provides for the segregated amounts to be fully reinstated when the alternate payee is located. [REA Senate Comm Report]

Q 30:14 How does a QDRO affect the qualified preretirement survivor annuity and qualified joint and survivor annuity requirements?

A QDRO (see Q 30:1) may provide that a former spouse will be treated as the participant's current spouse for some or all of the QPSA (see Q 10:9) and QJSA (see Q 10:8) requirements. [IRC § 414(p)(5); Treas Reg §§ 1.401(a)-13(g)(4)(i)(A), 1.401(a)-13(g)(4)(ii)]

To the extent a former spouse is treated as the participant's current spouse by reason of a QDRO, the actual current spouse will not be treated as the participant's current spouse. [IRC § 414(p)(5); Treas Reg § 1.401(a)-13(g)(4)(i)(B)]

Example 1. Assume Barrie is divorced from Larry, but a QDRO provides that Barrie shall be treated as Larry's current spouse with respect to all of Larry's benefits under a qualified retirement plan. Barrie will be treated as the surviving spouse under the QPSA and QJSA unless Larry obtains Barrie's consent to waive the QPSA or QJSA or both. The fact that Larry married Carrie after Larry's divorce from Barrie is disregarded. If, however, the QDRO had provided that Barrie would be treated as Larry's current spouse only with respect to benefits that accrued prior to the divorce, then Larry would need Barrie's consent to waive the QPSA or QJSA with respect to benefits accrued before the divorce, and Carrie's consent would be required with respect to the remainder of the benefits.

Example 2. Assume the same facts as in Example 1, except that the QDRO ordered that a portion of Larry's benefit must be distributed to Barrie rather than ordering that Barrie be treated as Larry's spouse. The QPSA and QJSA requirements would not apply to the part of Larry's benefit awarded Barrie. Instead, the QDRO would determine how Barrie's portion of Larry's benefit would be paid. Larry would be required to obtain Carrie's consent if Larry wanted to elect to waive either the QPSA or QJSA with respect to the remaining portion of his benefit.

Example 3. Assume the same facts as in Example 1, except that there was no QDRO and Larry died after marrying Carrie but never removed Barrie as his designated beneficiary. One court ruled that Carrie was entitled to one-half of Larry's plan benefits as his surviving spouse but that Barrie was entitled to the other half. [McMillan v Parrott, No. 89-611 (6th Cir 1990)]

If, because of a QDRO, more than one individual is treated as the surviving spouse, the qualified retirement plan may provide that the total amount to be paid in the form of a QPSA or survivor portion of a QJSA may not exceed the amount that would be paid if there were only one surviving spouse. The QPSA or survivor portion of the QJSA payable to each surviving spouse must be paid as an annuity based on the life of each respective spouse. If the QDRO splits the participant's benefit between the participant and a former spouse (either through separate accounts or percentage of the benefit), the surviving actual current spouse of the participant would be entitled to a QPSA or QJSA based on the participant's benefit reduced by the separate account or percentage payable to the former spouse. The calculation is made as if the separate account or percentage had been distributed to the participant. [Treas Reg § 1.401(a)-13(g)(4)(i)(C)]

If an alternate payee is treated pursuant to a QDRO as having an interest in the plan benefit, including a separate account or percentage of the participant's benefit, then the QDRO cannot provide the alternate payee with a greater right to designate a beneficiary for the alternate payee's benefit amount than the participant's right. The QPSA or QJSA provisions do not apply to the spouse of an alternate payee. If the former spouse who is treated as a current spouse should die prior to the participant's annuity starting date (see Q 10:3), then any actual current spouse of the participant would be treated as the current spouse, except as otherwise provided in the QDRO. [Treas Reg § 1.401(a)-13(g)(4)(iii)]

Q 30:15   Must an alternate payee consent to a distribution from a qualified retirement plan?

The general rules that apply to the distribution of benefits to a participant from a qualified retirement plan also apply to the distribution of benefits to an alternate payee (see Q 30:3) pursuant to a QDRO (see Q 30:1). (For exceptions, see Qs 30:6, 30:8, 30:14.)

If the distribution to the alternate payee does not exceed $3,500, the alternate payee's consent is not required. However, if the distribution exceeds $3,500, the alternate payee's consent is required (see Q 10:60).

In determining whether the present value of the benefit payable to the alternate payee exceeds $3,500, the present value of the participant's remaining benefit is disregarded. Similarly, for purposes of determining whether the present value of the benefit payable to the participant exceeds $3,500, the present value of the benefit payable to the alternate payee under a QDRO is disregarded. [TRA '86 Comm Reports]

Q 30:16   Does a QDRO affect the maximum amount of the participant's benefits under a qualified retirement plan?

Even though a participant's benefits are awarded to an alternate payee (see Q 30:3) pursuant to a QDRO (see Q 30:1), the benefits awarded to the alternate payee are still considered benefits of the participant for purposes of applying the limitations of Section 415 to the participant's benefits. See Chapter 6 for details. [Treas Reg § 1.401(a)-13(g)(4)(iv)]

Q 30:17   What are the income tax consequences of a QDRO to the participant?

If the alternate payee (see Q 30:3) pursuant to a QDRO (see Q 30:1) is other than the participant's spouse or former spouse (e.g., a child), any distribution from a qualified retirement plan to such alternate payee will be included in the participant's gross income for the year of distribution. If, however, any portion of the distribution represents a recovery of the participant's investment in the contract (see Q 13:2), that portion will be excluded from the participant's gross income. [IRC §§ 402(a), 402(e)(1)(A)]

The balance to the credit of an employee (see Q 13:5) does not include an amount payable to an alternate payee under a QDRO. So, an alternate payee's decision to receive payments in a form other than a lump sum will not affect the participant's eligibility for the special tax treatment afforded a lump-sum distribution (see Q 13:4) or the participant's eligibility to roll over a distribution from the qualified retirement plan. [IRC § 402(d)(4)(H); Ltr Ruls 8935041, 8743102]

See Chapters 13 and 28 for details on taxation of distributions and rollovers.

Q 30:18   What are the income tax consequences of a QDRO to an alternate payee spouse or former spouse?

If the alternate payee (see Q 30:3) is the spouse or former spouse of the participant, any distribution from a qualified retirement plan to such alternate payee pursuant to a QDRO (see Q 30:1) will be included in the alternate payee's gross income for the year of distribution. The participant's investment in the contract (see Q 13:2) must be apportioned between the participant and such alternate payee. The investment in the contract will be allocated on a pro rata basis between the present value of the distribution to the alternate payee and the present value of all other benefits payable with respect to the participant. [IRC §§ 72(m)(10), 402(e)(1)(A); Ltr Ruls 9138004, 9013007]

If a distribution of the balance to the credit of an employee (see Q 13:5) would be treated as a lump-sum distribution (see Q 13:4), then the payment under a QDRO of the balance to the credit of an alternate payee spouse or former spouse of the participant will be treated as a lump-sum distribution. The balance to the credit of the alternate payee does not include any amount payable to the participant. [IRC § 402(d)(4)(J)]

If there is no QDRO, the spouse or former spouse is not an alternate payee, and a distribution from the plan to the participant, who then gives the payment to such spouse, is included in the participant's gross income (see Q 13:1).

For details on taxation of distributions, see Chapter 13.

Q 30:19 Can an alternate payee roll over a distribution pursuant to a QDRO from a qualified retirement plan?

A distribution from a qualified retirement plan pursuant to a QDRO (see Q 30:1) to an alternate payee (see Q 30:3) who is not the spouse or former spouse of the participant (e.g., a child) may not be rolled over to another qualified retirement plan or to an IRA.

Since such alternate payee pays no income tax on the distribution, the ineligibility of the alternate payee to roll over the distribution is of no importance to the alternate payee. However, because the participant remains taxable on a distribution to a nonspouse or nonformer spouse alternate payee, this ineligibility to roll over will cause the participant to include the distribution in income. This remains true even if the participant receives, at the same time, a distribution from the plan eligible to be rolled over and does roll over such distribution (see Q 30:17).

If, however, the alternate payee is the spouse or former spouse of the participant and receives an eligible rollover distribution (see Q 28:8) pursuant to a QDRO, the alternate payee is eligible to roll over any portion or all of the distribution to an eligible retirement plan (see Q 28:16). [IRC §§ 402(c), 402(e)(1)(B); Ltr Ruls 9109052, 9013007]

An eligible rollover distribution made to an alternate payee spouse or former spouse may be subject to mandatory 20 percent income tax withholding (see Q 16:7). Since an alternate payee nonspouse or nonformer spouse pays no income tax on the distribution, the distribution will not be subject to the automatic withholding rules. [IRC § 3405(c)]

For details on rollovers, see Chapter 28.

Q 30:20 Does the 10 percent early distribution tax apply to a distribution made to an alternate payee pursuant to a QDRO?

The 10 percent tax on early distributions (see Q 13:39) from qualified retirement plans does *not* apply to any distribution to any alternate payee (see Q 30:3) pursuant to a QDRO (see Q 30:1). [IRC § 72(t)(2)(D); Ltr Ruls 9051041, 9013007, 8935041]

Because of this exception, the 10 percent early distribution tax will not be imposed on the participant if the alternate payee is a nonspouse or nonformer spouse (e.g., a child) (see Q 30:17) and will not be imposed on a spouse or former spouse alternate payee (see Q 30:18).

If a spouse or former spouse alternate payee rolls over to an IRA a distribution pursuant to a QDRO from a qualified retirement plan (see Q 30:19), the alternate payee can commence distributions from the IRA prior to age 59½ in a series of substantially equal periodic payments and avoid the 10 percent tax on early distributions (see Q 13:40). [IRC § 72(t)(2)(A)(iv); Ltr Rul 9109052]

Q 30:21 How does a QDRO affect the excess distribution tax and the excess accumulation tax?

To calculate an individual's distributions for excess distribution tax purposes, amounts paid to an alternate payee (see Q 30:3) who is not the spouse or former spouse of the individual (e.g., a child) from a qualified retirement plan pursuant to a QDRO (see Q 30:1) are included, but amounts paid to an alternate payee spouse or former spouse are disregarded. Any amounts paid to an alternate payee spouse or former spouse from a qualified retirement plan pursuant to a QDRO are includible distributions of the alternate payee for excess distribution tax purposes (see Qs 13:27–13:30). [Ltr Rul 9138004]

To calculate a decedent's aggregate interests for excess accumulation tax purposes, amounts paid to an alternate payee who is not the spouse or former spouse of the decedent (e.g., a child) from a qualified retirement plan pursuant to a QDRO are included, but amounts paid to an alternate payee spouse or former spouse are disregarded. Any amounts paid to an alternate payee spouse or former spouse from a qualified retirement plan pursuant to a QDRO will be includible distributions of the alternate payee for excess distribution tax purposes and, if rolled over to an eligible retirement plan (see Q 30:19), will be includible, to the extent not withdrawn during the alternate payee's lifetime, in the alternate payee's calculation of aggregate interests for excess accumulation tax purposes. However, if the alternate payee is the spouse, as opposed to the former spouse, of the decedent, a special spousal election will be available (see Qs 14:21–14:28). [Ltr Rul 9138004]

An individual whose total benefits in all retirement plans (see Q 13:31) on August 1, 1986, had a value in excess of $562,500 was eligible to elect a special grandfather rule. The grandfather election permits the individual to offset distributions received during the individual's lifetime by the portion of the initial grandfather amount recovered during the year of distribution. Furthermore, if the grandfather election was made, the decedent's aggregate interests may be reduced by the unrecovered grandfather amount on the date of the decedent's death. The effect of the special grandfather rule is the potential reduction of the excess distribution tax and/or the excess accumulation tax (see Qs 13:31–13:36; 14:24–14:26).

IRS has ruled that, if a portion or all of a participant's qualified retirement plan benefits are awarded to the participant's spouse or former spouse pursuant to a QDRO, there is no statutory authority for allocating to the alternate payee any portion, pro rata or otherwise, of the participant's unrecovered grandfather amount. Since there is no statutory authority for an allocation of the unrecovered grandfather amount, the participant's unrecovered grandfather amount is not reduced because of the distribution required by the QDRO. [Ltr Rul 9138004]

Example. Larry had qualified retirement plan benefits of $2,000,000 on August 1, 1986 and made the grandfather election. In 1994, Larry and Carrie are divorced and, under a QDRO, $1,000,000 of Larry's benefits is allocated to Carrie. If Larry has not recovered any portion of his initial grandfather amount, he retains the entire $2,000,000 initial grandfather amount.

Q 30:22   Are qualified retirement plan benefits subject to equitable distribution?

Some portion or all of a participant's benefits under a qualified retirement plan may be awarded to the participant's spouse pursuant to a QDRO (see Q 30:1). [Hamstead v Hamstead, No. 19529 (SCA W Va 1990); Givler v Givler, No. Ca-181 (CA Tenn, Eastern Division, 1990)]

At least one court has ruled that qualified retirement plan benefits accrued prior to the marriage are not subject to an equitable distribution of marital assets absent evidence of a gift or conveyance. [Zaborowski v Zaborowski, No. 88-1802 (DCA Fla, 5th District, 1989)] However, another court ruled that plan benefits accrued during the time a couple lived together before marriage were subject to division upon divorce. [Bays v Bays, No. 5-3635 (SC Alaska 1991)]

In a matter in which a couple separated and, during the separation but prior to the divorce, one spouse became covered under a new plan, the court ruled that the new retirement benefits were separate property and not community property and therefore the nonparticipant spouse had no entitlement to the benefits. [In re the Matter of the Marriage of Manry, 60 Wn App 146 (1991)] In another case, to accomplish a division of marital property, the court ruled that the value of the spouse's pension benefits should be based on present value and not the projected value at age 65. [In re the Marriage of Keedy, No. 90-598 (SC Mont 1991)]

Q 30:23   Can a QDRO be enforced by an attachment of the participant's monthly retirement benefits?

One court has held that an order made pursuant to the state domestic relations law that relates to alimony payments is a QDRO (see Q 30:1), which may be enforced by attachment of the participant's (husband's) qualified retirement plan benefits. The court determined that, since the state domestic law allowed attachment of the husband's income in any form, the attachment order against his qualified retirement plan benefits was a QDRO, which allowed the wife to recover amounts for alimony. [Taylor v Taylor, 44 Ohio St 3d 61 (1989)] Another court ruled that a garnishment judgment against a plan participant for failure to make required alimony and child support payments must satisfy the QDRO require-ments. [Arizona Laborers, etc. Local 385 Pension Fund v Nevarez, 8 EBC 2227 (D Ariz 1987)]

Even though an award of attorney's fees incurred by a spouse to obtain a QDRO for spousal support was not itself a QDRO, a court ruled that qualified retirement plan benefits could be used to satisfy the award. [In re the Marriage of Olivarez, 8 EBC 1263 (Cal Ct App 1986)]

Q 30:24   Can a QDRO be discharged in bankruptcy?

One court has held that a participant's obligation to pay one-half of his qualified retirement plan benefits to his former spouse as part of a divorce decree's property settlement was a "debt" under the U.S. Bankruptcy Code that was dischargeable in bankruptcy. The property settlement awarded the former spouse one-half of the participant's qualified retirement plan benefits as he received them. The par-ticipant filed a Chapter 7 bankruptcy petition and listed that obligation as a dischargeable debt. The Bankruptcy Code defines a debt as a liability on a claim and a claim as a right to payment, whether or not such right is contingent or unmatured. The court held that the former spouse had a claim for a share of future qualified retirement plan payments, however contingent or unmatured that claim may be. Although a debt for alimony, maintenance, or support is not dischar-geable under the Bankruptcy Code, the obligation in this case was a property settlement and, therefore, a debt that was dischargeable in bankruptcy. [Bush v Taylor, No. 88-2145 (8th Cir 1990); see also Anderson v Lifeline Healthcare Group, Ltd, No. 92-5076 (10th Cir 1993)]

However, another court ruled that since the wife had been awarded a part of the husband's pension fund, it had become her property and was not a dischargeable debt of the participant-husband when he filed a Chapter 7 bankruptcy petition. [In re Zick, No. 89-02388 (Bankr ED Wis 1990)]

Table of Internal Revenue Code Sections

[References are to question numbers.]

The Pension Answer Book

[References are to question numbers.]

IRC Sections

[References are to question numbers.]

[References are to question numbers.]

IRC Sections

The Pension Answer Book

[References are to question numbers.]

[References are to question numbers.]

[References are to question numbers.]

IRC Sections

IRC Sections

[References are to question numbers.]

[References are to question numbers.]

Table of Treasury Regulations

[References are to question numbers.]

[References are to question numbers.]

[References are to question numbers.]

[References are to question numbers.]

[References are to question numbers.]

[References are to question numbers.]

[References are to question numbers.]

[References are to question numbers.]

[References are to question numbers.]

[References are to question numbers.]

Treasury Regulations

[References are to question numbers.]

[References are to question numbers.]

Table of ERISA Sections

[References are to question numbers.]

[References are to question numbers.]

ERISA Sections

[References are to question numbers.]

Table of Revenue Rulings

[References are to question numbers.]

[References are to question numbers.]

Table of Letter Rulings

[References are to question numbers.]

[References are to question numbers.]

Letter Rulings

[References are to question numbers.]

Ltr Rul		Ltr Rul	
9043063	26:39	9119065	24:7
9044001	8:9	9119067	26:38
9045048	21:14	9120029	21:51
9046029	13:6	9122059	13:2
9046046	21:51	9124034	12:25
9046064	13:40	9124035	12:25
9047043	13:40	9124036	12:25
9047060	28:6, 28:32	9124037	12:25
9047065	28:6	9124038	24:12
9049047	28:34	9132024	24:12
9050030	26:39	9135059	24:10
9051041	30:20	9135060	13:40
9052015	11:11, 14:20	9136017	21:51
9052058	6:7, 11:19, 13:7	9137001	4:18
9102017	24:23, 24:30	9137037	13:7
9102021	24:23, 24:30	9137046	13:6
9102044	23:34	9138004	13:29, 30:18, 30:20, 30:21
9104020	26:39		
9104038	13:6	9138067	28:32
9106044	26:38, 26:39, 28:5	9139031	13:5
9107033	12:23	9138065	21:51
9108049	13:6	9141046	24:24, 24:31
9108057	28:36	9143013	24:24, 24:31
9109052	30:19, 30:20	9143078	13:7, 28:31
9110039	13:44	9144046	14:19
9111004	8:8	9145006	4:1
9111046	6:7	9145036	28:35
9114058	13:4	9145041	28:32
9114059	13:4, 13:21	9146005	8:25
9117035	24:22	9146045	28:36
9118001	20:1	9147053	13:17, 24:56
9118020	26:34, 28:39	9151024	28:36
9119002	20:1	9152041	13:40, 26:39, 28:34
9119007	2:17, 8:8, 12:18	9152044	13:40

Letter Rulings

[References are to question numbers.]

Ltr Rul		Ltr Rul	
9248042	8:20	9310050	8:20, 8:21
9248047	13:4	9310054	13:40
9249003	8:20	9311037	11:10
9249034	26:39	9311039	13:33, 14:26
9235058	28:6	9312035	26:39
9250002	8:8	9313029	8:20
9250040	28:6	9314007	24:6
9252034	13:8	9315031	28:1, 28:16
9252035	21:52	9316001	20:5
9253052	26:38	9316047	13:6
9253053	26:39	9316053	8:20
9253054	26:34	9317037	23:12
9302022	28:6	9317057	8:20
9302027	21:52, 23:50	9318035	21:51
9303023	13:29	9318043	26:39
9303031	28:6	9318044	28:34
9304003	24:12	9320006	13:1, 14:18
9304032	8:20	9320050	21:51
9304033	12:12	9321032	26:35, 26:36
9305025	28:6	9321035	26:35
9308049	8:20	9321065	24:12
9308050	28:3, 28:5	9321067	24:26
9309051	8:20, 8:21	9322005	26:35, 26:36, 26:38
9310026	11:19	9327080	24:31
9310035	13:2		

Table of Cases

[References are to question numbers.]

[References are to question numbers.]

Table of Cases

[References are to question numbers.]

Table of Cases

[References are to question numbers.]

Table of Cases

[References are to question numbers.]

Table of Cases

[References are to question numbers.]

[References are to question numbers.]

[References are to question numbers.]

[References are to question numbers.]

Table of Cases

Table of Cases

[References are to question numbers.]

[References are to question numbers.]

Table of Cases

[References are to question numbers.]

Table of Cases

[References are to question numbers.]

Glossary

The following is a list of terms (arranged in alphabetical order) that is intended to provide the reader with additional guidance in understanding the complex concepts that apply to qualified pension and profit sharing plans.

Acceleration Election: An election to increase the rate of recovery of the initial grandfather amount for excess distribution tax purposes from 10 percent to 100 percent if the discretionary method of recovery has been elected.

Accrued Benefit: A benefit that an employee has earned (or accrued) through participation in the plan.

In a defined contribution plan (e.g., a profit sharing plan), the accrued benefit of a participant is the balance in his or her individual account at a given time.

In a defined benefit plan, the accrued benefit is determined by reference to the benefit that will be provided to a participant when he or she reaches normal retirement age as specified by the plan.

The accrued benefit should not be confused, however, with the benefit (or portion thereof) that a participant has a right (nonforfeitable) to receive if he or she leaves prior to retirement. This benefit is determined by reference to the plan's vesting schedule and the years of service credited to a participant.

Actual Contribution Percentage (ACP) Test: A special nondis-crimination test applied to employer matching contributions and employee contributions.

Actual Deferral Percentage (ADP) Test: A special test designed to limit the extent to which elective contributions made on behalf of highly compensated employees may exceed the elective contributions made on behalf of nonhighly compensated employees under a 401(k) plan.

Actuarial Assumptions: Contributions to a defined benefit plan depend upon certain assumptions made by the plan's actuary, which may include mortality, investment return, employee turnover, retire-ment age, and salary scale.

Actuarial Equivalence: Two different sets of values are in an actuarial equivalence when they have an equal present value under a given set of actuarial assumptions.

Affiliated Service Group: Generally, an affiliated service group consists of two or more related service or management organizations, whether or not incorporated. Employees of the members of an affiliated service group are treated as employed by a single employer for plan qualification purposes.

Age-Based Profit Sharing Plan: A profit sharing plan that uses both age and compensation as a basis for allocating employer contributions among plan participants.

Alternate Payee: A spouse, former spouse, child, or other depend-ent of a participant who is recognized by a domestic relations order as having a right to receive all or a portion of the benefits payable under the qualified retirement plan with respect to the participant.

Annual Addition: Term used in connection with the limitation on the contributions that may be made for a participant under a defined contribution plan.

Annuity: A series of periodic payments, usually level in amount or adjusted according to some index (e.g., cost-of-living), that typically continue for the lifetime of the recipient. In contrast, an installment payment is one of a specific number of payments that will be paid

whether or not the recipient lives to receive them.
See also "Joint and Survivor Annuity."

Attained Age Method: The rate of recovery of the initial grandfather amount is calculated based on a formula that takes into account the individual's age both on August 1, 1986 and at the end of the year in which the retirement distributions are received.

Beneficiary: A person designated by a participant or one who, by the terms of the plan, is or may be eligible for benefits under the plan if the participant dies.

C Corporation: *See* "S Corporation."

Cash-or-Deferred Plan: A qualified profit sharing or stock bonus plan that gives a participant an option to take cash or to have the employer contribute the money to a qualified profit sharing plan as an "employer" contribution to the plan (i.e., an "elective deferral").
   These arrangements are often called "401(k) plans." *See* Chapter 22.

CB: Cumulative Bulletin. This is a government publication in which revenue rulings and other pertinent IRS pronouncements are published. The Cumulative Bulletin is published semiannually and incorporates the materials that were published weekly by IRS in its Internal Revenue Bulletins (IRBs).

Closely Held Corporation: A nonpublic corporation that is owned by a small number of shareholders.

Code: The Internal Revenue Code of 1986 (26 USC 1 et seq.), as adopted by TRA '86 (Pub L No 99-514). ("Former Code" refers to repealed provisions, including those in the previous Internal Revenue Code of 1954.)

Collectively Bargained Plans: Plans that provide retirement benefits under a collective bargaining agreement. Generally speaking, if more than one employer is required to contribute to the collectively bargained plan, the plan is treated as a multiemployer plan, subject to special rules. If only one employer (including affiliates) is required to contribute to the plan, however, the plan is treated in the same way that other plans that do not cover union employees are treated.

Combination Plans: The use of two or more plans in combination to provide retirement benefits for employees and their beneficiaries. A defined contribution plan (e.g., a money purchase plan) may be combined with a defined benefit pension plan or with another defined contribution plan (e.g., a profit sharing plan).

Limitations on contributions or benefits depend on the type of combination used.

Common-Law Employee: A person who performs service(s) for an employer, if the employer has the right to direct both the objective of the services and the manner in which they are performed.

Commonly Controlled Businesses: All employees of corporations that are members of a "controlled group of corporations" are treated as employed by a single employer for purposes of plan qualification. A comparable requirement applies to partnerships, sole proprietorships, and other businesses under common control.

See also "Controlled Group of Corporations."

Conduit IRA: *See* "Rollover IRA Account."

Contributory Plan: A pension plan under which employee contributions are required as a condition of participation.

Controlled Group of Corporations: There are three types of controlled groups: (1) the parent-subsidiary controlled group, (2) the brother-sister controlled group, and (3) the combined group.

Two tests must be met to have a "parent-subsidiary" controlled group: (1) stock equal to 80 percent of the combined voting power of each corporation, or at least 80 percent of the value of all outstanding stock of each corporation, is owned by one or more of the corporations of the group; and (2) the common parent corporation owns at least 80 percent of the voting power or value of at least one of the corporations in the group.

Two tests must be met to have a "brother-sister" controlled group: (1) five or fewer persons (individuals, estates, or trusts) own at least 80 percent of the combined voting power or value of two or more corporations; and (2) taking into account the ownership of each stockholder only to the extent that it is identical in each of the corporations involved, the five or fewer persons own more than 50 percent of the combined voting power or value of the corporations involved.

A "combined group" is a group of two or more corporations if: (1) each corporation is a member of either a parent-subsidiary group or a brother-sister group; and (2) at least one of the corporations is the common parent of a parent-subsidiary group and also is a member of a brother-sister controlled group.

All employees of corporations that are members of a controlled group of corporations are treated as employed by a single employer for plan qualification purposes.

Curtailments: The reduction of benefits or the augmenting of eligibility requirements so as to amount to a partial or a complete termination of the plan.

Death Benefits: Payments to a beneficiary of a deceased participant that may be provided under a qualified plan, but they must be incidental to the retirement benefits, which are the major purpose of the plan.

Defined Benefit Plan: A plan that is designed to provide participants with a definite benefit at retirement (e.g., a monthly benefit of 20 percent of compensation upon reaching age 65). Contributions under the plan are determined by reference to the benefits provided, not on the basis of a percentage of compensation.

Defined Contribution Plan: A plan that provides an individual account for each participant and in which benefits are based solely upon the amount contributed to the account (plus or minus any income, expenses, gain, and losses allocated to the account).

DEFRA: Deficit Reduction Act of 1984. Measure passed by Congress to reduce the budget deficit. One portion of the Act was the Tax Reform Act of 1984.

See also "Tax Reform Act of 1984."

Determination Letter: Letter issued by the IRS District Director's office determining that a plan submitted to it meets the requirements for qualification (or does not meet those requirements).

Direct Rollover: A distribution to an employee made in the form of a direct trustee-to-trustee transfer from a qualified retirement plan to an eligible retirement plan.

Discretionary Formula Plan: A profit sharing plan that provides that the amount of each year's contribution will be determined by the board of directors (or the responsible official(s)) of the sponsoring employer, in its discretion. (Contributions must be "recurring and substantial" to keep the plan in a qualified status.)

Discretionary Method: Under the discretionary method, 10 percent of the total retirement distributions received by an individual during a calendar year will be treated as a recovery of the initial grandfather amount. This method also allows an individual to elect to accelerate the rate of recovery to 100 percent of the distributions received.

Discrimination: A situation in which a plan, through its provisions or through its operations, favors officers, shareholders, or highly compensated employees to the detriment of other employees.

Disqualification: Loss of qualified (tax-favored) status by a plan, generally resulting from operation of the plan in a manner that is contrary to the provisions of the plan or that discriminates against rank-and-file employees.

See also "Discrimination."

Disqualified Persons: *See* "Party in Interest."

Distress Termination: The termination of a single-employer defined benefit plan covered by PBGC that is unable to pay all its benefit liabilities.

DOL: Department of Labor. The nontax (regulatory and administrative) provisions of ERISA are administered by the Department of Labor. The Department issues opinion letters and other pronouncements, and requires certain information forms to be filed.

Domestic Relations Order; DRO: A judgment, decree or order (including approval of a property settlement agreement) made pursuant to a state domestic relations law (including a community property law) that relates to the provision of child support, alimony payments, or marital property rights to an alternate payee.

Earmarking: Allowing a participant in a defined contribution plan to direct the investment of the amount in his or her account.

Elective Contribution: A contribution made to a 401(k) plan by the employer on an employee's behalf pursuant to the employee's cash-or-deferred election.

Elective Deferral: *See* "Elective Contribution."

Eligible Retirement Plan: An IRA and/or a qualified retirement plan.

Eligible Rollover Distribution: A distribution from a qualified retirement plan that may be rolled over to an eligible retirement plan.

Employee: An individual who provides services for compensation to an employer and whose duties are under the control of the employer.

Employee Contributions: *See* "Mandatory Employee Contributions" and "Voluntary Contributions."

Employee Stock Ownership Plan; ESOP: A profit sharing, stock bonus, or money purchase pension plan, the funds of which must be invested primarily in employer company stock. Unlike other plans, an ESOP may borrow from the employer or use the employer's credit to acquire company stock.
  See also "Stock Bonus Plan."

Employer Securities: For an ESOP, common stock issued by the employer that is readily tradable on an established securities market. If the employer has no readily tradable common stock, employer securities include employer-issued common stock that has a combination of voting power and dividend rights at least the equal of the class of common stock with the greatest voting power and the class of common stock with the greatest dividend rights. Noncallable preferred stock that is convertible into common stock that meets the requirements of employer securities also qualifies if the conversion price is reasonable.

Employer-Sponsored IRA: An IRA that is sponsored by the employer for purposes of helping its employees make a tax-deductible contribution to an IRA and to invest the funds in a particular type of investment.
  The employer-sponsored IRA should be distinguished from a simplified employee pension plan (SEP), which requires employer

contributions and must meet certain requirements with respect to participation, discrimination, withdrawals, and contributions.

Enrolled Actuary: A person who performs actuarial services for a defined benefit plan. His or her services include making a determination of how much has to be contributed to the plan each year to provide the stated benefits at retirement, and the preparation of a statement that has to be filed with the plan's annual return to IRS. Actuaries who perform these services are enrolled with the Joint Board for the Enrollment of Actuaries.

ERISA: Employee Retirement Income Security Act of 1974. This is the basic law covering qualified plans and incorporates both the pertinent Internal Revenue Code provisions and labor law provisions. ERISA is the basic law designed to protect the rights of beneficiaries of employee benefit plans offered by employers, unions, and the like. ERISA imposes various qualification standards and fiduciary responsibilities on both welfare benefit and retirement plans, and provides enforcement procedures as well. In the retirement area, it also provides standards for tax qualification.

ERTA: Economic Recovery Tax Act of 1981.

Excess Aggregate Contributions: The excess of the aggregate amount of employee contributions and matching contributions made on behalf of highly compensated employees for a plan year over the maximum amount of such contributions permitted under the ACP test.

Excess Contribution: The excess of the elective contributions (including qualified nonelective and matching contributions that are treated as elective contributions) made to a 401(k) plan on behalf of highly compensated employees for the plan year over the maximum amount of such contributions permitted under the ADP test for such plan year.

Excess Deferral: An employee's elective contributions for the taxable year in excess of $7,000 (increased for inflation).

Excess Distributions: A 15 percent excise tax is imposed on excess distributions. Excess distributions mean the aggregate amount of retirement plan distributions made with respect to an individual during a calendar year to the extent that such amount exceeds a threshold amount.

Excess Plan: A plan under which contributions or benefits are based on compensation in excess of the Social Security integration level.

Exclusive Benefit Rule: Plan fiduciaries must discharge their duties solely in the interest of participants and beneficiaries for the exclusive purpose of providing benefits to participants and beneficiaries and paying administration expenses.
 See also "Fiduciary."

FASB: Financial Accounting Standards Board; the body that sets uniform standards for treatment of accounting items. In the employee benefits context, FASB has prepared an exposure draft concerning disclosure of unfunded benefit liabilities.

FASB 87: The statement issued by FASB regarding employers' accounting for pensions.

Fiduciary: Any person who exercises discretionary authority or control over the management or disposition of plan assets or who gives investment advice to the plan for a fee or other compensation.

Fiscal year: A 12-month period used for accounting purposes.

5 Percent Owner: Any person who owns, directly or indirectly, more than 5 percent of the stock of the employer. If the employer is not a corporation, the ownership test is applied to the person's capital or profits interest in the employer.
 See also "Key Employee" and "Top-Heavy Plan."

Forfeitures: The benefits that a participant loses if he or she terminates employment before becoming eligible for full retirement benefits under the plan. For example, a participant who leaves the service of an employer at a time when he or she will receive only 60 percent of benefits forfeits the remaining 40 percent.

401(k) Plan: An arrangement (defined by Section 401(k)) under which a covered employee can elect to defer income by making pretax contributions to a profit sharing or stock bonus plan. A cafeteria plan may provide a 401(k) plan as a qualified benefit option. *See* Chapter 22.

Frozen Plan: A qualified pension or profit sharing plan that continues to exist even though employer contributions have been discontinued and benefits are no longer accrued by participants. The plan is "frozen" for purposes of distribution of benefits under the terms of the plan.

Funding Deficiency: The excess of total liabilities under a defined benefit, money purchase, or target benefit pension plan over total credits for all plan years. This amount is subject to an excise tax, unless IRS waives the tax. The technical term is "accumulated funding deficiency."

Grandfather Rule: An individual whose total benefits in all retirement plans on August 1, 1986 (initial grandfather amount) had a value in excess of $562,500 was eligible to elect the special grandfather rule. The special grandfather rule permits an individual to offset distributions by the portion of the initial grandfather amount recovered during the year of distribution. The election had to be made no later than the due date of the individual's timely filed 1988 income tax return.

Highly Compensated Employee: An employee who, during the year or the preceding year, is (or was): (1) a 5 percent owner, (2) receiving compensation in excess of $75,000 (adjusted for cost-of-living increases), (3) in the top-paid group of employees and receiving compensation in excess of $50,000 (adjusted for cost-of-living increases), or (4) an officer and receiving compensation greater than $45,000 (adjusted for cost-of-living increases).

H.R. 10 Plan: *See* "Keogh Plan."

Individual Account Plan: A plan that provides for an individual account for each participant and in which benefits are based solely on the amount contributed to an account and any income, expenses, gains, losses, and forfeitures allocated to the account.

Insured Plan: A plan funded exclusively by insurance contracts.

Integrated Plan: A plan that takes into account either benefits or contributions under Social Security. Social Security benefits are used to integrate a defined benefit plan; Social Security contributions are used to integrate defined contribution plans.

Interested Parties: Generally means all employees at the time the employer applies for a determination letter. IRS requires that interested parties be notified when the application is made.

IRA: An individual retirement account or an individual retirement annuity. Any working person and certain divorced spouses receiving alimony may establish IRAs and gain deductions for contributions to the IRAs and tax deferrals on the earnings.

IRB: Internal Revenue Bulletin. A weekly collection of materials published by IRS. *See also* "CB."

IRC: Internal Revenue Code of 1986. This is the basic federal tax law.

IRS: Internal Revenue Service: This is an agency of the Treasury Department, headed by the Commissioner of Internal Revenue, charged with primary responsibility for administering, interpreting, and enforcing the Code. (Note, however, that the Secretary of the Treasury—and not IRS—issues regulations under the Code.)

Joint and Survivor Annuity: An annuity paid for the life of the participant with a survivor annuity for his or her spouse. The survivor annuity must be at least 50 percent, but not more than 100 percent, of the annuity received by the participant during his or her lifetime. Also, the joint and survivor annuity must be the actuarial equivalent of a single life annuity that would have been paid to the participant.

Keogh Plan: A qualified retirement plan, either a defined contribution plan or a defined benefit plan, that covers a self-employed person. (Other employees might also be covered.)

Key Employee: A participant who, at any time during the plan year or any of the four preceding years, is (or was) (1) an officer who earns at least $45,000 a year, (2) one of the ten employees owning the largest interest in the employer and receiving annual compensation of more than $30,000, (3) a more-than-5 percent owner of the employer, or (4) a more-than-1 percent owner earning more than $150,000.

   See also "5 Percent Owner," "Officer," "1 Percent Owner," and "Top-Heavy Plan."

Letter Ruling: A private ruling issued by IRS in response to a request from a taxpayer as to the tax consequences of a proposed or completed transaction. Private letter rulings are published informally by several publishers. They are not considered as precedents for use by taxpayers other than the one that requested the ruling, but they do give an indication of IRS's current attitude as to a particular type of transaction.

Leveraged ESOP: An employee stock ownership plan that borrows to acquire employer company stock.
See also "Employee Stock Ownership Plan."

Lump-Sum Distribution: A type of distribution that is required for purposes of using the forward averaging method in computing the income tax that is due.

The basic requirements to qualify as a lump-sum distribution are (1) the distribution must be made within one taxable year of the recipient; (2) it must include the entire balance credited to an employee's account; and (3) it must be made on account of an employee's death, separation from service (except in the case of a self-employed person), or attainment of age 59 (or, in the case of a self-employed person only, on account of disability).

Mandatory Employee Contributions: Contributions made by an employee in order to become eligible to participate under a plan.

Master Plan: A retirement plan that is sponsored by a financial institution such as an insurance company, bank, mutual fund, or stock brokerage firm, and that may be adopted by an employer merely by executing a participation agreement.

Minimum Funding: The minimum amount that must be contributed by an employer that has a defined benefit, money purchase, or target benefit pension plan. The minimum is made up of amounts that go to cover "normal costs" (for the benefits earned by employees for the current year) plus other plan liabilities such as "past service costs"—liabilities for benefits that have been earned for services performed prior to the adoption of the plan. If the employer fails to meet these minimum standards, in the absence of a waiver from IRS, an excise tax will be imposed on the amount of the deficiency.

Minimum Funding Standard Account: An account that is maintained for a defined benefit, money purchase, or target benefit pension plan for purposes of keeping track of the plan's liabilities and credits. If the account shows a deficiency (excess of liabilities over credits), an excise tax is imposed on that amount.

Money Purchase Pension Plan: A defined contribution plan under which the employer's contributions are mandatory and are usually based on each participant's compensation. Retirement benefits under the plan are based on the amount in the participant's individual account at retirement.

Multiemployer Plan: A pension plan, maintained under a collective bargaining agreement, that covers the employees of more than one employer. Generally, the various employers are not financially related but rather are engaged in the same industry.

Named Fiduciary: A fiduciary who is named in the plan instrument or identified through a procedure set forth in the plan.

One of the distinguishing features of the named fiduciary is that he or she has the authority to designate others to carry out fiduciary responsibilities (e.g., invest the plan funds).

Noncontributory Plan: A pension plan under which employees are eligible to participate and receive accrued benefits without contributing to the plan.

Nonelective Contribution: A contribution to a cash-or-deferred arrangement other than an elective deferral. (An elective deferral is a participant-elected contribution that the participant could have chosen to receive instead as cash.) If the amount of the nonelective contribution depends on the amount of a participant's elective deferral, it is an "employer matching contribution."

Nonforfeitable Benefits: Benefits that cannot be lost by a participant even if he or she terminates service with the employer before qualifying for full retirement benefits. The nonforfeitable benefits are determined by applying the years of credited service to the vesting schedule used by the plan.

See also "Vested Benefits."

Notice of Intent to Terminate; NOIT: The 60-day advance notice to affected parties advising them of a proposed standard termination of a defined benefit plan covered by PBGC.

Notice of Plan Benefits: The notice to participants and beneficiaries to advise them of their benefits under a terminated defined benefit plan covered by PBGC.

OBRA '87: The Omnibus Budget Reconciliation Act of 1987 contained provisions affecting the minimum funding standards, including the Pension Protection Act of 1987. *See* "Pension Protection Act of 1987."

Officer: An administrative executive of a corporate employer who is in regular and continued service. One employed for a special and single transaction or one who has only nominal administrative duties is excluded.

Offset Plan: A plan that reduces the participant's benefit by an amount specified (i.e., by formula) in the plan.

Old Age, Survivors, and Disability Insurance; OASDI: Payroll tax imposed on employers that is equal to a set percentage of the wages paid to employees. The OASDI tax rate is used for purposes of integrating a defined contribution plan and a simplified employee pension (SEP). Social Security payroll taxes also include Medicare taxes.
See also "Integrated Plan."

1 Percent Owner: Any person who owns, directly or indirectly, more than 1 percent of the stock of the employer. If the employer is not a corporation, the ownership test is applied to the person's capital or profits interest in the employer.
A 1 percent owner is a key employee only if his or her annual compensation from the employer is more than $150,000.
See also "Key Employee" and "Top-Heavy Plan."

Owner-Employee: A sole proprietor or a partner who owns more than 10 percent of either the capital interest or the profits interest in a partnership.

Partial Termination: Reducing benefits or making participation requirements less liberal, although not amounting to a complete termination of the plan, may be considered a partial termination, resulting in the vesting of accrued benefits for at least part of the plan.
The typical types of partial terminations include: the employer closing a plant and thereby substantially reducing the percentage of employees participating under the plan, the reduction of benefits for participating employees, the substantial reduction of contributions to the plan, and the exclusion of a group of employees from participation after they were included in the plan.

Party in Interest: A party which, because of his or her or its relationship with the plan (e.g., as a fiduciary, provider of services, or the plan sponsor), is prohibited from entering into certain transactions with the plan.

See also "Prohibited Transactions."

Pension Benefit Guaranty Corporation; PBGC: A nonprofit corporation, functioning under the jurisdiction of the Department of Labor, that is responsible for insuring pension benefits.

Pension Protection Act of 1987 (PPA): Enacted as part of OBRA '87, legislation designed to protect the integrity of the federal pension system by, for example, raising PBGC premiums and tightening the plan termination requirements.

Plan Year: Any 12-consecutive-month period that has been chosen by the plan for keeping its records. The 12-month period may be the calendar year, a fiscal year, or a policy year (if insurance is used to fund all plan benefits). The plan year does not have to coincide with the employer's taxable year or begin on the first day of the month. Change of a plan year usually requires the consent of IRS.

Profit Sharing Plan: A defined contribution plan under which the employer agrees to make discretionary contributions (usually out of profits). A participant's retirement benefits are based on the amount in his or her individual account at retirement.

Prohibited Group: Officers, shareholders, or highly compensated employees. Discrimination in favor of the prohibited group may cause disqualification of a plan.

Prohibited Transactions: Specified transactions that may not be entered into (directly or indirectly) by a party in interest with the plan. Those include, for example, sales or exchanges, leases, and loans between the parties. The Department of Labor may exempt a specific transaction from the prohibited transactions restriction.

See also "Party in Interest."

Prototype Plans: *See* "Master Plan."

Prudent-Man Rule: The standard under which a fiduciary must act. The fiduciary is required to act "with the care, skill, prudence, and diligence under the circumstances then prevailing that a prudent man acting in a like capacity and familiar with such matters would use in the conduct of an enterprise of a like character and with like aims."

P.S. 58 Costs: Costs applied to current life insurance protection provided under the plan for purposes of determining the amount of the participant's tax liability for the coverage.

Qualified Cash-or-Deferred Arrangement: *See* "401(k) Plan."

Qualified Domestic Relations Order; QDRO: A court order issued under state domestic relations law that relates to the payment of child support or alimony or to marital property rights. A QDRO creates or recognizes an alternate payee's right, or assigns to an alternate payee the right, to receive plan benefits payable to a participant. The alternate payee may be the participant's spouse, former spouse, or dependent.

Qualified Election Period: The six-plan-year period beginning with the plan year after the first plan year beginning after 1986 in which the employee is a qualified participant and during which the employee can make a diversification election.

Qualified Participant: An employee who has completed at least ten years of participation in an ESOP and has attained age 55.

Qualified Pension Plan (Qualified Plan): A plan that meets the requirements of the Internal Revenue Code (generally Section 401(a)).

The advantage of qualification is that the plan is eligible for special tax considerations. For example, employers are permitted to deduct contributions to the plan even though the benefits provided under the plan are deferred to a later date.

Qualified Replacement Property: Any security issued by a domestic operating corporation that did not have passive investment income (e.g., rents, royalties, dividends, or interest) that exceeded 25 percent of its gross receipts in its taxable year preceding the purchase.

Qualified Securities: Employer securities that (1) are issued by a domestic corporation that for one year before and immediately after the sale has no readily tradable stock outstanding, and (2) have not been received by the seller as a distribution from a qualified retirement plan or pursuant to an option or other right to acquire stock granted by the employer.

REA: Retirement Equity Act of 1984. Among major changes made by the Retirement Equity Act: reduced the age requirement for participation in a plan; increased the period of service considered for vesting purposes; broadened the survivor-benefit requirements; allowed the assignment or alienation of benefits in divorce proceedings.

Replacement Period: The period beginning three months before the date of sale of employer securities to an ESOP and ending 12 months after the sale. The qualified replacement property must be purchased during this period.

Reportable Event: An event that may indicate that the plan is in danger of being terminated. ERISA requires plan administrators of certain defined benefit plans to notify the PBGC of the occurrence of such event so as to give the PBGC enough time to protect the benefits of participants and beneficiaries. The notice must usually be given within 30 days of the occurrence of the reportable event unless the PBGC waives notice.

A reportable event includes an occurrence such as: (1) disqualification of the plan for tax purposes; (2) benefit decrease by plan amendment; (3) substantial decrease (more than 20 percent) of the number of employees that are participating under the plan, if the present value of unfunded benefits equals or exceeds $250,000; or (4) an IRS determination that the plan has been partially or completely terminated.

Rev Proc: A revenue procedure issued by IRS. It is somewhat similar to a revenue ruling, but deals with procedural matters or details the requirements to be followed in connection with various dealings with IRS. Rev Procs also set forth (at times) guidelines that IRS follows in handling certain tax matters.

Rev Rul: A public revenue ruling issued by IRS. These rulings express IRS's views as to the tax results that apply to a specific problem.

Revenue Reconciliation Act of 1993 (RRA '93): Clinton Administration proposals sent to Congress on April 30, 1993 and enacted into law on August 10, 1993. RRA '93 increases income tax rates, repeals the Medicare base dollar limitation, and reduces the annual compensation limit affecting contributions, benefits, and tax deductions.

Reversion of Employer Contributions: A qualified plan (or trust) is prohibited from diverting corpus or income for purposes other than the exclusive benefit of employees. However, this prohibition does not preclude the return of a contribution made by an employer if the contribution was made, for example, by reason of a mistake of fact or conditioned on the qualification of the plan or the deductibility of the contribution.

Rollover: A tax-free transfer of cash or other assets from one retirement plan to another. An IRA account owner may shift assets from his or her present IRA to another. Certain payouts from a pension plan may also be rolled over to an IRA or to another employer's plan.

Rollover IRA Account: An individual retirement account that is established for the sole purpose of receiving a distribution from a qualified plan so that the assets can subsequently be rolled over into another qualified plan.

S Corporation: A corporation whose shareholders have elected not to be taxed as a regular (or "C") corporation, but like a partnership, with profits and losses passing through directly to the shareholders, rather than at the corporate level.

Salary-Reduction Arrangement: Under this type of cash-or-deferred arrangement, each eligible employee may elect to reduce his or her current compensation or to forgo a salary increase and have these amounts instead contributed to the plan on his or her behalf on a pretax basis.
See also "Cash-or-Deferred Plan."

Savings Plan: *See* "Thrift Plan."

Self-Employed Person: A sole proprietor or a partner in a partnership.

Settlement: An action taken to relieve a plan of primary responsibility for a pension benefit obligation.

Shareholder-Employee: A more-than-5 percent shareholder of an S corporation.

Simplified Employee Pension Plan; SEP: A retirement program that takes the form of individual retirement accounts for all eligible employees (subject to special rules on contributions and eligibility).

Split-Funded Plan: A plan that is funded in part by insurance contracts and in part by funds accumulated in a separate trusteed fund.

Spousal IRA: An IRA that is established for the nonworking spouse of an employee who qualifies for an IRA. A contribution of $2,250, instead of $2,000, is permitted, but the maximum contribution for either spouse is $2,000.

Standard Termination: The termination of a single-employer defined benefit plan covered by PBGC that is able to pay all its benefit liabilities.

Step-Rate Plan: A plan that provides different levels of benefits that are based on levels of compensation. For example, a contribution under a money purchase plan of 8 percent of compensation for amounts up to $15,300 and 13 percent of compensation for amounts in excess of $15,300. The step-rate plan is one of the ways of integrating benefits with Social Security benefits.

Stock Bonus Plan: A defined contribution plan that is similar to a profit sharing plan except that the employer's contributions do not have to be made out of profits and benefit payments generally must be made in employer company stock.

See also "Profit Sharing Plan" and "Employee Stock Ownership Plan."

Subchapter S Corporation: *See* "S Corporation."

Summary Plan Description; SPD: A detailed, but easily understood, summary describing a pension plan's provisions that must be provided to participants and beneficiaries.

Table 1: A table, found in the Treasury regulations under Section 79, that gives the monthly cost of providing $1,000 of insurance coverage, based on the employee's age. Table 1 is used to value coverage in excess of $50,000 that is provided to (and generates tax liability for) employees under a group term life insurance policy that qualifies under Section 79.

TAMRA: Technical and Miscellaneous Revenue Act of 1988. Contained many corrections to and clarification of OBRA '87 and TRA '86.

Target Benefit Plan: A cross between a defined benefit plan and a money purchase plan. Similar to a defined benefit plan, the annual contribution is determined by the amount needed each year to accumulate a fund sufficient to pay a targeted retirement benefit to each participant on reaching retirement. Similar to a money purchase plan, contributions are allocated to separate accounts maintained for each participant.

Tax Reform Act of 1984 (TRA '84): Tax measure signed into law on July 18, 1984. Among major changes made by the Tax Reform Act: delayed until 1988 cost-of-living increases in contributions and benefits; repealed the estate tax exclusion for death benefits from a pension plan or an IRA; allowed partial distributions from a pension plan to be rolled over to an IRA; applied restrictive distribution rules to 5 percent owners only.

Tax Reform Act of 1986 (TRA '86): The act that made such major changes to the Code that it renamed the Code as the "Internal Revenue Code of 1986." It was signed on October 22, 1986.

Tax Simplification Bill of 1993 (TSB '93): Legislation introduced on January 5, 1993, but not yet enacted. If enacted, will repeal certain tax advantages available for qualified retirement plan distributions, simplify the definition of highly compensated employee, and among other provisions, ease the nondiscrimination testing for 401(k) plans.

Taxable Year: The 12-month period used by an employer to report income for income tax purposes. The employer's taxable year does not have to coincide with the year used by the plan to keep its records.

TEFRA: Tax Equity and Fiscal Responsibility Act of 1982. Lowered limits on contributions and benefits for corporate plans; certain loans from plan to be treated as distributions; reduced estate tax exclusion for retirement plan death benefits to maximum of $100,000; repealed special Keogh plan and S corporation restrictions; added "top-heavy" plan requirements.

Threshold Amount: For excess distribution tax purposes, the threshold amount is either $112,500 (as adjusted for inflation), or

$150,000. The $112,500 adjusted threshold amount is used by individuals who elected the special grandfather rule, and the $150,000 unadjusted threshold amount is used by individuals who did not elect or were ineligible to elect the special grandfather rule.

Thrift Plan: A defined contribution plan that is contributory in the sense that employer contributions are geared to mandatory contributions by the employee. Employer contributions are made on a matching basis—for example, 50 percent of the total contribution made by the employee.

Top-Heavy Plan: Beginning in 1984, a plan that primarily benefits key employees is considered top-heavy and qualifies for favorable tax treatment only if, in addition to the regular qualification requirements, it meets several special requirements.
See also "Key Employee."

Treasury Regulations: Regulations promulgated by the U.S. Department of the Treasury. IRS is a part of the Treasury Department, and regulations interpreting the Internal Revenue Code are technically Treasury regulations.

Trust: A fund established under local trust law to hold and administer the assets of a plan.

Trustees: The parties named in the trust instrument or plan that are authorized to hold the assets of the plan for the benefit of the participants.
The trustees may function merely in the capacity of a custodian of the assets or may also be given authority over the investment of the assets. Their function is determined by the trust instrument or, if no separate trust agreement is executed, under the trust provisions of the plan.

Unemployment Compensation Amendments of 1992 (UC '92): Tax measure signed into law on July 3, 1992. Expanded rollover rules and introduced mandatory income tax withholding on certain plan distributions.

Unit Benefit Plan: A type of defined benefit pension plan that calculates benefits on the basis of units earned by the employee during his or her employment, taking into consideration length of service as well as compensation.

Vested Benefits: Accrued benefits of a participant that have become nonforfeitable under the vesting schedule adopted by the plan. Thus, for example, if the schedule provides for vesting at the rate of 10 percent per year, a participant who has been credited with six years of service has a right to 60 percent of the accrued benefit. If he or she terminates service without being credited with any additional years of service, he or she is entitled to receive 60 percent of the accrued benefit.

Voluntary Contributions: Amounts that a participant voluntarily contributes to a plan in addition to the contributions made by the employer. IRS permits "reasonable" amounts of employee contributions. Up to 10 percent of the employee's compensation is generally considered reasonable. Voluntary contributions, unlike employer contributions, are not deductible on the employee's tax return.

Year of Service: A 12-month period during which an employee is credited with at least 1,000 hours of service.

Index

[References are to question numbers.]

Index

nondiscrimination. *See* Nondiscrimination
nonforfeitable, 9:19
optional payment methods, 10:33
effective date of nondiscrimination rules, 10:39
employer denial of, 10:44
plan amendment pattern as, 10:43
plan amendment to change, 10:40
payment election by participant, 10:51
payment method, denial by qualified plan, 10:37
plan investor, defined, 19:20
plan termination
"all other benefits under the plan," 21:43
restrictions, 21:28
protected, 10:42
effective dates, 10:49
employer discretion amendment, 10:48
objective criteria for availability, 10:47
QDRO, earliest retirement age, 30:8
qualified plan, 1:22
choices, 2:31
equitable distribution under QDRO, 30:22
QDRO effect, 30:16
plan year, 6:23
recordkeeping, 16:4
reduction, Social Security payments and, 4:8
rollover, surviving spouse, 28:32
safe harbors, separate line of business, 5:41
stock bonus plan, 2:29
structure. *See* Prior benefit structure
timing, qualified plan, 5:20
top-heavy plan
annual retirement benefit, 22:38
average compensation, 22:40
early distribution, 22:39

employees receiving, 22:42
minimum requirement for defined benefit plan, 22:37
Social Security minimums, 22:47
vesting requirements, 22:34
underfunded plan, PBGC liability, 21:47
valuation, interest rate, 10:61
Board of directors, plan termination, 21:2
Borrowing. *See* **Loan**
Break in service, parental leave, 5:14
Business hardship. *See* **Hardship**
Business owners
affiliated service group
compensation limits, 6:24
defined, 29:31
plan qualification, 29:30, 29:32
benefits and contributions in favor of, 29:12
borrowing from plan
allowable, 29:25
business expenses, 29:24
choice of plan, 29:18
maximizing benefits, 29:19
normal retirement age earlier than 65, 29:20
closely held corporation
ESOP, 24:21, 24:22, 24:38
plan advantages, 1:1
plan benefits, 29:1, 29:2
prohibited transactions exemption, 20:11
commonly controlled businesses, 5:30, 25:17, 25:34
common ownership, 5:31, 5:32
contribution limits, 29:14, 29:15
employee-owner, defined, 29:35
five percent owner, 3:4
life insurance protection, 29:23
management corporation, 29:29
multiple corporations, 29:27
multiple, coverage requirements, 29:28

[References are to question numbers.]

[References are to question numbers.]

[References are to question numbers.]

[References are to question numbers.]

[References are to question numbers.]

[References are to question numbers.]

[References are to question numbers.]

I

[References are to question numbers.]

[References are to question numbers.]

[*References are to question numbers.*]

[References are to question numbers.]

[References are to question numbers.]

[References are to question numbers.]

[References are to question numbers.]

past service with former
employer, 5:13
statutory exclusions, 1:19
year of service defined, 5:8
separation from service defined,
13:9
**Severance from employment, early
benefit commencement, 10:56**
Shareholders. *See also* **Employee
Stock Ownership Plan; Securities**
ESOP benefits, 2:29
shareholder-employee, defined,
13:48
**Simplified employee pension (SEP)
plan**
advantages to business owner, 27:21
annual reporting requirements,
27:15
assets
management, 27:17
moving without penalty, 27:19
contributions
deductions, 27:7, 27:8
employee contributions,
taxability, 27:16
forfeitability, 27:5
IRA, 27:6
defined, 2:14, 27:1
discrimination, highly compensated
employee, 27:3
dissolved partnership, 27:14
distributions, taxation, 27:18
drawbacks, 27:22
elective deferrals, limitations, 27:10
vs. employer-sponsored IRA, 26:30
establishment, 27:12
model SEP, 27:13
participation, 27:2
permitted disparity, 27:4
rollover of qualified plan distributions, 27:20
SARSEP
adoption, 27:9
nondiscrimination test, 27:11

tax-favored status, 29:39
top-heavy, 22:7
**Single Employer Pension Plan
Amendments Act,** 21:11
**Single life annuity, present value cal-
culation,** 14:24
Small company, profit sharing plan,
2:27
Social Security
benefits
effect on deductible IRA contributions, 26:12
minimum benefit and contribution requirement, 22:47
and qualified plan, 2:30, 4:8
retirement age, 6:12
benefit commencement, 7:14
covered compensation tables, 7:22
defined benefit offset plan benefit
commencement, 7:19
wages, taxable wage base, 7:7
Sole proprietorship. *See* **Business
owners; Self-employed individual**
Spousal consent
antenuptial agreement, 10:22
participant waiver of QJSA or
QPSA, 10:21
plan document, 10:28
qualified plan loans, 10:12, 13:47
rules, effective date, 10:32
waiver of QPSA or QJSA
general consent, 10:26
as taxable gift, 10:27
Spouse. *See also* **Qualified domestic
relations order; Surviving spouse**
spousal IRA, defined, 26:18
Statutory exceptions
prohibited transactions, 20:7
qualified plan participation, 1:19

Statutory safe harbor. *See* **Safe harbor**

Stock. *See* **Employee Stock Owner-ship Plan; Securities; Stock bonus plan**

Stock bonus plan
active participant, 26:9
benefits, 2:29
defined, 2:12
vs. ESOP, 24:3
401(k) plan, 2:11

Straight life annuity, annual benefit, 6:9

Subsidiary, prohibited transactions, 20:5

Summary plan description
change in plan, 18:8
defined, 18:1
disclaimer clause, 18:6, 18:7
filing location, 18:3
foreign language requirement, 18:14
formal application for benefits, 10:62
information required, 18:4
legally binding, 18:5
material modification, 18:9
other documents obtainable by participant, 18:13
plan termination, 18:12
update deadline, 18:10, 18:11
when furnished, 18:2

Surviving spouse. *See also* **Beneficiary; Qualified joint and survivor annuity; Qualified preretirement survivor annuity**
aggregate interest rule, 14:26
death benefit, 14:1, 14:20
IRA
beneficiary, special rules, 26:37
rollover, 26:34, 28:6
lump-sum distribution, tax rules, 13:11
QDRO, 30:14
qualified plan benefits, distribution requirement, 10:1
rollovers, 28:15, 28:32

Survivor annuity
estate tax, 10:10
floor offset plan, 10:14

Survivor benefit requirement
annuity starting date, 10:4
benefits applicable, 10:18
effective date, 10:32
frozen or terminated plan, 10:16
participant waiver, 10:20
PBGC administration, 10:17
qualified plan, 10:6, 10:7
transferee plan, 10:13
unmarried participants, 10:5

T

Target benefit plan
active participant, 26:9
benefit timing, 5:20
defined, 2:5
minimum funding standards, 8:1
money purchase pension plan and, 2:5
nondiscrimination rules, 4:21

Taxation. *See also* **Deduction; Estate tax; Excise tax; Income tax; Internal Revenue Service; Penalty; Social Security; Taxation of distributions; Tax deduction rules**
death benefit payment, 14:18
employer contributions, qualified vs. nonqualified plan, 1:6
ESOP
distributions, 24:56
dividends, 24:14
excess contribution
distribution correction, 23:25
penalty, 23:22
recharacterization, 23:20
favorable tax treatment
401(k) plan, 23:4
plan coverage requirements, 5:15
plan termination, 21:7

[References are to question numbers.]

[References are to question numbers.]

[References are to question numbers.]